Oliver Scheiding, René Dietrich, Clemens Spahr (eds.)

A History of American Poetry

Contexts – Developments – Readings

WVT-HANDBÜCHER
ZUM
LITERATURWISSENSCHAFTLICHEN
STUDIUM

Band 19

Herausgegeben von
Ansgar Nünning und Vera Nünning

Oliver Scheiding, René Dietrich, Clemens Spahr (eds.)

A History of American Poetry

Contexts – Developments – Readings

 Wissenschaftlicher Verlag Trier

A History of American Poetry
Contexts – Developments – Readings /
Ed. by Oliver Scheiding, René Dietrich and Clemens Spahr. -
Trier: WVT Wissenschaftlicher Verlag Trier, 2015
      (WVT-Handbücher zum literaturwissenschaftlichen Studium; Bd. 19)
      ISBN 978-3-86821-610-3

Cover design: Brigitta Disseldorf

© WVT Wissenschaftlicher Verlag Trier, 2015
ISBN 978-3-86821-610-3

WVT Wissenschaftlicher Verlag Trier
Bergstraße 27, 54295 Trier
Postfach 4005, 54230 Trier
Tel.: (0651) 41503 / 9943344, Fax: 41504
Internet: http://www.wvttrier.de
E-Mail: wvt@wvttrier.de

TABLE OF CONTENTS

To the Reader   1

OLIVER SCHEIDING, RENÉ DIETRICH, CLEMENS SPAHR

I EARLY AMERICAN POETRY

1. Religious Poetry and New England Verse:
   Anne Bradstreet and Edward Taylor   7

   LUDWIG DERINGER

2. The Poetry of British America:
   Francis Daniel Pastorius and Richard Lewis   23

   OLIVER SCHEIDING

3. The Poetry of the New Nation: Joel Barlow and Philip Freneau   37

   JULIA STRAUB

4. Early African American Poetry:
   Phillis Wheatley and George Moses Horton   49

   ASTRID FRANKE

II ROMANTICISM AND NINETEENTH-CENTURY AMERICAN POETRY

5. Romanticisms in American Poetry:
   William Cullen Bryant and Ralph Waldo Emerson   65

   DAMIEN SCHLARB

6. American Romanticisms: Edgar Allan Poe and Herman Melville   79

   GERO GUTTZEIT

7. The Fireside Poets:
   Henry Wadsworth Longfellow and John Greenleaf Whittier   95

   MARGIT PETERFY

8. Native American Poetry in the Age of U.S. Expansion:
   Jane Johnston Schoolcraft and John Rollin Ridge/Yellow Bird   111

   RENÉ DIETRICH

9. Nineteenth-Century Women Poets:
    Lydia Sigourney and Sarah Morgan Bryan Piatt   125
    GUDRUN M. GRABHER

10. Modern Romantics: Emily Dickinson and Walt Whitman   141
    TIM LANZENDÖRFER

III AMERICAN MODERNISMS

11. The Country and the City in Modern American Poetry:
    Carl Sandburg and Robert Frost   157
    CLEMENS SPAHR

12. Variations on High Modernism: T.S. Eliot and Ezra Pound   171
    HEINZ ICKSTADT

13. American Modernist Poetry:
    Wallace Stevens and William Carlos Williams   187
    SIMONE KNEWITZ

14. Modernist Women Poets: H.D. and Marianne Moore   199
    TANJA BUDDE

15. The Harlem Renaissance: Claude McKay and Langston Hughes   215
    MAXIMILIAN MEINHARDT

16. The Objectivists: Louis Zukofsky and Charles Reznikoff   229
    MIRJAM HORN

17. Legacies of Modernism: Melvin B. Tolson and Robert Hayden   243
    MICHAEL BASSELER

IV POST-WAR POETRY AND POSTMODERN EXPERIMENT

18. American Post-War Poetry: Theodor Roethke and Elizabeth Bishop   261
    KORNELIA FREITAG

19. Black Mountain Poetry: Charles Olson, Robert Creeley,
    Robert Duncan, Denise Levertov, and Edward Dorn   275
    HELMBRECHT BREINIG

20. Beat Poetry and the Cold War:
    Lawrence Ferlinghetti and Allen Ginsberg   297
    PHILIPP LÖFFLER

21. Confessional Poetry and the 1960s: Robert Lowell and Sylvia Plath   311
     CARSTEN ALBERS

22. New Formal Languages: Frank O'Hara and John Ashbery   327
     ULFRIED REICHARDT

23. Performance Poetry: Anne Waldman and Saul Williams   341
     HARALD ZAPF

24. Language Poetry: Lyn Hejinian and Charles Bernstein   355
     KATHY-ANN TAN

     V   CONTEMPORARY AMERICAN POETRIES

25. Poetry of the Native American Renaissance and Beyond:
     Louise Erdrich and Joy Harjo   369
     HELMBRECHT BREINIG

26. African American Poetry: Amiri Baraka and Rita Dove   385
     ERIK REDLING

27. Contemporary Women's Poetry: Adrienne Rich and Harryette Mullen   397
     CHRISTIAN KLOECKNER

28. Asian American Poetry: Cathy Song and Theresa Hak Kyung Cha   413
     NASSIM W. BALESTRINI

29. Chicano/a Poetry: Rodolfo "Corky" Gonzales
     and Lorna Dee Cervantes   427
     ASTRID M. FELLNER

30. Disability Poetry: Jim Ferris and Cheryl Marie Wade   443
     MARION RANA

31. Twenty-first Century Poetry and Politics:
     Myung Mi Kim and Claudia Rankine   457
     ANGELA HUME

Index   473

List of Contributors   483

To the Reader

> The mecca Art is a babel city in the people's Shinar
> with a hundred gates
> and busybody roads
> that stretch beyond all dates . . .
> (Melvin B. Tolson, *Harlem Gallery*, 1965)

Looking at literary studies today, ours seems to be an age of handbooks and companions. An increasing number of guidebooks seek to provide students with continuously new surveys of the developments of American literature from the colonial period to the present (for the most recent examples in American poetry, see Bendixen/Burt 2014; Ashton 2013, Larson 2011). Editors and publishers justify their reassessments of American literature by pointing to the ongoing revisions of the canon, authors, and periods as well as the changes in our perception of literary history. Our view of American poetry in particular has been stirred deeply by current trends in literary and cultural theory, suggesting that we review America in light of a "global flow of people, ideas, texts, and products" (Fishkin 2005, 24). The reconceptualization of America in terms of transnationalism and globalization not only challenges earlier assumptions of origination and periodization in literary studies, it also raises questions about what counts as 'American' literature (see Levander 2013; Scheiding/Seidl 2014). Most recent anthologies, handbooks, and companions therefore reconsider American poetry by acknowledging the diversity of poetic practices, voices, and traditions that exist in the Americas across time and space. Moving beyond narrow generic classifications, scholars position American poetry in complex local and translocal contexts to demonstrate the simultaneous existence of multilingual and multiethnic poetic practices effective in any given historical period (see Marcus/Sollors 2009; Ramazani 2009).

Prevailing handbooks emphasize the dialogue between poetry and social life in both the private and public spheres, rediscovering a wide range of popular poetic forms that have, so far, been neglected (see Chinitz/McDonald 2014). In a similar manner, our handbook shows how the innovative potential of American poetry has resulted in an extremely fluid canon. Setting aside normative principles that have been used to classify American poetry according to strict formal principles, nationalist premises, or rigid period concepts such as Romanticism or Modernism, current handbooks propose ways to engage poetry with present scholarship conducted in gender, race, material and media studies (see Nelson 2012; Fredman 2005), and the history of the book, to name just a few prominent fields of activity in literary and cultural theory. In addition to the revisions of the modernist and postmodern canon, these approaches have also severely changed our way of understanding early American poetry. The former Anglocentrist focus on colonial poetry with its intellectual center in New England has been greatly expanded by exploring the multilingual and communal poetic traditions in both the Mid-Atlantic colonies and the South. Present anthologies show that the writing of poetry in regions besides New England, with its highly productive manuscript and print culture, also results from transatlantic networks of friendship, particular local institutions, and print markets meeting the needs of different communities at different times. Studies in the field of print cultures have similarly changed the ways in which we look at Native American literacy. Concurrent studies and textbooks reveal an unbroken tradition of verse in Native American literature that reaches back to the foundation of Harvard College in the 1630s and continues throughout the eighteenth into the nineteenth century—thus being effective long before the so-called Native American Renaissance of the 1970s (see Parker 2011).

Studying the expansive nineteenth-century periodical market discloses new forms of female agency in writing and publishing poetry, and it becomes clear that the multiple forms of lyric expression exceed by far the popularity of the novel and influenced reading habits and writing practices. Similar observations can be drawn from reexamining the period of High Modernism and its representative poets such as Ezra Pound and T.S. Eliot. Poetry appears less an elitist and more a cultural practice; it is not only encountered in the Modernists' little magazines, it abounds in a variety of material forms that derive from the poet's engagement in worldly affairs: verse written on greeting cards, advertisements, song lyrics, scrapbooks. But canon revisions are not restricted to earlier literary eras. While contemporary American poetry is often associated with specific movements that range from Confessional poetry to Language poetry as well as the poetic innovations among Latino, African American, and Asian American poets, it has found new outlets in various academic and non-academic poetic communities and their creative projects (see Beach 1999). Since poetry remains a site of cultural meaning, it is necessary to shed new light on the collective dimension of poetry and rediscover the writing of poetry as a political and social force in American intellectual life.

To capture the dynamic field of American poetry, current handbooks adopt a twofold approach that offers the reader both critical accounts of single poets and specific readings of representative movements and contexts. Following such an overview of major and emerging poets from the "beginnings" to the present, the editors of *The Cambridge History of American Poetry* (2014), for example, intend to show that poetry embodies the diversity of the American democratic experience in multiple ways. Interspersed thematic chapters on particular schools and settings fulfill the task of balancing literary analysis and literary history. *A History of American Poetry: Contexts—Developments—Readings*, however, offers a slightly different strategy in explaining to students the fluid canon of American Poetry. The guiding principle of this handbook derives from a belief in a context-based close reading. Placed in its specific historical context, a poem's formal, aesthetic, and thematic choices need to be understood before we can fully apprehend its cultural, political, and social function. The handbook's emphasis on "Contexts—Developments—Readings" proposes an interpretative method that allows both novice and expert readers to encounter and investigate the formal patterns and historically varying practices of poetic writing that define American poetry. Instead of producing content-based readings of representative authors and texts, *A History of American Poetry* asserts that the developments of American poetry are best understood as the result of aesthetic, linguistic, and rhetorical choices that occur in, and comment on, specific historical, ideological, and material contexts.

The method of reading and presenting poems is based on three principles:

1. Each chapter contextualizes the relevant practices of poetry in conjunction with prevailing poetics, literary conventions, and aesthetic norms that dom-

inate specific periods and are condensed in the formal experimentations of the poetic texts under discussion.

2. Each chapter will focus on two poets set into dialogue with each other, presenting paired readings of one representative text from each author. The poetic texts and authors selected for each chapter answer the canon revisions in American literary history over the past years. In addition to a number of familiar texts and names that are necessary for students to understand basic developments of poetry, the handbook offers chapters on multilingual colonial poetry, nineteenth-century Native American poetry, and contemporary experimental poetry.

3. Based on both textual analysis and dense contextualizations of poetic practices, each chapter reads poetry as sites of social and historical meanings condensed in the poem's form. In doing so, the handbook offers readers a wide spectrum of genres, styles, and conventions while tracing the changing practices of poetry from the colonial period the present.

Given the plurality of schools, movements, and settings, it is impossible to synthesize past and present developments of American poetry and provide one comprehensive narrative. An introduction that tries to do so would not be able to capture the dynamic of American poetry in all its facets over the last three hundred fifty years. We therefore decided to refrain from constructing one exemplary story, and want the handbook as a whole to serve as one way of tracing the creative vitality and diversity of American poetry. Until 1950, this history largely follows most handbooks and companions in dividing the field of poetic production into the major areas of poetry before 1800; Nineteenth-century poetry; and Modernist poetry until the 1950s. In order to account for the manifold innovations of poetry since the 1950s, the handbook further adds the less widespread division between postwar poetry/postmodern experiment, and contemporary developments up to the present (whose range the handbook can only suggest). Additionally, instead of offering a single chapter on High Modernism or Romanticism, the handbook examines the plurality of these canonical periods, drawing the reader's attention, for instance, to the "Modernisms" that mobilized the practices of poetry in the nineteenth and twentieth centuries (see Nicholls 2009). And in light of the multiple ethnic voices that have helped to constitute American poetry, it seems futile to offer an all-encompassing chapter on "ethnic poetries." Instead, the handbook contains numerous chapters on African American and Native American poetry in different historical periods as well as discussions of the more recent Asian American and Latino American poetry that analyze the diversity of ethnic poetries from the colonial period to the present.

Offering the reader diachronic readings of representative poetic texts and authors from the early Americas to the present, this handbook answers the student's need for fresh and informative readings of canonical and non-canonical poems. The thirty chapters engage revisionary trends and thus unfold a critical history of American poetry that challenges conventional interpretations and provides insightful new readings of well-known poems and writers as well as introductions to poets and texts that may be more unfamiliar. The paired readings of poems in each chapter also invite synchronic and interconnected lessons that make readers compare, for example, communal conventions in colonial poetry to collective poetics in contemporary performance poetry. The handbook encourages readings across and against literary periods, while annotated paired readings and additional reading suggestions should inspire students to analyze poems as particular sites of historical and political meaning. Being both a manual in terms of current theoretical directions in literary studies and a guide to practical criticism, *A History of American Poetry* helps students to further explore the diversity and multiple poetic traditions that make up American poetry in its intersections with historical contexts and other literatures.

***

The editors wish to thank those who made the publication of this handbook possible: first of all, the people who were willing to share their expertise and knowledge and took part in our project, and those who invested their invaluable energy and proficiency in the process of getting this volume ready for publication, notably Nida Naseer, Mareike Zapp, and Frank Newton. The editors also owe special thanks to Patricia Godsave and her eagle-eyed copy-editing as well as her steadfast advice from which both the editors and contributors profited greatly. Finally, we are indebted to Ansgar and Vera Nünning, the general editors of the Handbook in Literary Study Series, and the publisher, Erwin Otto, who encouraged us in seeing this book to print.

Mainz, July 2015   Oliver Scheiding, René Dietrich, Clemens Spahr

References

Ashton, Jennifer (ed.). 2013. *The Cambridge Companion to American Poetry since 1945*. Cambridge: Cambridge UP.

Beach, Christopher. 1999. *Poetic Culture: Contemporary American Poetry between Community and Institution*. Evanston: Northwestern UP.

Bendixen, Alfred and Stephen Burt (eds.). 2014. *The Cambridge History of American Poetry*. Cambridge: Cambridge UP.

Chinitz, David E. and Gail McDonald (ed.). 2014. *A Companion to Modernist Poetry*. Malden, MA. Wiley Blackwell.

Fishkin, Shelley Fisher. 2005. "Crossroads of Cultures: The Transnational Turn in American Studies." In: *American Quarterly* 57: 17-57.

Fredman, Stephen (ed.). 2005. *A Concise Companion to Twentieth-Century American Poetry*. Malden, MA. Wiley Blackwell.

Larson, Kerry (ed.). 2011. *The Cambridge Companion to Nineteenth-Century American Poetry*. Cambridge: Cambridge UP.

Levander, Caroline F. 2013. *Where is American Literature?*. Malden, MA: Wiley Blackwell.

Marcus, Greil and Werner Sollors (eds.). 2009. *A New Literary History of America*. Cambridge, MA: The Belknap P of Harvard UP.

Nelson, Cary (ed.). 2012. *The Oxford Handbook of Modern and Contemporary American Poetry*. Oxford: Oxford UP.

Nicholls, Peter. 2009. *Modernisms: A Literary Guide*. 2nd ed. New York: Palgrave.

Parker, Robert Dale (ed.). 2011. *Changing is Not Vanishing: A Collection of American Indian Poetry to 1930*. Philadelphia: U of Pennsylvania P.

Ramazani, Jahan. 2009. *A Transnational Poetics*. Chicago: U of Chicago P.

Scheiding, Oliver and Martin Seidl (eds.). 2014. *Worlding America: A Transnational Anthology of Short Narratives before 1800*. Stanford, CA: Stanford UP.

I Early American Poetry

1.

Religious Poetry and New England Verse

Anne Bradstreet's "Here followes some verses upon the burning
of our House" and Edward Taylor's "Huswifery"

Ludwig Deringer

1. The Diversity of Beginnings in American Poetry

The "very earliest extant poem written in the New World" is "Insula nomen habet
generosum matris amatae" (1522), a piece by Alessandro Geraldini (c. 1455-
1524) consisting of seven "elegiac couplets" about the Caribbean island of
Gratiosa (Kaiser 1972: 434). The poem exemplifies several paradigms defining
the early literatures of the Americas: their embeddedness in the contexts and
complexities of colonization and cultural transfer, their rhetorical and generic
variegation rather than normativity, and their multilingualism, including the
classical languages.

Understanding American literatures and cultures hinges upon the consideration of their origins in the Early Modern period. Irrespective of other givens, the
fact that American authors have always addressed America's literary and cultural beginnings is evidence enough. From the fifteenth century onward, a defining paradigm of American pluralism and multiculturality has been religion,
and throughout the seventeenth and early eighteenth centuries, the predominant variety of the American Dream is religious freedom. Another parameter of
diversity is region: on the North Atlantic seaboard, the distinctive settlement
areas are New England, the Middle Atlantic, and the Southern Atlantic colonies.

While early America is multilingual, multiregional, and multidenominational,
New England is characterized by the ethnic, linguistic, and religious homogen-
eity of English refugees seeking spiritual freedom as Puritans and followers of
the French Swiss Reformer Jean Calvin (1509-1564). As in New England, Calvinist culture prevails in neighboring Nieuw Nederland, and in both colonies,
literatures in Latin (see Kaiser 1982) as well as in the vernacular languages (see
Blom forthcoming) exist. Moreover, literary interrelations between Nieuw Nederland and New England are cultivated, as evidenced, for example, by the poetry
of Henricus Selijns (1636-1701) (see Murphy 1966 [1865]). Equally, the German
settlements in Pennsylvania can lay claim to a considerable body of poetry and
hymnody in the vernacular, influenced by late medieval, Reformation, and Baroque traditions (see Arndt/Eck 1989).

New England culture—in particular, New England Puritanism—has been
among the most influential traditions in America up to the twenty-first century.
Emily Dickinson, for one, even declared it a lasting impact on her world view: "I
see—New Englandly—" ("The Robin's my Criterion for Tune—", c. 1861). In intellectual history, New England provides the link between ancient Israel and
Protestant America, constituting the seedbed of the Judeo-Christian tradition in
the New World. Seventeenth-century New England Puritanism synonymizes the
attempt, communally and individually, at living a life with God. Puritanism
holds that a sense of order is reflected in *structure*, and that such order, as a
manifestation of meaning, does indeed exist—against any appearance to the

contrary—, even in the face of catastrophe. In essence, Puritan culture and literature are expressions of late medieval epistemes in transition to early modern
civilization. The world view of New England Puritanism is grounded in the theocentric-providential rather than the Cartesian-progressivist world view. All the
more is it ironic that even from its formative years, American Puritanism begins
to erode into an ideology of spiritual domination and imperialist oppression of
the Native American nations and their cultures.

Three transplanted hermeneutical systems of European thought and culture
that have shaped early America indelibly are providentialism, mysticism, and
rhetoric; all three lend themselves to actualization in the arts in general and
poetry in particular. As providentialism, mysticism, and rhetoric were part of
the standard university curricula in both Europe and the New World, there can
be no doubt that these traditions were known to, and applied by, colonial American authors, of the first immigrant generation and of subsequent generations
alike. To adequately interpret and historically place early American poetry, it
needs to be examined on its own terms; i.e., application of the theories under
which it was produced is a prerequisite.

Mysticism and rhetoric are transnational and intercontinental systems in
the age of colonial expansion. Mysticism designates a late medieval practice of
contemplation that aims for the union of the soul and God (*unio mystica*) and,
across the arts, generates a system of pictorial and verbal imagery particularly
favored by the poets of the Baroque and the Colonial Baroque. Rhetoric, a complex system of persuasive communication, originated in Classical Antiquity and
was further developed during both the Renaissance and Baroque periods, and
through Humanism, and New England Puritanism; it was considered the "universal science," a theoretical and technical edifice of which literary stylistics is
only one segment.

Poetry, in the beginnings of civilizations, emerges in cults and rites. Its character is manifested by the poet-priest in song or speech. From rite to rap, form
as music and condensed speech—emphasizing patterns of repetition and variation (but not necessarily rhyme)—is genre-constitutive to poetry of all ages and
cultures: primeval, autochthonous, 'Western,' global, and digital alike. From
Greek and Roman Antiquity to the early Middle Ages (c. 400-700 A.D.), poetry is
conceptualized as a type of communication with the gods. In ancient Israel,
poetic speech is religious speech, elemental to the individual and communal
communication between the people and their God, Jahwe. Hence, in the Judeo-
Christian tradition, the concept of the 'Word' comprises both human language
as well as Scripture, the Word of God in its ultimate physical and metaphysical
reality: Christ, the Word Incarnate (John 1:1). This explains the supremacy of
the 'Word' over icon and liturgy in the Reformation, and thus in Protestantism,
including the Lutheran, Reformed, and Calvinist (i.e., Puritan) churches in
Europe and America. Rhetoric—'the art of speaking/writing well'—is understood
as the most congenial frame of reference and expression of spiritual reality. On
the ontological status of rhetoric, Debora Shuger (2000) has put forth an astute
critique: she argues that philosophy—supposed by some to be purely "rational"
(52 passim)—is not the exclusive discipline aiming for "the True and the Good"
(60) but that rhetoric—supposed to be purely "emotional" (61 passim), hence
"unserious" (48)—in its own right is a "commitment to the . . . issues of human
existence, whether political or spiritual" (50).

In the theocentric-providential body politic, religion encompasses all forms of cultural expression. Religion and politics converge in the church-state, with rhetoric serving as a link between the spiritual and the public spheres. Consequentially, religious literature in the New England colonies is per se political literature, and vice versa. The Massachusetts Bay Colony was a society in which the most significant political speeches were sermons, as on Election Days or Public Fast Days. Due to its rootedness in the culture at large, rhetoric informs oratory and literature in a process of cross-mediality as seen, for example, in the epicedium as a dual genre: the funeral sermon and the funeral elegy. The foremost genres of colonial New England literature are nonfiction and poetry. In nonfictional prose, homiletics (the art of sermonizing), oratory, historiography, and life writing predominate. Poetry includes classic subgenres such as the ode, the hymn, the threnody, the meditation, the epitaph, the acrostic, and the anagram, but is not at all limited to prescriptive European poetics. Other representative poetic form types are the jeremiad (a call to repentance in the form of the 'long poem'), the song, travel writing in verse, and promotional, satirical, or occasional poems. A host of poets created a sizeable corpus serving functions both public and private that today are part of America's cultural memory. Some of the more prominent textual examples include "Good News from New-England," a piece of promotional writing in verse by Edward Johnson; "From my years young in dayes of Youth" ["Epitaphium Meum"] by William Bradford, the founding governor of Plymouth Plantation; "The Day of Doom" by the minister Michael Wigglesworth, a jeremiad; and the epigrammatic poems by Roger Williams, the founder of Rhode Island, which are interspersed in his linguistic study *A Key into the Language of America* (1643) as poetic commentaries on life in the colony, venting his criticism of intolerance and advocating respectful coexistence with the Native nations. According to Heather Dubrow (2000: 121-2), religious poetry does not constitute a genre per se, but in sixteenth-century English poetry already, the introspective vein of Protestantism is obviously conducive to the diversification of the lyric.

The most artistic poetries in New England verse are the oeuvres of Anne Bradstreet (c. 1612-1672) and Edward Taylor (c. 1642-1729). Bradstreet, a member of the Massachusetts Bay Colony elite as the daughter of Governor Thomas Dudley and the wife of Simon Bradstreet, later on himself Governor of the Colony, ranks superior among American women poets. Apparently she did not intend publication (McElrath, Jr./Robb 1981: xxviii). The two major collections of her poetry are *The Tenth Muse lately Sprung Up in America* (London, 1650) and *Several Poems* (Boston, 1678). While she wrote erudite conventional verse in her earlier period, such as the so-called "Quaternions" ("The Four Ages of Man," "The Four Monarchies," etc.), her most intriguing texts are devoted to her family or deal with her everyday life from a profoundly religious perspective, such as the love poem "To My Dear and Loving Husband"; her poems on the birth, or death, of several of her children and grandchildren, e.g., "On my dear Grand-child Simon Bradstreet Who dyed on 16. Novemb. 1669, being but a moneth and one day old"; a poem giving thanks "[For Delivere] From another sore fitt. etc."; "Here follows some verses upon the burning of our House" (to be examined below); the meditation "The Vanity of all worldly things"; or, anticipating her death, "As weary pilgrim, now at rest." An outstanding specimen of her art is the long poem "Contemplations."

Edward Taylor served as a Puritan minister in Westfield, Massachusetts from 1671 to 1725, where he wrote *Preparatory Meditations before my Approach to the Lords Supper* (also known as *Sacramental Meditations*) between 1682 and 1726, and *Christographia* (1701-1703), a series on fourteen cardinal Biblical verses, with each one treated in a sermon and an accompanying poem. Comparisons between a given sermon and the appertaining poem are most informative regarding Taylor's homiletics and poetics, while the genres of both the sermon and the poem were crafted on the basis of contemporaneous rhetorical theory and practice. "Huswifery," one of his few miscellaneous poems, will be compared to Bradstreet's "Verses" below. The two selections are among their authors' most frequently anthologized and analyzed pieces. Both texts thematize the tension between the empirical and the transcendent, yet differ markedly in attitude, mood, tone, diction, and imagery. Both employ the motif of the house and of life around the house but vary in poeticity and intent. As for structure, neither of the two samples is patterned on European form types.

"Verses" and "Huswifery" may be read as a stylized memoir and a prayer, respectively. Whereas Bradstreet's poem derives from a specific occasion and crisis, Taylor's is a meditation on universal matters of spiritual growth, a central issue in Puritan theology. Bradstreet—while not identifying her audience—appears to address her family, Taylor invokes God. The hallmark of both Bradstreet's "Verses" and Taylor's "Huswifery" is the fusion of art and Biblical faith.

2. Trying Faith, Living Faith: Anne Bradstreet's "Here followes some verses upon the burning of our House" (undated)

Anne Bradstreet's poem (Meserole 1972: 35-6) is a personal retrospective on the devastating experience of seeing one's family home go up in flames, and foreseeing the difficulties of a new start in a seventeenth-century colonial environment. The poem was left untitled and is among those poems that the editors, McElrath, Jr. and Robb, classify under the heading "In Simon's Hand" (213-37), with the transcriptions by the author's son. Current textual variants often include the title added by Simon Bradstreet: "Here followes some verses upon the burning of our House, July 10th, 1666. Copyed out of a loose Paper" (Meserole 1972: 35). When the fire consumed their comfortable mansion in Andover, Anne Bradstreet was about 54 years old. The tone at the beginning of "Verses" is panic; at the end, tranquillity. What accounts for this particular movement, and how is it presented?

Irrespective of variations in tone and intention, the poem on the whole is argumentative in stance. Argumentation constitutes the very essence of rhetoric, pertaining to all levels of the text (*oratio*): its theme (*inventio*), structure (*dispositio*), and style (*elocutio*). The structure of "Verses" reflects the changing sensibilities of the poet. Bradstreet's nine-stanza poem falls into three sections of three stanzas each. Functional rather than mechanical, this tripartite arrangement corresponds to three time levels and three tenses. Section 1 (st. 1-3) is a retelling, in the past tense, of the immediacy of the outbreak of the fire. Section 2 marks a transition from narrative to contemplation. The first part of section 2 (st. 4, l. 1; st. 5, l. 2) is still in the past tense but by now at further remove from the time of the fire ("When by the Ruines oft I past", st. 4, l. 3). The second part of section 2 (st. 5-6) is a lament on the dreariness brought upon the speaker by the catastrophe. Slight but meaningful, a change in perspective and time structure takes place in the fifth stanza: lines 1-2 are in the past tense, lines 4-5 in the future tense, while line 3 indicates a turning point as it employs the present tense ("lye"). Bradstreet's skillful handling of temporality and the tenses thus symbolizes her all-encompassing grief. Stanzas 5 and 6 constitute the crisis in the poem's ideational and emotional movement, in which the poet's grief is most intense (st. 6, l. 6). Significantly, the discourse in stanzas 5 and 6 is interior monologue.

Section 3 (st. 7-9) presents the spiritual assessment of the loss, thereby marking the climax of the poem: faith in the face of tragedy, one of the deep paradoxes of Christian existence. This section references the future in time and eternity and is again characterized by a change in perspective and the rhetorical situation. Whereas in stanzas 5 and 6 (st. 5, l. 5 to st. 6, l. 6) the poet addressed the *house* in interior monologue, in all of section 3 she turns to her innermost self—her *heart* (st. 7, l. 1)—in imagined interior dialogue. Section 3, in a nutshell, blends the three prototypical rhetorical speech/text types: the judicial, the deliberative, and the panegyric. Stanza 7 (ll. 1-4) represents an emphatical self-accusation of the speaker "chid[ing]" her heart, by way of three rhetorical questions (st. 7, ll. 2-4), the only questions in the poem:

> And did thy wealth on earth abide?
> Didst fix thy hope on mouldring dust,
> The arm of flesh didst make thy trust?

Self-reproach is followed by self-consolation (st. 7, ll. 5-6) with the single command in the poem: "Raise up thy thoughts above the sky" (l. 5). Consequentially, stanza 8 represents (self-)deliberation, serving as a reminder and a strengthening of the poet's faith through a series of reasons (lines 1-6), as in "Thou hast an house on high erect" (l. 1), emphasized by the "hast"/"high" alliteration. In conclusion, stanza 9 blends deliberation and panegyric: the soul's debate with itself and the poet's ensuing praise of God. Contemplating God's benevolence turns into gratitude, this meditative process thus revealing itself to be a form of spiritual clarification, composure being reflected in composition. In the third section, the concreteness of the first and middle sections is problematized in the light of Biblical imagery. In the final analysis, the poem's structure turns out to be of systematic and sophisticated crafting.

In combination with structure, it is style that organizes the argumentation, the individual figures and tropes functioning as structural units in their own right. Interconnecting religion and rhetoric, they enhance the poem's substance. Stanza form generally consists of three rhyme pairs in iambic tetrameter, with a given line pair expressing one particular idea. A number of representative passages will serve as illustrations of Bradstreet's technique.

While panic finds expression in hypotaxis and metrical irregularity ("I, starting up," st. 2, l. 1), prosodic regularity suggests the poet's regained inner stability by means of stichometry (the principle of one line consisting of one complete sentence), parataxis, and syntactic symmetry, in interplay with the metrical symmetry of isocolon (a parallel structure, here using medial caesura, monosyllabism and word repetition): "Yea so it was, and so 'twas just" (st. 3, l. 4). As section 2 reproduces the poet's observation of the house in "Ruines" (st. 4, l. 3), rhetorical devices vividly foreground the furnishings and the convivial atmosphere of the home against the gloom caused by the fire: adverbs of place, demonstratives, and again isocolon: "Here . . . that" correlated with "there that"

("Here stood that Trunk, and there that chest," st. 5, l. 1); *distributio*: "Trunk,"
"chest," "roof," "Table," "tale," "Candle" (running from st. 5, l. 1 to st. 6, l. 4); and
chiastic anaphora: "Nor" (st. 5, l. 6)—"No" (st. 6, l. 1)—"Nor" (st. 6, l. 2)—"No"
(st. 6, l. 3)—"Nor" (st. 6, l. 4). The series of five negations underscores the poet's
sense of negativity.

The former atmosphere of the house is suggested in overtones of melancholy
but never sentimentality. The poet admonishes herself to abstain from com-
plaint (st. 3, l. 5), and when grief is welling up anew, recollection does not give
in to resignation, with the speaker, literally, commending herself 'to God':
"Adeiu, Adeiu" (a concoction of Latin *deo* and French *à dieu*!). The exclamation
"All's vanity" (st. 6, l. 6), in end-stopped position, completes section 2; an omnipresent Baroque motif, literally echoing *Ecclesiastes* 1:2.

In literature as in oratory, the linkage between subject matter and style is
imagery. Protestant culture in general and New England Puritan poetics in particular discourage visual representation. Rather than the subjective imagination, the Bible and religious literature are the preferred sources of poetic and
cultural imagery. The measure of a poet's success, therefore, is the representation of experiential life in the light of Biblical tenets, eschewing conventionalism
at the same time.

Incorporated into the theme of the house and its destruction by fire, the two
structural image clusters in "Here followes some verses" are 'ownership' and
'justice,' expressing the relationship between God and humankind. The first
cluster is composed of two metaphorical patterns: 'the owner as giver' and 'the
owner as host.' From colonial times onward, 'ownership' has been a key concept
in American culture, and Bradstreet skillfully works into the poem a field of
Calvinist key words designating 'possessions,' both material and immaterial, in
varying connotations: "goods" (st. 3, l. 2), "store" (st. 5, l. 2), "pleasant things"
(st. 5, l. 3), "wealth" (st. 7, l. 2; st. 9, l. 3), "Prise" (st. 9, l. 1), "his Gift" (st. 9, l. 2),
"my Pelf . . . my Store" (st. 9, l. 4), "Treasure" (st. 9, l. 6). All denote concrete and
abstract values in antithetical, even polar, fashion. The *vanitas* motif becomes
evident through an anticlimax of commodities turned to "Ruines" (st. 4, l. 3)—
"ashes" (st. 5, l. 3)—"mouldring dust" (st. 7, l. 3). The epitomizing contrast of
empirical and eschatological possessions lies in the tension of "dunghill" (st. 7,
l. 6) and "Treasure" (st. 9, l. 6). Whereas the "I" had always *known* ownership to
be God's gift (st. 3, l. 2) as a result of her instruction, in the end she *understands* ownership to be a "Gift" (st. 9, l. 2) as a result of affliction ("his own"—
"not mine," st. 3, l. 5 and "his Gift"—"thine own," st. 9, l. 2). In this construction
each line individually carries two members of identical meaning: one that contrasts God and self in stanza 3, l. 5, and one in stanza 9, l. 2 where God's "Gift"
has by now become the poet's possession. The two lines are arranged in chiastic
order with "his own"—"thine own" and "not mine"—"his Gift" forming two antithetical pairs. Positioned toward the ends of sections 1 and 3, respectively, the
two lines—spanning the better part of the poem—mirror the relationship between God and self. Thus, from personal shock, Bradstreet develops a deliberation on a central creed of the Christian faith: God's gift of eternal life, drawing
on the New Testament imagery of Christ having "paid" for the sins of mankind
on the Cross, thus having "purchased" freedom as God's "Gift." Bradstreet enhances the meaning by various stylistic devices, such as triplicate alliteration:
"purchased"—"paid"—"Prise" (st. 8, l. 5; st. 9, l. 1); internal rhyme: "glory richly"

(st. 8, l. 3); and paradox (st. 9, ll. 1-2), suggesting the relation between the finite world and infinity: "A Prise so vast as is unknown" (st. 9, l. 1).

A paraphrase from the Book of *Job* in section 1 (st. 3, l. 2) of the poem—"I blest his Name that gave and took"—corresponds, in section 3 (st. 8, l. 1), to "Thou hast an house on high erect," intertextualizing Christ's words to his disciples before his Crucifixion: "In my Father's house are many mansions" (John 14:2). Incidentally, in 1709-1710, Taylor made this very passage the theme of his "94. Meditation (Second Series)" (Stanford 1977: 251-2). Evidently, the Biblical motif connecting Bradstreet's Andover house both to that of Job and to the 'house' that God has prepared for mankind holds far-reaching implications.

The second metaphorical pattern composing the cluster of 'ownership' is 'hospitality', employed in a historical and personal as well as a transhistorical and transcendent sense. The common denominator is again 'gift' (st. 5, l. 5; st. 6, l. 6). In this constellation the 'owner' figures as the 'host' to a 'visitor.' Bradstreet recalls past festivities enjoyed in her family home ("Under thy roof no guest shall sitt," st. 5, l. 5), the sociable atmosphere contrasting sharply with the deadening "silence" of emptiness (st. 1, l. 1; st. 6, l. 5). She imagines herself 'fleeing' (st. 8, l. 4) to heaven ("though this bee fled," st. 8, l. 4) to become a 'guest,' a 'resident,' and an 'owner' there herself, the antithesis of "dust" (st. 3, l. 3; st. 7, l. 3) and "permanent" (st. 8, l. 4) being crucial.

To a Christian poet like Bradstreet, *all* life—earthly and eternal—comes as a gift. To accept as a gift what is 'priced' "so vast as is unknown" (st. 9, l. 1) is a man's or a woman's ultimate justification, or "just[ice]" (st. 3, l. 4). At the same time, an individual's "just[ice]" is to acknowledge God's sovereignty and to set one's "trust" (st. 7, l. 4) and "hope" (st. 7, l. 3; st. 9, l. 6) solely in him. Consistently, the poet declares God's 'taking away' of her Andover house an act of justice ("just," st. 3, l. 4; "justly," st. 4, l. 1). With Bradstreet's reasoning encapsulating a Christian code of living, the poem's theological substance crystallizes in two rhyme pairs as strategic connectors: "dust"—"just" (st. 3, ll. 3-4) and "dust"—"trust" (st. 7, ll. 3-4). Scripture does not view as a weakness the fact that humans cannot accomplish anything of their own accord; it rather cherishes the idea that they find strength in their dependence on God. To Bradstreet, this is a foregone conclusion. At Jahwe's ordainment of the covenant with Israel, Abraham "believed in the Lord; and he counted it to him for *righteousness*" (emphasis added; Genesis 15:6). In Protestant theology, this is what constitutes "justification by faith"—the decisive concept in the emergence of the Reformation which is, to this day, a cornerstone of Protestantism (Martin Luther's *Rechtfertigungslehre*). To Bradstreet—a literary predecessor of Emily Dickinson—the finality of loss and the perseverance in faith are not mutually exclusive. On the contrary: not only does Bradstreet *not* draw this idea into question—she even affirms it. To her, doing so is not constraint but freedom. With Bradstreet, as with Job, it is neither the self nor a group that are autonomous but God.

Neither is Puritan aesthetics autonomous: *l'art pour Dieu* rather than *l'art pour l'art*. According to the Biblical "way of life," life in its entirety ideally is worship. The poet's initial despair eventually does not turn to rebellion or bitterness, but to acquiescence, out of her own free will, in tranquility. Bradstreet is certain that her existence is grounded, not in her earthly life, but in God. It is only with the dawn of Romanticism that the conception of the autonomous self will shape European and Transatlantic epistemology and literature.

3. For the Love of God: Edward Taylor's "Huswifery" (undated)

Perhaps the most demanding challenge to readers of Edward Taylor is the stance of one to whom the goodness of God is beyond argument. To be sure, Taylor's position is that of a personality grounded in faith that is experienced. The tranquility Bradstreet struggles for in "Verses" is a given for Taylor—in all his lyric poetry—from the outset. Taylor's argumentation is for spiritual growth, for the ability to praise God in the most appropriate way, and for the re-presentation of God's "Excellency"—a key motif in Taylor's oeuvre. His type of argumentation is, in short, a paragon of the panegyric as differentiated from the deliberative. Any approach to Edward Taylor must take into account that his ultimate goal is life with God, and that praising God is the purpose of his poetry. It is true that to praise God is a distinctive characteristic of Calvinism, given more emphasis here than by the other churches of Protestantism (Börger 1967 [1953]: 57; Calvin 1960, I: 764), but to Taylor lauding God is not a clerical exercise; it is the impulse and joy of his life.

Taylor's poetry, like Bradstreet's, exemplifies the fusion of spirituality, rhetoric, and art in seventeenth-century verse—a fusion of the pragmatic and the beautiful. From its first line to its last, "Huswifery" (Meserole 1972: 142-3) invokes God directly (*apostrophe*), without emotional turning points, shifts in perspective, or changes in the rhetorical situation. The tone is characterized by deep introspection. In form and attitude, "Huswifery" is not a lament in crisis, but a lyrical meditation on the desired personal union with God. By this rationale the poem falls into the mystical tradition in Western poetry full well.

The Puritanism—or Biblicality—of "Verses" and "Huswifery" lies in their respective awareness of the tension between the physical and the metaphysical, conceptualized as the polarity of "dust" and "glory" by Bradstreet, and as a development from "[in]compleate[ness]" (st. 1, l. 1) to "glory" (st. 3, l. 6) by Taylor. The latter consistently makes the juncture between a modest and the most sacred reality a pervasive configurational principle in "Huswifery." The technical languages of cloth-making and Biblical theology coalesce, thereby creating the poem's unique idiom. To Taylor and his parishioners, Westfield, Massachusetts embodies the American frontier. 'Housework,' i.e., chores like manufacturing textiles, is the daily routine on the settler farms and in the pioneer households. From his experiential reality, the poet derives his 'homely diction,' in "Huswifery" as in his oeuvre as a whole.

From the very beginning of the poem, Taylor uses cloth-making as a bold allegorical pattern, and in doing so, appears to be anticipating a credo in American literary history that is later voiced by William Carlos Williams: "No ideas but in things" (in "A Sort of A Song"). In stanzas 1 and 2 of "Huswifery," Taylor asks for transformation both in a figurative and a literal, personal, sense. He pictures God as a weaver and himself as God's "Spin[n]ing Wheele" (st. 1, l. 1) and "Loome" (st. 2, l. 1). The end product, i.e., the ornamented robe, will adorn the poet himself, thereby praising the "make[r]" (st. 2, l. 1), God. Thematic development, amplified in the work sequences of 'spinning' (st. 1), 'knitting,' 'weaving,' 'fulling,' 'dyeing' (st. 2), and 'clothing' (st. 3), delineates poetic structure. The techniques of web production and text production merge and mirror each other, to express the idea of intertwining both between theme and form and between God and the poet in the experience of *unio mystica* (on historical spinning and weaving cf. Rossi et al. 2009: 235-48).

The poem emerges in a set of correspondences between two detailed strings of key terms, one technical and allegorical, and the other religious and literary. The technical-allegorical series comprises objects and activities of cloth-making. The objects include fixtures: "Spin[n]ing Wheele" (st. 1, l. 1); "Distaff" (st. 1, l. 2); "Flyers" (st. 1, l. 3); "Spoole" (st. 1, l. 4); "Reele" (st. 1, l. 5); "Wheele" (st. 1, l. 6); "Loome" (st. 2, l. 1); and "Fulling Mills" (st. 2, l. 4) that are 'interwoven' with textile materials: "yarn" (st. 1, l. 6); "Twine" (st. 2, l. 1); "Web" (st. 2, l. 3); "Colours" (st. 2, l. 5); "Flowers" (st. 2, l. 6); "Holy robes" (st. 3, l. 6). Collocated to the corpus of activities, the corpus of textile materials is organized in a climax to reflect the work process: "reele the yarn" (st. 1, l. 6); "knit . . . this Twine" (st. 2, l. 1); "winde quills" (st. 2, l. 2); "Then weave the Web" (st. 2, l. 3); "Then dy the same" (st. 2, l. 5); "Then cloath therewith" (st. 3, l. 1). The motif of 'twining' (st. 2, l. 1) God and self is reinforced by the correspondences of the respective personal or possessive pronouns. Some of the more ingenious ones are: "Make me . . . thy Spin[n]ing Wheele" (st. 1, l. 1); "Thy Holy Worde my Distaff make," emphasized by internal rhyme (st. 1, l. 2); and "Make mine Affections thy Swift Flyers," underscored by assonance (st. 1, l. 3).

Each of the interrelations between the layers of technical-allegorical and religious-literal speech most poetically highlights a unique quality of the emerging closeness of self and God. All the human faculties—cognitive, pragmatic, affective—are involved: "Conversation" (st. 1, l. 5); "Understanding, Will, / Affections, Judgment, Conscience, Memory" (st. 3, ll. 1-2); "Words and Actions" (st. 3, l. 3); "My wayes" (st. 3, l. 4). In effect, the self as such is prepared by the Creator—his "Holy Worde" (st. 1, l. 2) and his "Holy Spirit" (st. 2, l. 2). Taylor's choice of individual images is exquisite, as when he allegorizes his soul to be the spool of the Lord's spinning wheel that accumulates "the yarn" (st. 1, l. 4), i.e., the yield, of God's working on the soul. If the "twine" and the "yarn" are the connecting lines between God and the "I," the completed "robe" signifies that all the self's identity has fused with God, and that he has conferred "sanctification" upon the speaker. The technical-allegorical process ends with the dyeing, or ornamentation, of the as yet coarse cloth. The emblematic "Heavenly Colours Choice" (st. 2, l. 5) and "Flowers of Paradise" (st. 2, l. 6) are the only evocations of colors and plants, suggesting transcendent—eternal—reality, or "perfection" ("56. Meditation. Second Series," st. 4, l. 4). The physical process of transforming fiber into fabric allegorizes, in rising order (a minore ad maius), the spiritual process of transforming imperfection into "glory," the poet envisioning "righteousness" in the theology of the Old Testament (Gen. 15:6) or "sanctification" in its New Testament equivalent (cf. Brumm 1973: 46-7). Focusing on the evolving mystical union, Taylor, on the lexical level, works with a contrast of etymologies; all of the mechanical fixtures occur as concretes of Germanic origin, most of the psychological and spiritual faculties as abstracts of Romance provenance.

As for structure, Taylor employs a subtle interplay of syntax, meter, and stanzaic composition in contouring "Huswifery." His most frequent sentence type is the imperative clause in the form of a petition to the Lord. Taylor accumulates eleven imperatives across the poem's eighteen lines, eight of which are alliterative and reiterative collocations using "make": anaphoric "Make me" (st. 1, l. 1; st. 2, l. 2); "make for mee" (st. 1, l. 2); "Make mine Affections" (st. 1, l. 3); "make my Soule" (st. 1, l. 4); "My Conversation make" (st. 1, l. 5); "make thy Holy Spirit" (st. 2, l. 2); and "Thine Ordinances make my . . . Mills" (st. 2, l. 4). When the weaving is complete, the quality of the product is appraised in a succinct statement, with the shortest sentence in the exact middle of the poem, line 9: "The yarn is fine." The statement is foregrounded by incisive caesuras—one preceding and one following it. All of the petitions designate God as the agent power. As a result ("that," st. 3, l. 3) of God's 'preparing' the poet, the latter is convinced in conclusion that "mine apparel shall display . . . / That I am Cloathd in Holy robes for glory" (st. 3, ll. 5-6). Only now is there a change in grammatical subject from God to "mine apparel" (st. 3, l. 3), while the speaker (Taylor himself) not even once figures as the grammatical subject, hence the agent power. No earlier than the very last line does the "I" come to the fore, yet even here it is not in the active voice: "I am Cloathd" (st. 3, l. 6). In this way the poet stresses that it is solely through *grace* that he is prepared for the action that is his life's essence to perform: to "display" God's "glory" (st. 3, l. 5; l. 6). As with Bradstreet, Taylor's ultimate 'activity' is, by way of receiving and reflecting, to laud God.

The poem's structural boundaries are further differentiated by a shift in sentence structure and sentence style. 'Simple' and compound sentences, resulting in parataxis, are used in stanzas 1 and 2; complex sentences, resulting in hypotaxis, predominate in stanza 3, namely, the purpose clause "that their shine may fill" (st. 3, l. 3), and the object clause "That I am Cloathd" (st. 3, l. 6). Syntactic variegation thus symbolizes the poet's progression toward union with the Lord. Adding to the cohesion of syntax and line, the coordinating conjunctions "And" (st. 1, ll. 4, 6; st. 2, l. 2) alternate with adverbs of time, "Then" (st. 2, l. 1; st. 2, ll. 3, 5; st. 6, ll. 1, 5), in an ongoing "And—Then" movement resembling the manufacturing process. For sonic variation, lines ending in metrical pauses alternate with end-stopped lines. Whereas the prosodic principle in stanzas 1 and 2 is stichometry, in stanza 3 the rhythm is accelerated by enjambements due to heightened emotionality.

As for style, "Huswifery" uses figures on the phonic, lexical, and syntactic levels to make for variation, structural cohesion, and thematic enhancement. On the phonic level, the six-line stanza in iambic pentameter, combining cross rhyme in lines 1-4 with pair rhyme in lines 5-6 (ababcc), is capacious and flexible enough to accommodate the intricate processes of production and of prayer. The concatenation of two cross rhymes and one rhyme pair in a closed couplet again aptly represents the idea of 'interweaving.' A net of 'interwoven' sound sequences permeating the poem is formed by alliteration and assonance. Some of the more effective alliterations are "Soule"—"Spoole" (st. 1, l. 4) and "pinkt"—"Paradise" (st. 2, l. 6). Among the most sonorous assonances, suggesting harmonious closeness with the Lord, are "me"—"Wheele"—"compleate" in the opening line; "reele"—"Wheele" (st. 1, l. 6); and, in the concluding line, a sequence symbolizing the ideas of gradation, union, and sublimity: the diphthongal "Cloathd"—"Holy"—"robes" (st. 3, l. 6). Occasionally, Taylor correlates internal rhyme pairs by using two different diphthongs, as in "my"—"thy" and "Soule"—"holy," which results in the phonic chiasmus "my Soule thy holy [Spoole]" (st. 1, l. 4).

On the lexical and syntactic levels, Taylor prefers figures such as parallelism (here, in the form of isocolon: "make my Soule thy holy Spoole," st. 1, l. 4); enumeration ("mine Understanding, Will, / Affections, Judgment, Conscience, Memory," st. 3, ll. 1-2), and repetition ("Wheele," st. 1, ll. 1, 6; "yarn," st. 1, ll. 6, 9; "Affections," st. 1, l. 3 and st. 3, l. 2; "Holy Worde," st. 1, l. 2; "holy Spoole," st. 1, l. 4; "Holy Spirit," st. 2, l. 2; "Holy robes," st. 3, l. 6). All remaining adjectives in the poem cohere with "holy" to create a semantic field of plenitude, namely, "compleate" (st. 1, l. 1), "neate" (st. 1, l. 3), "fine" (st. 2, l. 3), "Heavenly" (st. 2, l. 5), "pinkt" (st. 2, l. 6), and "Varnish't" (st. 2, l. 6). *Figura etymologica* ("weave the Web," st. 2, l. 3) and *polyptoton* ("thy Reele, / And reele the yarn," st. 1, ll. 5-6) add texture to the diction. A sophisticated instance of *polyptoton* is a frame suggesting the intimacy of *unio mystica* in the first and the final lines of stanza three, the latter of course constituting the closing line of the poem: "Then cloath" (st. 3, l. 1)—"That I am Cloathd" (st. 3, l. 6).

Imagery, as in Bradstreet's "Verses," serves to blend style and substance. One of the most subtle images in "Huswifery" is the motif of the reflected light, signifying the resplendence of God's glory in the "Words and Actions" of the "I." The motif unfolds in the speaker's wish "that their shine may fill / My wayes with glory and thee glorify" and is highlighted by *polyptoton* (st. 3, ll. 1-2). Whatever 'light' the poet in the end will be able to offer *to* God through his "Words and Actions" had originated *in* God, and if Taylor can only 'glorify' God by 're-flecting' God's splendor, it is evident to him that humanity cannot do or be anything—cannot exist—in a state of separation from the Lord. Separation from God, in the Christian as in the Hebrew Bible, is the quintessential meaning of 'sin.' In a theme-related poem, "Another upon the Same" (undated, Stanford 1977 [1960]: 468), Taylor submits a straightforward petition: "Cut off . . . my sins" (st. 2, l. 3), the "sins" pictured as refuse cloth on the loom. Here the poet openly names sin. He reiterates his plea as the weaver's shuttle turns into a weapon, with occupational jargon thus turning into religious discourse: "The shuttle shoot" (st. 2, l. 3). The metaphor, intensified by sibilant alliteration of the fricative, in onomatopoeic, near-synaesthetic expressivity, visualizes the discharge, by the shuttle, of the refuse of the poet's life, which is sin. Again, an antidote to this line is suggested in "94. Meditation (Second Series)" as the poetic persona exclaims: "Oh! that my Meditations all were frindg'd / With Sanctifying Gifts" (st. 4, ll. 1-2). Yet Taylor not only names that which damages, but also that which strengthens his life: "the web of *Grace* in mee" (emphasis added, "Another upon the Same," st. 1, l. 5).

The allusion to "Paradise" (st. 2, l. 5) once more makes for similarity between "Huswifery" and "Here followes some verses upon the burning of our House." In Jesus's parable of the Heavenly Wedding, an uninvited guest to the 'house' is denied entrance by the king because he lacks an appropriate 'robe': "Friend, how camest thou in hither not having a wedding garment?" (Matthew 22:12). In a related passage in the visionary Book of *Revelation*, John the Seer explains that "the fine linen is the righteousness of saints" (Rev. 19:8). Being dressed appropriately, i.e., being "justified" and "sanctified" by the acceptance of redemption in Christ, is the prerequisite for partaking of "glory," i.e., life in God—a life-long theme of Emily Dickinson. Taylor consistently uses a variant emblem on the "rich robes" (st. 5, l. 1) in "94. Meditation," the latter being addressed to Christ: "Dye them all . . . / Deep in thy blood" (st. 5, ll. 3-4), the sacrament establishing the most profound relationship between God and self. In the poem "Another upon the Same" referred to above, the symmetry of the isocolon: "My Life thy Web" (st. 2, l. 5), with linking verb omitted, cuts the mystical relationship in apodictic and epigrammatic compactness. Quite extravagantly, such life is imagined to be "this Gold-web of Glory to thy praise" (st. 2, l. 6), with "Gold" a variant symbol to "Heavenly Colours Choice" of "Huswifery."

As "Huswifery" ends, language has served its initial purpose of deliberation, and changes into "display[ing]" (st. 3, l. 5) God's greatness by virtue of the poet's existence. In "Huswifery," then, Taylor develops three concepts of 'web': the literal (the emerging textile), the spiritual (the emerging union of God and self), and the poetic (the emerging poem). Variations on this pre-Modern metapoetic motif in American verse are found elsewhere in Taylor's *Meditations*. The criterion of the artistic excellence of "Huswifery" is the interconnectedness of theme, structure, and style in its finesse. In their layering, the phonic, lexical, syntactic, stylistic and textual patterns "weave the Web" (st. 2, l. 3) that is the poem. "Huswifery," opening with a request and a reference to an everyday production instrument (cf. l. 1), concludes in vision and a reference to the end product: "Holy robes" (st. 3, l. 6). God's 'artisanship' as a weaver prefigures Taylor's craftsmanship as a poet; a humble frontierism foreshadows the "glory" of eternal life; rhetoricity transmutes into lyricism.

In the last analysis, "Huswifery" is all anticipation; its prayer is apostrophe writ large. The speaker's attempt at 'persuading' God to grant his grace defines the speech act as deliberative, melding into panegyric/epideictic, celebrating God's gifts and his holiness. Like Bradstreet's "Verses," Taylor's "Huswifery" rests on argumentation, not on the intuition of a later Romanticism. This self's 'desire' is not for union with a pantheist "Oversoul" (Ralph Waldo Emerson) or the "cosmic spirit" (Walt Whitman) but with the personal God of the Bible. As both Taylor and Bradstreet demonstrate, seventeenth-century American poetry is not yet associational but discursive and architectural.

4. Conclusion and Outlook

The stance of existential 'desire' pervades the history of American poetry from colonial Calvinism to the present. Of their own free will, Bradstreet and Taylor choose to be individualists in living the Christian faith. In doing so they are also voices of their Baroque age. Large-scale and in-depth comparisons of Anne Bradstreet, Edward Taylor and further colonial New England poets with Andreas Gryphius, Paul Gerhardt and other seventeenth-century German poets are long overdue. Since striking similarities in providential faith and rhetorical aesthetics exist between the New Englanders and the Germans in particular, the comparative approach would considerably add to our understanding of the Baroque religious lyric in Transatlantic perspective.

Public figures both, Bradstreet and Taylor write private poems representative of the poetry of colonial New England at large. An intimate lyric emerges from these poets' active involvement in the routines of everyday practical life. In "Verses" Bradstreet is coping with a challenge to her faith, while in "Huswifery" Taylor is at peace, even joyous. Whereas "Verses" enacts a Christian ethics on the basis of an actual calamity, "Huswifery" re-enacts the timeless reality of God's benevolence. Two features in which Taylor's poem differs from Bradstreet's are a higher degree of structural density and the poeticity of "Huswifery." While both poets draw on the house, it appears relevant that each one, in the deep structure of their respective texts, draws on the exact same eschatological passage from John 14:2, 'desiring' home and identity in eternity. Ultimately, the literary rank of both poems results from what current rhetorical theory terms "the rhetoric of sincerity" (van Alphen 2009). It is perhaps not amiss to call attention to the affinity of Bradstreet's and Taylor's poetry with a dictum of the early Imagists (with a side-glance at Dickinson along the way):

"Concentration is of the essence." Early American religious poets indeed practiced what was to become a guideline of the Moderns: 'Write about what you know best—from experience.'

As Puritan dominance is gradually superseded by the American Enlightenment from the early, and by American Romanticism from the late eighteenth century onward, the religious world view yields to the secular in a syncretism of intellectual and artistic paradigms. One of the manifestations of this process is New England Transcendentalism, which in itself includes a multiplicity of beliefs and agendas. Influenced by Calvinism, Neo-Platonism, German Idealism, and Eastern spirituality, Ralph Waldo Emerson formulates a philosophy and a poetry that are still rooted in the hermeneutics of Puritanism—reasoning by analogy and in "correspondences" between the empirical and the transcendent world—but in substance turn Pantheist. In contrast, Jones Very's poetry retains the unity of religion and rhetoric, representing a type of mysticism that fuses and epitomizes Puritan spirituality and the classic Shakespearean sonnet tradition ("The Fig Tree").

Emily Dickinson, in the post-Transcendentalist generation, takes American poetry beyond her Puritan heritage toward proto-Modernism. Her innovative poetry of philosophical pithiness and high lyricism is informed by a conflict of faith and skepticism ranging from inherited providentialism to sheer rebellion against it. To Dickinson's poetics of discontinuity, paradox comes naturally as the crystallization of her discursive-lyrical mode ("This World Is not Conclusion"). Symptomatically, Dickinson's 'house' has come quite a way from Bradstreet's and Taylor's, as in a poem whose first and last lines combined read as follows: "I dwell in Possibility— // . . . to gather Paradise—." "Paradise" still spells fulfillment of mind and text, yet it is no longer religious certainty but epistemological "Possibility" that sets the directions. While Ralph Waldo Emerson ("Waldeinsamkeit") and Walt Whitman ("Darest Thou now o Soul") celebrate cosmic optimism, Edgar Allan Poe in his poetry and poetics conceptualizes American Romanticism as pre-modern nihilism. According to Poe, religion and traditional philosophy can no longer provide meaning or a viable world view, and it is art that has to make up for meaning lost in experiential life while claiming autonomy as a consequence (Deringer/Hagenbüchle 1985: 205-9). The prevalent sensibility, therefore, is a death-in-life existence ("To One in Paradise"). The same holds true for the second half of the nineteenth century and into the twentieth century, as the disintegration of the traditional value system finds its reflexes in the disillusionment and pessimism of poets such as Herman Melville ("The Berg [A Dream]"), Frederick Goddard Tuckerman ("Sometimes I Walk where the Deep Water Dips"), and Edwin Arlington Robinson ("The Man against the Sky").

In the epistemological aftermath of World War I, it is T.S. Eliot who blends Christian and Humanist traditions of England and New England, especially after adopting British citizenship and converting to the Church of England in 1927. In poems like "The Waste Land" (1922) and the cycle Four Quartets (1935-1942), Eliot explores religious values in modern civilization, integrating Biblical and literary intertexts into a poetry of collage and association (Eliot's technique of the "objective correlative"). By the mid-twentieth century, the Christian religion, Western conceptions of art, and Humanist thought were declared defunct. They were ultimately discarded by the absolutist nihilism in the poetry of Wallace Stevens ("Conversation with Three Women of New England"), whereas a modern transformation of the meditation became the key genre of Stevens's richly philosophical lyric ("The World as Meditation"). On the other hand, Stevens's contemporary Robert Frost profoundly negotiates New England's religious-intellectual archaeology against the larger frameworks of American Modernism. Frost's philosophical and parabolic mode, the nexus of the particular and the universal, as well as his traditionalism in innovation offer brilliant reinterpretations of Puritan patterns and their resurgences in twentieth-century American life ("Provide, Provide!"; "Design"). The place and potential of religious forms and sensibilities in British and American verse now being defined by poets such as Geoffrey Hill, Jorie Graham, and others are becoming the subject of a new discussion in Poetry Studies (see Hart 2009).

Bibliography

Selected Primary Literature

Calvin[, Jean]. 1536, 1559 ff. *Institutes of the Christian Religion* [*Institutio Christianae religionis*]. 2 vols. John T. McNeill (ed.). Ford Lewis Battles (Translation and Index). Philadelphia: Westminster Press/London: S. C. M. Press, 1960.
An authoritative edition of Calvin's main work.

Grabo, Norman S. (ed.). 1962. *Edward Taylor's* Christographia. New Haven and London: Yale UP.

Johnson, Thomas H. (ed.). 1986. *The Poetical Works of Edward Taylor*. Princeton, NJ: Princeton UP.

Kaiser, Leo M. 1982. "A Census of American Latin Verse, 1625-1825." In: *Proceedings of the American Antiquarian Society* 91.2: 197-299.

McElrath, Jr., Joseph R. and Allan P. Robb (eds.). 1981. *The Complete Works of Anne Bradstreet*. Boston: Twayne.

Meserole, Harrison T. (ed.). 1972 [1968]. *Seventeenth-Century American Poetry*. New York: Norton.

Murphy, Henry C. 1966 [1865]. *Anthology of New Netherland or Translations from the Early Dutch Poets of New York with Memoirs of Their Lives*. Amsterdam: Israel.

Stanford, Donald E. (ed.). 1977 [1960]. *The Poems of Edward Taylor*. With a Foreword by Louis L. Martz. New Haven: Yale UP.

Selected Secondary Literature

Brumm, Ursula. 1973. *Puritanismus und Literatur in Amerika*. Darmstadt: Wissenschaftliche Buchgesellschaft.

Galinsky, Hans. 1995. "Verskunst als Lebenswerk einer Frau: Anne Bradstreet." In: Winfried Herget (ed.), *Aufbauphase im Nordosten: Neuengländisches Kolonialbarock (ältere Autorenreihe)*. Vol. 2 of *Geschichte amerikanischer Kolonialliteratur: Multinationale Wurzeln einer Weltliteratur in Entwicklungslinien und Werkinterpretationen (1542-1722)*. 1991-2000. 4 vols. Darmstadt: Wissenschaftliche Buchgesellschaft. 79-219.
An interpretative study of Bradstreet's oeuvre in the larger contexts of colonial American literatures and cultures, including detailed readings of representative poems.

Grabo, Norman S. 1988 [1961]. *Edward Taylor*. Boston: Twayne.

The first critical monograph on Taylor, by the editor of Christographia. *In the "Preface to the Revised Edition" Grabo concludes that the "winds of critical interest have . . . had little effect upon the main analysis of this study as it first appeared in 1961" (xi).*

Guruswamy, Rosemary Fithian. 2003. *The Poems of Edward Taylor: A Reference Guide*. Westport, CT: Greenwood.

A comprehensive and profound overview of the major fields and directions. Guruswamy and Hammond should be consulted in conjunction.

Hammond, Jeffrey A. 1993. *Edward Taylor: Fifty Years of Scholarship and Criticism*. Columbia, SC: Camden House.

An extensive review of research into all aspects. Hammond and Guruswamy should be consulted in conjunction.

Schulze, Fritz W. 1969. "Strophe, Vers und Reim in Edward Taylors 'Meditations'." In: Hans Helmcke, Klaus Lubbers and Renate Schmidt-von Bardeleben (eds.), *Literatur und Sprache der Vereinigten Staaten: Aufsätze zu Ehren von Hans Galinsky*. Heidelberg: Winter. 11-33.

A systematic study of Taylor's prosody.

Stanford, Anne. 1974. *Anne Bradstreet: The Worldly Puritan. An Introduction to Her Poetry*. New York: Franklin.

A chronological and critical study. Appends most helpful material such as "A Chronology of the Works of Anne Bradstreet," "Images in the Poetry: Frequency List," and "Books with which Anne Bradstreet Was Acquainted."

White, Elizabeth Wade. 1971. *Anne Bradstreet: "The Tenth Muse."* New York: Oxford UP.

A substantial biographical and critical study of Bradstreet's poetry and prose.

Further References

Alphen, Ernst van, Mieke Bal and Carel Smith (eds.). 2009. *The Rhetoric of Sincerity*. Stanford, CA: Stanford UP.

Arndt, Karl John Richard and Reimer C. Eck (eds.). 1989. *The First Century of German Language Printing in the United States of America: A Bibliography Based on the Studies of Oswald Seidensticker and Wilbur H. Oda*. 2 vols. Göttingen: Niedersächsische Staats- und Universitätsbibliothek.

Blom, Frans R. E. (ed.). *Nieuw Nederland: Representaties in pöezie en prosa*. Forthcoming.

Börger, Paul (ed.). 1967 [1953]. *Quellen zur Geschichte der Reformation*. Heidelberg: Quelle & Meyer.

Deringer, Ludwig and Roland Hagenbüchle. 1985. "Amerikanische Lyrik des 19. Jahrhunderts." In: Helmbrecht Breinig and Ulrich Halfmann (eds.), *Die amerikanische Literatur bis zum Ende des 19. Jahrhunderts*. Tübingen: Francke. 174-224, 296-303.

Dubrow, Heather. 2014 [2000]. "Lyric Forms." In: Virginia Jackson and Yopie Prins (eds.), *The Lyric Theory Reader: A Critical Anthology*. Baltimore: Johns Hopkins UP. 114-28.

Hart, Kevin John, presiding. 2009. "Contemporary Poetry and Prayer". Program arranged by the Division on Literature and Religion. Dec. 30. Session 616.

125th Annual Convention of the Modern Language Association of America. Philadelphia. Convention Program. In: *PMLA* 124.6 (Nov.): 2109.

Kaiser, Leo M. 1972. "The Earliest Verse of the New World." In: *Renaissance Quarterly* 25.4: 429-39.

Rossi, Cesare, Flavio Russo and Ferruccio Russo. 2009. "Spinning and Weaving." Ch. 13 of *Ancient Engineers' Inventions: Precursors of the Present*. By Rossi et al. N.p.: Springer. 235-48 [with illustrations]. Esp. 235-9.

Shuger, Debora K. 2000. "The Philosophical Foundations of Sacred Rhetoric." In: Walter Jost and Wendy Olmsted (eds.), *Rhetorical Invention and Religious Inquiry: New Perspectives*. New Haven and London: Yale UP. 47-64.

2.

The Poetry of British America

Francis Daniel Pastorius's "Epibaterium, Or a hearty Congratulation
to William Penn" (1699) and Richard Lewis's "Food for Criticks" (1731)

Oliver Scheiding

1. Reassessing Colonial Poetry

Only in the last decade has there been a reappraisal of the variety of forms and
themes as well as the multilingual sources that characterize the poetry written in
the North American colonies. In his seminal anthology, Harrison Meserole summarizes an attitude that many critics have shared up to this point and that has
shaped the public reception of colonial poetry for a long time: "One persistent
misconception about poets of early America has been that all of them were austere Puritan ministers writing pedestrian verses about a wrathful God" (1993:
xix). Meserole stands against such a widespread pejorative opinion that colonial
poetry has been written by people from all walks of life, ranging from servants to
the members of the landed gentry. Not only diverse in authorship, colonial poetry
is also transregional and cannot be exclusively narrowed down to New England
and its elite of well-educated ministers and laymen (cf. Galinsky 1991). The Atlantic world of the seventeenth and eighteenth centuries is one of literary traffic, in
which manuscripts, so-called scribal publications, and prints of all kinds migrated
back and forth between Europe and North America (cf. Love 1993; Scheiding
2012; 2015). In addition, some writers were trained at European universities and
took large libraries with them when they left for the New World, while others relied upon a circum-Atlantic network of correspondents and friends who were instrumental in circulating manuscripts, book catalogues, information on new
prints, and contacts to publishers and book sellers, as Hugh Amory and David
Hall show in their multivolume *A History of the Book in America* (2000-2009).

Investigations of English school curriculums, of early American library hold-
ings, of shipping lists of books sent to the colonies, as well as increasing documentation of direct influences discovered in literary works and letters, have led
in recent years to a general reassessment of colonial poetry. The view has been
dispelled that colonial America was a cultural backwater and that most colonial
poets were epigones who lacked imagination and thus only imitated English and
European verses. In contrast, one could even argue that poetry was the most
innovative of the literary types cultivated in colonial America, creating a rich
field of cross-pollination for thematic, linguistic, and aesthetic experimentations. Critics have frequently argued that these evolve out of experiences that
poets and occasional versifiers encountered in colonial America as well as out of
their own education and reading habits (cf. Spengemann 1994: 1-50). Poetic
topics thus not only focus on Puritan self-analysis and the wish to know whether
one is saved or damned, but go beyond such predestinarian anxieties and seek
to imagine the divine within the natural order, as can be seen in colonial German poetry and its Pietist lyricism (cf. Stoudt 1956). Additional themes that are
spelled out in colonial poetry are the arrival in the New World, the land, wildlife, Native Americans, the domestic sphere, plantation and slave life, gender, and

love, expressed through a wide variety of poetic forms such as elegies, epigrams, epics, meditations, odes, satires, sonnets, broadsides, ballads, and magazine verse.

There has been a lengthy debate on the question of whether the new settlers condemned poetry, or held it in great honor. The answer to this question, however, varies according to specific localized literary traditions and communities of readers, as becomes evident when one compares poems written in New England and the Middle and Southern colonies as well as those from the Caribbean dominions (cf. James Grainger's "The Sugar Cane: A Poem, In Four Books," 1999 [1764]: 166-260). Southern planters had an unadulterated admiration for classic poetry and standard English poets, whereas in New England, poetry was used to strengthen religious feeling. The Puritans honored poetry and considered it alongside rhetoric as belonging to both their religious upbringing and to their reading. New England Puritans admired the great poets and were fully aware of the possibilities and beauties of poetry. Anne Bradstreet, for instance, wrote poems on Philip Sidney (1554-1586) and acknowledged herself student to the French poet, Guillaume Du Bartas (1544-1590). Even renowned Puritan ministers such as Cotton Mather told the young that the "Soul" should not be wholly "*Unpoetical*," adding: "An Old *Horace* has left us an Art of Poetry, which you may do well to bestow a Perusal on. And besides your *Lyrical Hours*, I wish you may so far understand an *Epic Poem* that the Beauties of an *Homer* and a *Virgil* may be discerned with you" (*Manuductio ad Ministerium*, 1726: 39; original emphasis). And as Robert Dale Parker (2011) has recently shown, even Native Americans who were trained at Harvard College in the seventeenth century cherished classical poetry and wrote elaborate elegies in Latin. This brief survey demonstrates that critics refute the notion of a colonial lag in comparison to the metropolitan centers in Europe. Contemporary approaches to early American poetry move beyond the nationalist model and its conceptualization of a national literature in terms of 'origins' or as a canon of poets and specific texts.

In recent years early American studies has received new impulses by looking at "the discursive dimensions of American provinciality" (Shields 1997: xxix) and at the institutional forces at play in the production of colonial poetry: denominations, patronage, political factions and oppositions, conventicles, heterosocial groups, salons, societies, clubs, and the mixed print and manuscript practices that existed in the Atlantic world of the seventeenth and eighteenth centuries. One of the first anthologies that followed new trends in scholarship and considered early American poetry in the context of a complex Anglophone world in the eighteenth century was Myra Jehlen and Michael Warner's 1997 *The English Literatures of America, 1500-1800*. Although this new compilation of prose and poetry explained the rise of a colonial literary culture as a process of ramification and included many new voices, it overemphasized the importance of the English language as the historical ground of early American poetry. Since then, hemispheric approaches to reading colonial literary culture, and the anthologies produced in this context, stressed the multilingual, multiethnic, and translocal developments that characterize the writing of poetry in the colonial Americas (cf. Mulford 2002). In addition, an important step in re-evaluating colonial poetry resulted from the growing number of studies in the field of the history of the book. Literary and cultural historians called for a "social history of culture" (Hall 1996: 171). The focus of critical attention is now on the uses of poetry "at the intersection of the material conditions, social structures, and cultural values that give the written word its forms and meanings," as Joan Shelley Rubin aptly puts in her stimulating study *Songs of Ourselves: The Uses of Poetry in America* (2007: 3).

As valid as these approaches are in reconsidering the complex cultural work of print in the early modern Atlantic world, critics overlook the mix and circulation of manuscripts and printed matter in shaping the production, dissemination, and reception of poetry in the colonial Americas. In doing so, they frequently fail to recognize how aesthetic and cultural work interact, and thus overlook formal aspects of poetry in shaping social pleasure and emotional life while projecting private and public concerns. Literary and cultural historians such as David Shields (1994; 2007b) look at the production of colonial poetry and how it operates in specific social spaces, such as coffee houses and taverns. Extending existing studies, Shields examines the various uses of poetry within a range of discursive communities. To these communities belong the members of literary salons and circles, metropolitan-based intellectual groups, and the editor-printers of newspapers and periodicals, all of which grew in importance since the 1720s. Drawing upon the earlier work of such outstanding scholars of colonial literature as Leo Lemay (1972) and David Hall (1996; 2008), Shields brings back to life the "social aesthetics" of belles lettres or polite literature in the mid-Atlantic colonies and the South between 1690 and 1760 (Shields 1997: xxvii). Instead of a monolithic group of versifiers aping the great European masters, Shields's 2007 anthology, *American Poetry: The Seventeenth and Eighteenth Centuries*, collects a diverse body of social verse produced in North America. The anthology also demonstrates how colonial poetry interacts with baroque styles and neoclassicism as the dominant international systems of literary classification in the seventeenth- and eighteenth-century Atlantic world.

Current studies affirm the dynamic nature of baroque and neoclassicism as formal modes of writing (cf. Zamora/Kaup 2010: 1–35). To define the baroque is a difficult endeavor because its meaning differs widely. Coined by critics in the nineteenth century, the term found acceptance as a period concept to describe an artistic form and style that was predominantly used throughout Europe between the Renaissance (sixteenth century) and the Enlightenment period (eighteenth century). The baroque often invoked decadence in the arts, given its excessive compositional devices that deviated sharply from the classical rationality of Renaissance art. In the various romance languages, "baroque" or "barocco" means irregular, queer, and turgid. Today it refers less to a bombastic art-form, but rather it is reassessed as a transhistorical phenomenon that helps to understand contemporary developments in the arts. Critics are particularly interested in the baroque's theatricality, mediality, and its treatment of early modernity. In the English context, the baroque is frequently related to the metaphysical poets, a seventeenth-century movement with a strong taste for unusual imagery, paradoxes, and linguistic inventions. The term 'colonial baroque' includes the notion of literary traffic in the Atlantic world of the seventeenth century, and from it evolves a mixed literary baroque style in the Americas that is both regional and translocal. Neoclassicism has often been related to the cult of imitation of classical antiquity and the application of a normative poetics in the eighteenth-century arts. However the Augustan age, as it became known, cannot be restricted to notions of decorum and a rigid diction of conventions; rather, its polite imagination supports a theory of pleasure, universal taste, and communal sense. Neoclassical literature is like polite conversation, a form of sociability, and as such practices "mannerly conduct, styles of political publicity, and cultural mythology" (Shields 1997: 8).

Colonial poets adopt baroque and neoclassical elements to numerous practices and community narratives, ranging from sentimental moralism, evangelical
pietism, the speculative liberty of private society, to the merging of polite literature and civic humanism. Other writers, such as the African American poet
Phillis Wheatley, conflate political and religious themes and use the neoclassic
style to become a "manipulator of words," as Vincent Carretta puts it in his astute biography of a "Genius in Bondage" (2011: 137; cf. Wheatley's numerous
versions of her elegy on the death of George Whitefield, 1989 [1770]: 55-7; 132-
9). Contemporary studies also demonstrate that colonial poetry cannot be easily
classified by distinguishing between major and minor writers, as the writing of
poetry was a common means of correspondence within local and transatlantic
networks of communication. Thus categorizations in terms of an 'artful' composition that satisfies modern aesthetic criteria of finished textual products are
not helpful in understanding the changing functions of colonial poetry and the
formal experiments that go along with it. Literary historians have also shown
that the boundaries between private and public forms of publishing were fluent.
A handwritten manuscript, which was meant to be privately read and distributed, could also exert public influence, as autographs were funneled through literary networks, shared among like-minded correspondents, or ended up in a
print-shop often without the author's knowledge. Handwritten poems such as
elegies, for example, were ritual scripts shared among specific religious and civic
groups. As such, they shaped emotional life in terms of collective forms of reading and memory. Reconsidering the uses of colonial elegies, Jeffrey Hammond
concludes that their production, distribution, and reception forces "us . . . to
think of a poem in premodernist terms: as something that does rather than
something that *is*" (2000: 8; original emphasis).

What follows in this chapter suggests a reading of British-American poetry
in light of a social formalism by looking at two eminent colonial poets and their
poetic practices in producing poetry. Both writers exemplify the transition from
an earlier moment of scribal publications to printed magazine verse in North
America in the 1720s. Although these poets—Francis Daniel Pastorius (1651-
1719) of southern Germany and Richard Lewis (1699-1734) of Wales—come
from different cultural backgrounds, this chapter illustrates that they belong to
specific discursive communities in which "textuality and meaning developed
through communal affection and cooperation" (Erben 2012: 170). Both perform
for readers in whose lives poetry has a vital presence, and for whom reading and
writing poetry is a social act, whether in manuscript form or in print.

2. Francis Daniel Pastorius: Community and Scribal Publication

Francis Daniel Pastorius, the founder of Germantown near Philadelphia, emigrated to William Penn's newly chartered colony in 1683. As a believer in practical piety, he wished to participate in Penn's Holy Experiment. He converted to
Quakerism and became one of the leading public figures in Pennsylvania. In
1688 Pastorius wrote the first resolution and some verses against slaveholding in
North America (cf. Stoudt 1956: 4).

Like Cotton Mather in New England, he was a prolific writer of prose and
poetry, and—although only small parts of his literary penmanship made it into
print—he participated in an extensive network of communication, exchanging
book manuscripts, letters, and poems among his friends on both sides of the

Atlantic. He compiled an encyclopedic folio commonplace book, generally known as *The Bee Hive*, which contains—besides a vast gathering of texts—an anthology of poetry he had collected earlier in Europe as well as his own verses written in seven languages. Critics generally agree that the still unpublished commonplace book proves Pastorius to be one of the eminent experimenters of baroque and neo-Latin verse in the colonial Americas (cf. Jantz 1985).

Like other New England poets, Pastorius was also a prolific practitioner of occasional verse, composing numerous friendship, anniversary, welcome, and letter poems as well as countless epigrams (cf. Schweitzer 1981). In the context of a manuscript culture, his poetic production relied on textual exchange and personal interaction (cf. Pastorius 2007 [1714]). For example, young Jane Fenn Hoskens (1694-1764), one of the celebrities among the female Quaker missionaries, had sent him a sample of her own handwritten poems. Pastorius responded with a poem in which he cherished Hoskens's talent alongside the Greek poet Sappho and New England's Anne Bradstreet:

> *Jane Fenn* sent me the 5th of the 11th mo: 1717/8 a Sheet full of Rimes of her own Make; Upon which I answered her the next ensuing day etc.

> Loving Friend.
> Thy Rimes I read, and like them pretty well;
> For they do run, but run not parallel:
> One wants some Feet, the other does abound,
> which matters not, the Matter being Sound.

> Go thou but on! thou wilst <u>most of</u> thy Sex surpass,
> And be a Poëtress, as <u>famous</u> Sappho was.

> Mind, that each of these my two last Verses having two feet more than the former, are of a different race or species; But leave out the underlined words, and they'll be of due length.

> Finally I here shall set down the Names of some English and Scotch women, who well skill'd in Versifying left us divers good works behind, to wit 1. Jane Gray./. 2. Anne Askew./. 3. Mary Wroth./. 4. Catherine Philips./. 5. Margaret, Duchess of New-Castle./. 6. Mary, Countess of Pembroke./. 7. Elizabeth Carew./. 8. Mary Morepeth./. 9. Mary Molineux./. To these Nine Muses of Great Britain I shall add the Tenth sprung up in New England, viz. Anne Broadstreet [sic], etc. (2012 [1717/18]: 179-80; original emphasis)

In a manuscript culture, Pastorius's poems were frequently "created and re-created through the reception and response of the readers" (Erben 2012: 170). The poem's suggested metrical elisions demonstrate how the writer elicits a dialogue among like-minded persons by playing with formal irregularities. The poem blends the hexameter, generally considered to be unfit to the English language, into the English decasyllabic line, widely used in composing English couplets. In doing so, the metrical play exemplifies the communal function of poetry. Rather than being exclusive due to certain metrical restrictions in English prosody, creating a heteroglossic line "of a different race and species" highlights notions of mutuality and interdependence.

To illustrate the practice of manuscript poetry in the context of Pennsylvania's rocky history of diverse religious and ethnic communities, a good case in point is Pastorius's arrival poem (included in *The Bee Hive* folio) titled "Epibaterium, Or a hearty Congratulation to William Penn. Chief Proprietary of the Province of Pennsilvania etc. Upon his third Arrival into the same" (2007 [1699]: 209-14). William

Penn received a copy of it upon his return from England in 1699, where he had spent fifteen years entangled in numerous lawsuits and libel cases. To reveal his esteem and friendship for Penn, Pastorius used the *epibaterion*, a genre that was used throughout antiquity. When any person of condition and quality returned home after a long absence or journey to another country, he called together his friends and fellow citizens and presented them with a speech or some verses wherein he gave solemn thanks to the immortal gods for his happy return. The *epibaterion* is Homeric in origin, and examples abound in Homer's *Odyssey*.

There are two different forms of the arrival poem: the simple, and the formal *epibaterion*. The basic elements of both forms are the greeting to the land, the toils and miseries of going abroad and of the journey, the man's joy at returning, and expressions of love for his country and family. Whereas the simple form addresses a man's friends, the formal *epibaterion* addresses instead a polis or a collective of men. The returner usually illuminates his affection for his native city and its inhabitants in elaborate form. As such, it belongs to ceremonial oratory, or the praise-and-blame rhetoric (i.e., epideictic speech). The basic outline of a formal or public *epibaterion* consists of the following elements: praise of the founder and of the city, a laudatory description of the city's physical features, an account of the city's progress, a praiseful portrayal of the character of the inhabitants, a comparison to other cities, and an epilogue dealing with the city and its buildings.

Like Andrew Marvell's Horatian "Ode upon Cromwell's Return from Ireland" (wr. 1650), Pastorius's "hearty Congratulation to William Penn" is a poem of public concern. Pastorius did not use the form of the ode, however, because this genre was considered too massive in personal glorification. The often heroic exuberance of the genre contradicted Pastorius's adherence to Quaker humility and quietism. Instead, he chose the subtle narrative style and familial tone of the *epibaterion*, which also allowed him to put the speaker of the poem on equal footing with the addressee. The poem plays with the formal *epibaterion*, borrowing from it key elements such as the joy of homecoming, the address to the city, the returner's experiences abroad, and the epilogue. In addition, it contains religious instructions, autobiographical footnotes, allusions to the history of the Pennsylvania Quakers, and it also experiments with language and meter. Since Penn and Pastorius met for the first time in Pennsylvania in 1683, the poem highlights the two arrivals and unfolds a history of parallel lives: Penn the Proprietor of Pennsylvania, the founder of "the Metropolis (which Brother-Love they call)" (l. 35), and Pastorius, who "in [the province's] Infancy thy Face I first did see / The One and twenti'th of the Sixth Month, Eighty three" (ll. 33-4), was leader of the German-speaking emigrants to North America, founder of Germantown, and key office holder in church and state during Penn's long absence from the colony. The poem is thus less about praising the new arrival of Penn, and more concerned with the "Meeting" (l. 45) of two friends on equal terms.

Pastorius uses the *epibaterion* to make up a balance between the past and Pennsylvania's present state of affairs. Compared to its poor beginnings, Penn's province grew into a multilinguistic and religiously pluralistic "Country full of Folks" (l. 60), creating conflicts between the proprietary and the popular elements in the government. The speaker of the poem recalls the past, reminding Penn that "[w]e understood what things in Pensilvania were / Of good or evil use, to follow, or t'avoid" (ll. 47-8). The poem's subtitle signals Pennsylvania's progress as a Quaker "Province" within an Anglo-American Empire, and the ensuing couplets raise questions about the role of leadership, the tempting nature of power, and the condition of human fallibility. Given the *epibaterion*'s association with communal affinity and co-residence, the poem contains numerous exercises in translation to test Penn's understanding of Pennsylvania's peculiar civic and religious constitution. The exercises either revolve around the many repetitions of the number three in the poem or emerge as word-play. In the context of both men's multilingual training, the epilogue addresses Penn in lines written in German, playing with the ambivalent meanings of his last name.

> Penn heißt auf Welsch ein Haubt, auf Nieder Teutsch ein
> Feder,
> Die man zum schreiben braucht; das Haubt ersinn't entweder
> Gut oder Bös, womit die Königin paar Geldt,
> Durch Hülff der Feder Zwingt, die Gross und kleine Welt. (ll. 123-7)[1]

The triple meaning of Penn as "Friend," "head," and "feather" refers to three different layers of meaning in the poem. As a "Friend" he has gone through many ordeals, but now listens to the instructive couplets composed by the poet's feather-quill pen. As "head" of the government he can easily tip the balance of power on any issue, and like the king or queen, become an arbitrary ruler. The "feather" refers to two different forms of authorship: As proprietor, Penn's "feather" signs charters and revises constitutions that give the province's assembly full legislative powers. The speaker hints at it by pointing out: "The third time and the last, I question not, He will / Grant our Petition" (ll. 109-10), which Penn actually did by signing the "Charter of Privileges" in 1701 that codified the province's freedom of conscience until the outbreak of the American revolution. The "feather" also highlights the practice of social authorship. Critics claim that "[b]uilding community in Pennsylvania was an exercise in translation" (Erben 2012: 168). Accordingly, the poem refers to a common endeavor in which all language groups participate "to distill a mutually intelligible meaning [from] the discrepancy between languages and peoples" (ibid.). However, one should add that it also acknowledges—within the form of the *epibaterion*—the aesthetic and literary ingenuity of the poet's pen. It is he who symbolically remodels the social within the formal and the aesthetic. At the very end of the poem, Pastorius meditates upon the power of his "feather" and concludes:

> Nein, wanns hier Wünschens gält, so wolt ich, dass mein
> Feder
> Ein solchen Nach-druck hätt, damit sich Ja Ein jeder
> Als ein gehorsam Glied ergäbe Jesu Christ,
> Der da das Eintzig Haubt der wahren Kirchen ist;
> So wäre weder Heid, noch Jud; auch kein Papist. (ll. 128-33)[2]

The poem comes full circle, as the performed penmanship implies spiritual perfection within patterns of aesthetic or narrative form. The penman's power lies not so much in proposing a "common spiritual idiom" for leaders and members of the community to accept "different languages" (Erben 2012: 168), but in that

---

1   "Penn means in Welsh a head, in Low German a / Feather, / which one uses for writing; the Head devises either / Something Good or Evil, and with it the Queen / Forces both Rich and poor to pay her Money" (transl. in Shields 2007a: 909).

2   "No, if I was granted a Wish, I would that my / Feather / Had such an Impact that everyone would submit / As an obedient member to Jesus Christ, / Who is the only Head of the True Church; / Then, there would be no Heathen, no Jew, no Papist" (transl. in Shields 2007: 909).

it confronts social and linguistic divisions through a harmony of form. This becomes manifest not only in the selection of a specific genre, but also in the
poem's metrical outline. The poem translates English, French, and German
verse traditions into Greek and Latin hexameters, mixing prosodic and linguistic
differences to oppose the speaker's untainted "Rime" (l. 99) against the "thread-
bare Lie" (l. 99) and "vain words" (l. 54) of the three major public forces embodied by the press ("Gazetteers," l. 101), the church ("the stark-blind Apos-
tates," l. 53), and the government ("Königin [Queen]," l. 126).

The poem also contains numerous references to the writing of poetry. The
opening lines, which reverberate Anne Bradstreet's humble mocking of the male
heroic tradition in epic poetry, declare: "Let Heroic Poets Tote of War and warlike Men, / My Reed (shrill Oaten-Straw!) does Welcome Wm. Penn ("The Prologue," ll. 6-8). Similar to Bradstreet's tongue-in-cheek glorification of her "lowly
lines" and her "Parsley wreath" (1650: 4), the couplet contains a self-reflexive
statement about the role of scribal publications. The simple tools needed, the
"Oaten-Straw!" and the "Turky quill!" (l. 75), and their local material properties
finally bring to the fore the interdependence between the manuscript culture
and community building. As the following reading of Richard Lewis's poem will
illustrate, the literary practice of handwritten poetic experiments slowly changed
in the 1720s when colonial printers gradually transformed a scribal society into
a print-based one, although both ways of text-making existed throughout the
eighteenth and into the nineteenth centuries (cf. Weyler 2013: 10-8).

3. Richard Lewis: American Provinciality and Colonial Print Culture

While Pastorius preferred the 'public anonymity' of his network of friends and
like-minded correspondents for 'publishing' his works, Richard Lewis is the first
colonial poet whose poetry has to been seen in conjunction with the advent of the
printing press in the mid-Atlantic colonies in the 1720s. Lewis was well-known
during his time and "gave Maryland the best neo-classic poems in all the colonies" (Shivers 1985: 35; cf. Beyers 2002). His poetry was published in the newly
established colonial papers, and London's chief periodicals praised his mastery of
neoclassical verse, which Lewis used to translate "the meaning of the province—
its history, economics, and nature—to the metropolis" (Shields 1994: 329). His
widely read nature poem "A Journey from Patapsko to Annapolis, April 4, 1730"
(2007a [1730]: 386-96) appeared in print throughout the eighteenth century.
Alexander Pope duplicated some verses of Lewis's poem in his Dunciad (1742),
but ultimately condemned them as inferior to his own. Although Lewis's poetry
did not survive the rise of romanticism, his work was exhumed in the 1970s and
critics restored an interest in his nature poetry. Current studies read his poetry
in the context of the Augustan Age in America. He is frequently named in conjunction with Ebenezer Cook (1665-1732), another Maryland wit, who wrote the
immensely popular verse satire "The Sot-Weed Factor, or the Voyage to Maryland"
(2007 [1708]: 239-58), which makes fun of the crudeness of colonial life. Although Cook remained his rival for honor, Lewis turned out to be the province's
"civic archpoet" who was supported by a community of readers and thinkers developing around William Parks's book business in Maryland (Shields 1994: 328).
This circle of learned men also included the governor Benedict Calvert, who sup-

ported the foundation of literature in the colony and whom Lewis praised in a pamphlet hymn (cf. Parks 2012: 75-106; cf. Lewis 1733).

To argue that "colonial Augustan poetry provides the drama of writers attempting to take paradigms of gentility and culture that emerged from one society and transplant them in a very different society" (Beyers 2008: 193) fails to account for the local situation in which Lewis wrote his poetry, and how he and his circle exploited the interests of readers in England. Metropolitan audiences were fascinated by the idea of an empire by the seas and were eager to learn more about its economic and natural resources. Maryland's official printer, William Parks, therefore wanted to fill the void of mercantile information about the Chesapeake region and its staple products. In 1727 he began printing the *Maryland Gazette*. Modeling his newspaper after the tradition of English periodicals, he saw a good chance to increase his income in publishing not only factual accounts and instructive essays, but also by printing local voices. Residing in Annapolis, where Lewis was a schoolmaster, Parks published much of Lewis's poetry in his newspaper.

Richard Lewis's "Food for Criticks" appeared in Parks's *Maryland Gazette* in 1731 and was reprinted twice. The poem appeared in the *New England Weekly Journal* in the same year and was reprinted by Benjamin Franklin's *Pennsylvania Gazette* in 1732. Each reprint altered the local geographical features presented in the poem's opening lines; the editors of the *Pennsylvania Gazette* referred to the Schuylkill River, which joins the Delaware River in Philadelphia.

> Of ancient streams presume no more to tell,
> The fam'd castalian or pierian well;
> SKUYLKIL superior, must those springs confess,
> As *Pensilvania* yields to *Rome* or *Greece*.
> More limpid water can no fountain show,
> A fairer bottom or a smoother brow. (ll. 1-6; original emphasis)

Lewis's original version probably named the Severn River, which enters the Chesapeake Bay at Annapolis. Given its many references to American landscape and wildlife, the poem has been called the "best nature poem" prior to those written by Philip Freneau in the 1780s (cf. Lemay 1972: 150), and critics pay special attention to Lewis's sensitivity to the American environment. Similar to Pastorius's poem that revolves around the relationship between the poet's "Rime" and poetry's communal function, Lewis's poem is a meditation upon art and nature, a central issue for the writer in the context of an expanding mercantilist empire and its utilitarian ethos. In the context of the long tradition of topographical and loco-descriptive poems in English literature, which frequently mix pastoral, georgic, and panegyric elements, Lewis moves rural America into the center of critical attention. The poem's title thus derives from Lewis's participation in a variety of standard eighteenth-century poetic traditions, such as Virgil's *Eclogues* (a quotation from book ten serves as the poem's headnote), the uses of pastoral poetry, the interaction between man and nature, georgic norms such as cultivation and improvement (cf. Sweet 2002), and the idea of a postlapsarian world order referred to as the "age of gold" in the poem's concluding lines (l. 142).

The poem is divided into five sections. In the first and longest part (ll. 1-38), the poet-narrator contends that the river is superior to the classical sources of inspiration. He continues to describe the "groves and plains" (l. 8) as an enchanted and magic realm, a peaceful land, voiced by the "am'rous tunes" (l. 34) of America's wild birds. In the second part (ll. 39-66) the reader encounters the surrounding countryside and experiences the georgic prosperity brought about by the "reaper" and the "peasant" (l. 56). Like the opening lines of Alexander Pope's topographical poem "Windsor Forest" (1713), the poet-narrator highlights the interdependence between labor and nature by unfolding a panoramic canvas of natural resources securing Maryland's maritime role: "There open fields here mingled woods prevail: / Here lasting oaks, the hope of navies, stand" (ll. 50-1; cf. Lewis, 2007b [1730]). At the end of the section, he returns to the "stream" which "becomes a looking-glass" (l. 60) to review the past and present, as well as to envision the future. The third part (ll. 67-108) evokes the region's wilderness as a source of poetic inspiration. The appearance of the "indian prince" (l. 105) embodied as "swarthy ghost" (l. 104) is a haunting reminder of the burden of history. The fourth part (ll. 109-24) returns again to the "happy stream!" (l. 109) as the poet-narrator celebrates the abundance of nature found in the Chesapeake Bay. His long catalogue of fish and "flocks" (l. 123) echoes earlier travel accounts by Englishmen into this region. The final section (ll. 125-46) confronts the "poet's fire" (l. 74) with present developments symbolized by the sudden appearance of the hunter and his "fatal gun" (l. 124).

The hunter's presence recalls the reality of human agency—something that the poem's Arcadian "groves and plains" (l. 8) can hardly stand. The poet-narrator bemoans the damage wrought on nature:

> Hither oftimes th' ingenious youth repair,
> When Sol returning warms the growing year:
> Some take the fish with a delusive bait,
> Or for the fowl beneath the arbors wait;
> And arm'd with fire, endanger ev'ry shade,
> Teaching ev'n unfledg'd innocence a dread.
> To gratify a nice luxurious taste
> How many pretty songsters breath their last:
> Spite of his voice they fire the linnet down,
> And make the widow'd dove renew his moan. (ll. 127-36)

At first sight, the hunter's "artful harms" (l. 143) brings into the American Arcadia an elegiac despair because his "bait" (l. 129) will not yield to the Virgilian message "love conquers all," as promised in *Eclogue* ten, from which the poem quotes two lines in the headnote. A closer look reveals that the hunter assumes connotations beyond those usually attributed to him by the pastoral tradition and the Virgilian paradigm of a war against nature. The poem creates a dramatic contrast between the hunter's "artful harms" (l. 143) and the wild birds' "artless heavenly music" (l. 96). While the hunter's "Teaching" leads to destructive action, the wild birds' "winged choir" (l. 73) inspires contemplation and thus creates art: "For every verse a pattern here you have, / From strains heroic down to humble stave" (ll. 91-2).

Critics interpret the hunter as a "synecdoche for bad art" (Kropf 1980/81: 211) and maintain that the poem as a whole serves as a "systematic statement of neoclassical aesthetics in which the American landscape becomes a vehicle for exploring the proper relationship between art and nature" (ibid.: 205). As convincing as these readings are, one should also note the poem's strategic arrangements of parts and its condensed symbolism that provide a formal solution for the competing ideologies inherent in the pastoral tradition, namely, between labor and leisure, the Arcadian and imperial stance toward nature, and those pertaining to the "value of political and social stability nurturing the arts" (Patterson 1987: 8). In other words: Reading the American landscape in terms of pastoralism inevitably exposes the reader to historicity, the relationship between economy and environment, and the differences in creating human happiness. The concluding couplet—"[t]o leafy woods resort for health and ease, / Not to disturb their melody and peace" (ll. 145-6)—displays a sense of utopian sociability that has always been projected onto America's landscape. Given the hunter's intrusion into nature, the lines complicate the pastoral topoi such as an undisturbed retreat to nature, announced by the Latin headnote: "Here are cold springs, Lycoris, here soft meadows, / here woodland, here with thee, time alone would wear away" (trans. in Shields 2007a: 920). The hunter's possessive individualism raises questions about the function of human agency in its engagements with nature, and thus recovers the georgic tradition within pastoralism. The references to georgic elements of cultivation in the second part, particularly the "navies" built out of America's "lasting oaks" (l. 51), do not promote a separation of nature and civilization, or country and city. Instead, they concern a complex cultural engagement with the American environment that also includes the arts and poetry. Lewis's poem does not overpraise the superiority of America's natural scenery, as earlier critics contented. In the context of British North America, the poem is not counter-institutional, but through its loco-descriptive form exposes the environmental-economic ideology of a mercantilist Atlantic empire and its unsolved rival claims of labor and leisure, action and contemplation, commercial benefits and Arcadian desires.

4. Conclusion and Outlook

The poems under discussion make up two majors modes of poetic production in colonial North America prior to 1760. Pastorius's poetry stems from the rich practice of manuscript verse, either written and collected for members of his family or circulated among a growing number of friends. Seen from an aesthetic and formal perspective, Pastorius was an ingenious practitioner of baroque verse who experimented with form, content, and language. He drew upon the alexandrine (hexameter), introduced by Martin Opitz (1597-1639) into German poetry, and blended it with English verse to prove his poetic ingenuity and linguistic inventiveness. His themes recast the baroque antithesis of worldly vs. spiritual values. As a Quaker he favored a Christian ecumenism, for which he sought formal analogies in his serious poetry to balance an increasing sectarian splintering of society. Richard Lewis marks the other end of the literary spectrum in colonial North America. As an early embodiment of a civic poet in the colonies, his poetry demonstrates how the press and printing changed the status of poetry in the 1720s, when local print production shaped the context in which poetry was consumed and distributed. Similar to Phillis Wheatley and other eighteenth-century colonial writers, Lewis's poetry excels in combining an international writing style with the local conditions of production: specific politics; the personalities of local printers; authors and their patrons; and the interpretive framework of local communities.

Two vibrant areas of contemporary research—the history of the book and the study of the interconnected Atlantic world—extend the practices and politics of text-making into the field of colonial poetry to evidence the various uses of poetry and poetic form in locally diverse socio-economic, political, and religious contexts. In light of these critical trends, scholars frequently follow cultural studies approaches and focus on a broad variety of practices and discourses, acknowledging the creation of poets and the productions of their artifacts. As such, however, they tend to negate formal dimensions in the production, circulation, and reception of poetry. In general, most studies discuss historical, political, and gender issues when talking about early American poetry. Cultural historians spell out the social aesthetics of eighteenth-century polite literature, while they consider poetry along the lines of an "institutional history of manners" (Shields 1997: xxi). Accordingly, colonial poetry is relegated to performing acts of civility within processes of social figurations, such as elite circles or metropolitan clubs. To bridge the opposition between textualist and contexualist approaches to analyzing poetry, Rachel Blau DuPlessis suggests a "socio-poesis" (2012: 66), intending a social reading via poetic practices. A reading of colonial poetry crafted upon such an approach would not ignore the concurrence of social and aesthetic issues. Its focus on poetic forms and functions such as genre, arrangement of line breaks, or metrical devices exposes colonial poetry as a cultural text offering specific social and historical meanings distilled in the poem's aesthetic form and brought to light by a practice of close readings. It would finally also help reassess the value problem inherent in early American poetry and its long dependence on historical rather than literary considerations.

Bibliography

Selected Primary Literature

Bradstreet, Anne. 1650. "The Prologue." *The Tenth Muse Lately Sprung up in America or Severall Poems, Compiled with Great Variety of Wit and Learning, Full of Delight. Wherein Especially is Contained a Compleat Discourse and Description of the Four elements, Constitutions, Ages of Man, Seasons of the Year. Together with an Exact Epitomie of the Four Monarchies, viz. The Assyrian, Persian, Grecian, Roman. Also a Dialogue between Old England and New, Concerning the Late Troubles. With Divers Other Pleasant and Serious Poems. By a Gentlewoman in those Parts.* London: for Stephen Bowtell at the Signe of the Bible in Popes Head-Alley. 3-4.

Cook, Ebenezer. 2007 [1708]. "The Sot-Weed Factor; or, A Voyage to Maryland." In: Shields 2007a. 239-58.

Grainger, James. 1999 [1764]. "The Sugar Cane: A Poem, In Four Books." In: Thomas W. Krise (ed.), *Caribbeana: An Anthology of English Literature of the West Indies, 1657-1777.* Chicago: U of Chicago P. 166-260.

Lewis, Richard. 2007a [1730]. "A Journey from Patapsco to Annapolis, April 4, 1730." In: Shields 2007a. 386-96.

——. 2007b [1730]. "*To Mr.* Samuel Hastings, (ship-wright of Philadelphia) *on his launching the Maryland-Merchant, a large ship built by him at Annapolis.*" In: Shields 2007a. 380-6.

——. 2007 [1731]. "Food for Criticks." In: Shields 2007a. 396-400.

——. 1733. "A Description of Maryland, extracted from a Poem, entitled Carmen Seculare, addressed to Ld Baltimore, Proprietor of that Province, now there. By Mr. Lewis, Author of the beautiful Poem inserted in our 4th Number entitled, a Journey from Patapsco to Annapolis." In: *Gentleman's Magazine* III: 209-10.

Mather, Cotton. 1726. *Manuductio ad Ministerium.* Boston: Hancock.

Pastorius, Francis Daniel. 2007. [1699]. "Epibaterium, Or a hearty Congratulation to William Penn. Chief Proprietary of the Province of Pennsilvania etc. Upon his third Arrival into the same." In: Shields 2007a. 209-14.

—. 2007 [1714]. "A Token of Love and Gratitude." In: Shields 2007a. 200-2.

—. 2012 [1717/18]. "Jane Fenn sent me the 5th of the 11th mo: 1717/8 a Sheet full of Rimes of her own Make; Upon which I answered her the next ensuing day etc." In: Erben 2012. 179-80.

—. 1956 [1688]. "Protest Against Slavery." In: Stoudt 1956. 4.

Shields, David S. (ed.). 2007a. *American Poetry: The Seventeenth and Eighteenth Centuries*. New York: Library of America.

Wheatley, Phillis. 1989 [1770]. "On the Death of the Rev. Mr. George Whitefield." In: Julia D. Mason (ed.), *The Poems of Phillis Wheatley*. Rev. and enlarged Ed. Chapel Hill: U of North Carolina P. 55-7, 132-9.

Selected Secondary Literature

Beyers, Chris. 2008. "Augustan American Verse." In: Kevin J. Hayes (ed.), *The Oxford Handbook of Early American Literature*. Oxford: Oxford UP. 189-214.

A reliable survey of colonial poets such as Ebenezer Cook, Robert Bolling, and Richard Lewis in the context of the Augustan Age in British North America.

Erben, Patrick M. 2012. *A Harmony of the Spirits: Translation and the Language Community of the Spirits*. Chapel Hill: U of North Carolina P.

This is the first comprehensive study acknowledging not only Pastorius's role as a public figure in colonial Pennsylvania, but the book also gives stimulating insights into his poetry as well as colonial German-American literature.

Lemay, Leo J.A. 1972. *Men of Letters in Colonial Maryland*. Knoxville: U of Tennessee P.

Lemay's study is an early attempt to revive the rich literary tradition that existed in the mid-Atlantic British colonies prior to the American Revolution. It contains detailed close readings of the literature produced by poets, printers, and wits who established a society of polite letters in the colonies.

Shields, David S. 1997. *Civil Tongues and Polite Letters in British America*. Chapel Hill: U of North Carolina P.

This is the most trenchant study about the emergence of a "social aesthetics" in conjunction with the rise of belles lettres in British North America prior to 1760. The book should be read together with Shields's other studies on the literary culture in British America (cf. below 1994; 2007b).

Further References

Amory, Hugh and David D. Hall (eds.). 2000-2009. *A History of the Book in America*. 5 Vols. Chapel Hill: U of North Carolina P.

Beyers, Chris. 2002. "Maryland's 'First Essay of *Latin* Poetry in *English* Dress'." In: *Early American Literature* 37.2: 247-80.

Carretta, Vincent. 2011. *Phillis Wheatley: Biography of a Genius in Bondage*. Athens: U of Georgia P.

DuPlessis, Rachel Blau. 2012. "Social Texts and Poetic Texts: Poetry and Cultural Studies." In: Cary Nelson (ed.), *The Oxford Handbook of Modern and Contemporary American Poetry*. Oxford: Oxford UP. 53-70.

Galinsky, Hans. 1991. *Geschichte amerikanischer Kolonialliteratur: Multinationale Wurzeln einer Weltliteratur und Werkinterpretationen (1542-1722)*. 3 Vols. Darmstadt: Wissenschaftliche Buchgesellschaft.

Hall, David D. 1996. *Cultures of Print: Essays in the History of the Book*. Amherst: U of Massachusetts P.

—. 2008. *Ways of Writing: The Practice and Politics of Text-Making in Seventeenth-Century New England*. Philadelphia: U of Pennsylvania P.

Hammond, Jeffrey A. 2000. *The American Puritan Elegy: A Literary and Cultural Study*. Cambridge: Cambridge UP.

Jantz, Harold. 1985. "Baroque Free Verse in New England and Pennsylvania." In: Peter White (ed.), *Puritan Poets and the Poetics: Seventeenth-Century American Poetry in Theory and Practice*. University Park: Pennsylvania State UP. 258-73.

Jehlen, Myra and Michael Warner (eds.). 1997. *The English Literatures of America, 1500-1800*. New York: Routledge.

Kropf, C. R. 1980/81. "'Food for Criticks' as Aesthetic Statement." In: *Early American Literature* 15.3: 205-16.

Love, Harold. 1993. *Scribal Publication in Seventeenth-Century England*. Oxford: Clarendon P.

Meserole, Harrison T. (ed.). 1993 [1985]. *American Poetry of the Seventeenth Century*. 2nd printing. University Park: Pennsylvania State UP.

Mulford, Carla (ed.). 2002. *Early American Writings*. Oxford: Oxford UP.

Parker, Robert Dale (ed.). 2011. *Changing is Not Vanishing: A Collection of Early American Indian Poetry to 1930*. Philadelphia: U of Pennsylvania P.

Parks, Franklin A. 2012. *William Parks: The Colonial Printer in the Transatlantic World of the Eighteenth Century*. University Park: Pennsylvania State UP.

Patterson, Annabel. 1987. *Pastoral and Ideology: Virgil to Valéry*. Berkeley: U of California P.

Rubin, Joan Shelley. 2007. *Songs of Ourselves: The Uses of Poetry in America*. Cambridge, MA: Harvard UP.

Scheiding, Oliver. 2012. "Migrant Fictions and the Early Story in North American Magazines." In: *REAL—Yearbook of Research in English and American Literature* 28: 197-218.

— and Martin Seidl (eds.). 2015. *Worlding America. A Transnational Anthology of Short Narratives before 1800*. Stanford: Stanford UP.

Schweitzer, Christoph E. 1981. "Francis Daniel Pastorius, the German-American Poet." In: *Yearbook of German American Studies* 18: 21-8.

Shields, David S. 1994. "British-American Belles Lettres." In: Sacvan Bercovitch (ed.), *The Cambridge History of American Literature*. Vol. 1. *1590-1820*. Cambridge: Cambridge UP. 307-43.

—. 2007b. "Eighteenth-Century Literary Culture." In: Amory/Hall 2000-2009, Vol. 1. *The Colonial Book in the Atlantic World*. 434-76.

Shivers, Jr., Frank R. 1985. *Maryland Wits and Baltimore Bards: A Literary History*. Baltimore, MD: The Johns Hopkins UP.

Spengemann, William C. 1994. *A New World of Words: Redefining Early American Literature*. New Haven, CN: Yale UP.

Stoudt, John Joseph (ed.). 1956. *Pennsylvania German Poetry, 1685-1830*. Allentown: The Pennsylvania German Folklore Society.

Sweet, Timothy. 2002. *American Georgics: Economy and Environment in Early American Literature*. Philadelphia: U of Pennsylvania P.

Weyler, Karen A. 2013. *Empowering Words: Outsiders and Authorship in Early America*. Athens and London: The U of Georgia P.

Zamora, Lois Parkinson and Monika Kaup (eds.). 2010. *Baroque New Worlds: Representation, Transculturation, Counterconquest*. Durham, NC: Duke UP.

3.

The Poetry of the New Nation

Joel Barlow's "The Hasty-Pudding" and Philip Freneau's "The Wild Honey Suckle"

Julia Straub

1. Poetry of and for the New Nation

The poetry of the new nation was poetry for the new nation: poems written before, during, and in the aftermath of the American Revolution (1763-1783) are characterized by a strong public profile. "Poetry had a social identity," writes Michael Gilmore, it "enjoyed an intimate relation to national consciousness" (1994: 591, 594). The American Revolution was an incisive event in US-American history: it not only enabled political, economic, and cultural independence, but in the eyes of many it also marked the birth of an American literature. Literature plays a decisive part in processes of nation building as the concept of a national literature presupposes a consolidated, canonized body of works that reflect different facets or qualities of what is often called national character (cf. Corse 1991). Poetry has traditionally been a privileged genre in this context, most notably the subgenre of epic poetry (for example, the *Iliad*, the *Odyssey*, and the Old English *Beowulf*), which has been put in the service of chronicling heroic deeds and the rise and fall of nations, kingdoms, and empires since antiquity.

Poetry depended, like many other forms of Revolutionary discourse, on newspapers and magazines—the media that permitted the voicing of public opinion. Philip Freneau's partisan newspaper the *National Gazette*, a mouthpiece of the Republicans, is a good example here. It was published at the behest of Republican Party leaders Thomas Jefferson and James Madison and contained many pieces, albeit often published anonymously, by prominent Republicans. Ever since the Stamp Act of 1765, which enforced the use of tax-declared paper for the printing of legal papers, periodicals, and many other print products, the realm of print and publishing had become politicized. Scholars of early American literature, such as Trish Loughran and Michael Warner, have shown the importance of the printed word for the social and political processes leading to American Independence. The dissemination of periodicals, pamphlets, and other print products was crucial for the building of an "imagined community," to use the concept coined by Benedict Anderson (1983) in his eponymous study. In order to become a nation, Americans had to be able to imagine themselves as its citizens, the nation being a construct rather than a given entity.

Most poems written immediately during this period of political and social upheaval lack the historical and critical distance necessary to objectively discern and develop standards of such a new national literature. Instead, the poems reflect a noticeable topicality—a concern with current political and national matters. Party political struggles, public debates, and developments in Europe, particularly the French Revolution, stood center-stage. While in late eighteenth-century Britain the 'Graveyard Poets,' such as Thomas Gray and Edward Young, were anticipating the poetical gestures tied to their preferred themes of seclusion, sublime nature, and emotional exuberance that would shape Romantic concepts of literature for decades to come, their American counterparts were deeply rooted in their here and now and were acutely aware of their duties as citizens—and poets—of a new nation. The idea that literature should both teach and entertain was firmly inscribed into a neo-classical understanding of art that still informed much of the poetry from the American Revolution. At the same time, American poets did not remain immune to such new literary trends and debates spilling over from across the Atlantic, which explains the partly ambivalent formal and aesthetic qualities of Revolutionary poetry, as will be demonstrated below in the discussion of Freneau's "The Wild Honey Suckle."

One central poetic theme in this period is the celebration of future cultural achievement. Examples include John Trumbull's "Prospect of the Future Glory of America" (1770), Philip Freneau and Hugh Henry Brackenridge's "The Rising Glory of America" (1771), Joel Barlow's "A Poem, Spoken at the Public Commencement at Yale College, in New Haven" (1781), David Humphreys's "The Glory of America" (1783), and George Berkeley's well-known "On the Prospects of Planting Arts and Learning in America" (1752), where he elaborates the *translatio studii* theme of America's intellectual and artistic expansion toward the West. An appropriate form for the expression of patriotic sentiment was, for many, the epic; Joel Barlow's highly successful *The Vision of Columbus* (1787) and Timothy Dwight's "The Conquest of Canaan" (1785) are early American examples of this grand poetic subgenre, modeled on dignified precursory works from Europe.

Female writers were also actively involved in this discourse on America's bright future. They often embraced the cause of the American Revolution and wrote poems celebrating the Revolutionary spirit and praising the outlook for the future of the American nation. While kept from pursuing political careers themselves, poets such as Mercy Otis Warren ("To Fidelio, Long Absent on the Great Public Cause, Which Agitated All America," c. 1775) and Phillis Wheatley (America's first published African American author) paid homage to politics and the public sphere, their works representing female patriotism. In her poem "To His Excellency General Washington" (1776), Wheatley summons heavenly support in order to write her eulogy of America's first president: "Celestial choir! Enthron'd in realms of light, / Columbia's scenes of glorious toils I write" (Wheatley 1989 [1776]: 166). Hannah Griffitts's "The Female Patriots. Address'd to the Daughters of Liberty in America" from the year 1768 clarifies the priorities of America's women: "That rather than Freedom, we'll part with our Tea / And well as we love the dear Draught when a dry, / As American Patriots,—our Taste we deny" (Griffitts 2007 [1768]: 558, ll. 12-4). Inspired by a European discourse on artistic ingenuity, Americans painted visions of their nation as a place where the intellectual and artistic achievements of the Old World would be surpassed.

Puritanism had, of course, left its imprint on the American imagination. The belief that the Puritan settlers were God's chosen people in search of the Promised Land had shaped the literature of the seventeenth century. This quest for providential meaning, which had found numerous echoes in literary and non-literary writing in early America, also fed into the theme of America's 'rising glory' as political independence was achieved. But the poems listed above reflect a shift away from religious exceptionalism toward a self-portrayal of America as a fertile soil where the arts can prosper. These poems from the 1770s and 1780s act as miniature epics of the young nation. They were platforms where poets could air their patriotic feelings and loyalty to America's destiny and thereby give concrete shape to their belief that poetry ought to be useful for the public.

The quest for a distinctly American kind of writing expressed by the 'rising glory' poems took different forms. The use of epic patterns was one of them, but other, demonstratively unrefined genres were also in demand. The celebration and sometimes idealization of the life of the common man, embedded within a rural context, found its echo in popular songs and ballads. They included folk-loristic elements and were a backlash to forms and themes belonging to Euro-pean 'high culture' that had been exhausted by British writers. These poems, dealing with the life of the simple American and celebrating a plain lifestyle, were meant to foster a sense of patriotism disencumbered by foreign influences. The anonymous "Ballad of Nathan Hale" (1776) is a good example with its depic-tion of the eponymous devoted soldier; Francis Hopkinson's "The Battle of the Kegs" (1778), a propaganda ballad lauding the efforts of the rebel army in their fight against the British fleet, should be mentioned. Susanna Rowson's drinking song called "America, Commerce and Freedom" (1794), in which sailors praise America's wealth owed to seafaring and trade, adds an interesting and maybe unexpected facet to the body of works by this outstanding early American female novelist, the author of the bestselling sentimental novel *Charlotte Temple* (1791).

In the immediate post-Revolutionary period, however, there were also critical voices that uttered concern with the political and economic future of the United States—voices fuelled by an anxious anticipation of chaos. *The Anarchiad* (1786-1787), a poem that resulted from the cooperation of several Connecticut Wits—a group of poets who had met at Yale—was a satirical statement against Daniel Shays, a populist rebellion leader, and reflects the fear of social unrest in post-Revolutionary New England. The optimistic account of America's cultural destiny given in the 'rising glory' poems is complicated by at least two factors: the precariousness of being a writer in Revolutionary America, and the many debts to Europe in the fields of the arts and literature.

Poets in Revolutionary America had a primarily public function to perform, and it comes as no surprise that many of them played an active part in the sur-rounding political and administrative events and processes. Some of the poets whom we associate closely with the American Revolution, and whose works have become part of the American canon, held positions in the public arena. Joel Barlow and David Humphreys were diplomats; Barlow, among other things, helped ratify the Treaty of Tripoli between the United States and several North African States in 1797, thereby settling maritime conflicts that had led to several hostage crises during the eighteenth century. John Trumbull was a judge. Philip Freneau worked as a translator for Thomas Jefferson at the State Department and spent much of his life working as a captain at sea. Their lives and profes-sional multi-tasking reflect the close connection between political and poetic vocation at that time, and remind us of the realities of authorship as a pro-fession: most poets could not live off the money they earned with their poetry. While poetry was highly esteemed as a literary genre, it was rather difficult to find readers willing to spend money on it. As Emory Elliott has argued, writers had to fight hard to secure a respectable and financially rewarding position for themselves in a society that was undergoing revolutionary change and was thus averse to traditional figures of authority (1986: 47). As a consequence, author-ship often took on a collaborative dimension in Revolutionary America. The group of poets known as the Connecticut Wits is an outstanding example, in-cluding members such as John Trumbull, Timothy Dwight, Joel Barlow, David Humphreys, and lesser figures such as Lemuel Hopkinson, Richard Alsop, and

Elihu Hubbard Smith (who was also the editor of one of the earliest American poetry anthologies, entitled *American Poems: Selected and Original* from 1793). Their cooperation on poems and their collective self-identification as poets runs counter to the notion of the poet as the lonesome genius whose creativity unfurls in isolation, a predominant concept in European Romanticism.

While poets sketched visions of future success in the arts and placed a strong emphasis on the depiction of a distinctly American experience, the rhetorical means and traditions from which American writers drew were largely European. As studies by Leonard Tennenhouse and Elisa Tamarkin have shown, notions of cultural allegiance to Britain—both diaspora and 'Anglophilia'—persisted even after all political ties with the motherland had been cut.

European notions of 'taste,' literary fashions, and concepts of what is beautiful and 'good' poetry remained relevant yardsticks for American poetry in this period regardless of the urgency with which American themes were promulgated and the decisiveness with which political independence was entrenched. American poets were writing in line with European, particularly British, models and traditions as much as they were trying to write against them. Four sources of influence, which will be addressed in turn, are of particular importance: (1) Greek and Roman antiquity, (2) the seventeenth- and eighteenth-century neoclassical tradition, (3) contemporary writing, particularly nascent forms of Romanticism, and (4) imported debates on aesthetic theory.

(1) Due to their academic training at the New England colleges, several of which had been established as early as in the seventeenth century (Harvard was founded in 1636), many of the Revolutionary poets—the Connecticut Wits ranking as a prime example—were familiar with the works of Greek and Roman writers such as Cicero, Tacitus, and Plutarch, writers who placed a special emphasis on the Republic and Republicanism in their works. Many American poets were well versed in the formal and classical rhetoric that had been part of their scholarly training (cf. Hannemann 2008). Thus we find in numerous poems stylistic devices that reflect their knowledge of classical rhetoric; the "Hasty-Pudding" is a good example, as will be shown below. Genres such as the Georgics, going back to Virgil's *Eclogues*, or literary Pastoralism, as can be seen in works by Hesiod, Ovid, and Theocritus, also informed the writing about nature and the relationship between man and nature in America.

(2) The reception of the classics in America was not always first-hand but had been refracted by the reading of British poets who also made use of classical devices and genres. The names that need mentioning here are Alexander Pope, John Addison, Jonathan Swift, and John Dryden. While William Shakespeare and John Milton undoubtedly were the two major canonical authors in America, one has to acknowledge the influence of these eighteenth-century wits, particularly the adoration of Pope (cf. Giles 2011). Their works reflected the ideals of neo-classical writing with its strong emphasis on diction, rules, formal regularity, clarity, and control of feeling. It was from these authors that American writers gleaned their penchant for satire. Pope's *The Dunciad* (1728-1743) is a key text in this context as it reflects a mixture of elegance, formal correctness, learnedness, persuasiveness, humor, and provocation that suited a revolutionary context where writers would more often than not engage with each other in *guerres de plumes*. Examples are John Trumbull's mock epic *M'Fingal* (1775) and the anonymous *The Progress of Dullness* (1772), a satire of higher education in the American colonies.

(3) Late eighteenth-century literature in Europe was characterized by the transition from neo-classical modes of writing to a Romantic understanding of literature. Pre-Romantic writers in Britain include Edward Young, whose long poem *Night Thoughts* (1742-1745) introduced themes and moods that also defined the Gothic with its darker images of death and decay and a melancholic atmosphere, and Oliver Goldsmith, whose "The Deserted Village" (1770) dwells upon the contrast between urban and rural life. Pre-Romantic writers prepared major Romantic themes in their works, particularly the notion of nature as a refuge to which the tortured and isolated poetic self can withdraw for comfort and the ideal of an authentic experience of selfhood. Given their preference for an immediate expression of feeling and their quest for an unrepressed individuality, Romantic writers rejected the norms and dictates of neo-classical writing.

(4) Finally, Revolutionary writers were familiar with theoretical texts on literature and the aesthetics produced by European philosophers and theoreticians such as Lord Henry Home Kames (*Elements of Criticism*, 1762) and Hugh Blair (*Lectures on Rhetoric and Belles Lettres*, 1783). Their works were responsible for the importation of key concepts in aesthetic theory of the time such as 'the Sublime' or 'taste,' and for the emergence of *belles lettres* writing, i.e., literature that is intended to be entertaining and not primarily purposeful. Aesthetic theory also affected a transatlantic discussion on liberty and autonomy that played into Revolutionary discourse (cf. Cahill 2012).

2. Joel Barlow's "The Hasty-Pudding": A Recipe for America

"The Hasty-Pudding" (first published in *New York Magazine* in 1796) reflects several of the aspects mentioned above. The poem follows partly contradictory impulses: it milks poetic traditions and rhetorical conventions from the Old World but then parodies them. It also demonstrates serious concern with America's distinctiveness in cultural matters but ironizes these specificities. Still, it counts as one of the period's major poetic testimonies of literary independence by introducing themes that speak of an American sense of identity. As one of Barlow's most frequently anthologized poems, "The Hasty-Pudding" has persisted in the popular imagination where more foundational and programmatic (respectively cerebral) poems have receded from the public eye.

The poem describes simple American life by paying homage to 'hasty pudding,' coming closest to what is known today as polenta, a meal made of mushy corn. The poem consists of three parts that Barlow called "cantos," a term typically used to describe sections in long epic poems such as Dante's *Divine Comedy*. The fact that the poet calls these stanzas "cantos" can be seen as a playfully self-aggrandizing gesture: here is an American writer whose poetic subject is worthy of epic praise! Suffice it to look at the motto that preceded Barlow's "The Hasty-Pudding" to understand the poem's dominant tone of irony.

> *Omne tulit punctum qui miscuit utile dulci.*
> He makes a good breakfast who mixes pudding with molasses.
> (Barlow 2007 [1796]: 799; original emphasis)

Barlow's whimsical rendering of the Latin original hinges on the different semantic nuances of the Latin word *dulcis*. Whereas in Horace's *Ars Poetica* the sentence refers to the art of good writing, stating that a writer succeeds when he both instructs and entertains, Barlow ironizes this motto by punning on the notion of sweetness.

Canto 1 introduces the poem's central themes. It evokes the French Alps as a setting, a location far away from rural America but familiar to readers of Romantic literature at that time. The Alps counted as a sublime landscape par excellence, to use Edmund Burke's concept elaborated upon in *On the Beautiful and the Sublime* (1757): the grandeur of this scenery was considered awe-inspiring. In line 1, the speaker addresses the majestic Alps surrounding him in a somewhat colloquial fashion ("Ye Alps audacious"). Four lines later, however, he solemnly declares that it is not really the mountains' sublime effect that he wants to praise with this poem (l. 5: "I sing not you"). Thus, the poem begins on a note of defiance: exalted as this scenery might be presented by other writers, it does not elicit the speaker's admiration. Barlow writes instead about a topic which has received little attention so far, but warrants poetic consideration: the hasty pudding.

In the first eight lines alone, Barlow employs several stylistic devices that are typical of neo-classical writing and exhibit his poetic skillfulness. However, he also introduces the ironic tension that runs through the entire poem, which is caused by the discrepancy between his elevated style and the common subject. His highly artificial language and syntax stand in blatant contrast with the hearty, unsophisticated meal upon which he bestows any thinkable poetic gesture of reverence.

The first four lines represent what is known as *occupatio* in rhetoric: they state that with which the writer will not concern himself. The meter of these lines is iambic, but their regularity comes to an abrupt halt in line 5, which closes off syntactically the first four lines in the manner of a *zeugma*. Written in irregular spondees, "I sing not you" with its two long syllables interrupts the meter and signals a change of tide on the level of argument. What follows in the middle of the same line is a *caesura*, after which the speaker begins to unravel a new idea, the "virgin theme" (l. 6). There is an *anadiplosis* in the use of the word "theme" towards the end of line 5 and then again at the beginning of the next line. Furthermore, the adjective "soft" in line 5 is another hint at the texture of the hasty pudding. The opening eight lines anticipate some of the formal elements and themes that will shape the rest of the poem, and they reflect Barlow's dexterous but also tongue-in-cheek use of rhetorical devices and traditions.

It takes the speaker a few more lines to reveal to the reader his actual poetic interest. In the next lines (ll. 9-14) he turns to his fellow poets, those who evoke thunderous battlefields in their poems, praise the solaces of wine, extol the beauties of women, or contemplate elusive, unattainable joys. Thus, lines 9-14 take up the same thought as lines 1-5 in that they sketch conventions that other poets have followed in order for the speaker to single out his exclusive topic. He ostentatiously sets himself apart from the others by writing about a treat he knows well (l. 15), one that he enjoys every single day: "The sweets of Hasty-Pudding" (l. 17). Lines 15-6 contain a *chiasm*, a scheme that allows Barlow to very elegantly mingle sensory perceptions of the body ("the evening meal") with those of the soul ("morning incense") by crossing the syntactical structures of the two consecutive lines. Finally, in line 17 the actual object of this eulogy is named and addressed: "Come, dear bowl, / Glide o'er my palate, and inspire my soul" is a deeply humoresque line; the irony it contains is made overly conspicuous. The apostrophe of a "dear bowl" by itself, the explicitly physical description of the hasty pudding slithering down the speaker's throat and acting as a source of inspiration ridicules conventional poetic *topoi* (e.g., the praise of a beloved who is the speaker's muse).

The speaker depicts the preparation of hasty pudding in hyperbolic terms, tracing its origins back to Ceres, the Roman goddess of agriculture, who "[f]irst learn'd with stones to crack the well-dry'd maize" (l. 38). The pudding is compared to a "golden show'r" (l. 39) and shortly after its production is described in antithetical terms:

> The yellow flour, bestrew'd and stir'd with haste,
> Swells in the flood and thickens to a paste,
> Then puffs and wallops, rises to the brim,
> Drinks the dry knobs that on the surface swim; (ll. 41-4)

"Swells in the flood" implies some kind of grandeur (as does the overall mythological interpretation of the dish); one could think of a brutal force of nature about to unleash its power upon humankind. However, set against the thickening of the paste that follows, and the very colloquial "pugs and wallops" (the latter being onomatopoeic), the comic element is strong.

Throughout the poem Barlow maintains this ambivalent tone, i.e., he shows command of a refined and more colloquial linguistic register. In addition to the examples mentioned above, he uses the whole spectrum of stylistic devices to ennoble his poem formally: an onomatopoeic alliteration in l. 26 ("roll in substance, roll in rhyme"), key words of neo-classical thought and writing, such as "virtue" (l. 52 and l. 143), "clear" (l. 96), and the "rules of art" (l. 158), as well as multi-syllable words (e.g., "top-gallants," l. 229; "goose-egg-shell," l. 361). At the same time he employs plain and graphic language to describe the different textures and shapes of hasty pudding and connects it with the simplicity of rural life in America, praising it as a dish closely entwined with American culture (and popular with his own ancestors, l. 125). Hasty pudding is the Yankee's "abundant feast, / With simples furnish'd, and with plainness drest" (ll. 166-7).

One prominent semantic field that Barlow brings up in this canto and in other parts of his poem is that of harvesting: maize, the grain from which hasty pudding is made, is mentioned repeatedly, as is sun imagery (l. 71; l. 215), symbolizing fertility and growth. Thus, while the hasty pudding is its focus of attention, the poem touches upon a variety of topics, displaying myriad impressions from the American countryside, spotlighting a multitude of social settings, and also incorporating cosmopolitan glimpses. The poet stylizes himself as a world traveler who fails to fully enjoy the splendors of faraway places and falls homesick because he misses hasty pudding, looking for it abroad wherever he can and finding it under a number of different names. It is an utterly unpretentious meal, varieties of which appear in different parts of the world (cf. ll. 85-93). This passage positions the poem's domestic focus in relation to the world, since at the time Barlow was writing this poem, international trade was an important aspect of economic welfare and "a larger trajectory of global discovery" (Giles 2012: 142) that played into the perception of America as a nation.

Canto 2 further develops the panegyric of hasty pudding as a national dish. The speaker broadens his vision and that of his readers in order to provide a more panoramic view of American society. Sketching scenes of domestic life, Barlow represents hasty pudding as the food of humble American families who labor hard to earn their living and for whom it is a nourishing feast. The speaker then shifts his focus to the growing of maize and the annual cycle of farming and harvesting, describing in detail and rather poetically (note for example the comparison with a Corinthian column and the use of alliterations) the growth of the plant throughout the seasons: "Then start the juices, then the roots expand; / Then, like a column of Corinthian mould, / The stalk struts upwards, and the leaves unfold" (ll. 217-9). Barlow hereby takes up and parodies the traditional theme of nature's annual cycle as reflected also in *The Seasons* (1726), Scottish poet James Thomson's epic with which American readers were familiar. The poem further drifts into the genre of the pastoral because of its description of nature's progress: with the month of October the time of harvesting is reached, which the poem brings to life in emphatic terms, highlighting the plenitude of the "powder'd gold" (l. 260) that will see the farmers through the winter. The "well-pleas'd lasses and contending swains" (l. 287), who take part in the "frolic scenes" (l. 268) with which begins Canto 3, are stock characters in bucolic romance.

Canto 3 describes jovial farming customs such as "husking," the processing of corn where "[b]rown corn-fed nymphs, and strong hard-handed beaux" (l. 272) make the "corn-cobs crack" (l. 275). The speaker places the hasty pudding firm-ly amidst merry farming rites and domestic life, it being a "great resource in those black wintry days" (l. 313). Again, the praiseworthiness of the subject is rendered in hyperbolic ways:

> Blest-cow! thy praise hall still my notes employ;
> Great source of health, the only source of joy;
> Mother of Egypt's God,—but sure, for me,
> Were I to leave my God, I'd worship thee.
> How oft thy teats these pious hands have prest!
> How oft thy bounties prove my only feast!
> How oft I've fed thee with my fav'rite grain!
> And roar'd, like thee, to find thy children slain! (ll. 316-23)

These lines begin with a comic apostrophe of the hasty pudding as a golden cow. Hyperbole takes on several forms in this passage: it is represented on a formal level by the use of an *anaphora* in ll. 320-2 (the same words are repeated at the beginning of each line), and exclamation marks are used to add a sense of urgency. On the level of content, the quasi-religious veneration of the hasty pudding and the mock sentimentalism of these lines add to an effect of excess, as does the lengthy description, over the final lines of the poem, of the proper manner in which the hasty pudding should be eaten, including instructions re-garding the amount of pudding that should be scooped by a particular type of spoon for each bite (cf. ll. 342-5), so that "[t]he wide mouth'd bowl will surely catch them all" (l. 371).

While entertaining, Barlow's "The Hasty-Pudding" contains elements of so-cial criticism. It excels with its gaudy, but also very astute sense of irony: the good things about America manifest themselves first and foremost as the simple things. Old World sophistication is conjured up as a backdrop that, despite its luxuries and refinement, loses out against the plain but honest delicacy of the American national dish. The relationship between man and nature is also im-portant. In "The Hasty-Pudding" farming life plays an essential role, and Ameri-can identity is placed in close proximity to a nurturing nature. It is interesting to juxtapose Barlow's poem with Freneau's "The Wild Honey Suckle," which seems different at first sight given its brevity and focused argument, but invites comparison nonetheless.

3. Philip Freneau's "The Wild Honey Suckle": The Schizophrenia of American Poetry

Philip Freneau has been labeled the "poet of the American Revolution" (Wells 2008: 506). What earned him this epithet was his experience of captivity at sea in the hands of the British, which fed the strong anti-British sentiment that permeates much of his poetic work.

Freneau's poem "The Wild Honey Suckle" dates from the year 1786 and serves as a good example of the different, sometimes opposing aesthetic strains that pressed upon poets during this period of change. As stated above, poetry of this era had to follow a public, programmatic agenda. Whether alone or in groups, poets performed as a voice for the American nation as a whole. For these purposes the neo-classical rhetoric that was rooted in literary models from ancient Greece and Rome was a suitable means as it implied gravity and civic authority. At the same time, Revolutionary poets could not turn a blind eye to new aesthetic paradigms and demands. Their use of old neo-classical models that were neutral and impersonal (and thus suitable for depicting collective experiences relating to the new nation) clashed with new, rather 'Romantic' trends that stressed interiority and private experience. This has been described as a "schizophrenic" aspect of their writing (Gilmore 1994: 592).

Freneau's poetry embodies this tension: his poetry voices concerns of a public persona, but at the same time it deals with experiences that reflect a desire for solitude and private contemplation. In fact, Freneau liked to take the occasional 'time out' as a sporadic recluse who, it is well known, often set sail for remoter parts of the world, such as the West Indies.

"The Wild Honey Suckle" consists of four stanzas of six lines each, the meter being a regular iambic tetrameter. The rhyme scheme is ababcc, with a closing couplet concluding each stanza. This metrical and structural regularity and a clear, relatively simple diction endow the poem with a neo-classical quality: thoughts are rounded off in each stanza, and are thus under formal and logical control.

The speaker of the poem addresses a "[f]air flower" (l. 1) that grows in isolation, far away from civilization with its "roving foot and "busy hand" (ll. 5-6). It is beautiful, but tucked away, hidden and untouched (ll. 2-3). This idyllic vision of nature is evoked in contrast to the realm of humanity: in stanza two the flower's exceptional, isolated position is described as part of a personified nature's plan. Nature designed this exceptional place for the flower, which shuns "the vulgar eye" (l. 8) and whose white color signals vulnerability. Peace and tranquility are the conditions under which this flower thrives. The softness of nature summoned up in this stanza is disturbed by the hard, mono-syllabic adjective "[s]mit" (l. 13) with which the third stanza begins. Harshly, a new line of thought is introduced as the speaker becomes visible for the first time in line 14: behind the beauties he perceives, the speaker senses "decay" (l. 13). Stanza three thus opens up the major theme of the poem: *vanitas*. The flower and its idyllic surroundings will all fade away, victims of the changing seasons. A reference to the flowers in the Garden of Eden, which died because of human sinfulness, introduces a rich intertextual frame that exacerbates the poem's central conflict between innocence and corruption, nature and civilization, nature's beauty and brutality. Stanza four dwells on the idea of ephemerality, of which the flower becomes a symbol. Coming out of nothing, the flower returns to nothing; it exists only for a fleeting moment:

From morning suns and evening dews
At first, thy little being came:
If nothing once, you nothing lose,
For when you die you are the same;
The space between is but an hour,
The mere idea of a flower. (ll. 19-24)

The "Wild Honey Suckle" is not so much about a particular flower, but the flower gains universal meaning as a symbol. There is a noticeable gap between the speaker and the flower. In contrast to Romantic feeling, which aimed for a de-limitation of the self with regard to nature, the speaker here remains within the confines of his subjectivity, i.e., he does not seek transcendence. The poem equals an act of detached contemplation of the flower rather than an attempt at appropriating it in order to turn it into an extension of the self. Emotions are not effluent, but remain restricted because the formal rigidity of the poem re-flects the disciplined compassion of the speaker.

There is, however, a distinctly Romantic quality in the emphasis placed on the remoteness, the solitude, and the frailty of nature's beauty which needs to be protected from the presence of humans (while ultimately being inseparable from it). Nature in this poem comes across as a sphere of beauty and purity, where even the speaker is an intruder. Yet thanks to the human ability to praise the flower by virtue of poetry, and to thereby share its beauty with others, it can live on (cf. Elliott 1986: 169-70). Thus, the relationship between man and na-ture depicted in this poem is ambivalent: man is a threat, but he is also the one to perceive and relish nature's beauty. Only human *poesis* can ensure the sur-vival of perishable things like the flower. The formal regularity of this poem largely corresponds to the ideas it expresses which, too, remain under the speaker's control. However, there are obvious first stirrings toward the free-thinking and poetic liberation that define Romantic writing.

4. Conclusion and Outlook

With the turn of the century, satire in the vein of Barlow's "The Hasty-Pudding" subsided and poets increasingly devoted themselves to nonpolitical subjects. Poetry took on a more private quality. The cult of sentimentality and the aesthetic tenets of Romanticism reached America to the effect that much of the poetry from the early Republic meant to please and entertain, to blunt political or ideological edges. With print and distribution becoming easier, cheaper, and faster in the early nineteenth century, poetry turned into a commodity. Anthologies of Ameri-can poetry became an increasingly viable print product both in the United States and in Britain (an example is Samuel Kettell's voluminous *Specimens of American Poetry* from the year 1829), and while the question of what defined American lit-erature would remain hotly debated for many more decades, the body of poems available and the public interest necessary to sell it grew steadily. The work of the so-called "Fireside Poets" (Henry Wadsworth Longfellow, William Cullen Bryant, James Russell Lowell, Oliver Wendell Holmes, and John Greenleaf Whittier), who became the first prominent group of US-American poets to rival their British counterparts, reflects the growing autonomy of American poetry as well as the commercial viability of literature in the nineteenth century.

The contemplation of nature became a prominent theme that defined Ameri-can literature at its roots, in poetry and in other genres such as the novel and the short story. Freneau's works written after the Revolution reflect his interest in Romantic primitivism and in themes such as the noble savage, which originated from the writings of the French philosopher Jean-Jacques Rousseau. Freneau's depiction of nature as a secluded place to which the individual can withdraw proved to be influential for the development of the American Gothic, early representatives of which were the novelists Charles Brockden Brown and Washington Irving. The American Gothic dwells on the experience of the American wilderness as an uncanny place where the self is exposed to its 'other'; it can appear in the form of an experience with an indomitable nature or as an encounter with inscrutable Native Americans or other strangers. In the long run, many of the themes and sentiments broached by Freneau and other Revolutionary writers fed into the poetic and narrative works of Nathaniel Hawthorne, Edgar Allan Poe, and Herman Melville, where nature is often depicted in similarly ambivalent terms. Transcendentalists such as Ralph Waldo Emerson and Henry David Thoreau sought refuge in nature as a counterpoint to society, and Freneau's early Romantic understanding of nature can be placed in a line of tradition with these major authors of the later nineteenth century.

Bibliography

Selected Primary Literature

Barlow, Joel. 2007 [1796]. "The Hasty-Pudding. A Poem, in Three Cantos. Written at Chambery, in Savoy, January, 1793." In: Shields 2007. 799-808.

Brackenridge, Hugh Henry and Philip Freneau. 2001 [1771]. "The Rising Glory of America." In: Susan Castillo and Ivy Schweitzer (eds.), *The Literatures of Colonial America: An Anthology*. Malden: Blackwell. 559-67.

Freneau, Philip. 2007 [1786]. "The Wild Honey Suckle." In: Shields 2007. 742-3.

Griffitts, Hannah. 2007 [1768]. "The Female Patriots. Address'd to the Daughters of Liberty in America." In: Shields 2007. 558-9.

Humphreys, David, et al. 1967 [1861]. *The Anarchiad: A New England Poem*. Ed. Luther G. Riggs. Gainesville: Scholars' Facsimiles & Reprints.

Kettell, Samuel (ed.). 1829. *Specimens of American Poetry with Critical and Biographical Notices in Three Volumes*. Boston: S. G. Goodrich & Co.

Smith, Elihu Hubbard (ed.). 1793. *American Poems: Selected and Original*. Litchfield: Collier and Buel.

Trumbull, John. 2012. *The Satiric Poems of John Trumbull: The Progress of Dullness and M'Fingal*. Ed. Edwin T. Bowden. Austin: U of Texas P.

Wheatley, Phillis. 1989 [1776]. "To His Excellency General Washington." In: Julia D. Mason (ed.), *The Poems of Phillis Wheatley*. Rev. and enlarged ed. Chapel Hill: U of North Carolina P. 164-7.

Selected Secondary Literature

Bowden, Mary W. 1976. *Philip Freneau*. Boston: Twayne Publishers.
    While not a recent publication, this is an insightful study of Freneau, the poet and his life.

Dowling, William C. 1990. *Poetry and Ideology in Revolutionary Connecticut*. Athens: U of Georgia P.
    This is a seminal study of the lives and works of the Connecticut Wits and their intellectual New England context.

48 Julia Straub

Elliott, Emory. 1986. *Revolutionary Writers: Literature and Authority in the New Republic, 1725-1810.* New York: Oxford UP.

Elliott's influential monograph traces the emergence of American literary voices in opposition to political, religious, and cultural authorities.

Giles, Paul. 2012. "'To Gird This Watery Globe': Freneau, Barlow, and American Neoclassical Poetry." In: Eve T. Bannet and Susan Manning (eds.), *Transatlantic Literary Studies, 1660-1830.* Cambridge: Cambridge UP. 139-54.

Giles's recent discussion of Freneau and Barlow highlights the transatlantic dimension of their writing and the suitability of their works for a transnational approach to American literature.

Gilmore, Michael T. 1994. "The Literature of the Revolutionary and Early National Periods." In: Sacvan Bercovitch (ed.), *The Cambridge History of American Literature.* Vol. 1. Cambridge: Cambridge UP. 541-693.

Offers a concise, but comprehensive survey of Revolutionary poetry examining the main tendencies and crucial concerns of the period's poetic production.

Lemay, J. A. Leo. 1982. "The Contexts and Themes of 'The Hasty-Pudding.'" In: *Early American Literature* 17.1: 3-23.

Lemay's close reading is an accessible reading of thematic concerns and intertextual references in Barlow's poem.

Wells, Collin. 2008. "Revolutionary Verse." In: Kevin J. Hayes (ed.), *The Oxford Handbook of Early American Literature.* Oxford: Oxford UP. 504-24.

A useful survey article that works well in combination with Gilmore's chapter.

Further References

Anderson, Benedict. 2006 [1983]. *Imagined Communities: Reflections on the Origins and Spread of Nationalism.* London: Verso.

Buel, Richard Jr. 2011. *Joel Barlow: American Citizen in a Revolutionary World.* Baltimore: Johns Hopkins UP.

Cahill, Edward. 2012. *Liberty of the Imagination: Aesthetic Theory, Literary Form, and Politics in the Early United States.* Philadelphia: U of Pennsylvania P.

Corse, Sarah M. 1991. *Nationalism and Literature: The Politics of Culture in Canada and the United States.* Cambridge: Cambridge UP.

Giles, Paul. 2011. *Transatlantic Insurrections: British Culture and the Formation of American Literature, 1730-1860.* Philadelphia: U of Pennsylvania P.

Hannemann, Dennis. 2008. *Klassische Antike und amerikanische Identitätskonstruktion: Untersuchungen zu Festreden der Revolutionszeit und der frühen Republik, 1770-1815.* Paderborn: Schöningh.

Loughran, Trish. 2007. *The Republic in Print: Print Culture in the Age of U.S. Nation Building, 1770-1870.* New York: Columbia UP.

Shields, David S. (ed.). 2007. *American Poetry: The Seventeenth and Eighteenth Century.* New York: Library of America.

Tamarkin, Elisa. 2008. *Anglophilia: Deference, Devotion, and Antebellum America.* Chicago: U of Chicago P.

Tennenhouse, Leonard. 2007. *The Importance of Feeling English: American Literature and the British Diaspora, 1750-1850.* Princeton: Princeton UP.

Warner, Michael. 1990. *The Letters of the Republic: Publication and the Public Sphere in Eighteenth-Century America.* Cambridge: Cambridge UP.

4.

Early African American Poetry

Phillis Wheatley's "On Being Brought from Africa to America" and George Moses Horton's "On Hearing of the Intention of a Gentleman to Purchase the Poet's Freedom"

Astrid Franke

1. Early African American Poetry

Had they not been slaves, the poets Phillis Wheatley (1753?-1784) and George Moses Horton (1797-1883?) would have to be considered as belonging to different literary generations: beginning to publish poems in the years leading up to the American Revolution, Wheatley is a contemporary of Philip Freneau, Joel Barlow, and Benjamin Franklin. Unlike them, however, she was overtly pious and the Revolution proved to be a mixed blessing for her since it severed the ties to a transatlantic Methodist support network that had been crucial for the publication of her only volume of poems in 1773. Horton's poems began to appear in print in 1828 in newspapers and magazines, his books *The Hope of Liberty* (1829), *The Poetical Works of George Moses Horton* (1845), and *Naked Genius* (1865) make him contemporaneous with romanticists such as William Cullen Bryant, Ralph Waldo Emerson, and Edgar Allan Poe. To him, the end of the Civil War meant that he could finally publish what would be his last book as a free man.

As it is, Wheatley and Horton were first brought together by Margaretta Matilda Odell, whose third (1938) edition of *Memoirs and Poems of Phillis Wheatley* also contains poems by Horton, highlighting the shared circumstance of slavery. Together with African American slave poets Lucy Terry, Jupiter Hammond, and Francis Williams, the works of Wheatley and Horton illuminate what it takes to defy or circumvent the mechanisms of control that slavery exerted on poetic expression. A discussion of these slave poets sheds light on art under conditions of oppression and thereby contributes to an understanding of the connections between aesthetics and power. It inevitably also touches upon familiar problems in literary theory, such as the intention of the author, the connection between social and aesthetic affirmation in adherence to genre, the problems of periodization, and, more generally, the relation between literary history and 'history.'

Phillis Wheatley's original name is not known. "Phillis" was the name of the slave ship that brought her to America in 1761, and "Wheatley" the name of the Boston merchant family who bought her. Just as her English name conceals her origins, many of her texts obscure the experiences of her early life. The poem "On Being Brought from Africa to America" is a case in point; she may well have been asked what she remembered of that journey, since she was only seven years old at the time. Her owners and other people did take an interest in her: she was not only taught to read and write, but was also instructed in Christian doctrine, classical literature, Latin, and history. As her poems show, Phillis was given access to the books found in the libraries of educated people in Boston; she studied Milton and Pope, but also knew Virgil, Ovid, Horace, Terence, and

Homer, at least in translation, and she exchanged notes with clergyman Mather Byles (nephew of Cotton Mather), another poet in town. Most importantly, through her mistress Susanna Wheatley, Phillis became a part of the evangelical transatlantic network that centered on the famous preacher George Whitefield and his sponsor, the Countess of Huntingdon. This connection not only led to a funeral elegy that Wheatley wrote about Whitefield and addressed to the Countess, it also made her known on both sides of the Atlantic and helped to secure the necessary subscriptions for the publication of her book that the Wheatleys could not find in Boston alone (cf. Carretta 2011). Wheatley's trip to London was cut short by the illness (and subsequent death) of her mistress, and she may have been emancipated at this time, but she continued to live with John Wheatley and his daughter until their deaths in 1778. She composed a panegyric to George Washington in 1775 and celebrated the American Revolution in "Liberty and Peace, A Poem" in 1784. However, the new political elite did not take over the sponsoring function of the old transatlantic network of dignitaries: Wheatley's proposal for a second volume of poetry in 1779 failed, and she died in poverty in 1784.

George Moses Horton's family name is also that of his master; that he was sensitive to the power of naming can be deduced from the name he later gave his son: Free. From Horton's poetry, and also from letters and other historical documents, we know that two things were most important to him: personal freedom and recognition as a poet. While Wheatley was brought into an educated, wealthy family in a town dense with learning and socio-political debate, Horton was born into slavery on a small farm in North Carolina to a master who had no interest in education for either his slaves or the members of his own family. Horton grew up with the relative stability of a family consisting of his mother and his siblings; he taught himself to read and discovered poetry without any guidance or instruction. The nearest place of learning was the newly established University of North Carolina at Chapel Hill, about ten miles away, and by 1865 various people with ties to the university became Horton's connection to the world of literature and publication. Like Wheatley, he first made a name for himself by producing standardized occasional poems: white students paid him for composing love poems that Horton dictated while the students wrote down his words, later passing them off to their friends as their own. The wife of a professor, Caroline Hentz, helped him to publish his first book of poetry. Neither Susanna Wheatley nor Caroline Hentz—the women who acted as sponsors to Wheatley and Horton—were opposed to slavery; rather, they saw in their protégées a value that corresponded to their own commitments: religion in Wheatley's case and literature in Horton's.

An obvious similarity between Horton and Wheatley is that they both wrote under the close scrutiny of whites. Like many African American writers, they carried the burden of having to prove the humanity of their race: if blacks could master the intricacies of formal art and its universal truths, then—so the argument ran—they were presumably closely related to European people and were not, by nature, destined to be slaves (Gates 1988: x); this is why their work—whether it explicitly mentions and condemns slavery or not—was used for abolitionist purposes. But Wheatley and Horton also wrote for whites in the more specific sense of making a name for themselves by creating poems-on-demand that had to conform to accepted forms and conventions: the funeral elegy in Wheatley's case and the love poem, particularly the acrostic, in Horton's. Their poems, therefore, say a lot about a prevailing taste in poetry among specific groups of readers and demonstrate the social dynamics of genre conventions. The funeral elegies, for instance, which make up about one third of Wheatley's poems, were once the most flourishing poetic genre in New England. At Wheatley's time, however, elegies on cats and cows, and certainly Benjamin Franklin's "A RECEIPT to make a New-England Funeral ELEGY," had already expressed a certain weariness with the stereotyped lament (Franklin 1959 [1722], I: 25-6). Within the evangelical revivalist movement, however, the funeral elegy maintained its revered status. What made the genre attractive to Wheatley was its reliance on a presumably humble and pious voice, paradoxically authorized by its powerlessness in the face of God and death or by a kind of ventriloquism of the dead themselves.

Similarly, Horton's acrostic love poems are a time-honored kind of occasional poetry, not beneath the appreciation of an aesthete like Edgar Allan Poe but also enjoyed by educated gentlemen as a form of witty entertainment. Generally speaking, the somewhat rigid formal features and schemata of popular genres, an appreciation for clever imitation in combination with relatively low literary prestige, and a low premium on originality often allowed people on the margins of the literary field to demonstrate their skills and accomplishments. It is, therefore, no accident that popular culture often provides a kind of back entry for minorities to enter more elevated and thus more guarded spheres of literature and art. In this vein, the cultural aspects of Christianity were also crucial to early African American writers: genres such as the sermon, the hymn, the lamentation, or the psalm were 'popular' forms, the mastery of which could become the basis of recognition as a Christian. In addition, the wealth of figurative language in the Bible, narratives of slavery and oppression, salvation and redemption, and ideas about rewards for the lowly and the meek were widely known and yet ambiguous enough in their simultaneity of spiritual and political meanings to express a desire for freedom in a veiled fashion.

Finally, the term 'genius' is of interest, as both poets were advertised or advertised themselves as such and because the term provides insights into the politics and aesthetics of neoclassicism and proto-romanticism, both of which lay claim to the concept. While 'genius' originally referred to a kind of deity or demon, eighteenth-century poetics and aesthetics employed it as a key term in discussions on the relation of nature to art and the roles of imitation, of originality and the individual (cf. Bromwich 1985: 143). Following Joseph Addison, two understandings of 'genius' existed side by side, albeit in an uneasy relation to each other: one conception was the literary Augustinianism associated with Alexander Pope, with a reverence for imitation, translation, and adaptation of classical authors and learning; the other strove for a more 'natural' style by imitating not so much Homer and Horace but the 'native' authors Spenser, Milton, and Cowley. Natural description and the use of 'low' subject matter became a salient characteristic in the poetry of William Thomson, Richard Glover, John Dyer, and William Collins. The georgic is used for correcting idealized pastorals and for expressing an interest in a more 'realistic' rendering of rural life; for that purpose, autobiographical elements are increasingly acceptable in poetry as well. This context gives rise to a native primitivism, endorsing the idea that unknown poetic talent of a 'natural' kind resides among the simple peasant folk. That examples of genius may be found in the lower classes prompted members of the aristocracy to support and patronize several 'bards' and natural geniuses.

When Lady Huntingdon took up Wheatley as her protégée, she not only followed the evangelical urge to save the souls of the socially oppressed, she also complied with a tendency in literary taste that was manifest in the social practice of patronage. One of the ironies between Wheatley and Horton is that Wheatley—who is regarded as a natural genius—actually created herself through the manifold resources to which her learning gave her access, while Horton suffered from his own perceived lack of education and instruction. The title *Naked Genius* markets him, too, as a natural genius, but poems in that volume, such as "The Art of a Poet" or "The Obstruction of Genius," make it clear that he would rather be fully-dressed: he misses bitterly the support and cultivation that formal education and a group of peers might have given him.

2. Phillis Wheatley's Collective Voice in Poetry

"On Being Brought from Africa to America" (wr. 1768) is the only poem in Wheatley's *Poems on Various Subjects, Religious and Moral* (1773) that is presented as dealing with her personal experience. It is clear that abduction, enslavement, and the gruesome Middle Passage was, and still is, a highly charged subject, a traumatic experience beyond the scope of any existing poetic genre in the eighteenth century. This is all the more true in a neoclassicist poetic environment where displays of personal (and non-religious) sentiments and feelings are not common. It is hardly surprising, then, that the poem, tightly composed in heroic couplets, subsumes personal experience under a familiar religious idea that seems to leave no room for the individual, yet it does so to an extent that seems almost exaggerated. The title comes from her master's letter, which was inserted between the short Preface and the note "To the Publick," and begins "PHILLIS was brought from *Africa to America*, in the Year 1761, between Seven and Eight Years of Age" (Wheatley 1989 [1773]: 47; original emphasis). She borrows the euphemizing verb "brought," only to continue with a common justification of slavery, its stress being on a most unlikely word in that context: "mercy":

> 'TWAS mercy brought me from my *Pagan* land,
> Taught my benighted soul to understand
> That there's a God, that there's a *Saviour* too:
> Once I redemption neither sought nor knew. (ll. 1-4)

This religious argument was about to be supplanted by other reasons why Africans and African Americans were supposedly not fully human, and the idea that the conversion of pagans is a positive effect of slavery will persist well into the nineteenth century. The beginning of the poem is clearly a challenge to modern readers; one may be reminded of the grandfather's advice to the protagonist in Ralph Ellison's *Invisible Man*: "I want you to overcome 'em with yeses, undermine 'em with grins, agree 'em to death and destruction, let 'em swallow you till they vomit or bust wide open" (Ellison 1952: 13). Does Wheatley quote her masters to overcome them with agreement? Can she possibly really mean what she says?

It is important to realize that our tendency to acknowledge her humbling gesture only on the condition that her professed religious faith is feigned is just as problematic as the willingness to acknowledge her on the condition that she confesses to be a Christian. Since we cannot know the depth of her religious conviction, the best approach is to examine what these opening lines allow her to say: once the first quatrain with its emphasis on conversion is over, the "I" disappears.

> Some view our sable race with scornful eye,
> "Their colour is a diabolic die." (ll. 5-6)

With the beginning of line five, the speaker appears as a member of an un-named collective, most likely that of Christians in Britain and America, or perhaps even Christians in general, whose members display different attitudes toward "our sable race." This expression is significant for at least two reasons: in contrast to *my* sable race, "our" elevates the speaker into a wider group of humanity of which the sable race is only one; and through "sable" (denoting a highly priced fur) as one of the few positive words describing blackness, Wheatley introduces the focus for the rest of the poem—the false association of dark skin with moral depravity, which rests on the alignment of dichotomies such as light vs. dark, day vs. night, white vs. black, understanding vs. superstition, and finally, goodness vs. evil as it is summarized in the line quoting Christian racists: "Their colour is a diabolic die." With the concluding couplet—its significance further underlined by a regular iambic rhythm—Wheatley rejects this false attribution of moral meaning to skin color that threatens the unity of whatever community to which the earlier "our" refers:

> Remember, *Christians*, *Negros*, black as *Cain*,
> May be refin'd, and join th' angelic train. (ll. 7-8; original emphasis)

Like the poem as a whole, these last two lines chafe because they reintroduce the simultaneity of literal and metaphorical meanings of blackness that are part of the problem. Furthermore, because of the commas, (rather than a disambiguating colon after "Remember"), the line that begins "Remember, *Christians*, *Negros*" might, according to Erkkila, "be read doubly as an address to Christians about black humanity and an address to Christians and Negroes that links them both in the figurative image 'black as Cain'" (1993: 234). The two possible readings and the allusions to blackness and whiteness achieve a complex effect. First of all, the poem maintains the iconography of light and darkness but insists that it should be applied to matters of spirituality and not to skin color; thus, her soul was "benighted" (l. 2) when she was a pagan. The refinement, which in the context of processing sugar cane implies whitening, here refers to spiritual improvement that whitens those "black as *Cain*." The last two lines also foreground the very mechanisms with which spiritual matters and skin color are constantly linked: in biblical terms, Cain's mark is both a mark of a particular sin (the murder of his brother) and yet also a sign of God's special protection. "[B]lack as *Cain*" may therefore be understood in purely spiritual terms as referring to the state of sin, to be redeemed through Christ's sacrifice, even though the color of sin in the Bible is scarlet, not black. That Wheatley is well-aware of this color-code is shown by the line "Unmeasur'd vengeance Scarlet sins do cry" in the first draft for her unpublished poem "Atheism——," later to become "An Address to the Atheist, By P. Wheatley at the Age of 14 Years—1767—" (Wheatley 1989 [1772]: 118-21). Traditionally, however, the story of Cain (and especially the story of Ham, whose descendents were cursed to be slaves as punishment for his sin) was used to explain racial differences between Europeans and Africans, with the latter regarded as the descendants of either Cain or Ham. In this case, Cain's mark is regarded as literally black skin, so that all those with black skin may then be seen as literally and also spiritually 'black.' In a simultaneous address to Christians and Negroes, the exclusiveness of the spiritual meaning is clear; reading the line as an address to Christians alone, a reader may be tempted into a literal reading, but the last line emphasizes that any form of whitening is to be understood solely as spiritual improvement.

There is an impressive ascent in the position of the speaker in these eight lines, from the humble "'TWAS mercy" of someone who is grateful to be educated to someone who is now evidently an educator herself—one who teaches complex lessons. Paramount to her ascent is the public display of conversion in the first quatrain, as this experience is a prominent feature of evangelical theological convictions. Wheatley's self-humiliation enables her empowerment; that this transformation is carefully crafted can be seen in her sophisticated understanding of the Bible and religious doctrine as well as in her sensitivity to the multiple meanings and ambiguities of key words used in the poem. For example, "redemption" is a term of both religious and social significance; it refers not only to spiritual salvation but also to the legal possibility of buying the freedom of someone who has been sold into servitude. This second meaning originates in the Old Testament and was present in contemporary language and social practice in the eighteenth century where indentured servants (and occasionally black slaves) could buy their freedom and redeem themselves and their family. Considered in this light, the etymological origin of "mercy" in Latin (*merx, mercis*: commodity, goods) contributes to the subtext, as Wheatley was indeed brought from Africa to America as a commodity. Finally, the addition of "*Savior*" (l. 3; original emphasis) to "God" draws attention to various passages in the Old Testament where the word appears in the context of a deliverance from slavery, oppression, and enemies (cf. for instance 2 Kings 13:5; Nehemiah 9:27; Isaiah 19:20). The first quatrain thus seems to confirm that salvation is more important than liberty, but it also points to the fact that in Judeo-Christian thought, the two have often been linked.

Clearly, the subtle use of religious terminology is only discernable by fairly educated readers of the Bible, preferably those with some knowledge of Latin and an interest in fine semantic distinctions (such as members of the clergy), who figure prominently in the volume as addressees or otherwise having given occasion to her poems. Seven of these clerics sat on the committee that examined Wheatley to ascertain whether she really wrote the poems herself. Yet the voice she assumes in her poetry is frequently that of an equal as she, too, is preaching; the similarity between her voice and that of her presumed teachers is underlined by the fact that she uses their voices through quotation or ventriloquism.

A prominent example of this strategy to authorize herself is the poem with which she first gained a transatlantic reputation: her elegy "On the Death of the Rev. Mr. George Whitefield. 1770" (Wheatley 1989 [1773]: 55-7). The poem praises the itinerant preacher for his well-known dramatic skills while demonstrating Wheatley's own eloquence and dramatic skill in the alternating addresses to the dead preacher, her audience, and the Countess of Huntingdon, culminating in a final exhortation to rejoice in Whitefield's undoubted reward in heaven. Wheatley's skill is most salient when she gives us a 'direct' example of the preacher's style in quotation marks. Thus speaking through him, she can emphasize the doctrine of the "*Impartial Saviour*" (l. 35; original emphasis) who is willing to accept everyone, but prefers those who, in the eyes of the preacher as rendered by Wheatley, are in special need: sinners, Americans, youths, and Africans. Even before her elegy to Whitefield, Wheatley employed such dramatic devices as inserted dialogues and prayers (for example, in "On the Death of the Rev. Dr. Sewell. 1769"), but theatricality is most prevalent in the later "A Funeral Poem on the Death of C. E. an Infant of Twelve Months." Thus she gains authority by speaking with and through the voices of others, and then she uses this authority to speak for a larger collective as in "On Being Brought from Africa to America." The most explicitly political poem where Wheatley employs this strategy is "To the Right Honorable William, Earl of Dartmouth" (1773), where she speaks on behalf of all American colonists.

In the poems that open and conclude her volume—"To Mæcenas" (1773) and "An Answer to the *Rebus*, By the Author of these Poems" (1773)—Wheatley engages with readers who, being amateur poets themselves, appreciate the skillfulness of her verses and meet her as an equal. Ideally, her readers are well educated, comfortable with references to pagan gods and a highly allusive style, appreciative of the classics (if updated to suit a more softened, Christian atmosphere), and sensitive to the careful manipulation of feeling that balances the flights of fancy with a mournful and reflexive mood. Wheatley found an appreciative transatlantic audience in the years shortly before the American Revolution in the Boston dignitaries, especially the members of the clergy, and members of the English upper classes who corresponded to that portrait.

3. George Moses Horton and the Legacy of Slavery in American Poetry

In contrast to Wheatley's tightly composed poem, Horton's "LINES, On Hearing of the Intention of a Gentleman to Purchase the Poet's Freedom" (1837 [1828]: 21-2) seems more loosely organized. It, too, promises an insight into a slave's psyche, and here, too, the subject matter is delicate: too much gratefulness will offend his master and all adherents to slavery, yet not enough gratefulness might also offend the benevolent gentleman. As the title indicates, the poem promises to disclose a reaction to an intention that is as yet unfulfilled, and this is certainly one key to understanding the confusing sequences of hope and despair repeated throughout the poem. Using a sea journey as a metaphor for life in the first line: "When on life's ocean first I spread my sail," and the flight of the muse as another metaphor in the third: "And from the slippery strand I took my flight," the poet turns to the semantic field of weather as a major source of metaphors that conveniently fits both forms of travel. The first of the dramatic events are the "tyrannic storms" (l. 5) that unsettle the poet's journey to an extent that hope vanishes and, even worse, fear dominates; this is no condition for poetry. Stanzas three through eight seem to answer most directly to the announcement of the title with their varieties of joy, leading to "music breathed my gratitude to Heaven" (l. 32) as a climax.

Had the poem ended here, we would have a clear idea about the trajectory of Horton's life—"the clouds of fear" (l. 8, 31) would have been overcome twice—but the poem continues by turning again to stormy times. Attuning the harp hung among the willow trees ("osiers")—an allusion to Psalm 137 with its famous depiction of slavery and exile—also implies an end to weeping:

> The silent harp which on the osiers hung,
> Was then attuned, and manumission sung:
> Away by hope the clouds of fear were driven,
> And music breathed my gratitude to Heaven. (ll. 29-32)

And yet the very next stanza asks "Who could forbear to weep?" (l. 35). Is Horton looping back to expand on his misery before "hearing of the intention of a gentleman," or is he moving forward in time and relating a setback in his fate?

The repeated imagery of encouragement, assistance, and support is particularly confusing:

> At length a golden sun broke through the gloom,
> And from his smiles arose a sweet perfume—
> A calm ensued, and birds began to sing,
> And lo! the sacred muse resumed her wing.
>
> With frantic joy she chaunted as she flew,
> And kiss'd the clement hand that bore her through;
> Her envious foes did from her sight retreat,
> Or prostrate fall beneath her burning feet.
>
> 'Twas like a proselyte, allied to Heaven—
> Or rising spirits' boast of sins forgiven,
> Whose shout dissolves the adamant away
> Whose melting voice the stubborn rocks obey. (ll. 9-20)

While the "clement hand" suggests an individual, perhaps the gentleman of the title, some "philanthropic souls as from afar" (l. 41) implies a group of supporters. The first sign of help is announced by the sun breaking through gloom, and the very last line offers a "beam of hope" (l. 52). What, then, are the "tantalizing beams which . . . falsely promised all the joys of fame" (ll. 37, 39)? Was there something wrong with the first reaction? "Frantic joy" is not quite becoming to a "sacred muse," nor are "burning feet;" both might suggest that she was flying too fast. On the other hand, it is hard to find anything wrong with the following series of comparisons to capture the joy about the prospect of a new beginning, offering a fair overview of the different subjects and registers of Horton's writing: religion, nature, love, myth, and again, the Bible.

As in Wheatley's case, one is tempted to search for non-literary documents about the poet's life to find out what he might have meant—only to be further confused. The poem appeared first on October 7, 1828 in a North Carolina newspaper, the Raleigh *Register*, accompanied by a note reporting the North Carolina Manumission Society's interest in Horton. Nothing came of this interest, and it marked the end of a number of efforts to free Horton that had begun earlier in the summer when the New York *Freedom's Journal*, an African American antislavery newspaper, published some of Horton's poems accompanied by a short description of him. On August 29, a longer article revealed that a "philanthropic gentleman" associated with the Board of the University of North Carolina had attempted to buy Horton, but was refused because Horton's master claimed that he currently needed the slave, but it was possible, perhaps, that he might be bought later in the year. To that purpose, some $400 to $500 should be raised in the North, as it was illegal to do so in North Carolina. This, too, was apparently unsuccessful despite the two articles that appeared in September reminding readers of the campaign to free Horton. On October 3, the support of David C. Walker, a free-born African American who would become well known

the following year for his "Appeal to the Coloured Citizens of the World," was
announced—and that was the last time the *Freedom's Journal* reported on the
campaign. Two decades later, Horton claimed that it was the governor of North
Carolina himself, John Owen, who tried to negotiate with his master. Immediately following these frustrated efforts was another project by Horton, who set
out to publish his first volume of poetry, *The Hope of Liberty*, the proceeds of
which could be used to purchase his freedom—should his master consent (cf.
Sherman 1997: 11-9).

This does nothing to clarify whose efforts and purposes caused the various
sentiments in the poem; until he was freed by Union victory, Horton continued
to campaign, write, and plead repeatedly for his freedom, and he was repeatedly
disappointed. The five stanzas focusing on joy may therefore be as deceptive to
the reader as the "tantalizing beams" were to the poet. The more substantial,
more important emotional gesture may well be contained in the sobering last
four stanzas of the poem. Here there is neither muse nor flight; the mode of
travel is by foot, and the poet braces himself for difficult paths. The central
image is again a biblical allusion, harking back to the "burning feet": "He shod
my feet this rugged race to run" (l. 46) evokes a passage in Ephesians 6 which is
precisely about putting on armor to withstand the wicked. The wisest reaction
for a slave when hearing the good intentions of any white person, apparently, is
a complex exercise in emotional control: the good intention must be acknowledged, and exaggerated gratitude—"floods" of it—must be shown in response.
For sheer self-protection, the promise should not be entirely trusted, yet it must
be trusted to the extent that courage and energy can be summoned to take
measures accordingly, yielding to the "soft control" (l. 44) of the potential bene-
factor and always being careful not to offend anyone who might thwart the effort.

And so we get a poem that conceals as much as it reveals as it seemingly centers on joy and hope. The antagonist, we learn, is not just disillusionment, but
fear that leads to a loss of agency, indicated by passive constructions:

> Hard was the race to reach the distant goal,
> The needle oft was shaken from the pole;
> In such distress, who could forbear to weep?
> Toss'd by the headlong billows of the deep! (ll. 33-6)

The muse, as well as the compass needle, is shaken, and the poet is tossed by
waves. Walking "along the dismal path" (l. 48) is a rather bleak compromise, but
it is at least active and more 'substantial' than the various flights and sea jour-
neys. It provides an emotional middle ground, a determination that can act as a
protective shield and that requires control as well as a certain amount of deceit.
That this poem is about a complex reaction rather than a simple expression of
gratitude is further corroborated by an earlier poem of Horton's, first published
in the *Freedom's Journal* in July 1828. It is entitled "Slavery," and the first two
stanzas describe—as characteristics of his experience of slavery—the quenching
of hope, the deception by a "tantalizing blaze," and a friend who became a foe. It
is tantalizing and painful, and also dangerous; it is a pattern that accompanied
Horton all his life. For even with slavery abolished, white promises of support,
solidarity, and equality went only so far. In 1866 the *Christian Recorder* of Philadelphia printed Horton's "Forbidden to Ride on the Street Cars," which looks for-

ward to freedom "in full bloom" (1866: 1) when black and white people will be able to ride together.

4. Conclusion and Outlook

In the above readings, we can hardly separate the power relations between the African American authors and their predominantly white readership from the texts. Though this relation develops in the direction of greater equality, many of the issues persist over time and are discussed not only in poetry. The history of reception is a case in point, as the most famous dismissal of Wheatley's poetry is found in Thomas Jefferson's *Notes on the State of Virginia*:

> Misery is often the parent of the most affecting touches in poetry.—Among the blacks is misery enough, God knows, but not poetry. . . . Religion indeed has produced a Phillis Whatley [sic]; but could not produce a poet. The compositions published under her name are below the dignity of criticism. The heroes of the Dunciad are to her, as Hercules to the author of that poem. (Jefferson 1982 [1787]: 140)

As a Southern gentleman, slaveholder, and politician, as someone who regards himself as embedded in an Enlightenment tradition and is accused of atheism by his opponents, Jefferson's ideal of literature is oriented toward a secular, more 'manly' mode of writing—particularly satire in the vein of Alexander Pope. This is a far cry from Wheatley who, even though clearly inspired by Pope, differs markedly in that she does not employ satire—a style that would be at odds with both her subordinate and dependent positions and with her piety. This allows Jefferson to use Wheatley as proof for the superiority of whites in terms of "reason, and imagination" (ibid. 195).

Given that for a long time Africans and African Americans were stigmatized as non-Christians, and later—as the power of this argument lessens—as non-cultured, Jefferson's criticism illustrates a familiar mechanism in the justification of oppression that a character from Ralph Ellison's *Three Days Before the Shooting . . .* summarizes as he "*done changed the Rules*" on me (2010: 43; original emphasis). Something that counts as a marker of status and can thus serve as an explanation for exclusion (Christian faith, the ability to compose poetry, a Cadillac) loses this function as soon as the oppressed gain access to this marker. It shows the power of definition over the presumed prerequisites necessary for access to a certain class, clique, or even to humanity in general, but the fact that Jefferson entangles himself in a performative contradiction by criticizing something "below the dignity of criticism" (Jefferson 1982 [1787]: 140) also illuminates the important role of literary criticism and aesthetic values for social stratification.

The hopes for acknowledging the contribution of African Americans to a genuinely modern American art as voiced by Alain Locke in *The New Negro*, the debates surrounding any canon, and the recovery work that has brought to light poets like Wheatley and Horton are based on the insights sketched above. If art and its critique can support power structures, then efforts to change the terms and standards of the former may at least be a beginning to weaken the latter. But the cases of Wheatley and Horton also demonstrate that this process is fraught with difficulties. For LeRoi Jones/Amiri Baraka, like many other African American critics in the mid-sixties, Wheatley was too imitative of white poetry and ideology (cf. Jones 1963). While this seems surprisingly close to Jefferson's sentiments, it also highlights a troubling dilemma of any oppressed group when it comes to the question of a usable past: the creative works of an oppressed people will probably imply instances of resistance, critique, subversion, and even defiance, but in all likelihood they will also bear the marks of oppression, which includes signs of necessary adaptation, accommodation, and compromise, to say nothing about limited means and resources. To search for resistance is to search for an empowering tradition that contemporary artists could build upon; the latter might be analytically helpful, but what if that dichotomy does not entirely hold up?

Among the resources that Wheatley, Horton, and other early African American writers could draw upon, the Bible clearly played a crucial role. It was not only a respected book that was safe to use for intertextual references, it also deals extensively with the subject of slavery and oppression. The ways in which Wheatley and Horton draw attention to the political meanings of redemption and salvation align their texts with the spirituals—a powerful form of African American folk poetry. W.E.B. Du Bois, who was one of the first to point to the important social function religion had for slaves in the specific way they adopted it, writes that this new folk poetry was something Wheatley "never knew but always sensed" (Du Bois 1996 [1941]: 330). The different "voices" that Du Bois lists in his essay on Wheatley illustrates his meaning: the various phrases taken from the Bible not only allow African Americans to voice their longing for freedom, they are also an emotional outlet; through these biblical phrases, poets can express abandon and enthusiasm that stand in stark contrast to the constant fear-driven self-control they were forced to exert—a self-control to which both Wheatley's and Horton's poems testify. That we, like Du Bois, can sense something in or beneath the words of the poems is evidence of their complexity and perhaps also of our wishes; that the emotional tension is so well concealed and contained by an overall formal control reminds us of the constant close scrutiny to which both poets were subjected.

One of the most intriguing devices contributing to this concealment is a deliberate ambiguity, polysemy or structural confusion, or else a seemingly simple repetition of white notions and phrases. It is a sort of linguistic mimicry that might involve mockery, but one can never be sure. This device—like a mask— serves as a shield protecting poets from inquisitions about their 'real' thoughts and feelings. As a survival strategy that has its own price (elaborated on, for instance, by the psychoanalyst Frantz Fanon in *Black Skin, White Masks*), masking becomes an explicit topic in Paul Laurence Dunbar's "We Wear the Mask," Claude McKay's "Harlem Dancer," and Langston Hughes's "Minstrel Man", to cite but a few examples. That a black man would don a poetic white mask to write love poems to white women, however, is a form of masking quite unique to Horton, bringing together two contrasting forms of masking prevalent in black-white relations in the U.S.: when African Americans put on their masks, seemingly mirroring white projections, it is for purposes of hiding strong and potentially dangerous sentiments; when whites put on black masks they do so to create a framework for abandonment, spontaneity, enthusiasm, sentimentality, or passion, implying the pejorative assumption that African Americans have less self-control than whites. How wrong this assumption is, and how much it misidentifies the survival strategies of oppressed people, is one of the insights gained by a careful reading of African American poetry.

Bibliography

Selected Primary Literature

Franklin, Benjamin. 1959 [1722]. "A RECEIPT to make a New-England Funeral ELEGY." In: Leonard W. Labaree (ed.), *The Papers of Benjamin Franklin.* Vol. 1. New Haven: Yale UP. 25-6.

Horton, George Moses. 1997. *The Black Bard of North Carolina: George Moses Horton and His Poetry.* Ed. Joan R. Sherman. Chapel Hill: The U of North Carolina P.

——. 1837 [1828]. "LINES, On Hearing of the Intention of a Gentleman to Purchase the Poet's Freedom." In: *Poems by a Slave.* 2nd ed. Philadelphia: Lewis Gunn. 21-2.

——. 1866. "Forbidden to Ride on the Street Cars." In: *Christian Recorder* 10 November: 1, col. 1.

——. 1997 [1828]. "Slavery." In: Horton 1997. 56-7.

——. 1997 [1829]. "On Liberty and Slavery." In: Horton 1997. 75-6.

——. 1997 [ca. 1844]. "Acrostics." In: Horton 1997. 61.

——. 1997 [1845]. "The Division of an Estate." In: Horton 1997. 100-1.

——. 1997 [1865]. "George Moses Horton, Myself." In: Horton 1997. 122.

——. 1997.[1865]. "The Obstruction of Genius." In: Horton 1997. 156.

Jefferson, Thomas. 1982 [1787]. "Query XIV. Laws." In: William Peden (ed.), *Notes on the State of Virginia.* Chapel Hill and London: The U of North Carolina P. 130-49.

Wheatley, Phillis. 1989. *The Poems of Phillis Wheatley.* Revised and Enlarged Edition with an Additional Poem. Ed. Julian D. Mason, Jr. Chapel Hill and London: The U of North Carolina P.

——. 1989 [1772]. "An Address to the Atheist, By P. Wheatley at the Age of 14 Years—1767—." In: Wheatley 1989. 120-1.

——. 1989 [1773]. "John Wheatley's Letter to the Publisher in First Edition." In: Wheatley 1989. 47-8.

——. 1989 [1773]. "On Being Brought from Africa to America." In: Wheatley 1989. 53.

——. 1989 [1773]. "On the Death of the Rev. Dr. Sewell. 1769." In: Wheatley 1989. 54-5.

——. 1989 [1773]. "On the Death of the Rev. Mr. George Whitefield. 1770." In: Wheatley 1989. 55-7.

——. 1989 [1773]. "To the Right Honourable William, Earl of Dartmouth, His Majesty's Principal Secretary of State for North-America, &c." In: Wheatley 1989. 82-3.

——. 1989 [1773]. "A Funeral Poem on the Death of C. E. an Infant of Twelve Months." In: Wheatley 1989. 80-1.

——. 1989 [1773]. "To Mæcenas." In: Wheatley 1989. 49-51.

——. 1989 [1773]. "An Answer to the *Rebus,* By the Author of these Poems." In: Wheatley 1989. 111.

——. 1989 [1784]. "Liberty and Peace, A Poem." In: Wheatley 1989. 175-7.

Selected Secondary Literature

Du Bois, William Edward Burghardt. 1996 [1941]. "Phillis Wheatley and African American Culture." In: Eric J. Sundquist (ed.), *The Oxford W.E.B. Du Bois Reader.* New York: Oxford UP. 328-42.

A short, appreciative essay, using imagination to draw a portrait of the poet as a strange and lonesome figure.

Gates, Henry L. 2003. *The Trials of Phillis Wheatley: America's First Black Poet and Her Encounters with the Founding Fathers.* New York: Basic Civitas Books.

Gates uses intellectual history as an approach to illuminate the significance of Wheatley's poetry.

Richmond, Merle A. 1974. *Bid the Vassal Soar: Interpretive Essays on the Life and Poetry of Phillis Wheatley (ca. 1753-1784) and George Moses Horton (ca. 1797-1883).* Washington: Howard UP.

One of the few books available that treats the two poets together in one volume. Richmond compares them not side by side but portraits them one after another.

Sherman, Joan R. 1997. *The Black Bard of North Carolina: George Moses Horton and his Poetry.* Chapel Hill: The U of North Carolina P.

Sherman's introduction provides the reader with all we know about Horton, embedded in the historical context; it does not dwell on interpretations of the poems.

Shields, John C. 2008. *Phillis Wheatley's Poetics of Liberation: Background and Contexts.* Knoxville: U of Tennessee P.

The book argues that the problem of freedom is at the center of Wheatley's work and that she develops a proto-romantic conceptualization of it.

Stewart, Carole Lynn. 2007. "Slave to the Bottle and the Plough: The Inner and Outer Worlds of Freedom in George Moses Horton's Poetry." In: *Social History of Alcohol and Drugs* 22.1: 45-64.

The article focuses on Horton's classicist, republican ideas of freedom as tied to public distinction rather than in interiorized meaning of freedom. The article functions as a contrast to what Shields argues Wheatley strives for.

Further References

Bromwich, David. 1985. "Reflections on the Word *Genius*." In: *New Literary History* 17.1: 141-64.

Carretta, Vincent. 2011. *Phillis Wheatley: Biography of a Genius in Bondage.* Athens and London: The U of Georgia P.

Ellison, Ralph. 1952. *Invisible Man.* New York: Random House.

——. 2010. *Three Days Before the Shooting.* Eds. John F. Callahan and Adam Bradley. New York: Modern Library Edition.

Erkkila, Betsy. 1993. "Phillis Wheatley and the Black American Revolution." In: Frank Shuffelton (ed.), *A Mixed Race. Ethnicity in Early America.* New York: Oxford UP. 225-40.

Franke, Astrid. 2010. *Pursue the Illusion: Problems of Public Poetry in America.* Heidelberg: Winter.

Gates, Henry L. 1988. "Foreword. In Her Own Write." In: John Shields (ed.), *The Collected Works of Phillis Wheatley*. Oxford: Oxford UP. vii-xxii.

Jones, LeRoi. 1963. "The Myth of a 'Negro Literature.'" In: *Saturday Review* 20 April: 20-1.

Pitts, Reginald H. 1995. "'Let us Desert this Friendless Place': George Moses Horton in Philadelphia—1866." In: *The Journal of Negro History* 80.4: 145-56.

Rigsby, Gregory. 1975. "Form and Content in Phillis Wheatley's Elegies." In: *CLA Journal* 19: 248-57.

II Romanticism and Nineteenth-Century American Poetry

5.

Romanticisms in American Poetry

William Cullen Bryant's "The Prairies" and Ralph Waldo Emerson's
"The Rhodora: On Being Asked, Whence Is the Flower?"

Damien Schlarb

1. Early Nineteenth-Century Poetry: Movements and Poets

At the onset of the nineteenth century, poetry was already an omnipresent medium in American upper middle-class households. Marie Louise Kete observes
that "nineteenth-century Americans wrote and read poetry extensively and valued
it highly" as poetry attained cultural ubiquity (2011: 15). Poetry served to record
personal and moral reflections in diaries, was a source of spiritual inspiration
and development, and was used to express the still immaterial national character. Poems both domestic and foreign circulated in the numerous magazines and
newspapers, and published poetry was collected in keepsake books, given as gifts
alongside original productions of the gift bearer, and read aloud in family circles;
it thus derived its use value from its circulation in a vibrant gift economy (ibid.:
33). American poetry began exploring sentiment as a means of universalizing personal experience. Emphasizing "spontaneity and pure disinterestedness" as
markers of authenticity, poets adopted conventional objects and experiences as
themes to articulate a universal humanism (Larson 2011b: 2-3). This new aesthetics gradually displaced the neoclassical inclination towards elevated language, abstract topics, and privileging of didactic edifice over poetic edification. It
also enabled poets to champion alternative ways of knowing and helped to develop what Kete calls "the grammar and lexicon of shared emotions" (2011: 23).

Still, American poets struggled to unmoor from the haven of European literary tradition, both classicist and romantic. For scholarship, this American
struggle replicates (with a temporal lag) the dynamic dialectical movement that
characterized the transition from classicism to romanticism within European—
especially German—romantic literature, as noted by Leon Chai (1990: 376). Literary periods are not hermetic units, and the ideas and forms that connote one
movement are foreshadowed by those that precede it and referenced by those
that follow. For example, Transcendentalism employed many of the forms and
aesthetics of European Romanticism and Classicism. Perry Miller observes that
transcendentalism as an intellectual movement ultimately illustrated "the effect
upon an American provinciality of European sophistication with which it was
not entirely competent to deal" (1964: 121). Yet romantic poetry also labored
within a home-grown, sermonic tradition that infused poetic discourses of nationalism, individualism, environmentalism, and domesticity with what Stephen
Cushman has identified as a "Christian ethos" (2011: 91) of self-denial and
moral didacticism (cf. Larson 2011b: 2). Innovative inclinations notwithstanding, most popular poets still depended on Christian iconography, motifs, and
forms to versify their experiences.

While antebellum poetry continued to adhere to traditional forms, poets succeeded early in crafting original American themes and symbols, ranging from
the metaphysical significance of flowers and picturesque sceneries to pressing

social issues, such as the abolition of slavery, women's suffrage, and Indian territorial disputes. The political volatility of the age was reflected in the poetic landscape as women, African Americans, American Indians, and immigrant groups (also from annexed territories such as Texas and the Philippines) were brought into the fold by the many social reform movements.

The American poetic spectrum contained stylistic extremes: for instance, the "Fireside Poets"—Henry Wadsworth Longfellow, Oliver Wendell Holmes, John Greenleaf Whittier, and James Russell Lowell—were stylistically indebted to the English neo-classicists. Their poetry carried solemn, memorable rhyme schemes and featured didactic, pastoral, nationalist, and (after the Civil War) nostalgic domestic themes. Schoolchildren frequently had to memorize many of these poems, a practice that bestowed the moniker "schoolroom poets" on the group. Thematically (if not formally) more experimental, the transcendentalists—William Ellery Channing, Margaret Fuller, Ralph Waldo Emerson, Henry David Thoreau, and Jones Very—sought to express the symbolic character of nature with equally symbolic language. The transcendentalists' demand for a poet to put the essence of America on record would culminate in innovative forms later in the century: Whitman's democratic catalogs and fascination with the power of amative love or Emily Dickinson's terse style and poetic personae.

Writing poetry, however, was not perceived as a viable full-time occupation. The prevailing attitude was that "there is not wealth enough in this country to afford encouragement and patronage of merely literary men," as Longfellow's father tempered his son's poetic ambitions in the 1820s (Kete 2011: 27). Poets who did not have a pension to fall back on made a living as lawyers, clerks, ministers, housewives, editors, and literary critics. Accordingly, emerging professional occupations actively shaped American aesthetic sensibilities and vice versa. Eventually poetic production found publication outlets in popular magazines: William Cullen Bryant's *New York Evening Post*, *Harper's Magazine*, and the fast growing Christian press attested to the expanding literary market. Yet most poets continued to wear several professional hats and worked in various literary genres. Edgar Allan Poe, one of the most prolific literary critics and poets, also mentored emergent poets such as Sarah Helen Whitman. Herman Melville, originally considered an adventure novelist, created a substantial body of self-published poetry (e.g., *Battle Pieces* 1866; *Clarel* 1876). African American and women poets, such as Lydia Huntley Sigourney, Frances Osgood, Alice and Phoebe Cary, Frances Ellen Watkins Harper, Maria White Lowell, or Sarah Morgan Bryan Piatt, were among the most commercially successful writers of the period, and Native American poets, such as Jane Johnston Schoolcraft and John Rollin Ridge, also garnered circulation.

Scholarship has long deemed much of romantic poetry of moderate value because of its idealization of sentiment. The reinsertion of African American, Native American, immigrant, and women writers' poetic contributions into the canon have enabled discourses about the ways underprivileged, excluded, and subversive individuals resisted and influenced their roles in society. Nevertheless, the scholarly rehabilitation of nineteenth-century poetry is far from complete. For instance, American Renaissance poetry is not a mere transplantation of European values and forms into American soil. Like its European counterpart, American Romanticism receives and processes neoclassicism, preserving some of its forms while denying its stricter didactic themes. However, American Romanticism adds the complexity of simultaneously processing European romanticist forms and themes. It is thus rather a conglomeration of shifting sensibilities that work for, with, and against European influences, both classicist and romantic. Bryant and Emerson, for example, were influenced by Wordsworth and attempted to synthesize their idol's *topoi* in describing their own American realities. The spiritualization of nature, multifaceted historicisms, and social and political criticisms are results of this attempted synthesis. From this nexus of European romantic idealism and forms as well as from American living experience emerged a poetics that sought to versify the temper of living in a country that offered not only virtually unlimited geographic expansion and agrarian yield, but also the coequal promises of republican democracy and the fulfillment of uninhibited human potential.

2. William Cullen Bryant's "The Prairies" (1833)

Named the father of American song by contemporaries and biographers, William Cullen Bryant has been celebrated as one of the prototypical American poets. His poetry has since been widely anthologized and is still considered one of the pillars of American literature. Unlike Emerson, however, Bryant's enshrinement in the American literary canon has not produced continuous, vibrant scholarship. Bryant's political views, expressed in his editorial work for the *New York Evening Post* and in other periodicals, have impacted reviews of his poetry and lectures on literature in scholarship, on the one hand politicizing him for laboring towards a cohesive national form, and on the other hand condemning him as an apologist of imperialism due to his support of the 1830 Indian Removal Act. In addition, early over-exposure of his work in criticism and popular culture has long fatigued and debunked Bryant as a scholarly subject. Accordingly, scholars have stressed the need to "restore Bryant to his rightful place as a compelling and exemplary figure in American life and letters" (Muller 2008: viii) by putting him back into communication with contemporary scholarly conversations. Recent studies have problematized Bryant's attitudes towards politics, religion, and the environment, and have thus been able to reinvigorate scholarly debate about his poetry (cf. Gado 2006: viii; Galloway 2010: 741).

Immensely popular in his own time, Bryant first became known for his juvenile classic elegy "Thanatopsis" (1811, 1821), a contemplation of physical death that celebrates the subjectivity of sensory experience while controversially omitting the customary affirmation of an afterlife. He pursued contemplations of nature and art throughout his poetic career, as in his famous "To a Waterfowl" (1815, 1821), an optimistic pantheist Wordsworthian ode; or "A Forest Hymn" (1826), which similarly praises God's craftsmanship and benevolence; or "The Poet" (1864), in which Bryant versifies the poet as a fiery, emotional bard that emphatically sings the extremes of human experience. In his lecture "The Value of Poetry" (1825), Bryant suggests that the central mission of poetry is the excitement of emotion. He therefore deems poetry an "art which selects and arranges the symbols of thought in such a manner as to excite it [thought] the most powerfully and delightfully" (1964: 6). Bryant later adds: "the proper office of poetry was to fill the mind with 'delightful images' and to awaken the emotion" (Brown 1971: 489). Despite such conceptual conservatism, Bryant's poetry harbors complex and even conflicting attitudes toward ontology and the moral character of human history.

"The Prairies" (1833, 1834) marries the topics of sublimity in the American landscape and the sentimental construction of an American antiquity. The myth that remnants of a lost high culture exist in the soil of the American wilderness was a popular assumption in Bryant's day. Such fantasies allowed the fledgling American national literary project to take root in native soil, as opposed to importing the seedlings of European culture. This alleged American antiquity filled the dual need for a non-European past while rationalizing the immanent political issue of Indian removal. Bryant naturalizes expansionism by promulgating a utopian agrarian ideal for the emerging American empire. Anglo-Saxon America becomes the heir of a romanticized Hellenistic Classicism that predates the nomadic American Indians, a heritage consummated by European colonialism. Andrew Galloway argues that Bryant and his contemporaries construct this antiquity less for political reasons than out of an acute "anxiety about the fragility of their own cultural identity" (2010: 741). Bryant had expressed this anxiety in "An Indian at the Burial-Place of His Fathers" (1824), in which the Indian poetic speaker nostalgically contemplates the vanishing of his race, while also observing that the white race, too, may disappear "[a]nd leave no trace behind" (1967 [1824]: 1. 95). Considering the history of civilization in a cyclical fashion muffles moral apprehensions about displacing a primitive people because that displacement also foreshadows the fate of the Anglo-American civilization. "The Prairies" thus communicates an "element of incipient self-destruction," which David Moriarity exclusively restricts to Bryant's political poetry (1983: 216). Contrary to Moriarity's distinction though, Bryant realizes his increasing apprehensions about westward expansion through his contemplation of nature in "The Prairies."

The poem's epic blank verse gives it a somber, prosaic tone. The poetic speaker begins his journey through time and the prairies' panoramic vistas by stressing the "unshorn" appeal of the scenery ("Prairies" 1967 [1833]: 1. 2). Contrasting later assertions about the convergence of natural and cultural history, the landscape initially derives its aesthetic appeal from the absence of human civilization. The prairies seem to exist independently from history, and their naturalness connotes an era "ere man had sinned," as Bryant notes in a revised version of the poem published one year later (1834: 1. 3). Sight is the key sensation in these opening lines. Bryant emphasizes the melancholy, visually sublime landscape, as the prelapsarian world engulfs the speaker. The prairies' overwhelming vistas trigger a feeling of vertigo: the speaker's "heart swells" while the "dilated sight / Takes in the encircling vastness" (1967 [1833]: ll. 5-6). The poetic self fails to form a cohesive impression of the landscape. In fact, the scenery seems to move on its own volition by mirroring the cursory motion of the beholder's gaze. Bryant's ocean metaphor in the following lines expounds this optical illusion: the surrounding terrain appears like the "rounded billows" (ibid.: 1. 9) of the ocean, appearing "motionless forever" (1. 10) yet perpetually threatening. These petrified waves loom large with terrible destructive potential. Punctuation emphasizes this impression: two dashes frame the adjective "Motionless" (1. 10), forcing readers to linger over the word in the same way the speaker finds the landscape momentarily frozen in time. Only when a shadow cast by clouds "fluctuates to the eye" (1. 13) is mobility restored, and both the ocean metaphor and the speaker's stasis are dissolved. The speaker experiences the prairies' geographic extension as debilitating, acute absence of motion.

This conversion, expressed as the ocean metaphor, hinges on the poetic self's perspective as well as on his ability to switch perspectives. There is no physical interaction with the landscape; only shadows—the clouds' simulacra—touch the beholder's eyes. Addressing the speaker's perception, Alan Donovan usefully labels "The Prairies" a visionary poem that employs naturalist scenery to construct "a romantic vision which at its end signals the minuteness and loneliness of the individual perspective" (1968: 518). Bryant's bard is the focal point of two concentric gyral motions: the landscape's encircling stasis and his own circumspection. While physically threatening, such vistas cannot obliterate individuality (ibid.: 516), and it is this hesitancy to dissolve the poetic subject to uncover common natural origins that separates Bryant from the transcendentalists.

The ocean metaphor expands the biblical reference to God's creation of order from chaos (cf. Genesis 1:2, 4). Bryant's bard also performs world-constituting labor by poetically (re-)constructing the landscape he beholds. This composition continues with the speaker's address of the prairie hawk, whose elevated perspective enables him to fully appreciate the symbiosis of soil and sky. Ventriloquizing the hawk, the speaker judges the landscape a "Fitting floor / For this magnificent temple of the sky" (ll. 28-9). Several metaphors express the harmony and splendor of a creation that "Man hath no power in" (l. 24): the flowers' "glory and . . . multitudes / Rival the constellations!" (ll. 30-1); yet this rivalry holds no strife, for "The great heavens / Seem to stoop down upon the scene in love" (ll. 31-2). Indeed, the poet's description engenders the question as to what moral end humans may hope to utilize such a glorious landscape. Kinereth Meyer identifies the poem's idyllic vistas as strategically constructed "counter-landscape[s]" that depict the "poet's fears of his own destructive powers" (1993: 200); these poetic landscapes foreshadow the ecologically destructive results of westward expansion. Meyer contests that Bryant felt guilt at the thought that through his poetry he "participated in a similarly appropriative activity" (ibid.), but Bryant's speaker expresses a much more insidious outlook on the complicity of poetry in imperialism than Meyer gives him credit for. By establishing the natural landscape as aesthetic ideal, the speaker eliminates the possibility of a non-intrusive man-made aesthetics, including his *own* poetic production. Ergo, any poetic description of nature is a composition that subjugates the landscape to the spectator's sensibilities. Because "the poet . . . appropriates and shapes the land," the speaker also disqualifies himself as an accurate observer of the natural sublime (ibid.: 211). Any discussion of the moral dimension of land appropriation is moot, for all representations compromise their objects by substituting them for the subject's epistemological position.

Even humankind's fictive presence stains the speaker's perfectly shaped landscape and thus bars his recourse to the idyllic world he envisions. The schizophrenic anxiety of having lost an origin that never was propels the poet's contemplation forward. Having realized the factual inaccessibility of the past, the speaker begins constructing a fictitious antiquity by interpreting the hieroglyph-remnants of the mound-builders' civilization. He romanticizes these "dead of other days" as "disciplined and populous" contemporaries of the ancient Greeks, the founders of European civilization (ll. 40, 46). The speaker biasedly crafts the mound-builders as an agrarian society—very much the state of America at the time—who lived in symbiosis with nature. Even the yoked bison, "haply . . . lowed" by his stall, graciously following human commands, and the very landscape of the mound-builders "murmured with their toils" (ll. 52-4). As "twilight blushe[s]" over their existence, these ancient, mild-mannered people bring forth a high culture of "forgotten language and old tunes" played on "instruments of unremembered form" (ll. 56-7). Accordingly, after the "warlike and fierce" nomadic Indian tribes extinguish the mound-builders, a "solitude of centuries untold / Has settled where they dwelt," as the land mourns the loss of its benign custodians (ll. 59, 61-2).

The mound-builders' benign dominion and productive cultivation of the land make them proxies for claims of Euro-American cultural superiority. Connoting the term civilization with the European non-nomadic lifestyle was a popular counter-argument to the territorial claims of the nomadic Native American tribes in the debates about acculturation and displacement. Nature, though, seems less nostalgic than the speaker, as vibrant cities, places of worship, and military fortifications become "uncovered sepulchers" on which the "brown vultures of the wood" sit to feast "unscared and silent" (ll. 73-4). And if nature and history run on an iron rail, the eventual fall of Euro-American culture will occur equally unceremoniously.

Depicting the transition between civilizations, the poem's middle passage addresses miscegenation. The issue of racial inter-marriage was widely contested in nineteenth-century fiction. For instance, James Fenimore Cooper's *Leatherstocking Tales* hero Natty Bumppo frequently reiterates that he is not of mixed blood to asseverate his moral integrity. In Bryant's poem, the last mound-builder is assimilated into the Indian culture once the conquest is completed and "Man's better nature" prevails (l. 79). Although the outcast can never condone the rise of the "rude conquerors," his resentment does not lead to action (l. 80). The only obituary for the lost civilization is the speaker's ingenuous acknowledgment: "Thus change the forms of being" (l. 86). Contingency and imperialist strife, Bryant seems to suggest, characterize both history and human civilizations, which rise and fall with "the quickening breath of God" (l. 88). This providential concept of history could be traced to Bryant's Calvinist upbringing. Yet God's involvement in human history is notably subdued compared to "To a Waterfowl," for instance, where the speaker conceives of a world formed and kept in motion by a benevolent creator who will ultimately "lead [the speaker's] steps aright" (1967 [1818]: l. 32). The God of "The Prairies" instills no such confidence. His favor is capricious and fickle. This unstable divine patronage causes the poetic self to form a "laconic expression of the present" by expressing "a contradiction between the pastoral idyll of America's future and the poetic discourse of the American Sublime" (Haselstein 1998: 414). However, the speaker never actually comes to terms with the present in which he lives beyond feeling a tragic sense of loss at realizing that he is not privy to the secret organizing principle of nature. Bryant's poem thus illustrates the way romantic poetic meditation is restricted to either utopian or nostalgic representations.

Paul Newin finds Bryant's poetic self filled with regret at the end of the poem, as the speaker realizes that "the inevitable onslaught of the eastern settlers" ensures any "destiny manifested in America forever bear[s] the mark of a curse," namely that of the unstable temporariness of empire (1983: 33, 38). Nevertheless, the poem's central problem remains an epistemological one; the speaker's melancholy over God's negligence and humanity's restricted agency in historical events only compounds the problem of contingent epistemological access to the present. The latter sentiment especially illustrates the futility of both nostalgia and utopianism. Whatever regularity the speaker may discern from his observations of the land is ultimately a corrupt vision produced by an imperfect perception (cf. Haselstein 1998: 417). The poem's final lines emblemize these epistemological limitations: not only have the birds "learned the fear of man," but the bee, nature's original "adventurous colonist," also hides its nectar—its secret knowledge of the prairies' history—in tree stumps (ll. 106, 110). As the animals recede from human advances, the speaker is overcome with the melancholic realization that true insight into both history and nature is impossible.

Bryant ultimately illustrates the epistemological limitations of romantic meditation. His poetic speaker finds neither spiritual comfort nor transcendence in his reflections but is reminded of the illusory character of both his perception and contemplations. The speaker's identification with the past and the dead culture of the mound-builders does not enable him to understand the secrets he believes to reside in the recalcitrant, antisocial wildlife of the desert. After all, the animals, too, live in the ruins of the mound-builders and guard secret histories of their own. Contrary to Emerson, Bryant's speaker does not experience a universal connection with all of creation but is confined to speculating about the contingent processes of history manifested in his contrived romantic musings.

Adding to the speaker's dissociation, the new conquerors come not as discerning individuals but as an "advancing multitude," sweeping the continent and displacing the prairies' solitude with its "domestic hum" (ll. 116, 115). Although never mounting full-fledged criticism, Bryant seems to express apprehensions about modern civilization, a notion possibly derived from his editorial duties. But before the speaker can fully articulate a final verdict on his reflections, the "fresher wind" of an approaching future civilization violently "break[s]" his reverie: "All at once / A fresher wind sweeps by, and breaks my dream, / And I am in the wilderness alone" (ll. 122-4). The hypotactic structure of these lines emphasizes the abruptness with which the speaker is torn from his meditation, while the final adjective "alone" symbolizes his isolation. He observes history from the outside, not as part of the noisy multitudes, but as a harbinger who chronicles helplessly the advent and futility of empire in light of the prairies' secret history.

The history of civilization and nature is a record of violent and yet futile displacements in which the only constant seems to be the temporariness of human edifices. Contemplating the prairies teaches the poetic self that cultural history is contingent on the observer's perspective. In this context, Lawrence Buell points out that effective environmental fiction does not merely employ the non-human landscape as a *"framing device,"* but rather understands environment "as *presence that . . . suggest[s] that human history is implicated in natural history"* (1996: 7; original emphasis). In the case of "The Prairies," the land's metaphorical fabric teaches the bard about the instability of his vision. His attempts at mapping human history onto the soil ultimately deprive him of both the comfort of nostalgia and the humility of sublime experience. What is left is an unsettling apprehension of an evanescent, hieroglyphic, recalcitrant present, symbolized in the withdrawal of the animals and the simultaneous disembodied murmur of the oncoming multitudes. The speaker stands shiftlessly apart from either group.

3. Ralph Waldo Emerson's "The Rhodora: On Being Asked, Whence Is the Flower?" (1834, 1839)

Emerson proposes that poetry walks a *via media* between understanding (the retracing and regurgitation of pre-established ideas) and intuition (the spontaneous insights into the organization of the universe). Poetry stimulates the imagination, which to Emerson constitutes a "very high sort of seeing . . . by the intellect . . . sharing the path, or circuit of things through forms" (1983 [1844]: 15). By wielding "the universality of symbolic language" (ibid.: 10), the poet allows readers "to

escape from all frozen limitations of dogma to an ever fresh awareness of the multiple facets of the single Truth" (Matthiessen 1941: 43). True poetry therefore
challenges readers' imaginations and allows them to give themselves over, as
Emerson says in the poem "Each and All" (1839), "to the perfect whole" of nature
and to perceive universal connectivity as the structuring cosmic principle with
the immediacy and urgency of personal experience (2011 [1839]: l. 51). To enable
such perception, the poet must become what R. A. Yoder calls the Orphic "spirit
of revealed, syncretic truth" (1978: 7). Poetry must overcome "the discrepancy
between the world of fact and the world that man thinks" (Matthiessen 1941: 57).
Regardless of its theme, transcendentalist poetry must simultaneously dismantle
established aesthetics while proposing new ones in an act that Saundra Morris
describes as "both iconoclastic and . . . creative" (1999: 218).

The lyrical entity speaking in most of Emerson's poems strives to adhere to
this ideal of the Orphic synthesizer of opposites. Yet Emerson felt that no American poet (including himself) had yet managed to write with "sufficient plainness,
or sufficient profoundness" ("The Poet" 1983 [1844]: 21). "The Rhodora" practically illustrates this poetic program as well as its underlying problems. The
poet's chance encounter with the rhodora, a species of rhododendron native to
New England, yields the cosmic insight of beauty as the structuring principle of
nature. Different from Bryant's vistas of the prairies, Emerson's poet seeks meditative insights in an intimate setting. Later in Emerson's career, such intimacy
and "insulation from calamity" would come at the price of an increasing emotional detachment and aloofness from humanity (Whicher 1953: 286). Poems
such as "The Snow Storm" (1841) and "Terminus" (1867) encircle the poet-speaker
in narrow, meditative spaces and express an increasingly reclusive attitude.
Having found the flower, the poet becomes privy to its secret knowledge of beauty. In its ultimate extension, the flower symbolizes the purposeful arrangement
of the universe. Yoder usefully points out that "The Rhodora" structurally emulates the seventeenth-century meditation genre: meditation poetry first constructs "a concrete situation," stating a "spiritual problem therein dramatized,"
then analyzes the problem, and finally resolves it thorough colloquy, i.e., "intimate conversation and union between poet and the object of his spiritual exercise" (Yoder 1978: 82). In meditation terminology, the rhodora dramatizes beauty that exists independently of material utility, the primary register of thought
for the sages. The poet resolves this ideological conflict by realizing that the
common divine origin of flower and man expresses universal purposefulness.

The rhyme scheme formally supports the meditation structure: two couplets
(aa, bb) followed by an alternating rhyme (ab, ab) demark two meditative steps:
dramatization and resolution. Step one ("The Rhodora" 2011 [1834, 1839]: ll. 1-8)
describes the speaker's happening upon the flower, while step two (ll. 9-16) proposes the self-sustaining aesthetics the rhodora symbolizes. Contrary to Yoder's
assessment, however, Emerson does not simply exclude analysis from his meditation but rather relegates it to the sages' myopic questions. This strategy is consistent with Emerson's cosmology because analysis employs abstract terminology
and compartmentalized thinking to produce derivative knowledge. It is thus a variety of the understanding. The sages' analysis (by transcendentalist standards)
prevents any meaningful interaction, let alone synergy, between humans and nature. Such attempts by rationalizing minds to impose their notion of order upon a
universe that is already perfectly formed are obstructionist. Reason, while conceptually useful, is secondary to intuition. The poet does not need to concern

himself with such auxiliaries because his ability to intuit nature allows him to perceive beauty as a symbol of universal purposefulness of all life.

"The Rhodora" exemplifies both American Romanticism's engagement with everyday objects and events, as well as the movement's indebtedness to earlier poetic forms. Grammatically, the poem takes the shape of an explicative statement answering the question raised in the subtitle. This conversational frame gives the poem the poignancy of a spontaneous, anecdotal statement, a staple romantic ideal. The somber iambic pentameter evinces a settled, conversational mood; New England spring awakens both poet and flower: "In May, when sea winds pierced *our* solitudes" (l. 1; emphasis added). The first-person plural pronoun introduces the trope of shared experience between flower and poet. Roused from their respective winter isolation, aesthete observer and aesthetic object awaken and one sets out to find the other. These opening lines metaphorically evoke Emerson's own intellectual awakening during this time. In 1832 he had taken a stand against Unitarian dogma in his seminal lecture "The Lord's Supper," which eventually led him to even more radical statements in his "Divinity School Address" (1838). Escaping the chilling isolation of rationalist empirical ideology, Emerson wrote in his journal how, at the time of composing "The Rhodora," his inner poet learned to "lean without fear on [his] own tastes" (1964 [1834]: 317).

Growing out of a "damp nook," the rhodora seems without aesthetic purpose because it resides beyond the gaze of spectators (l. 3). Like the poet, the flower initially appears solitary. Its isolation, however, reveals the poem's original question to be a condensation of a set of underlying ontological problems: What is the purpose of unseen beauty? Why does this beauty exist? Where does such beauty come from? The poet's meditation thus explodes what initially seems a rather linear interrogation. Typical for Emerson, the poet's descriptions emphasize visual perception; striking color contrasts thematically guide the poet's observations. Plosive alliteration captures the minimalist aesthetic vista of the "purple petals" standing out against the water's black backdrop; the contrast intensifies the petals' hue (l. 5). What is more, the petals' 'fallen' state, like the color purple itself, evokes Adamic iconography. Yet even the flower's shattered petals befit such diametrically opposed landscapes as "desert and the sluggish brook," and thus symbolize synergetic integration rather than shameful, isolating abjection (l. 4). The structural inversion of the sentence emphasizes the visual effect of the petals' bestowing color and gayness to the lifeless "black water" (l. 6). The rhodora's invigorating properties reside even in her cast-off, unregenerate parts, a notion that symbolically foreshadows the poem's final assertion of universal purposefulness.

Deviating from the linear temporal scheme of his account, the poet next observes that a red-bird, or cardinal, may refresh himself in the pool (cf. l. 7). The cardinal, realizing the rhodora's superior aesthetic quality, courts the flower, whose beauty "cheapens his array" (l. 8). The bird's fiery plumage not only diversifies the scene's color scheme but also introduces an aesthetic hierarchy. The cardinal, instinctively drawn to the flower, underwrites the poet's reverence of the rhodora and illuminates its symbolic character as the aesthetic ideal of plainness. The rhodora thus represents a universal aesthetics of simplicity to which all of nature instinctively converges.

This idealized natural order, however, may also undermine the very transcendentalist project it propagates. In his essay "Experience" (1844), often considered the subversive counterpart to the essay "The Poet," Emerson warns against the illusions of sense perception and the infatuation it raises. If "dream delivers us to dream, and there is no end to illusion," all judgments based on visual sensations are contingent on the "succession of moods" we experience (2011 [1844]: 30, 32). The inclusion of the cardinal collapses the time span in which the poet observes the scene and arranges aesthetic objects in space. And while Emerson may argue that such composition faithfully depicts the inherent hierarchies found in nature, the red-bird sequence reveals a tension between the simplistic wholeness of ideal and the fragmentariness of observation. The passage therefore illustrates the office that imagination holds in Emerson's cosmology: starting from sensory experience, the poet slips into a reverie that grants insights about nature's symbolism, insights that the poet then translates into language by way of poetic symbolism.

Emerson eventually explores what befalls those who tip this delicate balance of perceptive and creative faculties, i.e., the sages. In the second part of the meditation, poet and flower confront the sages' dogmatic materialism. The poet-speaker hypothesizes skeptical learned men inquiring after the flower's aesthetic utility and proposing that its presence is "wasted on the earth and the sky" (l. 10). The sages are blind to imagination, and their anthropocentrism leads them to question the rhodora's aesthetic value due to its sequestered hideout. Ventriloquizing the rhodora, the poet responds, "if eyes were made for seeing / Then Beauty is its own excuse for being" (ll. 11-2). According to Morris, "ventriloquistic play characterizes [Emerson's] poetry and prose" (1997: 551). This mock interlocution with the skeptics dramatizes the poet's meditation and builds tension toward his direct address to the flower. Richard Tuerk points out that the poet's answer is "really no answer at all" (1990: 7). His casuistic, tongue-in-cheek reply equates the flower's aesthetic value to the faculty of sight, transferring connotations of naturalness and indispensability to the rhodora. Both sight and beauty are independent of volition and thus inexorably determine human consciousness. To Emerson, the nineteenth century was characteristically visual, a conviction that had him declare on numerous occasions: "our age is ocular" (in Matthiessen 1941: 51). The rhodora therefore derives aesthetic value from its presence in the world alone rather than from the presence of its beholder. Its ineffability and simple beauty, especially compared to its "rival," the rose—a more obvious and yet overdetermined romantic symbol—give the rhodora the quality of truth in the transcendentalist sense.

Terms of endearment, familial pronouns, and emotional interjections announce the poet's exuberance at uncovering the flower's symbolic meaning (cf. l. 13). He "never *thought* to ask" why the flower resides in this secluded place, a phrase that reasserts the exclusion of analysis from the meditative process (l. 14; emphasis added). The parallel structure of the main clause dramatizes his assertion to have never rationalized the rhodora's origin. The final answer to the poem's original question, therefore, is a response of the heart, given "in simple [read: truthful] ignorance" (l. 15). As his infatuation with the flower grows, so does his license to speak poetically because his knowledge is not based on rational but intuitive insight. So disarmed of his rational faculties, Emerson's poet can convey simple, Orphic truth. In this manner, the poet intuits his kinship to the flower (l. 15). Emerson frequently describes this license as the poet's representativeness in his essays. The poet alone "stands among partial men for the complete man, and apprises us not of his wealth, but of the commonwealth" ("The Poet" 1983 [1844]: 4). Indeed, only poetic sentiment can perceive the "self-same Power" that created and placed humans and plants in the world symbol-

ized in the rhodora. The attribute selfsame ambiguously refers to both the creations' shared origin and the Christian God creator's assertion of self-identity as
His quintessential attribute ("I am that I am," Exod. 3:14). The poet's dialectical
move eliminates all difference between himself and the object of his meditation.
Despite these emotional ripples, the meter remains unchanged, illustrating
Emerson's formal conservatism and his unwillingness to let content impact
form. In the transcendentalist's mind, however, such formal regularity reflects
the very order of nature that the poet uncovers in his meditation.

Barbara Packer argues that "The Rhodora" foreshadows Emerson's transcendentalist manifesto *Nature* (1836), which arguably absorbs the poem's assertions about beauty (2004: 93). In *Nature*, Emerson characterizes beauty as
"simple perception of natural forms" in chance encounters (1971 [1834]: 13).
The observer's ability to perceive beauty depends on his virtuousness, i.e., on
his willingness to accept natural beauty as the sole worthwhile subject of contemplation (ibid.: 15). In this way, beauty is "part of the final cause of the universe" because it exceeds myopic demands for immediate, material utility (ibid.:
16). The sages' skeptical bickering symbolizes the pitfall of compartmentalized
thinking, a trap Emerson's poet seeks to avoid through his aesthetic program.
The poet's intuiting of his kinship with the flower transfers the rhodora's aesthetic self-sufficiency to him. This is by no means a conventional notion for the
time. For instance, Lydia Huntley Sigourney's similarly themed "The Alpine
Flowers" (1827) depicts the poetic self's "rapt soul" as standing "in breathless
awe" at the potentially destructive power of the sublime symbolized by the
flower's placement at the edge of a ravine (1998 [1827]: l. 22). Sigourney's eighteenth-century notion of the sublime enforces the distance between the subject
and God. Morris calls Emerson's poems "entirely an answer to an antagonistic
question" (1997: 563). As it pertains to the sublime, Emerson's heroic answer
here consists of replacing a symbolic tradition of fearful, distant reverence with
one of comforting, simplistic, and intimate order.

4. Conclusion and Outlook

Both Bryant and Emerson attribute special authenticity and spirituality to contemplations of natural spaces. While Bryant never becomes as programmatically
dedicated to an ideal as Emerson, he does acknowledge the transcendental
quality of being in nature. Like Emerson, Bryant believes truth to be instantly
recognizable by virtue of its simplicity: the significance of the mound-builders'
tombs for future civilizations is apparent to those able to read the landscape's
historic symbolism. Both poets consider nature a multi-directional cipher revealing secret knowledge about the origins and fate of humanity.

Their congruence in theme notwithstanding, Bryant's and Emerson's considerations of nature vary in scope and direction. To Emerson's poet, the rhodora euphorically indicates humanity's metaphysical origins. Bryant sees the
inescapable fate of human civilization cataloged in the rolling hills of the prairies. Yet both Bryant's and Emerson's visions are only temporary. Bryant's poet-
speaker is roused from his reverie by the murmur of civilization's unstoppable
approach. While "The Rhodora" chronicles the poet's thought process, "The Prairies" more skeptically illustrates the world-constituting and self-deluding implications and contingencies of poetic language. The speaker's melancholic sense

of loss at being stirred from his vision complicates the cliché of Bryant's celebratory nationalism and communicates the mature insight that progress, however one chooses to define it, removes humans from the divine natural landscape as well as from one another. The speaker set adrift in the prairies at the end of Bryant's poem thus radically differs from Emerson's contented poet who rejoices in his discovery of metaphysical community with nature. Ironically, the flower depicts the same minuteness that Bryant's speaker faces at the end of his poem. But Emerson perceives this remoteness not as isolation but as a symbol of nature's all-inclusiveness.

Beyond the respective discourses about cultural historicism and phenomenological aesthetics, the common thematic denominator of the two poems seems to be their commentary on the romantic notion of pantheism, i.e., the idea of inferring God's character and work from natural phenomena. Bryant's poet-speaker is seized by feelings of vertigo upon beholding the prairies' geographical expanse. The panorama literally overwhelms (encircles and subsequently overruns) Bryant's speaker and causes him to contemplate the history of civilization in the same terms of perpetual cyclical motion that he finds in his experience of nature. Meanwhile, Emerson's is a God of flattened hierarchies, who takes equal care in planting a flower and creating humankind. Both poems address the relation of nature to humankind and dramatize the implication of natural landscapes as well as intimate scenes for civilization. Their contribution to American romantic poetry lies in their diametrically opposed approaches to this shared topic.

Bibliography

Selected Primary Literature

Bryant, William Cullen. 1834. "The Prairies." In: *Poems.* Boston: Russell. 39-43.
——. 1964. "Lectures on Poetry." In: *The Prose Writings of William Cullen Bryant: Essays, Tales, and Orations.* Ed. Parke Godwin. New York: Russell. 3-44.
——. 1967. *The Poetical Works of William Cullen Bryant.* Ed. Parke Godwin. 2 Vols. New York: Russell & Russell.
——. 1967 [1824]. "An Indian at the Burial-Place of His Fathers." In: Bryant 1967. Vol. 1: 93-6.
——. 1967 [1815, 1821]. "To a Waterfowl." In: Bryant 1967. Vol. 1: 26-7.
——. 1967 [1833]. "The Prairies." In: Bryant 1967. Vol. 2: 228-32.
Emerson, Ralph Waldo. 1964. *Journals: 1830-34.* Vol. IV of *The Journals and Miscellaneous Notebooks of Ralph Waldo Emerson.* Ed. Alfred Riggs Ferguson. Cambridge, MA: Belknap P of Harvard UP.
——. 1971 [1834]. *Nature.* In: *Nature, Addresses, and Lectures.* Vol. I of *The Collected Works of Ralph Waldo Emerson.* Ed. Robert Ernest Spiller and Alfred Riggs Ferguson. Cambridge, MA: Belknap P of Harvard UP. 3-47.
——. 1983. *Essays: Second Series.* Vol. III of *The Collected Works of Ralph Waldo Emerson.* Ed. Alfred R. Ferguson and Jean Ferguson Carr. Cambridge, MA: Belknap P of Harvard UP.
——. 1983 [1844]. "The Poet." In: Emerson 1983. 1-24.
——. 1983 [1844]. "Experience." In: Emerson 1983. 25-49.
——. 2011. *Poems: A Variorum Edition.* Vol. IX of *The Collected Works of Ralph Waldo Emerson.* Ed. Joseph Slater. Cambridge, MA: Belknap P of Harvard UP.
——. 2011 [1834, 1839]. "The Rhodora: On Being Asked, Whence Is the Flower?" In: Emerson 2011. 79.

——. 2011 [1839]. "Each and All." In: Emerson 2011. 14-5.

Sigourney, Lydia Huntley. 1998 [1827]. "The Alpine Flowers." In: Paula Bernat Bennett (ed.), *Nineteenth-Century American Women Poets: An Anthology*. Malden, MA: Blackwell. 4.

Selected Secondary Literature

Bercovitch, Sacvan (ed.). 2004. *Nineteenth-Century Poetry 1800-1910*. Vol. 4 of *The Cambridge History of American Literature*. Cambridge: Cambridge UP.

A detailed history of major currents and writers of the period. Its narrative chapters chronicle the authors' lives and weave readings of poems into biographical accounts.

Brodwin, Stanley and Michael D'Innocenzo (eds.). 1983. *William Cullen Bryant and His America: Centennial Conference Proceedings, 1878-1978*. New York: AMS.

The collection includes essays that investigate the aesthetic and professional dimensions of Bryant's poetic and editorial work.

Chai, Leon. 1990. *Romantic Foundations of the American Renaissance*. Ithaca, N.Y.: Cornell UP.

A thorough study that traces the philosophic and literary European heritage of American Romanticism.

Tharaud, Barry (ed.). 2006. *Ralph Waldo Emerson: Bicentenary Appraisals*. Trier: WVT.

This collection of essays re-assesses Emerson's contributions to a diverse array of discourses, such as ethnohistory and -geography, cultural progressivism, nationalism, and abolition.

Waggoner, Hyatt Howe. 1974. *Emerson as Poet*. Princeton, NJ: Princeton UP.

A standard work that records the stages of Emerson's development as well as his controversial critical reception as a poet.

Further References

Axelrod, Steven Gould, Camille Roman and Thomas Travisano (eds.). 2012. *Traditions and Revolutions, Beginnings to 1900*. Vol. 1 of *The New Anthology of American Poetry*. New Brunswick, NJ: Rutgers UP.

Bennett, Paula Bernat. 2003. *Poets in the Public Sphere: The Emancipatory Project of American Women's Poetry, 1800-1900*. Princeton, NJ: Princeton UP.

Brown, Charles Henry. 1971. *William Cullen Bryant*. New York: Scribner.

Buell, Lawrence I. 1996. *The Environmental Imagination: Thoreau, Nature Writing, and the Formation of American Culture*. 2nd ed. Cambridge, MA: Belknap P of Harvard UP.

Cushman, Stephen. 2011. "Transcendentalist Poetics." In: Larson 2011a. 76-93.

Donovan, Alan B. 1968. "William Cullen Bryant: 'Father of American Song.'" In: *New England Quarterly* 41.4: 505-20.

Gado, Frank (ed.). 2006. *William Cullen Bryant: An American Voice*. White River Junction, VM: Antoca.

Galloway, Andrew. 2010. "William Cullen Bryant's American Antiquities: Medievalism, Miscegenation, and Race in *The Prairies*." In: *American Literary History* 22.4: 724-51.

Gelpi, Albert. 1975. *The Tenth Muse: The Psyche of the American Poet.* Cambridge, MA: Harvard UP.

Haselstein, Ulla. 1998. "Seen from a Distance: Moments of Negativity in the American Sublime (Tocqueville, Bryant, Emerson)." In: *Amerikastudien/American Studies* 43.3: 405-21.

Kete, Marie Louise. 2011. "The reception of nineteenth-century American poetry." In: Larson 2011a. 15-35.

Larson, Kerry (ed.). 2011a. *The Cambridge Companion to Nineteenth-Century American Poetry.* Cambridge: Cambridge UP.

——. 2011b. Introduction. In: Larson 2011a. 1-11.

Matthiessen, F. O. 1941. *American Renaissance: Art and Expression in the Age of Emerson and Whitman.* New York: Oxford UP.

Meyer, Kinereth. 1993. "Landscape and Counter-Landscape in the Poetry of William Cullen Bryant." In: *Nineteenth-Century Literature* 48.2: 194-211.

Miller, Perry. 1964. "New England Transcendentalism: Native or Imported?" In: Carroll Camden (ed.), *Literary Views: Critical and Historical Essays.* Chicago: U of Chicago P. 115-29.

Moriarity, David J. 1983. "Bryant and the Suggestive Image." In: Brodwin/D'Innocenzo 1983. 209-22.

Morris, Saundra. 1999. "'Meter-Making' Arguments: Emerson's Poems." In: Porte/Morris 1999. 218-42.

——. 1997. "The Threshold Poem, Emerson, and 'The Sphinx.'" In: *American Literature* 69.3: 547-70.

——. 2006. "Poetic Portals: Emerson's Essay Epigraphs." In: Tharaud 2006. 255-78.

Muller, Gilbert H. 2008. *William Cullen Bryant: Author of America.* Albany, NY: SUNY P.

New, Elisa. 2009. *The Regenerate Lyric: Theology and Innovation in American Poetry.* Cambridge: Cambridge UP.

Newin, Paul A. 1983. "The Prairie and 'The Prairies': Cooper's and Bryant's Views of Manifest Destiny." In: Brodwin/D'Innocenzo 1983. 27-38.

Packer, Barbara. 2004. "American Verse Traditions, 1800-55." In: Bercovitch 2004. 11-145.

Pearce, Roy Harvey. 1961. *The Continuity of American Poetry.* Princeton, NJ: Princeton UP.

Porte, Joel and Saundra Morris (eds.). 1999. *The Cambridge Companion to Ralph Waldo Emerson.* Cambridge: Cambridge UP.

Schirmeister, Pamela J. 1999. *Less Legible Meanings: Between Poetry and Philosophy in the Works of Emerson.* Stanford, CA: Stanford UP.

Tharaud, Barry (ed.). 2010. *Emerson for the Twenty-First Century: Global Perspectives on an American Icon.* Newark, DE: U of Delaware P.

Tuerk, Richard. 1990. "Emerson and the Wasting of Beauty: 'The Rhodora.'" In: *American Transcendental Quarterly* 4.1: 5-11.

Waggoner, Hyatt Howe. 1968. *American Poets: From the Puritans to the Present.* Boston, MA: Houghton.

Whicher, Stephen E. 1953. "Emerson's Tragic Sense." In: *American Scholar* 22.3: 285-92.

Yoder, R. A. 1978. *Emerson and the Orphic Poet in America.* Berkeley, CA: U of California P.

6.

American Romanticisms

Edgar Allan Poe's "Dream-Land" and Herman Melville's "America"

Gero Guttzeit

1. Romanticism and Antebellum America

As early as 1924, the American historian of ideas, Arthur O. Lovejoy, pointed out the difficulties of defining Romanticism in its German, French, and British forms and suggested that "we should learn to use the word 'Romanticism' in the plural" (235). American varieties of Romanticism are at least as difficult to define, and the task is complicated by the complex transnational influence of earlier European Romanticisms within the United States in the period between 1800 and 1865. While the American situation does not evince the (relative) unity of the Romantics in England between roughly 1780 and 1830, romantic forms and motifs abound in early and mid-nineteenth century poems (and many other literary genres) in the United States. Most importantly, New England Transcendentalism is deeply saturated in Romanticism and is often called the American counterpart of European Romanticisms.

Antebellum poetry was shaped by the emerging literary market, the rise of literary nationalism, and the increasing political tension between the North and the South. The lack of an international copyright agreement meant that republishing British literature was much less expensive for American publishers than fostering national authors. In this "culture of reprinting," as Meredith McGill (2003) calls it, romantic and transcendentalist ideas were characteristically disseminated widely via the medium of the literary magazine. An increasing number of writers demanded that America have a literature of its own. Questions about what America was and should be were on the agenda and made urgent by westward expansion, the corresponding ideology of Manifest Destiny, and the opposition between the Southern and the Northern states. The war between the industrialized Union states in the North and the agricultural Confederate states in the South, whose political economy was based on slave labor, fundamentally changed conceptions and images of America. There is critical agreement that the military, political, and cultural clash of the Civil War marked the end of American Romanticism. Nevertheless, a variety of romantic elements survived in postbellum poetry, as will become apparent in Melville's case.

Both Edgar Allan Poe's and Herman Melville's writings differ in important respects from the main currents of American Romanticism and Transcendentalism, particularly with regard to their poetry. Often grouped together with Nathaniel Hawthorne, Poe and Melville are characterized as running counter to an American ideology of optimism and metaphysical transparency, and are viewed rather as exposing the dark and troubled aspects of personal identity and cultural ideology (see e.g., Harry Levin's classic study *The Power of Blackness* (1958)). Melville himself, in his enthusiastic review of Hawthorne's *Mosses from an Old Manse*, wrote: "this great power of blackness in him derives its force from its appeals to that Calvinistic sense of Innate Depravity and Original Sin, from whose visitations, in some shape or other, no deeply thinking mind is always and wholly free" (Melville 1987: 243). This field of political and artistic tensions in which Poe's and Melville's poems stand has been variously described as negative Romanticism (cf. Hoffman 1972: 19-29), dark Romanticism, or Gothic Romanticism. All of these concepts attempt to grasp the difference to the main characteristics of romantic poetry, which, as Jerome McGann (1983) has shown, is representative of the romantic ideology. Gary Richard Thompson explains that romantic writing "evokes an ideal world, infused with internal energy and dynamically evolving toward a yet higher state, in which the single, separate self seeks unity with nature, itself symbolic of the aesthetic harmony of the cosmos" (1974: 1).

Because of Poe's major influence on French poets from Charles Baudelaire to Paul Valéry, Poe's life and work were and are often viewed in terms of his influence on modernist rather than romantic poetry (see Eliot 1949). While Poe's early poetry was clearly influenced by Byronism, his later poems and his fiction in general are difficult to frame in terms of Romanticism. He published four collections of poetry in his lifetime: *Tamerlane and Other Poems* (1827), *Al Aaraaf, Tamerlane and Minor Poems* (1829), *Poems* (1831), and *The Raven and Other Poems* (1845).

Poe is often named as the prime example of the gloomy tradition of American Romanticism, yet the older literary tradition which feeds this type of literature is the Gothic, for a long time regarded as the inferior popular counterpart of Romanticism proper (cf. Botting 1996: 12). Recent research has rehabilitated the Gothic: Tom Duggett, for instance, argues that "the phenomenon known as Romanticism is a reform movement within the Gothic" (2010: 7; see Gamer 2000). The term 'Gothic Romanticism' also has the advantage of stressing the connections of Poe's poetry to both the earlier British and the American Gothic traditions, the latter usually thought to have reached its first heyday with the novels of Charles Brockden Brown around 1800.

Gothic romantic poetry reaches back to some of the most famous works often thought of as 'high' romantic such as Samuel Taylor Coleridge's "Rime of the Ancient Mariner" (1798) and "Kubla Khan, or A Vision in a Dream" (1816). Its themes and motifs are similar to the Gothic tradition in fiction (and architecture), which was associated with medieval times (and German horror writing), and depicted darkness, madness, and death. In the United States, Philip Freneau's "House of Night" (1779) is an early example of poetry that contains Gothic elements. While most authors entered the tradition to write but a few poems in it (e.g., Henry Wadsworth Longfellow), the majority of Poe's poems fall under the rubric of Gothic, the most famous by far being "The Raven" (1845), but also "The Haunted Palace" (1839), "The Conqueror Worm" (1843), "Ulalume" (1847), and "Annabel Lee" (1849). While almost all of Poe's poems employ elements of the Gothic—desolate landscapes, bereaved lovers, ghostly beings—one of the best examples of American Gothic in general is "Dream-Land" (1844).

The Gothic is also a strong presence in Melville's writings, the chief instance possibly being *Moby-Dick* (1851). Generally, Melville's writing is rooted in the traditions of Romanticism but also departs significantly from them: "The difference between the Melvillean and the Romantic quests is that, while reproducing the pattern of Romantic myth, Melville's quests thematically abort it: the ascending circle in Melville's writings is never completed . . ., the more inclusive unity never achieved" (Milder 2006: 31; cf. 41). The events of the Civil War, in particular, make both the earlier transcendentalist and Gothic varieties of Romanticism difficult for him to follow.

Melville's collection of poetry titled *Battle-Pieces and Aspects of the War* (1866), from which "America" is taken, is part of a large body of poetry about the Civil War. Older scholarship often dismissed Civil War era poetry because of its supposed inferior literary quality; Edmund Wilson, for instance, argued that Melville's *Battle-Pieces* were "versified journalism" (1962: 479). Thanks to recent scholarship, works by canonical writers—first and foremost Walt Whitman's *Drum-Taps* (1865) and its *Sequel* (1865-6) and Melville's *Battle-Pieces*, but also individual poems such as John Greenleaf Whittier's "Barbara Frietchie" (1863)—are now supplemented with works by African American poets, Southern poets, and previously unpublished material (cf. Miller/Barrett 2005). During this period, Shira Wolosky explains, "different sections of the country claimed the American language for their own interpretive interests, engendering variant forms of usage, emphasis, and intention" (2010: 52). Recited in front of large audiences or printed for even larger readerships, poetry often served predominantly rhetorical rather than aesthetic aims (ibid.: 64-5). The attempt to overcome the many political, ideological, and literary divisions after the war characterizes Melville's expressed project in *Battle-Pieces*.

Not only was the function of poetry a public one, but many writers metaphorically referred to America itself as a poem. For instance, Walt Whitman declared in the preface to *Leaves of Grass* that the "United States themselves are essentially the greatest poem" (1965 [1865-6]: 709). By examining mythic beings within American landscapes as scenes of conflict, both Poe's "Dream-Land" and Melville's "America" poetically and rhetorically negotiate what America means before and after the Civil War.

2. Poe's "Dream-Land": An American Antebellum Nightmare

A first reading of Poe's "Dream-Land" (1969 [1844]: 342-7) establishes an initial understanding of the depicted situation and its transformations. The poem consists of a speaker's retrospective description of a voyage in which he traveled through a land of dreams and nightmares. In the first stanza the speaker has arrived in lands that he later calls home, which becomes clear from the use of the present perfect at the beginning and the end of the poem: "I have reached these lands" (l. 5) and "I have wandered home" (l. 55). While it is not entirely clear whether this was his home originally, traveling to dream-land seems to mean, first and foremost, sleeping and dreaming. Thus, the speaker has left the waking world by sleeping, and the poem is the evocative description of what he saw while dreaming. The poem opens just as the speaker has returned to the waking world:

> By a route obscure and lonely,
> Haunted by ill angels only,
> Where an Eidolon, named Night,
> On a black throne reigns upright,
> I have reached these lands but newly
> From an ultimate dim Thule—
> From a wild weird clime that lieth, sublime,
>   Out of Space—out of Time. (ll. 1-8)

Beyond the title and the general setting, many individual elements speak in favor of this initial interpretation of the speaker's traveling as dreaming, which also helps to understand several poetic devices otherwise difficult to explain. The lands described show two aspects of dreaming: the nightmare and the soothing dream. Hence, despite its grotesque and terrible features, dream-land can be "a peaceful, soothing region" (l. 40). The presence of supernatural creatures such as the personification of Night ("an Eidolon, named Night," l. 3; *eidolon* is ancient Greek for 'phantom,' or 'specter') and the "ill angels" (l. 2) is typical of dreams. Individual phrases like the metaphor of "the fringed lid" (l. 48) also become clear: the lid with fringes which cannot be opened while someone is asleep is the eye. The general topic of dreams is arch-romantic and particularly popular in its Gothic tradition. This is perhaps nowhere as well exemplified as in Coleridge's "Kubla Khan," which he himself describes in a preface as the result of opium-induced sleep.

A substantial part of "Dream-Land" is devoted to topographical description. In his portrayal of the vast landscape in the second stanza, Poe makes use of adjectives with the suffix *-less* along with other types of grammatical negation:

> Bottomless vales and boundless floods,
> And chasms, and caves, and Titan woods,
> With forms that no man can discover
> For the dews that drip all over;
> Mountains toppling evermore
> Into seas without a shore;
> Seas that restlessly aspire,
> Surging, unto skies of fire (ll. 9-16)

The effect of this passage can be summed up with the term Poe uses in the first stanza in line seven: the awe-inspiring and grotesque picture of gigantic natural phenomena is sublime. While the origins of the sublime lie in ancient rhetoric, the term gained in importance during the second half of the eighteenth century. In his *A Philosophical Inquiry into the Origin of Our Ideas of the Sublime and Beautiful* (1756), Edmund Burke used it to describe the peculiarly positive physiological and mental experience of something terrible at a distance. Burke's definition linked the sublime closely to the terrible, and Ann Radcliffe, the English author who pioneered the Gothic novel, further developed this link in her dialogue "On the Supernatural in Poetry" (1826). The idea of the sublime relates not only to the nightmarish terror of the landscape but also to its vastness. At the heart of Immanuel Kant's definition of the (mathematical) sublime was the notion of boundlessness—that which makes it impossible to comprehend the object in its entirety (2003 [1790]: 248-60). Poe's poem has the phrase "forms that no man can discover" (l. 11), which encapsulates the paradox of the sublime: the speaker is experiencing and speaking about something which is so huge that it is virtually unspeakable.

As the middle part of the poem, the third and longest stanza diverges somewhat from the impressive vastness of the second, yet it reinforces the effect of terror. It describes the dreamscape in natural terms and progresses in the manner of the zoom shot in cinematography, moving from big to small, for instance, from *lakes* to *pools* to *nooks*. This is reinforced by the anaphoric structure of what is grammatically a single sentence, in which "by the" is repeated at the beginning of the subclauses:

By the lakes that thus outspread
Their lone waters, lone and dead,—
Their sad waters, sad and chilly
With the snows of the lolling lily,—
By the mountains—near the river
Murmuring lowly, murmuring ever,—
By the grey woods,—by the swamp
Where the toad and the newt encamp,—
By the dismal tarns and pools
    Where dwell the Ghouls,—
By each spot the most unholy—
In each nook most melancholy,—
There the traveller meets aghast
Sheeted Memories of the Past—
Shrouded forms that start and sigh
As they pass the wanderer by—
White-robed forms of friends long given,
In agony, to the Earth—and Heaven. (ll. 21-38)

At the end of this process of gradual magnification, the poem becomes once more supernatural. Up to this point, while the dreamscape in stanzas two and three offers a heightened and sublime description of nature, the negated elements of the landscape nevertheless make up a natural inventory of the wilderness: from vales and chasms to rivers and swamps (ll. 9-29). The line "Where dwell the Ghouls" (l. 30) is specially marked in several ways: it has only four syllables (as opposed to the usual eight), which makes it stand out typographically, and it is at the precise center of the middle stanza of the poem. This structural demarcation reinforces the semantic shift from the description of the sublime landscape (ll. 9-29) to the supernatural creatures peopling dream-land (ll. 30-50).

This supernatural second half of the stanza changes our conception of dream-land and also reintroduces the speaker in the third person as a "traveller" (l. 33) and "wanderer" (l. 36). Dream-land is apparently not merely the land of dreams and nightmares, but also that of the dead: Hades or Heaven. The ghouls (l. 30) and specters (ll. 34-8), which line the traveler's route, invoke not only darkness and sleep, but also the mythological brother of sleep: death. "White-robed forms of friends long given, / In agony, to the Earth—and Heaven" (ll. 37-8) describe ghosts who are no longer able to communicate with the living, even in their dreams. Moreover, the effect on the dreamer is described as terrifying or horrifying: he is "aghast" (l. 33). These motifs add to the sense of Poe's dream-land as a land of the dead through which dreaming people pass. In fact, the Gothic tradition in poetry began in England in the eighteenth century with so-called Graveyard Poetry by authors such as Thomas Parnell, Edward Young, and Thomas Gray. Aimed at "moral instruction rather than excitement," its principal motifs were "night, ruins, death and ghosts, everything, indeed, that was excluded by rational culture" (Botting 1996: 34, 32).

In contrast to such moral intentions of earlier Gothic poems, Poe's poetry, in general, is characterized by a strong opposition to edification or moral lecturing. In his critical writings, he dismissed anything close to what he called the "heresy of *The Didactic*" in poetry (Poe 1984 [1850]: 75-6): "Every poem, it is said, should inculcate a moral; and by this moral is the poetical merit of the work to be adjudged" (ibid.). Against this doxa, Poe posited his idea of the "poem written solely for the poem's sake," (ibid.) an idea which would become influential for literary modernity, particularly for the *l'art pour l'art* movement. The consequent moral indeterminacy also characterizes the fourth stanza of "Dream-Land":

> For the heart whose woes are legion
> 'Tis a peaceful, soothing region—
> For the spirit that walks in shadow
> O! it is an Eldorado!
> But the traveller, travelling through it,
> May not—dare not openly view it;
> Never its mysteries are exposed
> To the weak human eye unclosed;
> So wills its King, who hath forbid
> The uplifting of the fringed lid;
> And thus the sad Soul that here passes
> Beholds it but through darkened glasses. (ll. 39-50)

This stanza complicates our impression of dream-land as a vast, sublime land of ghouls and ghosts in that it offers consolation to melancholy people. But rather than provide ethical and intellectual answers to the questions raised by the land of dreams and the afterlife, the traveler catches only a glimpse of its secrets. The paradox is that to really grasp dream-land, one would have to be awake while dreaming of it. As with the "forms that no man can discover" (l. 11), "its mysteries" (l. 45) are never exposed to waking eyes. While night is often personified as a female figure, here it is likely that "King" refers to the night on its "black throne" (l. 54), making other interpretations, such as Death or the Christian God, less likely. The final metaphor reinforces the link between the land of dreams and the afterlife since "through darkened glasses" (l. 50) is an allusion to a biblical phrase in Paul's 1 Corinthians 13:12: "For now we see through a glass darkly, but then face to face," 'then' referring to the state after resurrection (King James Version, Mabbott in Poe 1969: 347).

This device points to the larger context of Poe's Gothic poetry which, as David Reynolds points out, made use of the techniques of the so-called visionary mode of religious writing: in Poe, the visionary mode "begins to be summoned into the human psyche, as dreams are no longer passively experienced for their religious lesson but rather are actively conjured up for their regenerating beauty" (2011 [1988]: 44). In Poe's "Dream-Land" the reader is not given a definite answer by an angel bringing the gospel as would have been the case in earlier visionary writing, but instead is faced with the impenetrability of the mysteries of the lands of the dreaming and the dead. The absence of religious certainty also distinguishes Poe's poetry from other American romantic poetry, such as Bryant's "Forest Hymn." Alan Shucard says that with Bryant, "there is always a heavenly, often patriotic, glow behind his clouds" (1990: 84) that is absent from Poe's writing. Generally, metaphysical uncertainty contrasted Gothic romantic writing from the "cosmic optimism of Romantic thinkers:" Thompson concludes that "the apprehension that there was a dark substratum to the rock of Romantic faith obsessed those Romantic writers who turned to the Gothic mode of terror and horror in an effort to express a complex vision of the existential agony confronting man since the Age of Faith" (1974: 5). "Dream-Land" thus draws in secularized fashion on ideas of the afterworld, but Poe's interest lies in the workings of the human psyche and its poetic representation.

The general effect of mystery in "Dream-Land" is amplified by the almost hypnotic sound texture of the poem. Poe makes extensive use of the technique of repetition with variation, which he often used and also theorized in his essay "The Philosophy of Composition" (1846). Taken together, the first and last stanza constitute a refrain, and an 1844 version of the poem had two additional repetitions of this refrain (cf. Poe 1969: 345). The varied repetition of the lines about the lakes (ll. 17-24) has a similar effect: the phonetic texture is often equivalent or identical both at the beginning of sound clusters (alliteration) and in the vowel sounds within the words (assonance). Where alliteration and assonance are combined (in such phrases such as "lolling lily," ll. 20, 24), they almost *lull* the reader into dream-land. This hypnotic effect is varied since the poem formally combines regular with irregular features as in the line "Where dwell the Ghouls" (l. 30). While not conforming to a rule-bound form such as the sonnet or the villanelle, the poem exhibits end rhymes and its lines are mostly written in trochaic tetrameter. It is remarkable that the formal regularity of the poem is not fractured by its disorderly content. While the mountains might topple into the shore, the rhythmic and semantic integrity of the lines describing it is conserved.

A first comparison of Poe's "Dream-Land" to Melville's "America" shows similar themes such as landscapes and dreams, but Melville's extended allegory of America suggests the necessity of a further examination of the historical conditions under which Poe composed his poem. In antebellum America, the centers of publishing were in the Northern states, and Poe, as a Southern writer, often criticized the literary coteries in the North. Despite Poe's involvement with the construction of a national American literature, the line "Out of Space—out of Time" from "Dream-Land" was for a long time taken as an apt self-description by Poe who was viewed as more of a displaced European than as an American writer (see Eliot 1949). While primarily a poem about the land of the dreaming and the dead, a reading of "Dream-Land" that takes into account the historical situation in antebellum America discloses links to the aforementioned ideological commonplace of America as a poem in its own right. Poe actually gives a further epithet to the wild, weird, and sublime land of dreams that is at once poetic and historically allusive:

> I have reached these lands but newly
> From an ultimate dim Thule—
> From a wild weird clime that lieth, sublime,
> Out of Space—out of Time. (ll. 5-8)

"Ultima Thule" is a commonplace in classical poetry used as a reference to "an island north of Britain," as Poe's editor Thomas Mabbott explains (Poe 1969: 345), or used figuratively as a catchword for a mythical place. On an ideological level America was viewed as an ultimate Thule in the sense that it fulfilled the utopian expectations connected to this mythical place. The most eloquent pronouncement of this topos was given in the prestigious Phi Beta Kappa oration at Harvard in 1824 by one of the most renowned orators of the nineteenth century, Edward Everett, who said about the United States: "the farthest Thule is reached; there are no more retreats beyond the sea, no more discoveries, no more hopes. Here, then, a mighty work is to be performed, or never, by mortals" (1850 [1836]: 42). This is a myth of an ultimate Thule that had been reached already and yet was still to be performed as "a mighty work" or, indeed, as a poem. Far from writing a nationalist poem in praise of America, as earlier epic poets such as Joel Barlow or Richard Emmons had tried to do, Poe's "Dream-Land" turns inward and shines a light on the nightmarish aspect of America as a "promised land."

3. Melville's "America": Dreaming of the United States after the War

In contrast to Poe, whose first collection of poetry appeared when he was eighteen years old, Melville published poetry only late in his career. After his early success with his autobiographical South Sea novels *Typee* (1846) and *Omoo* (1847), his later works, even *Moby-Dick; or The Whale* (1851), did not meet with public approval. Melville is often said to have abandoned prose for poetry because of his lack of success, yet he had studied poetry with a vigorous and systematic approach from early on (cf. Parker in Melville 2009: 330). In 1999 Lawrence Buell claimed that Melville's poetry "remains largely unread, even by many Melvillians" (135), but today scholars are reassessing the importance and influence of Melville's poetry, not only of *Battle-Pieces and Aspects of the War* (1866) and *Clarel* (1876), but also of his privately and posthumously published collections, *John Marr and Other Sailors* (1888), *Timoleon* (1891), and *Weeds and Wildings Chiefly, With a Rose or Two* (1924).

His first poetry collection, *Battle-Pieces and Aspects of the War*, was published almost immediately after the Civil War in 1866. The poems evince an occupation with romantic forms, but also include factual reports about the war (mostly taken from the newspaper articles collected in the *Rebellion Record*) and some formal experimentation. Despite its topic and its position as the last poem of the central section of the book, "America" is only rarely anthologized and has so far received comparatively little scholarly attention, partly due to the fact that Melville's poems have often been studied in isolation rather than in context (cf. Dryden 2004: 89). Robert Penn Warren went so far as to deny the poem any merit whatsoever, arguing that it was "written to resolve—no, gloss over—the very issues raised in the body of the book," and "as far as the virtues of 'America' as a poem, the less said the better" (in Melville 1970: 375). The poems in *Battle-Pieces* are generally arranged chronologically so that structurally "America" has a summarizing function: it can be called "a culminating point" (Garner 1993: 395).

In the four stanzas of "America," Melville describes the Civil War as a conflict with four stages: (1) a life of innocent happiness before the war (2) is interrupted by fierce combats, and only after (3) a nightmarish coma-like state can America (4) reawake at the end of the war as a wiser and more lawful country. The poem develops around a personification of America as a female figure much more individualized than any of the mythical beings in Poe's "Dream-Land." America's complexity is brought out by comparisons and contrasts to several mythical women, but is also compared to the flag as an emblem of national identity. The first stanza centers on the flag and introduces the main personification of America:

> WHERE the wings of a sunny Dome expand
> I saw a Banner in gladsome air—
> Starry, like Berenice's Hair—
> Afloat in broadened bravery there;

> With undulating long-drawn flow,
> As rolled Brazilian billows go
> Voluminously o'er the Line.
> The Land reposed in peace below;
>   The children in their glee
> Were folded to the exulting heart
>   Of young Maternity. (ll. 1-11)

This peaceful, romantic landscape, full of cosmic harmony, could hardly be more different from Poe's dream-land. Where Poe isolates the landscape and negates its individual features to create an effect of Gothic sublimity, Melville's stanza creates a pastoral atmosphere to depict the United States before the Civil War, using both idyllic imagery and harmonious sound patterns. One major contributing factor is the sound of the nautical simile of the "long-drawn flow" (l. 5) of Brazilian waves; the comparison is mirrored in the phonetic texture of lines 5-7, which adds to the fairly regular iambic tetrameter an abundance of similar /r/ and /l/ sounds. Alliteration and end rhymes as in "broadened bravery" (l. 4) and "glee . . . Maternity" (ll. 9, 11) further heighten the sense of idyllic lands that culminates in the harmonious unity between Mother America and her children.

Yet viewed historically, this romantic happiness is rather one-dimensional, especially since the identity of America's children is not specified. In the case *Dred Scott v. Sandford*, the Supreme Court had decided in 1857 that African American slaves were not citizens of the United States; this changed only through the process of the war, especially with the Emancipation Proclamation (1863) and the Thirteenth Amendment to the United States Constitution (1865). In Melville's "America" there is a strong tension between the actual historical situation and the counterfactual harmony, which results in a foreboding of danger at the sight of the picture of political unity.

At the center of this picture, the elevated flag is introduced by a comparison to Berenice, the first of several female figures to enrich the description of America. The allusive simile of Berenice's hair works on three interconnected levels: her hair is a constellation of stars ("Coma Berenices") named after the Egyptian Queen Berenice II (born after 270 BCE) who had consecrated her hair to Aphrodite for the safe return of her husband from war (Ameling 2002). Since the stars on the United States flag stand for the individual states (and the Civil War had seen many changes in both Union and Confederate flags), the connection to the constellation Coma Berenices imbues with mythical powers the relation between the individual states and America as a country. In depicting the flag, Melville evokes a conventional ensign of America, yet not as a sign of victory but as a complex and idealized index of antebellum political unity. The second stanza pictures the war as a violent interruption of this harmonic pastoral scene, turning the flag into an emblem of war:

> Later, and it streamed in fight
>   When tempest mingled with the fray,
> And over the spear-point of the shaft
>   I saw the ambiguous lightning play.
> Valor with Valor strove, and died:
> Fierce was Despair, and cruel was Pride;
> And the lorn Mother speechless stood,
> Pale at the fury of her brood. (ll. 12-19)

In describing allegorically a factual and recent historical conflict, the poem departs from earlier Romantic and Gothic poetry. Indeed, poets were acutely aware of the necessity to break with tradition, as becomes clear, for instance, in Whitman's poem on the first year of the Civil War, "Eighteen Sixty-One." In *Battle-Pieces* the allegorization of the war works via intertextual allusions to Milton's *Paradise Lost*, as Hennig Cohen points out: "Equating the Civil War with the Miltonic version of the War in Heaven amplified the earthly conflict and infused it with meaning" (in Melville 1964: 11-3, 279; cf. Dryden 2004: 90-2). What is decisive about the allegorical representation is that it prompts the reader to regard both sides in the war as equally valorous. Thus, the lyrical speaker does not take sides: "Valor with Valor strove, and died" (l. 16). In the "Supplement" to *Battle-Pieces*, Melville calls the actions in the war "reciprocal" and points to the fact that history is written by the victors: "had the preponderating strength and the prospect of its unlimited increase lain on the other side, on ours might have lain those actions which now in our late opponents we stigmatize under the name of Rebellion" (2009: 184).

The goddess-like figure of Mother America is elaborated on in the second stanza, standing speechless like a statue. The United States was often represented in statues: America (cf. Dryden 2004: 94), Liberty (as later in the nineteenth century with the Statue of Liberty), or Columbia (a Latinate designation for the United States based on Columbus's name). Since Melville had visited its architect, Robert Crawford, in Rome in 1857 (cf. Leyda 1969, II: 559), he was closely familiar with the Statue of Freedom, which still resides atop the United States Capitol Building. Hence, the "sunny Dome" in stanza one could refer metaphorically to the skies or intertextually to the dome in Coleridge's "Kubla Khan" (cf. Dryden 2004: 90), but it could also imply the Capitol, as the reference to the "Capitol Dome" in "The Scout Towards Aldie" makes most likely (Melville 2009: 140, cf. Fuller 2011: 198; Garner 1993: 395). In December 1863 the Statue of Freedom was installed on the top of the recently completed cast-iron dome so that for contemporary readers of "America," the Capitol Dome and the Statue of Freedom were still new signs of political power. In the context of *Battle-Pieces*, Melville brings out the ambivalence of this power by contrasting the sunny Dome in "America" with an "Iron Dome" in "The Conflict of Convictions." In the latter poem, "[p]ower unanointed" is represented by the "huge shadow" of the Iron Dome that endangers the American dream as it was conceived by the Founding Fathers of the United States (2009: 10).

The use of allegory and personification as figures of speech in literary and religious texts is most strongly associated with classical, medieval, and neoclassical texts rather than romantic texts. In this tradition, America's gender is in no way unusual. The ancient Roman rhetorician Quintilian had theorized the use of personification in giving a voice to large political bodies, stressing the possibility of making a state or nation speak (cf. 2001: 51). Significantly, America has lost this ability in Melville's poem: even when her children are fighting, she stands "speechless" (l. 18). In the third stanza, this muting of the female figure is escalated as America falls into a comatose state:

> Yet later, and the silk did wind
>   Her fair cold form;
> Little availed the shining shroud,
>   Though ruddy in hue, to cheer or warm.

A watcher looked upon her low, and said—
She sleeps, but sleeps, she is not dead.
  But in that sleep contortion showed
The terror of the vision there—
  A silent vision unavowed,
Revealing earth's foundation bare,
  And Gorgon in her hidden place.
It was a thing of fear to see
  So foul a dream upon so fair a face,
And the dreamer lying in that starry shroud. (ll. 20-33)

Like the whole of "Dream-Land," this stanza stresses the interconnectedness of sleeping, dreaming, and death. This connection had ancient mythological roots and reached a height in Romanticism. The motif of a death-like sleep recalls mythical female figures such as Brynhild (Brünnhilde) in the Volsunga saga and the Nibelungen or the fairy tale character, Sleeping Beauty. Extended poetic versions of the motif are frequent in Gothic romantic poetry, for instance in Poe's "The Sleeper" (1842) and Christina Rossetti's "Dream Land" (1862). Such associations work to contrast the positive personification of America with the dangers of terror, war, and rebellion.

"The terror of the vision" of America's dream is brought out through additional mythological female figures that embody revolution and chaos. The most important of these sources of terror is the "Gorgon" (l. 30)—whose name is that of the deadly sisters in Greek mythology with snakes for hair and a petrifying gaze. The most famous of the three Gorgons, Medusa, came to signify a revolutionary woman in the romantic era, outlined by Dennis Berthold as "one of the most powerful emblems of revolution and emergent feminism in the nineteenth century" (1997: 449). Medusa's decapitation by Perseus was connected to the guillotining in post-revolutionary France, so that the Gorgon embodied "conservative male fears of revolution conflated with misogyny" (ibid.). This dual fear of revolution and feminism also informs Melville's allusion (cf. l. 32) to the witches in *Macbeth*, whose speech in the very first scene of the play is a classic topos of a world in chaos: "Fair is foul, and foul is fair" (Shakespeare 2005 [1606]: 971). Both the witches' upending of the values of good and bad and Medusa's lethal glance contrast strongly with the mother-figure of America. There is a misogynistic aspect to America's passivity and speechlessness, yet these features also work to send a political message about the frailty of a union endangered by civil war.

It is easy to recognize in the Gorgon and the witches the contemporary view of the Southern states as rebels. Yet through its allusiveness the poem is far from attempting to pigeonhole the parties into good and bad. All of the images keep a certain distance and only indirectly describe the war and its ideological conflicts. Significantly, despite America's vision, Melville does not enter the visionary mode as Poe does, but introduces another character in the "watcher" who utters the only sentence spoken in the poem: "She sleeps, but sleeps, she is not dead" (l. 25). The nightmare that America has of revolutionary Medusa and the "earth's foundations bare" (l. 29) remains a temporary one. The flag has now become a "shroud" (ll. 22, 33), and yet America herself has narrowly escaped becoming a fatality of the Civil War. In the final stanza, the end of the war is not spelled out but likened to a mystical awakening, indeed a rebirth:

But from the trance she sudden broke—
    The trance, or death into promoted life;
At her feet a shivered yoke,
And in her aspect turned to heaven
    No trace of passion or of strife—
A clear calm look. It spake of pain,
But such as purifies from stain—
Sharp pangs that never come again— (ll. 34-41)

The "shivered yoke" at America's feet is the broken yoke of slavery, and her glance is directed toward heaven rather than earth or hell. While there are traces of pain visible in her face, even this pain is "such as purifies from stain" (l. 40): the pains of war are characterized as a necessary evil to reattain political union. The noun phrases that make up a large part of the stanza are as much descriptive as hortatory. The North is admonished to not mistreat the South and disregard the regained union; on America's face, there is pain:

And triumph repressed by knowledge meet,
Power dedicate, and hope grown wise,
And youth matured for age's seat—
Law on her brow and empire in her eyes.
So she, with graver air and lifted flag;
While the shadow, chased by light,
Fled among the far-drawn height,
And left her on the crag. (ll. 42-9)

This ending speaks against the way in which critics such as Robert Penn Warren have often viewed the poem as a simplistic celebration of postbellum America. Indeed, the last lines of the poem leave America in a potentially dangerous situation on a crag above an abyss. The phrase "promoted life" (l. 35) is ambivalent and might allude to such female mythical figures as the statue built by the ancient sculptor Pygmalion, which was given life by Venus (cf. Dryden 2004: 94); "promoted life" suggests an external source of life that might once again disappear. At the same time, Melville envisions a development of the United States, as suggested by the various metaphorical depictions of growing wise with age. This is particularly visible in the line "Law on her brow and empire in her eyes" (l. 45). Melville does not go so far as to question the concept of empire here (in his first novel, *Typee*, he had criticized commercial and religious imperialism to the extent that he had to censor later editions); but the nation is to be founded upon law. Robert Milder spells out the developmental connection between the individuals and the nation: "America will come to be an 'empire,' just as its citizens will become sober adults, but the character of 'empire' has shifted, for it now rests upon reasserted Law as tempered by tragic wisdom" (2006: 182).

In interpreting and evaluating "America" and all of Melville's *Battle-Pieces*, one should not lose sight of either the author's professed intent or the overall historical situation of the beginnings of Reconstruction after the Civil War. Melville's far from perfect solution to the political problems is one of moderation and compromise; thus he speaks against giving the vote to African Americans immediately and urges Northerners to forgo retribution on the South. He concludes his supplement to *Battle-Pieces*: "Let us pray that the terrible historic tragedy of our time may not have been enacted without instructing our whole beloved country through terror and pity" (2009: 188). The overall goal of *Battle-Pieces*, and of "America" in particular, is to persuade white Northerners to be moderate in their treatment of the South. As Robert Milder phrases it, "the aim of *Battle-Pieces* is persuasion, or the conversion of [terror and pity] into know-ledge and action" (2006: 181). To that end, Melville evokes a variety of conven-tional ensigns of the state, such as the Statue of Freedom and the U.S. Capitol, not to celebrate them but to infuse them with ambivalent meanings and make them emblematic of the ideological strife of war. Using classicist devices such as allegory, Melville paints a picture of America before, during, and after the Civil War, making it complex by the use of such romantically inflected imagery as the revolutionary Gorgon. While "America" urges its readers to 'write America' as a poem of wise law and constant moderation, *Battle-Pieces* as a whole is far from embracing a program of American imperialist exceptionalism: the ground on which the country moves—earth's foundation—remains dangerous to tread on, as Melville writes in "The Apparition": "Solidity's a crust— / The core of fire below" (2009: 116).

4. Conclusion: Beyond Romanticism

Both Poe and Melville refrain from romantic visions of unity between the indi-vidual and a higher order of nature, and Melville shares much of the Gothic ro-mantic outlook of Poe's writings. This holds true especially for *Battle-Pieces* due to the socio-cultural ruptures resulting from the Civil War. Where Poe continues to write in traditional forms, Melville often breaks from the traditional; but nei-ther poet shies away from classicist devices, making use of the sublime (Poe) and allegory (Melville), with Milton being a common reference point in their poetry. Both use the motif of the dream, yet approach the problems of American identity from different angles: whereas Poe depicts the sublimity and paradoxi-cal solace of American antebellum nightmares, Melville constructs a postbellum dream of America while remaining intensely aware of how imperiled it is. Mak-ing use of romantic elements and inflecting them through Gothic mirrors, Poe and Melville represent a major current in American poetry: fathoming the depths of personal and collective identity, interrogating religious certainties, and criticizing American exceptionalist ideologies.

After the Civil War Romanticism remained a reference point for American poetry. At the threshold of modernist poetry, Emily Dickinson and Walt Whit-man would make use of romantic materials throughout their poetry. While Whitman departed considerably from traditional verse forms and rhymes, his affirmative tone chimes in with earlier romantic writing. In contrast, Dickinson's poems often center on the bleak aspects of nineteenth-century domestic and spiritual life. Taking up the distinction between a darker, extroverted and a lighter, introverted side of Romanticism, Shucard argues that Dickinson "is not the blithe romantic at all," placing her in a tradition with Byron, Poe, Longfel-low, Melville, and Stephen Crane (Shucard et al. 1990: 3). In the twentieth cen-tury, William Sullivan argues, the romantic tradition "with its insistence on the ideal and the transcendent . . . would also be part of the modernist score," nam-ing Hart Crane, E. E. Cummings, and Robinson Jeffers as modernist romantic visionaries (ibid.: 172).

Although its direct influence was marginal, Melville's poetic work is part of the American tradition of "a poetry of intellectualized, cerebral bound form (rig-

orously disciplined accentually and/or syllabically, if not by rhyme as well),"
which Buell contrasts with the tradition of Whitmanian 'democratic' free verse
(1999: 152). While Melville's poetry is still in the process of being rediscovered,
Poe's poems have remained popular and have influenced symbolist and modernist poetry all over the world. Even T.S. Eliot had to admit that "one cannot be
sure that one's own writing has *not* been influenced by Poe" (1949: 327; original emphasis). In their poems, Poe and Melville probed the reflective and persuasive powers of American poetry and thus went beyond the major currents of
Romanticism.

Bibliography

Selected Primary Literature

Dickinson, Emily. 1999 [1861]. *The Poems of Emily Dickinson: Reading Edition.*
    Ed. R. W. Franklin. Cambridge, MA: Belknap P of Harvard UP.
Freneau, Philip M. 1786 [1779]. "House of Night." In: *The Poems of Philip Freneau.*
    Written Chiefly During the Late War. Philadelphia: Bailey. 101-23.
Longfellow, Henry Wadsworth. 1891 [1839]. "Hymn to the Night." In: Vol. I of
    The Standard Library Edition of the Writings of Henry Wadsworth Longfellow.
    Ed. Horace E. Scudder. Boston: Houghton, Mifflin & Company. 19-20.
Melville, Herman. 1964 [1866]. *Battle-Pieces and the Aspect of the War.* Ed.
    Hennig Cohen. New York: Yoseloff.
—. 1970. *Selected Poems.* Ed. Robert Penn Warren. New York: Random House.
—. 1987. *The Piazza Tales: And Other Prose Pieces, 1839-1860.* Vol. VIII of the
    Newberry Library Edition of *The Writings of Herman Melville.* Ed. Harrison
    Hayford et al. Evanston: Northwestern UP.
—. 2009. *Published Poems of Herman Melville.* Vol. XI of the Newberry Library
    Edition of *The Writings of Herman Melville.* Ed. Robert C. Ryan et al. Histori-
    cal Note by Hershel Parker. Evanston: Northwestern UP.
—. 2009 [1866]. "America." In: Melville 2009. 120-1.
—. 2009 [1866]. "The Apparition (A Retrospect)." In: Melville 2009. 116.
Miller, Cristanne and Faith Barrett (eds.). 2005. *'Words for the Hour:' A New*
    Anthology of American Civil War Poetry. Amherst, MA: U of Massachusetts P.
Piatt, Sarah Morgan Bryan. 2005 [1867]. "Giving Back the Flower." In: *Palace-*
    Burner: The Selected Poetry of Sarah Piatt. Ed. Paula Bernat Bennett. Urba-
    na: U of Illinois P. 7-8.
Poe, Edgar Allan. 1969. *Poems.* Vol. I of *The Collected Works of Edgar Allan Poe.*
    Ed. Thomas O. Mabbott. Cambridge, MA: Belknap P.
—. 1984. *Essays and Reviews.* Ed. Gary Richard Thompson. New York: Library
    of America.
—. 1969 [1844]. "Dream-Land." In: Poe 1969. 342-7.
—. 1969 [1845]. "The Raven." In: Poe 1969. 350-74.
—. 1984 [1846]. "The Philosophy of Composition." In: Poe 1984. 13-25.
—. 1984 [1850]. "The Poetic Principle." In: Poe 1984. 71-94.
Timrod, Henry. 2007 [1863]. "The Unknown Dead." In: *Collected Poems: A Vario-*
    rum Edition. Eds. Winfield Parks and Aileen Wells Parks. Athens, GA: U of
    Georgia P. 126-7.
Whitman, Walt. 1965. *Leaves of Grass: Comprehensive Reader's Edition. Collect-*
    ed Writings of Walt Whitman. Ed. Harold William Blodgett and Sculley Brad-
    ley. New York: New York UP.

——1965 [1865-6]. "When Lilacs Last in the Dooryard Bloom'd." In: Whitman 1965. 328-37.
——. 1965 [1865-6]. "Preface 1855." In: Whitman 1965. 709-29.

Selected Secondary Literature

Barrett, Faith. 2012. *To Fight Aloud Is Very Brave. American Poetry and the Civil War*. Amherst: U of Massachusetts P.

Contextualizes and interprets the rhetoric of voices in Civil War poetry; includes a chapter on Battle-Pieces.

Dryden, Edgar A. 2004. *Monumental Melville: The Formation of a Literary Career*. Stanford, CA: Stanford UP.

Study of Melville's poetry, including a chapter on Battle-Pieces.

Kennedy, J. Gerald and Jerome J. McGann (eds.). 2012. *Poe and the Remapping of Antebellum Print Culture*. Baton Rouge: Louisiana State UP.

Edited collection that represents the state of the art in Poe studies.

Larson, Kerry (ed.). 2011. *The Cambridge Companion to Nineteenth-Century American Poetry*. Cambridge: Cambridge UP.

This companion collects essays that deal with movements and individual authors in nineteenth-century American poetry, including a chapter on Poe.

Levine, Robert S. (ed.). 1999. *The Cambridge Companion to Herman Melville*. Cambridge: Cambridge UP.

Deals with a variety of topics in Melville studies and includes a helpful essay on Melville as a poet.

Milder, Robert. 2006. *Exiled Royalties: Melville and the Life We Imagine*. New York: Oxford UP.

Study of Melville from his early novels to the late poetry, including chapters on Melville's (post)romanticism and on Battle-Pieces.

Peeples, Scott. 2007. *The Afterlife of Edgar Allan Poe*. Rochester, NY: Camden House.

Helpful overview of critical perspectives on Poe and a good starting-point.

Richards, Eliza. 2004. *Gender and the Poetics of Reception in Poe's Circle*. Cambridge: Cambridge UP.

Examines Poe's poetry in relation to the work of contemporary female poets.

Wolosky, Shira. 2010. *Poetry and Public Discourse in Nineteenth-Century America*. New York: Palgrave Macmillan.

In-depth study of the public importance of poetry in the nineteenth century; includes chapters on antebellum poetry, Poe, and Battle-Pieces.

Further References

Ameling, Walter. 2002. "Berenice II." *Brill's New Pauly*. Ed. Hubert Cancik and Helmuth Schneider. Leiden: Brill. Web. 20 Apr 2014. <http://reference works.brillonline.com/entries/brill-s-new-pauly/berenice-e215400>.
Bailey, J. O. 1948. "The Geography of Poe's 'Dream-Land' and 'Ulalume'." In: *Studies in Philology* 45.3: 512-23.

Berthold, Dennis. 1997. "Melville, Garibaldi, and the Medusa of Revolution." In: *American Literary History* 9.3: 425-59.

Botting, Fred. 1996. *Gothic*. London and New York: Routledge.

Buell, Lawrence. 1999. "Melville the Poet." In: Levine 1999. 135-56.

Chai, Leon. 1987. *The Romantic Foundations of the American Renaissance*. Ithaca: Cornell UP.

Duggett, Tom. 2010. *Gothic Romanticism: Architecture, Politics, and Literary Form*. New York: Palgrave Macmillan.

Eddings, Dennis W. 1975. "Poe's 'Dream-Land': Nightmare or Sublime Vision?" In: *Poe Studies* 8.1: 5-8.

Eliot, T.S. 1949. "From Poe to Valéry." In: *Hudson Review* 2.3: 327-42.

Everett, Edward. 1850 [1824]. "The Circumstances Favorable to the Progress of Literature in America." In: Vol. I of *Orations and Speeches on Various Occasions*. 2nd ed. Boston: Little, Brown, 9-44.

Fuller, Randall. 2011. *From Battlefields Rising: How the Civil War Transformed American Literature*. New York: Oxford UP.

Gamer, Michael. 2000. *Romanticism and the Gothic: Genre, Reception, and Canon Formation*. Cambridge: Cambridge UP.

Garner, Stanton. 1993. *The Civil War World of Herman Melville*. Lawrence: UP of Kansas.

Hoffman, Michael J. 1972. *The Subversive Vision: American Romanticism in Literature*. Port Washington, NY: Kennikat.

Kant, Immanuel. 2003 [1790]. *Kritik der praktischen Vernunft. Kritik der Urtheilskraft*. Vol. 5 of *Kants Werke. Akademie-Textausgabe*. Berlin: de Gruyter.

Levin, Harry. 1958. *The Power of Blackness: Hawthorne, Poe, Melville*. London: Faber & Faber.

Leyda, Jay. 1969. *The Melville Log*. New York: Gordian.

Lovejoy, Arthur O. 1924. "On the Discrimination of Romanticisms." In: *PMLA* 39.2: 229-53.

McGann, Jerome J. 1983. *The Romantic Ideology: A Critical Investigation*. Chicago: U of Chicago P.

McGill, Meredith L. 2003. *American Literature and the Culture of Reprinting, 1834-1853*. Philadelphia: U of Pennsylvania P.

Quintilian. 2001. *The Orator's Education: Books 9-10*. Vol. IV of the *Loeb Edition of The Orator's Education*. Ed. by Donald A. Russell. Cambridge, MA: Harvard UP.

Reynolds, David S. 2011 [1988]. *Beneath the American Renaissance: The Subversive Imagination in the Age of Emerson and Melville*. Oxford: Oxford UP.

Shakespeare, William. 2005 [1606]. *The Tragedy of Macbeth*. In: *The Oxford Edition of The Complete Works of William Shakespeare*. Eds. Stanley Wells and Gary Taylor. Oxford: Clarendon Press. 969-95.

Shucard, Alan. 1990. *American Poetry: The Puritans Through Walt Whitman*. Amherst: U of Massachusetts P.

—— et al. 1990. *Modern American Poetry*. Amherst: U of Massachusetts P.

Thompson, Gary Richard. 1974. "Introduction: Romanticism and the Gothic Tradition." In: Gary Richard Thompson (ed.). *The Gothic Imagination: Essays in Dark Romanticism*. Pullman, WA: Washington State UP. 1-10.

Wilson, Edmund. 1962. *Patriotic Gore: Studies in the Literature of the American Civil War*. New York: Oxford UP.

7.

The Fireside Poets

Henry Wadsworth Longfellow's "A Psalm of Life" and John Greenleaf Whittier's "Barbara Frietchie"

Margit Peterfy

1. Authors, Characteristics, Contexts

The term 'Fireside Poets' is generally used to refer to four authors: Oliver Wendell Holmes, Sr. (1809-1894), Henry Wadsworth Longfellow (1807-1882), James Russell Lowell (1819-1891), and John Greenleaf Whittier (1807-1892). Occasionally, William Cullen Bryant (1794-1878) is included in the group, and two other designations—'Schoolroom Poets' and 'Household Poets'—have also been utilized in historical overviews (see Boswell 1983; Gioia 1993; Sorby 2005). In spite of the widespread occurrence of the terms, their exact origins are as yet unidentified. The authors mentioned above did not form a group on their own account, nor did they publish a common poetic manifesto. Consequently, there is no self-definition that would provide clear criteria for the inclusion or exclusion of certain poets. The classification 'Fireside Poetry' is thus a creation of literary historiography that has, in many ways, remained an "uninterrogated rubric" (Gruesz 1999: 51). But even though it is not entirely clear why and how the term was first used, the reading public has found it appropriate enough to describe a certain type of American poetry.

Since readers and critics were central in defining the Fireside Poets as a given group of writers, any analysis or interpretation must take into account both the conditions of the poems' historical reception and the formal features of the texts. This is particularly important because the Fireside Poets' reception is characterized by extremes; today they are considered minor poets, while in the nineteenth century they were tremendously popular and part of the core of American literary culture. A new source of information on the reception of these poets has recently become available: digital U.S.-American newspaper archives. Since newspapers were crucial for the development of nineteenth-century American culture and contained not just 'news', but also literary texts and commentary (see Starr 2004), contemporary reactions in print can help us to understand the historical success of the Fireside Poets and discover the reasons for the popularity of their texts.

In nineteenth-century American texts the attribute 'fireside' was frequently used in various combinations such as "fireside amusement," "fireside comfort," "fireside education," "fireside joys," and so on. Most importantly, 'fireside' had always a positive connotation with a metonymical association of domesticity that relied on values connected with the everyday conduct of family life as it took place in a home around a centrally located fireplace.

In spite of the name and its associations, the literary subjects of the Fireside Poets were by no means restricted to domestic topics, which implies that the term did not reflect the category of thematic choices, but rather the circumstances and conditions of the poems' reception. This also explains why the poets strictly avoided contents related to sexuality or eroticism, as these were deemed harmful for the moral development of the young, especially of young women. If love was depicted, it was always sublimated and of the most 'innocent' kind. All four poets wrote in a wide range of genres: narrative ballads, humorous pieces, lyrical works, and poems on American historical events, but they also wrote essays, short stories, and even novels. They were popular authors of 'occasional poems,' i.e., poems written for celebrations, anniversaries, and other festive public occasions, thus significantly contributing to the development of a collective memory culture of a still young 'United States of America.' While only Whittier can be described as an active abolitionist, all of these poets opposed slavery; they published poems with topical political messages, not just against slavery, but also about the threat to the political and territorial union of the 'Republic' and other political events (see Peterfy 2012).

All four writers felt their calling at an early age and began publishing their poems anonymously in local newspapers. This is significant because it has often been—wrongly—implied that the 'fame' of the Fireside Poets resulted from the pressures of compulsory school curricula (see Sorby 2005). However, Longfellow's and Whittier's literary breakthrough was not based on the institutional forces of education and patronage, but depended on two factors: one, on a genuine talent to capture the popular imagination (even with poems published anonymously) and two, on forces similar to the dynamics of the emergence of a popular product in a market economy. Once their names became 'brands,' they could sell their new works to magazines and reprint previously published poems in expensive "coffee-table" editions, further contributing to their prestige—and also to their bank accounts. Longfellow was the first American poet capable of making a comfortable living from his poetry; even more important was that his readers were aware of the fact that he had become an economically successful literary authority (cf. Charvat 1968: 155). Longfellow proved to the American public that a poet in the United States neither needed the patronage of a king, nor did he have to starve. Whittier followed suit after the Civil War with the profits from the sales of his long poem *Snow-Bound: A Winter Idyll* (1866). The other Fireside Poets (Holmes and Lowell) were also highly praised and well-known, but they did not command the sales figures of Whittier and Longfellow and relied instead on other professional pursuits for their livelihoods: Holmes was a medical doctor and lecturer; Lowell a professor of modern languages and literatures.

At their height of popularity, general opinion considered the Fireside Poets the first genuine American poets, not just native born, but also writing about native themes and addressing the American public with a truly American sensibility (Stedman 1885: 95,180). Nathaniel Hawthorne praised Longfellow as the first truly successful American poet: "Let him stand then, at the head of our list of native poets" (qtd. in Hoeltje 1950: 234). Such estimates were widespread, but they did not remain uncontested by other voices. Margaret Fuller and Edgar Allan Poe, for example, claimed that Longfellow was neither a 'real' poet nor 'American' enough because he lacked originality both in his general attitude and in the poetic execution of his ideas and themes (Fuller 1846: 132; Poe 1845: 250). Fuller's and Poe's criticism points to the question of how the adjective 'American' was to be defined in the nineteenth century: as an empirical reality or as an ideal? In other words: did this poetry already exist, unrecognized, or was it still waiting to be written? Corresponding to this distinction, there are two ways of interpreting American culture of the period: following Poe's and Fuller's lead, on the basis of normative criteria within which certain previously defined requirements are expected to be met, or descriptively, relying primarily on the judgment of former audiences and thus emphasizing the reception side of literary culture. The Fireside Poets' status is easily defined in the latter terms, applied, for example, to Longfellow by Robert Spiller:

> The perennial question with regard to Longfellow's 'Americanism' is not so difficult as it has been made to seem. Surely the best proof that a man belongs to his people is given when they accept him as their representative and beloved voice. By this test Longfellow is the most American poet that America has ever had. (1974: 595)

Spiller's description is not exaggerated, but the picture is not complete without Whittier. Whittier's popularity in the United States was similar to Longfellow's, especially after the Civil War. During the last decades of the nineteenth and the beginning of the twentieth centuries the inclusion of their poetry into school curricula led to a further growth of their fame and literary authority throughout the United States. Holmes's and Lowell's reputations rest on a number of popular poems, such as Holmes's "Old Ironsides," "The Last Leaf," or "The Chambered Nautilus" and Lowell's "To the Dandelion," "The Cathedral," and his satirical mock-epic of American writers, *A Fable for Critics*. But their fame was mostly limited to a middle- and upper-class readership and their popular appeal was never comparable to that of Longfellow or Whittier (cf. Hart 1950: 135).

As part of a literary tradition, 'fireside poetry' can be linked to a number of different predecessors. First of all, the intellectual climate of New England influenced all four poets. Although Puritanism had, by this time, already lost its grip on the intellectual life of the region, the stylistic preferences of the Fireside Poets had parallels to the earlier ideal of 'plain style' expression. 'Plain style' strives for simplicity and clarity, and although none of the Fireside Poets expressed any theoretical rejection of rhetorical ornament or artistry, their poems are in fact characterized by lucidity and a fluent, easily understood poetic diction. The appreciation of 'plain style' as a particularly sincere and favored way of expression becomes apparent in James Russell Lowell's comment—not on the Fireside Poets, but on another very popular American, Abraham Lincoln. Lowell admires "[t]he simple confidence, the *fireside plainness*, with which Mr. Lincoln always addresses himself to the reason of the American people" (emphasis added, Lowell 1871 [1864]: 174). "Plainness" here is not just a stylistic ideal, but a conceptual metaphor with a claim to American national distinction. The lucidity in expression parallels a simplicity, honesty, and authenticity in thought and communal life in a republic—values that, supposedly, were not to be found in Europe. A typical example—and precursor—is Joel Barlow's mock epic "The Hasty-Pudding," in which the decadence of Europe is placed against the healthy simplicity of America.

In spite of this claim to a specifically American position and a general patriotism, the Fireside Poets did not reject literary inspiration from Europe, and certain aspects of literary Romanticism became influential in various ways. First, Romanticism had an affinity to Republicanism with its conscious goal to reach the 'common man'—as expressed most famously by William Wordsworth, who emphasized in the "Preface" to his *Lyrical Ballads* the importance of simplicity and of "humble" themes (1974 [1800]: 124). In addition to this preoccupation with literature for the 'common man,' which was more dominant in the works of Whittier and Longfellow than that of Holmes and Lowell, the poets shared a preference for a poetic treatment of everyday life and objects. Lowell's "To the Dandelion" is such a text, as it celebrates the simplicity and beauty of a common flower. Last, but certainly not least, a love of the picturesque was assumed from earlier American writers, notably Washington Irving, which was readily greeted by the American reading public as a skill in creating 'word-pictures,' i.e., detailed and vivid descriptions of visual impressions. Other aspects of romantic literature, however, were rejected as unfit for American audiences, especially openly expressed sensuality.

Besides these common influences, there are also significant differences between the poets' educational backgrounds. Whittier was almost entirely self-educated, and the single most important literary influence for him was (after the Bible) Scottish poet Robert Burns, whose rural background resembled Whittier's origins as the son of Quaker farmers. Whittier's deeply felt piety was probably responsible for his repeatedly expressed conflicts when it came to the question of literary fame versus humanitarian or religious engagement. Commenting in 1828 on his two major occupations—his writing and his efforts toward the abolition of slavery—Whittier wrote: "I would rather have the memory of a Howard, Wilberforce, or a Clarkson [famous British abolitionists] than the undying fame of a Byron" (Pickard 1899, I: 71). Here we see the patterns of the old (whether Platonic, Puritan, or Quaker) controversy: art versus moral or religious pursuits. For many years Whittier's solution was to put his poetry into the service of his political goals, as he composed a steady stream of abolitionist poems attacking slavery from every side.

In the case of Longfellow, Lowell, and Holmes, whose privileged families had provided them with a university education, both in the United States and in Europe, literary influences were more varied and also crossed linguistic boundaries. Since their youth they had been exposed not only to the classical curriculum, but also to a wide range of more recent writers: Goethe, Schiller, Dante, Boccaccio, etc. (see Frank/Maas 2005). Longfellow was also a professor of literature and an avid translator and editor; his anthology *The Poets and Poetry of Europe* (1845) was a groundbreaking achievement that brought together translations of poems from many European languages.

Although the Fireside Poets did not have a poetic manifesto, Longfellow published a text in 1832 that comes close to a programmatic statement. He did not advertise it as such, however, but 'disguised' it as a review of Sir Philip Sidney's "Defence of Poesy" (1595). His reasons for not asserting himself more forcefully might be psychological—or perhaps strategic; he was thus able to present his ideas indirectly, in a diplomatic, more palatable way. The argument starts with his choice of a so-called "practical" man as his example. Sir Philip Sidney (1554-1586) was, besides a major English poet, a figure in public and political life and a military hero. Since Longfellow saw the greatest obstacles to American literary culture in the privileging of material and practical aspects of life over the artistic ones, he was keen on showing that there was no reason to reject one at the price of the other. He describes his motives: "As no 'Apologie for Poetrie' has appeared among us, we hope that Sir Philip Sidney's *Defence* will be widely read and long remembered. O that in our country, it might be the harbinger of as bright an intellectual day as it was in his own!" (1832: 59). In the course of the article, however, Longfellow leaves this 'literary mimicry' further and further behind as he develops an argument for the social utility of poetry—even in a society that values material progress above all else:

With us, the spirit of the age is clamorous for utility,—for visible, tangible utility,—for bare, brawney, muscular utility. We would be roused to action by the voice of the populace, and the sounds of the crowded mart . . . We are swallowed up in schemes for gain, and engrossed with contrivances for bodily enjoyments, as if this particle of dust were immortal,—as if the soul needed no aliment, and the mind no raiment. (ibid.)

Longfellow insists that Americans need poetry because it provides their souls and minds with spiritual nourishment and protection. In this sense 'Poetry' (or 'philosophy') is written not just for the vanity of idle artists or as a pastime for aristocrats, but is, or rather should be, available to every member of society.

Longfellow's theory of the 'utility' of poetry and of the other fine arts is also expressed in his poem "The Singers" (1849), where three different types of 'singers' (poets) fulfill their distinctive roles: the first is there "to charm," the second "to teach," and the third "to strengthen." These disparate responsibilities echo the classical functions of rhetoric: *delectare*, *docere*, and *movere*, as put forth, for example, by Cicero in his influential rhetorical manual *De oratore* (cf. Grube 1962: 235-7).

Since the collected works of the four Fireside Poets fill about forty volumes, it is questionable whether one can call two poems 'representative' of their oeuvre. The two poems selected here are rather 'exemplary' texts. They are relatively short, composed in simple diction, have a regular meter and rhyme scheme, and carry uplifting messages for their readers; and they were both extremely popular. These are the similarities. There are also some instructive differences: "A Psalm of Life" is a reflective, quasi-religious, personal poem, whereas "Barbara Frietchie" deals with a historical theme, claims to be of documentary character, and evokes patriotic emotions of national significance.

2. Henry Wadsworth Longfellow's "A Psalm of Life" as a Plea for Action

Longfellow's "A Psalm of Life" contains a *carpe diem* motif that can be found in many earlier texts, both American and European. *Carpe diem*, or 'seize the day,' is a maxim originating with Horace, a poet of classical antiquity, and it invites readers to enjoy life while they can (see Grimm 1963). Another influential *carpe diem* poem by an American is William Cullen Bryant's "Thanatopsis," but only Longfellow's variation on the theme has a distinctly American background. The epigraph is a motto: "What the Heart of the Young Man said to the Psalmist" (Longfellow 1904 [1838]: 18).

In New England churches, psalms were, starting with the Puritan settlements, the only acceptable songs or poems. The first original book printed and published in New England was, in fact, the *Bay Psalm Book* (1640), a new translation of the psalms into English.

The reference to the psalms of the Old Testament in this epigraph motto points to a significant difference between original audiences and present-day readers, since today the instant identification of Longfellow's intertextual reference would be the exception rather than the rule. This explains why the epigraph is often omitted in reprints—it is considered insignificant because it cannot readily be filled with significance. Nevertheless, the motto is important. Together with the first line ("Tell me not in mournful numbers"), it makes the stance of the speaker clear: it is one of contradiction, even rebellion against es-

tablished, rather gloomy ("mournful") convictions. The young man's "heart" rejects the teachings of "the Psalmist" and propagates instead a new message. In
order to understand the historical and cultural significance of this new teaching, we must first learn about the old, rejected one. Leafing through the Book of
Psalms we find Psalm 103:14-5 as a most probable target for the young man's
attack: "The life of mortals is like grass, they flourish like a flower of the field;
the wind blows over it and it is gone, and its place remembers it no more."
Psalm 103 warns against vanity and the pride of mortals, while it emphasizes
the futility of human actions on earth. A typical example of an interpretation of
this kind appeared in the newspaper *Columbian Register* in 1830:

> You forget that you are mortal, that you are dust, and that you must return to
> dust . . . Think on those, who, before you have performed a brilliant part on the
> theatre of human life. . . . Are they anything but ashes? Is their fame nothing
> but fable? Is not all their glory reduced to a small heap of monumental stones?
> ("Human Life," 1830: 4)

In opposition to this statement, the speaker in "A Psalm of Life" rejects the position that all human striving is futile and will soon be forgotten. Longfellow's persona claims that yes, indeed, there is meaning and visible consequence in human action, and one should always try to leave some "footprints" behind—not
just for one's own fame and glory, but for the sake of others who might profit
from learning about what had been achieved by fellow mortals. The most famous metaphor of the poem ("we can . . . leave behind us footprints on the sands
of time" (ll. 26-8)) allows not only for a more optimistic interpretation of life, but
also carries a number of practical implications for human conduct in general.

The climactic image around the "footprints," which occurs only in the last
third of the poem, is prepared by three premises in the first six stanzas. The
first premise establishes the foundation of the protest by a chain of negations
(in stanzas 1-3), containing the rejection of what the "young man" of the epigraph learned from "the Psalmist." The first objection goes against the notion
that life is just "an empty dream" (l. 2). If life was a dream, the consequence
would be that one goes through life in a state of slumber (l. 3), with a soul that
is not awake but in a death-like stupor, perceiving "things" in dreams that "are
not what they seem" (l. 4). Against this the young man insists that "Life is real!"
and not just an illusion and "Life is earnest!" and not just a fanciful, hedonistic
diversion (l. 5). The next major objection: "And the grave is not its goal" (l. 6)
points to the double meaning of the word "goal." Although all life on earth will
end with death, and in this sense, leads to the grave as a final destination, life's
purpose (the other sense of "goal") must lie elsewhere. Taking the "soul," rather
than the physical body, as the mainspring of human action, the young man
points out that "dust thou art, to dust returnest, / was not spoken of the soul"
(ll. 7-8).

The next stanzas continue to elaborate on the relationship between death
and life with a pun: "our destined end or way" (l. 10) of life; it is "to act that each
to-morrow / Find us farther than to-day" (ll. 11-2). With the verse "Art is long,
and Time is fleeting" (l. 13), Longfellow also refers to the classical adage, "Vita
brevis, ars longa" ("Life is short, art is long," meaning that one has only a short
span of life to accomplish something), and expresses his conviction that certain
creative exploits, not necessarily just fine art or poetry, but also other kinds of
human invention, will outlive their creators. By translating "Vita brevis" with

"time is fleeting," the persona emphasizes the aspect of urgency within his argument—typical for all *carpe diem* poems. In stanza four the semantic field of "Time" in the sense of musical rhythm is taken up again in the image of human hearts resembling "muffled drums, are beating / Funeral marches to the grave" (ll. 15-6).

Longfellow's skill in inventing metaphors shows itself in his ability to combine well-known subject matter with surprising associations. A beating heart is universally the sign of life and vitality, but Longfellow uses the familiar image of the heartbeat as a symbol for approaching death by drawing a parallel to the beating of drums in a funeral march. The poetic achievement—and the pleasant, aesthetic surprise—lies in the reinterpretation of a well-known topos and by emphasizing a new aspect of the theme. The poem thus confronts the reader with a fresh awareness of his or her mortality.

The last premise assumes that it is better to be a "hero" than to be "dumb, driven cattle" (ll. 20, 19). On the basis of this, and the two previous premises, the poem concludes in a plea for action:

> Trust no Future, howe'er pleasant!
>   Let the dead Past bury its dead!
> Act,—act in the living Present!
>   Heart within and God o'erhead! (ll. 21-4)

The introduction of "God" into the young man's thoughts is, at this point, unexpected and therefore seems like a mere concession to the mainstream religious establishment. However, "God" here is not the God of a specific religious community, but a reference to a transcendent being whose existence is acknowledged, who is "o'head" and hopefully benevolent, yet does not interfere.

The final three stanzas of the poem describe the usefulness of human action with the help of the image of the "footprints on the sands of time" (l. 28). The enormous popularity of this image is based on its simplicity and empirical accuracy. Readers of all ages are familiar with footprints in the sand and they can easily transfer their knowledge of such prints onto a more abstract level, i.e., to "footprints on the sands of time."

> Lives of great men all remind us
>   We can make our lives sublime,
> And, departing, leave behind us
>   Footprints on the sands of time;
>
> Footprints, that perhaps another,
>   Sailing o'er life's solemn main,
> A forlorn and shipwrecked brother,
>   Seeing, shall take heart again.
>
> Let us, then, be up and doing,
>   With a heart for any fate;
> Still achieving, still pursuing,
>   Learn to labor and to wait. (ll. 25-36)

According to the logic of this image, a person may create something during his lifetime that will endure for a while even after his death, as footprints in sand are still visible after somebody has walked away. In the next instance, these footprints (achievements and direction) can be seen and perceived by others walking by or, on the metaphorical level, by the next generation. Footprints in sand will gradually fade—but this is not a flaw in the image; it is rather the opposite. It does not deny that we, and humanity in general, will disappear, but the usefulness of these prints is given by their character as "signs"—signs for other humans—of earlier direction and development, of endurance and existence.

The image conjured up here has been sometimes criticized as mixed and insipid (cf. Buell 1986: 116-7), but as my reading above argues, this is not the case. Also, readers seem either to conceptualize the footprints as symbolical traces of somebody's actions, or they accommodate it easily enough in the realm of a more fantastic scenario: the beach, the footprints, the ocean, and the "shipwrecked brother" all inside a gigantic hourglass.

In 1836 Longfellow rejected the idea of fame and ambition in his unpublished journal: "The scholar should have a higher and holier aim than this: . . . when he writes it should be, not to immortalize himself, but to make a salutary and lasting impression on the minds of others" (qtd. in Anderson 2003: 5-6). We see here the beginnings of the image of the "footprints" in the dead metaphor of the "im-pression." Although the etymological source of this word is not a footprint but the physical trace of a stylus over a wax table, the basis for the images is the same. A major difference is that in his poem Longfellow removes the metaphor from the intellectual realm. He addresses not just the scholar or the poet; everyone who has ever heard of "great men" is being addressed: "We can make our lives sublime." This does not mean that everybody *will* make their lives sublime, but that nobody should feel excluded a priori from the possibility of achieving something 'im-pressive.' The poem is, in this sense, a republican and democratic statement that has a 'message' beyond a purely *carpe diem* motif.

The final stanza repeats the plea for action. The fact that we have been following a logical and not just rhetorical argument is made explicit by the word "then" in line 33. The very last words of the poem however, asking for endurance and patience, deflate the exalted atmosphere. They have been prepared for earlier by the mentioning of "God" and "fate," and they introduce a more mature aspect into the young man's reasoning: the generally unavoidable experience of setbacks and hindering moments in life. Although one might first wonder why Longfellow ended his poem on such a note, on second thought his concession even strengthens his argument, making it clear that although the speaker is young, he is not without common sense or empathy.

While "A Psalm of Life" does include aspects of U.S.-American 'self-made man mentality,' it was a poem that spoke to members of any modern society with middle-class notions of meritocracy, i.e., the belief in the possibility of personal and material betterment through individual action. It is eminently translatable as its major arguments rest on conceptual imagery related to human experiences known to all cultures and languages: the human body, agriculture, and war. The poem has indeed been translated into many languages, and there are many anecdotes about its success as a "self-help" poem (Gioia 1993: 70-2). Although Longfellow did not write it as a reaction to any particular political situation, it was well-received during the economic depression of 1837/38. And in 1852, the escaped slave and abolitionist Frederick Douglass used it in his famous oration, "What, to the Slave, is the Fourth of July?," urging his audience to concentrate on the present rather than complacently reflecting on the achievements of the past.

Toward the end of the nineteenth century, the poem's popularity manifested itself in countless parodies. Mimicking the rhetorical strategies and the characteristic structure of the poem, anonymous authors published their "Psalms" about various topics in newspapers across the country. A poem arguing for the advantages of oil production in 1865 started with the (by now) proverbial beginning "Tell me not . . .":

> Tell me not in mournful measure
>> Oil is but an empty show;
> For 'tis earth's deep hidden treasure
>> And a pump will make it flow. (ll. 1-4)

That such and similar parodies were part of newspaper print culture up until the Great Depression proves the former popularity of the poem (see historical newspaper databases, such as *19th-Century American Newspapers* or *America's Historical Newspapers*). The complete lack of such parodies nowadays reflects, on the other hand, the end of its influence with a general readership. This pattern of reception is equally valid for "Barbara Frietchie" by John Greenleaf Whittier, the second example of a Fireside poem.

3. John Greenleaf Whittier's "Barbara Frietchie" and the Poetic Vision of American Union

When we compare the private message of "A Psalm of Life" (1838) with John Greenleaf Whittier's Civil War poem "Barbara Frietchie" (1863), we can see some similarities but also substantial differences. Following a loosely trochaic rhythm, both poems are formally simple, "A Psalm of Life" presenting itself in quatrains, with a cross rhyme, while Whittier's "Barbara Frietchie" is in couplets, accordingly using pair rhymes. Whereas the rhythm is not perfectly consistent in Whittier's work, the rhyming is meticulously regular—just as in Longfellow's poem. The other similarity is their explicit didacticism: both poems address readers directly and conclude with clear instructions for further action.

The major difference lies in the subject of the texts; if we take "A Psalm of Life" to be a lesson in the maxims of life, "Barbara Frietchie" teaches civic values and patriotic sentiment. Whittier's poem describes a historical episode from the Civil War; at least this is what the poet thought he was doing after receiving a letter containing a story about Barbara Frietchie, an elderly "lady" from Frederick, Maryland, who had supposedly been waving the 'Stars and Stripes' while the Confederate army marched through her hometown. The accuracy of this anecdote was questioned soon after the publication of the poem and several alternative accounts were suggested as more truthful than Whittier's. The controversy around this poem is summarized, not in a work of literary historiography, but in the book *Origin and History of the American Flag*, where eight different testimonies are listed, each claiming to render the factual historical event (cf. Preble 1917: 482-93).

The lasting hero and protagonist of the poem and of the proto-historical episode is thus arguably not Barbara Frietchie, but the Union flag, the 'Star Spangled Banner.' Although Whittier's poem did not start the national veneration for the American flag—one of the central symbols of American civil religion (see Bellah 1967)—it certainly contributed to its adulation; an adulation that climaxed in the composition of "The Pledge of Allegiance" (to the flag) in 1892. For the poem's first 1863 printing in the *Atlantic Monthly*, a prestigious Boston literary magazine, Whittier received 50 dollars (about 800 dollars in today's currency) from the enthusiastic publisher James Fields. Newspapers all over the Northern states reprinted the work immediately afterwards. Its instant and lasting popularity was certainly due to the patriotic and touching anecdote, but a close reading of Whittier's literary construction shows that the poem is also a masterpiece of composition. Although many critics of the twentieth century rejected this and similar poems as sentimental doggerel, "Barbara Frietchie" serves as a good example for an effective 'public' poem that is also a carefully crafted literary work.

Whittier did not elaborate on his poetics beyond some cursory remarks in his letters. His individual aesthetics must be thus deduced from his literary production, and a close reading of this simple, but not simplistic, poem reveals indeed his most important poetic principles. It is an intricately constructed text with different levels of signification and self-contained symbolism. Whittier's most important compositional tools are depiction and visualization, both of which go back to the rhetorical tradition of ekphrasis. In its broadest and traditional sense, ekphrasis means simply "description." Its most important function is the creation of an effect of immediacy, as if the reader were there to see for him- or herself. Today, in a narrower sense, ekphrasis is also used to designate texts that describe visual or plastic works of art (cf. Krieger 1992: 1-28).

In the critical diction of the nineteenth century, individual descriptions of landscapes, people, and city streets were also called "wordpaintings" or "pen pictures." Such passages are characterized by the meticulous use of color, contrast, and spatial features, by a close attention to perspective and framing, and by a symbolic use of the elements of this literary 'sketch'. At the beginning of Whittier's poem (ll. 1-4) we have the very first example of a word-painting, seen from the perspective of hungry Confederate soldiers marching toward the town of Frederick:

> Up from the meadows rich with corn,
> Clear in the cool September morn,
>
> The clustered spires of Frederick stand
> Green-walled by the hills of Maryland.
>
> Round about them orchards sweep,
> Apple- and peach-tree fruited deep,
>
> Fair as a garden of the Lord
> To the eyes of the famished rebel horde,
>
> On that pleasant morn of the early fall
> When Lee marched over the mountain wall,—
>
> Over the mountains winding down,
> Horse and foot, into Frederick town. (ll. 1-12)

The sun has just risen and illuminates a paradisiacal landscape full of green trees, orchards, and fields "rich with corn." Several spatial attributes, such as "up," "round about," and "clustered" provide clear geometrical patterns, while details such as the "clear and cool September morn" or "apple and peach tree fruited deep" help to paint the scene. The "famished rebel horde," which is riding up toward Frederick, is personified as a single entity whose "eye" perceives this bountiful landscape to be as "fair as the garden of the Lord."

By presenting this word-painting to us through the perspective of the Confederate soldiers, Whittier achieves two things: first, we can clearly visualize the setting of the poem, and second, the soldiers are being indirectly characterized: they are hungry, they are "rebels," and they are wistful when seeing the quietly affluent order in and around Frederick. Nevertheless, there is no pilferage or any kind of unlawful behavior.

The next two stanzas of the poem take place in Frederick itself, containing two short word-pictures:

> Forty flags with their silver stars
> Forty flags with their crimson bars
>
> Flapped in the morning wind: the sun
> Of noon looked down, and saw not one. (ll. 13-6)

The anaphoras express the repeated, uniform presence of the flag as it could be seen all over Frederick on that morning. Its colors are described as "silver" and "crimson"—no ordinary hues, but "colors" in the sense of "insignia," as the sign and symbol for a *United* States of America. The emphasis on the stars is a further reference to the political background of the poem: the "War of Rebellion," as the Civil War was called in the North, was fought over these "stars" that represent the individual states.

The next stanzas (ll. 17-26) establish the conflict, represented by Barbara Frietchie and her flag against Stonewall Jackson and his soldiers. Here Whittier displays a spatial imagination full of symbolism: Barbara Frietchie takes up her flag and displays it. After the flag has been shot down, she takes it up again, this time holding it and expressing her determination to protect it, if necessary, with her life:

> She leaned far out on the window-sill,
> And shook it forth with a royal will.
>
> "Shoot, if you must, this old gray head,
> But spare your country's flag," she said.
>
> A shade of sadness, a blush of shame,
> Over the face of the leader came; (ll. 33-8)

Stonewall Jackson, whose name was, accidentally, highly appropriate with its metaphorical implications, is touched by Barbara Frietchie's extraordinary courage. We learn that "The nobler nature within him stirred" (l. 39) and this "stony" rebel turns out to be somebody who respects the patriotic sentiments of a defenseless, weak, old woman. This is, on the one hand, the trope of many sentimental scenarios in nineteenth-century literature: the reversal of attitudes—a conversion experience and thus the transformation from a negative into a positive character. On the other hand, for Whittier, a devout Quaker and pacifist, it was crucial to represent the Confederate forces as fellow Americans with humanity and similar values. Otherwise, the desired goal of the Civil War— a horrible war that was still raging at the time of the publication of the poem— would have been unattainable and probably also undesirable. Whittier was against the war in principle, but since it had already started, his only hope was that it would not last long and would lead to both the abolition of slavery and to

a reconciliation between North and South. Jackson's heroic image was heightened by the fact that he had died in May 1863, a fact alluded to in verses 52-4.

In the final part of the poem, the flag again takes a central role in a vision of
the future. Barbara Frietchie is dead, and the "Flag of Freedom and Union" waves
over her grave. Since we know that she was ninety years old ("Bowed with her
fourscore years and ten" (l. 18)), the fulfillment of this prophecy seems either to
be imminent or has already happened, and the poem thus closes with a triumphant vision of a peaceful re-United States.

> Over Barbara Frietchie's grave
> Flag of Freedom and Union, wave!
>
> Peace and order and beauty draw
> Round thy symbol of light and law;
>
> And ever the stars above look down
> On thy stars below in Frederick town! (ll. 55-60)

Just as with "A Psalm of Life," "Barbara Frietchie" became embedded in American
culture in various forms of adaptation. The poem was put to music, and the
climactic scene of the poem—with the confrontation between an old woman and
an army of men—invited many pictorial renderings and patriotic decorations.
The fact that a monograph on the *History of the Flag* dedicated more than ten
pages to the various versions of the "Barbara Frietchie" episode indicates the
significance of this poem for the historical imagination of American readers.

4. Conclusion: The Reception of the Fireside Poets

Most critics of the twentieth century found that Margaret Fuller's and Edgar
Allan Poe's positions showed more foresight than the opinions of the so-called
'ordinary Americans' who expected Longfellow's fame to last for centuries. In
1921 the author and critic Ludwig Lewisohn famously wrote: "Am I slaying the
thrice slain? Who, except wretched schoolchildren, now reads Longfellow?"
(1932: 65). And Hervey Allen maintained in 1926 that Longfellow was "the epitome
of what every ordinary man and woman in a democracy most desires in an artist: an ordinary person like themselves, who by industry, morality, education,
and the cultivation of talent produces the equivalent of genius. . . . Nature had
denied only one thing to Longfellow. It was that vague but significant thing
called genius" (1926: 361). It seems as though Longfellow's success worked
most damagingly against him. The influential, often sardonic journalist H.L.
Mencken also takes the general appeal as his target: "The poetry of Whittier and
Longfellow was democratic. It voiced the elemental emotions of the masses of
the people; it was full of their simple, rubber-stamp ideas; they comprehended it
and cherished it" (2000 [1919]: 54). And a couple of paragraphs later, ensuring
that his irony does not go undetected, the critic makes it clear that "no sound
art, in fact, could possibly be democratic" (ibid.).

During the first three decades of the twentieth century, the other Fireside
Poets also lost their status with critics and most of their readers, but most ferocious was the critical backlash against Longfellow. The critics' resentment is
difficult to understand unless one takes into account the degree to which Longfellow had been equated with "poetry" in the American imagination and how
trivial some of these usages seemed to more intellectual readers. Both Long-

fellow's and Whittier's poems had been used for advertising, as the basis for countless parodies, for adaptations as operas, songs, films, and tableaux vivants, and they were associated with countless commercial merchandise from raincoats to canned tomatoes (see Clapper 2002).

For today's student of American literature and culture, however, the idea of a popular poetry cannot be simply relegated to the realm of cultural embarrassment; it requires serious analysis and a more objective appreciation as a special kind of literature. In this sense Ezra Pound's statement reveals him to be a more perceptive and more neutral critic than many others. Commenting on popular American poetry he wrote: "I don't try to write for the public. I can't. I haven't that kind of intelligence" (Pound 1971: 6). Pound expresses here an awareness of a very specific skill, which is not just the sign of a lack of sophistication but an expression of a positive value. This is also resonant in Jorge Louis Borges's theory about the reasons for Longfellow's fall from favor: "I don't know why people look down on Longfellow. Maybe he was too much of a literary man, no?" (PBS Interview with William F. Buckley, February 18, 1977, qtd. in Calhoun 2004: 280.)

In most recent criticism, Longfellow has been reintroduced to the public as a substantial cultural figure of the nineteenth century (see Gioia 1993; Irmscher 2006), while Whittier, Holmes, and Lowell continue to be considered minor writers whose literary success was based on the genteel tastes and mediocre literary standards of the time and not on their technical mastery or individual achievement (see Friedl/Friedl 1987). However, high modernism—with its preference for irony, ambiguity, and self-referential signification—has recently begun to lose its grip on literary criticism, and this in turn may allow a way back into the canon for poets whose ideals lay in the putting forth of simplicity and empathy, and in the provision of spiritual usefulness for their readers.

Bibliography

Selected Primary Literature

Holmes, Oliver Wendell. 1892. *The Works of Oliver Wendell Holmes. In Thirteen Volumes*. Standard Library Edition. Boston and New York: Houghton, Mifflin & Co.

——. [1830]. "Old Ironsides." In: Holmes 1892. Vol. 1: 1-2.

——. [1830]. "The Last Leaf." In: Holmes 1892. Vol. 1: 3-4.

——. [1858]. "The Chambered Nautilus." In: Holmes 1892. Vol. 1: 393.

Longfellow, Henry Wadsworth. 1904. *The Complete Writings of Henry Wadsworth Longfellow. In Eleven Volumes*. Craigie Edition. Boston and New York: Houghton, Mifflin & Co.

——. [1838]. "A Psalm of Life." In: Longfellow 1904. Vol. 1: 18-20.

——. [1840]. "The Village Blacksmith." In: Longfellow 1904. Vol. 1: 72-5.

——. [1843]. *Evangeline: A Tale of Acadie*. In: Longfellow 1904. Vol. 2: 19-109.

——. [1849]. "The Singers." In: Longfellow 1904. Vol. 1: 320-1.

——. [1855]. *The Song of Hiawatha*. In: Longfellow 1904. Vol. 2: 113-298.

——. [1858]. *The Courtship of Miles Standish*. In: Longfellow 1904. Vol. 2: 299-371.

——. [1860]. "Paul Revere's Ride." In: Longfellow 1904. Vol. 4: 24-8.

Lowell, James Russell. 1892. *The Works of James Russell Lowell. In Eleven Volumes*. Standard Library Edition. Boston and New York: Houghton, Mifflin & Co.

——. [1848]. *The Biglow Papers*. In: Lowell 1892. Vol. 8: 1-375.

——. [1848]. *A Fable for Critics*. In: Lowell 1892. Vol. 9: 1-95

Whittier, John Greenleaf. 1892. *The Works of John Greenleaf Whittier. In Seven Volumes*. Standard Library Edition. Boston and New York: Houghton, Mifflin & Co.

——. [1850]. "Ichabod." In: Whittier 1892. Vol. 4: 61-2.

——. [1854]. "Maud Muller." In: Whittier 1892. Vol. 1: 148-51.

——. [1861]. "Barefoot Boy." In: Whittier 1892. Vol. 2: 126-9.

——. [1866]. *Snow-Bound: A Winter Idyll*. In: Whittier 1892. Vol. 2: 134-59.

Selected Secondary Literature

Arms, George. 1970. *The Fields Were Green: A New View of Bryant, Whittier, Holmes, Lowell, and Longfellow, With a Selection of Their Poems*. Palo Alto: Stanford UP.

The only existing scholarly monograph that is dedicated to the group as a whole.

Bell, Michael J. 1995. "'The Only True Folk Songs We Have in English': James Russell Lowell and the Politics of the Nation." In: *Journal of American Folklore* 108: 131-55.

Bell's essay contains a succinct examination of Lowell's literary nationalism.

Calhoun, Charles C. 2004. *Longfellow: A Rediscovered Life*. Boston: Beacon Press.

Calhoun's is the most recent biography of Longfellow.

Dowling, William C. 2006. *Oliver Wendell Holmes in Paris: Medicine, Theology, and The Autocrat of the Breakfast Table*. Lebanon: U of New Hampshire P.

This study interprets the various non-literary influences on Holmes's writing.

Friedl, Bettina and Herwig Friedl. 1987. "Dichtung als Institution: Die 'Fireside Poets' Bryant, Whittier, Longfellow, Holmes und Lowell." In: Rudolf Haas (ed.), *Die amerikanische Lyrik*. Berlin: Schmidt. 38-62.

The article examines the aesthetic value of selected works of the Fireside Poets and discovers serious flaws that explain the permanent loss of critical esteem.

Gioia, Dana. 1993. "Longfellow in the Aftermath of Modernism." In: Jay Parini and Brett C. Miller (eds.), *Columbia History of American Poetry*. New York: Columbia UP. 64-96.

Important essay, at the beginning of a revisionary view on Longfellow's status in American literary history.

Irmscher, Christoph. 2006. *Longfellow Redux*. Urbana: U of Illinois P.

Most recent comprehensive literary interpretation of Longfellow's major works and of some of his unpublished works.

——. 2009. *Public Poet, Private Man: Henry Wadsworth Longfellow at 200*. Amherst and Boston: U of Massachusetts P.

Irmscher presents the cultural contexts of Longfellow's literary career on the basis of original archival material.

Wagenknecht, Edward. 1967. *John Greenleaf Whittier: A Portrait in Paradox.* New York: Oxford UP.

This is the most recent modern monograph on Whittier as a writer and abolitionist.

Further References

Allen, Hervey. 1926. Review of *A Victorian American: Henry Wadsworth Longfellow* by H. Gorman. In: *Saturday Review of Literature* December 4: 361-2.

Anderson, Jill. 2003. "'Be Up and Doing': Henry Wadsworth Longfellow and Poetic Labor." In: *Journal of American Studies* 37: 1-15.

Bellah, Robert. 1967. "Civil Religion in America." In: *Daedalus* 96.1: 1-21.

Boswell, Jeanetta. 1983. *The Schoolroom Poets: A Bibliography of Bryant, Holmes, Longfellow, Lowell, and Whittier with Selective Annotation.* Metuchen et al.: The Scarecrow P.

Buell, Lawrence. 1986. *New England Literary Culture: From Revolution through Renaissance.* Cambridge: Cambridge UP.

Charvat, William. 1968. "Longfellow's Income from His Writings, 1842-52." In: *The Profession of Authorship in America, 1800-1870.* Columbus: U of Ohio P. 155-67.

Clapper, Michael. 2002. "'I Was Once a Barefoot Boy!': Cultural Tensions in a Popular Chromo." In: *American Art* 16: 16-39.

Frank, Armin Paul and Christel-Maria Maas. 2005. *Transnational Longfellow: A Project of American National Poetry.* Frankfurt am Main: Peter Lang.

Fuller, Margaret. 1846. "American Literature." In: Horace Greeley (ed.), *Literature and Art.* New York: Fowlers & Wells. 122-59.

Gale, Robert L. 2003. *A Henry Wadsworth Longfellow Companion.* Westport: Greenwood P.

Grimm, R. E. 1963. "Horace's 'Carpe Diem.'" In: *The Classical Journal* 58.7: 313-8.

Grube, G.M.A. 1962. "Educational, Rhetorical, and Literary Theory in Cicero." In: *Phoenix* 16.4: 234-57.

Gruesz, Kirsten Silva. 1999. "Feeling for the Fireside: Longfellow, Lynch, and the Topography of Poetic Power." In: Mary Chapman and Glenn Hendler (eds.), *Sentimental Men: Masculinity and the Politics of Affect in American Culture.* Berkeley: U of California P. 43-63.

Hart, James D. 1950. *The Popular Book. A History of America's Literary Taste.* New York: Oxford UP.

Hoeltje, Hubert H. 1950. "Hawthorne's Review of *Evangeline.*" In: *The New England Quarterly* 23: 232-5.

"Human Life." 1830. In: *Columbian Register* 28 Aug.: 4.

Krieger, Murray. 1992. *Ekphrasis. The Illusion of the Natural Sign.* Baltimore: Johns Hopkins UP.

Lewisohn, Ludwig. 1932. *Expression in America.* New York: Harper & Brothers.

Longfellow, Henry Wadsworth. 1832. "Defence of Poetry." In: *North American Review* 34: 56-78.

Lowell, James Russell. 1871 [1864]. "Abraham Lincoln." In: *My Study Windows.* Boston: Osgood. 150-77.

Mencken, H.L. 2000 [1919]. "The New Poetry Movement." In: Marion Rodgers (ed.), *Prejudices. First, Second, and Third Series.* Library of America. 48-56.

Peterfy, Margit. 2012. "Abraham Lincoln, Henry Wadsworth Longfellow, and the 'Ship of State': A Case Study in Presidential Rhetoric." In: Wilfried Mausbach, Dietmar Schloss and Martin Thunert (eds.), *The American Presidency: Multidisciplinary Perspectives*. Heidelberg: Winter. 211-28.

Pickard, Samuel T. 1899. *Life and Letters of John Greenleaf Whittier*. 2 vols. Boston: Houghton, Mifflin & Co.

Poe, Edgar Allan. 1845. "Review of Longfellow's Waif." Part 1. In: *Weekly Mirror* January 25: 250-5.

Pound, Ezra. 1971. *The Selected Letters of Ezra Pound: 1907-1941*. Ed. D. D. Paige. New York: New Directions.

Preble, Henry G. 1917. *Origin and History of the American Flag*. Philadelphia: Nicholas L. Brown.

"Psalm of Oil." 1865. In: *The Daily Cleveland Herald* Jan. 28: 1. *Infotrac Galegroup: 19th Century U.S. Newspapers*. Web. May 24, 2014.

Sorby, Angela. 2005. *Schoolroom Poets: Childhood, Performance, and the Place of American Poetry, 1865-1917*. Durham: U of New Hampshire P.

Spiller, Robert E. 1974. *Literary History of the United States*. New York and London: Macmillan.

Starr, Paul. 2004. "America's First Information Revolution." In: *The Creation of the Media: Political Origins of Modern Communication*. New York: Basic Books. 83-111.

Stedman, Edmund Clarence. 1885. *Poets of America*. Boston and New York: Houghton, Mifflin and Co.

Wordsworth, William. 1974 [1800]. "Preface to Lyrical Ballads." In: W.J.B. Owen and Jane Worthington Smyser (eds.), Vol. 1 of *The Prose Works of William Wordsworth*. Oxford: Clarendon Press. 118-59.

8.

Native American Poetry in the Age of U.S. Expansion

Jane Johnston Schoolcraft's "The Contrast" and John Rollin Ridge/Yellow Bird's "The Atlantic Cable"

René Dietrich

1. Early Native American Poetry Uncovered

Devoting a chapter to nineteenth-century Native American poetry in a history of American poetry would have been neither possible nor very plausible just a few years ago. In fact, it was not until 2011 that Robert Dale Parker's groundbreaking anthology *Changing Is Not Vanishing: A Collection of American Indian Poetry to 1930* retrieved a great number of texts from the archives and made them available to a present-day readership, showcasing the work of 83 poets and providing a bibliography of almost 150 authors. Until then, only a few texts by a handful of poets had been known, and only a few of those were represented in major anthologies. Through the anthology the field of nineteenth-century Native American poetry has begun to come into view so that literary histories now are able to consider it in its complexity and plurality (see Parker 2011c, 2012, Donohue 2007).

Together with recent studies on early Native literacies (see Bross/Wyss 2008, Rasmussen 2012, Jaskoski 1996), such scholarly efforts have helped to award the literary productions of American Indian cultures before 1900 a more prominent position within the field. Early Native American writing is generally associated with texts of various genres such as autobiography, sermons, speeches, and political essays, but not with poetry. Jane Johnston Schoolcraft and John Rollin Ridge are among the few poets who were known and included in anthologies prior to Parker's. Ridge, however, is known primarily as the first Native novelist, and Schoolcraft is also known mostly for her prose, while she is actually the first known Native American poet; but it is just recently that they have received attention as poets (see Whitley 2010 and Schneider 2008, respectively). Only the results of Parker's archival work—the aforementioned anthology and a collection of Schoolcraft's compositions (2007)—have brought to light the extent of Ridge's and Schoolcraft's poetic writing.

Parker's work has been instrumental in uncovering the scope of early Native American poetry and thus drawing attention to its diversity and richness. Such an endeavor also helps to correct, or at least to question, widespread assumptions about the status and literary quality of early Native poetic writing. In a chapter titled "America's Indigenous Poetry" in the *Cambridge Companion to Native American Literature* (2005), which is part of a series that aspires to represent the current standard of its field, Norma Wilson argues that "American Indian poets had come into their own by the late twentieth century" (2005: 145). This suggests a teleological Native American literary history in which figures such as Ridge or Schoolcraft are merely assigned the position of "predecessors" (ibid.) rather than being considered as poets in their own right. Their status in American Indian literary history is further downplayed when Wilson claims that early Native poets "have had less influence on Native poetics than have indigenous stories and songs" (ibid.). Such an assessment once again emphasizes the oral tradition over written texts by Native poets in the nineteenth century. Although different in intent, the effect of such an argument is similar to the result of non-Native anthropologists and poets transcribing and often freely translating or re-writing songs and stories of the oral tradition in verse and publishing them under the misnomer 'Indian poetry,' an earlier standard practice that is still strongly represented in major mainstream anthologies and has produced a genre that is neither poetry nor written by Indians (cf. Parker 2003: 80-100, 2011b: 8). The latter not only appropriates Native oral performance and imposes on it a dif-ferent cultural register, it also suggests that there is no written Native American poetry of this time—perpetuating the stereotype of illiterate American Indians—and that songs transcribed in verse can therefore claim instead the name and the place of 'Indian poetry.' Such a practice ultimately masks a failure to acknow-ledge the existent written poetic texts—a void that is supposedly compensated for by creating 'poetry' out of transcribed songs and stories, which in turns furthers the erasure of actual written poetry from cultural and literary history. Similarly, emphasizing the impact of oral traditions for "Native poetics" while downplaying the influence of nineteenth-century poets displaces their writing, suggesting a different genealogy for American Indian literary history from which they are either entirely excluded or in which they play only a subordinate part.

That this image of a handful of nineteenth-century Native American poets who have published only a few texts and figure merely as predecessors to latter Native poets has persisted for such a long time (even in recent surveys such as Wilson's essay) can be accounted for to some degree by the simple fact that the majority of texts rested all but forgotten in various archives. The willingness to accept this near absence of early Native American poets, however, has much to do with a continued deep-seated idea that Native American literature of note in genres such as poetry and fiction only really began with the publication of N. Scott Momaday's *House Made of Dawn* (1968), which heralded the so-called Na-tive American Renaissance, and that, conversely, nineteenth-century American poetry was almost solely a Euro-American affair. In this regard, Betty Booth Donohue's essay on "Teaching Nineteenth-Century American Indian Poetry" is one of the few to point out that apart from the few established names, "many more nineteenth-century American Indian poets . . . were published regionally in small presses or in newspapers and then forgotten," and posits that "[u]ndis-covered works of even more nineteenth-century American Indian poets have not yet come to light" (2007: 14). Parker's anthology showcases the work of 39 Native American poets writing in the nineteenth century and 44 more in the early twen-tieth century—some published and forgotten, some never published—and thus strongly underlines Donohue's point and unsettles the established narrative. These newly available texts highlight instead the diversity and plurality of nine-teenth- and early twentieth-century Native American poetic writing as well as their access to publication systems. In an early essay on American Indian poetry, contemporary Native writer Linda Hogan (1980) explained how concentrated ef-forts at assimilation severely limited publishing opportunities, particularly toward the turn of the century. And whereas it is crucial to take these conditions into account, particularly as a reason for many of these poets not finding the oppor-tunity to publish in the more prestigious and lasting form of a book, the recent findings show that Native poets found publication in the form of magazines and newspapers, generally a popular outlet for poetry at the time, and that large nations such as the Cherokee also created their own literary and journalistic forum, making them, in turn, strongly represented in Parker's anthology.

What the availability of a wider selection of authors also brings to the fore is not only the thematic diversity of early Native American poetry, but also how Native poets share certain issues, among them "colonialism and the federal government land, the condition of the world in general, nature, Christianity, and other Indian peoples" (Parker 2011b: 11). The more general themes on this list, which is of course by no means complete, show that Native and non-Native American poets wrote about similar topics such as love, death, and war. A number of others, most apparently poems about colonialism and the federal government such as Chickasaw poet James Harris Guy's "The White Man Wants the Indian's Home" (1871) and Delaware (Lenape) poet Richard Adams's "To the Delaware Indians" (1899), directly reflect and interrogate the situation of Indigenous peoples in relation to the Euro-American settlers and the recently founded and rapidly expanding United States. Poems about land stand in close relation to this situation as they clearly express how "narrative originates in the land" (Donohue 2007: 16) and illustrate how, as a result, the ancestral homelands of Indigenous peoples hold a position of crucial cultural and social significance. As Euro-American settlers continued to encroach on these lands, and various federal policies worked toward dispossessing American Indians of their lands, poems about land often reflect both the cultural centrality of land as well as point to the erosion of Native land rights due to Euro-American settler colonialism. And whereas some thematic occupations, such as nature, appear to be widespread among poetry of all kinds, nineteenth-century Native poems about nature often invite themselves to be read in two ways: as a dialogue with European traditions of Romanticism (very prominent in much of nineteenth-century American poetry) and as an engagement with Native perceptions of nature as animated and generative, part of an inherently relational worldview reflected in many Indigenous religions, and of course, again tied to issues of land (see, for example, Schoolcraft's "To the Pine Tree on first seeing it returning from Europe," pub. 2007, and Te-con-ess-kee's (Cherokee) "['Though far from thee Georgia in exile I roam']", 1848).

Renée Bergland has recently argued that "[w]riting about nineteenth-century Native American letters can be hazardous" (2006: 141) and that "the past is a great vexation to Native American studies" (ibid.). At the same time she points out the necessity for more of these studies despite the dangers of "displacing [Native Americans] from the present" and placing them within a largely Eurocentric concept of history (ibid.). A more thorough investigation of the Native American nineteenth century—for instance, considering previously neglected literary genres—can in fact help alleviate some of the dangers Bergland associates with nineteenth-century Native American Studies. Instead of displacing Native Americans from the present, a more sustained attention to nineteenth-century Native American writing can help correct a widespread oversimplified and romanticized static image of the 'Indian' of the past, the noble savage regrettably but inevitably vanishing under the onset of 'civilization.' The construction of this image benefitted the efforts at actually displacing Indigenous peoples—by means of removal, containment, elimination, and assimilation—from the present and from the future of the nineteenth-century settler nation-states of the U.S. and Canada. Countering such a neat narrative of Native disappearance, an investigation of the 'Long History of Native American Writing' (as a collection of essays recently called it) instead points out the plurality and diversity of Native cultures and peoples that were as impossible to homogenize then as they are today. An in-depth exploration of early Native American poetry illuminates the various roles Native poets assumed in this situation of U.S. expansion and Native reaction in the form of adaptation, resilience, or resistance, and examines the ways in which they were a part of the still-forming American society while being at odds with several national policies, and how they entertained multiple, often conflicting, loyalties. The attitudes expressed can range from, for example, a mournful confirmation of the myth of the vanishing Indian (uncomfortably so from a present-day reader's perspective) to a firm stance that points out how Native cultures were never static and that "Changing Is Not Vanishing" (Montezuma in Parker 2011a: 287-8) with many nuances in between. The following readings of Jane Johnston Schoolcraft and John Rollin Ridge/Yellow Bird take a closer look at two of the most prominent (and for the purpose of further reading and teaching, most readily available) Native American poets of the nineteenth century, while also investigating their positions within settler-Indigenous relations. In their own way, both of these poets defy easy classification and perhaps challenge what present-day readers might expect from Native American poetry and poets.

2. The Erosion of the Middle Ground in Jane Johnston Schoolcraft's "The Contrast"

Jane Johnston Schoolcraft (1800-1842), whose Ojibwe name, Bamewawagezhika-quay, translates as Woman of the Sound the Stars Make Rushing Through the Sky, was born in Sault Ste. Marie, present-day Michigan. Her mother Ozhagusco-daywayquay, whose English name was Susan Johnston, was an important leader, trader, and the daughter of war chief Waubojeeg; Schoolcraft's Scotch-Irish father, John Johnston, immigrated to North America as a fur trader, and later introduced his daughter to English literature through his extensive private library. As these circumstances alone indicate, Schoolcraft grew up in a mixed cultural, ethnic, and linguistic world, which is also characteristic of her larger social surroundings. In the Great Lakes area of the American Midwest, French, British, and Indian peoples lived together from the late seventeenth to the early nineteenth century, and while all of these groups exerted influence on this area, none were powerful enough to dominate. Thus, as historian Richard White has famously argued, they found new means of "accommodation and common meaning" (1991: xxv) and created something new, often from productive mis-understandings. They thus fashioned a "common, mutually comprehensible world" (ibid.), a *métis* world (French for 'mixed'). This "middle ground" (ibid.: xxvi) "was not so much half and half or bicultural as it was its own evolving and mobile space in the cultural landscape" (Parker 2007b: 4). With the founding of the United States republic and its increasing encroachment into the Midwest, this delicate balance no longer held. As this mutually comprehensible world broke down under colonialist pressure, Indian peoples were once again rein-vented "as alien, as exotic, as other" (White 1991: xxvi), and thus became objects for scientific study as well as obstacles to U.S. expansion that needed to be removed. Schoolcraft grew up during this shift that led to the erosion of the middle ground, and married Henry Schoolcraft, the first federal Indian agent of the area, a union that was born out of mutual affection and at the same time placed her in a prestigious social position. Since Henry Schoolcraft is also known today as one of the first American ethnographers, he was instrumental in the appropriation of both culture and land. Henry Schoolcraft published traditional tales of Indian peoples (particularly of the Ojibwe, with contributions from his wife and her extended family) to much acclaim, hardly crediting the individual Indians who provided him with the stories (Longfellow based his 1855 bestselling *The Song of Hiawatha* on some of these stories). Jane Schoolcraft never published her own writing, but her husband published a few of her poems after her death, and the fact that he saved many of her manuscripts and diaries allowed the eventual publication of many more (see also Parker 2007b, Bremer 1987).

In "The Contrast" (Parker 2011a: 53-4), Schoolcraft's speaker laments the abrupt changes in her surroundings by comparing her childhood world to the present, changes of which Schoolcraft's husband was an important agent. Fittingly, an earlier version contributes the changes and her ensuing confusion to falling in love and marriage, whereas the later version refers it to a larger historical context by naming "the arrival of the new republic" as the catalyst of change—an indicator for how Schoolcraft saw public and private histories as intricately intertwined and resulting in poems about multiple loyalties that are overlapping and sometimes incompatible.

While Johnston did not consider herself a writer in the sense that she sought publication, "The Contrast" begins by her assuming a writer's position: "With pen in hand, I shall contrast / the present moments with the past" (ll. 1-2) and specifies how this contrast applies foremost to an emotional level "weighed by feelings, joys and pains" (l. 4). The first 28-line stanza conveys the childhood world of the speaker's "earliest, happy days" (l. 6) in idyllic terms ("golden hours," l. 7, "bliss," l. 22, "warmed by love," l. 28). It is interesting to note what constitutes this idyll: "Calm, tranquil—far from fashion's gaze" (l. 5) as the line describing how the "happiest days" passed, transports a sense of serenity while making it clear that this tranquility is attained by a distance to a social setting that celebrates what is new, exciting, and maybe also profitable. What the speaker's family and social surroundings value instead is modesty, inclusiveness, and hospitality ("my father's simple hall, / Oped to whomsoe'er might call," ll. 9-10), peace of body and mind ("Pains or cares we seldom knew," l. 11), literature and fine arts ("Concerts," l. 13, "Books," l. 14), and a close circle of family and friends in which relations are defined by mutual consideration and love, unintentional hurts are soon mended, and admonishments are motivated by genuine care and concern (cf. ll. 16-28). It is interesting to note how communal values and close social and familial relations are highlighted as the fabric of this idyll and are connected to the contrast the poem sketches; this notion of a closely-knit community appears to be associated with a Native or *métis* social structure that is part of the past. It might then speak of the social importance of communal values integral to many Native cultures (while not exclusive to them) when Schoolcraft states, "My only wish, to gain the praise / Of friends I loved, and neighbours kind" (ll. 30-1) in a final celebration of the past that is soon contrasted with the present.

"But ah! how changed is every scene" (l. 35) begins the second part of the poem, emphasizing the contrast to be outlined by the combined means of a contrastive proposition, an exclamation, and the figure of inversion. With "Our little hamlet" (l. 36), "The long rich green" (l. 37), and the "breezy elm-wood shade" (l. 38), Schoolcraft's portrayal of "every scene" shows how her work continues in the Romantic and pastoral traditions while also expressing the close ties to na-ture and land that characterize the speaker and her Native/*métis* social sur-roundings. These ties are in danger since the "little hamlet" is no longer re-moved from the world, which, "full of strife and fear / hath sent its votaries here" (ll. 39-40). The poem describes the invaders with a term that suggests devotees to the world and thus the worldly things from which the community was previously kept apart, and also points to, through its religious implications, the work of missionaries, possibly implying a connection between Christianiza-tion and the entry into the modern world of market economy. The consequences to the natural environment are clearly stated: "The tree cut down—the cot re-moved, / The cot the simple Indian loved" (ll. 41-2). This speaks of the swift, even brutal efficiency—also transported through the clipped sentence and the line severed by the dash—with which nature is subordinated and traditional Na-tive living customs disrupted in the service of opposing interests.

From today's perspective, though, the point of view thus expressed is also problematic. Particularly lines such as "The long rich green, where warriors played" (l. 37) and "The cot the simple Indian loved" (l. 42) evoke long-standing stereotypical images of American Indians as both Romanticized and infantilized, 'noble savages' whose 'playing' represents an earlier, childlike state of humanity and whose "simple" ways cannot withstand the progress of civilization. One might ask whether Schoolcraft simply reproduces such a stereotype, and there-by adds to it, possibly aided by having the speaker associate the time of the 'playing warriors' with her own childhood. If one reads it as a conscious com-ment, however, the matter becomes more complicated because one can either see "the simple Indian" as an image of identification with Schoolcraft's Ojibwe heritage, or as a matter of distancing herself from an Indian imagined as simple because he or she *is* 'simple,' with all the implied positive and negative connota-tions, for not being part of the *métis* world but a traditional Native life exempli-fied through the "cot," and additionally not part of the social elite in which Schoolcraft grew up. Seen in still another light, one might also regard it, as Bethany Schneider argues for the inclusion of "the simple Indian" in "On the Doric Rock, Lake Superior" (cf. 2008: 133-5), not as a mere reproduction of Eu-ropean stereotype but as a repetition with a difference. In *The Middle Ground*, Richard White claims that the construction, or reinvention, of American Indian peoples as alien, other, and exotic in the context of the newly founded U.S. both led to and was a sign of the eroding middle ground at the beginning of the nine-teenth century when the new republic took hold and could dominate the terms of interaction. In that light, the 'playing warriors' and the "simple Indian" might not be Schoolcraft merely participating in this construction of Indians as other, but commenting on this process by making it part of her poem which depicts this erosion of the middle ground by contrasting the past with the present. Her usage of these terms might then echo somewhat ironically with the Euro-Ameri-cans whose reinvention of the Indian as simple and childlike, as opposed to Eu-ropean complexity and progress, underlined their effort of taking the land and eroding the autonomy of Indian peoples.

Then again, such a reading might say more about present-day expectations for the first known Native American poet writing in English—especially about the desire of reading a strongly anti-colonialist impulse in her compositions (see Parker 2009)—than it says about her actual work. Her use of 'playing warriors' and the "simple Indian" might be only the common idealization of Native peoples in the Romantic vein, in which Native peoples represent an innocent, unadulterated state of humanity in contrast to corrupt civilization. Schoolcraft's perspective does not necessarily share the currently widespread critical stance toward such an idealization; she might partake in this colonialist fantasy without seeing it for that, and without connecting this discourse to acts of dispossessing Indigenous peoples in the newly founded United States.

The point of considering various readings of a phrase such as "simple Indian" in Schoolcraft's poem is ultimately not to determine which one is 'right,' but to point out how her poetry is a multi-layered and complex composition that goes beyond one simple, clear-cut meaning, and how this ambiguity can, in turn, be read to reflect Schoolcraft's own position of multiple, contested loyalties and alliances that ultimately refuse simple categorization. And to take it a step further, the text itself has been copied by Henry Schoolcraft's hand, so he may have slightly revised it (as his wife invited him to do) or made changes as he had done with other texts when translating them from Ojibwe. Passages that strike present-day readers as problematic in their colonialist tone might be changes made by Schoolcraft's colonialist husband (see Parker 2009); or perhaps present-day readers are simply more comfortable making this assumption. Finally, the text itself may be regarded as the result of a collaboration, wittingly or unwittingly, so that it is not so much the question what Schoolcraft's position actually is, but how the text may be read to reflect its own historical position of contested meanings, conflicting intents, and mixed or opposing allegiances.

The continued evaluation of the present in contrast to the past is less ambiguous in the poem. With the advance of Euro-American settlers, the speaker sees community-based values replaced with the capitalist system of exchange value, so that efforts at accumulating wealth become imperative: "The busy strife of young and old / To gain one sordid bit of gold" (ll. 43-4). In the same way, instead of the leisure and freedom associated with entertaining social relations and following non-profit oriented interests, "lawsuits, meetings, courts and toil" (l. 46) dominate the everyday. And whereas this might generally be read as the speaker being drawn into society with the responsibilities and duties of adulthood, the historical moment of the poem refers to a wider context, to a different legal, economic, political, and social system that intrudes on and replaces the old as a consequence of colonialist pressures.

The final stanza, then, waves goodbye to the past ("Adieu, to days of homebred ease," l. 47) while holding on to something more fundamental.

> We trim our sails anew, to steer
> By shoals we never knew were here,
> And with the star flag, raised on high
> Discover a new dominion nigh,
> And half in joy, half in fear,
> Welcome the proud Republic here. (ll. 49-54)

As Bethany Schneider notes, "Schoolcraft imagines those who have experienced the shift from past to [synchronic] presence as travelers" who are on "a voyage of discovery in their own home" (2008: 139-40). Thus, the classic distribution of roles in which the old residents of a place more or less passively receive the discoverers, who bring with them the new, is reversed; or rather, the line between who is discovering and who is discovered becomes blurry. The travelers—if not fully Indian then very likely representing the *métis* community described before—discover something new "in their own home," as they are the ones who "Discover a new dominion nigh" by either sighting or raising for themselves "the star flag"; and this realization, having left the past behind to move on to the present and the future, enables them, with mixed feelings "half in joy, half in fear" to "Welcome the proud Republic here." In a way, it is only this acceptance and welcome that fully realizes the existence of the republic, now discovered in their home, "here," as a "new dominion." It is important to note how much depends on this "Welcome." The existence of the "new political order" (Schneider 2008: 140) is based on its acceptance by the old order, and therefore remains, in the poem's rhetoric, a conditional rather than an absolute entity.

The poem ends on the word "here," further demonstrating an affirmation of the ties of Indigenous peoples to the land and the place—or of the various groups making up Schoolcraft's *métis* world, depending on how one interprets the poem's 'we' (cf. ibid.). The travelers, while sailing into the present and the future, are not leaving their home, and in "Welcom[ing] the proud Republic here" they are, as Schneider states, "ready to leave days, not places" (ibid.: 139). The poem holds on to the "here," as the final word: succeeding, coming after, and maybe even imagined as outlasting the "proud Republic." One might read that, of course, as Schoolcraft giving over the place, the "here," to the new Republic and putting her faith, her mixed feelings, and her loyalties, "half in joy, half in fear" in this "new political order." Ending on the "here," however, the text is left open enough to suggest that while the middle ground may have been eroded due to the advance of the U.S. federal republic, one can still imagine the possibility of holding onto and standing one's own ground, even from within the "proud Republic." This, in turn, might be an indication for how Schoolcraft saw ways to imagine the possibility of cultural continuity in the midst of the drastic changes she experienced.

3. The Vision of a Common Ground in John Rollin Ridge/Yellow Bird's "The Atlantic Cable"

With John Rollin Ridge—also known as Yellow Bird, the translation of his Cherokee name Chees-quat-a-law-ny—the history of intra-tribal tensions and warring factions comes to light that play a vital part in the history of American Indians and settler-Indigenous relations within what is now the United States. This history is too often overlooked in the tendency to homogenize not only individual Indigenous nations but the entire population of American Indians. Ridge's father was one of the leaders who reluctantly signed the treaty that would order the removal of the Cherokees from their homeland east of the Mississippi to the Southwest, which made them traitors to the opposing party led by Chief John Ross. After having removed in 1836/37, two years before the infamous Trail of Tears that still stands metonymically for the inhumane suffering American Indians endured as a result of the removal policy, John Rollin Ridge's father and grandfather were brutally assassinated in front of him and his mother by members of the opposing Ross-party, forcing Ridge and his mother to flee to Arkansas, from where, after having murdered a member of the Ross party (probably in self-defense), Ridge again fled, finally moving to California in 1850 to join the gold rush and working as a journalist and newspaper editor. With this work, he could put to use some of the education he received at various schools where he studied Latin, Greek, classical literature, and law. In literary history, Ridge is primarily remembered for having written the first known novel by an American Indian, *The Life and Adventures of Joaquín Murieta, The Celebrated California Bandit* (1854), but as Edward Whitley points out, "to his contemporaries he was known first and foremost as a poet" (2010: 133). Apart from having various poems published during his lifetime in newspapers (often adding to his signature the town where they were written and 'C.N.' for Cherokee Nation), his wife published a book of his poems posthumously in 1868, simply titled *Poems*. Ridge also wrote articles about "Native American history, culture, and politics for mainstream periodicals" (ibid.: 124) in order to both correct widespread misassumptions about Indigenous peoples and to critically address the abuse they suffered at the hands of the federal government. Today Ridge is mentioned regularly among the few nineteenth-century American Indian poets known before Parker's anthology, and his work and life have received more recent attention (see Parins 1991, Whitley 2010).

Twice exiled, perceived as a traitor by an opposing faction of his own nation, educated in missionary schools and Euro-American institutions, and a firm antiabolitionist through the background of his family's slaveholding, Ridge is often conceived of as a 'civilized Indian.' As one example among many, Wilson's survey essay on Indigenous American poetry indicating his belief that technical progress would advance humanity as a whole is proof that "Ridge had bought into his assimilationist education" (Wilson 2005: 146); his biographer, James Parins, largely shares this perspective. Wilson, however, also concedes that such a pigeonholing of Ridge as being assimilated to Euro-American standards is complicated by the fact that he entertained an "increasingly . . . global" focus on "community" (ibid.). More recently, Edward Whitley closely examined Ridge's thought on the "universal amalgamation of races" (qtd. in Whitley 2010: 123) in relation to his poetry, and rather than seeing this as a synonym for assimilation (as Parins does in his biography), he intriguingly argues that Ridge sought for an understanding of humanity in which any difference based on nation or gender would be transcended and thus amalgamated into something new (cf. ibid.: 122-4). Given the painful and traumatic personal history that Ridge experienced due to differences between and within nations such as the Cherokee and the U.S., such a position is quite understandable from a psychological perspective, while from today's position it might seem incredibly naïve to believe that a merging of Euro-American and American Indian peoples would be possible without the erasure of American Indian identity as part of the dominant society of the United States. Before one too quickly psychologizes it or dismisses it as an embarrassingly misguided notion, it might prove fruitful to consider how the idea of an "amalgamation of races" might have offered Ridge a view of American society, or even of a 'global community' in which Europeans and American Indians were allowed the same space on a common ground, existing in unity and harmony, and in which both groups would come together on equal footing to the point that differences designated by European and Indian no longer mattered and something new was created instead. For this Anglo-Cherokee poet then, who both spoke out against the mistreatment of Native nations and praised the advance of Euro-American progress, the idea of "amalgamation" appeared to be a way to unite "the apparently contradictory goals of preserving Indigenous culture *and* spreading American civilization throughout the continent" (ibid.: 116). Firmly exhibiting such a progressivist stance, "The Atlantic Cable"—written as one of the "public verses that he was commissioned to write and recite at large public gatherings" (ibid. 138) on the occasion of laying the transatlantic telegraph cable—paints the picture of a unity that transcends all causes of separation and disunion, and in which technology becomes the catalyst for this development.

The very first lines of Ridge's 100-line poem (Parker 2011a: 88-90) state that the laying of the telegraph cable gives reason to rejoice since "that great work" (l. 1) makes "the Old and New World one" (l. 2). In a recognizable tone that was often used for odes of progress and human improvement (a prominent representative being Ridge's contemporary Walt Whitman), Ridge emphasizes how human technology can unite people and show how they, "Though Nature heaved the Continents apart" (l. 5), are defined not by what separates them but by that which they have in common: "She cast in one great mould the human heart; / She framed on one great plan the human mind" (ll. 6-7). With intellect and emotion being of the same kind across nations and cultures, the invention of the telegraph enables a connection that is already constitutive of humanity and allows closeness and equality between people to become manifest: "If there but be a carrier for the thought— / . . . man is nearer to his brother brought" (ll. 11, 13). While brotherhood between men is a staple of enlightenment thought, including the gender bias thus expressed, it is still notable how Ridge describes the relationship between people, the 'global community,' in terms of kinship. This is a crucial component of Native thought which, in both literal and metaphorical forms, bears such special significance on the social structures of many Native communities that the expression could be read to combine Ridge's European and Cherokee heritage.

The poem goes on to outline a history of communication across great distances, from "skin-clad heralds" (l. 17) to "beasts . . . tamed to drag the rolling car" (l. 20) to "wingéd ships, which . . . / Did skim the bosom of the bounding sea" (ll. 25-6), each time emphasizing an increase of speed. Importantly, sea travel allows contact and communication between populations previously separated: "Then, sea-divided nations nearer came, / Stood face to face, spake each other's name" (ll. 30-1). On the one hand, this account seems to forego the history of invasion and colonization of the Americas, enabled by Columbus's sea voyage, and the role of sailing ships in conquest and warfare. On the other hand, if one reads "sea-divided nations" in connection to the "Old and New World," which are now united through the transatlantic telegraph cable, then Ridge turns a history of discovering foreign lands, usually imagined as unpopulated, into a moment of contact between nations of equal status, such as between the British and the Indigenous nations of North America. Read in this way, Ridge does not perpetuate the colonialist fantasy of Europeans discovering America and its peoples, imagined as childlike savages, but instead stages a meeting of equals based on reciprocity, standing "face to face," speaking "each other's name," implying eye-level contact as well as the willingness of both sides to learn from the other culture. Strongly idealizing this first moment of contact between "sea-divided nations," the poem moves on to suggest that the ability to sail across the sea is foremost a means to realize how humanity, regardless of the nation to which one belongs, is essentially undivided: "Man is Man in every age and clime!" (l. 33). This can be identified easily as a universalistic humanist stance, integral to enlightenment thought and often used to project European standards and traditions as ultimately universal. But if one reads this within the background of the discourse of dehumanizing or exoticizing American Indigenous peoples—going back to Columbus's own accounts—Ridge's rhetoric offers another, more complex dimension in emphasizing how populations on either side of the dividing sea are equally human, and especially how both consist of nations having equal status. Only acknowledging this makes it possible to overcome differences and ultimately to cease being defined by any national or ethnic boundaries in a vision of "universal amalgamation."

The poem continues to the next innovation in speed of communication, "steam" (l. 36), before it names electricity "lightning's wondrous power" (l. 44), which is used by the telegraph to facilitate contact in a matter of minutes between people who are far apart. As suits the occasion for which the poem was written, "this great crowning deed of modern days" (l. 79) is celebrated. The patriotic tone with which Ridge's poem exclaims that it "was fitting that a great, free land like this, / Should give the lightning's voice to Liberty" (ll. 84-5) testifies to how the poem was written for a specific audience and a particular occasion, and thus sought to meet the respective expectations. At the same time it shows how Ridge saw himself as part of the America that had the potential to achieve his ideal of radical amalgamation as a liberty from all boundaries seemingly imposed by birth, which would also be an America that, by being true to this promise, would end the injustices committed against Indigenous peoples about which Ridge was equally outspoken in various journalistic articles.

The main hope in the poem connected to the possibility of "thought-swift" (l. 49) communication enabled through electricity is that this unlimited, immediate communication reduces the possibility of misunderstanding, of disagreement, and of any violent conflict that may arise from misconstruction. For Ridge, the merging of "Old and New World" by overcoming distance through communication technology once again prompts the realization of how humanity is one and, thus, how can there be no cause for disunity: "For Nation unto Nation soon shall be / Together brought in knitted unity, / And man be bound to man by that strong chain" (ll. 95-7). The poem offers a universal message of peace, which, in view of Ridge's activity as a Native rights advocate, may also imply a concrete hope for peace through the cessation of military aggression of U.S. federal forces against Indian nations, precisely in the way the poem reassesses the relations between peoples and nations in the history of human improvement. On the one hand, the poem recognizes difference in stating "Nation unto Nation," possibly including the Cherokee nations or other Indigenous nations in relation to the United States; on the other hand, the ideal relation between nations is not seen as oppositional or antagonistic, but one of "knitted unity." In this expression the praised oneness of humanity seems to appear in the form of a dense "knitted" web of entanglements, interdependencies, and interrelations. These connections then go as far as to create a sense of unity, an idea that resonates with the strongly relational worldview prominent among many Native peoples. The "strong chain" and the "throbbing heartstring of Humanity" (l. 100) of the Atlantic cable with which the poem concludes may be read as the manifestation of an ever-present connection and interrelation between all peoples and all people. This connection makes them one, or part of a greater communal whole, and through it they share a common ground of humanity that enables ongoing improvement to the point of transcending all differences.

Ultimately, Ridge might express nothing more than a very common trope of progressivism in which humanity is united through striving for improvement, usually a version of improvement defined by European or Euro-American standards. Such a view would make the poem almost the quintessential work of the 'civilized Indian,' an advertisement for the mythical American project of creating something new that transcends all differences of birth by investing in a new idea of unity. However, Ridge's poem, just as Schoolcraft's "The Contrast," also offers itself to a more complex reading that complicates a neat narrative of assimilation and Europeanization. Such a reading asks how a traditionally European or Euro-American version of progressivism and universalist humanism might be seen as being 'indigenized' by an Anglo-Cherokee poet. From this perspective the poem utilizes aspects of an Indigenous worldview, such as kinship relations and the emphasis on all-pervasive interrelations and connections, in order to create an image of oneness in humanity and an American society that is not based on one part being absorbed by the whole. Instead, connections and relations appear to become so strongly "knitted" that this process results in unity, a common ground for all peoples, Native and non-Native, from which something new can emerge. Whether any of this was perceived as such by the audience, and whether any of this was intended by Ridge, are different, and ultimately unanswerable, questions. These readings show, however, that poems by Native Americans of the nineteenth century, such as those written by Schoolcraft and Ridge, can be read as going beyond any clear-cut single meaning. Poems such as these thus challenge what one might expect from a nineteenth-century Native American poet when considering his or her circumstances or public image, and their analysis helps to illustrate the complexities of this specific period in the history of Native American poetic writing.

4. Conclusion

Schoolcraft and Ridge are two of the most prominent and (as far as we know) prolific early Native American poets. Both were entangled with colonialist and expansionist U.S. efforts, and both assumed a particular position that can seem contradictory from today's perspective, either by being married to an agent of a colonialism whose effects were often painfully felt, or by being both a Native rights advocate and a proponent of American civilizational progress. In one way their reception in literary history reflects the discomfort this might cause today. Schoolcraft's poetic aesthetics are easily dismissed as "imitative" in Wilson's *Cambridge Companion* essay (2005: 145), when her creativity and imagination should be seen within the Romantic traditions engaged in by so many other nineteenth-century poets. Ridge's poetics and attitude are also perceived as the product of his assimilationist education, as though he can be granted little to no agency of his own in developing a particular point of view. In both cases, such an assessment does little to acknowledge Schoolcraft and Ridge as poets or as important figures in the literary history of Native Americans in the nineteenth century. The complicated positions they inhabited and the consequences which one might trace in their writing are not cause to dismiss or diminish their writing, but need to be understood as part of the challenge in thinking through and analyzing the Native American poetic writing of this period. In comparison, poets of a later generation such as Alexander Posey and Zitkala-Ša, with the former writing a poem praising a Creek warrior fighting federal forces in 1910 and the latter commenting critically on enforced assimilation through federal boarding schools, are ultimately more easily integrated in a literary history of Native America and receive more appreciation for their skeptical attitude toward federal policies both in Hogan's early essay and in Wilson's *Cambridge Companion* essay from 2005.

Such a perspective might reveal one instance, however, in which today's views of Native poetry are projected onto earlier Native poets, so that contemporary expectations determine the reading and discussion of their poetry more than an attempt to understand the complex situations in which they found themselves, which they helped to shape for themselves, and navigated more or less successfully. Such an understanding of the complex navigations entails acknowledging that Native poets of the nineteenth century inevitably engaged various literary and cultural heritages and exhibited multiple and possibly conflicting loyalties and allegiances. To foster such an understanding it is essential to approach early Native poetry on its own terms, not as foils against which to measure the achievements of later poets, but as literary texts in their own right that offer their own distinct—even unexpected—contribution both to the history of Native poetry and to a more varied picture of nineteenth-century poetry. Work to this end might make the inclusion of nineteenth-century Native American poetry in future literary histories and anthologies not simply plausible, but a given.

Bibliography

Selected Primary Literature

Parker, Robert Dale (ed.). 2007a. *The Sound the Stars Make Rushing Through the Sky: The Writings of Jane Johnston Schoolcraft*. Philadelphia: U of Pennsylvania P.

—— (ed.). 2011a. *Changing Is Not Vanishing: A Collection of American Indian Poetry to 1930*. Philadelphia: U of Pennsylvania P.

Selected Secondary Literature

Donohue, Betty Booth. 2007. "Oktahutchee's Song: Reflections on Teaching Nineteenth-Century American Indian Poetry." In: Paula Bernat Bennett, Karen L. Kilcup and Philipp Schweighauser (eds.), *Teaching Nineteenth-Century American Poetry*. New York: The Modern Language Association of America. 13-25.

Helpful essay that outlines some characteristics and contexts of Native American nineteenth-century poets, and provides insightful readings of Alexander Posey and Pauline Johnson.

Parker, Robert Dale. 2007b. "Introduction: The World and Writings of Jane Johnston Schoolcraft." In: Parker 2007a. 1-84.

By outlining Schoolcraft's cultural world and personal life, and assessing her poetry and literary legacy, the introduction creates a differentiated picture of this writer, her historical context, and her work.

——. 2009. "Contemporary Anticolonialist Reading and the Collaborative Writing of Jane Johnston Schoolcraft." In: Simone Pellerin (ed.), *Before Yesterday: The Long History of Native American Writing*. Bordeaux: Presses Universitaires de Bordeaux. 47-52.

Heeds against projecting one's own contemporary position and anticolonialist sensibility on Schoolcraft's writing and asks instead to understand the complex situation of literary production and historical context.

——. 2011b. "A Garden of the Mind: An Introduction to Early American Indian Literature." In: Parker 2011a. 1-44.

Provides an overview of cultural and literary historical contexts of American Indian nineteenth-century poetry and identifies a number of major topics, offering short readings of several poems for each. Parker 2011c, and Parker 2012 follow this introduction closely.

Schneider, Bethany. 2008. "Not for Citation: Jane Johnston Schoolcraft's Synchronic Strategies." In: *ESQ* 54.1-4: 111-44.

Intriguing scholarly essay that provides detailed readings of a number of Schoolcraft poems and argues for the prominent position issues of land hold in her poetry.

Whitley, Edward. 2010. *American Bards: Walt Whitman and Other Unlikely Candidates for National Poet.* Chapel Hill, NC: U of North Carolina P.

In the chapter on John Rollin Ridge, Whitley argues how Ridge in his poetry sought to combine the advocacy of Native rights and his faith in Western civilization through the idea of 'universal amalgamation.'

Further References

Bergland, Renée. 2006. "The Native American Nineteenth Century: Rewriting the American Renaissance." In: *ESQ* 52.1-2: 141-54.

Bremer, Richard G. 1987. *Indian Agent and Wilderness Scholar: The Life of Henry Rowe Schoolcraft.* Mount Pleasant, MI: Clarke Historical Library.

Bross, Kristina and Hilary E. Wyss. 2008. *Early Native Literacies in New England: A Documentary and Critical Anthology.* Amherst, MA: U of Massachusetts P.

Brown Ruoff, A. LaVonne. 1998. "Early Native American Women Authors: Jane Johnston Schoolcraft, Sarah Winnemucca, S. Alice Callahan, E. Pauline Johnson, and Zitkala-Ša." In: Karen L. Kilcup (ed.), *Nineteenth-Century American Women Writers: A Critical Reader.* Malden, MA and Oxford: Blackwell. 81-111.

Hogan, Linda. 1980. "The Nineteenth Century Native American Poets." In: *Wassaja* 13.4: 24-9.

Jaskoski, Helen (ed.). 1996. *Early Native American Writing: New Critical Essays.* Cambridge: Cambridge UP.

Parins, James W. 1991. *John Rollin Ridge: His Life and Works.* Lincoln, NE: U of Nebraska P.

Parker, Robert Dale. 2003. *The Invention of Native American Literature.* Ithaca, NY and London: Cornell UP.

——. 2011c. "American Indian Poetry in the Nineteenth Century." In: Kerry Larson (ed.), *The Cambridge Companion to Nineteenth-Century American Poetry.* Cambridge: Cambridge UP. 36-53.

——. 2012. "American Indian Poetry at the Dawn of Modernism." In: Cary Nelson (ed.), *The Oxford Handbook of Modern and Contemporary American Poetry.* Oxford: Oxford UP. 71-95.

Rasmussen, Birgit Bander. 2012. *Queequeg's Coffin: Indigenous Literacies and Early American Literature.* Durham, NC: Duke UP.

White, Richard. 1991. *The Middle Ground: Indians, Empires, and Republics in the Great Lakes Region, 1650-1815.* Cambridge: Cambridge UP.

Wilson, Norma C. 2005. "America's Indigenous Poetry." In: Joy Porter and Kenneth Roemer (eds.), *The Cambridge Companion to Native American Literature.* Cambridge: Cambridge UP. 145-60.

9.

Nineteenth-Century Women Poets

Lydia Sigourney's "The Butterfly" and
Sarah Morgan Bryan Piatt's "The Funeral of a Doll"

Gudrun M. Grabher

1. Sentimental Poetry

With only Emily Dickinson looming large on the horizon of nineteenth-century American female poets, one may be tempted to assume that this very same nation and century managed to reject most other female voices inclined towards poetic self-expression. Even Dickinson waived the pursuit of the business of publication, facetiously snubbing it off as "the auction of the mind" (1960: 348) after only ten of her poems had been printed. But we would be totally wrong to assume that women did not write or publish their products "back then" (Stevens 2006: 1). The nineteenth-century literary landscape was anything but deplete of women poets; it was alive with many female voices who dared to sing: Elizabeth Drew Stoddard (1823-1902), Elizabeth Oakes Smith (1806-1893), Frances Sargent Osgood (1811-1850), Phoebe Cary (1824-1871), Elizabeth Akers Allen (1832-1911), to name but a few. In her 1977 book *The Poetry of American Women from 1632 to 1945*, Emily Stipes Watts counts more than eighty female poets who, between 1800 and 1850, published at least one volume of poetry, and at least twice that number who published their poems in journals (cf. Watts 1977: 65). But while those voices were heard and read at that time, by the early twentieth century they had faded away and soon fell into oblivion. Only through the efforts of (mostly female) critics have they been brought back to light. In the past couple of decades, critics such as "Emily Stipes Watts, Cheryl Walker, Alicia Suskin Ostriker, and Joanne Dobson [as well as others] have all challenged the earlier perception that nineteenth-century American women's poetry was a wasteland from which only Emily Dickinson emerged" (Okker 1993: 32). But restaging those female poets in this literary landscape has posed some major challenges and raises the following questions: What enabled these women to make their poetic output public? Why did their reputations as poets not survive the century of their lifetime? And most importantly, why have these poets stirred the interest of contemporary critics?

It is the "cultural politics of sentimentalism" (Larson 2011b: 3) in particular which has revived the interest in female verse of the nineteenth century, which witnessed a booming of literary journals and publications, as well as an increasing interest of the reading public in literary (and other) texts. In spite of a few female editors such as Sarah Hale, the publishing market remained in male hands, and it was men who made the decisions not only concerning what was going to be seen by the public but also the way it would be presented. In other words, the scope of poetic (self-)expression for women was clearly controlled. The first half of the century was marked by the Romantic aesthetic and its ideals, such as the glorification of individualism, the admiration of nature, the celebration of feelings and emotions, and an inclination towards the supernatural and the mystical. Apart from the focus on feelings and nature, however, those Romantic ideals applied to male rather than to female poets. In spite of being "so-

cially revered", "the poetess is bound by expectations of modesty, unassertive-
ness, and melancholy emotionalism" (Okker 1993: 33), and her poems, as argued by Annie Finch (1988) and other critics, seem to lack the presence and
authority of a poetic self. Emerson's profile of the (American) poet as seer,
namer, and sayer targeted only the male poet. Women, if they produced anything at all, were confined to "sentimental poetry." Rufus Griswold, famous journalist, editor, critic, and poet, published the first editions of *The Poets and Poetry of America* in 1842 and *The Female Poets of America* in 1848. Since he was
highly influential, most writers were eager to be included in his anthologies.
Griswold "contended that while men could poeticize conflict and intellectual
trials, women should properly only write sentimental lyrics about the joys and
tribulations of the domestic sphere" (Giordano 2006: 42); his opinion presented
the view of his time. Paula Bennett distinguishes between the "high sentimentalism" of the nineteenth century, where "the intuitions of the heart could serve as
reliable guides to moral and spiritual truths" (c. 1825-1850), and "low sentimentalism," which was, as it is still today, "loose, subjective, personal, [making] no
claims to knowledge, only to feeling." When practiced by women, high sentimentalism endowed them with considerable influence in the home and enormous power
as poets (Bennett 1995: 606). In the nineteenth century, it was this type of poetry—the sentimental kind—that readers wanted from female writers. This was a
time when people were hungry for words that could both express and evoke in
them feelings and sentiments, and women were believed to be masters in this
field. Moreover, with their poems addressed to the public, women were meant to
serve as moral guides and guardians. Male and female spheres were still separate, and would remain so, with the woman ruling the domestic realm as wife,
housewife, and mother. Within this sphere, and in particular in regard to her
role as mother, she began to expand her horizon because it was exactly this role
that connected the private and the public spheres. As a mother, woman was not
only her children's nurturer; she was, above all, their educator. Her goal was to
raise them to be mature, responsible, knowledgeable citizens, and in her identity as mother she was dependent on her success in this role (cf. Watts 1977: 87).
With the establishment of the new republic, the role of mother was regarded as
crucial and significant. The "angel in the house" ideology still determined the
identity of woman as both representative and teacher of the moral standards of
her society. The mother-child relationship is therefore in the foreground of many
nineteenth-century poems written by women. The death of a child was considered a failure on the mother's side, both in her own eyes as well as in the eyes of
society. With an extremely high mortality rate of both children and mothers during childbirth, it comes as no surprise that many poems were written on the
subject of infant and maternal death. But patriarchal society also made sure
that composing poetry would not take away too much of a woman's time and
energy and thus keep her from fulfilling her household chores and maternal responsibilities. If she did, or if there was concern that she might run the risk of
doing so, she was criticized for being "unfeminine," or worse, pronounced guilty
of causing her family to suffer. Women who showed an interest in intellectual or
literary matters and neglected their responsibilities prescribed for them by a
patriarchal society, were labeled "bluestockings" after the informal blue worsted
stockings worn by women who where less interested in fashion than intellectual
pursuits. The fear of competition was another (albeit unspoken) motive as women
writers were not supposed to rival the 'superior' male voices.

Sentimental, genteel poetry had to be beautiful and agreeable, using simple and direct language and preferably deriving its metaphors from nature or the domestic sphere; it should also adhere to a rhyme scheme and metrical pattern, usually iambic or trochaic tetrameter or pentameter. Because of the very definition of sentimental verse, women's poetry was not taken seriously in an aesthetic sense and "rests largely on negatives: the absence of a central poetic self and the avoidance of the unequivocal metaphorization of nature" (Finch 1988: 13). Finch continues to argue that good and serious poetry is characterized by the clearly perceivable authoritative poetic self. Since it is absent in sentimental poetry, the very notion of sentimental poetry is, according to Finch, "a contradiction in terms, a horrifying oxymoron" (ibid.: 3), at least from today's perspective. This verdict entails the question as to whether such poetry is still worth reading today, or whether it merely reflects the taste of its contemporary readership. "The Victorian poetess has become as important a figure in the late twentieth century as she was in the late nineteenth—perhaps because she seems now, as then, to have lapsed into the obscurity of literary history" (Jackson and Prins 1999: 521) and must be reclaimed because she was so popular at her time. At the same time, Virginia Jackson and Yopie Prins enhance the condemnation of the poetess as defined and characterized by "negations" when they argue: "One reason for the perpetual disappearance and reappearance of the Poetess is that she is not the content of her own generic representation: not a speaker, not an 'I,' not a consciousness, not a subjectivity, not a voice, not a persona, not a self" (ibid.: 523). While agreeing that "the absence of an individuated subjectivity or self in Poetess poems" accounts for the popularity of such poems (Bennett 2007: 270), Paula Bennett disagrees with the overall verdict by defending Lydia Sigourney and her peers as follows:

> [Scholars] have identified these poets in terms of a single set of generic parameters, be it those of the sentimentalist, elegist, nightingale, or Poetess. Worse, in doing so, these scholars have misrepresented the nature of poetry itself wherein what we call the author's "voice" or "self" has always and everywhere been mediated by the generic conventions he or she uses and is inseparable from them. (ibid.: 283)

I agree with Bennett that women poets of the nineteenth century found their own ways of undercutting the messages they were forced to produce, and Matthew Giordano (2006: 43) is also correct in emphasizing that one must recognize "the ways poets resisted, transformed, and negotiated with" the sentimental and genteel mode. The very fact that those female writers of the nineteenth century were rediscovered and reprinted in the past couple of decades seems to testify to this other perspective. As will be argued in the context of the analyses of the poems, there is much more to these sentimental outpourings than expected. Both Lydia Sigourney and Sarah Piatt are nineteenth-century poets who used the poetic conventions of their time to demonstrate that they had a voice and a consciousness of their own, a "self" to project.

2. Lydia Huntley Sigourney and Sarah Morgan Bryan Piatt: Nineteenth-Century American Poets before and after the Civil War

Lydia Huntley Sigourney, who wrote before the Civil War, and Sarah Morgan Bryan Piatt, who composed most of her work in the last quarter of the century, both represent the nineteenth-century American female poet. Their poems not only reflect the taste of their time, they also verbalize their frustration with the conventions and restrictions imposed on them by patriarchal society. Lydia Sigourney is said to have been the best-known and most famous American female poet of the nineteenth century and

> is most widely recognized as a singer of home and hearth. Although her poetic concerns are, in fact, much broader, Lydia Sigourney devoted much of her poetic career to celebration and examination of the woman's life—girlhood and education, marriage choice and maternity, religious life, and the joys and travails of the domestic sphere (Baker 1997: 69-70).

In her famous 1849 poem "The Unspoken Language" she celebrates the spontaneous language of the soul, but she is best known for her poems on mothers and children, for her numerous elegies on the death of infants and mothers, and for her poems of romantic content. One of the best-known examples is "The Death of an Infant," in which she emphasizes the continuity of the bond between mother and child beyond death, and celebrates the sentimental cult of motherhood. In her numerous "mourning" poems she often idealizes the bond between mother and child and expresses the hope of being reunited after death. While the death of the beautiful young woman served Edgar Allan Poe as the most poetic theme, the death of an infant or that of a mother haunted not only the poetic scope but also the reality of many female writers. As a common form of consolation, Sigourney compares death to sleep, thus removing the horror from death very much like Emily Dickinson did in her numerous death poems. But she also wrote about the deaf, the blind, and the insane, about missionary work, a large number of poems about the sea, for example "To the Ocean" or "Oracle for Seamen," and published numerous poems of political concern. Sigourney frequently deplores the inequality of Native Americans and African Americans. In *Traits of the Aborigines of America: A Poem* (1822), and later in *Pocahontas* (1841), for example, she accuses America of having slaughtered native Americans and robbed them of their land. "The Cherokee's Mother" is one of her best-known poems of revolt against the removal of Indians. In other poems she takes a critical stance on slavery, and questions the colonial expansionism of the American nation. She usually phrases those political concerns within a religious context. As Clark Lawlor has aptly remarked, "Sigourney's interest is to, like that of Hemans, feminize our perspective on these masculine histories" (2009: 20). For this and other reasons, Sigourney was often called the American Hemans in reference to the English poet Felicia Hemans (1793-1835). Since she was so well known as a poet (and writer) at her time, she was often commissioned to write poems for occasions such as weddings, funerals, birthdays, etc. In one of her most famous poems, "To a Shred of Linen," she enlarges a trivial object of the domestic sphere with a mythopoetic dimension and thus endows it with dignity, asserting herself as a poet (cf. Baker 1997: 69-71).

In the second half of the nineteenth century, Sarah Morgan Bryan Piatt was one of the most prolific poets. "Yet despite her productivity . . . she became, by the early twentieth century, as little known as most of her contemporaries. Brushed aside by modernists and New Critics as simply another sentimental poetess, she was erased from the dominant narratives of American poetic history" (Giordano 2006: 24) but is now present in both the Heath and Norton anthologies. During her six productive decades as a poet, Piatt received mixed, if not hostile reviews for the almost 500 poems that were published in books, periodicals and journals, such as *The Atlantic Monthly*, *Harper's*, *Scribner's*

Monthly, and others (cf. Bennett 2001b: xxviii). If she was praised, it was for her conservative celebration of the genteel style in the poems that "her period wanted" (ibid.: xxix). As Susan Grove Hall has observed, as a young poet, "Piatt expanded the subjective voice into a dramatic persona she constructed into a fragmentary consciousness of illusory psychic, moral, and spiritual identity. The alienation and despair of this persona, however, truthfully represent existence in a corrupt world" (Grove Hall 2006: 242). With time she began to venture away from the "poeticalness" propagated by her time and to disrupt the smooth metrical patterns and rhyming schemes, which were supposed to enable the poems to be sung, with rough rhythms and almost incomprehensible contents. Poets who refused to dwell on feelings and elicit sentiment with the graceful tools of genteel expression were, as Bennett has remarked, "roasted" by their reviewers (2001b: xxxi). When irony began to enter Piatt's tone, the verdict was final. Bennett therefore concludes that if Sarah Piatt was remembered at all as a poet, it was for her genteel products. But it is for her more daring ventures, her complexity of thought and style, that she deserves attention. Thematically, Piatt wrote poems about love and marriage, motherhood and children, religion, the Civil War, slavery and its prohibition, and about her time in Ireland and traveling in Europe. Bennett concludes that "Piatt pushed the limits of Victorian language and the Victorian female persona as hard as she could, staging in her language a multiply fractured persona instead, a persona divided not just between North and South, but between love and anger, dove and tiger, romanticism and cynicism, piety and apostasy, submissiveness and rank rebellion" (ibid.: xl). One of the most excellent examples in which she asserts this persona as a self-reliant and independent, self-determined subject is "The Fancy Ball," in which the speaker refuses any suggestion of a costume to mask her identity for the ball and instead states, at the end, that she will attend the ball as "Myself, I think," (Piatt 2001: 5). These last three words also stress the Cartesian principle of *cogito ergo sum,* thus emphasizing, "I think for myself." Throughout her life, death was a steady companion to Sarah Piatt. Her mother died when she was only eight, and later she would lose three of her own eight children in infancy or childhood.

3. Sigourney's and Piatt's Child Elegies:
Conventional and Subversive Strategies

While poems such as Sigourney's "To a Shred of Linen" or Piatt's "The Palace-Burner" have been frequently anthologized and commented on, a child elegy by each of these poets has been chosen to demonstrate two achievements of this kind of poem: On the one hand, it illustrates how the poet meets the demand for the sentimental within a certain stylistic scope and responds to the expectations of her readers to be consoled in their loss and grief, the religious context usually providing the metaphorical framework. On the other hand, each of these elegies opens up a hermeneutic horizon in which it can be read as a subversive comment on the role of woman and of the female poet in the Victorian age. Elizabeth Petrino argues that the child elegy contains not only a conservative but also a subversive side (cf. 1994: 330), and that "[n]egotiating between the prescribed means of expression and the desire to express themselves freely, nineteenth-century American women poets subtly altered the predominant image of women as pious and self-effacing" (1998: 4). Sigourney and Piatt knew very well what they owed their readers, and they offered what was wanted. But they also cleverly manipulated the terrain laid out for them by patriarchal society, daring to make a dash for a freedom beyond the constraints and restrictions imposed on them as both women and as poets. For these reasons they deserve to be resurrected from oblivion.

The elegy has a long tradition in America. In his book *American Elegy: The Poetry of Mourning from the Puritans to Whitman*, Max Cavitch differentiates between patriotic or nationalist elegies such as those for George Washington and Abraham Lincoln, and poems mourning the death of slaves or the slaughter of Native Americans (for example by William Cullen Bryant), a type of elegy that Sigourney had often produced in addition to her elegies on the death of children. Child elegies were especially popular in the nineteenth century and, for obvious reasons, were often composed by female writers. But contrary to the expectations raised by the emphasis on the sentimental, elegies written for children were not supposed to be merely "effusions," that is, emotional outpourings. On the contrary, they were meant to offer consolation within a religious context, convincing mourners that deceased children had escaped the sinfulness of earthly existence before they could be infected, that they are now angels rejoicing at the side of God, and that one day all family members would be reunited in heaven with those who had left prematurely.

Lydia Sigourney's poem "The Butterfly" is a consolation poem that complies with the readers' expectations, at least on a surface level:

> A BUTTERFLY bask'd on a baby's grave
> Where a lily had chanced to grow:
> "Why art thou here with thy gaudy dye,
> When she of the blue and sparkling eye
> Must sleep in the churchyard low?"
>
> Then it lightly soar'd through the sunny air,
> And spoke from its shining track:
> "I was a worm till I won my wings,
> And she whom thou mourn'st, like a seraph sings:
> Wouldst thou call the bless'd one back?" (1849: 150)

The poem first appeared in *The Ladies' Repository: A Monthly Periodical, Devoted to Literature, Arts, and Religion*, in Cincinnati, in April 1842. In this poem, Sigourney presents us with a dead baby, the mourner, and a butterfly, and she uses the butterfly as a "voice" of consolation. Finch has pointed out that "a typical Sigourney poem allows natural objects to speak in addition to the poetess" (1988: 6); she continues, however, by saying that unlike the typical Romantic poem, the Sigourney poem, especially this one, lacks the presence of a poetic self, a self with which the reader could identify. Although she contends that the views expressed in the poem are the poet's, she states that there is no authoritative subject-author in the poem. But her verdict, that "[t]his approach is consistent with Sigourney's artificiality," is too harsh (ibid.: 7). In a second approach to reading the poem, I will argue that there might be a purpose behind this strategy. On the obvious level, however, the message is clear: The infant, who was female (as revealed in the fourth line of the first stanza), has already been buried when a butterfly happens to visit her grave. The "gaudy" butterfly is juxtaposed with the sad and piteous image of the child, asleep below the earth in her cold grave, her beautiful and sparkling blue eyes no longer capable of seeing the world. The mourner seems to suggest that the butterfly has no right to disturb the melancholy ambiance of the gravesite: "Why art thou here . . .?"

The butterfly is unconcerned with the child's death and the mourning parents; it enjoys basking in the sun shining on the baby's grave. When its presence is questioned, the butterfly answers, gliding into the "sunny air," suggesting a parallel between its own existence and that of the child. As is well known, a butterfly undergoes a transformation. Having gone through larva to pupa (or cocoon) to butterfly, or, in the words of the poem, from "worm" to "wings," it has reached its full development, its destiny. The brightly colored butterfly also signifies joy, which is intensified by its ability to fly. The word "won" in "I won my wings" expresses a sort of triumph in this achievement as it "soars lightly" through the air, thus introducing an easiness to the dark and melancholy atmosphere of the poem that is emphasized by the phonetic change from the dark "o"-sounds (in soaring, worm, and won) to the much lighter "i"-sound in wings. The butterfly, gliding easily through the air, seems to suggest that the baby, too, has transformed from her earthly existence into a heavenly one, that of a seraph. The child is now far better off, singing in heaven. The mourner should not call her back from her "bless'd" existence. The child, too, has won her wings as an angel and deserves to rest in a peaceful celestial existence.

This elegy is thus in accordance with the consolation tradition of its time: There is no reason to mourn because the child has left behind this bleak and threatening life on earth and now sings and rejoices as a blessed creature in heaven. This message is accentuated by the lily growing on her grave, a flower that is used at funerals and at Easter as symbol of both death and of resurrection, at least in the context of the Christian belief system. Moreover, the lily stands for innocence and purity, reflecting the child's state of being immaculate and uncorrupted by life and human influences; she has escaped the tribulations of earthly life and enjoys a blissful existence in heaven. A girl with blue eyes conjures up the image of female beauty, but her blue eyes are also reminiscent of the color of the sky and may therefore suggest that she belonged in heaven, rather than on earth, in the first place. With her eyes closed, she has forever shut out the cruelties and atrocities of life on earth.

In Sigourney's "The Butterfly" a dialogue takes place between the mourner and the butterfly. The frequent use of dialogue in Piatt's poems, however, has been called a stylistic trademark of hers, a technique highly rewarding because it allowed her to introduce a voice other than her own. As Bennett remarks, Piatt uses a dialogue, a question, or a comment from real life as a starting point for her poems, thus anchoring them in time and place (cf. 2001b: xxxv); they serve as vehicles for communicative interaction (cf. ibid.: xxxvii). "Piatt's decision to build poems out of dialogue," however, "is better situated to receive a warm welcome from readers today than it was in her own period if only because it introduces into her poetry the very kind of intellectual challenges that modernism has taught us to value" (ibid.). Frequently the dialogue takes place between mother and child. In what is probably the most famous and most often anthologized poem by Piatt, "The Palace-Burner," the real-life occasion is a newspaper article about a woman who set fire to the palaces in Paris as a way of protesting against starvation, injustice, and oppression. In this poem, a child asks her mother if she, too, would burn palaces, which causes the mother to rethink her actions and question her own complacent attitude of obeying the rules while turning a blind eye on the injustices in the world around her.

Piatt gave birth to eight children and lost three of them. It is no wonder that she became almost obsessed with the death of children and began to explore "the much maligned and mocked 'child elegy' as exemplified by Lydia Sigourney and Henry Wadsworth Longfellow" (Elliott et al. 2009: 993), and challenged "the sentimentalization of the dead infant" (ibid.: 997). As a mother, Piatt knew that children were not always angels and cherubs but could be troublesome as well, and she was acquainted with the suffering caused by the loss of a child. In her poem "The Little Boy I Dreamed About" she ironically comments on the boy who is only perfect because he is dead. In poems such as "Her Blindness in Grief" or "No Help" she "rage[s] against the futility of the conventions of mourning" (Roberts 2011: 173). Piatt identifies with the desolate women whose maternal loss was "God's will," and certainly not that of the grief-stricken mothers. This is most strongly, even blasphemously, expressed in her poem "We Two," which she is said to have written in response to the death of two of her children. She refused to adhere to the sentimental tradition of the child elegy that offered consolation by rhetorically convincing the griever that the still-innocent child had left this world full of sinfulness and corruption, that it had been spared the hardships and sorrows of earthly existence, that it was going to heaven as an angel immaculate and unspoiled by civilization, and is now watching over the mourners and guiding them from the realm above. "Rampant in its self-destructive emotionalism, Piatt's absolute refusal to shed her grief and accept God's will radically differentiates her child elegies from those of her peers; and she was roundly criticized for them" (Bennett 2001b: xlvii); she clearly says 'no' to such glorification of the most painful experience any mother could undergo. In her poem "The Descent of the Angel," turning "descent" into the phonologically identical "dissent," she dismantles the "angel in the house" ideology. In the poem to be discussed here, she expresses not only dissent with this ideology but also the dissent of the angel to being identified as such.

Like Sigourney's elegy, "The Funeral of a Doll" works on more than one level. The first and most obvious is a dialogue between a mother and her daughter, a little girl who expresses her grief and mourning over the "death of her child," that is, the loss of her beloved doll. The mother, who is acquainted with maternal loss and pain, is supposed to console the "mother" of the doll. It is thus a dialogue between a mother and her child and between two "mothers" at the same time. While reading the poem, bear in mind that a "doll" is not only a girl's toy, but that the word is sometimes used to describe a nice little girl or even a sweet and pretty woman.

> They used to call her Little Nell
> In memory of that lovely child
> Whose story each had learned to tell.
> She, too, was slight and still and mild,
> Blue-eyed and sweet; she always smiled.
> And never troubled any one
> Until her pretty life was done.
> And so they tolled a tiny bell,
> That made a wailing fine and faint,
> As fairies ring, and all was well.
> Then she became a waxen saint.
>
> Her funeral it was small and sad.
> Some birds sang bird-hymns in the air.
> The humming-bee seemed hardly glad,
> Spite of the honey everywhere.

The very sunshine seemed to wear
Some thought of death, caught in its gold,
That made it waver wan and cold.
Then, with what broken voice he had,
The Preacher slowly murmured on
(With many warnings to the bad)
The virtues of the Doll now gone.

A paper coffin rosily lined
Had Little Nell. There, drest in white,
With buds about her, she reclined,
A very fair and piteous sight—
Enough to make one sorry, quite.
And, when at last the lid was shut
Under white flowers, I fancied—but
No matter. When I heard the wind
Scatter Spring-rain that night across
The Doll's wee grave, with tears half-blind
One child's heart felt a grievous loss.

"It was a funeral, mamma. Oh,
Poor Little Nell is dead, is dead.
How dark!—and do you hear it blow?
She is afraid." And, as she said
These sobbing words, she laid her head
Between her hands and whispered: "Here
Her bed is made, the precious dear—
She cannot sleep in it, I know.
And there is no one left to wear
Her pretty clothes. *Where did she go?*
———See, this poor ribbon tied her hair!"
(Piatt 1877 [1872]: 131-33; original emphasis)

Piatt gives us three stanzas of narrative on the doll and "her" funeral before she ends with the dialogue in the final fourth and last stanza. The first stanza introduces us to the appearance and character of the doll. Through the very description of the doll (she is, of course, female and white, as suggested by her blue eyes) she seems to come alive. In her book *Poets in the Public Sphere*, Paula Bennett offers an intriguing interpretation of this poem but argues that Piatt "gothizises" the doll, making her come alive even though all along she was a "dead" creature, a lifeless toy (Bennett 2003: 149). However, in any little girl's imagination, her baby doll is not only alive, it is perhaps more alive than many of the living beings that surround her. The girl's doll has a name, a personality, clothes, in short, a "life." And after all, the poem is about the doll's *funeral*, not about her *disposal*.

"They," presumably the children, used to call her "Little Nell," after the well-known and popular character of Charles Dickens's novel *The Old Curiosity Shop* (1840-1841). In the novel, Nell Trent, or Little Nell, as she is called, is a beautiful, virtuous, angelic young girl who, in the course of the plot, sickens, weakens, and dies in her teens. Just like Dickens's protagonist, the doll in this poem was a good creature, slight, still, mild, always smiling, never causing trouble, a pretty and nice little girl. But only through death does this saint-like creature turn into a real "saint," however "waxen." Again, this is part of the message of consolation poetry, trying to convince the bereaved that rather than feeling pity for the poor dead child, he or she should be envied for being an angel in the company of God's cherubs and seraphs.

The ceremony of the funeral is outlined in the second stanza. Obviously, Little Nell has been buried in the garden, with sadly singing birds and dolefully humming bees tuning in to the sorrow of the occasion; and even the sunshine is shivering with cold—an image that conjures up Emily Dickinson's celebrating the Sabbath in the garden, with birds as her choristers. The preacher, too, is overwhelmed with sadness, and it is with a broken voice that he warns the assembled mourners of a sinful life and its consequences—"With many warnings to the bad"—a message often delivered by ministers at funerals of the time. Along with her life, the doll's virtues have also passed away as we discover in the last line of the second stanza, where the "Doll" is mentioned for the first time. Capitalized as it is, the doll becomes an individual. Had the title of the poem not given away the identity of the one whose funeral is being described, the reader might have been tempted to assume that it was indeed the funeral of a little girl who was compared to a doll—with all the beautiful attributes that adorned the toy. In fact, the little girl and the doll are to a certain degree interchangeable, as will be argued later on.

In the third stanza, Little Nell is finally at rest in her coffin, dressed in white and with white flowers adorning the lid of her coffin. The "white woman" of the nineteenth century was a common metaphor for a woman being a blank page, lacking everything—especially an identity of her own—as defined by patriarchal society. With the absence of any color, this is a "piteous sight" indeed. And a storm rises to comment on this dreadful event. Is it in protest? It is a "Spring-rain" at night, scattered by the wind, that reminds us that this was a creature deprived of life in the "spring" of her existence; it is not "fair." And it is at night that the little girl, the doll's "mother," is most distressed, and she begins to moan, "half-blind" with tears. The emphasis here is on the funeral and, unlike "The Butterfly," it excludes the perspective of a redemptive heaven. In other words, the poet refuses to adhere to the rhetoric of the heavenly reward of the prematurely deceased. The doll's "mother" is inconsolable and she cannot accept the fact that her "child" is interred in a cold grave, deprived of the warmth, comfort, and the security of her little bed. The grave is located beneath the earth's soil and is clearly associated with darkness and imprisonment. Children are often afraid of the dark, and this little girl projects her own fear onto her little doll: "She is afraid." She is so afraid that she cannot sleep in that cold bed. The girl knows that her doll wants to be freed from her interment, her imprisonment below the ground. The only thing that is left of her child is her "pretty clothes," which are useless now because the one who wore them is gone. The question that she then raises in despair, "*Where did she go?*," is more a cry of painful loss than it is a query about her doll's whereabouts. This question, which is printed in italics, may well be a rhetorical question. The girl knows full well where her doll has gone: to her final resting place. The grave offers no consolation, it asks for rejection. It is a place where the doll cannot feel comfortable, and with the burial of the doll, everything that she meant to the little girl is gone. The child does not conceive of the doll as being endowed with a soul that may have risen to a happier place called heaven. The body of her doll was all she knew, the visible presence of her beloved companion. How could the soul, invisible by its very nature, be comprehensible to a young child? There are no words of consolation from the mother of the child responding to the exclamation of loss and grief and pain. What does the absence of an answer from her mother signify? That the mother knows very well that there is no consolation for anyone engulfed in the darkness of such deeply felt loss? Does her silence correspond with the protest of nature (expressed through the spring storm) against an inexplicable unfairness and the cruelty of fate? Or is she simply at a loss for words, being too familiar herself with the loss of a child?

On this first level of reading the poem, it seems to be yet another example of a comment on a mother who refuses to support the callous tradition of offering comfort in the face of a tragedy that is beyond consolation. The last line, however: "See, this poor ribbon tied her hair!", seems to 'untie' a different horizon of meaning. With the ribbon left behind, not only the doll's hair, but her whole being may have been 'untied,' freed. As I will argue in a second reading of this poem, the mother might be silent because she is not grieving at all. She does not empathize with her daughter but silently rejoices in the metaphorical death of the "angel in the house." Bennett has argued that this is one of many of Piatt's poems in which she "kills" the "angel in the house." In her poem "Shapes of a Soul" (1867) Piatt had mocked the male belief in woman's angelhood, which prevents him from recognizing the person she really is. In order to trace this act of 'murder,' we must return back to the very beginning of the poem.

While the first stanza does introduce the doll, her appearance, and her character, with a second glance we realize that the doll does not represent a unique personality but rather a type, the type of girl that is embodied by Little Nell, "Whose story each had learned to tell." The doll was named after this girl "in memory" of her; in other words, the "story" is meant to be not only remembered but to be kept alive and to be perpetuated. What story? The story of the Victorian woman as an angel, Coventry Patmore's "angel in the house," the story of woman as a pretty doll, a child who could be nothing but "lovely," "slight, still and mild," her virtuous character frozen in her eternal smile, her right to exist transformed into her kindness of never troubling anyone. Indeed, this type of woman was a "waxen saint" and much less alive than in our first reading of the poem. This doll is a puppet. As a child's toy, it is a lifeless object, and so was woman when defined as the "angel in the house." The mother's comment on this "fair and piteous sight" in the penultimate line of the second stanza is laden with irony: "enough to make one sorry, quite."

But this image of woman has now been buried. And thus the funeral turns into a ceremony of triumph, because it is "the virtues of the doll" that have been buried, the "virtues" imposed on woman by patriarchal society. The doll recumbent in her coffin is presented as the white woman, which in the nineteenth century signified the absence of an identity of her own. This white existence has now been sealed and put away. It is actually in the third stanza, after the lid of the coffin has been shut, that the mother has a thought: "I fancied—," but she refuses to verbalize that which has come to her mind by dismissing it as "but / No matter," seemingly suggesting that it is of no importance. Since Piatt elliptically separates the "but" from "No matter," the emphasis lies on "matter," or rather, on "No matter." If what she fancied is not of matter—not in the sense of not mattering but in the sense of matter standing for the physical, the "body" of the doll—then her fancy was about something spiritual; the death of an icon, perhaps? "Hurray!" she may be thinking; "We have finally buried the angel!" We may also read "Under white flowers" (which again is separated from the previous line) that it is not the lid of the coffin that was shut "under the flowers," but that she, the mother, fancied whatever thought she had about the whiteness of the flowers, suggesting that for a brief glimpse of a moment she looked under, or more deeply into, the meaning of those white flowers. With the doll buried, those flowers may now begin to bloom, their whiteness turning into colors. The child being "half-blind" with tears may imply that the child is as yet incapable of seeing, that is, understanding, what the mother understands: that the doll, representing the "angel in the house," was indeed "dead" in every sense of the word, and may become truly alive now that she has been buried. We are talking here of a different kind of promise of resurrection in the (silent) vow of a mother who knows that there is no reason to mourn the death of this creature. Rather, she and her daughter should rejoice in her burial. The doll, and her virtues, are gone. What is left is the "ribbon," the shackle, which has nothing left to tie. A tie can also be, according to the Merriam Webster dictionary, "a responsibility that limits a person's freedom to do other things." That the angel has finally escaped its confinement is, moreover, underlined by Piatt's use of meter. Throughout the whole poem, Piatt makes use of iambic tetrameter—her favorite metrical pattern. Her strict adherence to this pattern seems to enmesh and entangle the angel—the doll—in the inescapable web of conventions and restrictions. It is in the very last line of the poem that this pattern is interrupted: The long dash at the beginning of this line must be recognized for its significance. The use of dashes was one of Piatt's idiosyncrasies, and she "typically complicates formulaic rhymes and rhythms by loading her lines with caesuras, dashes, and parentheses" (Giordano 2006: 30). Here the dash forces the first spoken word to initiate a trochaic foot: "See," and the word "see" semantically invites the reader to "understand" that the ribbon is left with nothing to tie. The dash then might invite the reader to take a deep breath and utter a sign of relief, a sigh that freedom has been achieved. "The pretty life" of the angel is "done." Viewed in this light, the seventh line of the first stanza makes perfect sense. It is rather harsh to say that a life "is done," but if it pronounces the death sentence of the "angel in the house" as an imposition that is finally overcome, it perfectly fits. One might even go so far as to argue that this is a didactic poem between mother and daughter: The daughter needs to grow up before she can understand why her mother does not mourn the death of "Doll" and instead celebrates the burial of an icon in which woman was trapped, telling and living her story over and over again. Yet because this burial is of something that was pronounced dead from the very first moment of its existence, her burial is actually the beginning of her life, her resurrection from "the dead" in a metaphorical sense.

Having read Piatt's "Funeral of a Doll" as a celebration of the annihilation of the icon of the angel in the house, we may go back to Sigourney's butterfly poem and venture a more daring reading there as well. Contrary to Finch, who bemoans the lack of a poetic self in this poem, I would like to argue that the poet speaks 'as' the butterfly, since the only time we come across an explicit lyrical I is when the butterfly speaks in the second stanza: "I was a worm till I won my wings." The poet may be describing her own oppressed state of being in the first stanza, and her liberation in the second. Apart from the symbolical meanings described above, the butterfly also stands for creativity. This lyrical I proudly announces that it was a "worm" before it "won its wings." Worms, of course, conjure up death and the earth in which the corpse is buried, but also bring to mind a lowly creature that is often stepped on. And when used to refer to a human being, it describes a pitiable, weak, contemptible, even despicable person. A worm creeps and writhes just like a human being who is oppressed, forced to accept restrictions and conventions; it certainly never rises above ground level. Moreover, the worm semantically matches the word "low" in the first stanza, which, apart from meaning "dead and buried," also describes a humble person of inferior and insignificant status or character, lacking liveliness. "I was a worm" could then describe the state of being of the butterfly in the first stanza: It was barely alive, crawling unnoticed on—or even below—the ground. The "grave" of the first stanza then, just like in Piatt's poem, signifies the female poet's oppression, her confinement, darkness, coldness, the absence of color, the absence of joy, and even the absence of life. Her "blue and sparkling eye" is closed, and is therefore useless since it is forced to sleep: "must sleep." While blue eyes are considered a typical mark of beauty, the color blue is also associated with feeling downhearted and depressed, miserable and dispirited. This eye was sparkling—alive and shining with animation—until it was forced closed. Sleep is said to resemble death, and read in this context, it conjures up a state of total passiveness and inactivity, unawareness, even unconsciousness, making it impossible to move or respond. The lily that chanced to grow on this grave may suggest that there is potential for growth and life lurking within this gravesite and in the slumbering creature. It is interesting that the lily is not attributed a color; a white lily typically adorns the grave of a dead child, but this lily may be red or yellow, with the ability to bloom. And as an Easter flower, it promises resurrection. In the first stanza, the gaudily-colored butterfly initially contrasts with the slumbering creature below ground. It takes great pleasure in basking in the sun shining on the child's grave, which seems an insult to the fact that an innocent child has died. However, the butterfly's pleasure may come from waking up the slumbering child, lifting her above the ground. In the second stanza the butterfly has risen from sleep and is gliding through the air, easily, weightlessly, and effortlessly, as the verb "soaring" implies. Moreover, to soar is to rise powerfully, thus preparing for the self-assertive statement of the lyrical I that has powerfully risen above the ground. One might argue that the butterfly, which has spread its wings and is soaring through the air, stands for the super-ego of the poet whose subconscious voice raises the question: Would you want to return to the "bless'd" state of being a sleeping worm underneath the earth? The word "bless'd" is highly ambivalent. In the religious context, of course, it means holy, consecrated, and worthy of respect. One could therefore argue that if the woman (or the woman poet) behaved according to the norms of society—that is, if she crawled like a worm on the ground, unconscious of the potential lurking within her, content with her eyes closed—she deserved to be respected. What is interesting, however, is that "blessed" can also be used euphemistically for "damned," a figurative meaning that would aptly describe the state of being in the first stanza. The question that ends the poem refuses to offer an explicit answer, but the answer is clear nevertheless: The butterfly, the creative and self-assertive I, has left the earth and its ties behind and is speaking from its "shining track." Since a track is a mark, and since this track is shining, it obviously excels in quality. The poem itself may thus be read as such a shining track. Through the end rhyme, "wings" and "sings" are connected in the second stanza: The poet may sing, but the one who has emerged with wings is free to fly and leave the shining tracks. The poet does not want to sing like a seraph, predictably sweet and angelic, and if we read the question raised at the very end of the poem as uttered by the seraph (since it follows a colon), we may conclude that not even the seraph would want to go back to the blessed/damned state of being of the first stanza. Likewise, the word "back" at the very end of the poem contrasts with "track" in the second line: Going back would annihilate the butterfly's shining track that can be laid out up in the air. In the first stanza, the rhyming pairs work similarly. The sleeping eye is not capable of seeing the "gaudy dye" of the butterfly, but its color suggests a readiness for color. Simultaneously, the word "dye" is a phonetic reminder of "to die," and thus creates a juxtaposition of sight and death. The rhyming pair of "grow" and "low" also evokes an image of opposites: "grow" signifies a stretching and reaching into the air, while "low" emphasizes the earth. It is the final word of the first line of each stanza—"grave" and "air"—that does not rhyme with another word. From grave to air signifies the transition, even transformation, from the state of passivity to the state of freedom: from passivity to liveliness, from blindness to understanding, from sleep to creativity, from confinement to freedom, from death to life. The lily's promise of resurrection from the dead has come true: the "worm" has transformed into a "butterfly." Even the rhyme scheme of the poem supports this reading. In both stanzas the patterns are identical: a-b-c-c-b. While lines two through five (b-c-c-b) suggest inescapability, clasping the "worm" in their grip, the non-rhyming words in the first line of both stanzas ("grave" and "air") step out of this pattern and suggest that the worm will escape once it has "won its wings."

As has been illustrated, both poems can be read on a deeper level than that of the traditional elegy with its sentimental rhetoric of consolation. Each offers consolation in an additional sense, promising "resurrection from the dead" to the (female) poet and to woman, discarding the "virtues" imposed on both.

4. Conclusion: The Survival of Nineteenth-Century Female Verse

Even if Piatt's irony and her subtle use of dialogue anticipate the Modernist era, with the beginning of the twentieth century, Sigourney, Piatt, and other female poets of the previous century disappeared from the literary map, dismissed as unappealing both in regard to form and (sentimental) subject matter; the Modernist agenda had no space for such "scribbling" women. In the 1950s, however, with the blooming of the Confessional mode, a new obsession with death took center stage with female poets such as Sylvia Plath and Anne Sexton and may conjure up memories of the nineteenth-century celebration of the elegy. But while Plath perfects "the art of dying" as art for art's (and death's) sake, in the most literal sense of the phrase, nineteenth-century poets struggled with the reality of death, both in life and in their verse, in a different sense. Their poems on death served as a means of survival. Poems on this topic sold well, if they offered what the readers expected, and in return made their authors popular. But even though their metaphors were, necessarily, derived from the sphere of home and hearth, the female poets of the nineteenth century managed to transcend the glorious and, in particular, the inglorious aspects of this sphere by weaving statements of self-reflexivity into their masked verse of conventionalism. Those messages were, perhaps, not recognized, or even meant to be understood, by their contemporary readers, but have left behind a legacy worth "unearthing." According to Dorothy Z. Baker, "the self-reflexive poetry of Lydia Sigourney and Emily Dickinson [and Sarah Piatt] is expressive of the self-conscious and often conflicted response of the nineteenth-century woman to her double role as artist and 'angel in the home,' especially because these authors represent anomalies to both traditions" (Baker 1997: 82). Both Sigourney and Piatt managed to redefine their position of woman and of poet beyond the horizon laid out for them, and have therefore survived their central theme—death—by means of a "resurrection" that is consoling in more than sentimental terms.

Bibliography

Selected Primary Literature

Bennett, Paula Bernat (ed.). 2001a. *Palace-Burner: The Selected Poetry of Sarah Piatt*. Urbana and Chicago: U of Illinois P.
Piatt, Sarah Morgan Bryan. 1871. *A Woman's Poems*. Boston: James R. Osgood.
——. 1877. *That New World, & Other Poems*. Boston: James R. Osgood.
——. 1877 [1872]. "The Funeral of a Doll." In: *Poems in Company with Children*. Boston: D. Lothrop and Company. 131-33.
——. 1879. *Dramatic Persons and Moods, With Other New Poems*. Boston: Houghton, Osgood.
——. 1887. *Child's-World Ballads*. Cincinatti: Robert Clarke.
——. 1893. *An Enchanted Castle, and Other Poems: Pictures, Portraits and People in Ireland*. London: Longman's Green.
——. 1894. *Complete Poems*. 2 vols. London: Longman's Green.
——. 1906. *A Gift of Tears*. Cincinnatti: Western Literary.
——. 2001 [1866]. "The Fancy Ball." In: Bennett 2001a. 4-5.
Sigourney, Lydia Huntley. 1815. *Moral Pieces, in Prose and Verse*. Hartford: Sheldon and Godwin.
——. 1822. *Traits of the Aborigines: A Poem*. Cambridge: Cambridge UP.
——. 1835. *Zinzendorff; and Other Poems*. New York: Leavitt, Lord & Company.
——. 1841a. *Pocahontas and Other Poems*. London and New York: Harper & Brothers.
——. 1841b. *Poems, Religious and Elegiac*. London: R. Tyas.
——. 1849. "The Butterfly." In: *Illustrated Poems*. Philadelphia: Carey and Hart. 150.
——. 1852. *Voices of Home; or Poems for the Sea*. Hartford: P. Brockett.

Selected Secondary Literature

Baker, Dorothy Z. 1997. "Ars Poetica/Ars Domestica: The Self-Reflexive Poetry of Lydia Sigourney and Emily Dickinson." In: Dorothy Z. Baker (ed.), *Poetics in the Poem: Critical Essays on American Self-Reflexive Poetry*. New York: Peter Lang. 69-89.
    Baker illustrates how the use of the domestic icon allows the nineteenth-century female poet to convey her historical, spiritual, and aesthetic heritage.

Bennett, Paula Bernat. 2001b. "Introduction." In: Bennett 2001a. xxiii-lviii.
    This is an excellent introduction to Piatt and her development from a genteel to a subversive and ironical poet, with detailed analyses of individual poems.

Finch, Annie. 1988. "The Sentimental Poetess in the World: Metaphor and Subjectivity in Lydia Sigourney's Nature Poetry." In: *Legacy: A Journal of American Women Writers* 5.2: 3-18.
    The author discusses "sentimental poetry" as a contradiction in terms because of the absence of a poetic self.

Giordano, Matthew. 2006. "'A Lesson From' the Magazines: Sarah Piatt and the Postbellum Periodical Poet." In: *American Periodicals: A Journal of History, Criticism, and Bibliography* 16.1: 23-51.
    Giordano argues that the nineteenth-century periodical culture reflects the aesthetics of Piatt and other postbellum poets.

McCartin Wearn, Mary. 2006. "Subjection and Subversion in Sarah Piatt's Maternal Politics." In: *Legacy: A Journal of American Women Writers* 23.2: 163-77.
    In her analysis of Piatt's poems the author argues that Piatt protests against the 19th-century ideology of motherhood.

Roberts, Jess. 2011. "Sarah Piatt's Grammar of Convention and the Conditions of Authorship." In: Larson 2011a. 172-92.
Roberts closely analyzes Piatt's canny understanding of language and argues that she only seemingly adheres to conventions but critiques them in subtle and sophisticated ways.

Sigourney, Lydia Huntley. 1866. *Letters of Life.* New York: D. Appleton & Co.
The volume contains Sigourney's posthumously published autobiography.

Teed, Melissa Ladd. 2004. "A Passion for Distinction: Lydia Huntley Sigourney and the Creation of a Literary Reputation." In: *New England Quarterly* 77.1: 51-69.
Analyzes Sigourney's reputation against the background of the nineteenth-century literary market, including both critical voices and voices in praise of her.

Further References

Bennett, Paula Bernat. 2003. *Poets in the Public Sphere: The Emancipatory Project of American Women's Poetry, 1800-1900.* Princeton: Princeton UP.

——. 2007. "Was Sigourney a Poetess? The Aesthetics of Victorian Plenitude in Lydia Sigourney's Poetry." In: *Comparative American Studies* 5.3: 265-89.

——. 1995. "'The Descent of the Angel': Interrogating Domestic Ideology in American Women's Poetry, 1858-1890." In: *American Literary History* 7.4: 591-610.

—— and Mary G. De Jong (eds.). 2013. *Sentimentalism in Nineteenth-Century America: Literary and Cultural Practices.* Madison, NJ: Farleigh.

Cavitch, Max. 2007. *American Elegy: The Poetry of Mourning from the Puritans to Whitman.* Minneapolis: U of Minnesota P.

Dickinson, Emily. 1960. "Publication – is the Auction." In: Thomas H. Johnson (ed.), *The Complete Poems of Emily Dickinson.* Boston et al.: Little, Brown and Co. 348-9.

Elliott, Clare, Anne-Marie Ford and Theresa Saxon. 2009. "American Literature to 1900." In: *The Year's Work in English Studies* 88.1: 990-1009.

Grove Hall, Susan. 2006. "From Voice to Persona: Amelia Welby's Lyric Tradition in Sarah M. B. Piatt's Early Poetry." In: *Tulsa Studies in Women's Literature* 25.2: 223-46.

Haight, Gordon S. 1930. *Mrs. Sigourney: The Sweet Singer of Hartford.* New Haven: Yale UP.

Jackson, Virginia and Yopie Prins. 1999. "Lyric Studies." In: *Victorian Literature and Culture* 27.2: 521-30.

Larson, Kerry (ed.). 2011a. *The Cambridge Companion to Nineteenth-Century American Poetry.* Cambridge: Cambridge UP.

——. 2011b. "Introduction." In: Larson 2011a. 1-11.

Lawlor, Clark. 2009. "Liberation and Consumption: Disease, Imperialism, and the Conversion of the Heathen in Hemans, Sigourney and Stowe." In: Tristanne Connolly and Steve Clark (eds.), *Liberating Medicine, 1720-1835.* London: Pickering & Chatto. 11-26.

Okker, Patricia. 1993. "Sarah Josepha Hale, Lydia Sigourney, and the Poetic Tradition in Two Nineteenth-Century Women's Magazines." In: *American Periodicals: A Journal of History, Criticism, and Bibliography*: 32-42.

Petrino, Elizabeth A. 1998. *Emily Dickinson and Her Contemporaries: Women's Verse in America 1820-1885.* Hanover: UP of New England.

——. 1994. "'Feet so Precious Charged': Dickinson, Sigourney, and the Child Elegy." In: *Tulsa Studies in Women's Literature* 13.2: 317-38.

Stevens, Laura M. 2006. "'Women Didn't Really Write Back Then': From the Editor." In: *Tulsa Studies in Women's Literature* 25.2: 209-22.

Watts, Emily Stipes. 1977. *The Poetry of American Women from 1632 to 1945.* Austin and London: U of Texas P.

10.

Modern Romantics

Emily Dickinson's "I Like to See It Lap the Miles" and
Walt Whitman's "To a Locomotive in Winter"

Tim Lanzendörfer

1. Introduction: Poetic Themes and Formal Innovation in Whitman and Dickinson

The poetry of Emily Dickinson and Walt Whitman can be situated at the end of one literary development and at the beginning of another. On the one side, Dickinson and Whitman (in different ways) expand on the particularly American branch of Romantic thought that is Transcendentalism. Here, Whitman's conception of poetry and himself as a poet strongly resembles Ralph Waldo Emerson's belief that the poet is "representative of man" (1982: 448; cf. Allen 1975: 48), and Dickinson has been read as reacting and complicating Emerson's conceptions of the self (cf. Diehl 1981: 161-82). On the other side, their writings coincide with the beginning of great political and social transformations and technological developments in America. What might be said to make them 'modern' is their Romantic reaction to the shifting social forces and technological developments, their awareness of and engagement with the changes that were happening all around them.

Although both Dickinson and Whitman reacted to the same transformations and were influenced by the Romantic tradition, they are frequently read as deeply oppositional figures. Whitman lived a public life in large cities, a seeker of recognition and fame; Dickinson lived famously secluded in her parents' house in Amherst. These biographical facts seem to be traceable directly in their poetry: Whitman's poetry is certainly far more public-spirited than Dickinson's, more interested in and at home in the world; and Dickinson's writings can seem hermetic and wildly idiosyncratic. But to read their poetry based on their biographies alone is to obscure the fact that there was much that they shared. What connects Dickinson and Whitman despite their many fundamental differences are their experimental poetics, their shared recognition that theirs was the "time to do certain bold things in poetry" (Keller 1979: 266). Both reacted to cultural developments, yet they did so in different ways: Whitman celebrated progress and envisioned America's future; Dickinson was progress's ironic commentator. At heart, as Agnieszka Salska points out, "[d]espite their ostensibly opposing positions as 'public' and 'private' poets, Whitman and Dickinson respond fundamentally to the same philosophical and aesthetic problems" (1985: 189), but their poetic answers to these problems are quite different.

For Dickinson and Whitman both, poetry was a means to investigate questions about the self (one of the issues inherited from the Transcendentalists), and both were concerned with the relationship between society and poetry, between self and nature, and with the role of the self in society. Among the many possible examples for the centrality of the self to Whitman's poetry is the opening line of the first poem in Whitman's major work *Leaves of Grass*, the long

"Song of Myself," which seems clear about its agenda: "I celebrate myself" (1982 [1855]: 27, l. 1). For Whitman, however, this singing of himself was always also the singing of a type, of a representative figure. He sums up his poetic efforts in "One's-Self I Sing" in the final, 1892 version of *Leaves of Grass*: "One's-self I sing, a simple separate person / Yet utter the word Democratic, the word En-masse / . . . The Modern Man I sing" (1982 [1891-92]: 165, ll. 1-2, 8). Shira Wolosky has noted that "Whitman's 'I' stands not only for Whitman as an individual or even as a poet, but for the country as a personified figure" (2004: 364). In Whitman's poetry, the individual and the communal are always linked; the utopian potential of the nation is always in the foreground at the same time that he poeticizes the individual. Consequently, his major work, the consistently revised and expanded *Leaves of Grass*, was all-encompassing, and its central image, the eponymous leaves of grass, mirrored the way the communal—the "grass"—is always constituted by and indeed inseparable from the individual "leaves."

For Whitman, this vision of a simultaneity of individual and communal experience translated into a celebration of the United States, and he notes in the prose preface to the first edition of *Leaves of Grass* that "[t]he United States themselves are essentially the greatest poem" (1982 [1855]: 5). His concern with the political events in the United States, as well as its technical and social development, is powerfully evident throughout his oeuvre, and is one of the major differences between Whitman and some of his Romantic contemporaries. Whereas poets such as Longfellow remained rooted in the European tradition, Whitman was determined to find poetry in America: "As if it were necessary to trot back generation after generation to the eastern records" (ibid.: 6). America would be the source of a "new breed of poets . . . interpreters of men and women and of all events and things . . . They shall arise in America and be responded to from the remainder of the earth" (ibid.: 25). Here, too, is one of his greatest connections to Transcendentalism: if Emerson called for an autochthonous American poetry, Whitman was determined to deliver it.

Dickinson and Whitman both explored the question of how poetry could come to terms with the self. Their poetry shared a similar range of themes, responding to and commenting on the events of their times and investigating more timeless subjects as well; there is, therefore, ample reason to read them together as modern Romantic poets. Even as they shared common thematic interests and had a common underlying concern with the investigation of the self, the poetic forms in which they expressed their stances toward these questions did not coincide. In fact, Whitman and Dickinson offered radically different analyses for how a poet could respond to the world. In doing so, both also developed strikingly new poetic forms: Whitman's expansive free verse, and Dickinson's tight, dense, and intensely figural poetry.

Whitman's use of free verse was his major innovation, a poetic form he "all but invented" (Killingsworth 2007: 24). Free verse eschewed the conventions of contemporary poetry: it lacked a regular meter, relying on natural speech rhythms instead, and it forewent rhyme. Perhaps most notably, it allowed Whitman to write extremely long lines. The free verse form was ideally suited, as Whitman believed, to speak lyrically about United States democracy, and was capable of expressing the vast and multifaceted experience of America as he saw it. The line was one of the major stylistic choices here: its expansiveness was representative of America's own. Betsy Erkkila claims that "for Whitman the sources of language were in democratic culture" itself (1989: 85), and poetry conversely became a repository of that culture. Rhymeless, meterless, and modeled very much on the diction of everyday language, most of Whitman's poetry appears to roam freely from topic to topic, its formal freedom echoing the perceived political and social freedom of the United States.

If the general formal structure of Whitman's poetry was (with very few exceptions) free verse, this freedom did not mean a lack of structure. Whitman's poems abound in description, in the repetition of words, lines, and sounds, in catalogues and lists, and—as representations of an unruly society—they rather resist unification: instead of permitting the reader to recognize them as parts of a coherent whole, Whitman's poetry points out the incoherence of a democratic society as its greatest strength. For him, the future potential of the United States, socially and politically, and its radically "new breed of poets," necessarily went hand in hand with the development of new poetic forms, including the resistance to regularizing rhyme and meter. In this sense, Whitman's free verse expressed formally what the poems also expressed thematically, and what he perceived as his role as America's unofficial laureate: his "poetic revolution"—that is, the tremendous innovation which his development and particular use of free verse constituted—"is closely connected to other revolutions, in technology, in science, in industry, in communications" (Wolosky 2004: 384).

Whitman's poetical themes were as broad as the American vista that unfolded before him. He wrote affirmatively about his own body and sexuality, but his poems also discussed the Civil War, the wonders of industrialization and the promise of urbanity, westward expansion, and everyday life. Whitman preferred to see the positive, community-building aspects of modern society, a cheerful view that often sat in stark contrast with the "growing impoverishment in American cities" (Erkkila 1989: 256). In "Crossing Brooklyn Ferry," the poet sees the urban masses as a "simple, compact, well-join'd scheme, myself disintegrated, every one disintegrated yet part of the scheme" (1982 [1891-92]: 308, l. 5); in "Mannahatta," Manhattan is celebrated for its "[n]umberless crowded streets, high growths of iron, slender, strong, light, splendidly uprising toward clear skies" (ibid.: 585, l. 7), inhabited by a "million people—manners free and superb—open voices—hospitality—the most courageous and friendly young men" (ibid.: l. 18). Although Whitman, a former journalist, was well aware of the difficult living conditions experienced in urban slums, as a poet he preferred to see these problems as perhaps unfortunate now, but likely to be corrected. What he was after was not a poetic description of America as it is, but rather the promise of a future America, a future in which grand political subjects play a more decisive role than social problems. What ultimately united his concerns was the way each contributed to Whitman's "cumulative" (Salska 1985: 45) self, a poetic persona that was capable of holding the different thematic concerns Whitman's poetry evinces together around one center (cf. Waskow 1966: 3).

The problem of identifying a coherent theme is much greater in Emily Dickinson's poetry. It explores, often with fine irony, such very personal subjects as death and grief, but also broader themes such as the significance of nature for the imagination, the experience of the divine, and the role of poetry in elucidating all of the above—a spectrum of topics which she could discover around herself, or even within herself. David Porter suggests that in "the unruly body of her poetry there may be found a theme to fulfill every critic's disposition" (1998: 183), yet uniting most of her poetry is a concern for "individual consciousness" (ibid.: 194). Dickinson did not develop a poetic vision that was as broadly concerned with society as Whitman's. Perhaps she removed herself from society, as Judith Farr maintains, in order to be "free to write poetry" (1992: 31), but certainly her seclusion was coincident with the focus on interiority with which she investigated the self. As opposed to Whitman, Dickinson did not desire to foreground the lyrical potential of the United States as a society; on the contrary, her vision of poetry was to find the new precisely in interiority, in self-reflection:

> Soto! Explore thyself!
> Therein thyself shalt find
> The "Undiscovered Continent"—
> No Settler had the Mind (1999 [1864]: 359, #814)

The speaker's argument echoes throughout Dickinson's work: genuine discoveries can be made not in expeditions into the heart of uncharted territory, such as Hernando de Soto's through the American southeast, but through investigations into one's own "Mind."

Despite this poetic emphasis on individual consciousness, however, it would be a mistake to assume that Dickinson's physical seclusion at Amherst meant that she was not attuned to the social changes occurring around her (see St. Armand 1984). Dickinson's poetry was engaged with a number of societal issues including the role of women, the technological progress of the United States, westward expansion, and the Civil War (see Wolosky 2004). Perhaps most notably, Dickinson was deeply engaged with the religious developments of her time, schooled as she was at Trinitarian Amherst Academy and Mount Holyoke Seminary, having a Puritan family background, and being a witness to the various religious revivals of the 1840s. Her poetry, however, reflects an ironic distance from religious faith; maybe she "refused faith" (Wolff 1986: 104), but certainly she remained doubtful about many aspects of her family's Congregationalism in particular and religious beliefs in general. Yet her criticism was largely playful, acknowledging her doubt rather than resolutely affirming a stance. Religion was, as Linda Freedman has recently argued, a "source of poetic enrichment" (2011: 2) and a major thematic concern. The final stanza of "The Brain is wider than the Sky," for example, suggests a comparison between the psychological individual—and perhaps poetry as one of the brain's products (see Sielke 2008)—and the divine:

> The Brain is just the weight of God—
> For—Heft them—Pound for Pound—
> And they will differ—if they do—
> As Syllable from Sound— (1999 [1863]: 269, #598, ll. 9-12)

One of the most important themes for Dickinson was the writing of poetry itself. For Dickinson, poetry was a realm of literary opportunity: "I dwell in Possibility— / A fairer House than Prose" (1999 [1862]: 215, #466, ll. 1-2). Poetry here is not just a tool of expression for Dickinson; it is a place of habitation, at once exclusionary and delimited (with "Chambers as the Cedars— / Impregnable of eye—", ll. 5-6), and yet open to the "Sky" and "the fairest" guests (ll. 8-9). Poetry permitted Dickinson to explore the entirety of existence, and many of the themes she picked up otherwise became conflated with the discussion of poetry's reach. "I reckon—when I count at all— / First—Poets—Then the Sun—" (1999 [1863]: 242, #533, ll. 1-2), as she had it elsewhere, "Then Summer—then the Heaven of God / And then—the List is done" (ll. 3-4). Dickinson privileges the experience of nature—the sun and summer—over God's heaven and the ineffable afterlife. But more importantly the poem suggests that the poet "seems / To Comprehend the Whole" (ll. 5-6)—not just everything else she has listed, but the whole of life itself.

For Whitman, the free verse form was representative of the promises of democracy; for Dickinson, a similar relationship between poetic form and poetic message existed. David Porter points out that in Dickinson's poetry the use of vernacular language—exhibited, for example in word choice and in what Porter calls a "talking" (1981: 225) poetical speech—encounters great formal innovativeness, combining into "revolutionary" (ibid.: 226) poetry. This poetry "defied all [contemporary] poetic rules" (Martin 2007: 41): while it did not abandon rhyme and meter, it played with both, producing slant rhymes and irregular scansion. Where Whitman's poetry was often almost epic in scope, Dickinson's poetic expression is tightly reined in. But in this brevity, she was ceaselessly innovative. She eschewed regular capitalization and punctuation, often using dashes of varying lengths instead of commas (which may also have had different meanings: whole monographs have been written on the dash in Dickinson; see Crumbley 1997). Her syntax is often convoluted and irregular, using verbs and adjectives in the place of nouns. But like Whitman's free verse, Dickinson's poetic language fixes formally the relationship between a complex and disorderly world—an outside world—and the representation of that world in poetry (cf. Budick 1985: 14). Her poetics are summed up in her exhortation to "Tell all the truth but tell it slant / Success in Circuit lies" (Dickinson 1999 [1872]: 494, #1263, ll. 1-2). Her densely figural language obscures her revelations as a safeguard for an audience too unprepared to grasp the full truth of existence—it must "dazzle gradually / Or every man be blind—" (ll. 7-8). Dickinson's often complicated and ambiguous imagery must be read against this recognition that poetry's truth must be cushioned for an unprepared readership.

2. Emily Dickinson's Poetics of Irony: "I Like to See It Lap the Miles"

To juxtapose the two poems this chapter will discuss, Whitman's "To a Locomotive in Winter" (1982 [1876, 1881]: 583) and Dickinson's "I Like to See It Lap the Miles" (1999 [1862]: 176, #383), is already to interpret them: they are read together here on the assumption that they have the same subject, a locomotive, which is quite obvious in Whitman, but rather well concealed in Dickinson. In Dickinson's opening line "I like to see it lap the Miles—" we already find reflected much that is important about her poetry in general. Opening on "I," the poem foregrounds the personal, subjective view characteristic of almost all of her writing. But the poem then immediately veers off into a description of the things that the speaker likes to see "it" do—without clearly specifying who or what "it" is. Notably, Dickinson's speaker never explicitly names her object. Indeed, it may justly be asked why we should take this object to be a train, when a train is never explicitly mentioned, and we might with as much justification say that the poem reflects upon the speaker's experience of a free-roaming horse. Dickinson's notion of poetry as telling everything "slant" comes through here: throughout the poem, the speaker conflates train and horse, horse and train, using words that might as easily refer to one as to the other, and, crucially, never settling easily into a simple reading of one as metaphor for the other.

Why then, do critics read the poem as speaking about trains, rather than horses? While Dickinson did not give her poems titles, some early editors, following poetic convention, have done so, giving this poem the title "The Railway Train" (cf. Franklin 1998: 409). As we will see, it makes good sense to read the poem as being ultimately about a train: for one thing, Dickinson plays off the already well-established motif of the train as an 'iron horse.' This privileges a reading of the train as tenor of the metaphor to which the horse is vehicle. So, of course, does the context of Dickinson's poem. Riding through dust clouds and barren wastes, galloping hard on the plains of the West, the advent of the steam locomotive as the primary mode of American transportation had signally transformed the United States. For this reason too, Dickinson's poem was more likely to comment on the new technology of the train rather than on horses. The issue, however, is more complicated than that: nothing in the poem requires us to read it as commenting metaphorically on a train; we could insist on an interpretation that sees even the less oblique references to the railroad as metaphors for horses.

From the first line on, the speaker treats her object as though it is alive: it laps, it licks, it feeds. The first hint we get that "it" might be a train is in line 3: it stops "to feed itself at Tanks—" as a train would fill up its water from tank towers at stations. But then the poem returns to describing its object's movements: it steps "Around a Pile of Mountains" (l. 5), peers into shanties, pares a quarry, crawls along, and finally chases "itself down Hill—" (l. 13). The speaker's words make the train-horse appear almost exuberant, dashing to and fro in ceaseless activity. At the same time, however, the word choice would be puzzling if it referred only to a horse's movements: the dimensions seem off in the "Pile of Mountains," while the two lines "And then a Quarry pare / To fit it's sides" (ll. 8-9) suggests the cut made for the passage of a railroad through a mountain—also giving a meaningful reading to the crawling "between" (l. 10) of the next line.

In the second stanza, the "Shanties—by the sides of Roads—" (l. 7) suggest railroads as much as normal roads; in the third, the "horrid—hooting stanza" (l. 12) of complaints sounds more like a train's whistle than a horse, yet the fourth stanza's first line contains "neigh" (l. 14)—something which we are more likely to read as the sound made by a horse. This line is more complex, however: it reads, in full, "And neigh like Boanerges—" an oddly intrusive biblical reference that echoes the generally critical view of the previous lines, as well as highlighting Dickinson's religious learning and willingness to ironize it. Boanerges, "sons of thunder" or perhaps "windbags," was the nickname given to James and John by Jesus for their vociferous demands for divine punishment of Jesus's critics, punishment which they would be unwilling to mete out by themselves. The train here appears overly noisy and ineffectual, and its loud "complaining" (l. 11) as it negotiates the difficult parts of the railroad tracks must seem unnecessary because the complaints have no effect. But besides this purely formal analysis of the metaphor, the mere fact that the speaker deems the biblical reference a useful comparison indicates the remarkable status the train has attained, adding religious overtones to its sheer power to fit the landscape to its demands.

The final stanza's last three lines reaffirm this reading of the train's latent power, possibly with the same religious undercurrent. "Then—prompter than a Star" (l. 15) the speaker sees it "Stop—docile and omnipotent / At it's own stable door—" (ll. 16-7). The stable door invokes again the idea of the horse, and hints at the engine shed in which a locomotive would be 'stabled,' or the train station where it would stop. But at the same time, the train goes beyond nature: it is "prompter" than a star and, most tellingly, "docile and omnipotent." The speaker here takes us back to the religious reference of the first line of the stanza, but expands it: the train comes to appear almost as a break with nature and religion both, and as much a menace as a promise. Helen Vendler suggests that the "Star" might even be the Christmas Star, which, like the train, stops at a stable (cf. 2010: 178). God-like, it is "omnipotent," but unlike Him, it is "docile." It appears in this next to last line as an object willing to be controlled and capable of everything. For the speaker, much of what the train is capable of in surpassing both nature (over-coming in this reading the horse with which, metaphorically, it shares so much) and religion remains potential only. It ends the poem "At it's own stable door—," apparently domesticated and yet lingering as a potentially "omnipotent" entity. The final lines thus pick up on a larger theme: its depiction of the train's power to alter the natural landscape is rendered ambivalently throughout the poem. It "pares" the quarry, thus shaping the land for its needs, but at the same time it pares the "quarry," a man-made feature, while it leaves the "hill" well alone.

Despite its uncharacteristic topic, "I Like to See It Lap the Miles" is exempla-ry of Dickinson's poetic method. The poem's message, indeed its symbolism, remains doubtful and open to interpretation. Rather than insisting on the ne-cessity to read the poem as presenting a horse metaphorically for a train, the poem depends on continuously allowing a reading of the observed object as both horse and train. Some commentators have suggested that in the "horrid—hooting stanza" Dickinson alludes to the writing of poetry (cf. Mitchell 2000: 43), or they read the poem into the historical Amherst context as a commentary on the social developments in the town and the Dickinson family's role in it (cf. ibid.: 42). Dickinson's complex comparison between horse and train, between animal and machine, nature and technology, bends the train's potential back to older forms of transportation and lets the train's journey end before "it's own stable door," suggesting that there are limits to the transformative potential of new technologies. Certainly we may read Dickinson's conflation of train and horse, and her refusal to privilege one over the other in what might pass for an early Romantic meditation on nature, as a level of ironic commentary on a mod-ern belief in the superiority of technology. In such a commentary, neither horse nor train is privileged: nature and technology can equally be grasped and tamed in poetic diction. Domnhall Mitchell maintains that "there are contradictions in the poem and these contradictions mirror Dickinson's own ambivalence toward the social forces she symbolizes in the poem" (ibid.: 40). Yet despite this fact, it is only a connection of the poem to the social context—the ascendancy of train over horse, and perhaps the coming of the railroad to Amherst itself—that en-ables a collapse of the metaphorical relationship between train and horse and a clear reading of the circumspect poetical language.

Crucially, the speaker's insistence that she "likes" all that she describes later on clashes with the words she chooses: the train's peering into the (rail)road-side (workers') shanties is "supercilious"—haughty and proud—perhaps suggesting the ways in which railroad construction was applauded in the abstract, but that the workers who labored in the effort were often second-class citizens, Irish or Chi-nese immigrants. Likewise, the "horrid—hooting stanza—" of complaints breaks with the easy "liking" that the speaker has for her object. The train's poetry (its "stanza") is not musical to the speaker's ear, its complaints, as noted above, ap-parently uncalled for, and she deftly ironizes her object still more in describing the train chasing "itself down Hill—," a rather solipsistically pointless activity.

It is important to recognize the poetic method Dickinson employs in the very difficulty of reconciling the poem's complex allusions. The poem rather straightforwardly affirms its subjectivity: it is, in simple terms, sufficient that the speaker "likes" all the things she mentions, recognizing that poetic reconciliation of all of a poem's contradictions would be artificial—it would tie a neat bow around a complex mental process. "My business," Dickinson wrote about the same time in a letter, "is Circumference" (Johnson 1958: 412): like her insistence that "success in circuit lies," the notion of poetical circumferences that implies more than it states outright embodies her poetical stance, a stance fully in evidence in "I Like to See It Lap the Miles."

3. Walt Whitman's Progressive Poetics: "To a Locomotive in Winter"

In Dickinson's poem, the first difficulty is teasing out what is being described; Whitman's poem "To a Locomotive in Winter" leaves us in no such doubt. It begins with an apostrophe, an identification of the poetical object, and a description of the poem itself as a particular poetic and musical form: "Thee for my recitative" (1982 [1891-92]: 583, l. 1). The word 'recitative' itself is onomatopoetic: its repetitive plosives already suggest the rumbling of the train on the tracks. But the word also lifts the locomotive into a higher poetic realm, even into religious terminology, recitatives being constituent parts of opera (in which Whitman was interested) and religious oratorios. Taking the locomotive as his recitative, the speaker elevates the locomotive almost to the level of worship. Whitman's word choice shows how far removed from so-called common language he could be: the archaic use of 'thee' and 'thy,' the "sweetness debonair" (l. 22), and the idea of the recitative itself, all remove the poet from the realm of common expression, but the language clearly supports the greater theme. Its vocabulary is distinctively public: Whitman's call for the locomotive to become his "recitative" is at once pleading, as though he were begging it for permission, and couched in terms of a religious musical performance. He transforms the observation of an object, through an extrapolation of its possibilities, into a vision.

Successive lines build upon this situation: initial "th" connects the first eleven lines in which the speaker describes in elaborate and lyrical detail the locomotive itself. Whitman's poem is very much a visual celebration, its first lines indulging in a detailed description of the appearance of the locomotive, a description in which incessant movement plays a major role: "thy beat convulsive," the "gyrating, shuttling" movement of the rods, the "swelling" and "tapering" of the locomotive's sounds, the smoke-clouds "out-belching" and the "twinkle" of the wheels. In Whitman's verses, one feels the piston scraping, the steam breaking on his brow; the locomotive is impressively massive: "black," "ponderous," "great," "long," and "dense" (ll. 3-10). The descriptive passage, the technological elaboration on what is clearly a machine (in contrast to Dickinson), segues into an interpretative extension of the observation. For Whitman's speaker, the locomotive is a "Type of the Modern—emblem of motion and power—pulse of the continent" (l. 13). If the previous lines have been descriptive, the recitative's bare if poetical content here is the reason for the celebration: the locomotive is representative of technological advancement, but also already embraces the wide vistas of the entire continent. The locomotive represents progress, a progress that is impossible to stop—not that Whitman would want to stop it. If the "driving storm" (l. 2) is not enough, it cannot come as a surprise that "[b]y day" as much as "[b]y night," the locomotive warns of its approach by "ringing bell" or "silent signal lamps" (ll. 16-7), but never halts. Indeed, whatever observations Whitman has made about the locomotive, they are the characteristics of the modern age, itself "steadily careering" (l. 12)—steadily making progress—whether fast or slow, towards the future United States. The poem's speaker becomes almost suppliant, calling for the locomotive to pay attention to him: "For once come serve the Muse and merge in verse" (l. 14). As we have seen, Dickinson's speaker keeps an ironic distance; in her ability to "like" what she sees, she also implicitly encodes the possibility to dislike, and to disregard. It is the speaker who, voluntarily, pays attention to the train. By contrast, Whitman's speaker not only addresses the locomotive directly, but is forced to do so because it exists fully and primarily outside his poetry; it must deign to "merge in verse" rather than be created in it.

The second section of Whitman's poem again begins with an apostrophe:

Fierce-throated beauty!
Roll through my chant with all thy lawless music, thy swinging lamps at night,
Thy madly-whistled laughter, echoing, rumbling like an earth-quake, rousing all, Law of thyself complete, thine own track firmly holding,
(No sweetness debonair of tearful harp or glib piano thine,) (ll. 18-22)

But now, instead of a descriptive section, the speaker continues the transfiguration of the locomotive into something larger than itself. "[R]ousing all" (l. 20), the locomotive even seems to leave behind the musical metaphor the speaker has built for it: "(No sweetness debonair of tearful harp or glib piano thine,)" (l. 22); rather, its "trills of shrieks" (l. 23) are the honest manifestation of the age. The locomotive's sounds themselves are made into a form of musical expression, a modern and especially apropos kind of sound that leaves behind older conceptions of what is musical. Shrieks, rumbles, whistles are simply the right sounds for the age, as opposed to the falsely tuneful sounds of piano and harp—they may not be musical as such, but at least they are appropriate. The speaker notably rejects the harp—symbolic of Romantic poetry at least since Samuel Taylor Coleridge's "The Eolian Harp"—as unsuitable for the present, modern moment. The poem seems to suggest that traditional musical forms must make way before the music of technological progress, just as British-derived Romantic poetry cannot fully mediate the experiences of incipient American modernity, demanding Whitman's formal experiments.

Whitman's poem ends with an opening of vista, sending the locomotive into an unceasing forward movement in which its sounds, and with its sounds the locomotive itself, become part of the country and its future: "Thy trills of shrieks by rocks and hills return'd, / Launch'd o'er the prairies wide, across the lakes, / To the free skies unpent and glad and strong" (ll. 23-5). The speaker has only a momentary glimpse of the locomotive, as he notes twice in the poem—"even as here I see thee" (l. 14), "in the driving storm, even as now" (l. 2)—and that in peculiar circumstances, but it opens for him the broad expanses of the West. The locomotive becomes symbolic of the American progress, "rousing all!" (l. 20) to its promises, promises with a distinctly rural slant: open prairies for America's agricultural democracy. In Whitman's poem, the locomotive becomes an embodiment of both current and prospective technological progress.

Dickinson's and Whitman's poems share an idea of the power of the new technology, whether it is "omnipotent" as in Dickinson (1999 [1862]: 176, l. 15), or "lawless" (Whitman 1982 [1891-92]: 583, l. 19), a "law upon thineself complete," and "unpent and glad in strong" as in Whitman (ibid.: l. 21). While that power is clearly a cause for celebration in Whitman's poem, Dickinson is more ambivalent. Her "docile and omnipotent" train seems to have the potential, at least, to embody the destructive side of technology and progress, and the sheer pointlessness and self-sufficiency of a train that chases "itself down Hill" contrasts with the purposefulness of Whitman's locomotive with its "train of cars behind, obedient, merrily following" (l. 11). In Whitman's poem, the celebration of the train as a mechanism, as an intricate assemblage of parts, produces a well-ordered vision of technological and societal progress in which human sensibilities—embodied, for example, in tuneful music—will find future benefit in the logic of technology. Dickinson's poem, by contrast, both naturalizes and personalizes the train she encounters: it seems to possess its own idiosyncratic motivations, irreducible to either its parts or an overarching logic of progress.

The contrast between the broad vista opened by Whitman's poem and the narrow conclusion of Dickinson's may not be all that far from a useful general observation about the respective poetics of the two writers. Both poets apparently react to a visual impulse, even though it becomes impossible for either to read their poems as a spontaneous reaction, as immediate experience transformed into a meditation. Agnieszka Salska has noted, Dickinson "tends to focus her poems on single moments" (1985: 47). This does not mean that a particular real moment becomes transformed into poetry; it means that her poetry itself is momentary and somewhat transitory. Some of Dickinson's shortest poems possess a condensed quality almost like Imagist poetry. By contrast, Whitman seems to situate his meditation on the locomotive at a specific point in time, but just as his speaker comes to stand as much for the whole nation as for himself, so does this chronological pinpointing become transformed into a general observation about the progress of the United States as a whole.

A final comparison is in order here. In an undated poem, Dickinson once more sums up poetry's relation to the world:

> To make a prairie it takes a clover and one bee,
> One clover, and a bee,
> And revery.
> The revery alone will do,
> If bees are few. (1999 [n.d.]: 632, #1779)

For Dickinson, the poetic act, encoded here as "revery," can supplant the reality of nature—it "will do" in a pinch, though it neither necessarily must nor, in this reading, necessarily should. Crucially for our purposes, the action at hand is "to make a prairie," literally a creative act. No such act of creation is possible in Whitman's poem: the "prairies wide" (l. 24), just like the locomotive, pre-exist the poem. They become an object of the train's conquest, symbolic of the potential that lies in the future of the United States, yet not themselves a realm of poetic possibility. Dickinson's poetry points back to the poetic act; Whitman's points outward, to the future and to the nation.

4. Conclusion and Outlook

In recent years the act of writing and publishing poetry has come under increasing scrutiny in both Dickinson and Whitman. The majority of Dickinson's poems existed as handwritten text only, and much discussion has been engendered by the question whether the particular handwritten forms her poems take on the page are themselves meaningful, since they often resist breakdown into stanzas and an easy transfer to the printed page. The majority of Dickinson's poems were published after her death; Dickinson had sewn some of them together by hand in fascicles. Dickinson's editors since her death have usually disaggregated these packets and put the poems in topical or chronological order, yet the possibility remains that the fascicles themselves were a part of a formal arrangement Dickinson sought for her poetry, possibly as thematic clusters. Ralph W. Franklin's publication in 1981 of Dickinson's poems in a facsimile edition rekindled interest in the form of her poems, and in the process of getting her into print (see Christensen 2008; Oberhaus 1995; Werner 1995); even her idiosyncratic punctuation has been the topic of a monograph (see Crumbley 1997).

Whitman's *Leaves of Grass* is similarly being more heavily investigated as a literary product (cf. Miller 2010), even though, as well as we can possibly expect, we know how Whitman intended his poetry to be read: his *Leaves of Grass* remained a work in progress, appearing in constantly expanding and changing editions under the careful direction of the author until his death in 1892. Whitman rearranged the sequence of his poems numerous times, even going so far as to add individual lines, the most famous probably being the extension of the first line of "Song of Myself" to read "I celebrate myself, and sing myself" (1982 [1891-92]: 188, l. 1). The formal arrangement of his poetry, the way it would be delivered to the readership, thus remained a constant concern for Whitman.

Current scholarship on Whitman and Dickinson has emphasized a wide variety of topics. Whitman especially has seen a number of studies that are inflected specifically with questions of gender and sexuality (see Schmidgall 1998; Pollak 2000; Brasas 2010), and there has also been greater concern with placing Whitman more firmly in the cultural contexts of his time, emphasizing his relationship with the politics of his day (see Erkkila 1989; Lawson 2006; Stacy 2008; Seery 2011) and the Civil War (see Genoways 2009; Roper 2008); he has also begun to be read ecocritically (see Killingsworth 2004). If current Whitman scholarship focuses on the larger contexts of Whitman's work, much of the scholarly work on Dickinson still focuses on Dickinson's own thematic concerns and poetic method, including investigations of her religious imagery (see Freedman 2011) and of her poetical identity (see Oeldorf 2002). There is also criticism that seeks to investigate in greater detail Dickinson's social relations with her friends (see Wineapple 2008) and family (see Benfey/Liebling 2001; Gordon 2010), but also with the social world of Amherst (see Mitchell 2000). Readers interested in a broader survey of Dickinson criticism should consult Klaus Lubbers's *Emily Dickinson: The Critical Revolution* (1968) and Fred White's *Approaching Emily Dickinson: Critical Currents and Crosscurrents since 1960* (2008), which usefully complement each other.

Given the vast amount of output on both poets, it is not surprising that no single scholarly view exists of Whitman and Dickinson—rather, there is "a complex layering of perspectives" (Killingsworth 2007: 122). If there is no agreement about the details of interpretation—and, as I have intimated above, for Dickinson this may well be an intentional result of a particular poetic method—there is agreement about the importance of Dickinson and Whitman's shared place in American literary history. They stand, in the words of Dana Gioia, "at the beginning of modern American literary consciousness" (1993: 67). Whitman's themes, his free verse and diction, were important precursors to the poetry of American Modernism that find their echoes, for example, in Carl Sandburg's poetry, in Allen Ginsberg, and in John Berryman. Ezra Pound found him so oppressive as a lyrical presence that he made a poetical "Pact" with him, admitting that "It was you that broke the new wood," but insisting that it would be he doing the "carving" (in Perlman et al. 1998: 111), suggesting at once his indebtedness to Whitman's innovations as well as his belief that Whitman had left much unsaid and undone.

Dickinson, very much unlike Whitman, barely sought publicity. A mere handful of her poems saw print in her lifetime, although, as Lena Christensen points out, the wide circle of acquaintances who received poems in letters constituted at least some form of publication (cf. 2008: 16-7). The first major scholarly edition of her poetry came in 1955 with Thomas Johnson's *The Poems of Emily Dickinson*. Since then she has been placed both within the history of American poetry at large as well as within the history of American women's poetry, becoming important both formally and as a person and author for such later writers as Adrienne Rich and Susan Howe. This lasting influence is testament to the way in which Whitman and Dickinson—he unaware of her poetry, she aware of but apparently uninterested in his—independently of each other found ways of addressing a changing society in poetry and revolutionized poetic form.

Bibliography

Selected Primary Literature

Dickinson, Emily. 1955. *The Poems of Emily Dickinson*. Ed. Thomas Johnson. Cambridge, MA: Belknap P of Harvard UP
——. 1958. *The Letters of Emily Dickinson*. Ed. Thomas Johnson. Cambridge, MA: Belknap P of Harvard UP.
——. 1999. *The Poems of Emily Dickinson*. *Reading Edition*. Ed. R.W. Franklin. Cambridge: Belknap P of Harvard UP.
Emerson, Ralph Waldo. 1982. *Essays and Lectures*. Ed. Joel Porte. New York: Library of America.
Folsom, Ed and Kenneth M. Price (eds). *The Walt Whitman Archive*. Web. 20 April 2014. <http://www.whitmanarchive.org/>.
Franklin, Ralph W. (ed.). 1981. *The Manuscript Books of Emily Dickinson*. Cambridge, MA: Belknap P of Harvard UP.
—— (ed.). 1998. *The Poems of Emily Dickinson*. *Variorum Edition*. 3 vols. Cambridge: Belknap P of Harvard UP.
Whitman, Walt. 1982. *Poetry and Prose*. Ed. Justin Kaplan. New York: Library of America.

Selected Secondary Literature

Keller, Karl. 1979. *The Only Kangaroo Among the Beauty: Emily Dickinson and America*. Baltimore: Johns Hopkins UP.

Usefully traces the affinities between Dickinson and a number of predecessors, such as Anne Bradstreet, and contemporaries, such as Walt Whitman.

Reynolds, David S. 1995. *Walt Whitman's America. A Cultural Biography*. New York: Alfred A. Knopf.

Extremely thorough and highly informative book situating Whitman in the context of his times.

Salska, Agnieszka. 1985. *Walt Whitman and Emily Dickinson: Poetry of the Central Consciousness*. Philadelphia: U of Pennsylvania P.

A comparative reading of the two poets that situates them as respondents to Transcendentalist philosophy, especially that of R.W. Emerson.

Sewall, Richard B. 1991. *The Life of Emily Dickinson*. Cambridge: Harvard UP.

Sewall's is an astute biography of Dickinson.

Vendler, Helen. 2010. *Dickinson: Selected Poems and Commentaries*. Cambridge, MA: The Belknap P of Harvard UP.

Provides readings of individual Dickinson poems—good resource for interpretive suggestions.

Further References

Allen, Gay Wilson. 1975. *The New Walt Whitman Handbook*. New York: New York UP.

Barker, Wendy. 2002. "Emily Dickinson and Poetic Strategy." In: Martin 2002. 77-90.

Benfey, Christopher and Jerome Liebling. 2001. *The Dickinsons of Amherst*. Hanover: UP of New England.

Brasas, Juan A. Herrero. 2010. *Walt Whitman's Mystical Ethics of Comradeship: Homosexualtiy and the Marginality of Friendship at the Crossroads of Modernity*. New York: SUNY P.

Budick, E. Miller. 1985. *Emily Dickinson and the Life of Language: A Study in Symbolic Poetics*. Baton Rouge: Louisiana State UP.

Callow, Philip. 1992. *From Noon to Starry Night: A Life of Walt Whitman*. Chicago: Ivan R. Dee.

Christensen, Lena. 2008. *Editing Emily Dickinson. The Production of an Author*. New York and London: Routledge.

Crumbley, Paul. 1997. *Inflections of the Pen: Dash and Voice in Emily Dickinson*. Lexington: U of Kentucky P.

Dickinson, Emily. 2003 [1894]. *The Letters of Emily Dickinson*. Ed. Mabel Loomis Todd. Mineola, NY: Dover Publications.

Diehl, Joanne Feit. 1981. *Dickinson and the Romantic Imagination*. Princeton: Princeton UP.

Erkkila, Betsy. 1989. *Whitman: The Political Poet*. New York and Oxford: Oxford UP.

Farr, Judith. 1992. *The Passion of Emily Dickinson*. Cambridge, MA: Harvard UP.

Freedman, Linda. 2011. *Emily Dickinson and the Religious Imagination*. Cambridge: Cambridge UP.

Genoways, Ted. 2009. *Walt Whitman and the Civil War: America's Poet during the Lost Years of 1860-1862*. Berkeley: U of California P.

Gioia, Dana. 1993. "Longfellow in the Aftermath of Modernism." In: Jay Parini (ed.), *The Columbia History of American Poetry*. New York: Columbia UP. 64-96.

Gordon, Lyndall. 2010. *Lives Like Loaded Guns: Emily Dickinson and Her Family's Feuds*. New York: Viking.

Killingsworth, M. Jimmie. 2007. *The Cambridge Introduction to Walt Whitman*. Cambridge: Cambridge UP.

——. 2004. *Walt Whitman and the Earth: A Study in Ecopoetics*. Iowa City: U of Iowa P.

Lawson, Andrew. 2006. *Walt Whitman and the Class Struggle*. Iowa City: U of Iowa P.

Martin, Wendy (ed.). 2002. *The Cambridge Companion to Emily Dickinson*. Cambridge: Cambridge UP.

—. 2007. *The Cambridge Introduction to Emily Dickinson*. Cambridge: Cambridge UP.

Miller, Matt. 2010. *Collage of Myself: Walt Whitman and the Making of* Leaves of Grass. Lincoln: U of Nebraska P.

Mitchell, Domnhall. 2000. *Emily Dickinson: Monarch of Perception*. Amherst: U of Massachusetts P.

Oberhaus, Dorothy Huff. 1995. *Emily Dickinson's Fascicles: Method and Meaning*. University Park: Pennsylvania State UP.

Oeldorf, Heike. 2002. *Positionen poetischer Identität in Gedichten Emily Dickinsons*. Frankfurt am Main: Lang.

Perlman, Jim et al. (eds.). 1998. *Walt Whitman: The Measure of His Song*. Duluth: Holy Cow! P.

Pollak, Vivian R. 2000. *The Erotic Whitman*. Berkeley: U of California P.

Porter, David T. 1981. *Dickinson: The Modern Idiom*. Cambridge, MA: Harvard UP.

—. 1998. "Searching for Dickinson's Themes." In: Gudrun Grabher et al. (eds.), *The Emily Dickinson Handbook*. Amherst: U of Massachusetts P. 183-196.

Reynolds, David S. 2002. "Emily Dickinson and Popular Culture." In: Martin 2002. 167-190.

Rich, Adrienne. 1984. "Vesuvius at Home." In: Paul J. Ferlazzo (ed.), *Critical Essays on Emily Dickinson*. Boston: G. K. Hall & Co. 175-95.

Roper, Robert. 2008. *Now the Drum of War: Walt Whitman and His Brothers in the Civil War*. New York: Walker.

Schmidgall, Gary. 1998. *Walt Whitman: A Gay Life*. New York: Plume.

Seery, John E. (ed.). 2011. *A Political Companion to Walt Whitman*. Lexington: UP of Kentucky.

Sielke, Sabine. 2008. "'The Brain—is wider than the Sky—' or: Re-Cognizing Emily Dickinson." In: *Emily Dickinson Journal* 17.1: 68-85.

St. Armand, Barton Levi. 1984. *Emily Dickinson and Her Culture. The Soul's Society*. Cambridge: Cambridge UP.

Stacy, Jason. 2008. *Walt Whitman's Multitudes: Labor Reform and Persona in Whitman's Journalism and the First* Leaves of Grass, *1840-1855*. New York: Lang.

Werner, Marta L. (ed.). 1995. *Emily Dickinson's Open Folios: Scenes of Reading, Surfaces of Writing*. Ann Arbor: U of Michigan P.

White, Fred D. 2002. "Emily Dickinson's Existential Dramas." In: Martin 2002. 91-106.

—. 2008. *Approaching Emily Dickinson: Critical Currents and Crosscurrents Since 1960*. Rochester, NY: Camden House.

Waskow, Howard J. 1966. *Whitman: Explorations in Form*. Chicago and London: U of Chicago P.

Wineapple, Brenda. 2008. *White Heat: The Friendship of Emily Dickinson and Thomas Wentworth Higginson*. New York: Knopf.

Wolff, Cynthia Griffin. 1986. *Emily Dickinson*. New York: Knopf.

Wolosky, Shira. 2004. "Poetry and Public Discourse, 1820-1910." In: Sacvan Bercovitch (ed.), *The Cambridge History of American Literature, Vol. 4: 1800-1910*. Cambridge: Cambridge UP. 147-480.

III American Modernisms

The Country and the City in Modern American Poetry

Carl Sandburg's "Chicago" and Robert Frost's "Out, Out—"

Clemens Spahr

1. The Country and the City in Modern American Poetry

Carl Sandburg and Robert Frost were both immensely popular poets in the early twentieth century. Sandburg made his name as the poet of urban Chicago, and Frost was known as the poet of rural New England. In many ways, these categories aptly describe their poetry, although they require a few caveats. Biographically, the seemingly neat division is complicated by the fact that Sandburg grew up in the small town of Galesburg, Illinois before moving to Chicago, whereas Frost, who spent the majority of his life in New England, was born and raised in San Francisco and spent a considerable amount of time in England. Nor were the country and the city—both geographically and economically—distinct spheres at the turn of the century. The late nineteenth and early twentieth centuries were characterized by dramatic changes in all areas of life: a growing urbanization, rapid technological and medical progress, social and political upheavals, new forms of mass communication, and revolutions in the arts (see Berman 1988). While these developments were more readily discernible in a metropolis like Chicago, they thoroughly affected rural America as well. William Cronon has shown that the nineteenth-century American Midwest was characterized by an "expanding metropolitan economy creating ever more elaborate and intimate linkages between city and country" (1992: xv). Indeed, thoroughly aware of this interrelation between the country and the city, Sandburg wrote a great number of poems on the rural American Midwest, most notably those collected in *Cornhuskers* (1918). Conversely, Frost's pastoral poetry addressed what one critic has called the "city's exported dangers" (Hass 2014: 117). The city and the country therefore provided exemplary portraits of the expansive economic and social processes that shaped the United States at the beginning of the twentieth century.

Both Sandburg and Frost were faced with the question of how to confront a rapidly unfolding modernity, but they chose, and came to be associated with, different poetic modes and genres. Sandburg's city poems employed free verse to carefully balance the city's eerie side with its expansive promises; he saw free verse as the most suitable means to channel the unleashed energies of modernity into a form of expression adequate to the promises and threats of the early twentieth century. Although Sandburg's city poems—through their use of free verse—are in form more immediately discernible as modern experiments, Frost's poems equally reinvent traditional forms and deal with the consequences of modernity. Frost's poetry is a rewriting of the pastoral tradition; what he sought in nature was not to recuperate a lost past or to find an alternative to the challenges of modernity. His poetry rather seeks out instances of moral guidance in an age that often uncritically celebrated progress as a value in itself. As Frost puts it in "The Black Cottage," a poem from his second collection titled *North of Boston* (1914): "Most of the change we think we see in life / Is due to truths being in and out of favor" (1995 [1914]: 61). While Frost was not one to condemn modern achievements, he questioned the physical and spiritual consequences of human progress.

Sandburg's and Frost's careful appreciation of modern developments formed a counterpoint to other varieties of modern art. The Italian Futurists, for instance, celebrated modernity as a new age of civilization that would also usher in a new era in the history of art. In his "Futurist Manifesto" (1909), Filippo Tommaso Marinetti declared that "this wonderful world has been further enriched by a new beauty, the beauty of speed. A racing car, its bonnet decked out with exhaust pipes like serpents with galvanic breath . . . a roaring motorcar, which seems to race on like machine-gun fire, is more beautiful than the Winged Victory of Samothrace" (2006 [1909]: 13). While Marinetti proposed Futurism as a way to absorb the technological and industrial progress of modernity into art, Ezra Pound and T.S. Eliot, although more skeptical about modernity's progress, similarly embraced an aesthetics that broke with tradition. Pound, for instance, equally demanded a revolution in the arts but rejected a naïve celebration of technology which often produced only "a prose kinema, not, not assuredly, alabaster" (2004: 550)—that is, a prosaic, decidedly unpoetic mass-produced form of art. As Peter Nicholls has it, the High Modernists' poetry "issued a call to order in the name of values which were explicitly anti-modern, though it did so by developing literary forms overtly modernist" (2009: 164). Despite their differences, the Modernists agreed that to express the experience of modernity, a new, experimental form of poetry was needed.

Frost and Sandburg did not disagree; what most distinguished them from the canonized Modernists, however, was that they grounded their poetic vision in the language and experience of 'the people.' While both poets differed significantly with regard to their choice of poetic form and subject, they shared an interest in the vernacular of the people as a resource that could be used to understand and organize the forces of modernity. What Sandburg stated as the aim of his long poem, *The People, Yes* (1936), can be taken as one of his fundamental poetic principles: "Affirmative of swarming and brawling Democracy, it attempts to give back to the people their own lingo" (1991: xxv). When Sandburg writes about the architecture of the modern city, the buildings are made up of the people who inhabit the city. As he says in "Skyscraper": "It is the men and women, boys and girls so poured in and out all day that give the building a soul of dreams and thoughts and memories" (ibid.: 31). Just as the people's thoughts, dreams, and labor constituted the city for Sandburg, for Frost, rural America was the result of lived experience rather than a static space readily available for literary representation. Frost saw the people's experience of a modernized natural landscape as an important resource for a poetics that tried to get a handle on the modern world. His aim was to hear Californians "Talk California" (1995 [1923]: 151)—to record the experience of the new century in words that are the result of lived experience. Frost's portraits of country people were often detached, ironic case studies, while Sandburg's poems affectionately celebrated the people's creativity. And yet they tried to preserve the vernacular of the people in an age where both the country and the city underwent dramatic changes that threatened to obliterate the individual. As we will see, this poeticization of the people's language was not an organic, natural process, but depended on particular philosophical and political views.

2. City of the Big Shoulders: Carl Sandburg's "Chicago"

By the end of the 1910s Carl Sandburg was a prominent if contentious poet who had been widely discussed ever since the 1914 publication of "Chicago" in the avant-garde magazine *Poetry* put him on the literary map. It is hard to overestimate *Poetry*'s relevance for the development of modern American literature (cf. Newcomb 2012: 26-53), as Harriet Monroe's Chicago-based magazine was instrumental in promoting the work of such seminal Modernist poets as Ezra Pound, Amy Lowell, and T.S. Eliot. In 1913 for example, *Poetry* featured H.D.'s "Hermes of the Ways," Ezra Pound's "In a Station of the Metro," and also Pound's programmatic essay "A Few Don'ts by an Imagiste," thus helping to initiate the Imagist movement that is often credited as the founding moment of Modernist poetry. In 1915 it would see the publication of Eliot's "The Love Song of J. Alfred Prufrock." The publication (after a number of rejections) of "Chicago" and other poems in *Poetry* magazine, and the subsequent publication of *Chicago Poems* with a major publishing house, marked Sandburg's transition from an unknown Chicago journalist to one of the most prominent voices of modern American poetry. The youthful Langston Hughes dedicated a poem to Sandburg and later spoke of him as a "guiding star" (1993 [1940]: 29) while readers and critics alike celebrated his poetic portraits of twentieth-century America. But there were also those who saw Sandburg as the sentimental champion of the people, a poet whose oversimplified, trite verse depicted an ungraspable amorphous mass rather than give literary expression to lived experience. Cultural critic William Braithwaite, for instance, criticized *Chicago Poems* (1916) as "a book of ill-regulated speech that has neither verse or prose rhythms" (in Yannella 1996: 70). And Karl Detzer states that in the late 1910s Sandburg's poetry "stirred minor tempests in academic teacups from coast to coast. Defenders and detractors broke inky lances on the pages of the book supplements. Admirers proclaimed him a latter-day Walt Whitman. Objectors cried that their six-year-old daughters could write better poetry" (in Callahan 1987: 89).

Perhaps the most significant contemporary assessment came from Imagist poet Amy Lowell. While in her review of Sandburg's *Smoke and Steel* (1920) Lowell would disapprove of what she saw as an increasingly propagandistic dimension in his poems, a few years earlier she had nothing but praise for Sandburg's *Chicago Poems*, calling it "one of the most original books this age has produced" (in Callahan 1987: 81). For Lowell, the collection's city poems struck just the right balance between "tenderness" and "virility" (ibid.), thus capturing the modern city's dual character. In his emphasis on the city, Sandburg exemplifies the dominant strain in Modernist literature. Malcolm Bradbury has stressed the relevance of the city's virility for Modernist literature and art: "In many respects the literature of experimental Modernism . . . was an art of cities, especially of the polyglot cities which, for various historical reasons, had acquired high activity and great reputation as centres of intellectual and cultural exchange" (Bradbury 1991 [1976]: 96). For Sandburg, however, the city was not only an intellectual center, but also represented one of the great achievements of the people. Sandburg's early portraits of the city remained ambiguous: if the city's virility promised to initiate a new age, it was also the token of a threatening force of potential destruction.

"Chicago" stands in a long tradition of American Modernist city poems that deal with the city's destructive nature and its simultaneous promise of technological and cultural progress. These poems include Eliot's "The Love Song of J. Alfred Prufrock," Claude McKay's "Harlem Shadows" (1922), Hart Crane's epic poem *The Bridge* (1930), and Langston Hughes's towering achievement "Air Raid Over Harlem" (1935). Chicago was an apt subject for depicting the hopes and failures of modernity. Having recovered from the Great Chicago Fire in 1871, the city hosted the World's Fair in 1893 and became a center of cultural activity, with Theodore Dreiser's *Sister Carrie* (1900) and Upton Sinclair's *The Jungle* (1906) standing as testimonies to Chicago's prospering literary life. While Sandburg's "Chicago" may at first sight appear to be an impressionistic ode to Chicago that celebrates the city's achievements, it in fact develops the contradictory logic of the modern city. The poem can be loosely divided into three parts: the speaker's opening apostrophe to the city; his presentation of what others see as the city's fierceness and its merciless destruction of individuals; and, finally, his response to these objectionable attributes in the course of which he develops a vision of the city as both a place of human suffering and a redeeming space of social interaction. The first lines present a majestic modern metropolis:

> Hog Butcher for the World,
> Tool Maker, Stacker of Wheat,
> Player with Railroads and the Nation's Freight Handler;
> Stormy, husky, brawling,
> City of the Big Shoulders: (1991 [1914]: 3, ll. 1-5)

The first three lines provide a catalog of nouns that sets the scene for an ambiguous portrait of Chicago and the modern city in general. In this first section, the "City of the Big Shoulders" (l. 5) emerges as strong and noisy, full of the vibrancy of everyday life, and an important player in national and global economic affairs. The apostrophe to Chicago (addressed and described as if it were a person) serves to illustrate that the city is more than simply an environment in which individuals are situated. Instead, the city itself has agency and becomes the poem's protagonist. Of course, the poem's ultimate point is that the city's value lies with the people who constitute and permanently recreate it, even though it has partially assumed a life independent of human actions and certainly beyond the control of the individual. The city's sheer metropolitan power will figure as the source of human creativity, but it will also turn out to be a force that mercilessly devours its inhabitants.

Although not as experimental as Eliot's "The Waste Land," which employs a multiplicity of voices instead of a controlling lyrical speaker, "Chicago" uses different perspectives to capture the city's complexity. The corresponding shifts in perception are illustrated through the poem's arrangement on the page and through changes in the style and form of the three sections. The first part introduces the image of a gargantuan city, which is set off from the next section through spacing and the colon after the phrase that establishes Chicago as the "City of the Big Shoulders." Although it is clear from the outset that there is a speaker who sings this ode, it is only after the colon that the poem's speaker starts referring explicitly to himself. Throughout the poem's second section, the speaker continues to address the city itself but now relates what others experience as the metropolis's destructive effect on their lives ("And they tell me you are brutal," l. 8). What seemed a celebration of the city in the first part—or at least a depiction of its sheer power—now seems to be put into perspective by the opinions the speaker reports: "They tell me you are wicked and I believe them,

for I have seen your painted women under the gas lamps luring the farm boys"
(l. 6). Indeed, there is no shortage of problems: the city is "wicked," most evidently so with its "painted women" and city lights drawing innocent country boys into a corrupting yet fascinating city experience. On a more sinister level, the prostitutes exemplify not the ambiguous fascination the city radiates, but represent a cruel form of exploitation. In this second section, the city emerges not only as a place of vice, but also of exploitation, violence, and hunger. Its "brutal" side shows in the "faces of women and children" in which the speaker sees "the marks of wanton hunger" (l. 8). Significantly, the poem here also switches to the use of long lines typical of free verse poems at least since Whitman. More restricted, traditional versification, it seems, can no longer capture the city's expansive, contradictory character.

Fully aware of the city's problems, the speaker then embraces the potential of the modern metropolis. The city is not only a place of destruction and exploitation but also of creativity, labor, and progress. Immediately after the three long lines that raise objections to the city's destructive nature, the poem provides a fuller picture of Chicago: "And having answered so I turn once more to those who sneer at this my city, and I give them back the sneer and say to them: / Come and show me another city with lifted head singing so proud to be alive and coarse and strong and cunning" (ll. 9-10). The first line of this rejoinder is connected to the objections through the anaphoric use of "And." Yet whereas so far the long lines have been complete sentences, the praise of the city now defies the constraints even of the long line:

> Fierce as a dog with tongue lapping for action, cunning as a savage pitted against
>   the wilderness,
> Bareheaded,
> Shoveling,
> Wrecking,
> Planning,
> Building, breaking, rebuilding,
> Under the smoke, dust all over his mouth, laughing with white teeth,
> Under the terrible burden of destiny laughing as a young man laughs,
> Laughing even as an ignorant fighter laughs who has never lost a battle,
> Bragging and laughing that under his wrist is the pulse, and under his ribs the
>   heart of the people,
>   Laughing!
> Laughing the stormy, husky, brawling laughter of Youth, half-naked, sweating,
>   proud to be Hog Butcher, Tool Maker, Stacker of Wheat, Player with Railroads and Freight Handler to the Nation. (ibid.: 3-4, ll. 12-23)

The poem's final section is interrupted only by an exclamation point before the last long line. The lines build a muscular image of Chicago as a pinnacle of human labor and interaction that is juxtaposed against the "little soft cities" (ibid.: 3, l. 11). Just like in the beginning of the poem, the city is not only the product of human action and performance, but also an active force (it is "[p]lanning") by itself—a force that can easily become a monstrosity that devours its inhabitants. At times the city seems arrogant, laughing as an "ignorant fighter laughs who has never lost a battle."

In its final long line, the beginning of the poem is repeated almost verbatim but omits the reference to the "Stormy, husky, brawling, / City of the Big Shoulders" (ibid.: 3, ll. 4-5). The last lines rewrite the city's economic and social power through the process of human labor and social interaction that make up the city in the first place. By now, the people have been introduced as constitutive of the city described as a bragging young man: the people's pulse beats under the city's wrist, its "heart" under the city's "ribs." Sandburg's emphasis on the people is also echoed in the poem's diction. The list of words one would not expect in poetry ("Bareheaded, / Shoveling, / Wrecking, / Planning,") serves to underscore the agency of the people who created and constantly recreate the living organism that is the city. The apostrophe of the city in the poem's first lines has now been formally rearranged as one long free verse line; it has been spread out into a free verse celebration of the city's potential greatness—a greatness that is achieved through the labor and the creativity of the people. The last line of Sandburg's poem, then, not only embodies the promise of the modern city but also captures social energies which, if unchecked, might easily overrun humanity. As such, this final line concludes a poem that creates an image of a city full of tensions, a place of progress and development that simultaneously threatens to overwhelm and destroy the individual person. To talk of "Sandburg's ambivalent but mainly celebratory 'Chicago'" (Alexander 1973: 68) is not wrong, but fails to notice how this celebration is inextricably linked to Chicago's threatening underside. While "Chicago" primarily celebrates the people who constitute the city, it is equally concerned with the adverse conditions they have to overcome.

Sandburg remained a champion of 'the people'—who continued to figure as the most important collective signifier in his poetry—and often staged himself as such, most evidently in his programmatically titled long poem *The People, Yes* (1936). Although Sandburg offered complex portraits of the people as a "tragic and comic two-face: / hero and hoodlum" (1991 [1936]: 616), critics took issue with what they saw as an often schematic emphasis on the people as a political force. At mid-century, William Carlos Williams claimed that "*Chicago*, his first brilliantly successful poem should have been his last" (1951: 346), for Williams believes Sandburg's subsequent poetry to be an endless repetition of places and persons which eventually "sums it up, *The People, Yes*, and lets it go at that" (ibid.: 347). Since 'the people' would indeed become an often formulaic term in Sandburg's poetry, it is easy to miss how the phrase had distinct class overtones for him in the 1910s and 1920s. Recent scholarship has commented on how his later reputation "as the adulatory biographer of Lincoln and as a folksy, silver-haired singer of ballads and reciter of poems has obscured the radically innovative and oppositional character of his earlier poetic work" (Van Wienen 1991: 89). Philip Yannella even states that "[d]uring the crucial, watershed years surrounding World War I, when the future of American domestic and foreign policy was being shaped and the circumstances of the common people were as much a subject of fierce public debate and confrontation as they were at any moment in American history before or after," there was another Sandburg who "believed that America was a faithless monster of a country" (1996: xiv).

Chicago was not simply a monstrosity for Sandburg; the city emerges as the product of real socioeconomic contradictions, and it is important to remember that "Chicago" was written at a time when Sandburg was active in socialist politics and was writing for the *International Socialist Review*. For Sandburg, the people were mostly 'the masses.' When he refers to the people at this stage of his career, he means America's multi-ethnic working-class population as portrayed in "Masses," in which the speaker wanders the mountains, thinking of the "Great men, pageants of war and labor, soldiers and workers, mothers lifting their children" only to discover "one day" that there are "millions of the Poor . . . all broken, humble ruins of nations" (1991 [1914]: 4-5). "Chicago" and *Chicago Poems* in general clearly address social injustice and class inequality while simultaneously celebrating the people's attempt to overcome these hostile conditions. Chicago becomes the "city of the big shoulders" that engages with people and presses them to resolve its material contradictions. Sandburg's embrace of the people's diction should therefore also be considered a much more concrete political statement than the generalizing phrase 'the people' might suggest if read out of context.

3. Modernity and Nature: Robert Frost's "Out, Out—"

Robert Frost was born in San Francisco and spent the first years of his childhood there. But it was in New England that he found his literary inspiration, and he became a noted voice among modern poets for his depictions of New England life in *North of Boston* (1914) and *Mountain Interval* (1916). In Frost's pastoral poems, modernity is as much a reality as it is in Sandburg's city poems, and he is equally concerned with capturing the diction of the people. As a consequence, one of Frost's fundamental organizing poetic principles was sound because the "speaking tone of voice," he said, "is all that can save poetry from sing-song, all that can save prose from itself" (1995 [1929]: 713). To capture the importance of sound for poetry, Frost spoke of the "imagining ear." The poet has to address the reader's visualizing ear thereby "bringing in the *living* sounds of speech" (1995 [1915]: 687; original emphasis). As Frost put it in a letter to cultural critic William Braithwaite, his aim was to evoke "reading tones" different from those to which the audience is accustomed: "We must go out into the vernacular for tones that haven't been brought to book. We must write with the ear on the speaking voice. We must imagine the speaking voice" (ibid.: 685). But where Sandburg was often willing to let the rhythm of the people's speech flow, Frost applied a stricter, more philosophically charged poetic frame. He believed that some organizing rules were necessary in order to express how rural New England was beautiful and earthy, but also harsh and cold. Although Frost was not a champion of rigid formal patterns, he felt that poetry's true task was to reconcile form and everyday diction: "I should be as satisfied to play tennis with the net down as to write verse with no verse form set to stay me" (1995 [1934]: 735). Poetry, for Frost, was a way to organize the experience of modernity.

Frost's "Out, Out—" was originally published in *McClures's Magazine* and subsequently appeared in his collection *Mountain Interval* (1916); the very title suggests an interval of recovery away from the urban centers. If "[l]ocality gives art" (Frost 2006 [1919]: 183), the sound of that locality is key to representing it. While for Frost that sound was always the sound of the people's speech, in the 1910s it was also the sound of what Leo Marx has famously referred to as the machine in the garden (see 2000 [1964]). In "Out, Out—" the machine is the force that mercilessly determines the course of the workday and eventually kills a boy. The poem's dramatis personae, however, will enter only later in the poem. Initially, the reader listens to the sound of a landscape altered by modern technology:

The buzz saw snarled and rattled in the yard
And made dust and dropped stove-length sticks of wood,
Sweet-scented stuff when the breeze drew across it.
(1995 [1916]: 131, ll. 1-3; emphasis added)

The use of consonance opens a range of connotations here. In the first line, it lends the machine attributes that turn it into a snarling, rattling, unsettled animal, just as Chicago became a fierce dog with sharp white teeth. The second line links the sound of the buzz saw to the products of its work. The "stove-length sticks of wood" are the regulated product of the machine that also produces sawdust—a "Sweet-scented stuff." While the machine processes nature into a product, it is only through a breeze—through nature—that our senses become alert to the fragrance produced solely by the joint contribution of nature and machine. In the end, the poem will have unfolded the cruel logic of a routine workday. It is consistent with this logic that the poem's final word "affairs" (l. 34) picks up the sound of the machine in the beginning, telling the reader that the country workers return to the affairs of their routinized workday without much time to ponder the loss of the boy.

"Out, Out—" is written in blank verse, although the meter is frequently suspended and varied. Frost's flexible use of blank verse captures the tension between the structured workday and the industrialized labor processes on the one side, and the spontaneity and beauty of rural New England life on the other. But Frost does not offer a simple dichotomy between a redemptive nature and a corrupting society. Nature can no longer be considered apart from the regulated work patterns and objectified human relations that have permanently changed it. While Frost's poetry is characterized by a "willed resistance to mutability, to any external efforts to produce change" (Parini 2000: 119), he is not blind to the advancement of technology and industrialization. A reference to the unmitigated beauty of the New England landscape appears only once in the poem, contrasting sharply with the individuals' experience of regulated work patterns. "Five mountain ranges one behind the other / Under the sunset far into Vermont" (ll. 5-6) can be seen only by "those that lifted eyes" (l. 4), with the implication that the characters of the poem are too much involved in their work routine to appreciate nature's beauty.

Given the centrality of technology for modernity, it is logical that the machine, and not nature, is driving the plot of "Out, Out—." Right after the brief view of the mountain range (as it were, a 'mountain interval'), the poem returns to the sounds of the wood-cutting machine, now emphasizing darker sounds ("the saw snarled and rattled, snarled and rattled," l. 7; emphasis added) and a brooding tone that announces a dramatic turn of events. At this point, halfway through the poem, it still seems that the poem is primarily a description of yet another dull workday: "And nothing happened: day was all but done" (l. 9). It appears that the workers will return to their homes or linger to enjoy the beauty of the Vermont landscape after they end their workday. In the next lines, however, the poem's dramatic climax is announced more explicitly. Without further explanation, it moves from the description of the scenery to individual protagonists affected by the workplace. For the first time, the poem's speaker (to whom we will return) refers to himself and introduces "the boy," with the definitive article suggesting that the reader is already acquainted with this boy:

Call it a day, I wish they might have said
To please the boy by giving him the half hour
That a boy counts so much when saved from work. (ll. 10-2)

Through the use of alliteration ("him," "half hour," l. 11) the boy's leisure time is connected to his very being. Instead of taking some time off after what seems an exaggerated amount of labor, the boy continues to work and meets his final fate. It is significant that Frost uses the phrase "saved from work," since in "Out, Out —" human labor does not exemplify a more original relation with nature and the universe, nor is labor the foundation for a monumental effort as in "Chicago." Routinized labor is what literally kills the individual.

In the poem's climactic scene, the buzz saw jumps at the boy's hand and inflicts what will turn out to be a fatal wound. While the story itself is straightforward, the poem's description of the persons and objects involved raises intricate epistemological and moral questions:

His sister stood beside him in her apron
To tell them 'Supper.' At the word, the saw,
As if to prove saws know what supper meant,
Leaped out at the boy's hand, or seemed to leap—
He must have given the hand. However it was,
Neither refused the meeting. But the hand! (ll. 13-8)

Frost plays with the question of agency here. It is not clear what initiated the event—the sister's call to supper, the boy's inattention, or the buzz saw itself. The poem foregrounds an indeterminacy of meaning and responsibility that is characteristic of Frost's work. With the explicit reference to the speaker, the poem introduces a normative moral perspective ("I wish," l. 10). But it is precisely this speaker who remains ambiguous in his description of the scene. He first refuses to specify the sister's role: potentially she is the distractive force that interrupts the boy at work—but this is never spelled out. The speaker then shifts the agency to the saw itself, which actively 'responded' to the sister's words "[a]s if to prove saws know what supper meant" (l. 15). This impression, in turn, is qualified by the statement that the saw only "*seemed* to leap" (l. 16; emphasis added) and that the boy must have reached into the buzz saw himself: "He must have given the hand" (l. 17). In the end the speaker contents himself with holding in suspension these multiple perspectives. "However it was" (l. 17), he says, deliberately avoiding a clear causality of events, "the meeting" is characterized by a peculiar fatality, for neither the boy nor the buzz saw "refused the meeting" (l. 18). These lines shift the question away from considerations of individual guilt. Every person and object simply fulfills their roles in this setting.

As if using the accident primarily as a representative case study of modern life in the rural area, the poem maintains its serene, detached tone even in the depiction of the boy's death. We are told that the boy holds up his severed hand "[h]alf in appeal, but half as if to keep / The life from spilling" (ll. 21-2). Just as the "appeal" is immediately balanced by the boy's intention to stop the wound from bleeding, the witnesses are first shocked, but quickly accept the fact that there is nothing to be done:

And then—the watcher at his pulse took fright.
No one believed. They listened to his heart.
Little—less—nothing!—and that ended it.
No more to build on there. And they, since they
Were not the one dead, turned to their affairs. (ll. 30-4)

Even though there is a sense of compassion and an incredulity about the severity of the boy's injury, once the boy has died the community quickly turns away from his fate. It seems that any meaningful form of coexistence in "Out, Out—" has become problematic—not only in the urban centers of modernity, but in the rural space itself. The poem consciously refrains from depicting any act of solidarity; we do not even learn the sister's reaction, being told instead that everyone returns to "their affairs." Even worse, the pastoral retreat seems to have become dysfunctional; it seems that "nature is indifferent to man's sufferings" (Pratt 1996: 119). Frost's poetry often describes the countryside as "retreat, rather, than escape from universal chaos as a way to reflect upon and strengthen the self" (Faggen 2001: 50), and yet "Out, Out—" forms a counterpoint in this respect. When the speaker comments on the boy's moment of death by saying "that ended it" (l. 32), he means quite literally that for the bystanders, the affair has ended. Mourning and commemoration are surrendered to routine.

Rural space in "Out, Out—" becomes a scene for investigating the forms of alienation and the destruction of community associated with modernity. The poem portrays a group of individuals that is held together mostly through routinized labor processes. When, in an epiphanic moment before his death, the boy "saw all— / Since he was old enough to know, big boy / Doing a man's work, though a child at heart— / He saw all spoiled" (ll. 22-5), he recognizes the meaninglessness of a world determined by work and machinery. In fact, the question of meaning underlies the entire poem, as indicated by the title's reference to Shakespeare's *Macbeth*. After his wife's death, Macbeth ponders the meaninglessness of his life and human actions:

> Out, out, brief candle!
> Life's but a walking shadow, a poor player
> That struts and frets his hour upon the stage
> And then is heard no more. It is a tale
> Told by an idiot, full of sound and fury
> Signifying nothing. (Shakespeare 1997 [1606]: 153, 5.5.23-8)

This is the moment when Macbeth ponders the failure and ultimate futility of his political intrigues and his attempt to challenge the late medieval order. Macbeth asks what his actions mean in a world that ultimately seems to have lost all stable meaning. His life eventually amounts to "[s]ignifying nothing." This phrase is picked up in "Out, Out—" by the poem's speaker when he describes how the boy dies after he has been etherized: "Little—less—nothing!—" (l. 32). Just as for Macbeth, the larger question is whether meaning exists at all; the boy's epiphanic vision spells out the other characters' general behavior. In the remainder of the poem the speaker reports the bystanders' response in a coldly detached manner: "No more to build on there" (l. 33). There is not much to be done; all that remains is to note how the transition from innocence to experience coincides with death.

If the poem works as an indictment of an industrialized landscape and objectified work relations, it is primarily concerned with how to deal with these problems. The poems in *Mountain Interval* in general "reflect a sense of choice, an awareness both of the options among which a choice must be made and the very action of choosing itself" (Bieganowski 1984: 259). They exemplify what Richard Poirier has called Frost's "work of knowing." For Poirier, Frost's "ultimate subject is the interpretive process itself" (1990: xxiii). In "The Road Not

Taken," the first poem of *Mountain Interval*, the protagonist must choose between two roads, one "just as fair" as the other (Frost 1995 [1916]: 103, l. 6). In the end he states that while he "shall be telling this with a sigh / Somewhere ages and ages hence" (ll. 16-7) it was his *choice* in taking the road "less traveled by" (l. 19)—rather than any characteristic of the two roads—that made the difference. Frost's famous poem might be read as an allegory of the modern world in which one decision is as good as another and where the poetic imagination must come to terms with the unavailability of stable meaning in a rapidly changing world. The same epistemological questions are addressed in "Out, Out—." Although there is little choice available to the poem's characters, readers are forced to choose how to judge the characters' situation. Giving expression to the structural conditions of rural life and the epistemological consequences of a modernity characterized by the absence of stable meanings, it creates a problematic with which readers must grapple.

As such it is a typical example of what Frost considered the purpose of poetry. For Frost, poetry does not explain the world by offering neat blueprints, but rather "ends in a clarification of life—not necessarily a great clarification, such as sects and cults are founded on, but in a momentary stay against confusion" (1995 [1939]: 777). If the pastoral is a "type of didactic poetry extolling hard labor and a scientific approach to nature" (Faggen 2001: 49), Frost redefines the pastoral as a form that thrives on ambiguity rather than teaching moral lessons. This ambiguity is part of his response to the conditions of modernity. In "The Figure a Poem Makes," Frost asserts that poetry "will have the more charm for not being mechanically straight. We enjoy the straight crookedness of a good walking stick. Modern instruments of precision are being used to make things crooked as if by eye and hand in the old days" (1995 [1939]: 777). While Frost is more frequently interested in epistemological and philosophical consequences, and Sandburg leans more toward politics and social agency, their poetry still touches upon the same issues. Frost equally elevates the people's language and experience to poetic heights: "We write of things we see and we write in accents we hear. Thus we gather both our material and our technique with the imagination from life: and our technique becomes as much material as material itself" (1995 [1914]: 682). True, as opposed to Sandburg's often normative use of the people as a collective that will channel the forces of modernity in the right direction, Frost often entertained a more detached relationship with his 'poetic material.' And yet by contrasting "the boy's death against regal tragedy" (Bieganowski 1984: 264), he grants him the aura of a truly poetic subject. It is this subtle sense of the dignity of life that underlies the destructive machinery driving "Out, Out—." The boy's insight into life's meaninglessness and cruel irony is also structurally related to the poem's other epiphanic moment noted only by the speaker: Vermont's beautiful mountains (cf. Frost 1995 [1916]: 131, l. 6). This is an important contrast in a poem that addresses the cruelties of a technological age when progress comes with the exploitation and destruction of the individual.

4. The Road Not Taken

Sandburg's and Frost's fame and popularity increased long after their seminal poetry had been published. In 1940 Sandburg would win the Pulitzer Prize for his six-volume biography of Abraham Lincoln, only to be awarded a second Pulitzer in 1951 for his *Complete Poems*. In Chicago, a 1961 urban renewal project neighborhood was named "Carl Sandburg Village." His name is still closely linked to the history of the city, and "Chicago" stands as a poem that gives expression to a dialectic vision of hope and despair that would continue to haunt the twentieth century. In other words, by the mid-twentieth century Sandburg was an achieved, publically recognized poet. The same was true for Frost, who would read his poem "The Gift Outright" at John F. Kennedy's inauguration in 1961—an unprecedented event in American cultural history. And yet their academic reputation has not fared overly well. Despite, or perhaps because of, their popularity, these "popular modernists" (Newcomb 2012: 5) were often marginalized by an academic criticism that canonized the experimental Modernist tradition.

Although neither Sandburg nor Frost belonged to a particular school of poetry, it bears remembering that Eliot, Frost, Pound, and Sandburg lived in the same world, were involved with the important publication sites of modern American poetry, and addressed the same problems, although often with radically different forms and from different political positions (see Cooper 2014). While the experimental tradition came to dominate academic teaching of American poetry, in the first half of the twentieth century there was a much more diverse sense of what modern, experimental American poetry was. "Chicago" was not only printed in *Poetry* magazine, but used on the magazine's first page as a quasi-editorial statement for experimental art. Answering the various attacks on the poem, *Poetry*'s editors decided to award a prize to Sandburg's poem and thereby "reasserted its commitment to the radically modern values and styles Sandburg represented" (Newcomb 2012: 42). As Cary Nelson has argued, "one set of coherent aesthetic criteria will not even encompass the variations within canonical modernism, let alone the whole range of poems recovered in recent decades" (2001: 164). Both Frost and Sandburg sought to 'make it new' in their own ways, and their poetry shows that modern American poetry took different roads in the early twentieth century. What sets them apart from many Modernists is not so much their rather cautious experimentalism, but their emphasis on the people, their language, and their experience. Frost's rewriting of the pastoral tradition was forged from the diction of New Englanders; Sandburg's free verse city poems embraced the people as a force that could give direction to an inchoate modernity. As such, they tried to create a poetics of the people and to ask how one could meaningfully speak of community and human interaction in an age increasingly characterized by alienation and objectified human relations.

Bibliography

Selected Primary Literature

Frost, Robert. 1995. *Collected Poems, Prose, and Plays*. New York: Library of America.

——. 2006. *The Notebooks of Robert Frost*. Ed. Robert Faggen. Cambridge, MA: Harvard UP.

Hughes, Langston. 1993 [1940]. *The Big Sea: An Autobiography*. New York: Hill and Wang.

Marinetti, Filippo Tommaso. 2006. "The Foundation and Manifesto of Futurism." In: *Critical Writings. Filippo Tommaso Marinetti*. Ed. Günter Berghaus.

Trans. Doug Thompson. New ed. New York: Farrar, Straus, and Giroux. 11-6.

Pound, Ezra. 2004. *Poems and Translations*. Ed. Richard Sieburth. New York: Library of America.

Sandburg, Carl. 1914. "Chicago." In: *Poetry* 3.6: 191-2.

——. 1991. *The Complete Poems of Carl Sandburg*. Rev. ed. New York: Harcourt, Brace, and Company.

Shakespeare, William. 1997 [1623]. *Macbeth*. Ed. Kenneth Muir. London: Arden.

Williams, William Carlos. 1951. "Carl Sandburg's Complete Poems." In: *Poetry* 78.6: 345-51.

Selected Secondary Literature

Berman, Marshall. 1988. *All That Is Solid Melts Into Air: The Experience of Modernity*. New ed. New York: Penguin.

Still an important and accessible study of the social and cultural environment of modernity.

Callahan, North. 1987. *Carl Sandburg: His Life and Works*. University Park: Pennsylvania State UP.

Accessible biography that is weak on interpretation but presents an excellent overview of the reactions to Sandburg's poetry at the time. Callahan also provides an important account of Sandburg's career in journalism.

Parini, Jay. 2000. *Robert Frost: A Life*. New York: Picador.

Together with Pritchard 1993, the standard biography of Frost's life and works. Parini also provides good readings of individual poems.

Poirier, Richard. 1990. *Robert Frost: The Work of Knowing*. New ed. Stanford: Stanford UP.

Important pragmatist study of Frost's poetry which contains excellent readings. Poirier shows how Frost's poems stage their own process of meaning-making.

Yannella, Philip R. 1996. *The Other Carl Sandburg*. Jackson: UP of Mississippi.

Important reading of Sandburg's early poetry within the context of early twentieth-century socialism. Yannella shows how Sandburg's poetry seems much more politically radical if read in the appropriate contexts of the early twentieth century and in light of Sandburg's political engagement of the time.

Further References

Alexander, William. 1973. "The Limited American, the Great Loneliness, and the Singing Fire: Carl Sandburg's 'Chicago Poems'." In: *American Literature* 45.1: 67-83.

Bieganowski, Ronald. 1984. "Robert Frost's Sense of Choice in 'Mountain Interval'." In: *College Literature* 11.3: 258-68.

Bischoff, Volker. 1983. *Amerikanische Lyrik zwischen 1912 und 1922: Untersuchungen zur Theorie, Praxis und Wirkungsgeschichte der "New Poetry."* Heidelberg: Winter.

Bradbury, Malcolm. 1991 [1976]. "The Cities of Modernism." In: Malcolm Bradbury and James McFarlane (eds.), *Modernism 1890-1930*. Repr. New York: Penguin. 96-104.

Cooper, John Xiros. 2014. "Robert Frost and Modernism." In: Mark Richardson (ed.), *Robert Frost in Context*. Cambridge: Cambridge UP. 85-91.

Cronon, William. 1992. *Nature's Metropolis: Chicago and the Great West*. New York: Norton.

Faggen, Robert. 2001. "Frost and the Questions of Pastoral." In: Robert Faggen (ed.), *The Cambridge Companion to Robert Frost*. Cambridge: Cambridge UP. 49-74.

Hass, Robert Bernhard. 2014. "'Measuring Myself against all Creation': Robert Frost and Pastoral." In: Mark Richardson (ed.), *Robert Frost in Context*. Cambridge: Cambridge UP. 114-22.

Lynen, John F. 1960. *The Pastoral Art of Robert Frost*. New Haven: Yale UP.

Marx, Leo. 2000 [1964]. *The Machine in the Garden: Technology and the Pastoral Ideal in America*. New York: Oxford UP.

Nelson, Cary. 2001. *Revolutionary Memory: Recovering the Poetry of the American Left*. New York: Routledge.

Newcomb, John. 2012. *How Did Poetry Survive? The Making of Modern American Verse*. Urbana: U of Illinois P.

Nicholls, Peter. 2009. *Modernisms: A Literary Guide*. 2nd ed. New York: Palgrave Macmillan.

Pratt, William. 1996. *Singing the Chaos: Madness and Wisdom in Modern Poetry*. Columbia: U of Missouri P.

Pritchard, William. 1993. *Frost: A Literary Life Reconsidered*. 2nd ed. New York: Oxford UP.

Van Wienen, Mark. 1991. "Taming the Socialist: Carl Sandburg's *Chicago Poems* and its Critics." In: *American Literature* 63.1: 89-103.

12.

Variations on High Modernism

T.S. Eliot's "The Love Song of J. Alfred Prufrock" and Ezra Pound's *Hugh Selwyn Mauberley*

Heinz Ickstadt

1. Introduction: Literary Modernism

Like all major literary movements, Modernism was an international phenomenon. It issued from a cultural conflict between generations: the radical break of sons—obsessed by ideas of the New—with the repressive culture of their Victorian fathers. It was therefore essentially the product of the modernizing societies of the West (including western Russia) and its favorite environment—the locus *par excellence* of all modernizing processes: the contemporary metropolis. Paris, London, Berlin, Milan, St. Petersburg, and New York were its centers. It began well before World War I with the literary and cultural rebellion of the avant-gardes against the cultural complacency of the bourgeoisie: with Futurism in Italy (Marinetti, Boccioni, and many others) and Russia (Chlebnikow and Majakowski), early Surrealism in France (Jarry and Apollinaire), Expressionism in Germany (Georg Heym and Gottfried Benn), with Dada in Switzerland (Tristan Tzara) and Germany (Hugo Ball), Imagism and Vorticism in England (Ezra Pound, Wyndham Lewis, T.E. Hulme, Hilda Doolittle, and Richard Aldington). But the horrors of World War I changed modernism fundamentally. Although the avant-gardes did not disappear, the 1920s saw the rise of modern masters and the creation of new master works: James Joyce and *Ulysses*, T.S. Eliot and *The Waste Land*, Ezra Pound and *The Cantos*.

Modernism gave artistic expression to a cultural discontent that Freud, at almost the exact same time, expressed in psychoanalytical terms. Accordingly, it drew its creative energy from the liberation (and symbolic taming) of the cultural repressed—of the dark, primitive, identity-dissolving 'Other' of Western civilization. The ambivalence of this fascination led to highly diverse, contradictory, and often questionable practices and political alliances. Modernism explored the dark Other of European and American culture by integrating 'feminine' regions of the psyche (at the same time that it propagated an aesthetic ideology of 'maleness'); or it indulged in fantasies of ethnic and racial otherness that allowed for the creative integration of the culturally 'primitive' without questioning existing social and racial hierarchies. It was anarchic and revolutionary *vis-à-vis* the dominant conventions and expectations of the bourgeoisie, but it was also obsessed with a quasi-religious search for a spiritual order or 'wholeness' it could not find in the wasteland of a modernized, commercialized, and fragmented society. Modernism welcomed (and contributed to) the decay of bourgeois values and thus acted in alliance with social forces accelerating that decay: the energies (and products) of modern technology and also the revolutionary or reactionary prophets of a New Society. In its early phase, modernism revolted with anarchist fervor against 'Art' and the institutionalized High Culture of Victorianism in an effort to level the division between Art and Life, between High and Low. But during the post-World War I era, the insistence of the Masters on form and

craftsmanship became increasingly directed against the democratic formless-
ness of mass culture (thus eventually creating a High Culture of its own).

Although modernism is a cosmopolitan phenomenon, it is yet marked by national differentiations. American modernism was more than a provincial imitation
of European developments. It was rather the product of an intercultural exchange
in which new concepts and practices of innovation were adapted to a social and
cultural tradition of democratic self-definition. To be sure, the modernism of the
early twentieth century was a European invention; it seemed natural, however, to
transplant and adapt it to a country that saw itself as the champion of the technological modern, and certainly as a vanguard among modernizing nations. Even
though, in her effort to become a modern writer, Gertrude Stein felt compelled to
leave America for the culturally more congenial ambience of Paris, she was nevertheless convinced that modernism had its natural home in the United States
since the U.S. had entered the spirit of the twentieth century earlier than any
other nation. If to be modern was already implicit in America's self-interpretation,
then modernism did not have to radically break with American ideals and realities. Rather it meant to uncover what was in front of everyone's eyes, or to rediscover and work out what was always inherently there. American modernism
thus made its search for genuine self-expression a national project that drew its
energy from several sources. For William Carlos Williams, for example, the project
of American modernism—like John Dewey's project of democracy—was open-
ended, an ongoing linguistic revolution, a process of constantly re-making and
working out what was originally given in the continental fact, the local soil, the
democratic idea—in short, the spiritual essence of America. Expatriate poets such
as Pound, H.D., and Eliot looked for and discovered such 'essence' elsewhere, but
in doing so they strangely fulfilled a vision of the young Henry James who had
been similarly engaged in a process of cultural absorption and transformation: It
"seems to me," he wrote to his friend Thomas Sargent Perry in 1867,

> that we are ahead of the European races in the fact that more than either of them
> we can deal freely with forms of civilization not our own, can pick and choose and
> assimilate and in short (aesthetically etc.) claim our property wherever we find it
> . . . American writers may yet indicate that a vast intellectual fusion and synthe-
> sis of the various National tendencies of the world is the condition of more im-
> portant achievements than any we have seen (James 1974, I: 77).

Yet the sharp distinction that has been frequently made between those cosmopolitan American artists and writers who—like Stein, Pound, H.D., and Eliot—left
the United States to become founders and promoters of a transatlantic modernism and those who—like Robert Frost, Wallace Stevens, Hart Crane, Marianne
Moore, and William Carlos Williams—stayed at home to cultivate the local is not
entirely justified. There was a constant going back and forth: Not only did American artists and writers frequently travel from New York to Paris (or London), but
under the impact of World War I European avant-gardists—artists like Marcel
Duchamp, Francis Picabia, and Edgar Varèse, or the poet Mina Loy—also left
Paris or London for New York. During the teens and twenties, little magazines
sprouted up in New York (or were later transplanted to Rome, Paris, or Berlin because publishing was less expensive there). They were filled with texts of the various European avant-gardes translated from Italian, French, and German.

Particularly in its early phase, the preferred genre of avant-gardist literary expression was poetry rather than fiction. The novel, mediated through the literary
market, depended on a larger reading public. In comparison, poetry was a mar-

ginal and therefore a more independent medium, addressing a select audience—
an audience more or less confined to readers of small and short-lived journals.
When Pound left America for London in 1908, he was bent on promoting a new
poetic style that he had yet to translate into his own poetic practice. His poetry—Anglo-Saxon poetry in general (the linguistic experiments of Stein went
practically unnoticed)—was marked by the influence of French symbolism and
the preciousness of *fin-de-siècle* aesthetics; and Pound, too, was, as David
Perkins writes, still an "Edwardian poet" (1976: 454). In the process of modernizing himself, Pound discovered the "new" by appropriating—via translation—
traditions of poetic expression (Provençal, Latin, Chinese, and Japanese) that
helped him shed established conventions and develop an idiom at once econom-
ical (i.e., non-rhetorical), musical, and visually precise.

Pound's Imagism (as documented in his "A Few Don'ts" of 1913) was not only
the earliest but also the most influential 'movement' of modern American poetry.
It has even been argued that modernism in literature has been haunted by the
spirit of Imagism. Perhaps one could say with equal justification that modernism
has been 'haunted' by Emerson's figure of the "transparent eye-ball" (1990
[1836]: 6) in which the 'mere' eye of everyday perception is transcended in the all-
encompassing grasp of visionary seeing. Indeed, whether acknowledged or not,
Emerson's ideas have left a visible trace in the rhetoric of American modernism,
not only his linking of the I (as self-reliant subject) to the Eye as its main instrument of perception and cognition, but also his connecting the act of seeing with
the act of knowing, and connecting both with an effort to construct the world by
(re)naming it—a world always already there and yet to be made new through its
visual and sensuous reconstruction in language. The Imagists would presumably
have rejected the implied vagueness of Emerson's idealizing vision—as much as
they would have separated the 'I' from the 'Eye' since, in their notion of the act of
seeing, they shifted emphasis from the subject to the object of perception.

For Pound and his friends, Imagism was a double counter-discourse: On the
one hand, it evoked a classical tradition of Greek marble, thus setting the notion
of a clear and hard image (partly in alliance with French Symbolists and English
Pre-Raphaelites) against the ornamental and emotional vagueness of late-
Romantic and Victorian verse. On the other hand, the concept of an image as
hard and solid as marble also set the stillness of the classic against contemporary culture's voracious demand for moving images. The postulate of a "direct
treatment of the thing" (Flint/Pound 1970 [1913]: 41; cf. "It's straight talk,
straight as the Greek!," Pound 1971: 11) was part of an anti-subjectivist project
(as was Eliot's 'objective correlative,' or Hemingway's 'iceberg theory') that tried
to avoid any direct articulation of emotion by finding its 'sensory equivalent' in
the objective and visually concrete image. However, the very evocation of classic
stillness implied an aesthetic ideal of the statuesque which seemed, in its very
stylization, conventional and academic. Therefore Pound very soon went from
'Imagism' to what he and his friends Wyndham Lewis and Henri Gaudier-
Brzeska called 'Vorticism,' and argued for a more dynamic notion of the image.
He had become aware that the new developments in literature and the arts went
with and not *against* the dynamics of modernity.

With several interruptions—trips to Italy, the U.S., and France—Pound
stayed in London for twelve years. During that time he published several volumes of poetry and translations, joined a circle of artists and intellectuals
(among them William Butler Yeats, D.H. Lawrence, Ford Madox Ford, Wyndham

Lewis, and T.E. Hulme), and learned his first lessons in economic theory from Major C.H. Douglas, the founder of the Social Credit movement. Although he was, in many ways, the center of these circles—instigating literary movements, supporting literary magazines, discovering and promoting individual talents like that of H.D., Joyce, and the as yet little-published Eliot—he found the intellectual climate during the war, and especially in post-war London, increasingly suffocating. Many of his friends and artistic collaborators (like Hulme and the sculptor Gaudier-Brzeska) had died during World War I, but the political and economic establishment Pound held responsible for the death of millions was unshaken. Together with Lewis and Gaudier-Brzeska he founded 'Vorticism' as an English answer to Italian *Futurismo*. But the movement did not survive the first years of the war and died as fast as its magazine, *Blast*, where its "Manifesto" and a major article by Gaudier-Brzeska—"written from the Trenches"—had been published. Pound realized that the center of artistic and literary innovation (if it ever had been in London) was now elsewhere. In December 1920 he left London for Paris, but before leaving he published a cycle of poems he called *Hugh Selwyn Mauberley: Contacts and Life*—a bitter good-bye to his previous poet-self/selves as well as to a stifling culture. Pound's *Mauberley* and Eliot's "The Love Song of J. Alfred Prufrock" (which Harriet Monroe had reluctantly published in her 1915 journal, *Poetry*, on Pound's insistent recommendation) are generally considered the most important poems of early Anglo-Saxon modernism—until they were both overshadowed by Eliot's *The Waste Land* in 1922.

2. Avant-Garde Eliot: "The Love Song of J. Alfred Prufrock"

Eliot began writing "Prufrock" while still studying at Harvard. Influenced by Arthur Symons's *The Symbolist Movement in Literature* (1899), he immersed himself in the work of Jules Laforgue whose self-ironic, even self-deprecatory mode taught him, as Eliot later wrote, "the poetic possibilities of my own idiom of speech" (in Perkins 1987 [1976], I: 493). Eliot continued working on "Prufrock" during a prolonged stay in Paris and again in 1911 after returning to Harvard. He also took it with him when he went to England in 1914. First readers thought the poem was "absolutely insane . . . the morbid ravings of a madman" (Gordon 1977: 47), whereas Pound, in his letter to Harriet Monroe, called it the best poem he had yet seen from an American. Without Eliot's knowledge, Pound borrowed money to finance its publication in 1917 as part of a first collection of Eliot's poems, *The Love Song of J. Alfred Prufrock and Other Observations* (ibid.: 67-8).

Like much modern music, Eliot's 'maddening' dissonances no longer shock our ears. On the contrary, the music of his verse—what Northrop Frye once called its "mnemonic adhesiveness" (1981 [1963]: 28)—makes certain passages (as, for instance, its famous opening lines) haunt our memories:

Let us go then, you and I,
When the evening is spread out against the sky
Like a patient etherised upon a table;
Let us go, through certain half-deserted streets,
The muttering retreats
Of restless nights in one-night cheap hotels
And sawdust restaurants with oyster-shells:
Streets that follow like a tedious argument
Of insidious intent

To lead you to an overwhelming question . . .
Oh, do not ask, "What is it?"
Let us go and make our visit. (ll. 1-12)

The melodious surface of rhyme in the first three lines (I, sky) and assonance—
[ai] [ee] [i] [e]—smoothes over the shocking metaphoric linkage of a nature image
(evening) with sickness or surgery. Not only is the abstract "evening" spatialized
and made concrete in the "spread out . . . upon a table," the "etherised" that goes
with "patient . . . upon a table" (the anesthesia used in preparation of surgery)
also evokes (and mocks) the familiar "ether" of Romantic nature poetry. Ironic
defamiliarizations such as these—the coziness of an image coating the ugliness of
the subject matter (shabby cheap hotels and grubby restaurants, with "oyster
shells" continuing the dreary sexual connotations of "one-night cheap hotels")—
mark a text that draws poetic 'beauty' from the ugliness of the contemporary
scene, the tedium of its social life, and the general *ennui* of existence. The sound
structure of the subsequent lines—the dominant sequence of [ee] and [i] in "retreats," "street," "tedious" and "insidious intent," "is it," "visit"—underlines the
trivial repetitiveness and cheapness that is expressed on the semantic level.

The discrepancy between Romantic expectation and the impossibility of
achievement (or the lack of will and energy to achieve) pervades the poem from
beginning to end and is anticipated in the title. "The Love Song of J. Alfred
Prufrock" raises expectations that the poem by no means fulfills: It is neither a
song about love, nor is it addressed to anyone with whom the speaker is in love.
It is a monologue of self-doubt and hesitation. Narcissistically preoccupied with
himself, the speaker considers "an overwhelming question" that betrays melancholic self-indulgence more than a quest for knowledge. For all quests are taint-
ed with futility from the start: the tediousness of what is always already known
and familiar, the routine behavior at social salons where "women come and go /
Talking of Michelangelo," and the empty rituals of courtship and lovemaking.
The "you" addressed by the "I" in the very first line is thus not an addressed
Other in conversation, but the "I" as an object of its own reflection, the mind's
shadow—or, possibly, even the reader ("You, hypocrite lecteur!—mon semblable,—
mon frère!," as Eliot quotes Baudelaire in *The Waste Land*). Prufrock, the poet's
mask (not Eliot who, when he wrote "Love Song," was a young man of twenty-
three) is an aging alter ego in midlife crisis, a joke to himself and others, afraid
of time and death as much as of life and love, melancholically resigning himself
to mediocrity. In her discussion of Prufrock (both the figure and the poem), Marjorie Perloff quotes Charles Altieri's essay on Eliot's "Symbolist subject": "There
is far too much of the fool in the character for the author to be content with the
identification." Thus, "we find ourselves entering a sensibility so fluid and eva-
sive that it makes classical distance necessary, but at the same time renders it
impotent" (Altieri in Perloff 2002: 24).

The poem is full of rhetorical gestures of a romantic desire that cannot reach
beyond the limits of timid self and tepid social life: "Do I dare / Disturb the universe?" (ll. 45-6); "I have measured out my life with coffee spoons" (l. 51); Should
I, after tea and cakes and ices, / Have the strength to force the moment to its
crisis?" (ll. 79-80). Throughout, the speaker not only makes himself the object of
his own reflection but imagines and dramatizes himself as an object in the eyes
of others, especially in the eyes of women whose expectations and appreciations
he feels as a threat to his (social) existence:

> And I have known the eyes already, known them all—
> The eyes that fix you in a formulated phrase,
> And when I am formulated, sprawling on a pin,
> When I am pinned and wriggling on a wall,
> Then how should I begin
> To spit out all the butt-ends of my days and ways?
> And how should I presume?
> . . . .
> Is it perfume from a dress
> That makes me so digress? (ll. 55-61; 65-6)

The presumed "Love Song" is thus rather the digression from a love song, listing everything that prevents Prufrock from singing it. It is not until the end, when the speaker seems to take off his Prufrock-mask, and the poem contracts to the more conventional form of the last two tercets, that it seems to follow the more audible pattern of the ten-syllabic pentameter line. The tercets may also suggest—however vaguely—the convention of a poetic form (Dante's, for instance, in his *Divina Commedia*) that the poem fails to achieve, just as it fails to be the "Love Song" promised in its title.

> Shall I part my hair behind? Do I dare to eat a peach?
> I shall wear white flannel trousers, and walk upon the beach.
> I have heard the mermaids singing, each to each.
>
> I do not think that they will sing to me.
>
> I have seen them riding seaward on the waves
> Combing the white hair of the waves blown back
> When the wind blows the water white and black.
>
> We have lingered in the chambers of the sea
> By sea-girls wreathed with seaweed red and brown.
> Till human voices wake us, and we drown. (ll. 122-31)

In these highly ambivalent and deliberately inconclusive final lines, the poem seems to leave behind the reality of the raw urban scene as well as the civilized *ennui* of the bourgeois salon in favor of the romantic nature world of sea and imagination, a "wish-fulfillment world," as Frye has it (1981 [1963]: 58), of dream, poetry, and fairy-tale.

The voice who wonders whether he shall "dare to eat a peach" is clearly Prufrock's. But who are the "mermaids" he has heard singing—the ladies in the salon who, he knows, will not "sing to me?" Or are they creatures and messengers of a realm to which the speaker (the poet in the mask of Prufrock) secretly belongs via the very qualities (his sensitivity and otherworldliness) that make him unfit for the social world he has left behind (at least in metaphor)? If so, Prufrock's "Love Song" might also be taken as an ironic allusion to Baudelaire's "L'Albatros," that strange bird—an image of the alienated poet—who does not fit into the society from which he cannot escape except into his true element, the air—the realm of poetry and the imagination. And yet Prufrock, "strange" as he may be, is by no means also a higher being (as Baudelaire's albatross is): a creature, ugly and clumsy on earth, yet majestic in flight. Rather, he is socially formed, has "measured out his life with coffee spoons" and is, to that extent, part of the world that he rejects.

One might further ask whether this introverted dreamer and jaded master of ironic (self-)reflection is secretly at home "in the chambers of the sea" and "drowned" only when forced into a state of awareness through the eyes and voices of others. Is Prufrock's "love song" addressed to mermaids and sea-girls of the deeper world to which he periodically surrenders? Is the 'drowning' the promise of an eventual wakening, and death the final fulfillment of and liberation from futile desire? Or is this only the ultimate turn in his self-ironic introspection, as Marjorie Perloff assumes in her discussion of the poem (2002: 25)? Who is the "we" and "us" in the last tercet? Is it the "I" and "you" of the opening line now conceived as unity in doubleness? Does it evoke a community of the like-minded, of *fin-de-siècle* sensibilities? Does it include the reader in an embrace of mutual understanding so that a whole generation could—as in fact it did—recognize, but also critically assess, itself in Prufrock's self-involved and world-weary aestheticism?

The poem, although mocking romantic conventions of the poetic, also evokes and thrives on them. It stages, in abrupt juxtapositions of the incongruous and in metaphoric combinations of the concrete and the abstract ("hands that lift and drop a question on your plate," "I have measured out my life in coffee spoons"), a state of consciousness that is embodied with remarkable precision in clear and sensuous images.

This visual suggestiveness via image and metaphor—an early practice of what Eliot later called "objective correlative"—is continued in the musical structure of the poem, its sound and rhythmic patterns in their subtle variations. The function of rhymes (end rhymes and interior rhymes, consonance and assonance) changes throughout the poem; they mark the comic or ridiculous, or the elevated and poetic ("I have seen them riding seaward on the waves"); or they evoke whispers of threat or sexual invitation ("one-night cheap hotels / And sawdust restaurants with oyster-shells: / Streets that follow like a tedious argument / Of insidious intent"). Rhythmically, the poem expands and contracts, shifts from complex syncopated patterns ("Asleep . . . tired . . . or it malingers") to banal regularity ("Advíse the prínce; no dóubt an éasy tóol"), all on the basis of a variably used iambic/trochaic scheme or even a ten-syllabic pentameter.

Even if the poem's fractured idiom ironically subverts the romantic and conventional (as annunciated in its very opening lines) and rejects the female world of "culture" (together with the adored woman that a "love song" might be expected to address), it is nevertheless linguistically committed to the non-rational (although it may be quite rationally constructed): to the fluid, the preconscious or subconscious realm—those "chambers of the sea" that Julia Kristeva has associated with the semiotic and the feminine. The "mermaids" may not sing to Prufrock, but they certainly sing to the poet and—through his poem—to the reader.

3. Pound's Farewell to London: *Hugh Selwyn Mauberley*

Although Eliot's poem was originally published before the war, it was republished in a wartime context: Eliot dedicated his *Prufrock and Other Observations* (1917) to the memory of his friend Jean Verdenal, a Parisian who had been killed in 1915. Pound's *Hugh Selwyn Mauberley: Contacts and Life* was published three years later in 1920 and shows more immediately the impact of World War I which made him ultimately turn away from aestheticism. The war shocked Pound into a critical assessment of his past career, of his social function as a poet, of the state of the art of poetry, as well as of the pre-war and post-war literary scene in London. As Eliot wrote in his introduction to the 1928 edition of Pound's selected poems, *Mauberley* is "compact of the experience of a certain man in a certain place at a certain time; and it is also a document of an epoch; it is genuine tragedy and comedy . . ." (Pound 1968 [1928]: 20). This "tricky poem" (Kenner 1985 [1951]: 165) has provoked much literary exegesis without solving its ambivalences or bringing light to its obscurities. Most of these are connected with Pound's confusing play with masks (or personae) of which one is called "E.P.," and the other "Mauberley." *Personae* (1926) is also the title of Pound's collection of his shorter poems in which *Hugh Selwyn Mauberley* was subsequently published.

The poem cycle consists of two almost symmetrically constructed parts—the first comprising twelve poems (including an opening poem bearing the title "E.P. Ode Pour L'Élection de son Sépulchre"), plus a valedictory "Envoi (1919)." The ambivalences begin right here: The edition of Pound's *Selected Poems* (1968 [1928]) has "E.P. Ode Pour L'Élection de son Sépulchre" as the title of Part I, the whole section consisting of twelve poems (some marked by numbers, others by individual titles) plus the "Envoi." In his extensive analysis of the cycle, John Espey takes the "Ode" as the title of the first poem of Part I and not as the title of the whole section. (He is followed in this by the 1990 revised edition of *Personae*, on which Sieburth bases his version of Pound's text.) Espey understands the "E.P." of the title as marking not only the object of the ode but also the name of its creator. The first poem of Part I would then be Pound mocking his critics in his own mock-epitaph. (In a comment, Pound had written: "*Mauberley* buries E.P. in the first poem; gets rid of all his troublesome energies," 2010: 301). The critical irony of the subsequent sections of Part I would then be, so Espey claims, of a different kind. The second part, "Mauberley 1920," is much shorter and consists of only five poems with the last one, "Medallion," corresponding to the "Envoi" of the first part. The question of the extent to which the cycle can be called autobiographical—which of these masks and voices, if any, might be taken as the face and voice of Ezra Pound—has led to diverse and conflicting interpretations. Pound later famously asserted that "I'm no more Mauberley than Eliot is Prufrock" (ibid.: 301).

Hugh Selwyn Mauberley offers a brilliant intertextual display of changing poetic styles and aesthetic poses from post-Symbolism and the Pre-Raphaelites to early modernism, through the various masks the poet wears (and discards) as he labors to find identity. Dedicated to an idea of beauty, he is yet failing in his effort to mediate between what "the time demanded" and his commitment to aesthetic achievements of the past. But does "Mauberley" succeed where "E.P." has failed? Are both (self-)critically discarded as protagonists of failed poetic endeavors? Or is "Mauberley" a version of the kind of poet Pound envisions he might have become had he chosen to stay in London? Hugh Kenner points out that the title page's footnote of the American edition marks the poem cycle "a farewell to London" (1985 [1951]: 169).

The first poem of Part I, "E.P. Ode Pour L'Élection de son Sépulchre," has been taken as self-deprecatory parody—Pound dismissing an earlier version of his identity as poet. But could it also be understood as a sarcastic self-assertion against the verdict on "E.P." ("wrong from the start") as pronounced by London's stodgy critical establishment or one of its mouth-pieces?

> For three years, out of key with his time,
> He strove to resuscitate the dead art
> Of poetry; to maintain "the sublime"
> In the old sense. Wrong from the start—
>
> No, hardly . . . ("E.P. Ode": ll. 1-5)

As Jo Brantley Berryman suggests, the whole first part could be seen as the work of a limited poet, called "Mauberley," as his epitaph for the poet "E.P.," whom he considers limited in his poetic response to the times (1983: xii). The second part, "Mauberley," would then be the work of "E.P.," dedicated to critically unravel the limits of a poet called "Mauberley"—both parts (and poets/masks) thus mirroring each other in their limitations.

Throughout the twelve poems of Part I, however, it is difficult to locate the critical perspective; it seems to be constantly shifting between a critical perception of "E.P." and "E.P.'s" critical perception of his critics. Therefore, it is as problematic to identify the critical voice of Part I as that of "Mauberley" as it is to assume that the voice critically assessing "Mauberley" in Part II is that of "E.P." In his memoir, *Gaudier-Brzeska*, Pound writes about this early period of experimentation that culminates with *Hugh Selwyn Mauberley*:

> In the 'search for oneself,' in the search for 'sincere self-expression,' one gropes, one finds some seeming verity. One says 'I am' this, that, or the other, and with the words scarcely uttered one ceases to be that thing. I began this search for the real in a book called *Personae*, casting off, as it were, complete masks of the self in each poem. I continued in long series of translations, which were but more elaborate masks. (1970 [1916]: 85)

The opening "Ode" reads "E.P." through the eyes of his critics as much as it sets his aesthetic commitment stubbornly against their limited perspective: "Bent resolutely on wringing lilies from acorn" (l. 8). If his stubbornness resembles the hubris of Capaneus, who challenged the gods as arrogantly as "E.P." challenged the gods of criticism, he did so for the sake of an aesthetic ideal of verbal economy and precision as represented by Flaubert's objective and dispassionately analytic style that had been rejected on moral grounds by much English criticism of the period:

> His true Penelope was Flaubert,
> He fished by obstinate isles;
> Observed the elegance of Circe's hair
> Rather than the mottoes on sun-dials.
>
> Unaffected by "the march of events,"
> He passed from men's memory in *l'an trentuniesme*
> *De son eage*; the case presents
> No adjunct to the Muses' diadem. ("E.P. Ode": ll. 13-20; original emphasis)

"The elegance of Circe's hair"—i.e., the hair of the woman whose seduction turned men into swine—may be an aesthetic/sexual distraction on "E.P.'s" Odyssey-like journey toward the goal of his aesthetic desire, yet it is still more meaningful than observing the platitudinous wisdom written on sun-dials or the slogans that accompany the "march of events." Like François Villon—that early case of *le poète maudit* forgotten by the public in his thirty-first year—"E.P." indirectly claims (through Villon's voice) the immortality that Villon nevertheless achieved, his work long recognized as an "adjunct to the Muses's diadem"—an attribute critics denied "E.P."

The second poem of Part I deals with the pressures of the era on a poet committed to a classical ideal of beauty and craftsmanship ("Attic grace", l. 4; "'sculpture' of rhyme", l. 12)—pressures of the commercial and the fast-produced: "plaster . . . not assuredly, alabaster" (l. 11). The same topic is pursued and intensified in the subsequent poem and its attack on the commercialization and democratization of beauty: "We see το καλόν [to kalón] / De-creed in the market place" (ll. 15-6; as Richard Sieburth explains: "'To Kalon' [i.e., the good and the beautiful] was an American brand of port wine around the turn of the century," 2010: 301). The fourth and fifth sections are dedicated to the horrors of war and the deception of a whole generation into patriotic self-sacrifice for the sake of a "botched civilization" (poem v, l. 4). The subsequent poems of this first part ("Yeux Glauques" and "Siena mi fe', Disfecemi Maremma") go back to the ravage worked on the Pre-Raphaelite avant-garde and their cele-bration of sensuous beauty by the bourgeois establishment ("Yeux glauques" being Théophile Gautier's metaphor for the green-gray glaze "common in the eyes of Pre-Raphaelite portraits of women," Sieburth 2010: 302) and the damage done to intellectual promise by the established culture. It made Brennbaum (perhaps the critic and caricaturist Max Beerbohm) "impeccable" through his cultivation of style and the "stiffness" of manners he assumed to repress "the heavy memories of Horeb" (his Jewish heritage; "Brennbaum": ll. 3, 5). Or it caused the deterioration of a once promising novelist, Mr. Nixon (perhaps Arnold Bennett), who became rich by compromising his "art" and, like any member of the bourgeois establishment, now admonishes the artist to be useful to society and not rebel against accepted opinion: "The 'Nineties' tried your game / And died, there's nothing in it." ("Mr. Nixon": ll. 23-4)

Similar pressure has moved the "stylist" (perhaps Ford Madox Ford) into rural exile, "unpaid, uncelebrated," in poem x of Part I, ll. 2-3. The degradation of a mythological past ("Daphne with her thighs in bark," poem xii, l. 1) is made conspicuous in the Prufrock-like banalities of social life, as in the "stuffed-satin drawing-room" where "I await The Lady Valentine's commands" (xii, ll. 3-4). (It is the only time when the cycle's impersonal rendition is interrupted by the intru-sion of the personal pronoun). The last poem of Part I, "Envoi 1919," presents an example of "E.P.'s" aesthetic ideal (a song in the manner of Edmund Waller addressed to the muse)—"a triumphant vindication" (Kenner 1985 [1951]: 176) of his labors in quasi-exile and—since it is a "dumb-born book"—his gift to a future generation of readers to be remembered and celebrated by. It is also a liberation from the constraints of the hard-edged image and the rhymed quat-rain (as practiced by Théophile Gautier and Tristan Corbière) and a re-invention (in the spirit of "making it new") of the musical flow of post-Elizabethan verse:

> Go, dumb-born book, . . .
> Tell her that goes
> With song upon her lips,
> But sings not out the song, nor knows,
> The maker of it, some other mouth,
> May be as fair as hers,
> Might, in new ages, gain her worshippers,
> When our two dusts with
> Waller's shall be laid,
> Siftings on siftings in oblivion,
> Till change hath broken down
> All things save Beauty alone. (ll. 1, 17-26; original emphasis)

Part II, "Mauberley 1920," returns to the "firmness" of the quatrain and deals with the representation of beauty and the poet's response to what "the age de-manded," but this time not in terms of "sculpture" and "alabaster" but of metal and porcelain: "his tool / The engraver's" (ll. 7-8). Yet the first poem of this second part of the cycle seems to mark "Mauberley's" austere "firmness" as a limitation of his art: since it "[t]urned from 'eau-forte / Par Jacquemart" (ll. 1-2)—an allusion to Gautier's *Émaux et Camées*—"[t]o the straight head / Of Messalina" (ll. 3-4) as seen on Roman coins, engraved in profile. Like "E.P.'s," Mauberley's "true Penelope / Was Flaubert" (ll. 5-6)—an allusion to Part I that is marked as a quotation. His art, however, is "but an art / In profile; / Colourless / Pier Francesca" (ll. 11-4)—a painter otherwise celebrated for his color. It is also associated with that of the early-Renaissance portraitist Pisanello, famous for his portrait medals and his medallic art in general, e.g., his medallion of Sigismondo Malatesta, one of Pound's heroes in *The Cantos*. Does the voice that seems to criticize him for not having the "skill / To forge Achaia" (i.e., to initiate a Renaissance of the Greek spirit; ll. 15-6) belong to "E.P." or to that of established criticism? And could it also be understood as praising him for resisting a fashionable imitation of Greek models?

The second poem of Part II is preceded by a quotation in French by "Caid Ali" and addresses again—as did several sections of Part I—the frustrations and deviations of the poet in an environment hostile to the advancement of art:

> For three years, diabolus in the scale,
> He drank ambrosia,
> All passes, ANANGKE prevails,
> Came end, at last, to that Arcadia.
>
> He had moved amid her phantasmagoria,
> Amid her galaxies,
> NUKTOS AGALMA (poem ii: ll. 1-7)

According to Sieburth, Caid Ali is a pseudonym for Pound, and the quote is made to sound like his mentor Remy de Gourmont: "What do they know of love, and what can they understand? If they cannot understand poetry, if they have no feeling for music, what can they understand of this passion, in comparison with which the rose is coarse and the perfume of violets a clap of thunder?" (in Sieburth 2010: 303). The "three years" go back to the first line of "E.P.'s" Ode and his effort "to resuscitate the dead art of poetry." But the number three also refers to the tritone, a musical interval made up of three whole tones. Just as the tritone was avoided or even ruled out in medieval music and music theory, the poem's speaker becomes the "diabolus [the devil] in the scale." The drinking of ambrosia points back to poem iii of the first part where it is associated with Dionysos. "Anangke" (fate, necessity) may be an allusion to the "march of events" and with it to the loss of an aesthetic culture—a loss that makes the poet's striving for beauty in the manner of Bion (the Greek pastoral poet and his address to the Evening Star: "Nuktos Agalma," Jewel of the Night) a mere "phantasmagoria." After the loss of that "arcadia," he drifts in confusion, merely taking a measurement of beauty ("to convey the relation / Of eyelid and cheek-bone / By verbal manifestation," ll. 22-4), confining himself to creating a series "Of curious heads in medallion" (l. 26). And in doing so, he misses—in a state of mental "anaesthesis" (l. 31)—the "diastasis" (l. 30), the characteristically wide-apart eyes of Aphrodite as Botticelli envisioned and painted her (and as the French art historian Salomon Reinach showed her in his *Apollo: An Illustrated Manual of Art throughout the Ages*).

The third poem of Part II, which explicitly refers back to poem ii of Part I ("The Age Demanded") shows Mauberley's responding to those demands in successive movements of withdrawal from the world into himself, at the same time that such withdrawal increases his own sense of social irrelevance: "The glow of porcelain / Brought no reforming sense / To his perception / Of the social inconsequence" ("The Age Demanded": ll. 5-8). Seeking protection in a pose of aloofness and "Olympian" passivity, he restricts himself to the "[r]efinement of medium, elimination of superfluities" (l. 48) and to the stale and impotent "conservation of the 'better tradition'" (l. 47). However, to his own eyes (or to the eyes of his critics?), all this is a self-delusional "down-float / Of insubstantial manna," the "faint susurrus / Of his subjective hosannah" (ll. 52-5). So that, judged by the critics—those "self-styled 'his betters'"—he sees himself as finally excluded "from the world of letters" (ll. 58-61).

Poem iv enacts Mauberley's deterioration and final dissolution, "washed in the cobalt of oblivions" (l. 9), his epitaph written on an oar stranded on an "unforecasted beach" (l. 19): "I was / And I no more exist; / Here drifted / An hedonist" (ll. 22-5). Sieburth points out that in *Blast* I (June 1914), "Pound defined hedonism as 'the vacant place of the Vortex, without force, deprived of past and future'" (2010: 303). This raises again the question of who is voicing the critical judgment on Mauberley and his work: dominant critical opinion, or E.P., or the one as mediated through the other?

The closing "Medallion" is Mauberley's gift to the world as "E.P.'s" "Envoi" was at the end of Part I. If "Envoi" was written in the spirit of Waller's verbal music, Mauberley's "Medallion" is conceived in the spirit of a Bernardo Luini portrait. "Luini in porcelain!" (l. 1) seems, however, faintly self-ironic since it suggests a much too static frame for the "profane / protest" (ll. 3-4) of song it stages, the singer's "sleek head" rising "[f]rom the gold-yellow frock" like Venus in Botticelli's painting (ll. 5-8). The final stanza thus enacts a raw and dynamic apparition of Beauty in a contemporary setting ("half-watt rays", l. 15)—full face, not as a "face in profile"—combining music (song) and engraved image in a statement of art that merges the best that *one* poet (in two different masks) has to offer, the aesthetic object defiantly set to survive his "contacts and life" against all critical judgment:

> The face-oval beneath the glaze,
> Bright in its suave bounding-line, as,
> Beneath half-watt rays,
> The eyes turn topaz. (ll. 13-6)

In *Modernisms*, Peter Nicholls identifies the singer in "Medallion" as the soprano Raymonde Collignon whom Pound admired. "No one has a more keen perception than she has of the difference between art and life," wrote Pound. "As long as this diseuse was on stage she was non-human; she was, if you like, a china image; there are Ming porcelains which are respectable; the term 'china' is not in this connection ridiculous" (in Nicholls 1995: 192)—not as ridiculous as, presumably, "Luini in porcelain!" In the *Cantos*, "topaz" is a color associated with sexual union and—like "golden" and "copper" (orichalchi)—with Aphrodite, who is here re-embodied in the image of the singer.

4. Conclusion and Outlook

It is fascinating to see how both Eliot and Pound, in the two most important poems of this early phase of Anglo-Saxon modernism, stage a complex game of

masks in order to mirror—not mimetically but in a sequence of broken-up mir-
rorings—the deviations and confusions of their alter egos as well as the tensions
and conflicts of a period of increasing social and spiritual fragmentation. Although "The Love Song of J. Alfred Prufrock" may have seemed more maddening
than *Hugh Selwyn Mauberley* to the contemporary reader in its radiance of obscure suggestiveness, it is, in retrospect, the more accessible, the more unified
in mood and mode, in its haunting musicality and metaphorical brilliance.
Prufrock's dilemma, pushed to its ultimate extreme in *The Waste Land*, is finally, perhaps "logically," overcome by Eliot's metaphysical leap into faith. But the
manner of his meditative style, while becoming less dazzlingly innovative in the
range of its metaphoric fusions, remains intensely focused in its reflective manner and is thus an easily recognizable signature.

   Pound's *Hugh Selwyn Mauberley*—through its lack, or refusal, of meditative
inwardness—is much more diffuse, more difficult, and devious in its effort to
counter any temptation toward the subjective by elaborate strategies of self-ob-
jectification and by its dramatization of perspective. His brilliant display of poetic masks and styles, his almost claustrophobic insistence on verbal economy
and precision (echoed in the self-imposed discipline of quatrain and rhyme), his
dedication to "Anadyomene/Aphrodite" (and his growing awareness of the limits
of such dedication), will eventually lead Pound to a new definition of the poet's
role and social function in *The Cantos*. But there too, the tension between his
commitment to "Beauty" on the one hand, and his didactic commitment to
shape the reader's consciousness on the other, will remain ultimately unre-
solved. Dembo concludes that "Pound, at best, vacillated between the ironic and
heroic views of the poet and his capacity to deal with social reality . . . The social
vision in the *Cantos*, in one sense a positive response to the dangers revealed in
Mauberley, actually did nothing more than magnify Pound's conception of reality while preserving its basic paradoxes" (Dembo 1966: 167). His determination
to work an inherent Form—a quasi-transcendent Order (to kalón)—out of an
ever-increasing mass of diverse material will eventually lead Pound, battered by
age and the burden of his "contacts and life," to the final recognition that nothing coheres, and to a stoic acceptance of what is: "Do not move / Let the wind
speak / That is paradise" (Pound 2012: 1188).

Bibliography

Selected Primary Literature

Dante Alighieri. 2000 [1321]. *Inferno*. Trans. Robert Hollander and Jean Hollan-
    der. New York: Anchor Books.
Eliot, T.S. 1954. *Selected Poems*. London: Faber & Faber.
Emerson, Ralph Waldo. 1990 [1836]. "Nature." In: *Ralph Waldo Emerson: A Crit-
    ical Edition of the Major Works*. Ed. Richard Poirier. Oxford and New York:
    Oxford UP. 2-36.
Flint, F.S. and Ezra Pound. 1970 [1913]. "From 'Imagisme'." In: J.P. Sullivan
    (ed.), *Ezra Pound: A Critical Anthology*. Harmondsworth: Penguin Books. 40-1.
James, Henry. 1974. *Letters*. Vol. 1. Ed. Leon Edel. Cambridge: Harvard UP.
Pound, Ezra. 1968 [1928]. *Selected Poems*. Ed. with an introduction by T.S. Eliot.
    London: Faber & Faber.

——. 1926. *Personae: The Collected Poems of Ezra Pound.* New York: Boni & Liveright.

——. 1990. *Personae: The Shorter Poems of Ezra Pound.* Eds. Lea Baechler and A. Walton Litz. New York: New Directions.

——. 1971. *The Selected Letters of Ezra Pound,* 1907-1941. Ed. D.D. Paige. New York: New Directions.

——. 2010. "Hugh Selwyn Mauberley." In: *Ezra Pound: New Selected Poems and Translations.* Ed. Richard Sieburth. New York: New Directions, 109-23, 303-4.

——. 2012. *Die Cantos: Zweisprachige Ausgabe.* Trans. Eva Hesse. Eds. Manfred Pfister and Heinz Ickstadt. Hamburg: Arche.

——. 1970 [1916]. *Gaudier-Brzeska: A Memoir.* New York: New Directions.

Selected Secondary Literature

Bradbury, Malcolm and James McFarlane (eds.). 2012 [1976]. *Modernism: A Guide to European Literature 1890-1930.* Penguin Books.

Still an excellent introduction to modernism as a many-faceted international phenomenon as it discusses the scope of its ideas, the range of its artistic innovations, its main figures, and movements as well as its national variants.

Frye, Northrop. 1981 [1963]. *T.S. Eliot: An Introduction.* Chicago: U of Chicago P.

Although one of the oldest analyses of Eliot's work, it is still worth reading and impressive in its insights.

Ickstadt, Heinz. 2010. "Die amerikanische Moderne." In: Hubert Zapf (ed.), *Amerikanische Literaturgeschichte.* Stuttgart: Metzler. 217-81.

Ickstadt analyzes the different conditions, tensions, and formations of American modernism specifically.

Kenner, Hugh. 1985 [1951]. *The Poetry of Ezra Pound.* Lincoln: The U of Nebraska P.

During and after World War II, critical appreciation of Pound had declined because of his allegiance to Mussolini's fascism. Kenner's insightful book made Pound and his importance for modern poetry again a topic worthy of critical discussion.

Nicholls, Peter. 1995. *Modernisms: A Literary Guide.* London: Macmillan.

Bradbury and Nicholls offer an excellent survey and discussion of the modernist literary and artistic movement in general.

Perloff, Marjorie. 1985. *The Dance of the Intellect: Studies in the Poetry of the Pound Tradition.* Cambridge UP.

Perloff offers an excellent analysis of the role of Pound's poetry and its lasting impact on the poetic developments of modernism and post-modernism.

——. 2002. *21st-Century Modernism: The "New" Poetics.* Oxford: Blackwell.

Especially in the first chapter of her book, Perloff discusses the innovative, the "avant-garde" aspects of the early Eliot that later became overshadowed first by his elevation to the rank of literary master of modern poetry and subsequently by his demontage.

Further References

Berryman, Jo Brantley. 1983. *Circe's Craft: Ezra Pound's Hugh Selwyn Mauberley*. Ann Arbor: UMI Research P.

Dembo, L.S. 1966. *Conceptions of Reality in Modern American Poetry*. Berkeley: U of California P.

Eliot, T.S. 1934. *Selected Essays*. London: Faber & Faber.

Espey, John. 1955. *Ezra Pound's Mauberley: A Study in Composition*. Berkeley: U of California P.

Gordon, Lyndall. 1977. *Eliot's Early Years*. Oxford: Oxford UP.

Grover, Philip (ed.). 1978. *Ezra Pound: The London Years*, 1908-1920. New York: AMS.

Hamilton, Scott. 1992. *Ezra Pound and the Symbolist Inheritance*. Princeton UP.

Kenner, Hugh. 1971. *The Pound Era*. Berkeley, CA: The U of California P.

Kristeva, Julia. 1984. *Revolution in Poetic Language*. New York: Columbia UP.

Perkins, David. 1976. *A History of Modern Poetry: From the 1890s to the High Modernist Mode*. Vol. 1. Cambridge: Harvard UP.

——. 1987. *A History of Modern Poetry: Modernism and After*. Vol 2. Cambridge: Harvard UP.

Pound, Ezra. 1954. *The Literary Essays of Ezra Pound*. Ed. with an introduction by T.S. Eliot. London: Faber & Faber.

13.

American Modernist Poetry

Wallace Stevens's "A High-Toned Old Christian Woman" and William Carlos Williams's "The Red Wheelbarrow"

Simone Knewitz

1. American Modernism's Redefinition of the Romantic Imagination

William Carlos Williams and Wallace Stevens represent what poetry scholar Hugh Kenner called a "homemade" modernism (1975: xvi). Unlike the many American avant-garde writers who lived as expatriates in Europe at the beginning of the twentieth century—Ezra Pound, T.S. Eliot, Gertrude Stein, or Ernest Hemingway—Williams and Stevens developed their poetics in their home country, at a distance from the movements in Europe. In many respects, the poetic careers of Williams and Stevens are almost parallel: both authors moved in the same circles of the New York poetry scene; both pursued a professional career apart from their writing—Williams as a physician, Stevens as an insurance agent and eventually vice-president of an insurance company. And both became canonical poets of modernism and achieved major critical recognition of their work at a relatively late point in their lives. Most significantly, the poetry of Stevens and Williams shares a number of thematic and formal concerns, which the current book section sets out to explore. However, the following exemplary analysis of Stevens's "A High-Toned Old Christian Woman" and Williams's "The Red Wheelbarrow" will also show that despite some common assumptions, both authors developed divergent, almost opposite aesthetics, more often differing than agreeing on questions of poetics.

Like many other modernist poets, Williams and Stevens aspired to transform the sound of English language poetry (cf. Longenbach 2007: 79). Yet their writing was also profoundly influenced by the ideas of the English and American Romanticist tradition, which reveals itself particularly in their insistence on the primacy of the imagination. In the Romantic period, Samuel Taylor Coleridge had defined the imagination as the supreme cognitive faculty, instituting it as the individual's intuitive insight into divine transcendence. Aptly describing the common denominators of Stevens's and Williams's poetics, Albert Gelpi suggests that "Stevens and Williams considered the chief challenge to the Modernist poet—one of life-or-death urgency—to be the redefinition of the function of the imagination," seeking to reinvigorate its power in the face of the psychological and social contexts of modernity (1985: 5).

Crucial within the Romantic conception was the presence of a divine and spiritual order. For Coleridge, as well as for the American Romanticists Ralph Waldo Emerson and Walt Whitman, the imagination created a synthesis between the perceiving individual subject and the objects of reality, allowing the subject to penetrate "to the essential reality and transcendental interrelatedness of the objects of experience" (ibid.). Unlike their Romanticist predecessors, Williams and Stevens do not base their claims for the imagination on metaphysical or mystical grounds. While the Romantic poet strove to find a language to express his mystical experience of the world, the anti-idealist, anti-mystical modernist attempts "to compose the fragments of impression and response into an autotelic art-object" (ibid.: 8).

Within their common epistemological assumptions, there are substantial differences between Williams's and Stevens's modernist aesthetics, which play out in the particular forms of their poems. If both explore the relationship between the imagination and an objective external reality, Stevens is more interested in the subjective end of this relation while Williams reaches out toward the objective. In other words, Stevens contrasts Williams's concern with an "image of the world" with the "world of the image" (ibid.: 14). For Williams, the poem constitutes an art-object that assumes a place within nature; Stevens sees art as a rival of nature and posits it against nature. In his preface to Williams's *Collected Poems*, Stevens suggested that Williams's work was drawn to the "anti-poetic" (1957: 255)—a description Williams found offensive, but one that captures the simplicity of his language as well as his focus on ordinary subject matters, such as the everyday life of his fellow citizens in Rutherford, New Jersey, or the common wildflowers of the American locale. Stevens's texts, in contrast, are philosophical, of a symbolist aesthetic complexity that often seems to risk escapism.

Four years Williams's senior, Wallace Stevens was born in Reading, Pennsylvania, in 1879. His family belonged to the Dutch Reformed Church, which gave him the opportunity to study Greek and Latin at an early age. Later he attended Harvard University, where he gained recognition as a prolific writer for the *Harvard Monthly*. He left Harvard without a degree to pursue a career as a journalist for the *New York Evening Post*, but soon became dissatisfied with journalism. He then enrolled in the New York School of Law and was admitted to the New York Bar in 1904. Subsequently, he worked for various law firms in New York City before accepting a job at the American Bonding Company, an insurance firm. In his early professional life, Stevens did not write poetry, but was involved in New York's artistic community, which also included William Carlos Williams and Marianne Moore. In 1916 he left New York for Hartford, Connecticut, to work for the Hartford Accident and Indemnity Company, where he would remain employed for the rest of his working life.

Around the same time, Stevens also returned to writing poetry and publishing individual pieces in the literary magazine *Poetry*. His first volume of poetry, *Harmonium*, was not published until 1923. Though today considered to contain some of his best poems, including "Sunday Morning" and "Thirteen Ways of Looking at a Blackbird," the volume was not enthusiastically received at first. Stevens did gain some recognition after the publication in 1935 of his second volume, *Ideas of Order*. In subsequent volumes Stevens would further concentrate on writing poetry conceived as the synthesis between reality and imagination, making much of his work poetry about poetry. The long poem "Notes Toward a Supreme Fiction" (1942) goes at greatest length to explore the nature of poetry. In 1950 Stevens published his last collection of original work, *The Auroras of Autumn*. By that time he had become one of the most renowned American poets, and with his philosophical abstractions he began to exert profound influence on other writers. Shortly before his death in 1955, Stevens was awarded the Pulitzer Prize and a National Book Award for *The Collected Poems of Wallace Stevens*.

Similarly to Stevens, William Carlos Williams achieved critical acclaim only late in his life. For more than forty years Williams served as a doctor in the small town of Rutherford, New Jersey, the city in which he was born and grew up as the son of an English father and a Puerto Rican mother. John Keats and Walt Whitman were the poetic heroes of his early writing life. Williams studied medicine at the University of Pennsylvania where he became acquainted with Ezra Pound and Hilda Doolittle—later known as the poet H.D.—as well as with the painter Charles Demuth. Pound quickly became a mentor for Williams's poetic aspirations, and through his friendship with Pound and H.D., Williams was a close observer of the emerging Imagist movement, although never himself fully a part of it. After the publication of his first volume of poems, *The Tempers*, which was very much indebted to the Romanticism of Keats, his three pivotal volumes of his early career were *Al Que Quiere!* (1917), *Sour Grapes* (1921), and *Spring and All* (1923), constituting his distinct contribution to American modernism and the beginning of his search for poetry that reflected the "American idiom" (see Williams 1976).

Williams's poetry would undergo several transformations, but throughout his poetic career he drew inspiration from the American locale; he found his subject matter in the people of Rutherford, and particularly in his patients. In contrast to modernists like T.S. Eliot, who from Williams's point of view conformed to English tradition instead of attempting to "make it new," Williams strove to use a poetic diction that was insistently American and engaged the American environment. It was his conviction that every historical era needed to express itself in its own forms. In his work, this implied the purging of rhyme, meter, and traditional forms of figurative language, and an intense focus on the medium of language itself. Williams considered Eliot's work to be a setback in the development of a modernist aesthetics, especially the publication of *The Waste Land*, which he thought was not revolutionary, but dwelling in outdated traditions. His own volume, *Spring and All*, can be read as an answer to *The Waste Land*. After *Spring and All*, Williams did not publish a volume of poetry for ten years, but wrote several prose texts, and his late career was dominated by his work on the multi-volume epic *Paterson*. Despite failing health, Williams remained productive until the end of his life. His last volume of poems, *Pictures from Brueghel*, won him a Pulitzer Prize in 1963, the year of his death.

In their conceptions of modernist poetry, Stevens and Williams were both profoundly influenced by developments in the arts. By the beginning of the twentieth century, painters had already challenged all conventions of their craft, asserting that "painting was first and foremost a matter of paint upon canvas—not a 'mirror up to nature' or 'a window on the world'" (MacGowan 1984: xv). Artists such as Paul Cézanne, Marcel Duchamp, and Wassily Kandinsky rejected the representation of an external reality as the function of art, focusing instead on aesthetic strategies that revolved around the essential properties of their medium: the two-dimensional space of the canvas. Both Williams and Stevens followed the work of the modern artists in the contemporary New York art scene; the famous New York Armory Show of 1913 took place at a point in their early career at which they developed their distinctive poetics. For Williams, his friendship with American artists Charles Demuth and Charles Sheeler would have a significant impact on his early work. Stevens was intrigued with the impressionists, as well as with Cézanne and Paul Klee and many other painters whose work emphasized the modes of perception rather than what is actually being seen (cf. Costello 2007: 167).

Critics have often placed Williams and Stevens in two divergent traditions of modernism, linking Williams with Pound "along the imagist-objectivist line of modern poetry, in which language is meant to achieve the status of an object itself" (Longenbach 2007: 77). Stevens, in contrast, is related to the symbolism represented by William Butler Yeats, "in which language is meant to be suggestive, invoking associations beyond itself" (ibid.). While this distinction in its absoluteness would be too schematic, it helps to understand some of the differences in their aesthetics. Of the two, Williams's work may seem more radically modern, while Stevens's texts appear at once traditional and experimental. Stevens's poems are characterized by an extraordinary vocabulary, technical and thematic complexity, abstraction, and philosophical argument. Williams's texts are often minimalist and refute abstraction; they employ the diction of the realm of spoken language and tend to avoid multi-syllable words. A comparison of Williams's and Stevens's early poems "The Red Wheelbarrow" and "A High-Toned Old Christian Woman" brings into relief the commonalities as well as the differences in their poetics.

2. Poetry as Supreme Fiction: Wallace Stevens's "A High-Toned Old Christian Woman"

One of the dominant topics of Stevens's work is the fate of religious belief in a modern secular age and the empowerment of the poetic imagination as a vital alternative to Christian mythology. "Sunday Morning" (1978 [1915]: 66-70), one of his best-known poems, presents one of Stevens's first attempts to find substitutes for Christianity in natural religion, or paganism. In this poem two voices argue with each other—a woman longing for spirituality beyond the pleasures of the world, and a second voice assuring her that the world is all there is, and needs to be enough. "A High-Toned Old Christian Woman" (1978 [1923]: 59), which Stevens published along with "Sunday Morning" in his first volume *Harmonium* in 1923, engages with a similar theme.

Stevens's poem is a dramatic monologue written in a mocking and rather humorous tone: the speaker addresses the Christian woman of the title in an apostrophe, calling her "madame" three times throughout the text. The (presumably male) speaker, about whom we learn almost nothing, takes on the role of an objective, though ironical, observer. In contrast, the woman—whom the lyrical I characterizes as a straight-laced, haggard prude and who thus becomes the object of his ridicule—does not get the opportunity to voice her views. Conceiving religion as a form of fiction, the speaker challenges the Christian belief system, which the woman represents to him, countering religion with an alternative, hedonist fiction and suggesting that the poetic imagination possesses a superior way to explain reality.

The first line—"Poetry is the supreme fiction, madame"—can be read as a programmatic statement; in fact, this is the first time that Stevens uses the phrase "supreme fiction," which would later assume a central position in his poetics, and which he would try to define more extensively in his late long poem "Notes toward a Supreme Fiction." Stevens's claim that poetry is the "supreme fiction" was inspired by George Santayana, a philosopher at Harvard when Stevens studied there. For both Santayana and Stevens, the God of religion is a product of the poetic imagination and thus of the mind's attempt to overcome the subject's estrangement from objective reality. In his work *Interpretations of Poetry and Religion* (1900), Santayana argues that both poetry and religion were fictive forms expressing human values and thus identical in origin. Yet, inasmuch as they fabricate specific belief systems and entail ethical values, they differ in their practical effects. Traditional Christian religion and its accompanying mythology may thus prove distasteful or obsolete as a fiction for modern times and in need of being replaced by a different, secular one.

In the following lines, Stevens projects two "fictions": a Christian one illustrating the alleged belief system of the woman, and the speaker's pagan one, in which each aspect of the Christian image is replaced with an earthly one. The speaker contrasts the "moral law" (l. 2) that represents the woman's rigid ethical code with a less definite "opposing law" (l. 7) relating his own attitudes. To this end Stevens uses a number of metonymies: the moral law assumes its concrete form in the architecture of a nave, whereas the speaker's frame of mind is associated with a "peristyle" (ll. 2, 7). Thus, the speaker contrasts the Christian church with a Greek temple, representing a pre-Christian period of artistic achievement. The nave is associated with a "haunted heaven" (l. 3) suggesting an afterlife haunted by regrets, or perhaps by the repression of worldly desires. Heaven is certainly not pictured as a state of purity or salvation. With the image of the "haunted heaven," the text critiques those Christian doctrines that teach restraint and defer joy and happiness to an allegedly better life after death. In distinction, the "opposing law" takes on the architectural form of the peristyle, which is then further associated with a "masque" (l. 8): the masque recalls ancient theater performances, which could stand as a pagan counterpart to the solemnity of the Mass in the Christian church (cf. Lensing 1972: 45). The image of heaven is further contrasted with the projection of the masque "[b]eyond the planets" (l. 9), thus replacing the abstract idealization of heaven with a material image of a cosmic dimension.

The extension of the nave into heaven is followed by the first conversion: "The conscience is converted into palms" (l. 4). The peristyle's extension leads equally to a conversion of "our bawdiness" into palms (ll. 9-11). The palms in the first instance call up the reeds waved in homage to Jesus; in the second instance they may refer to the palm of "tropic pleasure" (Litz 1972: 116), and in the third instance they may denote the palms of the hands ("And palm for palm", l. 12). The first conversion is associated in a simile to "windy citherns hankering for hymns" (l. 5): obsolete instruments that are either no longer used or whose sound is not musical. That they are "windy" links them back to the "haunted heaven." The second conversion relates to the much livelier, "[s]quiggling" saxophones (l. 12), which we can associate with modern, more physical, jazz music. One could think perhaps of Mardi Gras festivities, in which the hedonism of life becomes apotheosized after death rather than ". . . purged by epigraph" (l. 10).

In the second half of the poem, the speaker again addresses the Christian woman, asking her to allow her own "disaffected flagellants" to dance in the "planetary scene" and indulge in physical pleasures, letting them celebrate their earthly existence in a parade (ll. 14-6). The term "flagellant" denotes a person who castigates himself by religious discipline; "disaffected" may refer both to their alienation from the world and their dissatisfaction with their own state. Giving up their penance and religious fervor, the speaker envisions the flagellants indulging in gluttony, "[s]macking their muzzy bellies" and, instead of scourging themselves, "whip[ping] from themselves / A jovial hullabaloo" (ll. 16, 19-20). Significantly, the poem here increasingly employs onomatopoetic language. The previous images of the "windy citherns" and the "[s]quiggling . . . saxophones" already alluded to music; the flagellants' parade, however, appears less musical and more like a noisy turmoil: "tink and tank and tunk-a-tunk-tunk" (l. 18). Emphasizing sound rather than referential meaning by onomatopoeia and alliteration, the poem here turns toward its own poetics and linguistic play.

In the final two lines, the speaker suggests that the blasphemous spectacle he envisions will make "widows wince" (ll. 21-2). He alludes to the woman as a "widow," stereotypically associating widowhood with barrenness and the rejection of physical desires, as well as a Christian conservatism. Referring to the works of the imagination as "fictive things" (l. 21), the final lines of the poem return to its beginning and the notion of poetry as a supreme fiction. Here the speaker self-referentially emphasizes that the projected images are works of his imagination; they are a "wink," meant as a provocation, but not as a damning of the woman's views. And the provocation is most effective when it works, or "when widows wince" (l. 22). The last two lines are particularly strong in using assonance, alliteration, repetition, and half rhyme. With these poetic means, the text again draws attention to its own poetics. The wink of the fictive may thus also be considered a wink toward reality.

Significant for the text's poetics is its humorous tone, which is also underlined by Stevens's use of variations in meter; like many dramatic monologues in the Romantic and Victorian tradition, "A High-Toned Old Christian Woman" employs blank verse—unrhymed iambic pentameter. Yet not all its lines are regularly iambic; the first line, as well as lines 2, 12, 14, 16, 17, 19, 21 and 22, begin with metric inversions; lines 6, 7 and 20 contain additional unstressed syllables. These are hardly accidents; these inversions become meaningful when related to the content, as they occur precisely at those points at which the speaker seems to most explicitly resist the traditions the Christian widow represents. In this sense, the "opposing law" also works against traditional metrics; the poetic imagination, "[s]quiggling like saxophones," cannot be fully contained by the rigidity of iambic pentameter.

As the preceding interpretation has shown, Stevens's poem "A High-Toned Old Christian Woman" is primarily a poem about poetics. Not only its imagery, metonymies, and similes support this interpretation, but also the way in which the text employs alliteration and assonance, rhyme and half rhyme, repetition and internal rhyme, and onomatopoetic language. With these often playful devices Stevens draws the reader's attention to the aesthetics of his text, and to the work of language itself. In this sense, "A High-Toned Old Christian Woman" is a performative poem, meaning that it enacts what it is about: a dramatization of the role of "fictive things" in the creation of poetry (cf. Lensing 1972: 47).

Having discussed the text in some depth, we may want to revisit the first line. In what way, then, could poetry be considered the "supreme fiction"? Does Stevens equate fiction with the unrestrained bawdiness of his poem's speaker? Such a reading might equate the author with the lyrical I of the text and imply that the speaker's hedonistic image constitutes poetry. Yet as the speaker projects two opposing images—one Christian and one earthly—the text more strongly suggests that the imagination as a creative faculty can be put to different uses and envision all kinds of fictional worlds: those that are restrained puritanical as well as those considered world-affirming and hedonistic. And the poem exemplifies the workings of the imagination with its two opposing projections. Yet to the extent that Christianity insists on a particular, absolutist fiction that rejects the validity of alternative worldviews, Stevens's text claims poetry to be the superior form of fiction: "Underlying the poem's self-conscious verbal play and shrewd irony, however, is the serious issue of poetry and fictions forced into confrontation with a world that often stubbornly prefers the widow's wince to the poet's wink. To 'pick a fight' with that reality was Stevens' earnest and continuing preoccupation as a poet" (ibid.: 48).

3. No Ideas But in Things: William Carlos Williams's "The Red Wheelbarrow"

Stevens argues that our knowledge about the world is fictive by necessity, and that it embraces the marvelous world of the imagination, a world of ideas rather than things. Williams, in contrast, feeling closer to Pound's Imagist principles, would famously claim: "no ideas but in things" (1995: 6). Striving for a "direct treatment of the 'thing'" (Pound 1968: 3), Williams focused on the concrete objects of visual experience, avoiding metaphors and symbolism. "The Red Wheelbarrow" originally appeared in his experimental volume of poetry and prose *Spring and All*, published in 1923, the same year as Stevens's *Harmonium*. The poems in *Spring and All* are untitled, given only numbers; "The Red Wheelbarrow" is therefore labeled "XXII" in the volume (Williams 1991: 224).

Easily accessible to the reader, this short text is certainly Williams's most famous poem. It projects a rural scene: the image of chickens next to a wheelbarrow after rainfall. Though the poem does not contextualize the image spatially or temporally, we may imagine this as a common scene of American rural life. The objects presented here are not specifically poetic, but appear common and ordinary. The first of the four couplets, however, adds an enigmatic quality to the text, because what "so much" refers to remains undefined and "depends / upon" the visual image described here (ll. 1-2). Thus, we may begin to speculate about the text's meaning. If we think of agriculture as the fundamental form of human production, we may interpret "so much" as possibly referring to more complex forms of industry and culture which would not be sustainable in the absence of the more basic products of farming. We may also recall that the wheelbarrow represents an elementary technology which was already employed in antiquity.

But it would be too simple to stop our interpretation of the text at this point. For one thing, merely looking at its content does not take into account the particular visual arrangement of the poem on the page. Syntactically and semantically, Williams's poem is one grammatically correct sentence: "So much depends upon a red wheelbarrow glazed with rainwater beside the white chickens." Yet this is not the way Williams chooses to arrange the words. We have to consider how the materiality of the words on the page contributes to the meaning of the text. At first glance—before even beginning to read "The Red Wheelbarrow"—we notice its minimal diction and lack of punctuation. Our initial impression of the poem therefore is a visual one: the lines do not break according to their meaning. Williams's guiding principle is the number of words: four stanzas with two lines each, the first line with three words, the second line with only one word. Williams also chooses not to capitalize any of the words (e.g., at the beginning of the lines) nor does he include any punctuation marks. Each word seems as important as the next; none is subordinated to another. Considering the words in their grammatical functions, however, we should notice differences. Within the

sentence, "so much" constitutes the subject, "depends" is the only verb or copu-
la, and the three last couplets constitute the object of the sentence. Kenner, in
this respect, reminds us that the verb "depend" has Latin roots, meaning "to
hang from" (1975: 58); taken literally, the whole meaning of the poem "hangs
from" the first couplet and our interpretation of it.

The immediate contrast to Stevens's "A High-Toned Old Christian Woman" is
striking: Stevens's poem uses an extensive vocabulary that includes many terms
which are uncommon in everyday usage: "citherns," "hankering," "masque,"
"flagellants," "hullabaloo"; Williams's "Red Wheelbarrow" employs basic terms of
the English language that often refer to concrete material objects. By using enjambment to break apart compound words like "wheelbarrow" into "wheel / bar-
row" (ll. 3-4) or "rainwater" into "rain / water" (ll. 5-6) Williams further divides
language, as well as the objects the words refer to, into more elementary components. Stevens once referred to Williams's poems as being "mobile-like arrangement[s]" (1966 [1953]: 801): the words, or perhaps the couplets themselves, become objects in space and are defined by their visual arrangement more than by
their actual referential meaning.

Enjambment in this context is also an important device in Williams's poetry because its function is primarily visual. "The Right of Way," for instance,
poem XI *Spring and All*, ends with the following couplet:

> I saw a girl with one leg
> over the rail of a balcony
> (Williams 1991 [1923]: 206, ll. 27-8)

Here, Williams does not break apart a compound word, but the example illustrates how the enjambment determines our reading process: as we perceive only
the first line, we picture the image of a girl with only one leg; only as we read the
next line do we understand that the girl does indeed have two legs, only one of
which is placed over the rail of a balcony. In this instance, the lines may also
reflect the visual perception of the poem's speaker, who, driving by in his car (as
the poem tells us), may initially see a one-legged girl before recognizing the details of the situation. Williams here also self-reflectively plays with enjambment,
as the French word "enjamber" literally means "to straddle," just as the girl here
straddles the balcony (cf. Dolin 1993: 34).

Williams thereby subordinates meaning and sound to visual form. This is a
principle both reminiscent of and also distinct from, for instance, Marianne
Moore's use of syllabic verse in her poetry. Consider this excerpt from Moore's
"The Fish":

> All
> external
>   marks of abuse are present on this
>   defiant edifice—
>   all the physical features of
>
> ac-
> cident—lack
>   of cornice, dynamite grooves, burns, and
>   hatchet strokes, these things stand
>   out of it; the chasm side is
>
> dead.
> (Moore 1968 [1935]: 38, ll. 26-36)

Like Williams, Moore works with enjambment, sometimes even cutting apart non-compound words, as here in the case of "ac- / cident," subordinating meaning to the number of syllables in each line. Moore's poems thereby also create a visual, non-audible impression on the page. In the case of "The Fish" we may even attribute the form of the stanzas with a figurative meaning and associate them with the scales of a fish.

My reading makes it apparent that "The Red Wheelbarrow" is a poem as much about language itself as it is "about" its ostensible content, the visual image of chickens next to a wheelbarrow that is still wet from the rain. And this brings us back to the initial observation about Williams's concern with the relationship of imagination and reality. In fact, the whole volume of Spring and All, in which Williams published "The Red Wheelbarrow," engages with the tension between objective reality and the reality and materiality of the poem. Spring and All wavers between two conflicting goals: the wish to overcome the "cleavage" between the poet's imagination and the material reality, and the desire to create the poem as a thing in itself. Williams stresses time and again that poems should not copy nature, but must become nature (cf. 1991 [1923]: 208). It is in that way that we also have to understand Williams's "The Red Wheelbarrow"; as J. Hillis Miller suggests, the wheelbarrow "does not stand for anything or mean anything. It is an object in space dissociated from the objects around it, without reference beyond itself. It is what it is. The aim of the poem is to make it stand there for the reader in its separateness, as the words of the poem stand on the page" (1965: 307).

4. Conclusion

In his preface to Williams's Collected Poems 1921-1931, Stevens classified Williams as a "romantic poet" and asked:

> What, then, is a romantic poet now-a-days? He happens to be one who still dwells in an ivory tower, but who insists that life would be intolerable except for the fact that one has, from the top, such an exceptional view of the public dump and the advertising signs of Snider's Catsup, Ivory Soap and Chevrolet Cars; he is the hermit who dwells alone with the sun and moon, but insists on taking a rotten newspaper. (1957 [1934]: 256)

As Gelpi points out, Stevens's depiction of "the romantic as idealistic solipsist" in a modern commercialized society may be a more fitting self-portrait of Stevens himself than a characterization of Williams. Of the two, Stevens would be the poet in the ivory tower, gazing at the scene from above, while Williams would prefer to sit in the middle of the "public dump" reading the rotten local newspaper (cf. 1985: 11). Both authors engaged with the contexts of modernity in their own ways, and aspired to translate their experience into their distinctly modernist poetics. Though Williams and Stevens are interested in the relationship between imagination and reality, they conceived of this relationship in quite different fashions and pursued radically different poetics. If both poets believed that the "thing in itself" remains inaccessible to the mind, and that what we know of the world has been fabricated by the structures of consciousness, they drew remarkably different consequences for their aesthetics from this insight. Stevens celebrates the beauty of the workings of the imagination expressed in language; Williams turns to the materiality of the poem, establishing the poem itself as a material object whose materiality rivals that of an external, objective reality.

Contemporary poetry scholars recognize Williams and Stevens as two central modernist American poets whose works have acquired canonical status. *Spring and All* and *Harmonium* are considered the major achievements of the poets' respective early careers and would also come to influence poets of later generations. Important assessments of their work, like Hugh Kenner's *A Homemade World*, J. Hillis Miller's *Poets of Reality*, or Harold Bloom's studies evaluated their poetics in explicit distinction from the avant-garde writers in Europe, suggesting that their work needs to be considered distinctly 'American.' More recent criticism has challenged such dichotomous views, reevaluating their transatlantic ties and the interconnectedness of different modernist movements.

Though Williams and Stevens have often been studied in conjunction with each other, the differences in their poetics have been responsible for a divergent critical heritage. Of the two, Stevens has been a favorite of poetry critics of all generations and turns of critical theory. He received much appreciation for his early poetry from the New Critics of the 1940s and 50s, who saw their ideas about linguistic complexity and ambiguity reflected in his poems; in turn, his work was influenced by their theories (cf. McCann 1995: 140). Indebted to this critical tradition, book-length studies in the 1960s and 70s such as Joseph Riddel's *The Clairvoyant Eye* (1965), Helen Vendler's *On Extended Wings* (1969), and A. Walton Litz's *Introspective Voyager* (1972) made important contributions to the analysis of Stevens's poetry. Subsequently, deconstructionist critics claimed Stevens's later work for postmodernism. Since the 1990s, many studies have also attempted to demonstrate the connectedness of Stevens's writings with the political and social contexts of his era, employing approaches of new historicism.

The appreciation of Williams's poetry surged in the 1960s, when he was discovered by a younger generation of poets who perceived his writings as an alternative form of modernism to those of Pound and Eliot. His poetics have exerted considerable influence on the beat poetry of Allen Ginsberg, the writing of Robert Lowell, and the Black Mountain poets of the 1950s and 60s, particularly Robert Creeley. At the same time, literary critics seeking to distinguish themselves from the approaches of the New Critics, among them Linda Welshimer Wagner, Thomas R. Whitaker, and James Guimond, began promoting Williams's inclusion into the modernist canon, picturing Williams as a democratic, nonintellectual, 'American' author. Since then, Williams's work, like Stevens's, has been interpreted from various perspectives, including postmodernist and cultural studies approaches. Over the years, Williams has come to be the most influential of the modernists for the development of American poetry.

Bibliography

Selected Primary Literature

Moore, Marianne. 1968 [1951]. *Collected Poems*. New York: Macmillan.
——. 1968 [1935]. "The Fish." In: Moore 1968. 37-8.
Pound, Ezra. 1968. "A Retrospect." *Literary Essays of Ezra Pound*. New York: New Directions. 3-14.

Stevens, Wallace. 1957. *Opus Posthumous*. Ed. Samuel French Morse. London: Faber and Faber.

——. 1966. *Letters of Wallace Stevens*. Ed. Holly Stevens. New York: Knopf.

——. 1978 [1954]. *The Collected Poems of Wallace Stevens*. New York: Knopf.

——. 1978 [1923]. "A High-Toned Old Christian Woman." In: Stevens 1978. 59.

Williams, William Carlos. 1976. "The American Idiom." *Interviews with William Carlos Williams: "Speaking Straight Ahead."* Ed. Linda Wagner. New York: New Directions. 52-60.

——. 1991. *The Collected Poems of William Carlos Williams*. Vol. I, 1909-1939. Ed. A. Walton Litz and Christopher MacGowan. New York: New Directions.

——. 1991 [1923]. "XI." In: Williams 1991. Vol. 1. 205-6.

——. 1991 [1923]. "XXII." In: Williams 1991. Vol. 1. 224.

——. 1995. *Paterson*. New York: New Directions.

Selected Secondary Literature

Axelrod, Steven Gould and Helen Deese (eds.). 1995. *Critical Essays on William Carlos Williams*. New York: G.K. Hall.

A collection of historical reviews of selected writings by Williams as well as critical essays by renowned Williams scholars.

Bloom, Harold. 1977. *Wallace Stevens: The Poems of Our Climate*. Ithaca: Cornell UP.

A comprehensive study of Stevens's poetry which relates his work to the tradition of American Romanticism.

Copestake, Ian D. 2010. *The Ethics of William Carlos Williams's Poetry*. Rochester: Camden House.

A most recent and well-informed reading of Williams's poetry which traces his writing to Unitarianism and Emersonian thinking.

Litz, A. Walton. 1972. *Introspective Voyager: The Poetic Development of Wallace Stevens*. New York: Oxford UP.

One of the foundational studies of Stevens's early poetry.

Lowney, John. 1997. *The American Avant-Garde Tradition: William Carlos Williams, Postmodern Poetry, and the Politics of Cultural Memory*. Lewisburg: Bucknell UP.

Examines William Carlos Williams's importance for postmodern poetry and his role in the formation of the American poetry canon.

MacGowan, Christopher J. 1984. *William Carlos Williams's Early Poetry: The Visual Arts Background*. Ann Arbor: UMI Research P.

A classic study on the relationship of Williams's early work to modern painting.

Mariani, Paul. 1981. *William Carlos Williams: A New World Naked*. New York: Norton.

The standard biography of William Carlos Williams.

McCann, Janet. 1995. *Wallace Stevens Revisited: "The Celestial Possible."* New York: Twayne.

A comprehensive chronological study of Stevens's poetic oeuvre.

Ragg, Edward. 2010. *Wallace Stevens and the Aesthetics of Abstraction*. Cambridge: Cambridge UP.

A most recent study analyzing Stevens's interest in abstraction throughout his work in detailed close readings.

Serio, John N. (ed.). 2007. *The Cambridge Companion to Wallace Stevens*. Cambridge: Cambridge UP.

A current collection of introductory essays on major themes in the poetry of Wallace Stevens.

Sharpe, Tony. 2000. *Wallace Stevens: A Literary Life*. London: Macmillan.

A recent biographical study of Stevens.

Vendler, Helen. 1969. *On Extended Wings: Wallace Stevens' Longer Poems*. Cambridge: Harvard UP.

A seminal study of fourteen longer poems by Wallace Stevens, among them "Sunday Morning" and "Thirteen Ways of Looking at a Blackbird."

Further References

Costello, Bonnie. 2007. "Stevens and Painting." In: Serio 2007. 164-79.

Dolin, Sharon. 1993. "Enjambment and the Erotics of the Gaze in Williams's Poetry." In: *American Imago* 50.1: 29-53.

Gelpi, Albert. 1985. "Stevens and Williams: The Epistemology of Modernism." In: Albert Gelpi (ed.), *Wallace Stevens: The Poetics of Modernism*. Cambridge: Cambridge UP. 3-23.

Kenner, Hugh. 1975. *A Homemade World: The American Modernist Writers*. New York: Knopf.

Lensing, George. 1972. "'A High-Toned Old Christian Woman': Wallace Stevens' Parable of Supreme Fiction." In: *Notre Dame English Journal* 8.1: 43-9.

Longenbach, James. 2007. "Stevens and His Contemporaries." In: Serio 2007. 76-86.

Miller, J. Hillis. 1965. *Poets of Reality: Six Twentieth-Century Writers*. Cambridge: Belknap P.

Riddel, Joseph N. 1965. *The Clairvoyant Eye: The Poetry and Poetics of Wallace Stevens*. Baton Rouge: Louisiana State UP.

14.

Modernist Women Poets

H.D.'s "Sea Violet" and Marianne Moore's "The Fish"

Tanja Budde

1. Literary Modernism and Female Poets

"I, too, dislike it; there are things that are important beyond all this fiddle" proclaims the speaker in the first line of Marianne Moore's poem titled "Poetry." After such a harsh initial statement, readers may be surprised to learn, as the poem unfolds, that the speaker does not dislike all poetry, but only certain kinds. The speaker rejects insincere fiddle so "derivative as to become unintelligible" (l. 8) and poems that aim at "a high-sounding interpretation" being "put upon them" (l. 7), while arguing in favor of poetry that does not "discriminate against 'business documents and school-books'" (ll. 17-8) and that reserves a place for "the genuine" and the "raw material of poetry in all its rawness" (ll. 26-7). Starting with a confession of dislike to arrive at a refutation of the initial claim, the poem is a self-reflective discussion of the role of poetry in a changing world. It displays an integral feature found not only in Moore's work, but also in H.D.'s: a commitment to modernism's effort to redefine poetry or, to use Ezra Pound's famous phrase, to 'make it new.'

The modernist desire for innovation stems from a profound sense of discontent with preexisting modes of literary expression. In his 1921 essay "The Metaphysical Poets," T.S. Eliot writes: "We can only say that it appears likely that poets in our civilization, as it exists at the present, must be difficult. Our civilization comprehends great variety and complexity, and this variety and complexity, playing upon a refined sensibility, must produce various complex results" (65). In other words, the modern world calls for new, complex, and difficult forms of writing that reflect the complex and often difficult times; the early twentieth century was indeed a time in which many of the cultural developments that had started at the end of the nineteenth century came to the fore. Growing urbanization, rapid development of new technologies that led to new forms of transportation and communication, crucial developments in the fields of philosophy and psychology (Sigmund Freud's *The Interpretation of Dreams* was published in 1900), and the experience of a devastating world war conspired to call old certainties into question. The sense of discontent expressed in the short excerpt from Eliot's "The Metaphysical Poets" is thus not only a discontent with established literary forms, but also alludes to a deep-felt cultural crisis.

While a desire for innovation in light of these dramatic changes is characteristic of virtually all modernist poets, the extent to which they break with established practices of writing and the ways in which they do so are varied. And while the umbrella term modernism usefully points to key characteristics of modernist poetry, it often involves simplification and neglect of particularities. Given that male modernist poets tended to stage their endeavors 'to make it new' as "the radical break of sons . . . with the repressive culture of their Victorian fathers" (Ickstadt, this volume, p. 171), and given that "the invention of modernist form by male authors was in part an attempt to 'rescue' literary writ-

ing from what they saw as the 'effeminacy' of late-nineteenth-century literature"
(Beach 2003: 72), H.D., Marianne Moore, and other female modernist poets face
an obvious problem: how were they to write poetry in a literary culture that was
predominately misogynistic, and how where they to respond to a literary tradition that privileges male authors?

The complexities of the situation for female modernist poets are reflected in
the names that Moore and H.D. used and to which they are still commonly referred. That Hilda Doolittle received her pen name from Ezra Pound is a well-
known and oft-repeated tale. H.D. recalls the day Pound first read her work and
told her:

> "[T]his is poetry." He slashed with a pencil. "Cut this out, shorten this line.
> 'Hermes of the Ways' is a good title. I'll send this to Harriet Monroe of Poetry.
> Have you a copy? Yes? Then we can send this, or I'll type it when I get back. Will
> this do?" And he scrawled "H.D. Imagist" at the bottom of the page (in Pondrom
> 1990: 87).

While this account underlines Pound's impact on H.D.'s career, it also points to
the gendered nature of modernist literary culture. First, it is the male poet who
declares "this is poetry"; second, the name he devises and which she continued
to use, makes the poet's gender ambiguous, emphasizing androgyny instead of
femininity. Marianne Moore, as she became increasingly successful and well
known, was regularly referred to as 'Miss Moore.' This, of course, indicates and
even highlights the fact that she never married and continued to live with her
mother. At first blush such a reference seems to stand in contrast to the androgyny inherent in Hilda Doolittle's pen name, yet as Victoria Bazin has argued, "the critical construction of 'Miss Moore' as chaste and pure reinforces an
idealized and transcendent femininity detached from what are perceived as the
sordid and corrupting influences of modernity" (2010: 33). Since these names
cast the poets in a light that went against what was considered an effeminized
and sentimental tradition and norm, it offered them ways to participate in the
cultural production of high modernism, which had fashioned itself as hard,
technical, and unsentimental. At the same time, however, these constructions—
of modernism and both H.D.'s and Moore's identities as poets—clearly "replicate
existing cultural models" and binaries (ibid.).

Despite the complex position female modernist authors had to negotiate, it is
important to note that the literary marketplace was changing and women were
entering it not only as writers but also as editors of periodicals. Harriet Monroe,
for example, was founder and long-time editor of the highly influential *Poetry: A
Magazine of Verse*. Printing texts that were often deemed too experimental by
established publishing houses, such magazines played an important role in the
shaping of modernism; in fact, the history and success of modernism is largely
connected to periodical publication: "without magazines from *291* to *The Little
Review*, or *Poetry* to *Pagany*, the contours of American modernism, and indeed
also the transnational character of modernism, would not be as we know it
today" (Thacker 2012: 1). Many of the now canonical texts were first published
in one of the numerous little magazines founded in the first half of the twentieth
century. The changes in the publishing world allowed the development of a
"useful support system for women writers" that "facilitated the publication of
writing by women" (Bazin 2010: 35). Having begun to write poetry during her
time at Bryn Mawr College, from which she graduated in 1909, Moore began

publishing her poems in magazines such as *Poetry*, *Others*, and *The Egotist*. Through these magazines, but most importantly through her position as editor of *The Dial* from 1925 through 1929, Moore made "important and influential friends early in her career" and became "one of the most respected and powerful writers in the United States" (ibid.). Yet at the beginning of her career, before her move to New York City in 1918 and her work for *The Dial*, it was H.D. who provided support and proved to be an important contact to the world of expatriate poets in London. Having become involved in avant-garde circles after her move to London, it was H.D. who, together with her partner Winifred Ellermann (known as Bryher), published a first edition of Moore's *Poems* in 1921.

2. Modernist Revisions: H.D.'s "Sea Violet"

In 1913 Harriet Monroe's influential magazine *Poetry* printed three poems by H.D.: "Priapus," "Hermes of the Ways," and "Epigram"—the poems mentioned earlier that Pound signed for Doolitte with "H.D. Imagiste." Three years later they were published in H.D.'s volume *Sea Garden*. Ever since then the name H.D. and the term imagism have been closely intertwined, and H.D.'s early poems are often seen as exemplifying the imagist mode at its most successful. Working together with other poets such as Richard Aldington, Amy Lowell, and H.D, Pound coined the term imagism and propounded several principles for this new kind of poetry:

> Use no superfluous word, no adjective, which does not reveal something.
>   Don't use such an expression as "dim lands *of peace*." It dulls the image.
> It mixes an abstraction with the concrete. It comes from the writer's not
> realizing that the natural object is always the *adequate* symbol.
>   Go in fear of abstractions . . . (in Pondrom 1990: 88).

Defining imagism by way of a polemical attack on 'the old,' Pound by implication stresses imagism's novelty. The verbosity and ornate diction of nineteenth-century verse must be avoided in favor of sparse and precise language, which in turn shifts the focus to that which is of upmost importance: the image. The poetic image must be "hard and clear, never blurred nor indefinite," i.e., it should eschew abstraction and vagueness while trying to "find the closest possible connection between the words used and the objects being described" (Beach 2003: 81). Free from abstraction and other 'dulling' elements, the poems should not represent emotions and experiences, but instead evoke 'bright' experiences of precise and discrete images.

   Sea Garden (1916), H.D.'s first volume, portrays with great precision a landscape located, "where the sea grass tangles with / shore grass," as it is put in the poem "Hermes of the Ways" (1983: 37-9, ll. 53-4). While the twenty-seven poems depict different aspects of this natural world—some describe places, others are invocations to natural forces and gods; many poems are associated with the sea and several with the land—the volume is nevertheless highly cohesive as it is held together by a variety of recurring images and motifs: the poems consistently employ imagery from the natural world, emphasizing at the same time abundance, lushness, regeneration and the destructive powers of the elements; images of fruits and flowers abound, and the boundary between land and sea and the mingling of the elements is emphasized continually. The world of *Sea Garden* is not that of an urban, modern wasteland but rather "set in a symbolic

green world removed from conventional space and time" (Friedman 1990: 51).
Devoid of ordinary human life, *Sea Garden* is, as Beach summarizes, "inhabited
by the gods, goddesses, and other human and mythological characters of ancient Greece" (2003: 81). Like many modernist poets, H.D. was captivated by
and attracted to ancient Greek myths. The lyrical fragments of Sappho held a
particular fascination for the poet; "adopting her as the authorizing muse,"
Sappho "empowers [H.D.] to write her own lyrics" (ibid.; cf. also Gregory 1990).
Sea Garden is infused with allusions to Sappho's island world of female passion
and creativity, and her choice of fruits—pears, melons, and quince, but no
apples—makes it clear that *Sea Garden* does not depict, despite its many references to gardens, a Christian garden of Eden.

The volume is also held together by the consistent use of free verse and
sparseness of language. The five flower poems in particular—"Sea Rose," "Sea
Lily," "Sea Poppies," "Sea Violet," and "Sea Iris"—exemplify this imagistic reduction of language and concentration on the image, as it is here that the reader
would perhaps expect the most 'flowery' language. In its three stanzas, "Sea Violet" revolves around the juxtaposition of two kinds of violets: the "white violet"
(1983: 25-6; l. 1) and the "greater blue violets" (l. 8). Stanza one describes the
white violet as "scented on its stalk" (l. 2), "fragile as agate" (l. 4), and "fronting
all the wind / among the torn shells / on the sand-bank" (ll. 5-7). The language
is clear and precise, and there is, as Pondrom has remarked on another of
H.D.'s early poems, a "total absence of words which describe an emotion or state
of being" (1990: 95). In this first stanza, the contradictory phrase "fragile as
agate" stands out and lays bare the poem's thrust against conventional depiction. While "fragile" evokes predictable associations of flowers with delicacy and
fragility, the reference to agate—a colorful gemstone often found in volcanic
rock—immediately negates this notion. The description of the sea violet as
"scented on its stalk" further emphasizes that its outstanding characteristics
are not outward beauty and elegance, but strength and beauty that lie within.
Seemingly fragile on the outside, it holds its precarious position "on the sand-
bank" (l. 7), i.e., on the place where land and sea meet and where it lies exposed
to the force of the elements.

The first two lines of stanza two continue the description, now focusing on
the "greater blue violets" about which readers are given only minimal information. As opposed to the single white violet in stanza one, the blue violets are
depicted as a group, with information conveyed simply through the plural 's.'
They are "greater," but information as to why they might be deemed so is not
provided. Line two of this stanza describes the blue violets as "flutter[ing] on the
hill" (l. 9); in contrast to the white violet, the blue violets are located at a remove
from the sea, with the verb "flutter" suggesting a mild breeze and not the storm
of stanza one. Lines ten through twelve develop into a question that asks "who
would change for these / who would change for these one root of the white sort?"
The question remains unanswered, and at this point it is not entirely clear
whether the question is why anyone would change these greater violets for one of
the "white sort" or if it is an expression of wonder at the number of people who
would do so. In other words, it is left open whether the question valorizes the
white "sort" or the blue violets.

Stanza three returns to the white violet, but this time without the epithet
"white." Lines thirteen through fifteen echo the imagery of stanza one, reinforcing the precariousness of the violet's location on the sand-hill through the

addition of the words "on the edge" (l. 15). The poem ends with what Eileen Gregory calls an "ecstatic image" reflective of a move that takes place in many poems in *Sea Garden*, but especially the flower poems: they "end with an exalted movement, a movement upward" (1990: 141). Although "Sea Violet" does not as, for example, "Sea Rose" describe an actual movement upward ("you are lifted," l. 11), it still valorizes the delicate but resilient flower by addressing it and describing it as "catch[ing] the light" (l. 16). The poem's sudden move away from the world of sea and sandbanks in the last line is enigmatic: "But you catch the light— / Frost, a star edges with its fire." In these last two lines, H.D. juxtaposes two images without explaining the connection between them—a movement that resembles Pound's famous imagist poem "In a Station of the Metro" (1913) which, in its two lines, also presents two seemingly unconnected images. As with Pound's poem, it is the surprise of initial dissimilarity that creates the tension and energy that forces the reader to consider the connection between and significance of the images. How does this line relate to the rest of the poem? Does it in any way describe the sea violet? While the initial reaction evoked by the abrupt transition from "light" to "frost" might be one of disorientation, a closer look reveals several surprising connections between the sea violet and the poem's last image of frost and fire: "fire"—the poem's closing word— recalls the light caught by the sea violet; "edges" refers back to the phrase "edge of the sand-hill" (l. 15) and thus to the sea violet's vulnerability. It also evokes the "torn shells" (l. 6) and their presumably sharp edges; the word "frost" alludes to the sea violet's white color; and the words "frost" and "fire," positioned at the beginning and the end of the line respectively, recall the elemental forces of wind and water evoked in stanza one.

Considering these connections, it becomes clear that the last line, like the rest of the poem, works toward a renewed vision of the white violet: the image of the violet, stripped bare of conventional associations, appears in a new light. If the last line paradoxically conjoins frost and fire, the violet similarly combines (but does not suspend) opposite qualities. While it might be delicate and exposed, its strength lies in exactly this exposure to the elements. Unlike the blue violets that gently flutter in a mild breeze, the white violet is tossed and torn by the wind, yet it is this exposure that also allows it to "catch the light." Additionally, the violet is often associated with delicacy and modesty, but by isolating the flower's name in line 13, the poem draws attention to its similarity with the word violence. Endurance and resilience in the face of violent storms and its ability to endure extremes turn out to be the white violet's most striking characteristic and its strength.

The poem's reduced and concentrated language that is "cleansed of Victorian and Georgian excesses" ("H.D. 1886-1961," n. pag.), its avoidance of sentimentality and descriptions of emotion in favor of a focus on the natural object, and an emphasis on sudden transformation and revelation make "Sea Violet" a prototypical imagist poem. However, a reading of H.D.'s poems in *Sea Garden* merely as exemplars of the imagist mode tends to obscure other elements of these unique poems. Friedman points out that the landscape of *Sea Garden*, while "overly genderless," is "covertly gendered"; the poem is an "encoded text in which techniques of the impersonal imagist both reveal and conceal a forbidden gendered rebellion and eroticism" (1990: 56). Flowers, delicacy, and modesty are, of course, terms frequently associated with women in general and the Victorian 'poetess' in particular, and it is easy to see how the depiction of the sea vio-

let as outwardly delicate, but strong and resilient on the inside can also be read
as a comment on the position of the female poet in a patriarchal world that sees
women and women poets as fragile and often negligible: the poem warns not to
underestimate the sea violet's resilience. Her strength and beauty lies, like the
female poet's, in her ability to persist in and negotiate a hostile environment.
This emphasis on the flower's strength in the face of its exposure to this environment also suggests, as Beach has pointed out, "two very different choices
for the woman artist" (Beach 2003: 82). "Sheltered Garden," a poem that is linked
to "Sea Violet" through the use of frost imagery, spells this out most directly:

> Have you seen fruit under cover
> that wanted light
> pears wadded in cloth
> protected from the frost,
> melons, almost ripe,
> smothered in straw? . . .
>
> it is better to taste of frost—
> the exquisite frost—
> than of wadding and of dead grass. (ll. 18-23, 37-9)

The opposition is clear: on the one hand there is the "'sheltered garden' of traditional femininity" (Beach 2003: 82) with its delicate flowers and pears, wadded
and protected; it is a garden of "beauty / without strength [that] chokes out life"
(ll. 40-2). On the other hand there is the speaker's desire to "blot out this garden" and "to find a new beauty / in some terrible wind-tortured place" (ll. 56-8)
where pears are allowed to "taste of frost" and which promises "a newer, more
innovative, and more daring aesthetic" (Beach 2003: 82) that 'uncovers' underlying strength.

H.D. developed this feminist strain of *Sea Garden* in her later poems, many
of which take up ancient mythology and engage what Alicia Ostriker calls "revisionist mythology" (cf. 1986: 210-38). In her poem "Eurydice," for instance, H.D.
rewrites the story of Orpheus and Eurydice from Eurydice's perspective, thereby
transforming and rejecting "the image of Eurydice as the passive object of her
heroic husband's quest, allowed, while Orpheus charms the underworld with
his music, no creative voice of her own" (Sword 1995: 186). Emphasizing Eurydice's desire to tell her own story and again connecting flowers with strength,
the first lines of the last stanza serve well as concluding words for this section:
"At least I have the flowers of myself, / and my thoughts, no god can take that"
(1983: 55).

3. Modernism and Nature in Marianne Moore's "The Fish"

Marianne Moore's poetry is highly idiosyncratic, and although it is distinctly
modernist in its focus on formal and linguistic innovation and in its break from
traditional poetic forms, it cannot easily be classified as belonging to any particular movement or school, nor does it owe much to the influence of any particular author (cf. Beach 2003: 86). Moore shares with the Imagists a desire for
precision and clarity of language and a strong rejection of the sentimental, but
she puts more emphasis on a non-hierarchal and non-discriminatory approach
to poetic language. For example, her poetry does not privilege elevated or 'poetic'
language over the ordinary. Quite to the contrary, many of her poems are con-

versational and prosaic in tone while also employing erudite and Latinate diction. The reader will also encounter words from a wide variety of contexts and sources: Latinate names for animals, for example, stand next to words taken from the realm of the newly emerging consumer culture, and a quotation from a classic Greek text might be placed beside excerpts from a pamphlet or magazine.

The first seven lines of Moore's highly ambitious poem "Marriage"—Beach argues that it "can be read at least in part as a response to such poems as [T.S. Eliot's] *The Waste Land* and [Ezra Pound's] *The Cantos*" (2003: 91)—exemplify her poetic style:

> This institution,
> perhaps one should say enterprise
> out of respect for which
> one says one need not change one's mind
> about a thing one has believed in,
> requiring public promises
> of one's intention to fulfill a private obligation: (1994: ll. 1-8)

The language here is formal, even expository, and the sentence is studded with insertions. Reading these lines aloud, one would not necessarily assume them to be part of a poem. As is often the case with Moore, it is interesting to consider what the poem does not say, what it withholds. If, given the title of the poem, we expect a love poem or a poem that praises a long-lasting relationship, we will be sorely disappointed. Flowery language and a sentimental attitude are nowhere in sight. As these first lines indicate, this poem is a tour de force of a variety of different perspectives on marriage. Is it an institution or an enterprise, and what's love got to do with it? Asking what "Adam and Eve think of it by this time," the poem offers—in its 289 lines—an "extended portrait of the relationship between the sexes" (Miller 1995: 118). Moore's interest in the complexities of relationships—in this case, the relation between man and woman, between men and women, between love and the institution called marriage, and between public and private—is not only a pronounced feature in this late work but is a concern in Moore's poetry in general. A good way to approach her idiosyncratic and often riddle-like poems is to pay attention to the relations or relationships foregrounded and consider the often unconventional way readers are asked to look at them.

"The Fish," one of Moore's many nature poems, is a case in point. If the title leads us to expect that this poem is about fish, the first two lines—"wade / through black jade"—work to revise this impression by instantly moving our focus to the fishs' surroundings. Syntactically the title is part of the poem's first sentence. This tactic of running the title into the text reflects on a formal level what the first lines describe: the focus is not so much on the fish themselves, but on how they relate to their environment and move through the water. In short, the poem shows us an undersea world—another sea garden—and focuses our attention throughout on how the different elements of this world relate to one another.

The blurring or merging of title and text immediately plunges readers into the poem and asks us to "wade" through this undersea world. What we encounter there is strange and extraordinary, and so is the form of this poem. The first five stanzas read as follows:

wade
through black jade.
   Of the crow-blue mussel-shells, one keeps
   adjusting the ash-heaps;
      opening and shutting itself like
an
injured fan.
   The barnacles which encrust the side
   of the wave, cannot hide
      there for the submerged shafts of the
sun,
split like spun
   glass, move themselves with spotlight swiftness
   into the crevices—
      in and out, illuminating
the
turquoise sea
   of bodies. The water drives a wedge
   of iron through the iron edge
      of the cliff; whereupon the stars,
pink
rice-grains, ink
   bespattered jelly fish, crabs like green
   lilies, and submarine
      toadstools, slide each on the other. (ll. 1-25)

What immediately catches our eye is the unconventional way in which the lines are arranged on the page. Even though the stanzas are clearly demarked, they do not follow a traditional form. Moreover, the coherence of the stanzas is undermined by the almost continuous use of enjambment: stanzas one through five comprise three sentences, and only the ending of the third sentence coincides with the stanza's conclusion. At first sight, then, the poem seems to thwart form, but a closer look reveals quite the opposite: the poem conforms to its own strict rules. It is written in rhymed syllabic verse, i.e., its form is determined by the number of syllables per line rather than by the alternation of stressed and unstressed syllables. The syllabic pattern for each stanza of "The Fish" is 1, 3, 9, 6, 8.

Such a structure has several effects. Together with the enjambment, this strict form creates a sense of ongoing motion and flux, mirroring the "in and out" of the sea. Additionally, both syllabic verse and enjambment work to isolate individual words, only to then immediately draw the reader's attention to the relationship between these words and to the relationship between the undersea world creatures and elements the words describe. For example, "like," the last word of stanza one, arrests our attention and keeps us guessing, if only for a second, what the mussel-shells will be compared to. In this way, the poem's unique structure works like a focusing device. Much like a camera—gliding in slow-motion past one element, zooming in on another, and then swiftly moving on—it guides the reader's attention.

Using a camera metaphor is apt as "The Fish" is indeed intensely visual and foregrounds questions of perception in a variety of ways. Just as in H.D.'s *Sea Garden*, we are not provided with descriptions of the speaker's emotional response to this undersea world. Instead the poem focuses with precision and discrimination on the depiction of sea life. What is particularly interesting is how the poem's imagery constructs the details of this world: the fish of the poem's first stanza do not swim through blue or clear water, but "wade through black jade," suggesting movement that is not swift and smooth, but slow and ponderous. The opaqueness evoked through the reference to jade calls attention to the dark mystery of the sea. One becomes aware that this is a world that we usually cannot or do not see. Yet refracted sunlight illuminates this world as indicated by the enjambment between stanzas two and three and by the prominent position of the word "sun" as the only word in the first line of the third stanza. Shafts of light move with "spotlight swiftness," and—like the enjambment and the syllabic verse—focus the reader's attention while simultaneously hinting at the idea that while the sunlight illuminates certain aspects of this sea world, others are left in the dark.

What is it that the poem casts light on and urges us to 'see'? Taffy Martin argues that Moore's poems often "warn against uncritically accepting surface appearances and first impressions" and that "The Fish" in particular "should warn readers that images in poems are not always what they seem to be" (1986: 95). What we are urged to see below the surface of the water, as the quotation above suggests, might not be what we are led to expect. The imagery of the first five stanzas presents a strange and yet strangely familiar world: the mussel-shells of the first stanza are "crow-blue" and are compared to "an injured fan"; the sea is "black like jade"; jelly-fish are "ink-bespattered"; crabs are compared to "green lilies"; the reader encounters "rice grains" and "stars." In short, throughout the poem, but most prominently in stanza five, the imagery presents sea life in terms of land life. Additionally, the poem continuously emphasizes how the different creatures or elements influence each other, working together or against each other. The first stanza describes crow-blue mussel-shells depicting them as a mass of creatures. Out of this "ash-heap" (another depiction in terms of land life) Moore singles out one mussel and emphasizes how its movements affect its environment. Similarly, stanza four describes how one element acts on another: "the water drives a wedge / of iron through the iron edge / of the cliff." The words "drive," "iron," and "wedge" stress the relentlessness of the waves. This force, as the enjambment between stanzas four and five suggests, cannot easily be contained. Stanza five continues to illustrate the impact of the waves, shifting the focus from the relation between water and cliff to how the waves influence sea life—how jelly fish, crabs, and starfish "slide each on the other."

Unlike stanzas one through four, the fifth stanza does not run into the next. The colorful ("pink," "ink-bespattered," "green") depiction of nature and the abundance of life in stanza five stands in stark contrast to the strong focus on destruction, decay, and violence that begins with stanza six and shapes the last three stanzas of the poem. These stanzas speak of the physical features of abuse and accident, with the word "accident" broken in half:

All
external
    marks of abuse are present on this
    defiant edifice—
        all the physical features of
ac-
cident—lack (ll. 25-33)

Where the first part of the poem hinted at the world above the sea by depicting sea life in terms of land life, the idea of human presence becomes more pronounced in stanzas seven and eight: the words "accident," "dynamite grooves," "burns," and "hatchet strokes" (ll. 33-4) all strongly imply human agency. The poem's last stanza, however, returns to nature and the depiction of the relationship between cliff and sea. If we expect resolution or a conclusion that spells out how one is to understand the relationship between the different elements we have encountered in the poem, i.e., between sea life and land life, or between cliff and waves, we are in for disappointment. Taffy Martin argues that

> Moore ends many of her poems by irrevocably undermining her readers' expectations and by presenting enigma, imbalance, and incongruity. In fact, the most consistent quality of Moore's poetry is instability. Her images promise specificity, but they dissolve as soon as one tries to visualize them. Her epigrammatic endings fly off into abstraction instead of offering resolution that they seem to promise. (1986: 93)

The last lines of "The Fish" are certainly enigmatic, but they do not fly off into abstraction as much as into obfuscation:

> Repeated
>   evidence has proved that it can live
>   on what can not revive
>   its youth. The sea grows old in it. (ll. 37-40)

While these lines return to the relationship between cliff and sea, the exact nature of the interrelationship is left deliberately vague. This ambiguity is achieved through the repetition of the pronoun "it." Contiguity suggests that the first "it" refers to the cliff, but this contradicts the preceding statement: if the chasm-side of the cliff is dead, how can "repeated evidence" have proven that "it can live / on what can not revive its youth"? (cf. Martin 1986: 94-5).

Instability, as Martin puts it, or lack of certainty are useful terms in connection with "The Fish," for it is not only the last stanza but the entire poem that raises questions and makes high demands on its readers. What might the sea stand for? Is it a place of abundance and life, as stanza five would suggest, or is it a place of darkness, decay, and injury? Does the poem strike a balance between light and darkness, or does it favor one over the other? Is this a poem about the force of nature or about the human capacity for destruction? Or could it be, as John Slatin suggests, a war poem that depicts "A Graveyard" (the title of another of Moore's sea poems) and "mourn[s] a loss which it is as helpless to restore as it has been helpless to prevent"? (1986: 75) Or, given the poem's play on the notions of surface and depth, does the sea in this poem stand for the human subconscious?

"The Fish" does not offer complete insight and, given its almost unyielding stance, it seems useful to take this ambiguity seriously and spend a moment asking what exactly it is that the poem does *not* do. Many critics have pointed to what Cristanne Miller calls Moore's "anti-poetic mode of expression" (1995: 17), and "The Fish" is no exception. The poem's organization into syllabic verse units (apart from guiding the reader's attention) runs counter to many notions that are ordinarily associated with poetry. Instead of presenting itself as the "spontaneous overflow of powerful feeling" (this is, of course, William Wordsworth's famous wording from "The Preface to Lyrical Ballads," 361), "The Fish" calls attention to its own constructedness and artificiality, creating a strong contrast to the natural world that it purports to describe. Looking at the page, one cannot help but notice its idiosyncratic form, which leads directly to another observation about Moore's poetry: "Her poems are not for the voice," Hugh Kenner points out; "in response to a question she once said that she wrote them for people to look at" (1970: 211). In other words, they work counter to the tradition of song that is connected to the idea of lyric poetry. Moore's poems are written for the page: we would not be aware of the 'violence' done to the word "ac- / cident" in stanza seven if we heard this poem being read out loud without simultaneously seeing it on the page.

Of course not all of Moore's poems are written in syllabic verse, but one finds this "anti-poetic mode of expression" in her free verse poems as well. This is achieved through her deliberate play with different registers, but is most notable through her idiosyncratic use of quotations: she inserts quotations from a variety of sources into many of her free verse poems. "The Octopus," for example, is a poem about Mount Rainier that makes references to Milton's *Paradise Lost* while at the same time drawing heavily on the brochures of the National Parks Service. In "Marriage," the "series of voices, all on the [topic of marriage], but all pulling in slightly differing directions, demonstrates why Moore's longer quoting poems are so difficult, presenting the greatest challenge to the reader who wants to find out what they 'mean'" (Diepeveen 1993: 105). Even without going into detail, it becomes clear that Moore's use of quotations has an effect similar to her poetic strategies in "The Fish": multi-vocality and multi-perspectivity are privileged over one unified voice or unified perspective, and the reader is urged to put the quotations in relation to one another and to the rest of the poem. Syllabic verse and use of quotation are also distancing devices, working to undercut "the tradition of the lyric poem as a form of self expression" (Bazin 2010: 63).

For a better understanding of Moore's poetic strategies in "The Fish," it is also illuminating to compare it to other nature poems. Like the idea of lyric poetry as songlike self-expression, the notion of nature as an object of poetic contemplation is connected to Romantic and post-Romantic poetry. Wordsworth's "Lines Written a Few Miles above Tintern Abbey" and the "Ode: Intimations of Immortality" come to mind, both of which "present a determinate speaker in a particularized, and usually localized, outdoor setting" (Abrams 1984: 76). Working to define "the greater Romantic Lyric," M.H. Abrams delineates the movement or structure shared by "Tintern Abbey" and the "Immortality Ode" as well as other Romantic poems:

> The speaker begins with a description of the landscape; an aspect or change of aspect in the landscape evokes a varied but integral process of memory, thought, anticipation, and feeling which remains closely intervoled with the outer scene. In the course of this meditation the lyric speaker achieves an insight, faces up to a tragic loss, comes to a moral decision, or resolves an emotional problem. Often the poem rounds upon itself to end where it began, at the outer scene, but with an altered mood and deepened understanding which is the result of the intervening meditation. (ibid.: 77)

The "Immortality Ode" begins with a sense of loss and crisis; a tree, a single field, and a little pansy "speak of something that is gone" (l. 54). The speaker mourns the ability to intuitively respond to nature and to perceive its immanent beauty and glory—an ability that is connected, throughout the poem, to childhood. Facing up to the loss, the speaker arrives at the end of the poem with a sense of reconciliation. Loss is transformed into gain. In its last lines the poem returns to the image of a small flower that now "give[s] / thoughts that do often lie too deep for tears" (ll. 207-8). The speaker is again, albeit differently, able to respond to nature.

Moore's nature poem is strikingly different. While the sea is full of life, it is most certainly not purely benevolent. The water, for example, is a massive force working on the cliff and the sea. Moreover, "The Fish" does not chronicle a movement from loss to gain, or from disconnection to connection. If anything the poem moves in the opposite direction. A closer look reveals that even this movement—from light to darkness, from a focus on life in the first stanzas to a focus on destruction in the last stanzas—is not as unambiguous as it could be. The mussel-shells are described as "ash-heaps," thus suggesting decay and destruction amidst life in the first stanza, and the phrase "the turquoise sea of bodies" might, on a second look, also assume a more sinister meaning. Does this phrase refer to the fish and other sea life, or does it suggest that the sea is also a grave? Conversely, while the focus of the last three stanzas clearly lies on destruction, the poem describes the cliff as a "defiant edifice" (l. 29) and the final line positions the word "youth" adjacent to "growing old." Like the creatures the poem depicts, endurance and destruction, abundance and lack, innocence and experience, the natural and the mechanical "slide each on the other."

Moore's poem undoubtedly shares with Wordsworth's a sense of crisis, but hers is not a poem of personal crisis. Like many of Moore's and also H.D.'s works, it withholds the 'I' and does not register any explicit emotional responses. The speaker instead emerges more as an 'eye,' an observer who guides the reader's attention. In both Wordsworth's "Immortality Ode" and "Tintern Abbey," the speaker stands at a distance looking onto a natural scene and is therefore able to reflect on it. "The Fish," in contrast, does not allow a distanced view but hints in many ways at a crisis of perception. The poem immerses the reader in the ocean—an inhospitable place for humans—and the first five stanzas present an array of close-ups; the spotlight image calls attention not only to what we can see, but also to what is left in the dark. Through emphasizing fragmentation and instability over coherency and closure, the poem illustrates that the sea, and thus nature, forcefully resists being reduced to only one meaning. "The Fish," as Christian Reed puts it, "refuses to be caught" (2006: n. pag.); it raises the question of how one can approach and represent nature, and it does so while, almost contradictorily, evoking the natural world in extraordinary detail. In other words, the poem remains elusive and continues to ask the reader to engage in a constant shift of perspectives. The poem's 'submerged' play on the words 'see' and 'sea' is no "fiddle," but is central to it.

4. Conclusion and Outlook

Despite obvious differences between the two poets, H.D. and Moore share many similarities. Both celebrate the power of precise observation—Moore's first American-published volume was, in fact, called *Observations* (1924)—and both show an acute awareness and critical engagement with literary tradition as well as with their modernist contemporaries. Both are now recognized and canonized as influential modernist poets. The trajectories of their careers, however, were to develop differently. Although a "touchstone for modern poetics" (Connor 2004: 33), imagism, as a literary movement, was short-lived—Pound abandoned it in favor of vorticism—and H.D.'s reputation suffered with its decline. Her success in the imagist mode with her early poems overshadowed her later works, and many of her novels were published only posthumously. Her later poems such as *Trilogy* (1944-46) and *Helen in Egypt* (1961) started to gain scholarly attention only in the late 1980s and 1990s. In contrast, Marianne Moore's later years were increasingly characterized by academic honors and "by the kind of public adulation that led to her being asked, at one point, to throw out the ball that would open the Brooklyn Dodgers' baseball season" (Gilbert/Gubar 1996: 1448). She received the Pulitzer Prize in 1951 and the Bollingen Prize two years later. Scholarly attention has shifted from a focus on, or rather a construction of, Moore's "poetics of purity" (Bazin 2010: 34) to an increased emphasis on how her poetry responds to and is shaped by her experience of and reaction to the modern world (e.g. Bazin 2010).

H.D.'s and Moore's importance for other twentieth-century poets is without question, and there is a significant number of publications that acknowledge their influence. Black Mountain School poet Robert Duncan's *H.D. Book* (written between 1959 and 1964 but published in 2011), for instance, is part personal tribute and part critical reevaluation of literary modernism, and the collection *Critics and Poets on Marianne Moore: "A Right Good Salvo of Barks"* (2005) collects not only essays written about Moore's poetry but also poetic responses to her work. Many works of twentieth-century American women poets—in their exploration and representation of female subjectivity—display the influence of H.D. and Moore. To mind comes Elizabeth Bishop, to whom Moore was both friend and mentor and whose "The Fish" and "To the Fishhouses," like Moore's "The Fish," meditate on the relationship between aesthetics and perception. Adrienne Rich's "Diving into the Wreck" (1973) employs the trope of immersion so evident in Moore's poem to depict the speaker's perilous descent into the sea to explore an old ship and "the damage that was done" (l. 55). In its exploration of the 'wreck' of civilization, Rich takes up Moore's attempt to investigate that which is usually left in the dark and often remains unacknowledged while also engaging H.D.'s "revisionist mythology" or "Writing as Revision" (1972) as one of Rich's essays puts it. "Diving into the Wreck" is one of many poems that attest to the lasting importance of H.D.'s and Moore's poetic explorations into the nature of perception.

Bibliography

Selected Primary Literature

Bishop, Elizabeth. 2008 [c. 1969]. "Efforts of Affection: A Memoir of Marianne Moore." In: *Poems, Prose, and Letters.* Ed. Robert Giroux and Lloyd Schwartz. New York: Library of America.

Duncan, Robert. 2011. *The H.D. Book.* Berkeley: U of California P.

Eliot, T.S. 1975 [1921]. "The Metaphysical Poets." In: *Selected Prose of T.S. Eliot.* Ed. Frank Kermode. New York: Farrar.

H.D. 1981. *HERmione.* New York: New Directions.

——. 1983. *Collected Poems 1912-1944.* Ed. Louis L. Martz. New York: New Directions.

——. 1985 [1961]. *Helen in Egypt.* Introduction by Horace Gregory. Manchester: Carcanet.

Moore, Marianne. 1994. *Complete Poems.* New York: Macmillan.
—. 1998. *Selected Letters.* New York: Macmillan.
—. 2008. *A-Quiver with Significance: Marianne Moore: 1932-1936.* Ed. Heather Cass White. Victoria: ELS.
—. 2012. *Adversity and Grace: Marianne Moore 1936-1941.* Ed. Heather Cass White. Victoria: ELS.
Rich, Adrienne. 1993. *Poetry and Prose.* Ed. Barbara Gelpi and Albert Gelpi. New York: Norton.
Wordsworth, William. 1998 [1921]. "Lines Written a Few Miles above Tintern Abbey, on Revisiting the Banks of the Wye During a Tour, 13 July 1798." In: Wu 1998. 265-69.
—. 1998 [1802]. "Preface to Lyrical Ballads." In: Wu 1998. 357-66.
—. 1998 [1807]. "Ode. Intimations of Immortality from Recollections of Early Childhood." In: Wu 1998. 375-80.
Wu, Duncan. 1998. *Romanticism: An Anthology.* 2nd ed. Oxford: Blackwell.

Selected Secondary Literature

Bazin, Victoria. 2010. *Marianne Moore and the Cultures of Modernity.* Farnham: Ashgate.

Bazin reads Moore's poetry as shaped by and responsive to the forces of modernity and newly emerging consumer culture and argues against a construction of Moore's poetry as immune to the pressures of modernity. It offers many detailed readings of Moore's poems, while also providing a comprehensive overview of scholarly writing on Marianne Moore.

Connor, Rachel. 2004. *H.D. and the Image.* Manchester: Manchester UP.

This study explores the H.D.'s interest in the image by giving attention to H.D's preoccupation with European avant-garde cinema and emerging theories of montage.

Friedman, Susan Stanford and Rachel Blau DuPlessis (eds.). 1990. *Signets: Reading H.D.* Madison: U of Wisconsin P.

Important collection of essays on H.D. that covers her entire oeuvre. Includes several detailed readings of Sea Garden.

Heuving, Jeanne. 1992. *Omissions are Not Accidents: Gender in the Art of Marianne Moore.* Detroit: Wayne State UP.

First feminist book-length study of Moore's poetry. Arguing that Moore's poetic achievement can be better understood when taking into account how gender structures her work, it gives a chronological overview of Moore's work.

Sielke, Sabine. 1997. *Fashioning the Female Subject: The Intertextual Networking of Dickinson, Moore, and Rich.* Ann Arbor: U of Michigan P.

A study of the poetry of Emily Dickinson, Marianne Moore, and Adrienne Rich that engages these three paradigmatic American poets in dialogue with one another and traces the historical transformations of female subjectivity.

Slatin, John M. 1986. *The Savage's Romance: The Poetry of Marianne Moore.* University Park: Pennsylvania UP.

An important study of Moore's early poetry that places Moore beside Pound, Eliot, Williams, and Stevens. It traces Moore's engagement with her contemporaries as well as literary tradition.

Further References

Abrams, M.H. (1984). "Structure and Style in the Greater Romantic Lyric." In: *The Correspondent Breeze: Essays on English Romanticism*. New York: Norton.

Beach, Christopher. 2003. *The Cambridge Introduction to Twentieth-Century American Poetry*. Cambridge: Cambridge UP.

Christodoulides, Nephie J. and Polina Mackay (eds.). 2012. *The Cambridge Companion to Teaching H.D.* Cambridge: Cambridge UP.

Debo, Annette and Lara Vetter (eds.). 2011. *Approaches to Teaching H.D.'s Poetry and Prose*. New York: MLA.

Diepeveen, Leonard. 1993. *Changing Voices: The Modern Quoting Poem*. Ann Arbor: U of Michigan P.

Erickson, Darlene Williams. 1992. *Illusion is More Precise than Precision*. Tuscaloosa: U of Alabama P.

Friedman, Susan Stanford. 1990. *Penelope's Web: Gender, Modernity, H.D.'s Fiction*. Cambridge: Cambridge UP.

Gilbert, Sandra M. and Susan Gubar. 1996. "Marianne Moore." In: *The Norton Anthology of Literature by Women: The Traditions in English*. Ed. Sandra M. Gilbert and Susan Gubar. 2nd ed. New York: Norton. 1446-8.

Gregory, Eileen. 1990 [1986]. "Rose Cut In Rock: Sappho and H.D.'s *Sea Garden*." In: Friedman/DuPlessis 1990. 129-54.

"H.D. 1886-1961." N.d. *Poetryfoundation.org*. Web. 10. Sept. 2014.

Kenner, Hugh. 1970. "The Experience of the Eye: Marianne Moore's Tradition." In: Jerome Mazzaro (ed.), *Modern American Poetry: Essays in Criticism*. New York: McKay.

Leavell, Linda, Cristanne Miller and Robin G. Schulz (eds.). 2005. *Critics and Poets on Marianne Moore: "A Right Good Salvo of Barks."* Cranbury: Associated UP.

Martin, Taffy. 1986. *Marianne Moore: Subversive Modernist*. Austin: U of Texas P.

Miller, Cristanne. 1995. *Marianne Moore: Questions of Authority*. Cambridge: Harvard UP.

Ostriker, Alicia. 1986. *Stealing the Language: The Emergence of Women's Poetry in America*. Boston: Beacon.

Pondrom, Cyrena N. 1990. "H.D. and the Origins of Imagism." In: Friedman/DuPlessis 1990. 85-109.

Reed, Christian. 2006. "On 'The Fish.'" *Modern American Poetry*. University of Illinois. Ed. Cary Nelson and Bartholomew Brinkman. Web. 10. Sept. 2014.

Schulman, Grace. 1986. *Marianne Moore: The Poetry of Engagement*. Urbana: U of Illinois P.

Sword, Helen.1995. *Engendering Inspiration: Visionary Strategies in Rilke, Lawrence, and H.D.* Ann Arbor: U of Michigan P.

Thacker, Andrew. 2012. "General Introduction: 'Magazines, Magazines, Magazines!'" In: *The Oxford Critical and Cultural History of Modernist Magazines*. Volume 1: Britain and Ireland 1880-1995. Ed. Peter Brooker and Andrew Thacker. Oxford: Oxford UP.

15.

The Harlem Renaissance

Claude McKay's "The Harlem Dancer" and Langston Hughes's "The Negro Speaks of Rivers"

Maximilian Meinhardt

1. Harlem Renaissance Reconsidered

In his 1940 autobiography *The Big Sea* Langston Hughes writes: "The 1920's were the years of Manhattan's black Renaissance . . . It was the period when the Negro was in vogue" (1963 [1940]: 223, 228). These two sentences epitomize the ambivalence constitutive of "the first significant literary and cultural movement in African American history" (Bernard 2007: 28), today known as the Harlem Renaissance. Hughes, "the veritable icon of the Harlem Renaissance" (Sanders 2007: 107), not only designates the 1920s as the heyday of the "black Renaissance," but moreover characterizes this era as a time in which African Americans were fashionable as artists and when African American culture was popular subject matter for artistic expression. This trendsetting popularity appealed to "[w]hite people" who "began to come to Harlem in droves" (Hughes 1963 [1940]: 224). Hughes's terms "black Renaissance" and "in vogue" do not contradict each other because a rebirth (the etymological meaning of a renaissance) naturally draws attention to and creates interest in its genesis; yet the transience of trends—of being "in vogue"—seems hardly reconcilable with the emergence of a "Negro Renaissance" (ibid.: 228). This complexity between rebirth and the ephemerality of being in vogue is visible in today's assessments of the movement and figures in scholarly discussions about the movement's place in literary history (see Bernard 2007). In fact, the question of whether the Harlem Renaissance was an influential but ephemeral phenomenon, or whether it was truly the founding moment of modern African American culture, continues to be one intricate point of contention within the field of Harlem Renaissance scholarship.

If the literal meaning of the term 'Harlem Renaissance' suggests a number of problems, temporal demarcations for and definitions of the movement are even more contested. George Hutchinson clearly expresses this problem of scholarly inconsistency and vagueness in his introduction to *The Cambridge Companion to the Harlem Renaissance*:

> The Harlem Renaissance—what a complex and conflicted aura the term evokes! People can scarcely agree on what it means. A vogue. A blossoming. A failure. A foundation. A few stars. A movement of black self-assertion against white supremacy, connected with anticolonial movements world-wide, or a local phenomenon gradually co-opted and destroyed by white voyeurs, cultural colonialists taking advantage of black naifs, opportunists, or weak-kneed bourgeois artists. A post hoc invention of cultural historians, now abundantly exploited by publishers, New York tour guides, and even, of late, real estate inventors. (2007: 1)

This list of diverse designations and interpretations seems to suggest that we can pick and choose. Hutchinson's plethora of opposites ("failure/foundation," "world-wide/local") captures the "complex and conflicted aura" which permeates

Harlem Renaissance scholarship. Depending on the social, historical, and political context of its readers and critics, different labels have been attributed to the movement. In these processes, critical assessments have changed from understanding the Harlem Renaissance as an emancipatory cultural movement to assuming that it was created by "weak-kneed bourgeois artists." Although "a general consensus remains that it took form after World War I and continued well into the 1930s" (ibid.: 6), scholars often either expand or narrow their periodization of the Harlem Renaissance and especially argue about the movement's contribution to and stance in American modernist writing (see Lewis 1994: "Introduction"; Tracy 2004b; Baker 1987).

Providing a pertinent periodization, David Levering Lewis subdivides the movement into three phases that coincide with the publication of major texts. For Lewis, the "first phase, ending in 1923 with the publication of Jean Toomer's unique prose poem *Cane*, was deeply influenced by white artists and writers" (1994: xv). The mid-twenties, then, were "a period of interracial collaboration," whereas the "last phase, from mid-1926 to the Harlem Riot of March 1935, was increasingly dominated by the African American artists themselves" (ibid.: xv-xvi). Alain Locke's groundbreaking anthology *The New Negro* (1925) functions as a transitory text, as it stands for the increasing self-empowerment of African American artists. Locke proclaimed the necessity "to register the transformations of the inner and outer life of the Negro in America that have so significantly taken place in the last few years" (1970: xv), and his anthology contains works of creative expression which record considerable changes in African American identity and art. While this explosion of creative output was not limited to literature alone (see Thaggert 2010), literary achievements in various genres make up the most part of the Harlem Renaissance artistic corpus. Lewis thus concludes: "The movement . . . was above all literary and self-consciously an enterprise of high culture well into its middle years" (1994: xvi).

2. The Harlem Renaissance: Form and Literary Context

As important as such discussions about periodization are (see Tracy 2004b), they often ignore the significance of form for Harlem Renaissance artists. Against this backdrop, Houston A. Baker, Jr. has introduced the concepts of "mastery of form" and "deformation of mastery" (1987: 15). According to Baker, key figures of the movement adopted traditional poetic forms to be recognized in the field of literary expression, and then they deformed these conventions to bring about an ideological change. While Baker's readings of the Harlem Renaissance have often been criticized (see Hutchinson 1995), his idea of the "mastery of form" provides a starting point for investigations into the cultural function of form and its relationship to content. Indeed, considering the bulk of shape-shifting assumptions in Harlem Renaissance scholarship, it seems effective to shed light on certain crucial forms of expression that influential figures of the movement employed, and ask how they understood the relationship between literary expression and cultural/social context. Instead of trying to place the Harlem Renaissance into a clear-cut time frame, or delving into abstracted socio-historical examinations, this essay (after briefly sketching contextual characteristics of the movement) provides a close reading of two canonized poems: Claude McKay's "The Harlem Dancer" (1917) and Langston Hughes's "The Negro

Speaks of Rivers" (1921). As early examples of poetic expression in the movement—according to Lewis "1917 [is] traditionally cited as the natal year of the Harlem Renaissance" (1994: xiii)—these poems, albeit distinctly differing in form, comprise leitmotifs reverberating in later Harlem Renaissance works. Employing and discussing key concepts first verbalized by W.E.B. Du Bois, such as the African American "double consciousness" (2007 [1903]: 8), both poems facilitate an understanding of ideas, problems, and aesthetic approaches to the dilemmas which the African American (artist) faced in the first decades of the twentieth century.

The prolific literary production of the 1920s was closely connected to and dependent on the foundation of numerous new magazines. For African American writers in particular, *The Crisis* and *Opportunity* provided entry points to participate in discussions of African American self-expression. As official journals of the National Association for the Advancement of Colored People (NAACP) and the National Urban League (NUL), these publications were highly conducive to sparking literary careers. W.E.B. Du Bois and Charles S. Johnson—two influential African American intellectuals and sociologists—spearheaded the magazines as the respective editors of *The Crisis* and *Opportunity*. The vital connection between similar publications, their editorial agendas, and eminent literary figures of the Harlem Renaissance like Hughes and McKay, is consequently one point of analysis in the following close readings. These interpretations employ Rachel Blau DuPlessis's concept of "social philology or socio-poesis," a "reading method" which "respects the verbal complexities, formal particularities, and aesthetic intricacy of the poetic text while analyzing the ideologies and social meanings that are condensed in and propelled by these linguistic and rhetorical choices" (2012: 66). These choices are especially significant for the Harlem Renaissance poets discussed here, since their formal choices are also a comment on how to define African American literature and culture against the backdrop of modernity.

3. Claude McKay's "The Harlem Dancer" and the Sonnet Form

In October 1917, Waldo Frank and James Oppenheim published two poems by Claude McKay under the pseudonym Eli Edwards in their *Seven Arts* magazine. In contrast to his earlier volumes of Jamaican-dialect poems that were published in Jamaica as *Songs of Jamaica* and *Constab Ballads* in 1912 (see James 2000; Tillery 1992), McKay's first literary output to appear in the United States was composed in Standard English. His Petrarchan sonnet "Invocation" and Shakespearean sonnet "The Harlem Dancer" were accepted for publication by the staff of *Seven Arts*, a short-lived little magazine considered the "most lyrical of the city's [New York's] leftist journals" (Maxwell 2004: xv). In their manifesto, the editors of *Seven Arts*, convinced that they were "living in the first days of a renascent period, a time which means for America the coming of that national self-consciousness which is the beginning of greatness," called for literary "self-expression without regard to current magazine standards" (Oppenheim 1916: 52-3). Both McKay poems, grouped in *Seven Arts* under the heading "Two Sonnets," engage with such ideas of "a renascent period" and "self-expression . . . through a joyous necessity of the writer himself" (ibid.). In McKay's sonnets, however, the aspect of joy is less prominent than the actual need to express the juncture of the poet's "world and race" (1917a: l. 14).

This juncture is immediately evident in "Invocation," which pleads for a return of the black, "[a]ncestral spirit" to "[l]ift" the poet-speaker "out if this alien place" so that he, as "exiled counterpart," might become the "worthy singer of [his] world and race" (ll. 1, 12-4). This plea is further accentuated by the end rhymes of the concluding sestet, which point to questions of race and belonging. McKay rhymes "heart/art/counterpart" (ll. 9, 11, 13) and "face/place/race" (ll. 12, 14, 16), thus binding together sounds and nouns which evoke concepts of alienation, emotional detachment, and duality. These key terms constitute the life of black westerners in a world after "the white God said: Let there be light" (l. 8). In deploying these terms, McKay engages with one of the most influential texts of African American culture, Du Bois's *The Souls of Black Folk*, which, as McKay states in his autobiography *A Long Way from Home*, "shook [him] like an earthquake" (2007 [1903]: 90). Racially defined by his "sable face" (l. 10) and emotionally detached from "this alien place" of "modern Time's unnumbered works and ways" (ll. 12, 2), the speaker of "Invocation" personifies what Du Bois famously defined as "double-consciousness" (2007 [1903]: 8): "One ever feels this two-ness,—an American, a Negro; two souls, two thoughts, two unreconciled strivings; two warring ideals in one dark body, whose dogged strength alone keeps it from being torn asunder" (ibid.). In McKay's sonnet, then, this dual condition of African American identity is poetically discussed in the speaker's striving to come to terms with modernity from an alienated perspective.

The poet-speaker is a part of modernity yet feels out of place, alienated, "exiled" (1917a: l. 13). By appealing to the African spirit to "[b]ring ancient music to [his] modern heart" (l. 9), he strives to cope with "two warring ideals in one dark body" (Du Bois 2007 [1903]: 8). As the last line of the poem suggests, this duality, one of "the highly personal yet broadly representative problems of black identity" (Cooper 1987: 82), can best be approached by artistic self-expression and self-affirmation. The speaker's and, in logical extension, McKay's aspiration to become the "worthy singer of [h]is world and race" (1917a: l. 14) echoes and aims to realize Du Bois's belief that the "Negro race . . . is going to be saved by its exceptional men," skilled with "intelligence, broad sympathy, knowledge of the world that was and is, and of the relation of men to it" (2007 [1903]: "The Talented Tenth" 189). But in order to sing, to artistically express one's self and soul, the obstacles blocking the way toward the creation of self-consciousness need to be known.

In a similar way, McKay's "The Harlem Dancer" embraces two elements impeding the condition of "the Negro," namely that he is "born with a veil" into this "world which yields him no true self-consciousness, but only lets him see himself through the revelation of the other world" (Du Bois 2007 [1903]: 8). The metaphor of 'veil' as well as the African American duality of mind, poetically represented in the concept of seeming/appearance versus being/reality, permeate McKay's sonnet on multiple levels. Supposedly set in a nightclub or bordello in Harlem, the poem depicts a scene of interaction between the eponymous dancer, her aroused audience, and the poet-observer. The first two lines of the poem introduce the reader to the erotic atmosphere and set the tone for the following dance within the dichotomous field of seeming/being: the reader encounters the Harlem dancer through a glimpse of the audience characterized by youth and sex ("youths," "young prostitutes"; McKay 2004: 172, l. 1). Pleased with what these "wine-flushed, bold-eyed boys, and even the girls" behold (l. 11), they eagerly follow the movements of the female dancer's "perfect, half-clothed body"

(l. 2). This juxtaposition of adjectives thereby not only discloses the half-re-
vealed, beautiful body of the dancer, but additionally highlights the seemingly
paradoxical word combination of "perfect" and "half." The undisturbed sequence
of iambs in this end-stopped line stresses the first syllable of "perfect" as well as
the "half" in "half-clothed." Thus, McKay metrically accents the concept of duality and ambiguity that underpins his sonnet. Halved perfection and imperfect
perception surface here for the first time in the poem.

With regard to content, the initial description of the audience ("Applauding,"
"laughed," l. 1) depicts how they perceive the dancer: She is physically attractive, seminude, and in motion ("sway," l. 2). These characteristics of her
outer appearance are palpable and concrete, yet the portrait of the dancer remains incomplete without her essential second half. Tellingly, the second half of
the first quatrain mentions "[h]er voice" (l. 3). Although the title of McKay's sonnet does not hint at singing, the Harlem dancer also entertains her audience
vocally. The sound of her voice, however, seems to be ineffable, beyond words,
which results in a simile evoking the bucolic idyll of "a picnic day:" "Her voice
was like the sound of blended flutes / Blown by black players upon a picnic
day" (ll. 3-4). The dancer's voice is here compared with musical harmony created
by multiple flutes; one vocal expression finds its poetic counterpart in the con-
cord of flutes "[b]lown by black players." By choosing this simile for his sonnet,
McKay ushers in a distinctly racial component which resonates in the reference
to the dancer's "swarthy neck" upon which fall her "black shiny curls" (l. 9).
While the first quatrain of "The Harlem Dancer" contrasts the concrete, factual
description of audience and dancer (ll. 1-2) with the poet-observer's rendering of
the dancer's voice (ll. 3-4), alliterations bind together the quatrain's halves.
Sound patterns link audible applause and the imagined blowing of flutes.

In the first quatrain, onomatopoeia underscores the tension between lascivi-
ous applause and bucolic harmony. The series of bilabial plosives beginning
with "blended" (l. 3), intensifying with alliterations on 'b' ("blown by black," l. 4),
and culminating in three forceful 'p' sounds ("players upon a picnic," l. 4) harks
back to the very first word of the poem "applauding" (l. 1). But the clapping of
hands combined with lewd laughter and hissing, which onomatopoetically resonates in four cacophonous fricatives in the first two lines ("youths laughed,"
"perfect, half-clothed"), is not the only suffused sound to be heard. The "blended
flutes / Blown by black players upon a picnic day" also reverberate in this
amalgamation of 'b/p' sounds. The fourth line with its change from three alliterations on 'b' to three stressed 'p' sounds illustrates the (con)fusion of lustful
applause and euphonious flute-playing. The sound of flutes, evoked by simile
and traditionally associated with pastoral harmony, blends into the clamor of
the nightclub into which the second quatrain returns. This mixture of sounds
exemplarily shows how the tension between external perception and the
dancer's internal striving for harmony is prefigured on the level of form.

This subtle formal contrast between harmony and disharmony becomes
more explicit as the poem proceeds. Similar to the first two lines of McKay's
sonnet, lines five and six describe the dancer's actions ("She sang and danced
on," l. 5) as well as her attire (the "light gauze hanging loose about her form,"
l. 6). Yet contrary to the initial rendering of her as a "half-clothed" beauty, words
like "gracefully and calm" (l. 5) extol the female dancer and separate her from
the eroticism surrounding and defining her body's sway in the second line.
Likewise, the adjective "half-clothed" soon develops from a prosaic, hyphenated

word combination into an elevated version: the dancer's "form" (l. 6), echoing "her perfect, half-clothed body" (l. 2), is draped in a "light gauze hanging loose about her" (l. 6). Again, McKay's equivocal word choice challenges the reader to see through the verbal veil. "The light gauze," which at first glance and with regard to content might seem to be only a description of the gauze's quality, in fact contains a number of ambiguities. Stressed through its position in the poem's iambic metrical pattern, the adjective "light" also illuminates by association the homonymous noun 'the light' and hence evokes radiance and brightness. However, this light can only be apprehended through the "gauze," the veil. This dual aspect of 'light' is further emphasized in the pairing of the adjectives "black shiny" in line nine, as well as in the complementary sonnet "Invocation" where the black poet-speaker pleads: "Let fall the light upon my sable face" (1917a: l. 10). Thus, both meanings inherent in the word 'light' support the dancer's ambiguous and incomplete identity. Formal details in "The Harlem Dancer" harmonize with the concept of duality in the Harlem dancer.

McKay's use of the word "gauze" in his depiction of the dancer promotes the notion that there is always something more behind a mask, a veil, a word. In addition to being a transparent fabric, 'gauze' also denotes and evokes a bandage used for covering wounds. Similar to the homonymous 'light' immediately preceding 'gauze,' this second meaning is supported by a conjoining reference in a subsequent line. In the last lines of the third quatrain, the poet-observer characterizes the "eager, passionate gaze" (l. 12) of the "wine-flushed, bold-eyed boys, and even the girls" (l. 11) with a strong and vivid verb: they "devoured her shape" (l. 12). Interestingly, the original version of "The Harlem Dancer" published in *Seven Arts* does not contain the word "shape," which was added in McKay's 1922 volume of poetry *Harlem Shadows* (cf. Maxwell 2004: 327). Including this noun in "The Harlem Dancer," however, seems perfectly appropriate, as it is the dancer's outer appearance rather than her personality which the aroused audience ravenously eyes. Their predatory gaze pierces "her form" (l. 6), wounds "her shape" (l. 12), and consumes "her self" (l. 14). The medical meaning of 'gauze' consequently suits the invasive atmosphere of the Harlem nightclub. On a verbal level, the "light gauze" in which the dancer is dressed captures the complexities and ambiguities with which African Americans have to deal.

Beyond epitomizing the general African American cultural situation of the time, the Harlem dancer is also an artist figure. Therefore it is only logical that the poet-observer, distanced from the young and sexually titillated audience, has a deeper understanding of and emotional connection to the dancer. In line seven, at the juncture of the sonnet's halves, the speaker enters the poem explicitly: "To me she seemed a proudly-swaying palm." With McKay's Jamaican background in mind, Wayne Cooper regards the image of the "proudly-swaying palm" as a reference to the poet's native island, which he left for America in 1912: "Momentarily she swept him back to his own tropical past" (1987: 83). More important than such a biographical interpretation, however, is the fact that the palm tree has "[g]rown lovelier for passing through a storm" (l. 8). As Cary Nelson remarks, this line "reaches beyond her [the Harlem dancer's] skilled triumph over the dance hall setting to reverberate throughout black history . . . and the dancer's pride and beauty stand for everything black Americans have won from adversity" (1996: 337). In Nelson's interpretation, the storm sweeping over the palm resembles the perpetual hardship "black Americans" have endured in their history. Despite these adversities and animosities, the Harlem dancer, as a metonym for "black Americans," proudly persists which is clarified by the repetition of "sway" in her as well as in the palm's movement ("body sway," "proudly-swaying palm," ll. 2, 7). In fact, "passing through a storm" results in development ("Grown") and renders the palm/dancer even "lovelier," a connection that is emphasized by the rhyme pair "Blown/Grown." Introducing the last line of the first and second quatrain respectively, these rhymed words bring the "black players" and the dancer as "a proudly-swaying palm" closer together. Pride and artistic expression in the face of obstructive circumstances characterize their common history. And yet the expression of this African American artistic identity seems only partially possible in Harlem, as the last two lines of the second quatrain transcend the oppressive nightclub atmosphere and, similar to the third and fourth lines of the sonnet, raise issues of race. The idyll of a "picnic day" might then be one place where the poet-observer imagines "her self" to be rather than "in that strange place" (ll. 4, 14).

As the concluding rhyming couplet suggests, the speaker senses the Harlem dancer's alienation. Observing her, the speaker unveils the discrepancy between perfection and "double self" (Du Bois 2007 [1903]: 8), while the audience carries on "tossing coins in praise" (l. 11). The volta, introduced in line thirteen with a classically conventional "But," draws attention to the subjective perspective of the speaker, who sees through the dancer's "falsely-smiling face." This hyphenated word combination reveals that the Harlem dancer is literally putting on a show, a notion that echoes Paul Laurence Dunbar's famous poem "We Wear the Mask," and in particular its first line: "We wear the mask that grins and lies" (2006 [1896]: 107). In a conscious act of wearing the mask, and thus tricking others into believing that the mask resembles their true identity, African Americans, in Dunbar's rondeau, "smile" (l. 4), "sing" (l. 12), and "let the world dream otherwise" (l. 14). Similarly, the Harlem dancer's "falsely-smiling face" ("the mask that grins and lies") hides "her self." By "looking at her" facial expressions however, the 'I/eye' of the sonnet penetrates this façade: "I knew her self was not in that strange place" (ll. 13-4). As in his "Invocation," McKay rhymes "face/place" and uses a semantically similar phrase to verbalize the out-of-placeness pervasive in his sonnets: "this alien place" (1917a: l. 12), "that strange place" (1917b: l. 14). "[S]able face" and "place" do not go well together (1917a: ll. 10, 12). Not surprisingly, the third, rhyming constituent "race" of the sestet in McKay's sonnet, though not explicitly mentioned, resonates in "The Harlem Dancer"/the Harlem dancer, too. Sonnet and dancer, restricted and limited as they are in both space (fourteen lines, strict rhyme scheme) and place (Harlem nightclub), reach beyond their formal and formative realities. The sonnet is not merely an exercise of formal expertise, but with its conventional confinements and ambiguities, it is a poetic counterpart of the African American condition.

McKay continued to use the sonnet form throughout all phases of his career. His affection for the fourteen-line formula has led critics to diagnose a "form-content schizophrenia" in his sonnets (Maxwell 2004: xxx), which Cary Nelson, for instance, sees in "The Harlem Dancer." He considers it "somewhat compromised by its unselfconsciously judgmental opening and closing lines (and by a formalism that does not altogether serve [its] subject well)" (1996: 338). While this, and other similar interpretations that "a seven-hundred-year-old design clashe[s] with his [McKay's] racial interests, if not his racial identity" might have a point with regard to the poem's audience at the time, William Maxwell's notion that McKay was persistently interested "in *collaborating* with the sonnet" (2004:

xxxiv-v) seems more productive. Maxwell builds on Baker's idea that "McKay's 'sonnets,' like Cullen's 'ballads,' are just as much mastered masks as the minstrel manipulations of Booker T. Washington and Charles Chesnutt are" (Baker 1987: 85). But what Baker designates as *the mastery of form* and *the deformation of mastery*" (ibid.: 15) is only one strategy applicable to McKay's sonnets. By mastering the convention-loaded fourteen lines of this poetic form, McKay not only denigrates "the sonnet's upright white mask" but, according to Maxwell, collaborates with the sonnet "as a fellow vagabond equipped with centuries of worldly advice on living through the century of the color line" (2004: xxxv-vi). Two years after the publication of "Invocation" and "The Harlem Dancer," this 'cooperation' would produce the violent Shakespearean sonnet "If We Must Die," a seminal poem about the 1919 race riots. With its fearless, exclamatory, and ferocious rhyming couplet "Like men we'll face the murderous, cowardly pack, / Pressed to the wall, dying, but fighting back!" (2004: 177-8, ll. 13-4), the sonnet form helps condense complex questions about race and politics, thus continuing McKay's project of adopting traditional forms for his own purposes. The fact that the poem was well-received by African Americans (Maxwell 2004: xxi) shows that McKay's fierce formalism did not prevent him from winning "a permanent place in the memory of a beleaguered people" (Cooper 1987: 101).

4. Langston Hughes's "The Negro Speaks of Rivers" and the Freedom of Form

Compared to McKay, Hughes's career as a poet was more intricately bound to and propelled by his first publication in an American magazine. While the older Jamaican poet, whom Hughes praised as "the best of the colored poets" (in Cooper 1987: 241), did not use his real name and was published in the last issue of *Seven Arts*, Hughes's signature poem, "The Negro Speaks of Rivers," appeared in June 1921 in the NAACP's official journal, *The Crisis*. Under the editorship of Du Bois, who co-founded the NAACP in 1910, *The Crisis* had a circulation of approximately 100,000 copies in the 1920s, which guaranteed Hughes a huge, politically interested and race-conscious audience from the start. As indebted to Du Bois's writings and his ideas as McKay was, Hughes dedicated his poem to the African American sociologist in *The Weary Blues* (1926). Decades later, in a brief tribute to Du Bois, Hughes verbalized the importance and influence that this "*Black Titan*" had on him: "My earliest memories of written words are those of Du Bois and the Bible. My maternal grandmother in Kansas . . . read to me as a child from both the Bible and *The Crisis*. And one of the first books I read on my own was *The Souls of Black Folk*" (Hughes 1970: 8). Spiritual and social texts concerned with the analysis of "that deadweight of social degradation partially masked behind a half-named Negro problem" thus introduced Hughes to literature and impacted his early writings (Du Bois 2007 [1903]: 12).

"The Negro Speaks of Rivers" (1995 [1921]: 23), in particular, poetically elaborates on Du Bois's definition of the "history of the American Negro" as "this strife,—this longing to attain self-conscious manhood, to merge his double self into a better and truer self" (2007 [1903]: 8-9). To successfully "attain self-conscious manhood," certain criteria for creating an African American self, however, should be respected: "In this merging he [the Negro] wishes neither of the *older selves* to be lost. He would not Africanize America, for America has too much to teach the world and Africa. He would not bleach his *Negro soul in a flood* of white Americanism, for he knows that *Negro blood has a message for the world*" (ibid.: 9; emphasis added). These specifications seem to have influenced Hughes's first nationally published poem. African as well as African American history ("older selves"), "Negro soul" and "blood," and aquatic analogs ("merging," "flood") resonate throughout "The Negro Speaks of Rivers" (cf. Onwuchekwa 1976: 103).

The title of the poem hints at the representative function which the speaker embodies in the following thirteen lines: it is not an indefinite article preceding the subject, but the definite and definitive "The." "The Negro" speaks as an advocate of and for his people. This representative figure of the title then merges into the 'I,' a speaker whose voice is particular and universal at the same time. As critics like Hutchinson have pointed out, Hughes's speaker resembles the all-encompassing, democratic 'I' in Whitman's poems. According to Hutchinson, Hughes "sensed the affinity between the inclusive 'I' of Whitman and the 'I' of the spirituals" and fused these two voices into the 'I' of "The Negro Speaks of Rivers" (1995: 415). DuPlessis adds Carl Sandburg, who Hughes later called "my guiding star" (in Rampersad 2001: 207), as an influence on Hughes's speaker and considers the "'I' strongly indebted to Whitman as mediated by Sandburg, and with a diction drawn from spirituals" (2001: 95). In his description of how, when, and where his poem originated, Hughes himself stresses the ambivalence of 'I' and 'our.' Mexico-bound on his way to his father, whose "strange dislike of his own people" Hughes had been pondering "[a]ll day on the train," the eighteen-year-old poet, while crossing "the Mississippi, slowly, over a long bridge," reflects on the meaning of rivers. Hughes recalls:

> I looked out the window of the Pullman at the great muddy river flowing down toward the heart of the South, and I began to think what the river, the old Mississippi, had meant to Negroes in the past. . . . Then I began to think about other rivers in our past—the Congo, and the Niger, and the Nile in Africa—and the thought came to me: "I've known rivers." (1963 [1940]: 54-5)

In Hughes's recollection, the "I" looking upon the "great muddy river," a phrase that in his poem echoes in "I looked upon the Nile" (l. 7), is connected to a collective African American tradition and surpasses its sole identity. The Mississippi links Hughes to the history of "Negroes in the past"; a past which he then tellingly specifies as "our past." In Hughes's episode, as in the poem, knowledge of history connects the African American individual to the African motherland metonymically captured in "the Congo, and the Niger, and the Nile." "The Negro Speaks of Rivers," however, digs even deeper into the past and "goes back to a pre-'racial' dawn and a geography far from Africa that is identified with neither blackness nor whiteness" (Hutchinson 1995: 415). The first four lines elucidate that "[t]he Negro" has, in fact, fathomed rivers older than any race.

The first line of the poem ends with a colon ("I've known rivers:"), which draws attention to the following characterization of the rivers. They are "ancient as the world and older than the / flow of human blood in human veins" (ll. 2-3) and predate human life and existence. These primordial, deep rivers flowed and left their mark on "the world" long before "human blood" began to pulsate and flow "in human veins." Prior to human beings, prior to "blood" (a conventional determinant and image of race), the rivers of the first three lines epitomize primeval time. Thus, the speaker's first statement that his/her "soul has grown deep like the[se] rivers" implies knowledge of a past which goes back to the origin of the world (l. 4). Soul growth here coincides with the depth of timelessly flowing, but still unnamed rivers.

This universal reflection on ancient, unspecified streams is then qualified by a list of particular rivers in lines five through ten. Facilitated by a paratactic style and simple diction, this central section sheds light on specific African and African American experiences of and in the past. Beginning in line five, the speaker localizes and names four rivers that impacted and formed the African and African American self throughout history. In anaphoric enumerations, the "Euphrates," "the Congo," "the Nile," and "the Mississippi" are connected to the "I" (ll. 5-8). The Euphrates, in which the "I bathed . . . when dawns were young," and the Mississippi enclose the rivers situated in Africa (l. 5). As the "origin of civilization and the site of the Jewish captivity in Babylon" (Hammer 2007: n.p.), the Euphrates geographically stands for "the cradle of all the world's civilizations" (Hutchinson 1995: 415). Yet the biblical history of the river also implicates oppression and confinement: themes which, though not explicitly articulated, also resonate in the raising of the pyramids and the "singing of the Mississippi" (l. 8). Nonetheless, natural harmony defines the first two river settings. Bathing "when dawns were young" and being "lulled . . . to sleep" point to the maternal qualities characterizing the Euphrates and the Congo (ll. 5-6). The mentioning of the pyramids in Egypt, however, disturbs these pastoral, free-flowing settings. The line "I looked upon the Nile and raised the pyramids above it" (l. 7) suggests both spatial distance (instead of bathing in or building a "hut near" the Nile, the speaker looks upon it; ll. 6-7) and vertical fixation, as the pyramids point to the sky. The African(-American) 'I,' physically involved in the raising of these archetypal structures, thus labored to erect static monuments, while the Nile continued its timeless flow toward its estuary: motion and motion fixed in place side by side.

In contrast to the pyramids pointing upward, Abraham Lincoln's journey on the Mississippi is associated with a downward movement: "I heard the singing of the Mississippi when Abe Lincoln / went *down* to New Orleans, and I've seen its muddy / bosom turn all golden in the *sunset*" (ll. 8-10; emphasis added). The beginning of the journey ("when dawns were young," l. 5) through sites of African American history terminates on American soil with the Mississippi's "muddy bosom turn[ing] all golden in the sunset." This image of change (mud to gold) metaphorically mirrors Lincoln's decision to end slavery, which is further highlighted by a (grammatical) time shift at this pivotal point of the poem. Up to this moment of the catalog, the speaker listed specific rivers and events connected to their geography in the simple past ("bathed," l. 5; "built," l. 6; "lulled," l. 6; "looked," l. 7; "raised," l. 7; "heard," l. 8; "went," l. 9). With Lincoln traveling by boat down the Mississippi to New Orleans, times and tenses change: "and I've seen." The present perfect tense, which was first used at the beginning of "The Negro Speaks of Rivers" ("I've known" in lines one and two, and "My soul has grown" in line four), proceeds here from the grammatically simple, but historically complex past. Yet this time shift does not obliterate the past, as the present perfect tense, grammatically speaking, combines the past and its effect on the present. As the sequence of tenses in Hughes's poem suggests, this simultaneity of past and present is also necessary for a truly African American identity. Thus Lincoln's resolution to abolish slavery breaks the simple past, but the shift back to the present perfect, at the same time, points to the significance which this past still has. It is a past that is still active and (a) current in the "shining rivers of the soul!" (Hughes 1995 [1923]: "Jazzonia" 34, l. 2).

Hughes's eleventh and thirteenth lines then do not merely echo the first and third lines of the poem. Instead, they affirm the speaker's knowledge of his people's specific history. The speaker has "known rivers ancient as the world and older than the / flow of human blood in human veins" (ll. 2-3) and has also, and more importantly, experienced history associated with four localized and temporalized rivers. Wisdom and the soul grow out of these historical experiences. The fact that Hughes reduces the second line of his poem to "Ancient, dusky rivers" (l. 12) emphasizes this depth gained by particular experiences in particular times. With "dusky" reverberating "dawns" (l. 5) as well as "all golden in the sunset" (l. 10)—words and images positioned in the first and last lines of the simple past section—the final line encompasses a soul wisdom of both the universal and the particular: "My soul has grown deep like the rivers" (l. 13).

Like Whitman and Sandburg, and in contrast to McKay's favorite style of versification, Hughes composed "The Negro Speaks of Rivers" in free verse. Instead of a consistent meter or rhyme scheme, repetitions of words and sounds connect lines and rivers throughout the poem. Both Hughes's recurrent "I've known rivers" and the refrain-like line "My soul has grown deep like the rivers" consist of words with long 'o' sounds ("known," "soul," "grown"); a vowel that also occurs in the second syllable of "Negro," which Hutchinson regards as "a word of pride, of strong vowels and a capital N" (2007: 1). Interlinked by assonance, and especially audible in the rhyme "known/grown," Hughes's sound devices carry over into the listing of specific rivers. The long vowels in "Congo," for instance, onomatopoetically contribute to the calming, lullaby-like effect which the river had on the speaker: "I built my hut near the Congo and it lulled me to sleep" (l. 6). Adrian Oktenberg hints at this underpinning function of sound patterns when she states that "[m]ost of the consonants—*d*'s, *n*'s, *l*'s, *s*'s— are soft, and of the vowels, long *o*'s reoccur, contributing by sound the effect of an ancient voice" (1987: 95-6). The importance of this "ancient voice" and sound in general becomes explicit if one listens to Hughes reciting "The Negro Speaks of Rivers." The track "I Have Known Rivers" on *Harlem in Vogue: The Poetry and Jazz of Langston Hughes* features Hughes briefly introducing and then reading his poem. In the course of his recitation, he lengthens syllables made up of strong vowels (e.g., "soul," "dawns," and "Orleans") with a stress on the last syllable) and consciously overemphasizes sounds. The most striking example of his exaggerated pronunciation underscores the pivotal point of the poem "when Abe Lincoln / went down to New Orleans" (ll. 8-9). Hughes stresses "all golden" by prolonging the pronunciation of the two strong vowels contained in these words. This dual emphasis is amply justified, as the metamorphosis of "muddy bosom" into "all golden in the sunset" coincides by implication with the end of slavery. Sound and musicality ("the singing of the Mississippi," l. 8) harmonize with the content of "The Negro Speaks of Rivers." In Hughes's poem, the voice of the African American past and the African American vernacular tradition are synthesized by musical expression.

In his later writings Hughes continued to develop and refine this key concept of fusing music and poetry while simultaneously celebrating "the low-down folks, the so-called common element" (2010 [1926]: 1193); it is a celebration of the African American 'I' which his signature poem already projects. In his groundbreaking essay "The Negro Artist and the Racial Mountain" published, like

The Weary Blues, in 1926, he explicitly links African American musical forms like jazz and the blues to "these common people [who] will give to the world its truly great Negro artist, the one who is not afraid to be himself" when he states that "[t]heir joy runs, bang! into ecstasy . . . and jazz is their child" (ibid.). For Hughes, jazz "is one of the inherent expressions of Negro life in America" and a musical form which, like the blues, provides a pathway to the African American "soul-world" (ibid.: 1195). Both musical styles are, "for the American Negro artist," constituents of "a great field of unused material ready for his art" (ibid.: 1193). By synthesizing poetry and distinctly African American music, such as in his poem "The Weary Blues," Hughes added new forms of vernacular speech to poetry. Hughes's poetic method of bringing "the meanings and rhythms of jazz" into poetry (ibid.: 1195) and "poeticizing the blues in his zeal to represent the Negro masses" (Cullen 1974 [1927]: x) is commonly considered his most innovative contribution to American modernist literature (see Jones 2011; Tracy 1998).

5. Conclusion and Outlook

McKay's "The Harlem Dancer" and Hughes's "The Negro Speaks of Rivers" are frequently included in anthologies and, given their canonicity, have become benchmark poems of the (early) Harlem Renaissance. Both poets later became more involved in leftist politics: McKay co-edited *The Liberator* and left for Russia in 1922, Hughes traveled to Russia in 1932 and had to testify before McCarthy's Senate subcommittee in 1953. The anti-capitalist diction of Hughes's later poem "Advertisement for the Waldorf-Astoria" exemplifies this shift. Their inaugurating poems, however, remain emblems of formally different approaches in coming to terms with "modern Time's unnumbered works and ways"—"works and ways" that transcend the locus of Harlem (McKay 1917a: l. 2).

Even though Harlem was no longer the epicenter of the movement after the Harlem race riot in 1935, its repercussions still reverberate in contemporary poetries. African American poets like Amiri Baraka ("Harlem is vicious / modernism. BangClash. / Vicious the way its made. / Can you stand such beauty? / So violent and transforming," 1995: ll. 1-5) or Rita Dove ("I like how the sonnet comforts even while its prim borders . . . are stultifying; one is constantly bumping up against Order," 1995: "Foreword," n.p.) continue to build upon the Harlem Renaissance approach to African American vernacular tradition and forms of expression, though their uses of form differ considerably from one another (see Sanders 2007). Similarly, rap music harkens back to ideas of race-conscious, musical self-expression that have roots in the Harlem Renaissance, particularly in Hughes's synthesis of music and poetry. In fact, rap provides a fruitful field for further investigations into the afterlife of the Harlem Renaissance. Peruvian-American rapper Immortal Technique, for example, participates in the discussion of the movement's legacy in his song "Harlem Renaissance" and supplements scholarship with contemporary music. He utilizes the Harlem Renaissance to show that it is necessary to redefine its notions for today's multi-ethnic societies: "Harlem Renaissance—a revolution betrayed / Modern day slaves thinking that the ghetto is saved" (2008: 3, ll. 30-1). While (Harlem) vogues come and go, Harlem Renaissance concepts of African American self-assertion, self-expression, and self-definition live on in various forms.

Bibliography

Selected Primary Literature

Du Bois, W. E. B. 2007 [1903]. *The Souls of Black Folk*. Oxford: Oxford UP.

Hughes, Langston. 1921. "The Negro Speaks of Rivers." In: *The Crisis* (June 1921): 71. *The Modernist Journals Project*. Web. 27 Feb. 2013.

——. 1926. *The Weary Blues*. New York: A.A. Knopf.

——. 1963 [1940]. *The Big Sea: An Autobiography*. New York: Hill and Wang.

——. 1995. *The Collected Poems of Langston Hughes*. Ed. Arnold Rampersad. New York: Vintage.

——. 2010 [1926]. "The Negro Artist and the Racial Mountain." In: Vincent B. Leitch (ed.), *The Norton Anthology of Theory and Criticism*. New York: W.W. Norton & Co. 1190-6.

Lewis, David Levering (ed.). 1994. *The Portable Harlem Renaissance Reader*. New York: Penguin.

Locke, Alain. 1970 [1925]. *The New Negro*. New York: Atheneum.

McKay, Claude. 1917a. "Invocation." In: *The Seven Arts* (Oct. 1917): 741. *The Modernist Journals Project*. Web. 27 Feb. 2013.

——. 1917b. "The Harlem Dancer." In: *The Seven Arts* (Oct. 1917): 742. *The Modernist Journals Project*. Web. 27 Feb. 2013.

——. 1922. *Harlem Shadows: The Poems of Claude McKay*. New York: Harcourt, Brace.

——. 2004. *Complete Poems*. Ed. William J. Maxwell. Urbana: U of Illinois P.

——. 2007 [1937]. *A Long Way from Home*. New Brunswick: Rutgers UP.

Selected Secondary Literature

Baker, Houston A., Jr. 1987. *Modernism and the Harlem Renaissance*. Chicago: U of Chicago P.

Though heavily criticized by Hutchinson, this study remains essential for an understanding of the role which the Harlem Renaissance plays in American modernism. Baker's concepts like the "mastery of form" and the "deformation of mastery" are still influential and important in Harlem Renaissance studies.

James, Winston. 2000. *A Fierce Hatred of Injustice: Claude McKay's Jamaica and His Poetry of Rebellion*. New York: Verso.

This study of McKay's Jamaican poetry facilitates a deeper understanding of the poet, his politics, and his poetics.

Jones, Meta DuEwa. 2011. *The Muse is Music: Jazz Poetry from the Harlem Renaissance to Spoken Word*. Urbana: U of Illinois P.

This interdisciplinary study contains numerous 'close listenings' of African American (poetic) expressions and traces the Jazz tradition from the first decades of the twentieth century to today's spoken word poetry.

Thaggert, Miriam. 2010. *Images of Black Modernism: Verbal and Visual Strategies of the Harlem Renaissance*. Amherst: U of Massachusetts P.

Highlighting the importance of visual elements in Harlem Renaissance works of art (including photography), Thaggert expands the scope of traditionally literature-focused scholarship of the movement.

Tillery, Tyrone. 1992. *Claude McKay: A Black Poet's Struggle for Identity*. Amherst: U of Massachusetts P.

This study uses McKay's conflicted life to shed light on the complexities and contradictions which black intellectuals faced in their struggle for identity.

Further References

Baraka, Amiri. 1995. "Return of the Native." In: Jay Parini (ed.), *The Columbia Anthology of American Poetry*. New York: Columbia UP. 684-5.

Bernard, Emily. 2007. "The Renaissance and the Vogue." In: Hutchinson 2007. 28-40.

Cooper, Wayne F. 1987. *Claude McKay: Rebel Sojourner in the Harlem Renaissance. A Biography*. Baton Rouge: Louisiana State UP.

Cullen, Countee (ed.). 1974 [1927]. *Caroling Dusk: An Anthology of Verse by Negro Poets*. New York: Harper & Row.

Dove, Rita. 1995. *Mother Love*. New York: W.W. Norton.

Dunbar, Paul Laurence. 2006 [1896]. "We Wear the Mask." In: Arnold Rampersad (ed.), *The Oxford Anthology of African-American Poetry*. Oxford: Oxford UP. 107.

DuPlessis, Rachel Blau. 2001. *Genders, Races, and Religious Cultures in Modern American Poetry, 1908-1934*. Cambridge, MA: Cambridge UP.

——. 2012. "Social Texts and Poetic Texts: Poetry and Cultural Studies." In: Cary Nelson (ed.), *The Oxford Handbook of Modern and Contemporary American Poetry*. Oxford: Oxford UP. 53-70.

Hammer, Langdon. 2007. "Lecture 15: Langston Hughes." Yale U: *Open Yale Courses*. Transcript. <http://oyc.yale.edu/english/engl-310/lecture-15.>

Hughes, Langston. 1970. "Tribute." In: John Henrik Clarke et al. (eds.), *Black Titan: W. E. B. Du Bois*. Boston: Beacon P. 8.

——. 2011. "I Have Known Rivers." *Harlem in Vogue: The Poetry and Jazz of Langston Hughes*. Fingertips Records. CD.

Hutchinson, George. 1995. *The Harlem Renaissance in Black and White*. Cambridge, MA: Belknap P of Harvard UP.

——. (ed.). 2007. *The Cambridge Companion to the Harlem Renaissance*. Cambridge, MA: Cambridge UP.

Immortal Technique. 2008. "Harlem Renaissance." *The 3rd World*. Viper Records. CD.

Lewis, David Levering. 1994. "Introduction." In: David Levering Lewis (ed.), *The Portable Harlem Renaissance Reader*. New York: Penguin. xiii-xli.

Maxwell, William J. 2004. "Introduction: Claude McKay—Lyric Poetry in the Age of Cataclysm." In: William J. Maxwell (ed.), *Complete Poems*. Urbana: U of Illinois P. xi-xliv.

Nelson, Cary. 1996. "The Fate of Gender in Modern American Poetry." In: Kevin Dettmar and Stephen Watt (eds.), *Marketing Modernisms: Self-Promotion, Canonization, and Rereading*. Ann Arbor: U of Michigan P. 321-60.

Oktenberg, Adrian. 1987. "From the Bottom Up: Three Radicals of the Thirties." In: Marie Harris and Kathleen Aguero (eds.), *A Gift of Tongues: Critical Challenges in Contemporary American Poetry*. Athens, GA: U of Georgia P. 83-111.

Onwuchekwa, Jemie. 1976. *Langston Hughes: An Introduction to the Poetry*. New York: Columbia UP.

Oppenheim, James. 1916. "*The Seven Arts*: An Expression of Artists for the Community." In: *The Seven Arts* (Nov.): 52-6. *The Modernist Journals Project*. Web. 27 Feb. 2013.

Rampersad, Arnold. 2001. "Langston Hughes." In: William L. Andrews, Frances Smith Foster and Trudier Harris (eds.), *The Concise Oxford Companion to African American Literature*. Oxford: Oxford UP. 207-8.

Sanders, Mark A. 2007. "African American Folk Roots and Harlem Renaissance Poetry." In: Hutchinson 2007. 96-111.

Tracy, Steven C. 1998. *Langston Hughes and the Blues*. Urbana: U of Illinois P.

——. (ed.). 2004a. *A Historical Guide to Langston Hughes*. New York: Oxford UP.

——. 2004b. "Introduction." In: Tracy 2004a. 3-22.

16.

The Objectivists

Louis Zukofsky's *"A" (11)* and Charles Reznikoff's
Testimony: The United States, 1885-1890 (Recitative)

Mirjam Horn

1. Introduction: Historical Context and the Objectivists

In his "Comment" on the program of the Objectivists, the poet Louis Zukofsky introduced selected definitions of

> *[a]n Objective: (Optics)—The lens bringing the rays from an object to a focus. (Military use)—That which is aimed at. (Use extended to poetry)—Desire for what is objectively perfect, inextricably the direction of historic and contemporary particulars.* (Zukofsky 1931a: 268; original emphasis)

As the guest editor for a special issue of *Poetry* magazine on Objectivist writing in 1931, Zukofsky attributed to poems a rather unusual quality: that of being objects, things, practical material entities. Similar to a lens in optics or the target in military affairs, verse was meant to focus on the world and its "historic and contemporary particulars," since this is what counts as "objectively perfect."

Beginning with the *Poetry* issue of 1931, the contested term Objectivism defines a poetic program that peaked in the early 1930s, but that saw a rise of shared interests already in the 1920s as well as an expansion and specialization well into the 1970s, with the later reprise due to the 1978 publication of *"A"* and *Testimony*, two enormous volumes of longer Objectivist poetry. The movement only comprised a couple of "persistently underknown and undervalued" second-generation modernist writers (DuPlessis/Quartermain 1999: 2) whose work followed that of proto-modernist authors such as T.S. Eliot, Ezra Pound, and William Carlos Williams. When some of the more eminent artists, such as Eliot and Pound, left the United States for Europe or elsewhere during and after World War I, the Objectivists filled a small though significant lacuna in the literary scene and qualified for one of the diverse variants of American Modernism.

The Objectivists consisted of a loosely knit group of predominantly Jewish American poets who were located primarily in New York City. While Louis Zukofsky (1904-1978), Charles Reznikoff (1894-1976), George Oppen (1908-1984), Carl Rakosi (1903-2004), as well as British poet Basil Bunting (1900-1985) are nowadays considered the most important representatives, Lorine Niedecker, Muriel Rukeyser, and Kenneth Rexroth among others often rank as later or associated members (see e.g., McAllister 1996; Perloff 1995). All of them started writing under the strong impression of ideas and poetic forms promoted by Imagist poets such as H.D., Richard Aldington, William Carlos Williams, and, most of all, Ezra Pound—"still for the poets of our time / the / most important" according to Zukofsky (1975 [1932]: "Dedication"). Pound and Williams provided Objectivist poets in general and Zukofsky in particular with valuable criticism and contacts in the literary scene of magazines and book publishers.

Louis Zukofsky can be seen as the most influential figure both in terms of Objectivist poetry and its programmatic formation. After the *Poetry* issue had laid the foundation of the Objectivist project, the following year saw the publication of *An "Objectivists" Anthology* that assembled the works of both Objectivists and high modernist writers. The anthology's title points to a distinctive feature in that the noun 'objectivism' was dismissed in favor of the adjective 'objectivist': despite biographical backgrounds, themes, motives, and forms shared by these authors, Zukofsky insisted that they were addressed as 'Objectivists' while he rejected the unifying umbrella term 'Objectivism' (cf. McAllister 1996: 10). In denying this systematic label, Zukofsky indicated the challenges of the Objectivist project as well as its inevitable inconsistencies and paradoxes involved in coining a poetic movement that emphasizes consistency and common ground.

An investigation of the general formal and thematic characteristics of this movement therefore proves to be a complex endeavor. The Objectivists suggested a continuation of high modernist claims: that an intellectual statement about the world was first of all possible in literary language and that a poem in itself carried some total significance for each and every reader. While Pound and the Imagists opted for the "[d]irect treatment of the 'thing,' whether subjective or objective" and to "use absolute no word that did not contribute to the presentation" (Pound 1954 [1913]: 3) in order to "render particulars exactly" (Aldington 1915: vi), Zukofsky stressed a "[d]*esire for what is objectively perfect, inextricably the direction of historic and contemporary particulars*" (Zukofsky 1931a: 268; original emphasis). With Imagism as a direct precursor, Pound's claims certainly influenced Objectivist form and method. In a qualitative assessment of the Objectivists' literary program, Barry Ahearn summarizes this determination in his approach to Zukofsky's *"A"* as "[c]lear seeing, [with an] emphasis on the mundane, feats of mental gymnastics, [and] abstract organization" (1983: 31).

In amplifying Imagist straightforwardness, these new poets introduced material that is not necessarily understood as symbolic or even 'literary,' but that possesses a distinctly documentary, factual quality. Their processing of newspaper clips, legal reports, and census records suggests an entry of the everyday, a heightened "emphasis on the mundane," of social, material reality into the poetic world and word. Consequently, both a report on rising food prices and a witness report in court were considered valuable for the literary endeavor as they provided the most direct access to material reality, a reality in turmoil. Under the influence of several historical developments, the rise of social movements, and the changes of political ideologies with Marxism and Socialism, the purpose of poetry for the Objectivists followed due as these poets "regard[ed] their formalism as a material agent within the social" (Davidson 1997: 239). Emphasis on the everyday complemented the experience of societal turmoil and the necessity to re-structure it, and allowed the poet (and the reader) to investigate how the bigger picture effected the personal lives of human beings, "[t]he immediate scene" (Ahearn 1983: 31) that meets the eye. This agency certainly involved a call for individual and communal commitment that led to a parting from traditional, reactionary models of society and the body politic as evidenced with the re-sorting of political powers after World War I. What still seemed possible with the high modernists' belief in the power of innovation faded with the Objectivists' poetics assuming a quality that was "anti-sublime, anti-transcendent" (DuPlessis/Quartermain 1999: 6). The hazy symbolism of the Romantics as well as the elitist introspection of high Modernism was discarded in favor of direct access and the poem's social relevance.

Particularly with respect to this call for precision and direct treatment it must be noted that the term 'objectivist' does not address the objective quality of a poem;

it does not have the ability to neutralize subjective impressions and unify them in the quest for a detached, stable truth and ultimate perspective on the real world. The poem itself was treated as an object, and a useful one at that. In his essay "Sincerity and Objectification," Zukofsky explicated this notion of usefulness. He asked the poet to deny "*symboliste* semi-allegorical gleam" (1931b: 273; original emphasis) as the "entire matter involves the process of active literary omission and a discussion of method finding its way in the acceptance of two criteria: sincerity and objectification" (ibid.). What matters most is paying attention to the particulars of sincere observation: "Writing occurs which is *the detail, not mirage*, of seeing, of thinking with the things as they exist" (emphasis added; ibid.), with "each word possessing remarkable energy as an image . . . as action" (ibid.: 275). The word assumes a powerful role since it enables us to 'see' and 'think'—activities that are unspoiled by "mirage" or by illusions of reality that foreclose agency and intervention. This approach leads to "perfect rest . . . objectification—the apprehension satisfied completely as to the appearance of the art form as an object" (ibid.: 274). Thus, 'objectification' as a poet's activity is dedicated to arriving at the comprehensive, 'satisfying' treatment of material reality in poetic form.

Obviously, this "perfect rest" does not occur as either a natural or ideal state, as Zukofsky himself concedes; the facts a word can convey are usually "not sufficiently explicit to warrant a realization of rested totality such as might be designated an art form" (ibid.). He stresses the poem's privileged capacity to this warrant: "Yet the objectification which is a poem . . . may exist in a very few lines" (ibid.), and he finally stipulates that "no verse should be called a poem if it does not convey the totality of perfect rest" (ibid.: 276). In sum, the poetic method of aiming for objectification in general favors sincerity and preciseness over sentimentality and symbolism: "The disadvantage of strained metaphor is not that it is necessarily sentimental . . . but that it carries the mind to a diffuse everywhere and leaves it nowhere" (ibid.: 278). Things, facts, and phenomena can be described anew in the poem's emphasis on precise form and on content that constantly acquires new, historically charged meanings. It therein adopts the Imagist focus on the elementary, the economy of expression, avoiding syntactical hierarchies with subordinate clauses and omitting language decorum to the end that "information, not ignorance, remains" (ibid.: 283).

Yet in exaggerating this language economy of its direct literary predecessor, the Objectivist project likewise exhibits a heightened solidification of the 'ordinary' as evidenced by the reproduction of oral everyday speech, mundane settings, and the power of sometimes tedious triviality. These writers' interest in the social everyday often resulted in either the close chronicling of quotidian events (as in Zukofsky's *"A"*) or the faithful reenactment of functional texts of everyday use (as in Charles Reznikoff's *Testimony*) thereby "recording and objectifying good writing wherever it is found" (ibid.). Although the potential of objectification was acknowledged to "exist in a very few lines," these major works of Objectivist poetry provided for rather extensive readings, to put it mildly. The following case studies offer readings of selected parts from both volumes.

2. Kin and Cosmos: Louis Zukofsky's *"A" (11)* (1978 [1950])

Louis Zukofsky was born in 1904 into a family of religious orthodox Jews who had emigrated from Lithuania to New York City shortly before his birth. His first language—Yiddish—and his upbringing on New York's Lower East Side brought a daily confrontation with what Ahearn calls a "linguistic goulash" (1983: 5). This stew contained, among other things, bits of German, Polish, Irish, and Russian, causing the young second-generation immigrants to abandon the naïve idea of a 'native' language. Once in school, English became the main language of conversation, and the teenager's first canonical literary influence was Shakespeare's Elizabethan dramas. With this mixed cultural and linguistic background, a precocious Zukofsky enrolled at Columbia University at the age of sixteen and graduated four years later with majors in philosophy and English. While at Columbia Zukofsky wrote his first poems which were published in student magazines. After considering significant influences in Guillaume Apollinaire's work and what he identified as "composition as action" (Zukofsky 1934: 19) in the French writer's work, Zukofsky became interested in eroding the division between the poet and the poem s/he produces, i.e., between the social being and the artifact. Adopting this dissolution of boundaries between artist and artifact paved the way for Zukofsky's later poetic agenda. However, the biggest impact for the young poet was Imagism and especially his long-lasting friendship with Ezra Pound, who also acted as Zukofsky's patron. Pound was the main contact of the Objectivists to Harriet Monroe, the influential founder of *Poetry* magazine in Chicago, who invited Zukofsky to organize the special issue that contained the essay "Sincerity and Objectification" and which marked the movement's conceptual initiation to literary publicity.

Bearing in mind the foundations of Objectivist poetry outlined above, it is imperative to see Zukofsky's work as subject to a variety of sometimes corresponding, often conflicting influences. These conflicts arose from basic oppositions: between the autobiographical self and the artwork, the concrete material world and how it is processed by the poetic mind; the potential of personal, fragmented stories shaped by local events and actions versus a depiction of the total view on a unified history. It is this interest in exploring conflicts and the disjointedness of poet and poetry that also emphasizes Zukofsky's Objectivist program as bridging the generational gap between Modernism and Post-Modernism (see Hatlen 1997).

Zukofsky's oeuvre is comprised of 49 books of poetry, short prose, and literary criticism. His early lyrical endeavors include "Poem Beginning 'The'" (1928), a long poem of 330 lines in six so-called movements. This collage features a variety of attending paratexts—acknowledgments, dedications, and an epigraph—as well as quotations by modernist authors such as James Joyce, T.S. Eliot, E.E. Cummings, and D.H. Lawrence. It was considered Zukofsky's "The Waste Land" in an "attempt to surpass Eliot" (Ahearn 1983: 36).

Yet it is the monumental volume *"A"* that defined Zukofsky's literary career. It is 826 pages long and took over 50 years (from 1927 until Zukofsky's death in 1978) to write. Since the creation of this poem spanned a time period that covered a major part of the 20th century, determining both its scope and literary relevance as a specimen of Objectivist art is quite a challenge. As a result, scholars disagree about the thematic structuring of the poem's 24 sections that Zukofsky continued to call "movements." For example, Barry Ahearn's comprehensive analysis of the poem identifies four topical units: movements 1-7 are captioned "The Resurrectionist" and tackle "the self cut loose from the family circle and an ancient, cohesive culture" (1983: xii); movements 8-12 outline "The Art of Appropriation" (written between 1935 and 1951) as "connections between past and present, specifically the relation of [Zukofsky] and his poem to history and literary tradition" (ibid.: xii); movements 13-20 are titled "The Recluse" and negotiate the intensified literary processing of autobiographical details, i.e., Zukofsky's experience of his son Paul distancing himself from the family; and movements 21-24, summarized as "Rich and Strange," provide "a final accounting of those things he loves best and place[] them in the context of history" (ibid.: xii). Other scholars employ a more basic, two-part division and identify overtly political passages in sections 1-11, followed by a focus that shifts to family and intimacy in sections 12-24. In his detailed biography of Zukofsky (2007), Mark Scroggins discusses the sections according to their time of publication. Whichever structure readers choose to utilize, it is clear that the question of unity—with the 24 movements corresponding to the 24 hours of the day—also occupied Zukofsky's thoughts during the creation of his life's work; he stated that "writing . . . which is an object or affects the mind as such . . . may be simply described as the arrangement, into one apprehended unit, of minor units of sincerity—in other words, the resolving of words and their ideation into structure" (1974 [1931]: 13).

Following Ahearn's four-part structure, the second topical unit titled "The Art of Appropriation" (*"A" 8-12*)—which includes *"A" (11)*, the focus of this reading—epitomizes the practice of objectification. This section is particularly rich with quotations that create a dense fabric of associated poetic images, forms, and histories that, in turn, become interrelated with the lyrical autobiographical I 'Zukofsky.' In this vein, the poem as object frequently resonates within *"A" (8-12)* when text 're-appears.' This happens first in the sense of poetic form when *"A" (8)* recreates the compositional principle of the fugue and again in *"A" (11)*, the early modern Italian *ballata*. Second, objectification is evident whenever Zukofsky adopts or channels material from other authors, for example Karl Marx' *Capital* (1867/1885/1894; cf. Zukofsky 1993 [1978]: 45-8, 106) and Friedrich Engels' *On Historical Materialism* (1892), that are employed as material movable pieces of the canonical scenery, themselves objects that designate intertextuality and their own literary historicity. Additional examples include the adaptation and processing of historical events and accounts such as Henry Adams' experience of travelling in the 19th century as depicted in his *The Degradation of the Democratic Dogma* (1919) or the Adams brothers' *Chapters of Erie* (1886) in which they unfold the capitalist exploitation of the American railroad system (cf. Zukofsky 1993 [1978]: 71-8). The practice of objectification is also apparent in the quoted words of close family members and friends, or in conversations overheard on the street that reemerge to allegedly counterpoint the other texts' heaviness and historicity with mundane immediacy. All of these forms become appropriated and leveled, equally rated as appropriate materials for literary negotiation as long as they fit the Objectivist design.

At first glance, *"A" (11*; 1993 [1950]: 124-5) seems to retreat from actual historical and literary intertexts and zoom in on the private life of the immediate Zukofsky family: the poet himself, his wife Celia, and their son Paul. The first indicator of this shift toward the personal is the movement's dedication: *"for Celia and Paul"* (ibid.: 124; original emphasis). Suggesting familial intimacy in the midst of modernist chaos presents a caesura, delimiting the preceding plethora of obvious intertexts. Yet this inside view does not ease the former movements' hermeticity, and it certainly does not meet any voyeuristic interests on the part of the reader. Formally, the five stanzas of the movement (each comprised of ten lines, except for the first stanza, which has only six), all feature irregular rhyme schemes, and each ends with the same word: "honor." Through this structure *"A" (11)* adopts that of "Perch'i' no spero di tornar giammai" ('Because I do not hope to turn again'), a *ballata* by Italian poet and philosopher Guido Cavalcanti (c. 1255-1300), who was a contemporary of Dante Alighieri and became a strong influence for anglophone Modernism through Pound's translations (1936) and T.S. Eliot's adaptation of the opening line of "Perch'i' no spero" in his "Ash Wednesday" (1930). Both poems deal with the vanishing man/poet who wants to send a message to his beloved ones, in Zukofsky's case his immediate family. Thus, even below the surface of domestic motifs, the impact of literary history is felt. In *"A" (11)* this vanishing becomes obvious in the anticipated death of "Zukofsky" in the first stanza. The lyrical I has crossed a "River that must turn full" (l. 1) and orders his wife and son to move on from "grief to music" "after I stop dying" (ll. 2, 1). Paul, a violinist wunderkind, shall play "Sounds of light, stay in her keeping / And my son's face—this much for honor" (ll. 5-6). Anxious of leaving the "wrangling" (l. 4) wife and son behind, the first stanza is concerned with managing the lyrical I's legacy: "this much for honor" (l. 6). 'Honor' herein serves as an abstraction from the family's everyday conduct, an overriding principle that involves great esteem, moral consciousness, and privileged position—all sentiments easily lost in quotidian conflicts between family members.

The notion of honor also permeates stanzas two and three, which clearly borrow from Spinoza's *Ethics*. According to the 17th-century philosopher, as individual family members we must learn to moderate our passions—those inconsiderate impulses that keep us from becoming virtuous and happy, from following our "desire of honour" although "under the burden of blame we can scarcely endure it" (Spinoza 1970 [1677]: 177; pt. 4/prop. 52n). In *"A" (11)* this advice resounds as follows: "Freed by their praises who make honor dearer / . . . draw speech from their nature or / Love in you . . . purer / Gold than tongues make without feeling" (ll. 7-12). Mutual respect arrives from praising each other, a mode of speech that produces honor far better than words ("tongues") devoid of empathy. This manner of speaking resumes the first stanza's command to "raise grief to music" in that it is transformed into "song," and even into the family's signature instrument, the violin: ". . . thread gold stringing / The fingerboard pressed in my honor" (ll. 15-6). The praise of mutual respect resonates with the violin's strings that testify to the father's legacy.

The third stanza of the movement continues this advice and underpins the complexity of the domestic unit. The family is acknowledged as a contentious space, yet the lyrical I also conjures its potential: ". . . delight knowing / We overcome ills by love . . ." (ll. 17-8). In this forced unit of three people, "ills"—conflicts and misunderstandings as much as misfortune and harm—can be met by an intimacy that "nourish[es]" (l. 18), allowing its members to "Flourish / By love's sweet lights and sing" (ll. 20-1). The poem again accounts for the fragility of this construct in linguistic ambiguity: ". . . For the flowing / River's poison where what rod blossoms" (ll. 19-20). The flowering "rod" as an ambivalent signifier becomes a useful object to illustrate the hard-fought nature of the family: on the one hand, 'rod' denotes a big stick that indicates destructive authority—think of how Moses used the rod to turn the water of the Nile into blood (cf. Ex. 7:14-25); on the other hand, the botanical species Aaron's rod comes to mind: a tall biennial plant that has been used as both an organic torch and to predict the winter's intensity according to its inflorescence. The rod becomes an indicator of both destruction and fertility and locates the proximity of these qualities in the family. The complex interrelations and the potential to either destroy or to allow its members to flourish cannot be compared: "No, song, not any one power / May recall or forget, our / Love to see your love flows into / Us. If Venus lights, your words spin" (ll. 22-5). The blossoming rod, the flowing power, and lighting love that makes words spin in the third stanza buoys up the fragile construct that is family.

The fourth stanza signals the opening of the nuclear unit to the world, an opening that will become further developed in *"A" (12)*: "I, dust—raise the great hem of the extended / World that nothing can leave" (ll. 28-9). The border between private and public, the nucleus and its bigger picture, becomes permeable yet stable since still "nothing can leave." As the outer world, that is, material reality, has already found its way into the family by means of canonized texts, the present "great hem" is just as necessary for the spheres to cooperate: the individual, the family, and the cosmos. When "Zukofsky" turns to his son and says, "If your father offended / You with mute wisdom, my words have not ended / His second paradise . . ." (ll. 30-2), it is the early modern alchemist and philosopher Paracelsus who provides textual background: "The striving for wisdom is the second paradise of the world" (1951 [1583]: 65). The microcosm of the human being who is co-defined by an exchange with others (here muted), reflects in the greater structure, the universe as a whole.

The remaining lines of the stanza, which are further complicated by the breaking of the syntactic unit through numerous enjambments, return to the two people closest to the lyrical I:

> His second paradise where
> His love was in her eyes where
> They turn, quick for you two—sick
> Or gone cannot make music
> You set less than all. Honor (ll. 32-6)

The epistrophe "where" keeps the line running before someone quickly turns for Celia and Paul. Then the weak rhyme "sick"/"music" takes over, accentuating their lagging behind and Paul's/the family's incapacity to play music/pay respect because—remember Cavalcanti's 'I do not hope to turn again'—they are separated. The verb "set," pointing to a musical collection of pitches as well as the adjustment of an object, is also a homophone to 'said,' which again indicates the lack of communication, or of miscommunication, within the family and among humans in general.

With the fifth stanza, the poem pores on the theme of interconnectedness of systems:

> . . . the river's turn that finds the
> Grace in you, four notes first too full for talk, leaf
> Lighting stem, stems bound to the branch that binds the
> Tree, and then as from the same root we talk, leaf
> After leaf of your mind's music, page, walk leaf
> Over leaf of his thought, sounding
> His happiness: song sounding
> The grace that comes from knowing
> Things, her love our own showing
> Her love in all her honor.' (ll. 37-47)

The poem's ending acquires a musical, and thereby conciliatory, quality with the epistrophe and in-line repetition of "leaf" and with the syllabic rhyme "sound-

ing"/"knowing"/"showing." The family is permanently joined to the bigger picture: the "notes" relate both to musical notation and to the various intertexts
underlying, or annotating, the poem; the leaves represent the violinist's sheet
music, the family tree's organs that are connected to the stem, to the branch,
and to the root, the material book pages of the intertexts, and, from a poetical
meta-perspective, *"A"* itself as Zukofsky's life poem ("leaf / Over leaf of his
thought"). The ambiguity of 'leaf' resonates in particular with "Grace" as God's
blessing, which keeps the promise of salvation. This blessing "comes from knowing / Things," the final poetic curtsy to the Objectivist program of treating "minor
units of sincerity" (Zukofsky 1974 [1931]: 13). The goal of Zukofsky's monumental volume is anything but the composition of a life poem. *"A"* is the poet's long-
term project to come to terms with his own self, his position within the material
world, and the excess of impressions, experiences, and affects. Although short in
length and incorporating relatively few canonical intertexts, *"A" (11)* allows
readers to grasp the Objectivist poet's attempt to represent his surroundings
anew. The poem neither falls back on idealized symbolism that obscures the verbal objects nor does it simply continue the Imagist's imperative of a minimalist
'treatment of the thing.' The heavily loaded intertexts by Cavalcanti, Spinoza, and
Paracelsus enhance Zukofsky's sometimes esoteric, sometimes simplistic remarks on the nature of family in general, and his own in particular. The reciprocity of the family's microcosm and (literary) history's macrocosm enables
"Zukofsky" to fulfill the Objectivist demands of "information, not ignorance"
(1931b: 283) and to meet the challenge of "the totality of perfect rest" (ibid.: 276).

3. Reenacting History: Charles Reznikoff's *Testimony: The United States, 1885-1890 (Recitative)* (1978/79 [1965/68])

Like Louis Zukofsky, Charles Reznikoff was a poet with a second-generation immigrant background. Born in 1894 to Russian immigrant parents living in a
Jewish neighborhood in Brooklyn, he studied journalism for a year, then
entered New York University's law school in 1912, graduated four years later,
and briefly practiced law. Reznikoff soon changed his profession to become a
writer for a publishing house where he composed summaries of court transcripts for legal reference books. Here he found a non-literary model for the
proper way of dealing with language: like a legal transcript, poetic form and content had to be reduced to the most relevant pieces of information and the elements of the cases must be stated clearly.

Reznikoff started writing poetry in his youth and, along with Zukofsky and
George Oppen, founded the publishing company To Publishers and the Objectivist Press in order to guarantee the steady publication of their works. After receiving favorable reviews for his novel *By the Waters of Manhattan* (1930), Reznikoff
featured prominently in Zukofsky's coinage of the Objectivists in the latter's "Sincerity and Objectification." Despite the early honors he garnered from this poetic
manifesto, broader recognition among critics and readers eluded Reznikoff until
the 1960s when independent publishers like New Directions, San Francisco
Review Books, and Black Sparrow Press put his work back into print.

Another analogy between Zukofsky and Reznikoff is the complex publication
history of their major works. Published in a 'final' version as late as 1978 by
Black Sparrow Press, the editor Seamus Cooney explains that *Testimony: The*

United States, 1885-1915 (Recitative) (*T* in the following) "originally was prepared in four parts" (in Reznikoff 1978 [1965]: 7). The first part covers the years 1885-1890 and was published by New Directions in 1965; the second, privately released as a run of only 200 copies in 1968, focuses on the years 1891-1900; the years 1901-1910 build the third part which was prepared for publication by Reznikoff just before his death in 1976; and the fourth part (1911-1915) comprises a short typescript that was posthumously found among the author's private notes. The first collected edition was not published until 1978 (volume 1) and 1979 (volume 2). After a brief examination of the poem's paratexts—title, author's note, and epigraph—and of Court poetry as the text's overriding genre, the remainder of this chapter investigates *Testimony*'s Objectivist features by centering on the coherent first part (1885-1890) available from the first of two Black Sparrow volumes (Reznikoff 1978 [1965]: 11-110).

The title of the two-volume poem indicates a clear connection to authoritative discourses, namely those of law and religion. In the first case, Reznikoff's edited testimonies as comprehensive 'witness reports' comprise not only the subjective experience and the personal knowledge of a singular (criminal) event, but in their entirety of 500 pages suggest a panoramic perspective on the United States. In addition to opening up a vast, yet limited spatial unit, the poem offers historical coordinates that further determine the testimonies' temporal situatedness at the turn of the 19th to the 20th century. In the second case, 'testimony' refers to the religious discourse we encounter as the declaration of a believer's creed or a remarkable spiritual experience; it not only acknowledges the existence and potency of God as the ruling power but professes this conviction for others to see. Both volumes additionally include a note from the author who assures his readers: "All that follows is based on law reports of the several states. The names of all persons are fictitious and those of villages and towns have been changed. C.R." (ibid.: 9). While acknowledging the appropriation of historical court records, this note highlights that necessary changes have been made to prevent voyeurism and testifies to an authorial intervention that marks the transition from the legal to the literary context.

Finally, the poem is preceded by an epigraph from the epistle to the Ephesians in the English Revised Version of the Holy Bible from 1885: "Let all bitterness, and wrath, and anger, and clamour, and railing, be put away from you, with all malice" (ibid.: 12; Eph. 4:31). Lifted from the tenth book of the New Testament, this quotation refers to its source's concern with the church as 'the body of Christ' and with the lives of all Christians in peaceful community. As a central book of the Bible that gives practical advice in leading this kind of life, its last chapter closes with the verse: "Be kind to one another, tenderhearted, forgiving one another, as God in Christ forgave you" (Eph. 4:32). Contrasting the legal dimension of the title and the author's note with the religious insistence on loving Christian conduct in the epigraph, these paratexts prepare readers for the text to come, text that can be qualified as so-called Court poetry.

The genre heading of Court poetry, which also attracted Muriel Rukeyser (e.g., in "Absalom" 1938) and M. NourbeSe Philip ("Zong!" 2008) comprises text recovered from legal records and/or transcripts that becomes translocated and rearranged in the literary environment, thereby changing the material's genre and purpose from law to literature. In this line, the 500 pages of *Testimony*'s two volumes provide an alternative history of the United States over a period of 30 years as reconstructed from extant court records. This recovery encompasses 150 volumes compiled throughout the 19th century in the federal and state reporter system with which Reznikoff came in contact during his day job working on the *Corpus Juris Secundum*, an encyclopedia of United States law. These texts had already been through several acts of translation and transcription: from oral witness report (in first person) to court transcript to case report (in third person).

As a legal writer Reznikoff diligently compiled the vast material; as a poet he selected the most telling passages for his project: "It occurred to me that I should go through all the case books. I might go through a volume of a thousand pages and find just one case from which to take the facts and rearrange them so as to be interesting" (in Sternburg/Ziegler 1984 [1973]: 132). Although Reznikoff clearly edited the found records "so as to be interesting," he collected them to build an archive of all published case decisions, and roughly maintained the structure of the source text, arranging them to correspond with the seven regional districts of the United States (Pacific, North Western, South Western, North Eastern, Atlantic, South Eastern, and Southern). Reznikoff's selection first of all concerns the source material's vastness and integrity. Following the court records' regional divisions in the part covering 1885-1890, readers encounter three main sections named after three of the cardinal directions of the compass: "The South" (1978 [1965]: 13-41), "The North" (ibid.: 43-90), and "The West" (ibid.: 91-110). Each of these regional areas is again divided into various subchapters (in Roman numerals) and often further into individual scenes (in Arabic numerals). At times the subchapters come without additional details; others are captioned thematically: "SOCIAL LIFE" (cf. ibid.: 15, 46, 99, 113, 172), "DOMESTIC SCENES" (cf. ibid.: 22, 51, 100, 118, 183), "MACHINE AGE" (cf. ibid.: 30, 88, 237), "PROPERTY" (cf. ibid.: 33, 64, 154, 218), "NEGROES" (cf. ibid.: 39, 76, 134, 212), and "RAILROADS" (cf. ibid.: 84, 159, 247). These subdivisions emphasize the multiplicity of voices while also underlining the object-ness of individual witnesses: the appropriated records both reflect and subsume the individuals of that time.

With the poem's overall structure imitating that of the *Corpus Juris Secundum*, the reader encounters a series of individual vignettes that correspond to the legal text's statements of facts. These statements, already abstractions from the first-person accounts, usually report vice: gruesome force and abuse, murderous assault, bodily harm inflicted by industrial machinery or through acts of racism, acts that are fuelled by greed, theft, and sadism. These overriding themes affect the reader all the more when 'innocent' individuals like children or the weak are involved: The orphan "Tilda was just a child / when she began to work for the Tells . . . / When, as is the way of women, / her monthly sickness first began, / she was frightened / and told Mrs. Tell about it: / 'That is bad . . . / and dangerous: you might go crazy and die. / There is only one thing to do: / work hard! / Work as hard as you can, and you may still get well!'" (ibid.: 60, ll. 68-82). The scene testifies to allegations of hard child labor at the end of the 19th century when there were few health and safety regulations, a decided lack of care that should have been Mrs. Tell's duty, and a propensity for sadism and torment that affect a child who "did the work / two stout girls had done" (ibid.). With every new account, we expect more vicious deeds, gruesome details, and impulsive violence from the parties involved: the pointless beating of a horse with an iron rod (ibid.: 44); the torturing of two boat hands by their captain on an oyster trawler (ibid.: 45-6); the quickly escalating fight of two men who compete over a farmer's daughter (ibid.: 46-8); a wife's extramarital affair with her piano teacher (ibid.: 52-3); the domestic violence that ends in murder for an immigrant couple from Italy (ibid.: 53-5).

Under the impression of this omnipresent greed and violence, most striking is the continuous listing of the ruined lives of people at the lower end of society—those "destroyed by things (machines, circumstances, and economy) out of their control: again, the neglected, the overlooked" (Bernstein 1999 [1993]: 234). Here the railway assumes a particularly lethal role: A newsboy is pushed off a moving train by the conductor and is run over by the following car (1978 [1965]: 58); a man with a horse and sleigh is crushed by a train while crossing railroad tracks during a snowstorm because "no bell was rung, no whistle blown" (ibid.: 84); a black woman and her baby are thrown from the train and abandoned in the middle of the tracks (ibid.: 86). The ongoing repetition of neglect, abuse of power, and mindless destruction places the reader in a spiral of violence with neither escape nor relief: "The weak and the helpless in these pages attract the sadistic and the evil like magnets . . . The cruelty may be purposeful, but just as often it may exist for its own sake (like art) and appease some incurably corrupt and vicious streak in human nature itself" (Hindus 1977: 25).

Returning to the nature of the pre-text, this "corrupt and vicious streak" becomes closely tied to the history of the still-young United States during industrialization, and the exhibition of court records as poetry contributes to the picture of a young nation's identity in transit: "These [court writings] would illuminate the transition in America from an agricultural to an industrial society and, presumably, the impact of that transition on particular individuals" (Simon 1984: 241). *Testimony* invites the reader to acknowledge the omnipresence and necessity of violence for the country's progress, the fulfillment of Manifest Destiny to expand U.S. territory from the east to the west coast, and the cost exacted for the benefits of modern infrastructure. This acknowledgment is not achieved by referring directly to these abstracted events, but by reproducing individual fates via the court cases: "to found America means to find it, which means to acknowledge its roots in violence, to tell the lost stories because unless you find what is lost you can found nothing" (Bernstein 1999 [1993]: 236).

In transferring the legal text into the literary sphere, *Testimony*'s achievement is twofold: in terms of its situatedness, the poem exhibits the everyday world without further decoration or heightened symbolism (synchronic dimension of representation); as a historical object, the poem enables a look back at a changing society at the turn of the century (diachronic dimension of text as archive), as "a kaleidoscopic vision of American life" (Auster 1984: 159). Yet this vision could only be represented far from complete. National identity in the United States may only be constituted by a variety of often contradicting voices, a multiplicity of witnesses that testify to the project of the new world beyond unified narratives such as the American Dream. The text attempts to "'brush history against the grain' [to paraphrase Walter Benjamin] by reading American history not as a narrative of Adamic discovery and perfectability but as a material record of diverse constituencies" (Davidson 1997: 140).

Having 'ordinary' people speak in non-symbolic ways assists the split identities of the Objectivists of European origin to connect to a young unstable American heritage, translating it into and archiving it in literature. What becomes obvious is the diversity of a changing society in the enclosed space of a courtroom that becomes represented in the backgrounds of both the various victims and witnesses: it is "revealing the grating isolation in which each of the victims and their aggressors were living in a country dedicated to unity within diversity. There was plenty of diversity but little or no unity" (Ignatow 1984: 74).

In an early move toward a democratization of the literary artifact, the poem as found object speaks for itself and has the reader judge both the case and the implications of legal documents as poetic text: "Instead of judgment, there is a sense of great detachment, a kind of moral spaciousness that the reader must cross. It is not that there are gaps of information—everything is given. Yet, as with few other contemporary bodies of verse, the reader must discover in himself the attitudes he has toward the material" (Heller 1984: 171). The reader becomes a witness not only to the translocation of legal text into the literary environment and to the historical kaleidoscope emanating from the court documents, but also to confirm or withdraw a sense of appreciation: "there is, by usual standards, nothing of literary value, nothing quotable or memorable, or even ironic . . . by the affected reader. Shorn of entertainment value, of sentiment, this work seems to place a curious demand on the modern reader" (ibid.: 174). This partiality reveals another parallel in Zukofsky's and Reznikoff's work in that both poets bridge the gap between modernist and postmodernist concerns. While recognizing the potential of multiple perspectives to give an idea of the bigger picture, both *"A"* and *Testimony* expose the incompleteness of reality and history by supposedly exhibiting the thing itself; in the case of *Testimony*, this includes the witness report as well as both the poem and the language of which it is made.

Testimony's detailed structuring of the enormous text corpus and the sense of an ending the reader encounters at the conclusion of page 528 do not hide the fact that the narrative of this extensive poem appears curiously frayed and incomplete. While constantly reinforcing the Objectivist claim to unity and wholesomeness, this meticulous ordering may never fully level out the plurality of local voices and limited perspectives. If we return to a testimony's religious connotation as a personal, reaffirming promotion of God's presence and efficacy in this world, this failure also ironically denounces as futile that act of witnessing. God as an ordering transcendental source and authority exists no more than do neutral grounds in the assessment of what has happened at a crime scene: The truth of a testimony in the legal sense runs parallel to the understanding in the religious discourse. The literary environment, itself marked as a forum for lies and imagination, renders this analogy all the more prevalent in the translocation of legal text into poetry.

4. Outlook

These second-generation modernist writers helped to bridge the lacuna between literary activities eminent before and during World War I and the post-war sentiment and literary developments of confessional poetry and language experiment after 1945. The Objectivists "laid down an alternative history of writing whose precision, nerve and exploratory impetus ensure that it is still a viable model" (McAllister 1996: 15), and their impact becomes all the more apparent if we look at how their poetic heritage resonates with contemporary poets. In Post- or Neo-Conceptual writing by Kenneth Goldsmith, Vanessa Place, and Robert Fitterman, for example, especially the practice of appropriating the everyday in the form of 'factual' texts and translating or transferring them into the literary environment has caught on. These writers renegotiate Objectivist claims in a similar encyclopedic fashion and therein translate their interest in 'sincerity and objectification' for the 21st century.

Bibliography

Selected Primary Literature

Bunting, Basil. 1966 [1965]. *Briggflatts: An Autobiography.* Golden, CO: Fulcrum Press.

Niedecker, Lorine. 1969. *T & G: Collected Poems 1936-1966.* Winston-Salem: Jargon Society.

Oppen, George. 1968. *Of Being Numerous.* New York: New Directions.

——. 1975. *The Collected Poems of George Oppen, 1929-1975.* New York: New Directions.

Philip, Marlene NourbeSe. 2008. *Zong!* Middletown: Wesleyan UP.

Rakosi, Carl. 1967. *Amulet.* New York: New Directions.

——. 1995. *Poems 1923-1941.* Los Angeles: Sun and Moon Press.

Reznikoff, Charles. 1975. *Holocaust.* Santa Barbara: Black Sparrow Press.

——. 1978 [1965]. *Testimony: The United States, 1885-1915. (Recitative).* Vol 1. Santa Barbara: Black Sparrow Press.

——. 1979 [1968]. *Testimony: The United States, 1885-1915 (Recitative).* Vol 2. Santa Barbara: Black Sparrow Press.

——. 1996. *Poems 1918-1975: The Complete Poems of Charles Reznikoff.* Ed. Seamus Cooney. Santa Rosa: Black Sparrow Press.

——. 2005. *The Poems of Charles Reznikoff 1918-1975.* Ed. Seamus Cooney. Boston: Black Sparrow.

Rukeyser, Muriel. 1938. *U.S. One.* New York: Covici, Friede.

Zukofsky, Louis. 1931a. "Comment Program: 'Objectivists' 1931." In: *Poetry: A Magazine of Verse* 37.5 (Feb.): 268-72.

——. 1931b. "Sincerity and Objectification: With Special Reference to the Work of Charles Reznikoff." In: *Poetry: A Magazine of Verse* 37.5 (Feb.): 272-85.

——. 1934. "The Writing of Guillaume Apollinaire." In: *The Westminster Magazine* 23.1 (Spring): 7-46.

——. 1971. *All: The Collected Short Poems, 1923-1964.* New York: Norton.

——. 1974 [1931]. "An Objective." In: *Prepositions: The Collected Critical Essays.* Berkeley and Los Angeles: U of California P. 12-8.

——. 1975 [1932]. *An "Objectivists" Anthology.* Folcroft, PA: Folcroft Library Editions.

——. *"A."* 1993 [1978]. Baltimore and London: The Johns Hopkins UP.

Selected Secondary Literature

Ahearn, Barry. 1983. *Zukofsky's "A": An Introduction.* Berkeley [u.a.]: U of California P.

Ahearn's analysis provides a substantial structuring of "A" and a helpful discussion of the poem's themes, motifs, and historical background. He unearths the intertexts Zukofsky incorporated and offers parallel readings to cut through the text's density. Beginners, however, may be easily overwhelmed since Ahearn leaves the volume's 'introductory' nature behind.

DuPlessis, Rachel Blau and Peter Quartermain (eds.). 1999. *The Objectivist Nexus: Essays in Cultural Poetics.* Tuscaloosa: U of Alabama P.

This well-edited anthology comprises crucial perspectives on Objectivist writing and provides valuable insights into the context, poetic program, and aftermath through literary critics and fellow contemporary writers.

Hindus, Milton. 1977. *Charles Reznikoff: A Critical Essay.* Santa Barbara: Black Sparrow Press.

——. 1984. *Charles Reznikoff: Man and Poet.* National Poetry Foundation/University of Maine at Orono.

> *Both books by Hindus, one an influential essay, the other a comprehensive collection of interviews, analysis, and "testaments," provide substantial material about Reznikoff and his relation to the Objectivist program and other writers.*

Stanley, Sandra Kumamoto. 1994. *Louis Zukofsky and the Transformation of a Modern American Poetics.* Berkeley: U of California P.

> *Stanley identifies Zukofsky as a formative literary figure of modern poetics very much in the line of Pound and Williams. She accounts for his complex involvement with modernism and convincingly argues for Zukofsky being the all-important link between American modernism and post-modernism.*

Further References

Aldington, Richard. 1915. "Preface." In: *Some Imagist Poets: An Anthology.* Boston: Houghton Mifflin. vi-vii.

Auster, Paul. 1984. "The Decisive Moment." In: Hindus 1984. 151-65.

Bernstein, Charles. 1999 [1993]. "Reznikoff's Nearness." In: DuPlessis/Quartermain 1999. 210-39.

Davidson, Michael. 1997. *Ghostlier Demarcations: Modern Poetry and the Material Word.* Berkeley: U of California P.

Dembo, L. S. 1969. "Charles Reznikoff." In: *Contemporary Literature* 10.2 (Spring): 193-202.

Hatlen, Burton. 1997. "From Modernism to Postmodernism: Zukofky's 'A'-12." In: Scroggins 1997. 214-29.

Heller, Michael. 1984. "The Modernity of Charles Reznikoff." In: Hindus 1984. 167-75.

The Holy Bible, English Revised Version. 1885. Oxford: Oxford UP.

Ignatow, David. 1984. "Charles Reznikoff: A Memoir." In: Hindus 1984. 69-76.

McAllister, Andrew. 1996. *The Objectivists.* Newcastle upon Tyne: Bloodaxe Books.

Paracelsus. 1951 [1583]. "De vita longa." In: Jolande Jacobi (ed.), *Paracelsus: Selected Writings.* Princeton: Pantheon Books.

Perloff, Marjorie. 1995. "'Barbed-Wired Entanglements.' The 'New American Poetry,' 1930-1932." In: *Modernism/modernity* 2.1 (Jan.): 145-75.

Pound, Ezra. 1954 [1913]. "A Few Don'ts by an Imagiste." In: T.S. Eliot (ed.), *The Literary Essays of Ezra Pound.* London: Faber & Faber. 4-6.

Quartermain, Peter. 1992. *Disjunctive Poetics: From Gertrude Stein and Louis Zukofsky to Susan Howe.* Cambridge: Cambridge UP.

Scroggins, Mark. 1998. *Louis Zukofsky and the Poetry of Knowledge.* Tuscaloosa: U of Alabama P.

——. 2007. *The Poem of a Life: A Biography of Louis Zukofsky.* Emeryville: Shoemaker & Hoard.

—— (ed.). 1997. *Upper Limit Music: The Writing of Louis Zukofsky.* Tuscaloosa: U of Alabama P.

Sharp, Frederick Thomas. 1982. *"Objectivists" 1927-1934: A Critical History of the Work and Association of Louis Zukofsky, William Carlos Williams, Charles Reznikoff, Carl Rakosi, Ezra Pound, George Oppen.* Diss. Stanford University.

Shevelow, Kathryn. 1982. "History and Objectification in Charles Reznikoff's Documentary Poems, *Testimony* and *Holocaust.*" In: *Sagetrieb* 1.2: 290-306.

Simon, Linda. 1984. "Reznikoff: The Poet as Witness." In: Hindus 1984. 233-50.

Spinoza, Baruch. 1970 [1910/1677]. *Ethics and On the Correction of the Understanding.* Trans. Andrew Boyle. New York: Dutton/Everyman's Library.

Sternburg, Janet and Alan Ziegler. 1984 [1973]. "A Conversation with Janet Sternburg and Alan Ziegler." In: Hindus 1984. 127-36.

17

Legacies of Modernism

Melvin B. Tolson's "Dark Symphony" and Robert Hayden's "Middle Passage"

Michael Basseler

1. Whose modernism, who's modernist? African American writers and the (problems of the) modernist legacy

To define 'modernism' is an endeavor that has occupied generations of literary critics and historians and thus goes far beyond the confines of a short chapter, let alone an introductory paragraph. Most scholars agree, however, that the core idea of modernism is nicely captured in Ezra Pound's famous dictum 'Make it New.' Virtually all of the proponents of literary modernism felt a strong desire for renovation as they were often dissatisfied with the artistic practices of previous generations and disillusioned by the social and historical developments of their time. In this sense, modernism refers to a collective feeling of discontent, leading to a critical reflection of the very foundations of Western culture and civilization and, consequently, the search for new models and practices of literary expression. Modernism is thus a more or less direct response to the collapse of authority and security in all spheres of private and public life, posing the most basic questions about morality, human relationships, politics, aesthetics, art, science, human consciousness, and psychology.

'Modernism' is no doubt one of those abstract, shorthand terms in literary history and theory whose explanatory power comes at the expense of a great degree of homogenization, simplification, and exclusion. Whenever the term is used in order to label authors and works, this labeling implies questions of—and decisions about—cultural belonging and hierarchy, of who's in and who's out as well as who's on top of the game. Well into the late twentieth century, there had been a certain tendency to associate modernism primarily with western, white (and usually male) authors, a tendency that is already reflected in book titles such as Hugh Kenner's *The Pound Era* (1971). Such a narrow understanding of modernism, however, has recently been criticized from various perspectives (feminist, postcolonial, etc.), resulting in an expansion of the very meaning of 'modernism':

> [I]nstead of letting one or two poets define an era, surveys of the modernist *period* are now a patchwork of different poets, styles and groupings around places and publications. All of them are linked, many of them overlap, but none of them has priority, as if poetic history itself resembled the non-linear structure of one of Eliot's poems. (Howarth 2012: 187)

One should keep in mind, though, that this idea of a non-hierarchical, non-linear, and democratic 'patchwork modernism' is a rather recent—or postmodern—notion which conceals the fact that modernist discourse was actually quite clearly defined in terms of centers and margins, of 'high' and 'low.' In this regard it is interesting, of course, that in a statement which seems to propagate the necessity to broaden our notion of modernism and which draws our attention to the cultural exclusiveness that has shaped the modernist discourse for many decades, Peter Howarth (perhaps inadvertently) backslides to the grand narrative that firmly reasserts T.S. Eliot (and thus a white male perspective) at its center. What the above quote obscures, in other words, is that for many writers 'from the margins,' modernism did not mean a sudden emancipation from cultural, let alone social, hierarchies but a double-edged sword, promising the possibility of 'making it new' yet also highlighting their place outside the center and thus forcing them into a liminal cultural position. In fact, the very privilege to become 'modern'—i.e., to liberate oneself from the clutch of tradition and to 'make it new'—was withheld from writers who did not fit neatly into the cultural mainstream, be it because of their ethnic background or societal role (cf. Howarth 2012: 191).

For African Americans in particular, modernism's legacy has been problematic and even burdensome in many ways. To begin with, the sense of the decay (or waste land) of Western civilization was both mirrored and redeemed in a widespread fascination for the supposedly 'primitive,' and it is in this context that Africa became the dominant metaphor for the unknown, unconscious, or stigmatized areas of society and self (cf. Ickstadt 2004 [1996]: 225), so powerfully at work in texts such as Joseph Conrad's *Heart of Darkness*. In this regard, modernism has been interpreted as the release and symbolic domestication of the hitherto repressed, particularly the abysmal, primitive, and threatening 'dark other' of Western culture. Hence, part of the modernist endeavor was to explore the taboo zones—the tensions and ruptures of Victorian culture—by turning to the cultural other. In the United States, this kind of 'othering' became particularly visible during the Harlem Renaissance in the "vogue in things Negro" (Hughes 2000 [1926]): when, as Rudolph Fisher (1995 [1927]) put it, 'the Caucasian stormed Harlem' in search of exotic entertainment and cultural renewal. The modern investment in the 'primitive' thus culturally showcased and marginalized African Americans at the same time.

Moreover, modernism in America eluded African Americans, as almost none of the writers of the Harlem Renaissance regarded themselves as part of a modernist literature if that meant the kind of writing promoted by writers like Pound, Eliot, H.D., and Wallace Stevens. Instead, they were either "enthralled by traditional forms of verse as established by the major British and American Romantic poets" (Rampersad 2004: 956) or looking for more 'authentic' forms of cultural expression, rooted in African American folklore and dialect. Highlighting the latter strand of African American modernism, critic Houston Baker (1987: xvi) has claimed that there are fundamental differences between a 'white' and a 'black' modernism.

Quite similarly, the historical events and socio-economic situation, especially in the wake of World War I, which contributed to the emergence of modernism in a transnational Western context have only limited explanatory value with regard to the specific social circumstances of African Americans. It has been argued that in a way the modernist feeling of a fragmentation of life connected to the loss of certainty and the belief in a stable reality has always been an integral part of the African American experience *per se*:

> Confronted with the conditions of life facing most migrants to the industrial cities of the Northeast, the Great Lakes region, and, slightly later, the West Coast, black modernists certainly shared the general sense of psychic and social

alienation. Their sense of the origins, meaning, and possible responses to the malaise, however, grew directly out of the specific circumstances of African American history. Far from being a new experience, fragmentation had been the organizing element of black life since Middle Passage. Uprooted from their geographical, cultural, and linguistic homes, slaves were forced to adapt to a world in which nothing could be trusted. (Werner/Shannon 2011: 242-3)

As a result of these tensions and cultural specificities, African American modernism (alternatively named 'Afro-Modernism' or 'Afro-Modernity') has been described as a special case of American modernism, a literature that occupies "a rhetorical space in at least two canons" (Bérubé 1992: 205). What is more, notions of racial identity connected to certain forms of expression that have dominated discussions of 'black art' at least until the 1970s have created a kind of doubleness for those few African American writers attracted by a modernist style. Melvin B. Tolson was well aware of this problem, as Matthew Hart reminds us: "This doubleness exists, Tolson suggests, because of a cultural dichotomy that reinforces received definitions of 'Negro' language and culture by erecting a wall between modernist artifice and African-American speech" (2010: 144). Consequently, writers like Melvin B. Tolson and Robert Hayden (or, to a lesser extent, Gwendolyn Brooks) had to work "at the crossroads of cultural traditions," paying homage to while at the same time subverting white modernism, as Werner and Shannon put it (2011: 245), and they had to navigate the problematic "assumption that African-American modernism's relation to Euro-American modernism can only be secondary, whether in resistance or imitation" (Bérubé 1992: 164). This chapter will explore this double-edged legacy that modernism posed for African American writers of the mid-twentieth century by focusing on two exemplary works by Tolson and Hayden.

2. He, too, sings Black America: Melvin B. Tolson's "Dark Symphony"

Melvin B. Tolson's significance for American literature has not yet been adequately fathomed, and he is blatantly underrepresented in works of (African-) American literary history. There are only a handful of book-length studies dedicated to his work (see Russell 1980), and the small number of articles seems piteous if compared to other African American writers of his era such as Langston Hughes, Zora Neale Hurston, and Richard Wright. It is only in recent years that Tolson has gained wider scholarly recognition. In the *Norton Anthology of African American Literature*, for instance, the editors remark that "[r]eading Tolson allows one to explore modernist poetics from an African American cultural stance" (McDowell/Spillers 2004: 1368), an assessment that echoes Aldon Nielsen's assertion that Tolson's poems are "an assault upon Anglo-American modernism's territorial designs, but they have been little read" (1992: 254). Despite his somewhat minor role in (African-)American literary history, however, Tolson's poems "have been read to great effect" (ibid.), exerting their influence on a number of African and African American thinkers and politicians.

Melvin Beaunorus Tolson was born in 1898 in Moberley, Missouri, as the oldest son of the itinerant Methodist pastor Alonzo Tolson and Lera Tolson, who was of Cherokee descent (cf. Flasch 1972: 20). He studied at Fisk and, like Langston Hughes, at Lincoln University in Oxford, Pennsylvania (formerly Ashmun Institute, named after Jehudi Ashmun, the founder of the Republic of

Liberia), as well as at Columbia University. Tolson gained wider public recognition during his years as an instructor of English and speech at Wiley College, Texas, where he coached a debate team, the legendary Wiley Forensic Society—an episode from his life that was (mis-)portrayed in Denzel Washington's *The Great Debaters* (2007). People who knew Tolson well described him as an extraordinarily gifted and dedicated teacher, orator, and writer, who, as his biographer Robert Farnsworth puts it, "loved an argument, and . . . seldom backed off from controversy" (1988: 167).

During his lifetime Tolson published only three volumes of poetry, partly due to his massive teaching load and dedication as a debate team coach, and partly due to the reserved public reactions to his work. After his first book of poetry, "A Gallery of Harlem Portraits" (a work he had begun as an M.A. student at Columbia and which was only published posthumously in 1979), had been rejected by several publishers, Tolson was so disheartened that he put the manuscript in a trunk and stopped writing until he received an invitation to the National Poetry Contest sponsored by the American Negro Exposition (which took place in Chicago in 1940). The piece he submitted for the contest was "Dark Symphony," and it won the first place, bringing Tolson national recognition as a poet (cf. Flasch 1972: 30; Tolson, Jr. 1990: 397). After its appearance in *Atlantic Monthly* in 1941, the magazine's editor, Mary Lou Chamberlain, coaxed Tolson into writing a whole volume, and in 1944 his most accessible work, *Rendezvous with America*, was published.

Despite some initial skepticism and prejudices against modern poetry (cf. Flasch 1972: 33), Tolson soon fully embraced the poetics of high modernism: "When T.S. Eliot published *The Waste Land* in 1922 . . . the victory of the moderns was complete . . . The modern idiom is here to stay—like modern physics" (Gates/McKay 2004: 1365). Apart from Eliot, he was heavily influenced by a whole range of early and high modernists, from Charles Baudelaire through Edgar Lee Masters and Hart Crane. Moreover, Tolson's poetics was strongly influenced by Marxist literary and political thought, an influence that showed most clearly in *Harlem Gallery* (see Spahr 2007). And while these influences and his belief in modernist aesthetics are even more obvious in his later works, "Dark Symphony" already contains many of the elements that are typical for Tolson's poetry; it also illustrates where Tolson deviates from the high modernists: "Instead of looking backward to the decaying civilizations of the European past, Tolson embraced Africa and its rich, vital heritage" (Beaulieu 2001: 397).

In the first sustained and systematic discussion of Tolson's oeuvre, Joy Flasch has aptly described the overall theme of "Dark Symphony": it deals with "the black man's contribution to his country, despite years of abuse from the white man, and the black man's gradual evolution to his place in the sun" (1972: 59). Structured like a symphony (it was actually set to music by composer Earl Robinson), the poem is subdivided into six parts, each of which is entitled with a certain musical tempo. Taken together, the six parts chart some three centuries of African American history in a more or less chronological manner. The symphony embraces darkness in at least two different yet interrelated ways: first in the sense of being gloomy, since it explicitly addresses the dire chapters of the past that were so often absent from American history books, and second in the sense that it constitutes an ode on the humanity, strength, and endurance of black people in America and beyond and thus praises those with dark skin.

Part I, "Allegro Moderato," introduces the theme of Black agency in American history by pointing out the role of Crispus Attucks, the slave famously credited for being the first man to be killed in the Boston Massacre in 1770 and thus inciting the Revolutionary War. Part II, "Lento Grave," is dominated by allusions to several Negro Spirituals (especially "One More River to Cross," "Steal Away to Jesus," and "Go Down, Moses"), acknowledging the vernacular's function of providing psychological relief from the cruelties of slavery and oppression, thereby maintaining the slaves' humanity and moral integrity. The third part, "Andante Sostenuto," asks "Oh, how can we forget?" (l. 56), lamenting the "Three hundred years we slaved" (l. 45) and asking how one copes with these collective memories. Moreover, it juxtaposes Christ's suffering at Golgotha with the 'crucifixion of manhood' experienced by black people in the American diaspora. In the fourth part, "Tempo Primo," the poem strikes a more optimistic note by celebrating the "New Negro" identity forged out of the historical examples of slave revolters and abolitionists like Nat Turner, Joseph Cinquez, Frederick Douglass, Sojourner Truth, and Harriet Tubman. The New Negro, of course, is a reference to Alain Locke's eponymous manifesto that jump-started the Harlem Renaissance. In it Locke champions a new identity based on self-respect and self-dependence that strips off the image of the passive 'Old Negro,' who is described as a "stock figure perpetuated as an historical fiction" and who is therefore "more of a formula than a human being" (Locke 2004 [1925]: 984-5). What Tolson, through this reference to Locke, emphasizes and celebrates is thus the agency of black people in American history and society, underscored by a whole series of action verbs like 'plant,' 'build,' 'erect,' 'harvest,' and 'fight'. Part V, "Larghetto," then, points out the moral superiority of "black men" (l. 94) by alluding to the white man's inhumanity and failures, manifested in a number of historical atrocities. This part reinforces the rhetoric of 'us versus them' introduced in Part III, indirectly accusing 'them' (i.e., the white Americans) of ruining the economy by causing the stock-market crash (l. 107), "counterfeit[ing] . . . Christianity" (l. 109), and "bring[ing] contempt upon Democracy" (l. 110). The poem closes with the quite prophetic section entitled "Tempo di Marcia" that identifies the African American "waste lands" (l. 125) and conjures up images of black resistance to, and survival in, a world of historical denial, oppression, poverty, and segregation: "We advance!" (l. 126). In theme and tone, this part anticipates similar later poems like Maya Angelou's "Still I Rise" (1978). More importantly, however, through its generic marker (march) and the stoical insistence on black resilience, the section also portends to the Civil Rights and Black Power movements of the 1960s, especially the "March on Washington for Jobs and Freedom" of 1963 during which Martin Luther King, Jr. delivered his famous "I Have a Dream" speech.

Although usually regarded as an example of African American modernism, on a formal level "Dark Symphony" harks back to rather conventional stylistic devices and generic forms, even if Tolson's handling of those devices can be considered innovative. The most striking formal feature is probably the poem's musical structure, implying several changes in intensity, meter, pace, and rhythm (as already indicated by the headlines) that undergird the thematic content and culminate in the strong, regular rhythm of the closing march. Influenced by music and art, during the 1930s Tolson developed his formula of what he called the 'three S's of Parnassus,' meaning the interplay of the *sight* of the words on the page, their *sound* as well as their *sense*, i.e., the appeal of the verbal images to the senses (cf. Flasch 1972: 48). In its versatile structure, "Dark Symphony" perfectly exemplifies this formula. Whereas, for example, the fractured line placement (e.g., in Part I) attracts the eye (ibid.: 59), the poem also places great emphasis on its acoustic qualities (e.g., through its rhythmic/metric variations or alliterations like "white world," l. 20, "shadow-shapes," l. 22, and "torture tombs," l. 24) as well as its sensational images. Together with its use of free verse, catalog technique (the listing of the New Negro's achievements), and parallelisms, the vivid imagery in Part IV highlights the emancipatory and triumphant spirit of this passage and serves to elicit emotional responses on the part of the reader:

> The New Negro,
> Hard-muscled, Fascist-hating, Democracy-ensouled,
> Strides in seven-league boots
> Along the Highway of Today
> Toward the Promised Land of Tomorrow! (ll. 88-92)

There is an ongoing debate around the question of whether Tolson assimilated into the Anglo-American modernist mode and therefore sold out his African American identity as a poet, or whether he challenged and subversively undermined that very tradition, especially in his later works. For instance, Tolson was repeatedly confronted with the notion that he attempted to 'outpound Pound,' even at a time when Pound had already been outdated (cf. Hart 2010: 147), or with the accusation that because of his learned, technical, and often hyperallusive style he could not speak to a black community. What this debate boils down to, of course, is the problematic legacy of modernism described in the introductory section of this chapter. For Tolson himself, however, racial identity and artistic integrity and responsibility were not reducible in such easy terms, even if this alienated him from both black and white literary circles. He therefore believed in the 'vertical audience' of future readers to understand and appreciate his work but also to carry on the "struggle against socioeconomic and cultural racism" (Tolson 1990: 395) that had occupied him during his career. According to Hart (2010: 144), Tolson fully achieved an African American modernism (or, as Hart puts it, "Afro-Modernism") which refused simple racial dichotomies and insisted "that blackness is equal to poetic modernity and that modernist form is no barrier to blackness" in his later works, especially in the *Libretto for the Republic of Liberia* (1953).

3. Modern 'waste lands' and the collective trauma of slavery: Robert Hayden's "Middle Passage"

Born Asa Bundy Sheffey in 1913, Hayden grew up in a foster family (the Haydens) in a ghetto on Detroit's East Side, but he also had regular contact with his mother, a constellation that led to many conflicts and deeply affected the young boy. A rather frail child whose impaired vision required him to wear almost absurdly thick glasses, Hayden became an outsider who dedicated his interest to books early on. After some years at Detroit City College (today Wayne State University), he worked for the Federal Writers' Project, researching black history and folklore (cf. Jones 1988: 77; Williams 1987: 16-22). It is probably during those years that Hayden first developed his poetics of history and memory that would later become characteristic of his work. In 1942 he went to the University of Michigan where he took classes with W.H. Auden, who gave Hayden "personal advice as well as valuable criticism of his poems, which Hayden credited with helping him to develop his own individual style" (Jones 1988: 77). His other influences include, among others, Carl Sandburg, Ezra Pound, William Carlos Williams, Langston Hughes (Hayden's mentor in the early stages of his career), Richard Wright, Wallace Stevens, and Rainer Maria Rilke, but it was probably Auden who had the greatest impact on his writing and shaped Hayden's belief that "art was a concern more timeless than race or social condition" (Williams 1987: 27). And although during his lifetime Hayden never had the popularity of Langston Hughes or Countee Cullen, he is now widely acknowledged as one of the most complex, innovative, and technically sophisticated African American poets of the twentieth century.

Accustomed to being an outsider from his early years on, Hayden never quite fit into any fixed group or category—partly due to his racial background and partly due to his personality as a writer and intellectual. When he took up his first teaching position at the University of Michigan in the 1940s, he was the first black member of the English faculty. Later, at black Fisk University where he taught for some twenty years, "Hayden was . . . burdened by the straitlaced, southern black middle-class environment of Fisk, which did not quite know what to make of an avant-garde Negro intellectual from the North" (Jones 1988: 79). Thus embodying a peculiar version of Du Boisian double-consciousness, Robert Hayden—who described himself as "a romantic who has been forced to be realistic" (ibid.: 87)—occupied a middle space between the African American and the high modernist tradition. Like Countee Cullen before him, Hayden conceived of himself primarily as a writer, not as a writer "with a particular racial identity" (Williams 1987: 10), although both Cullen and Hayden dealt extensively with racial themes.

The year 1966 is crucial for understanding Hayden's conflicted position between the traditions. Having worked as an associate professor at Fisk without any major critical or commercial successes (cf. Conniff 2003 [1999]: 6), he received the *Grand Prix de la Poesie* at the Third World Festival of Negro Arts in Dakar, Senegal for his work *A Ballad of Remembrance* (1962). Despite this international accolade, Hayden was faced with relentless criticism and even outright rejection at the first Black Writers' Conference held at Fisk in the same year, since he did not fit into the then dominant paradigm of a 'Black Aesthetic.' Hayden's liberal, non-instrumental notion of art, his high-modernist aesthetics and reverence for Western literary tradition, and his integrationist views were diametrically opposed to the Black Arts movement's notion that "all art must reflect and support the Black Revolution" (Karenga 1971 [1968]: 33). Larry Neal claimed that the Black Arts movement "is radically opposed to any concept of the artist that alienates him from his community" and that it "is impossible to construct anything meaningful within [Western aesthetic's] decaying structures" (2004 [1968]: 2039). Opposing Neal, Hayden "refused to subordinate art to race even during the turbulent 1960s" (Jones 1988: 76), and consequently, he was ostracized as an 'Uncle Tom' by the younger generation. Ironically enough, Tolson was among Hayden's harshest critics, even though he shared with him a fascination for the possibilities of modernist expression beyond nationalistic propaganda and simplistic didacticism. As for Hayden, he "had to live with the knowledge that a group of people whose heritage he shared, and indeed had celebrated powerfully in poem after poem, were attacking him simply because he believed that any artist should feel free to approach his materials as a man of unique sensibility and a craftsman of integrity" (Williams 1987: 32).

Although Hayden's poetic oeuvre is marked by a sustained engagement with issues of race and racism as well as the troubled position of African Americans in history, he arguably transcends those narrow categories, mainly due to his formal complexity and universalistic vision. For Philipp Richards, the "central drive" of Hayden's poetry is the "projection of his own imagination and psychological insight across the whole realm of the human condition" (1999/2000: 611). As a Bahá'í, Hayden believed in the unity of a transcendent humanity (or "universal humanism," Williams 1987: xviii), the idea of a brotherhood of mankind and, consequently, the possibility to overcome all divisiveness in terms of race or creed (see Kuroszczyk 2013). Accordingly, he rejected all positions which sought to exploit literature and especially poetry for ideological purposes and "acknowledged the impossibility of aesthetic separatism" (Broeck 2011: 366).

Today Hayden is almost unanimously credited for developing a suggestive and influential model of the history poem, "a poem that searches personal or public past for a significant truth that the poet might present to his audience" (Richards 1999/2000: 611). His works thus constitute a pioneering example of the role of African American literature in re-visioning and reclaiming an often shameful and traumatic past in order to integrate it into a more positive cultural self-image and collective memory (see Basseler 2008). In this regard, Hayden's poems both anticipate and pave the way for a later generation of writers for whom the act of a poetic and imaginative rewriting of African American history and memory became the most central concern. Illustrating how Hayden engages with historical personages, events, and historical documentation, Scott Howard argues that history "conditions Hayden's poems, which, in turn, constitute their own terms of figurative confrontation with the known world in order to form a contiguous reality, or what I will call *figural historicity*" (2006: 134; original emphasis). He claims that especially Hayden's elegies "intervene (as a work of mourning) in the entanglement among personal recollection, cultural memory, and official historical discourse" (ibid.: 146).

"Middle Passage" perfectly exemplifies both Hayden's achievements in the sub-genre of the history poem and his role as a cultural go-between, an artist who deeply cared for issues of black life but for whom questions of 'racial identity' were secondary as far as poetic traditions and styles are concerned. First published in the journal *Phylon* in 1945 (not, as several scholars have claimed, in 1941), Hayden repeatedly revised the poem over the course of two full decades, a fact that reveals much about his self-criticism and perfectionism. The major historical backdrop of the poem is the mutiny on board the slave ship *Amistad* in 1839 and the subsequent U.S. Supreme Court case, which soon turned into an international *cause célèbre* and a milestone in the abolitionist movement (see Kutzinski 1986 for a concise summary of the case). Furthermore, "Middle Passage" was inspired by Stephen Vincent Benét's 1928 epic poem *John Brown's Body*, whose contrapuntal style and multiperspectivity it echoes, yet with a strong foothold in historical facts meticulously researched by Hayden himself during his stay at the New York City Public Library's Schomburg Collection in Harlem (cf. Conniff 2003 [1999]: 14). The result of this blend of historical accuracy and poetic imagination is a text rich in complexities and ambiguities, "a poem whose linguistic surfaces are as varied as its voices and ultimately as deceptive as the references to calm seas in the slavers' logbooks" (Kutzinski 1986: 182).

The rather long poem (177 lines in the 1962 version) is subdivided into three parts, each of which provides a slightly different perspective on the theme of the Middle Passage, i.e., the transatlantic slave trade triangle between West Africa, Europe, and the Americas. Part one consists of "the sometimes uneasy, sometimes complacent thoughts of slave ship officers" (Jones 1988: 80) presented in the form of logbook entries and interspersed with the ironical names of slave ships ("*Jesús, Estrella, Esperanza, Mercy*," Hayden 2004 [1962a], l. 1; original emphasis) as well as lines from sailor's hymns and variations on "Ariel's Song" from Shakespeare's *The Tempest* (1611). Part two presents the crude recollections of a former slave trader who, after some twenty years of 'harvest' from the "black fields," was forced to retire due to "the fevers melting down my bones" (l. 93). Part three, finally, tells the story of the slave mutiny aboard the *Amistad* and the "Voyage through death, / voyage whose chartings are unlove" (ll. 102-3), comprising a long oral argument by one of the surviving Spanish masters of the *Amistad* who demands "to return to Cuba / with our slaves and there see justice done" (ll. 169-70). Whereas the Spaniard denounces Cinquez—the African prince and leader of the slave uprising—as a "surly brute" (l. 138) responsible for butchering "bodies of / our men, true Christians all, like so much jetsam" (ll. 144-5), the poem closes on the lyrical I's appraisal of Cinquez as the embodiment of African resistance, dignity, and humanity in the face of death and humiliation:

The deep immortal human wish,
the timeless will:

> Cinquez its deathless primaveral image,
> Life that transfigures many lives.

Voyage through death

> to life upon these shores. (ll. 172-7)

The poem's most dominant formal characteristic is probably its collage-like structure and particularly its multiperspectival, polyphonic style. In juxtaposing such various discursive elements as ship's logs (e.g., ll. 8-13, 26-41), chanteys (ll. 20-1, 25, 47), prayers (ll. 22-4), yarns (Part II), and courtroom statements (ll. 120-71), and combining them with the lyrical voice of the speaker, Hayden effectively uses the interdiscursive potential of literature (see Link 1992): Structured around the collective symbol of the Middle Passage as a "voyage through death to life," Hayden develops "an experimental poetics that could examine racism, directly and specifically, by telling an episode of its history in a number of contending voices," thereby also challenging "the modernists' sense of social crisis and giv[ing] voice to his personal doubts about modernism's moral limitations" (Conniff 2003 [1999]: 10). Additionally, because of the multiperspectivity it creates, poetry even becomes a more appropriate means of telling history as it serves to critique the ways in which historiography tends to monolithic representations. In this 'figural historicity' (Howard 2006: 134), personal memories, collective memories, and historical discourse merge with poetic imagination, raising the question of how to remember the past. As Vera Kutzinski aptly puts it:

> Resituated in a new context, the texts Hayden purports to quote lose not their appearance of authenticity but their historical authority. Broken up into textual

fragments, they are no longer capable of offering a coherent, unified historical narrative. They become voices among many other, competing voices, or better perhaps, images of language, of the discourse of slavery, without claims to representational authority and historical truth. (1986: 174)

While this multiperspectival, fragmented style is reminiscent of the high modernist poetics of Pound or Eliot, the poem's dense symbolism, its mythic allusions and rich intertextuality lend themselves to further comparisons and discussions. The central symbol of Hayden's piece, of course, is that of the Middle Passage itself. More than a mere historical reference, it becomes the signifier of African diasporic experience and identity, a technique similar to that of Hart Crane's "The Bridge" (1930). In Crane's masterpiece, the bridge becomes the key symbol of modern America's identity, whereas in Hayden it is the Middle Passage around which an African American identity symbolically centers (cf. Williams 1987: 79).

Furthermore, this key symbol comprises rich water imagery and structures of in-between-ness that are evocative of the modernist poem with which "Middle Passage" has been frequently compared—T.S. Eliot's *The Waste Land* (1922). For instance, Brian Conniff has suggested that Hayden explores Eliot's "theme of cultural 'schizophrenia'" (2003 [1999]: 17) and establishes a narrative framework in which historical sources are used "to turn Eliot's own poetics against his restricted vision of cultural decline" (ibid.: 21). Where Eliot sees Western civilization's demise by turning to its own cultural remnants—the "fragments I have shored against my ruins" ("The Waste Land," l. 431)—in a rather self-absorbed manner, Hayden reminds his readers of the troubled, haunting presence of Africans in Western history. A closer look at an intertextual reference that both poems share—Shakespeare's *The Tempest*—may serve to further illustrate the way in which Tolson's poem employs and at the same time undermines Eliot's modernist poetics of cultural decline.

In *The Waste Land*, water is a symbol of both life and death in the numerous images of, and allusions to, rivers and lakes (both real and mythic), rain, death by drowning (e.g., the "drowned Phoenician Sailor," l. 47), and in the human activities connected with water in some way or another (e.g., sailing, fishing, weeping). Part of this theme is a line taken from *The Tempest* in act 1, scene 2, where the "airy spirit" Ariel delivers her famous song that commemorates the water death of the King of Naples (Ferdinand's father): "Those are pearls that were his eyes" ("The Waste Land," l. 125). In Eliot's poem, this line is merely another fragment in the cultural and emotional wasteland it describes, void of any particular meaning or significance. In "Middle Passage," Hayden also draws on Ariel's song, but he varies the spirit's lines and thus turns them into a scathing indictment of the hypocrisy and twisted morality of a culture that simultaneously brought forth a great bard famous for his love sonnets *and* the cruel Atlantic slave trade that treated millions of human beings as economic goods:

> *Deep in the festering hold thy father lies,*
> *of his bones New England pews are made,*
> *those are altar lights that were his eyes.*
> . . .
> *Deep in the festering hold thy father lies,*
> *the corpse of mercy rots with him,*
> *rats eat love's rotten gelid eyes.* (ll. 17-9, 108-10; original emphasis)

Compare the original lines from Shakespeare:

Full fathom five thy father lies;
Of his bones are coral made;
Those are pearls that were his eyes:
Nothing of him that doth fade,
But doth suffer a sea-change
Into something rich and strange. (Shakespeare 2008: 1.2.397-402)

While Eliot warns, "Fear death by water" ("The Waste Land," l. 55), the fate of the slaves seems far worse than drowning: corpses rot in the "festering hold," blurring the lines between the living and the dead. Furthermore, through the allusion to "New England pews," the poem decries the Christian legitimization of slavery (this also resonates in another of the poem's intertexts, the sailor's hymn "Jesus, Savior, Pilot Me"). And whereas the ancestor in Shakespeare is transformed "into something rich and strange" by the regenerative forces of water, with his eyes becoming precious pearls, the slaves are doomed to putrefy alive. Hayden thus signifies on both Shakespeare and Eliot, as this passage "parodies the European civilization's great poet while it extends Shakespeare's text to emphasize the profound rage of the enslaved" (Potter 1981: 51).

4. Conclusion

For Tolson and Hayden, the legacy of modernism was a difficult one in many ways: On the one hand, their racial or cultural identity as African Americans denied them full membership in the club of high modernism, and even when critics credited them for their achievements, this often implied cultural biases and a certain condescension (e.g., in Allen Tate's preface to Tolson's *Libretto*). Moreover, both writers could not be easily absorbed into the white modernist canon, as their work questions many of the basic tenets of this movement, especially by pointing out the presence of Africa within Western cultural history. On the other hand, during their lifetime both writers were marginalized within the African American intelligentsia, particularly during the 'Black Aesthetic' phase with its rejection of Western tradition, its nationalist agenda, its emphasis on direct communication to the masses, and its propagandist framework. Dissatisfied with the kind of modernism practiced by the writers of the Harlem Renaissance, yet unwilling to sacrifice artistic autonomy for a Black nationalist ideology, Tolson and Hayden represent a middle generation of (African-)American writers whose significance could be understood only with some delay. Both are highly technical, experimental writers who have sometimes been ostracized as "library poets" and "intellectual exhibitionists" (McDowell/Spillers 2004: 1364) pining for white recognition, but this assessment hardly does justice to the depth and complexity of their poetic vision.

Both authors—and the poems discussed here at some length—display the diasporic literary consciousness which Werner and Shannon describe as a major factor in the formation of an African American modernism (2011: 258). Whereas in "Heritage" (1925), Countee Cullen expressed a bitter irony about the "difficulty of finding real information about Africa" (Werner/Shannon 2011: 258) and thus about coming to terms with the cultural heritage, Tolson and Hayden have re-examined the question "What is Africa to Me?"

For Hayden, the key to answer this question lies in the historical perspective of his poetry. Several of his works continue and expand the central themes of "Middle Passage" as in, for instance, "Runagate Runagate" (1962), "Tour 5" (1962), and "The Dream" (1970; see Potter 1981), and celebrate black historical figures in works such as "A Letter From Phillis Wheatley" (1978), "Frederick Douglass" (1962), "Homage to the Empress of the Blues" (1962, Bessie Smith), and "El-Hajj Malik El-Shabazz" (1970, Malcolm X; for the persona poem in African American poetry see Scheiding 2010). It is particularly this historical dimension that makes Hayden such an important writer, and one can hardly overestimate the literary significance and cultural work of his poetry, especially since it was produced in an era that precedes the widespread interest in African American history. As Sabine Broeck reminds us, "Middle Passage" interrupted the "national amnesia about the slavery trade," and it did so "without the benefit of years of Black Studies research that would follow, without years of public debates about the scandalous absence and suppression of slavery and the slave trade in American collective memory" (2011: 365). More particularly, the relevance and importance of the Middle Passage as a site of collective (and contested) memory and identity is reflected in such poems as Clarence Major's "The Slave Trade: View from the Middle Passage" (1994) and Elizabeth Alexander's *American Sublime* (2005) as well as in fiction (e.g., Charles Johnson's 1990 novel *Middle Passage*).

As far as Tolson is concerned, recent criticism has almost unanimously agreed that his late works, *Harlem Gallery* (1965) and *Libretto for the Republic of Liberia* (1953) are not only his most complex, but also his most aesthetically compelling works, as they attempt to deterritorialize modernism (see Nielsen 1992) and overcome such narrow dichotomies as Eurocentric/Afrocentric by "occupying a paradoxical zone of difference" (see Hart 2010). Peter Howarth even goes so far as to state that "[i]t wasn't until Melvin B. Tolson's remarkable *Libretto for the Republic of Liberia* (1953) that African American verse really took on the dizzying cross-cultural allusions and montage perspectives of modernism" (2012: 193), yet this assumption again relies on the problematic cultural dichotomies sketched out above.

In order to fully come to terms with the significance and innovativeness of both writers discussed in this chapter, particularly with regard to the question of how they created new spaces and possibilities for African American writers, one needs to look at the following generations in whose works Tolson's and Hayden's achievements are reflected. For example, Derik Smith's claim that the stark opposition in which Hayden's work is usually seen in comparison with the poetry of the Black Arts movement is misleading (see 2010), since this view both reduces the diversity of the movement and obscures Hayden's influence on writers like Michael Harper, Jay Wright, Yusef Komunyakaa, Brenda Marie Osbey, Melvin Dixon, Elizabeth Alexander, Rita Dove, and many others (cf. Conniff 2003 [1999]: 27-8; Richards 1999/2000: 608; Scheiding 2010: 301-17). Thus, to explore the meanings of the modernist legacy for, in, and through the poetry of Melvin Tolson and Robert Hayden is to provide an immensely interesting point of departure for renegotiating the well-established boundaries and categories of (African-)American literary history.

Bibliography

Selected Primary Literature

Gates, Henry Louis Jr. and Nellie McKay (eds.). 2004. *The Norton Anthology of African American Literature*. New York: Norton.

Hayden, Robert. 2004 [1948]. "Homage to the Empress of the Blues." In: Gates/McKay 2004. 1519-20.

———. 2004 [1962a]. "Middle Passage." In: Gates/McKay 2004. 1520-4.

———. 2004 [1962b]. "Frederick Douglass." In: Gates/McKay 2004. 1528.

———. 2004 [1962c]. "A Ballad of Remembrance." In: Gates/McKay 2004. 1528-30.

———. 2004 [1962d]. "Runagate Runagate." In: Gates/McKay 2004. 1526-8.

Tolson, Melvin B. 2004 [1944]. "Dark Symphony." In: Gates/McKay 2004. 1371-4.

———. 1953. *Libretto for the Republic of Liberia*. New York: Twayne.

———. 1965. *Harlem Gallery: Book I, The Curator*. New York: Twayne.

Selected Secondary Literature

Conniff, Brian. 2003 [1999]. "Answering 'The Waste Land': Robert Hayden and the Rise of the African American Poetic Sequence." In: Harold Bloom (ed.), *African-American Poets: Robert Hayden Through Rita Dove*. New York: Chelsea House. 5-34.

Discusses Hayden's poetry as "one of the most persistent forces moving poetry in the direction of the post-traditional" and explains why it is Hayden's struggling with traditions and social orders that has made him unpopular among his contemporaries, both black and white.

Farnsworth, Robert M. 1988. "Melvin B. Tolson." In: Trudier Harris and Thadious M. Davis (eds.), *Afro-American Writers, 1940-1955*. Vol. 76 of *Dictionary of Literary Biography*. Ann Arbor, MI: Gale. 164-73.

Very informative and concise overview of Tolson's life and work, including short exemplary analyses of some of his poems.

Flasch, Joy. 1972. *Melvin B. Tolson*. New York: Twayne.

A pioneering work and the first book-length study on Tolson when it came out, Flasch's work still offers numerous valuable close readings of several of his poems.

Kutzinski, Vera M. 1986. "Changing Permanences: Historical and Literary Revisionism in Robert Hayden's 'Middle Passage'." In: *Callaloo* 26 (Winter): 171-83.

Kutzinski explores the links between the historical and literary revisionism of Hayden's most famous work, discussing the poem's intertextual relations as well as the differences between the 1945 version and Hayden's later revisions of the poem.

Nielsen, Aldon L. 1992. "Melvin B. Tolson and the Deterritorialization of Modernism." In: *African American Review* 26.2: 241-55.

In this dense essay, Nielsen discusses Tolson's relationship to the Western modernist tradition with a particular focus on the Libretto.

Richards, Philipp M. 1999/2000. "Robert Hayden (1913-1980): An Appreciation."
     In: *The Massachusetts Review* 40.4: 599-613.

*Richards argues that despite, or maybe because of, Hayden's outsider status,
his poetry achieved a complexity and cosmopolitan perspective not available
to the ideologically confined vision of the Black Arts Movement, and paved the
way for the coming generation of African American poets.*

Smith, Derik. 2010. "Quarreling in the Movement: Robert Hayden's Black Arts
     Era." In: *Callaloo* 33.2: 449-66.

*In this stimulating essay, Smith shows how an appreciation of Hayden's sig-
nificance complicates established, monolithic notions of New Black Poetry.*

Williams, Pontheolla T. 1987. *Robert Hayden. A Critical Analysis of His Poetry.*
     Urbana and Chicago: U of Illinois P.

*Contains a comprehensive, well-researched chapter on Hayden's biography,
which also succinctly points out the literary influences that shaped Hayden's
work.*

Further References

Angelou, Maya. 2004 [1978]. "Still I Rise." In: Gates/McKay 2004. 2156-7.

Baker, Houston A. 1987. *Modernism and the Harlem Renaissance.* Chicago: U of
     Chicago P.

Basseler, Michael. 2008. *Kulturelle Erinnerung und Identität im zeitgenössischen
     afroamerikanischen Roman. Theoretische Grundlegung, Ausprägungsformen,
     Entwicklungstendenzen.* Trier: WVT.

Beaulieu, Elizabeth Ann. 2001. "Tolson, Melvin B." In: William L. Andrews et al.
     (eds.), *The Concise Oxford Companion to African American Literature.* Oxford:
     Oxford UP. 396-7.

Bérubé, Michael. 1992. *Marginal Forces/Cultural Centers: Tolson, Pynchon, and
     the Politics of the Canon.* Ithaca: Cornell UP.

Broeck, Sabine. 2011. "Geographies of the Modern: Writing Beyond Borders and
     Boundaries." In: Maryemma Graham and Jerry W. Ward (eds.), *The Cam-
     bridge History of African American Literature.* Cambridge: Cambridge UP
     2011. 356-76.

Eliot, T.S. 2007 [1922]. "The Waste Land." In: Nina Baym (ed.), *The Norton An-
     thology of American Literature.* New York: W.W. Norton. 1587-99.

Farnsworth, Robert M. 1984. *Melvin B. Tolson, 1898-1966: Plain Talk and Poetic
     Prophecy.* Columbia: U of Missouri P.

Fisher, Rudolph. 1995 [1927]. "The Caucasian Storms Harlem." In: David Lever-
     ing Lewis (ed.), *The Portable Harlem Renaissance Reader.* New York: Penguin.
     110-17.

Hart, Matthew. 2010. *Nations of Nothing But Poetry: Modernism, Transnational-
     ism, and Synthetic Vernacular Writing.* Oxford: Oxford UP.

Howard, W. Scott. 2006. "Resistance, Sacrifice, and Historicity in the Elegies of
     Robert Hayden." In: Eric Haralson (ed.), *Reading the Middle Generation
     Anew: Culture, Community, and Form in Twentieth-Century American Poetry.*
     Iowa City: U of Iowa P. 133-52.

Howarth, Peter. 2012. *The Cambridge Introduction to Modernist Poetry.* Cam-
     bridge: Cambridge UP.

Hughes, Langston. 2000 [1926]. "The Negro Artist and the Racial Mountain." In: Winston Napier (ed.), *African American Literary Theory: A Reader*. New York: New York UP. 27-30.

Ickstadt, Heinz. 2004 [1996]. "Die Amerikanische Moderne." In: Hubert Zapf (ed.), *Amerikanische Literaturgeschichte*. Stuttgart und Weimar: Metzler. 218-80.

Jones, Norma R. 1988. "Robert Hayden." In: Trudier Harris (ed.), *Afro-American Writers, 1940-1955*. Ann Arbor, MI: Gale. 75-88.

Jones, Sharon Lynette. 2007. "The Poetry of the Harlem Renaissance." In: Alex Davis and Lee M. Jenkins (eds.), *The Cambridge Companion to Modernist Poetry*. Cambridge: Cambridge UP. 195-206.

Karenga, Ron. 1971 [1968]. "Black Cultural Nationalism." In: Addison Gayle (ed.), *The Black Aesthetic*. Garden City, NY: Doubleday. 32-8.

Kenner, Hugh. 1971. *The Pound Era*. Berkeley: U of California P.

Kuroszczyk, Miriam. 2013. *Poetic Brokers: Robert Hayden, Melvin B. Tolson, and International Modernism in African American Poetry*. Trier: WVT.

Link, Jürgen. 1992. "Literaturanalyse als Interdiskursanalyse. In: Jürgen Fohrmann and Harro Müller (eds.), *Diskurstheorien und Literaturwissenschaft*. Frankfurt/M.: Suhrkamp. 284-307.

Locke, Alain. 2004 [1925]. "The New Negro." In: Gates/McKay 2004. 984-93.

McDowell, Deborah E. and Hortense Spillers. 2004. "Realism, Naturalism, Modernism, 1940-1960." In: Gates/McKay 2004. 1355-67.

Neal, Larry. 2004 [1968]. "The Black Arts Movement." In: Gates/McKay 2004. 2039-50.

Nicholls, Peter. 2007. "The Poetics of Modernism." In: Alex Davis and Lee M. Jenkins (eds.), *The Cambridge Companion to Modernist Poetry*. Cambridge: Cambridge UP. 51-67.

Potter, Vilma Raskin. 1981. "A Remembrance for Robert Hayden: 1913-1980." In: *MELUS* 8.1: 51-5.

Rampersad, Arnold. 2004. "Harlem Renaissance, 1919-1940." In: Gates/McKay 2004. 953-62.

Russell, Mariann. 1980. *Melvin B. Tolson's "Harlem Gallery": A Literary Analysis*. Columbia and London: U of Missouri P.

Scheiding, Oliver. 2010. "Inszenierung einer afroamerikanischen Gedächtnispoetik am Beispiel der Lyrik Rita Doves." In: *Literaturwissenschaftliches Jahrbuch* 51: 301-17.

Shakespeare, William. 2008 [1611]. *The Tempest*. Oxford: Oxford UP.

Spahr, Clemens. 2007. "A Babel City with a Hundred Gates: Concepts of Space in Melvin Tolson's *Harlem Gallery*." Gerhard Stilz (ed.), *Territorial Terrors: Contested Spaces in Colonial and Postcolonial Writing*. Würzburg: Königshausen und Neumann. 239-60.

Tolson, Melvin B., Jr. 1990. "The Poetry of Melvin B. Tolson." In: *World Literature Today* 64.3: 395-400.

Werner, Craig H. and Sandra G. Shannon. 2011. "Foundations of African American Modernism, 1910-1950." In: Maryemma Graham and Jerry W. Ward (eds.), *The Cambridge History of African American Literature*. Cambridge: Cambridge UP. 239-67.

IV Post-War Poetry
and Postmodern Experiment

18.

American Post-War Poetry

Theodore Roethke's "The Lost Son" and
Elizabeth Bishop's "At the Fishhouses"

Kornelia Freitag

1. Introduction: Roethke and Bishop in the Post-War Poetry Scene

At Woodlawn I heard the dead cry;
I was lulled by the slamming of iron,
A slow drip over stones,
Toads brooding wells.
All the leaves stuck out their tongues;
I shook the softening chalk of my bones,
Saying,
Snail, snail, glister me forward,
Bird, soft-sigh me home,
Worm, be with me.
This is my hard time. (Roethke 1966 [1948]: ll. 1-11)

A Gothic and somewhat murky tableau opens Theodore Roethke's five-part sequence "The Lost Son" from his collection under the same title, which was published in 1948. In clipped, short lines—each one containing exactly one proposition—the reader encounters the speaker, most likely the eponymous 'lost son'
who is huddled in a decidedly uncanny, i.e., wet ("dripping") and hard ("iron,"
"stones") place, with—of all possible fellows—a bunch of slimy creatures
("toads," "snail," "worm") and a moaning fowl ("Bird, soft-sigh") for company.
Assistance is solicited by an incantation of the skeletal "I" which, after shaking
the "softening chalk of [his] bones," implores in lines eight to ten the animal inhabitants of the surface of the earth ("snail"), the sky ("bird"), and the ground
("worm") to aid him in his "hard time."

This thrillingly surreal, mythic opening announces in no uncertain terms
Roethke's strong anti-realist, highly symbolic thrust, signaling the poem's relation to some of the hallmarks of the tradition of high modernism that was se-
curely established at the time of its publication. Shortly after the end of World
War II, modernists T.S. Eliot, H.D., Marianne Moore, Ezra Pound, Wallace Stevens, and William Carlos Williams were writing and publishing their later work,
and readers of poetry would have immediately detected the modernist artifice,
allusiveness, and anti-traditional originality of Roethke's poem. They would have
spotted even more quickly its spectacular violation of the modernist law of "depersonalization" as laid down by Eliot in "Tradition and the Individual Talent,"
his "Impersonal theory of poetry" (1932: 18). Roethke's painfully serious, obsessive, and lengthy self-searching was a clear deviation from the polished self-
irony of a T.S. Eliot. It violated his dictum that a poet should be only a "catalyst," his "passions" just the "material" (ibid.) to be forged into an "impersonal"
(ibid.: 22) work of art. As Charles Molesworth put it, Roethke's "The Lost Son"
was "a daring exploration," a "plunge into his own psyche" (1979: 23), an early

example of a spectacular embrace of and obsession with *the personal* in an important part of post-World War II poetry.

At roughly the same time, a poet of about the same age as Roethke published a poem that also deals with a mundane place, with animals, and with a speaker who tries to find a place in the world. Elizabeth Bishop's "At the Fishhouses" was published in 1947 in *The New Yorker* before it appeared in her collection *Poems: North & South—A Cold Spring* (1955). It is also written in short verses, yet comprises only 83 lines, often not end-stopped, and is arranged in three stanzas of unequal length. The first sentence, stretching over six lines, sets the tone for the rest of the poem:

> Although it is a cold evening,
> down by one of the fishhouses
> an old man sits netting,
> his net, in the gloaming almost invisible,
> a dark purple-brown,
> and his shuttle worn and polished. (ll. 1-6)

The contrast between two poems could hardly be greater. The mythical and anguished opening of Roethke's "Lost Son" is nothing like the precise and perfectly restrained introduction of Bishop's "At the Fishhouses." The specification of time ("cold evening"), place ("down by the fishhouses"), and protagonist ("old man . . . netting") are crystal clear; and the scene is rendered in words that evoke a vivid picture of the fisherman expertly mending a net in the cool twilight of an evening at the seashore. Yet what is most conspicuous in comparison to "The Lost Son" is the complete absence of any personal touch. Not only does the speaker refrain from uttering fears or pleas, but Bishop's speaker is, in fact, introduced late in the poem and very composed.

Bishop's lines, much more than Roethke's, recall modernist traditions. The vividness and precision are reminiscent of Ezra Pound in the 1910s lauding the "direct treatment of the thing" (1918: 95) and the poetic "Image" as "that which presents" an intellectual and emotional complex in an instant of time" (ibid.: 96). The clear rendering of the beauty and meaning of mundane reality brings to mind William Carlos Williams's poems about a "red wheelbarrow / . . . beside / the white / chickens" (1986 [1923]: 224) or a "young housewife / mov[ing] about . . . behind / the wooden walls of her husband's house" (ibid.: 57). And the very reticence of Bishop's speaker seems to honor Eliot's claim that "Poetry is not a turning loose of emotion, but an escape from emotion; it is not the expression of personality, but an escape from personality" (1932: 21). As Molesworth describes Bishop's way of handling the self in poetry, it is a "for[m] of self-removal" (1979: 11), the expression of the "desire for a sort of anonymity" (ibid.: 20). And yet, on closer inspection Bishop's flaunting of markers of modernism is just as much a revolt against the practices and theories of high modernism as is Roethke's open defiance of impersonality. Both younger poets were united in the effort to develop a new poetry and a poetics to succeed modernism.

A particular version of modernism dominated U.S. and British literature up until the 1960s. Marjorie Perloff describes the standard that characterized the poetry scene at the time, playing upon Pound's rebel stance against what the "Age Demanded" in his *Hugh Selwyn Mauberley* of 1920:

In 1960, the Age Demanded that a poem be self-contained, coherent, and unified: that it present, indirectly to be sure, a paradox, oblique truth, or special
insight, utilizing the devices of irony, concrete imagery, symbolism, and structural economy . . . The speaker was "dramatized"—a persona, whose relation to
the author was "hidden," the norm was show not tell, as Cleanth Brooks and
Robert Penn Warren repeatedly pointed out in their *Understanding Poetry.*
(1996: 107)

These were the demands faced by Theodore Roethke (1908-1963) and Elizabeth
Bishop (1911-1979), who belonged to a group of poets born early in the twentieth century that also included John Berryman (1914-1972), Randall Jarrell
(1914-1965), Robert Lowell (1917-1977), Howard Nemerov (1920-1991), and
Richard Wilbur (b. 1921). They all grew up with modernism, had learned from it,
and experimented with it. Yet as writers coming into their own in the 1940s and
1950s, they also felt that the modernist ways of writing had hardened into a
dogma somewhat comparable to the one against which the modernists themselves had rebelled at the beginning of the century.

Not only did the young poets chafe at the restrictions of modernist dogma,
they also felt stifled by rampant post-war materialism and political conservatism. The America that had emerged from World War II was in many respects
different from the one that had entered it; the new postwar America differed
even more from the nation where, in the beginning of the century, modernism
had begun. In the war against Hitler and his allies, America had established itself as the strongest Western power. In the late 1940s and throughout the
1950s, the U.S. was assuming its role as the most important political, military,
economic, and financial global player. It quickly re-fashioned itself from a war
ally of the Soviet Union to its most important, and somewhat paranoid, antagonist. The world became split into Eastern and Western Blocs, and a balance of
power—or rather of atomic and political terror—was struck in what became
known as a "Cold War" which lasted until the end of the 1980s. The new post-
war world order, with the United States in a prominent position, was mirrored
within the country by economic and financial affluence, rabid anti-Communist
sentiments, and extreme militancy against political dissenters. On the one
hand, the G.I. Bill offered thousands of demobilized soldiers from modest backgrounds an academic education, and for the first time in history, poets were
hired by universities to teach the reading and writing of literature in Creative
Writing courses, which added considerably to the professionalization and
academization of poetry and would be crucial to its position in the latter half of
the twentieth century. On the other hand, the dominant atmosphere inside as
well as outside academia was conservative and intellectually cramped, and New
Critical normative standards, such as those Perloff describes, were widespread
and often strictly maintained. Conformism was the order of the day. Public discourse—in the first years after the end of World War II not yet significantly disturbed by dissenting black, female, or gay voices—was uniformly hollow and
manipulative.

Robert Lowell (a contemporary poet whom Roethke perceived as his biggest
rival but who became a good friend of Bishop) captured his whole generation's
dissatisfaction with the suffocating atmosphere in America in 1959 in the memorable lines "These are the tranquilized *Fifties*, / and I am forty. Ought I to regret my seedtime?" (1959: xx). Critic Charles Molesworth spells out some of the
reasons for the contempt and unease:

[T]he postwar economic recovery was producing an American form of capitalism based on unlimited credit, trust in unlimited resources, and the drive toward unfettered consumption. Official morality was content to reassert the vindication of its system, of individual enterprise over the mass hysteria of Nazism and to promise that the same system would prevail against the equally collectivist evil of communism. The American heights of the species was well on its way to using four-fifths of the globe's supplies. (1979: 3)

This is the situation in the history of the Unites States and its poetry, when the generation of writers, represented here by Theodore Roethke and Elizabeth Bishop, began to work on redirecting American Poetry. Wedged between an overbearing modernist poetic tradition of "depersonalization" and a depressing postwar public discourse of red scare and consumerism, they began to forge early postmodern poetry: a poetry that finds ways to go against or circumvent the debasement of "official morality" (ibid.) and that uses, in one way or another, the 'personal' to do this.

Roethke's and Bishop's poems represent some of the first postmodern poetic attempts to challenge what the modernist and postwar "Age Demanded." Instead of drawing on world and literary history like Eliot and Pound, they restricted the setting of their poetry to contemporary time and to places with which they were familiar: that Bishop travelled while Roethke stayed in the U.S., makes her an early poet and critic of globalization while Roethke is today also seen as regionalist (see Kearful 2000). Both manipulated the poetic speaker in order to focus on new ways of seeing and envisioning the world. Bishop apparently bowed to the rules of "self-contain[ment]" and "indirect[ion]" (Perloff 1996: 107)—yet as I will show in what follows, she strategically positioned a linguistic alter ego in order to ground textual efforts to reach out to and confront an Other. Otherness took different forms in the course of her poetic career: it is often nature, as in "At the Fishhouses," but also the other person, environment, class, race, or nation. Roethke, in contrast, was anything but "self-contained"; he unashamedly staged himself and his innermost fears and longings in a poetic mode that is extremely private and confronts the inner self—and yet his view into the workings of the psyche turns out to be closely connected to the poetic traditions of modernism and Romanticism. His blunt personalizing and psychologizing of poetry led to much attention and popularity in his lifetime, while Bishop's poetic reticence and references to mundane reality seemed much less spectacular. Hence, it took some time before her poems found a wider audience. Since her death in 1979, however, critical attention to her work has grown immensely and by now she has been read—among other things—as an "American nature poet," "an erotic poet, a political poet, a travel poet, a poet of childhood," "across the spectrum of feminist poetics," "in the tradition of a postcolonial, multicultural critique," "as a neopragmatist, a neoformalist, and a postmodernist" (Travisano 1995: 926).

2. Theodore Roethke's "The Lost Son" (1948): Returning to the Childhood Self

Theodore Roethke was born to German-American parents in 1908 in Saginaw, Michigan (for Roethke's biography see Seager 1991). His grandfather, an immigrant from Prussia, bequeathed a big greenhouse to Theodore's uncle and his father, Otto. The poet later remembered his father as hard-working, "stern and short-tempered" (Seager 1991: 26). As Roethke recalled, his father's "chief interest [was in] the growing of . . . flowers" and the family "lived in a frame house which was in front of the greenhouse" (in ibid.: 12). Early on Theodore, like everybody else in the family, had to lend a hand in the business. He spent much time in the greenhouse but also in the surrounding fields and woods, all of which figure prominently in his later writings. His father died of cancer when he was fifteen, and the loss or absence of a father would become a recurring theme in his poetry. Roethke graduated from the University of Michigan and went to Harvard graduate school for a short time. This was also when his first poems were published and he decided to become a writer. He left Harvard in 1931 because of financial difficulties caused by the Great Depression and subsequently started a teaching career which lasted throughout his life. He turned out to be an exceptionally gifted teacher but had difficulties holding positions because of bouts of manic depression and heavy drinking that led to a number of breakdowns and hospitalizations. He was finally hired by the University of Washington, Seattle, in 1947, where he taught until the end of his life. *The Lost Son and Other Poems* (1948) was his second book of poems. It was followed by six further collections. He died in 1963 as a venerated teacher and poet at the height of his fame.

In *The Lost Son and Other Poems* Roethke sketched out the basic topics and developed the intense and symbolic style which would characterize his later poetry. The book was completed during a sabbatical at his family home in Saginaw and is a return to Roethke's childhood, yet a highly over-determined one at that. "The Lost Son" works through, or rather re-works, the loss of his father by turning it into a universal quest for ultimate knowledge and spiritual meaning. It is an exploration of the self that has been read as "psychological death and rebirth in the context of a landscape imagery symbolizing access to the unconscious" (Applewhite 1987: 109), as "anchored in the world of myth" and demonstrating "the contrast between innocence and experience in the mental development of a youth" (Ahrends 1986: 153; my translation), as "the struggle of the self to circumscribe itself, fighting off the equally tempting but equally fallacious notions of solipsism and determinism" (Molesworth 1979: 25), and "bring[ing] into being the existence of the experiencing self and its emotional states never more fully than during the immediate moment of experience" (Sundahl 1988: 45).

The exploration of the self is performed in four parts: "The Flight," "The Pit," "The Gibber," and "The Return," which lead to a final, untitled section. The sequence "follows a narrative line" (Roethke 2001 [1950]: 50) similar to what Joseph Campbell described in a study published in 1949, one year after the publication of Roethke's *The Lost Son*, as "monomyth":

> A hero ventures forth from the world of common day into a region of supernatural wonder: fabulous forces are there encountered and a decisive victory is won: the hero comes back from this mysterious adventure with the power to bestow boons on his fellow man. (2008 [1949]: 23)

As the assessment by the various critics quoted above makes abundantly clear, the heroic quest narrative in Roethke's poem is focused not on the social but on the self. In his text, personal and concrete details are turned into signs of more general and deeper psychological, anthropological, and philosophical meaning; as Roethke put it, they are "at once literal and symbolical" (2001 [1950]: 51).

Thereby his poetry is related to Romantic symbolism, which he—at times—clearly plays upon.

I will exemplify this poetic method in a short reading of part I of "The Lost Son," which is, in Roethke's own words, "a terrified running away—with alternate periods of hallucinatory waiting" of a "protagonist" who "goes in and out of rationality" (ibid.: 50). The poem starts (see quotation at the beginning of this essay) by introducing the burial place of Roethke's father as well as Roethke's alter ego, the speaker of the poem: "At Woodlawn I." Yet, with the four concluding words of the first verse, the biographical significance of the real-life place—which hints at the early loss of Roethke's father—is turned immediately into something transcending reality and biography, passing into another realm: "At Woodlawn *I heard the dead cry*" (l. 1; emphasis added). Accented by an internal rhyme that stresses personal pain ("I"—"cry"), the speaker is endowed with supernatural sensory perceptions that connect him with the world of the dead, and he is turned into a mythic hero. In the next two lines, the realm of the dead is merged with Roethke's childhood reminiscences of "lull[ing]" greenhouse noises like "the slamming of iron / A slow drip over stones" (ll. 2-3), which at the same time encapsulate mythic ideas of hell and the netherworld. The animal query (ll. 8-11) indicates multiple directions for the quest: "forward" (l. 8) and back ("home," l. 9), and, as indicated by the addressees "bird" (l. 8) and "worm" (l. 11), further up and further down.

The quest is turned inward in the second stanza to express the pain felt by the self: "Fish(ing) in an old wound" (i.e., the loss of the father, l. 12). Here, and in the next three stanzas, which play upon poetic tradition, no answer is given to the self, anxiously searching and in isolation. "The soft pond of repose" (l. 13) is not stirred; the "empty house" (l. 16) is not filled; the "silence" (l. 20) remains undisturbed.

> Sat in an empty house
> Watching shadows crawl,
> Scratching.
> There was one fly.
>
> Voice, come out of the silence.
> Say something.
> Appear in the form of a spider
> Or a moth beating the curtain. (ll. 16-23)

The "one fly" is more an ironic reminder of the profanity of life (and death) than the vainly hoped-for consoling "voice . . . out of the silence" (l. 20). It seems related to the ghastly creature that in Emily Dickinson's mid-19th-century "I heard a fly buzz when I died" (1955 [1862]: #465) aggravates pain and punctuates the moment of death. While her contemporary Walt Whitman found consolation in "a noiseless, patient spider" (1983 [1868]: 371), which symbolized and expressed the workings of the soul, and while the more skeptical Dickinson could still celebrate natural beauty in "a moth the hue of this" (1955 [1864]: #841), Roethke's speaker cannot avail himself of the Romanticist consolation of "a spider / Or a moth" (ll. 22-3), both of which keep their distance. Line 25 voices the central question of the heroic quest in this and every other actualization of the "monomyth": "Which is the way to take?" And the answers re-situate a rational layout of life choices as, for example, in Robert Frost's famous poem "The Road Not Taken" (1916), in the irrational realm of nonsense and dream language.

Tell me:
Which is the way I take;
Out of what door do I go,
Where and to whom?

Dark hollows said, lee to the wind,
The moon said, back of an eel,
The salt said, look by the sea,
Your tears are not enough praise,
You will find no comfort here,
In the kingdom of bang and blab. (ll. 24-33)

In a playful fairy tale scenario—mind the twisting and interlocking of words and
rhyme by anagram ("lee"—"eel," ll. 28-9), alliteration ("salt, said, sea," l. 30;
"lee," "look," ll. 28-9; "bang," "blab," l. 33), or assonance ("lee," "eel," "sea,"
"tears," "here," ll. 28-32)—the escape from rationality and conscious choice is
prepared. "Comfort" is said not to be found "In the kingdom of bang and blab"
(l. 33)—neither in the real-life and rational world of coerced conformism and
public discourse in post-war America nor in its high modernist poetry scene.

For the rest of the first part of the sequence, the title-giving "Flight" of the
eponymous "Lost Son" is staged. It moves "over" and "toward" the alternative, if
incomprehensible and shifting realm: the discourse of the unconscious, the
"spongy ground" (l. 34) and "the quick-water, wrinkling and rippling" (l. 39). By
emulating the patterned and associative speech of children's rhyme and mythical incantations, authenticity is artfully fabricated—while staying as much out
of reach as knowing oneself and one's way. As the end of part I indicates, this
knowledge is

. . . sleek as an otter
With wide webby toes
Just under the water
It usually goes. (ll. 58-61)

The search for self-knowledge continues through the following four sections. In
the nine-line second section "The Pit," the speaker's search for "roots" (sec. 2,
l. 1) is expressed in Freudian imagery. Part III, "The Gibber," next to expanding
an Oedipal scenario, takes up the biblical overtones of the title in asking:

Hath the rain a father? All the caves are ice. Only the snow's here.
I'm cold. I'm cold all over. Rub me in father and mother.
Fear was my father, Father Fear.
His look drained the stones. (sec. 3, ll. 14-7)

Roethke asserts that the "line 'Hath the rain a father?' is from Job—the only
quotation in the piece. (A third of a line, notice—not a third of a poem.)" (2001
[1950]: 50). Here he underlines his difference from Eliot's or Pound's compositions with their extensive use of quotations.

The fourth section, "The Return," turns back to Roethke's childhood memories. It has "Papa . . . coming," and his harsh German demand for "Ordnung!
ordnung!" (sec. 4, ll. 21-2) interrupts the comfortable atmosphere—"Pipe-knock.
/ Scurry of warm over small plants" (sec. 4, ll. 19-20)—of the family greenhouse.
Finally, in the last section, Campbell's "boons" that Roethke's hero has earned
"to bestow . . . on his fellow man" are, according to the poet, "the illumination,
the coming of light suggested at the end of the last passage" (2001 [1950]: 51):

Light traveled over the wide field;
Stayed.
The weeds stopped swinging.
The mind moved, not alone,
Through the clear air, in the silence.

Was it light?
Was it light within?
Was it light within light?
Stillness becoming alive,
Yet still? (sec. 5, ll. 11-20)

The list of questions indicates that the meaning of the light remains unclear. In fact, the unmotivated change of speaker in the last five lines (note that they cannot be spoken by the speaker who saw the light and wondered what it was and meant) indicates Roethke's longing for insight and transcendence. The wise speaker (God? the Author?) of the last lines admonishes:

A lively understandable spirit
Once entertained you.
It will come again.
Be still.
Wait. (sec. 5, ll. 20-5)

Poised between vision ("light") and the promise of understanding (which "will come again"), Roethke's poem ends.

In a letter to William Carlos Williams (for his relation to Williams, see Kusch 1999) Roethke claimed that the sequence used "the accent of native American speech," just like Williams's poetry did, and was "not the meditative T.S. Eliot thing" (in Seager 1991: 154-5). While the plain language and the abstinence from learned allusions and lengthy speculation make for a very different style than Eliot's, Roethke was obviously striving for the same kind of transcendence and sublimity. The poet Richard Eberhart summarized Roethke's aim in writing in a speech on the occasion of the first anniversary of the poet's death:

[H]e tried to penetrate the ideal essence behind the mask of time; he tried, at first through writing of newts and worms and later and last through mysticism, to penetrate the heart of life and to give, through sensuous, sometimes sensual images, the feel of nature as most sensitively apprehended by him. (1965: 619)

Hence, as the following excerpt from a contemporary review in *The New Yorker* by Louise Bogan shows, Roethke's in-your-face rebellion against what the "Age Demanded" could and was easily contained and expressed in the very terms of modernist writing (italicized in the following quotation):

In the long poem that gives the book its title, he plunges into the subconscious as into a pond, and brings up all sorts of clammy amorphous material. He often *frames* it in the language of the adage, the proverb, the incantation, and the nonsense rhyme . . . "The Lost Son" is written with complete conscious *control*. The effects have been *manipulated* as all art is manipulated, but the method aids in *understanding* of the material *instead of befogging* it. Throughout true emotion gives the chosen *style* coloration and shape. (Bogan in Seager 1991: 157-8; emphasis added)

Or, in the words of Eliot in "Tradition and the Individual Talent" (who contradicts Wordsworth's famous definition of poetry in the Preface to *Lyrical Ballads*):

[I]t is neither emotion, nor recollection, nor, without distortion of meaning, tranquility. It is a concentration, and a new thing resulting from the concentration, of a very great number of experiences which to the practical and active person would not seem to be experiences at all; it is a concentration which does not happen consciously or of deliberation. (1932: 21)

In his autobiographical poetry Roethke "discovered the seeds of several modes that were later to dominate contemporary poetry: confessionalism, neosurrealism, deep images" (Molesworth 1979: 23). At the same time and despite his explicit resistance against Eliot, however, the way in which the depth psychology of his poetry can convincingly be phrased in the critical vocabulary of Eliot's modernism indicates how complex Roethke's relation to modernism ultimately was and that he, in some ways, continued modernism more than challenged it.

3. Elizabeth Bishop's "At the Fishhouses" (1956): Self-Reflexively Documenting Everyday Life

Elizabeth Bishop was born in 1911 in Worcester, Massachusetts (for Bishop's biography see Millier 1993). Her father died when she was only eight months old and, subsequently, her mother developed a mental disorder which prevented her from caring for her daughter. Elizabeth spent her childhood and youth with her maternal grandparents in Nova Scotia, Canada, then with her paternal grandparents in Worcester and, after having developed a depression and a chronic case of asthma, with an aunt in Boston. She studied from 1930 to 1935 at Vassar, where she received the intellectual and literary background for her later career as a poet but also started to relieve stress by drinking. While at Vassar, her first poems were published and she contacted and met Marianne Moore, who became an important mentor and friend. After college, financially independent by a small income from her father's estate, she started to travel—to Europe, Florida, Mexico, and back to her childhood home in Nova Scotia. In 1951, on what was planned as a world tour, she stopped and stayed in Brazil to live with her friend Lota de Macedo Soares, only resettling back in the United States after the death of Soares in 1967. She started teaching late in her career, and her first appointment at the University of Washington in 1966 was, incidentally, a replacement for the late Theodore Roethke. In 1970 she took over the teaching position of the departing Robert Lowell at Harvard. Her first book of poetry was published in 1946, and in 1947 she was awarded a Guggenheim Fellowship, the same year she first met Robert Lowell. The famous confessional poet became an important friend and confidant, although she "In general . . . deplore[d] the 'confessional'" while acknowledging nonetheless that it was "perhaps . . . a necessary movement, and it helped make poetry more real, fresh, and immediate" (in Millier 1993: 462). Bishop was named poetry consultant to the Library of Congress for 1949-50 at Lowell's suggestion. Her second book of poems, which contained "At the Fishhouses," came out in 1956 and won the Pulitzer Prize that year. She published *Questions of Travel* in 1965 and *Geography III* in 1976, which are both marked by her experiences in Brazil. In between the two collections, in 1970, she was awarded a National Book Award. Bishop died in 1979, known mostly to other poets—"a writer's writer's writer" as John Ashbery (1977: 8) put it—but her fame has increased dramatically ever since.

"At the Fishhouses" was begun during a tour to Nova Scotia in 1946, sixteen years after Bishop had last been there, and it turns out to be based as much on personal experience as is Roethke's "Lost Son." It reworks her visit to a small port on the Atlantic coast—and the dreams she had of it. As she explained later in a letter: "Quite a few lines of "At the Fishhouses" came to me in a dream, and the scene—which was real enough, I'd recently been there—but the old man and the conversation, etc., were all in a later dream" (1994 [1955]: 308).

Far from defying the modernist urge for formal rigor and depersonalization, however, Bishop processed her personal experience as if taking "Tradition and the Individual Talent" for her blueprint. A notebook entry, made shortly after she had left college in 1934, shows her agreement with rejecting, in Eliot's words, "a turning loose of emotion" and "the expression of personality" (1932: 21). This is what she wrote:

> It's a question of using a poet's proper materials, with which he's equipped by nature, i.e., immediate, intense physical reactions, a sense of metaphor and decoration in everything—to express something not of them—something, I suppose, *spiritual*. But it proceeds from the material, the material eaten out with acid, pulled down from underneath, made to perform and always kept in order, in its place (in Millier 1993: 65; original emphasis).

This shows the influence of her poetic models—the devotional poets George Herbert and Gerard Manley Hopkins, as well as the modernists T.S. Eliot, Wallace Stevens, and Marianne Moore (and also suggests why neo-formalists would laud her today). There are, however, a number of notable differences in this enumeration of the poet's "materials" in comparison to the ones of her modernist forebears: "physical reactions" and "a sense of metaphor and decoration" are much more modest and technical than "emotion" or "personality." And her aim of writing—before it is hesitantly ("I suppose") translated into the somewhat religious "spiritual"—is simply "to express something not of them." In other words, she wishes to get deeper insights into the world by working hard on the ways to represent it. And she wishes to catch "something not of them" (transcendence) not by looking through the "materials" but by vigorously manipulating them: "eat[ing] out with acid, pull[ing] down, mak[ing] . . . to perform." This led to precise, this-worldly, and socially aware poetic texts that are highly self-conscious (and often self-ironic) explorations of knowledge and its limits. "At the Fishhouses" is a perfect early example of this.

Bishop reworked the scene at and/or dream of the fishhouses at Nova Scotia into a poem that stages, enacts, and acknowledges an encounter with nature as Other. She starts with the mundane scene of the fisherman by the sea which was discussed at the beginning of this essay. The resulting image is intensified by specifying—in one sentence each—the smell (ll. 7-8), the outward appearance of the fishhouses (ll. 9-12), and the "silver" color of the fish scales that spreads over and connects the sea, the boats, and the houses (ll. 13-20), the color which is mirrored in

> The big fish tubs . . . completely lined
> with layers of beautiful herring scales
> and the wheelbarrows are similarly plastered
> with creamy iridescent coats of mail,
> with small iridescent flies crawling on them. (ll. 21-5)

The "iridescent" scenery is then set off against "an ancient wooden capstand / cracked" on a "little slope" (ll. 26-31), while in the rest of the first stanza, the— until here implicit—basic relation between man and nature is made more explicit. A short "talk" between the speaker (who enters the poem at this point) and a fisherman on "the decline in the population / and of codfish and herring" (ll. 34-5) precedes the concluding sober observation on the fisherman's work:

> He has scraped the scales, the principle beauty,
> from unnumbered fish with that black, old knife,
> the blade of which is almost worn away. (ll. 38-40)

While the laconic turn from the declining population of people (l. 34) to the one of fish (l. 35) ironically flattens out the difference between human and animal "population," the image of "that black, old knife" (l. 39) illuminates an imbalance of power that underlies the apparently peaceful bond between man and nature—as well as the violence that grounds the silvery beauty paraded in the preceding lines. In the following line (l. 40), though, the human advantage over nature resting in men's "knife" becomes reversed. In another turn of the ecological screw, the deadly instrument is shown to be severely eroded, "almost worn away" by the effort to wrest life and beauty from the powers of nature.

These acute observations on the uneasy and multilayered interplay of men and their natural environment are continued and taken to another sphere— "tree trunks" as "ramp" (ll. 41-6)—in the one-sentence, six-line second stanza. Yet far from culminating in an eco-critical manifesto (even if the poem might be read to support one), the last stanza takes a final, epistemological turn. It focuses on the sea, following a logic which has led from the fishhouses on land (stanza 1) over the ramp (stanza 2) to the ocean (stanza 3), yet it starts in a completely different register. In prophetic language the sea is characterized as absolute Other and great danger to men: "Cold dark deep and absolutely clear, / element bearable to no mortal, / to fish and to seals . . ." (ll. 47-9; original ellipsis).

The apparently objective speech act (note that the speaker is nowhere in sight) is literally broken off in the middle of line 49 when the feeling and meaning of the sea to marine creatures is about to be put into words. Stopping short of this pretense of knowing not just 'the other mind' (a famous philosophical problem) but even the 'mind' of another species, the tenor of the sentence is transposed into the language of everyday, concrete experience and, what is more, tied back to a concrete perceiving subject: "to fish and to seals . . . One seal particularly / I have seen here evening after evening" (ll. 49-50). This is the point in the poem at which the speaker enters the text as "I" (in the speaker's first short appearance as interlocutor of the fisherman, the use of the first person singular was avoided). For the next seventeen lines of the third stanza, what "I" sings (funnily enough "Baptist hymns" and "A Mighty Fortress Is Our God," ll. 53-4) and sees (a "seal," "water," "firs," ll. 49, 61-2) is related. This is not to make the poem more personal, subjective, or psychological; in fact, the speaker's inscription into the text serves to *disclose* the personal, subjective, psychological quality of *every* speech act, no matter what register is used.

The disclosure of 'disinterested' knowledge as illusion is played upon directly by a reversal of the gaze in this section of the last stanza. The observer becomes the observed as the—anthropomorphized—seal is said to have been "curious about me" (51), to have "regarded me / steadily" (ll. 55-6), and been as nonplussed as the speaker. The following word-for-word repetition of line 47, "Cold dark deep and absolutely clear," in line 60 has lost its universal ring and refers no longer to some abstract "element" (l. 48) but to "the clear gray icy water . . . Back, behind us" (l. 61). The sea water connects "us," the seal (in it) and the speaker (at its edge). Only after this—and a number of further permutations of perspectives on the sea "indifferently swinging above the stones, / icily free above the stones, / above the stones and then the world" (ll. 68-70), painful to touch and drink—does the poem move to its final insight:

> It is like what we imagine knowledge to be:
> dark, salt, clear, moving, utterly free,
> drawn from the cold hard mouth
> of the world, derived from the rocky breasts
> forever, flowing and drawn, and since
> our knowledge is historical, flowing, and flown. (ll. 78-83)

With multiple qualifiers ("like," "imagine") this conclusion about knowledge as something strikingly real yet absolutely alien and always elusive is itself very tentative. At the same time, though, the only definite statement of this sentence, "our knowledge is historical," demonstrates how Bishop's poetical investigations are tied to ever shifting but concrete social and historical realities. Knowledge is "flowing and drawn"; it exists in motion and has to be extracted by hard work; it is "flowing, and flown"; it develops and will not be arrested in an epiphany.

While Bishop's poem with its concluding quasi-definition of (historical) knowledge is still more conclusive than later Language poetry or deconstructive criticism, it goes some way to a self-reflective analysis and critique of the traditions of representation in poetry and epistemology that later came to characterize these discourses.

4. Conclusion

Like Roethke, Bishop used an autobiographically and locally based self in her poems yet it is not meant as a vehicle for confession but to keep in mind the standpoint and context-dependence of any insight. In Bonnie Costello's words:

> Bishop's . . . visual experience and the spatial and visual poetry which com-
> municates it do not resist history and diversity but rather disclose it, challeng-
> ing her position as a detached creative subject. She sets her eyes not on the
> transcendental fade-out or on the modernist fixed object, but on the panorama
> and minutiae of a changing world which she tentatively orders and interprets.
> (1991: 2)

Like Roethke, Bishop yearned for knowledge, yet she did not look for it within the psyche but outside the self. While Roethke used poetry to perform, and thereby explore the ego, which is described as constantly slipping away like "an otter," Bishop took poetry to be the record and means to investigate the changing social order, such as "the decline in the population / and of codfish and herring." Adrienne Rich wrote that Bishop "was critically and consciously trying to explore marginality, power and powerlessness" (1983: 17), and James McCorkle has observed that Bishop's "concordances of possibilities, impressions, and glimpses . . . unsettle the given order" (1989: 7).

Both Theodore Roethke and Elizabeth Bishop drew on the traditions of American poetry to grapple with the reality and the poetry scene in the postwar

United States. Roethke personalized his poetry to resist the "kingdom of bang and blab" in an effort to reach a new spirituality through poetic explorations of the psyche, while Bishop heightened the self-reflexivity of her poetic investigations of everyday life, "At the Fishhouses" or elsewhere, in order to catch glimpses of the workings of the social. Both poets highlighted the ephemeral nature and precariousness of vision or knowledge, foreshadowing the idea that "transcendent truths seem forever out of reach" (Bertens 1994: 11) and thereby betraying their connection to later postmodern developments in the history of American poetry.

Bibliography

Selected Primary Literature

Ashbery, John. 1977. "Second Presentation to the Jury." In: *World Literature Today* 51.1: 8-11.

Bertens, Hans. 1994. *The Idea of the Postmodern: A History.* New York: Routledge.

Bishop, Elizabeth. 1994. *One Art: Letters, Selected and Edited by Robert Giroux.* New York: Farrar, Straus & Giroux.

——. 2011 [1947]. "At the Fishhouses." In: *Poems.* London: Chatto & Windus. 62-4.

Dickinson, Emily. 1955. *The Poems of Emily Dickinson.* Cambridge: Belknap.

Eliot, T.S. 1932. "Tradition and the Individual Talent." In: *Selected Essays.* London: Faber & Faber. 13-22.

Lowell, Robert. 1959. "Memories of West Street and Lepke." In: *Life Studies.* New York: Farrar, Strauss & Cuhady.

Pound, Ezra. 1918. *Pavannes and Divisions.* New York: Knopf.

Rich, Adrienne. 1983. "The Eye of the Outsider: The Poetry of Elizabeth Bishop." In: *Boston Review* 8 (Apr.): 15-7.

Roethke, Theodore. 1966 [1948]. "The Lost Son." In: *The Collected Poems of Theodore Roethke.* New York: Doubleday. 50-5.

——. 2001 [1950]. "Open Letter." In: *On Poetry and Craft.* Port Townsend, WA: Copper Canyon. 49-54.

Williams, William Carlos. 1986. *The Collected Poems: 1909-1939.* Vol. I. Ed. A. Walton Litz and Christopher McGowan. New York: New Directions.

Whitman, Walt. 1983 [1868]. "A Noiseless Patient Spider." In: *Leaves of Grass.* Toronto: Bantam. 371.

Selected Secondary Literature

Ahrends, Günther. 1986. "Die Suche nach dem fernen Feld: Theodore Roethke und die romantische Dichtungstradition." In: Karl Joseph Höltgen and Lothar Hönnighausen (eds.), *Tradition und Innovation in der englischen und amerikanischen Lyrik des 20. Jahrhunderts.* Tübingen: Max Niemeyer. 150-62.

A brief and useful overview on Roethke's work as continuation of the Romantic quest.

Costello, Bonnie. 1991. *Elizabeth Bishop: Questions of Mastery.* Cambridge: Harvard UP.

An excellent discussion of Bishop's oeuvre that concentrates on its negotiation and renewal of a long tradition—devotional, romantic, modern—of visual and spatial poetry.

Millier, Brett C. 1993. *Elizabeth Bishop: Life and the Memory of It.* Berkeley: U of California P.

An informative and detailed biography that connects the life of the poet to her writings.

Molesworth, Charles. 1979. *The Fierce Embrace: Of Contemporary American Poetry.* Columbia: U of Missouri P.

An early but still greatly informative and illuminating study of the post-war poetry scene with an excellent discussion of Roethke's works.

Seager, Allan. 1991. *The Glass House: The Life of Theodore Roethke.* Ann Arbor: U of Michigan P.

A new edition of Seager's 1968 standard biography of Theodore Roethke with an illuminating personal introduction by the renowned U.S. poet Donald Hall.

Further References

Applewhite, James. 1987. "Theodore Roethke: Death and Rebirth in a Modern Landscape." In: Harold Bloom (ed.), *American Poetry 1947 to 1965: The Critical Cosmos.* New York: Chelsea House. 109-21.

Campbell, Joseph. 2008 [1949]. *The Hero with a Thousand Faces.* Novato, CA: New World Library.

Eberhart, Richard. 1965. "On Theodore Roethke's Poetry." In: *Southern Review* 1 (Jul.): 612-20.

Kearful, Frank. 2000. "Regions of the Self: Theodore Roethke's *North American Sequence.*" In: Lothar Hönnighausen (ed.), *Regional Images and Regional Realities.* Tübingen: Stauffenburg. 249-69.

Kusch, Robert. 1999. *My Toughest Mentor: Theodore Roethke and William Carlos Williams (1940-1948).* Lewisburg, Pennsylvania: Bucknell UP.

McCorkle, James. 1989. *The Still Performance: Writing, Self, and Interconnection in Five Postmodern American Poets.* Charlottesville: U of Virginia P.

Perloff, Marjorie. 1996. "Whose New American Poetry? Anthologizing in the Nineties." In: *Diacritics* 26.3-4: 104-23.

Sundahl, Daniel James. 1988. "Theodore Roethke's 'The Lost Son': Solipsism and the Private Language Problem." In: *Essays in Arts and Science* 17 (May): 41-61.

Travisano, Thomas. 1995. "The Elizabeth Bishop Phenomenon." In: *New Literary History* 26.4: 903-30.

19.

Black Mountain Poetry

Charles Olson, Robert Creeley, Robert Duncan,
Denise Levertov, and Edward Dorn

Helmbrecht Breinig

1. The Black Mountain School and Charles Olson's "Projective Verse"

In the 1950s, the most culturally stimulating spot in the U.S. outside New York and San Francisco was a tiny college in North Carolina. Black Mountain College was founded in 1933 by John Andrew Rice and others as a pedagogical experiment promoting interdisciplinary, coeducational education free of hierarchies and competitiveness, centered on the arts as stimuli for the development of creative personalities. In a second developmental phase the emigrated Bauhaus couple Josef Albers, the painter, and his wife Anni, a textile artist, took over, bringing Bauhaus ideas of renewing the arts and crafts. Under their leadership the college turned into a hot spot for the fine arts. In a final phase before its demise for financial reasons in 1956, poets became the dominant members. The leading figure, Charles Olson (1910-1970), who had taught at Black Mountain College since 1948, became rector in 1953. There were never more than a hundred students, yet the list of teachers and alumni (including those of the summer schools) reads like a Who-is-Who of avant-garde post-war (plus some pre-war) American (and to a certain extent European) arts and ideas. The list includes painters like the modernist Lionel Feininger; Robert Motherwell, Franz Kline, and Willem de Kooning, all commonly associated with American Abstract Expressionism that became the dominant post-World War II movement before the advent of Pop Art, whose forerunner Robert Rauschenberg also studied at Black Mountain College and whose "combines" of found objects helped break the dominance of abstraction; and the Color Field artist Kenneth Noland. Noted persons from other fields are the psychologist Erwin Straus, the architects Walter Gropius, founder of the Bauhaus, and Buckminster Fuller, systems theorist and inventor of the geodesic dome; the composers David Tudor and John Cage, who was to become the most iconoclastic innovator of the idea of music; and the radical experimental dancer and choreographer Merce Cunningham.

Among the best-known people associated with Black Mountain College were those poets who became known as the Black Mountain School of Poetry, some connected to the college only by contributing to the *Black Mountain Review* edited by Robert Creeley from 1954 to 1957. Besides Olson and Creeley, the most prominent poets are Robert Duncan, Denise Levertov, Edward Dorn, Jonathan Williams, Paul Blackburn, Larry Eigner, and John Wieners. The college's central idea—the close collaboration of people from different fields—led to a burst of creativity. For instance, in 1952 Black Mountain College was the scene of what is often regarded as the first "happening"—a multi-disciplinary performance or event—involving as participants Cage, Tudor, Olson, Rauschenberg, and Cunningham, that is, music, text, art, and dance. Such collaboration led to the development of an aesthetics of chance and openness, the rejection of formal and genre conventions, the transgression of the borders into other arts and disciplines, and the suspension of the opposition of art and reality. In this way Black Mountain College became a hotbed of beginning postmodernism.

Although not all the poets listed liked to be identified as "Black Mountain Poets," it became an established term notably through Donald Allen's 1960 anthology *The New American Poetry 1945-1960*, where the Black Mountain School is distinguished from what Allen called the New York School and the San Francisco Renaissance, although all three share certain tendencies, as did the Beat Poetry of the same period. Black Mountain poets did not have a common set of prosodic or content elements, but subscribed to an aesthetics of what became known as "open form"; the group is therefore sometimes linked with others under the term Open Form Poetry. More common is the term Projectivist Poetry, which refers to Charles Olson's seminal essay "Projective Verse" (1950).

"Projective Verse" was the most significant poetic theory of its time, influencing not only the Black Mountain poets, but also Allen Ginsberg and other Beats as well as poets of both the New York and San Francisco movements. William Carlos Williams, although belonging to an older generation, found it so important that he included major parts of it in his *Autobiography* (1951), thus indicating how lyrical modernism might develop into postmodernism. Olson was one of the most universally yet eclectically educated people of his time. He turned to literary work after becoming disillusioned with the political machinery (even among the Democrats) when he worked with the American Civil Liberties Union for the benefit of ethnic minorities under the Roosevelt administration. Absorbing a magnitude of ideas from philosophy, the sciences, history, social and political science, archaeology, anthropology, and literature, he turned his disappointment with American competitive individualism into a concept of human solidarity and community ("polis") in harmony with the natural world, and formulated these ideas into his most important essay, "Human Universe" (1951). He rejected most philosophical and political ideas from ancient Greece to the present as too logocentric, and called for a return to more archaic, tribal, and mythical ways of approaching reality, emphasizing the unity of body and mind. Other important essayistic works include the notes making up "Proprioception" (wr. 1959-62), reflecting upon the body as the locus of awareness of the psychic and the exterior world, and *Mayan Letters* (1954), the result of a five-month stay in Yucatán that served to provide him with insights into a non-western and pre-modern approach to reality.

In his letters to Creeley in the early 1950s, Olson often uses the term "postmodern" (see Butterick 1980), which had been coined just a few years earlier by historian Arnold Toynbee, and indeed, Black Mountain poetry is often grouped with other innovative tendencies considered postmodern. Lyrical postmodernism differs, however, from what was known under this term in fictional literature from the 1970s on. While the border between literature and life there leads to a textualization and fictionalization of reality, for Olson and his followers the inverse takes place: the text becomes part of reality and is closely entwined with the physics of both the poet and the macrocosm. It has often been said that Olson was much rather a late modernist than a postmodernist, radicalizing modernist tendencies he found in Ezra Pound and William Carlos Williams while rejecting T.S. Eliot as too cerebral, academic and detached from the physical, breath-line aspect of poetic writing. In his poetic thinking and practice Olson was influenced by Pound's cumulative technique and his use of contrasting images as well as by Williams's emphasis on the syllable as the smallest poetic unit and his preference for non-literary American English. However, Olson understood Pound's *Cantos* and Williams's *Paterson* as open poetic sequences without predictable structure, organically following the flow of ideas, thereby ignoring the older poets' striving for some comprehensive order. He quotes Creeley's dictum that "FORM IS NEVER MORE THAN AN EXTENSION OF CONTENT" (Olson 1966 [1950]: 16; original emphasis) and insists on a radical openness and immediacy of writing. The first major poem in which he exemplifies his philosophy, social thinking, and poetics is "The Kingfishers" of 1949.

Projectivist poetry is part of a critical and literary reaction to the ideals of closed form and internal tension propagated by the New Critics. The Black Mountain poets, like the Beats, opposed this with their own ideal of an open form that develops organically with the content, an idea familiar from Romanticism but now executed with much more radical formal freedom. For Olson and Duncan, reality cannot be profoundly understood because to human perception it appears as incoherent, fluid, and constantly changing. Both assume, however, that the universe is in truth a coherent, organic albeit dynamic system. In his essay "Projective Verse," Olson finds an image for this idea in the concept of the field as it is used in physics: a field of energy characterized by movement (as in electric waves) and thus openness, but held together by tension (like electric tension), a coherence that is quite different from the tension of elements in a closed structure as propagated by the New Critics. (For a good analysis of Olson's poetics see Schiffer 1972.) Micro- and macrocosm, including the human mind and body, function according to this model of the field, just as the poem— a product of the energy of the universe—is transported through mental attention and biological rhythms (like pulse and breath) to paper, and from there to the reader. In this process the energy is transformed, but it is not—and this is a criterion for poetic quality—diminished. In transmitting the dynamic-kinetic nature of the universe the poet is as much an instrument as an active participant. During the "COMPOSITION BY FIELD" (Olson 1966: 16) the poet is therefore supposed to follow his intuitions spontaneously and rapidly: "ONE PERCEPTION MUST IMMEDIATELY AND DIRECTLY LEAD TO A FURTHER PERCEPTION" (ibid.: 17; original emphasis).

The poet is involved as a subject, but not autobiographically as with the contemporary Confessional Poets because he is part of a super-personal nature. Subjectivism is therefore replaced by "objectism" (not to be confused with *objectivism*): "the getting rid of the lyrical interference of the individual as ego" (ibid.: 24), the "kind of relation of man to experience which a poet might state as the necessity of a line or a work to be as wood is . . . to be shaped as wood can be" (ibid.). Poetic language is free of all metrical, grammatical, and syntactical norms, but by its participation in the rhythms of nature it is not arbitrary. In "Human Universe," Olson says, echoing Novalis: "he who possesses rhythm possesses the universe" (ibid.: 61). The freedom of the poem to change its direction begins at its smallest units, since the syllable is considered as semantically significant, be it through its sound associations or its etymology. All elements— syllables, words, rhythms, and ideas—are readily available; the poet only has to listen with intense attention to grasp the right particles of the field and write them down. Olson claims that the syllable, received through the ear which in turn is closely connected with the brain/mind, is a basic unit of sound and meaning that can unfold in an open sequence. The line that is shaped by the unit of breath and thus depends on the heartbeat is the result of the physical side of writing and also an element of control, a natural measure as proposed in the late theory of William Carlos Williams. The invention of the typewriter gives the poet the ability to devise a notational system on the page (similar to a musical score) that indicates breath lengths, hesitations, the progress of sound, and thought units. Again and again Olson uses metaphors like that of the dance (adopted from Pound) or playing for the tension between total freedom and openness on the one hand and controlling, 'measuring' elements on the other.

2. Charles Olson: Poetry and the New World in "I, Maximus of Gloucester, to You"

Olson's ideas of poetry are best realized in his own œuvre in the monumental series of *The Maximus Poems* that make up the most voluminous part of his lyrical writing (for his other poetical work see his *Collected Poems*). He probably did not initially intend to expand the opening poem into the huge book that was posthumously composed of three previously published volumes (1960, 1968, 1975). "I, Maximus of Gloucester, to You," published in 1950 and thus very close to "Projective Verse," may have been meant as a letter, but in the series it functions as an introduction of the speaker, the place, and some principal themes. "Maximus" refers to the second century Greek eclectic philosopher Maximus of Tyre and thus represents the stance of a thinker vis-à-vis the human world (see George F. Butterick's indispensable *A Guide to* The Maximus Poems *of Charles Olson*, 1978). Gloucester, Massachusetts, Olson's hometown at the time, embodies this world as did the ancient Tyre/Tyros. Maximus is also a self-projection; Olson was a huge man who, by addressing both his city and the reader, perceives himself as a seer and interpreter of signs:

> Off-shore, by islands hidden in the blood
> jewels & miracles, I, Maximus
> a metal hot from boiling water, tell you
> what is a lance, who obeys the figures of
> the present dance (Olson 1983: 5, ll. 1-5)

In this passage Maximus assumes the position of the early sailors and explorers who encounter America, a stance he takes up in later poems as well. It is particularly appropriate because Gloucester is a fishing town in constant interaction with the sea.

Outer and inner reality are inseparable ("islands hidden in the blood"), macro- and microcosm are seen in analogy. In calling himself a lance—a weapon and instrument—he acknowledges his function in society. Yet "a metal hot from boiling water" also alludes to the harpoon that Captain Ahab has had made for himself in chapter 113 of Melville's *Moby-Dick* (1851), a phallic symbol that changes gender when removed from the pole and turned upside-down, as Ahab has his harpooneers do in chapter 36, using the harpoon-heads as drinking vessels—chalices, as it were. This convertibility of male and female images will remain relevant in "I, Maximus." The harmony of contrasting elements, their interplay in the field of energy as envisioned in "Projective Verse," is made obvious in the image of the "dance" and its rhyme with "lance." The participants in the dance "obey" its figures, but they are also active, shaping parts of it. The metaphor of the dance as the unity of space and movement found in Pound's famous definition of "logopeia" (the kind of poetry dominated by connotative language) as "the dance of the intellect among words" (1968: 25), was adopted by the Black Mountain poets but used beyond the intellectual, in a much more physical sense. Thus, the very opening lines define the speaker's bodily and intellectual position and hint at what is to come: the constant transformation of opposites like mind and body, inside and outside, material ("jewels") and immaterial ("miracles"), male and female, active and passive.

After these introductory lines, the poem consists of six sections of irregular length and form. The text is distributed over the page using the whole breadth of the paper, with some lines beginning near the right margin. The author makes use of the tab stop opportunities offered by the typewriter, as Olson explains in his essay, to make his "composition by field" immediately visible. Although not quite as wildly expressive as some of the later poems where the author uses additional symbols and even slanted or circular printing lines, the poem gives an idea of his concept of energy spontaneously and immediately transferred to paper and should, therefore, be looked at in its entirety.

Section 1, which provides a good example of the arrangement on the page, further develops the ideas of the introductory lines:

the thing you're after
may lie around the bend
of the nest (second, time slain, the bird! the bird!

And there! (strong) thrust, the mast! flight

> (of the bird
> o kylix, o
> Antony of Padua
> sweep low, o bless

the roofs, the old ones, the gentle steep ones
on whose ridge-poles the gulls sit, from which they depart,

> And the flake-racks

of my city! (ll. 6-17)

The "thing you're after" refers to what is to be created: nest, ship, love, poem, ideal polis. The immediate "around the bend" is transformed from the temporal to the spatial, the nest pushing the second into second place, and therefore time is slain. Yet as "second time" the situation also alludes to a rebirth, a second chance, including the old notion of America as mankind's second chance that may have been wasted. The open parenthesis is a popular sign that Olson uses to indicate openness, the open process of what is to follow. All of the images refer to Gloucester: gulls, nests, and masts that are linked by spontaneous association. From the female sexual image of the nest arises the male thrusting mast and the flight of the birds, which is connected with what comes from above: the kylix, the stemmed bowl (in itself both feminine and masculine), the grail that was sent from heaven and is associated with Antony of Padua, the patron saint of the Portuguese fishermen who settled in Gloucester long ago. The subsequent series of contrastive images and semantic/acoustic elements— "gentle"/"steep," "ridge-poles," "sit"/"depart," "flake-racks" (used to dry fish)— achieve a kind of balance. One should also note the many exclamation marks in this expressive, gestural kind of poetry, demanding that the reader see, understand, and mend his or her ways. Sometimes the text is almost staccato, evoking the sex act ("And there! (strong) thrust, the mast!"). Alliterations, assonances,

repetitions, and exclamations form the aural side of the rapid semantic development. Olson's idiosyncratic punctuation and the uneven distribution of the
text on the page are meant to point to nuances of speed and emphasis of the
language.

Section 2 develops the idea of love as creating form that is also content—the
idea of organic form—in the image of the bird's nest from section 1:

> feather to feather added
> (and what is mineral, what
> is curling hair, the string
> you carry in your nervous beak, these
>
> make bulk, these, in the end, are
> the sum (ll. 22-7)

Love and procreation are thus linked with the creation of art that always requires emotional engagement, attention to the tiniest detail, and esteem. For
Olson, birds are the quintessence of attentiveness, care, mobility, and energy—
not only in his poetry but also in his essays and in the travel notes of his *Mayan
Letters*. What is also constructed is the community, or polis, for which the figure
of "my lady of good voyage" is important:

> in whose arm, whose left arm rests
> no boy but a carefully carved wood, a painted face, a schooner!
> a delicate mast, as bow-sprit for
>   forwarding (ll. 28-32)

This significant figure on the central façade of Gloucester's Portuguese church,
a secularized madonna, an embodiment of the female principle, holds a ship as
the symbol of trade and fishing: another chalice, as it were; another female geni-
tal image that balances the male energy of the "beak" and yet already reproduces this energy in the shape of the mast, a dynamic process that carries city,
trade, the poem, and its message "forward."

Section 3 declares sex and money to be "facts" (l. 34), albeit "uncertain"
(l. 33), that must "be played by . . . the ear" (ll. 36-8). Although commercialization has made listening difficult, since "all, even silence, is spray-gunned . . .,
when sound itself is neoned in" (ll. 42, 45), art keeps its transformative power in
the beautiful image of the evening seen across the bay:

> when, on the hill, over the water
> where she who used to sing,
> when the water glowed,
> black, gold, the tide
> outward, at evening
>
> when bells came like boats
> over the oil-slicks, milkweed
> hulls (ll. 46-53)

Art can make even the inattentive—"a man slumped, / attentionless, / against
pink shingles" (ll. 54-6) part of the tapestry of visual impressions and the music
of poetic language.

However, this is not enough. The negative forces in capitalist society, what
Olson calls "pejorocracy" (l. 73) in section 5 (echoing Pound's *Pisan Cantos*),
have to be marked and combated. The three fairly regular stanzas of section 4,
printed as descending stair steps like Williams's late "variable foot" lines, repre-

sent such opposition by celebrating form as the result of love and birth, of care for the detail: "street-pickings, . . . weeds / you carry in, my bird" (ll. 64-5), culminating in the transformations

> of a bone of a fish
> of a straw, or will
> of a color, of a bell
> of yourself, torn (ll. 66-9)

Section 5 dwells on the difficulty of such activity in the face of current superficialities that "offend / a black-gold loin" (ll. 75-6)—a sexualized echo of the evening image in section 3—and detract from the traditional skills like that of the swordfish harpooner spending the evening with "mu-sick, mu-sick, mu-sick" (l. 80). What is called for is a return to ancient, even pre-literal, cultural values as evoked in the sounds and semantic associations of "as faun and oral, / satyr lesbos vase" (ll. 92-3), only to be turned into a call for action that imitates the cry of the sea-gull:

> o kill kill kill kill kill
> those
> who advertise you
> out) (ll. 94-7)

The sixth and last section returns to the image of nest or boat or art building as a (pro-)creative alternative and proclaims with increasing speed and intensity:

> in! in! the bow-sprit, bird, the beak
> in, the bend is, in, goes in, the form
> that which you make, what holds, which is
> . . . what you are, what you must be, what
> the force can throw up, can, right now hereinafter erect, (ll. 98-102)

which is also the message that Maximus, returning to the words and images from the beginning of the poem, "deliver[s]" (l. 111) "over the waters" (l. 106): "a feather . . . a jewel, / it flashing more than a wing, / than any old romantic thing . . . than anything other . . . than that which you / can do!" (ll. 109-21). Nothing is more important than what is demanded by the next moment, than what one is capable of doing and contributing to a "human universe."

This opening poem, which develops a set of central images and deals with certain "facts," also exemplifies Olson's method of constantly adding new details, listening to new sounds, and exploring the possibilities of meaning. While the end refers back to the beginning, the series as a whole is open, "projective," characterized by enormous energy and associative creativity but also accumulating references to more and more elements of reality, of "facts," often from history, but with the tendency of actualizing them and revealing their importance for the present. Olson incorporates quotations from historical texts and geographic descriptions, even imitating the shape of coastlines. Such material refers to the history of discovery, the early settlers, but also to contemporary events. Physical space is and remains of central importance because it is the key experience of the New World, as Olson points out in his study of Herman Melville, *Call me Ishmael.* Therefore, much geographical information enters the poems, as do Maximus's quarrels with contemporary society and culture. Not all poems have the same intensity, but on the whole this is one of the most impressive and powerful reading experiences twentieth-century American poetry has to offer.

3. Robert Creeley and the Search for Art in "The Door"

Robert Creeley (1926-2005) discontinued his studies at Harvard University shortly before taking his B.A. degree and lived as a freelance experimenter with writing and lifestyles. He moved with his wife and three children first to France and then to Mallorca, where he wrote and started Divers Press (a publishing press for innovative literature of such authors as Olson and Duncan), when Olson called him in 1954 to teach at Black Mountain College. While this step reveals the informality of the college and the unconventional policy of its rector, it also testifies to Olson's ability to see and attract genius. Although he was considerably older than Creeley, he immediately accepted the younger man as his equal when Creeley initiated a correspondence that continued for many years, often on a daily basis, and developed into one of the most significant collections of letters in American literature. Through this exchange Creeley became an active partner in the formation of ideas that Olson finally put down in "Projective Verse." While in Mallorca, Creeley had written a novel, *The Island* (1963), and the short story collection *The Gold Diggers* (1954); he continued to write essays and other prose works throughout his life. He later pursued a regular academic career, teaching at SUNY Buffalo and Brown University, but his fame rests on his poetry, which he continued to publish in numerous volumes and that earned him the Bollingen Prize and many other honors.

Reading Creeley alongside Olson feels like looking at minimalist art next to the high-energy action painting of a Jackson Pollock. And yet Creeley subscribed to Olson's notion of the poem as a field of energy creating a tension of its elements that—and here Creeley follows his other mentor Williams—function with the absolute necessity of the parts of a machine. The selection, or rather, the discovery of the individual word (and syllable) is a crucial process, but even more important is the line that is not to follow any syntactic or traditional pattern but, as in Olson, the breath of the poet.

Breath carries what for Creeley is at the heart of poetry: emotion. The psychological, the physical (breath), and the mental association of ideas come together in dealing with

> some imminence of occasion that has not as yet become literal. I have never . . . anticipated the situation of my own writing in the sense of what I was about to say. It is certain enough that preoccupations recur—"themes," as Duncan has called them—but how these might gain statement as writing could not be proposed except as the literal writing then found means. I was struck by a comment Franz Kline once made: "If I paint what I know, I bore myself. If I paint what you know, I bore you. So I paint what I don't know . . . ." I write what I don't know. (Creeley 1970: 57)

Creeley continues to find kindred spirits in Pollock and in the Olson of "Projective Verse." He sees writing poetry as analogous to driving: "The road, as it were, is creating itself momently in one's attention to it, there, visibly, in front of the car" (ibid.: 58). Such attention to what follows occupies the mind: "Mind, thus engaged, permits experience of 'order' far more various and intensive than habituated and programmed limits of its subtleties can recognize" (ibid.: 58). It is no coincidence that one of Creeley's poems quoted most often, "I Know a Man," from his early volume *For Love* (1962), uses exactly this analogy of speaking/writing/thinking/feeling with driving in exploring the depths of a banal, everyday situation:

As I sd to my
friend, because I am
always talking,—John, I

sd, which was not his
name, the darkness sur-
rounds us, what

can we do against
it . . . (1982: 132, ll. 1-8)

What is immediately apparent is the hesitant, stumbling manner of speaking. If the line corresponds to the unit of breath, with Creeley this often means a bated breath. The a-syntactical line breaks with the slowing down of the last word/syllable, and the emphasis on the first word of the next line, create accents of attention, as it were: "my," "friend," "am," "name," in the case of "rounds" even achieving a more positive, optimistic reversal of meaning, as if the disassembling of language uncovered new ways of overcoming the existential crisis in which the speaker finds himself. His Beat-like tentative escape: "or else, shall we & / why not, buy a goddam big car" (ll. 8-9), the latter line with its 8 syllables breaking the pattern of 3-6 syllables per line and thus reflecting the sudden verbose acceleration, is only a superficial, misleading way out of the crisis and into capitalist consumerism. The answer is given by "John" and signalizes the need to focus on what is immediately ahead, whether in driving or writing:

drive, he sd, for
christ's sake, look
out where yr going. (ll. 10-2)

Of course, this may also mean that the speaker's exploration by arbitrary language ("which was not his name!") should not be allowed to swerve, to get unfocalized.

As Creeley says in "Notes Apropos 'Free Verse,'" the "rhythmic possibility," the "inherent periodicity in the weights and durations of words" (1970: 58) that comes most naturally to him is a pattern of four, reminding him of the "'foursquare' patterns" (ibid. 59) he heard in the Bebop jazz of Charlie Parker. This rhythm is apparent in the four stanzas, and also in the four lines of which a stanza consists. Given Creeley's insistence on the explorative nature of language, his adherence to short, song-like forms reveals the tension between intellectual openness and the contracting physical rhythms echoing internal anxieties, doubts, and wishes. In later poems this pattern is replaced by sequences of mini-poems or -stanzas sometimes consisting of only two lines. His poetry is rarely descriptive or narrative. The typical situations with which Creeley engages are very personal: love, anxiety, loneliness; there is often, however, a good deal of self-irony in the emotional complex driving the text forward. Yet as Creeley insists again and again,

poems are not referential, or at least not importantly so. They have 'meaning' in that they do 'exist through themselves' . . . I do feel poems to involve an occasion to which a man pays obedience, and which intentions alone never yield . . . I think I first felt a poem to be what might exist in words as primarily the fact of its own activity. Later, of course, I did see that poems might comment on many things, and reveal many attitudes and qualifications. Still, it was never

what they said *about* things that interested me. I wanted the poem itself to exist
and that could never be possible as long as some subject significantly elsewhere
was involved. There had to be an independence derived from the very fact that
words are *things* too. (1970: 54; original emphasis)

Both the non-referentiality and the existence of layers of meaning can be discovered in Creeley's poem "The Door," which was first published in 1959 and is
dedicated to Robert Duncan. This makes sense, since it is an unusually symbolic
poem for Creeley, unusually long, unusually circular. And yet in many aspects it
is typical of Creeley's work in his collection *For Love*, where it was printed. The
poem consists of 21 four-line stanzas of the short line length Creeley so often
used, most frequently between 7 and 9 syllables long, but sometimes emphatically shorter, down to the 3 syllables of "Where were You" (l. 49), and sometimes
longer, up to 13 syllables: "Come toward me from the wall, I want to be with You"
(l. 40). If we remember Creeley's close association of breath and line, this makes
for a strong modulation of speed and creates a variable rhythm highly charged
with emotion, particularly in the stair-like growth of line length of stanza 13:

> Where were You.
> How absurd, how vicious.
> There is nothing to do but get up.
> My knees were iron, I rusted in worship, of You. (1982: 200, ll. 49-52)

In this case, the four lines are also four sentences of growing length, concluded
by periods and not by the question marks or exclamation points one might expect, a common technique with Creeley who thus forces us to leave the beaten
path of semantic expectations. Creeley's sentence, quoted by Olson in "Projective Verse," "Form is never more than an extension of content" (1966: 13), also
works the other way around, as Creeley was to realize later: content is never
more than an extension of form, and in "The Door" this means that the regulari-
ties and occasional (remember Creeley's idea of poetry as arising out of the occasion) irregularities of the stanzas that mark the slow progression of the search
and escape attempts that the speaker tells about stand in tension with the emotional intensity of the process.

The content here is the desire to escape from a closed-in situation or condition into an area of longing, a garden, a *locus amoenus*, a paradise associated
with a dominant "Lady" who is an embodiment of feminine allurement and
superiority. Since Creeley often speaks of his wife or lover as "the lady," it is
tempting to see the relationship explored in this poem in connection with some
personal situation; but this would be reductionist. The personal situation of
longing for a woman, but also longing for escape, may provide the emotional
material, but the text is much more than a traditional love poem. Rather, it presents a series of explorations of the basic situation and its implications. The
first components of this situation are presented in stanzas 1-3:

> It is hard going to the door
> cut so small in the wall where
> the vision which echoes loneliness
> brings a scent of wild flowers in a wood.
>
> What I understood, I understand.
> My mind is sometime torment,
> sometimes good and filled with livelihood,
> and feels the ground.

But I see the door,
and knew the wall, and wanted the wood,
and would get there if I could
with my feet and hands and mind. (ll. 1-12)

The unexpected is there right from the start. Why is it hard to go "to" rather
than through the small door? Could it be "small" only because this rhymes, because it echoes with "wall"? The "vision," what little can be seen through the
door, synaesthetically brings a scent rather than a view. Could the vision be just
a projection? The many rhymes on "wood" ("understood," "good," "livelihood,"
"would," "could") create a pattern of echoes that begin with the solid and end
with the wistful. The situation is permanent: "What I understood, I understand,"
but not without variation, the mind being "sometime torment, / sometimes
good," and the "livelihood" it provides indicates a living or a state of vivacity. The
same minute and disturbing variations and irregularities occur with tempus.
"But I see the door, / and knew the wall": what do present and past tenses
imply? Is not the past always also present? Does "would get there" refer to a
past habit or to wishfulness?

The Lady, who the speaker is afraid might "banish" him and to whom he
pledges obedience: "Lady, I follow" (ll. 13, 16), and with whom he may have had
a love affair: "I walked away from myself, / I left the room, I found the garden, /
I knew the woman / in it, together we lay down" (ll. 17-20), may be the poet's
muse, as Ford has argued (1978: 86-7), the goddess of poetic fertility whom the
speaker tries to follow and obey. Yet she may also be associated with Kore, the
ancient fertility goddess who has to spend the winter in the underworld, reduced to a memory: "Dead night remembers. In December / we change, not
multiplied but dispersed, / sneaked out of childhood, / the ritual of dismemberment" (ll. 21-4), alluding to the lover Kore chooses in summer and who will
be sacrificed in winter to ensure the return of fertility (1978: 86). Again, one
wonders whether the sequence "remembers," "December," "dismemberment" is a
chain of associations resulting primarily from the internal rhyme. The remembered or imagined ("I walked away from myself") unity of two lovers, or of mother
and child, is destroyed by the winter separation. But the Lady is in command of
great power, as stanza 7 points out with startling trochees quite unusual in
Creeley: "Mighty magic is a mother" (l. 25); one is tempted to juggle the three
alliterated terms around and change the sequence to see what happens. For
Creeley, words are objects that create their own reality: "in her there is another
issue / of fixture, repeated form, the race renewal" (ll. 26-7). That is, the Lady as
the archetypal Great Mother may have other themes or other offspring in her,
the topic of regeneration being strangely linked to "fixture," the immutable law.

The poem continues to explore the mutabilities of the speaker-Lady relation,
the repeated attempts to get away, the interchangeability of inside and outside
("Inside You would also be tall," l. 38), the frustration of her unreachableness.
There is the temptation of "the Graces in long Victorian dresses" (l. 59), representing former (aesthetic) values: "History sings in their faces / . . . / and you
follow after them also / in the service of God and Truth" (ll. 61, 63-4), but this is
a wrong lane to take:

But the Lady is indefinable,
she will be the door in the wall
to the garden in sunlight.
I will go on talking forever. (ll. 65-8)

The garden cannot be (permanently?) reached except through her. She becomes the door as a metaphor; that is, she becomes a metaphor, but is there really a difference between the "real" and the "figural" in a text whose reality consists of words as objects? In any case, passing through her will only lead to a further, endless search. Going to the garden now seems to offer no solution because that would mean only a return to worn-out romantic forms of thinking and writing: "I will go to the garden. / I will be a romantic. I will sell / myself in hell, / in heaven also I will be" (ll. 77-80), but the Faustian pact is not satisfactory, either. And thus the poem ends on the tone of longing on which it began:

> In my mind I see the door,
> I see the sunlight before me across the floor
> beckon to me, as the Lady's skirt
> moves small beyond it. (ll. 81-4)

Art—and we may now identify the Lady as symbol and reality of that, whatever else she may stand for—can be realized as in the musical beauty of these lines, but it can never be pinned down. But again, this cannot be more than an attempt to distil a message from a text that is an object in itself: "poems . . . have 'meaning' in that they do 'exist through themselves'" (Creeley 1970: 54), and thus the poem cannot be contained by the "almost rhetorical term of argument" that Creeley ascribes to it in an interview (in Davies 1996: 312). When he sent the poem to Duncan the day after it had been written, he called it "a long rambling 'sight' of the Lady, influenced like they say I think by you." He goes on to wonder how useful his digressive form may have been:

> But the form no matter allows me to play rhymes the way I enjoy to, loosely, and 'punctually' to obtain insistence, etc. The thing started after breakfast . . ., talking of 'images,' and this one I always remember, I must have had it as a kid, etc., of the little door in the wall, and the garden one could see through it, all sunlight, and the sounds of voices and happiness, and the warmth of a woman there too. Like those doors in Alice In Wonderland, I think. A sort of peep hole into heaven. (unpublished letter, 2 Jan. 1959; in Davies 1996: 313)

This is a perfect description of an "occasion" in memory, stocked with emotion, being turned by the poet into an exploration of where the mind—the conscious and subconscious, memory and creativity, the physical and the mental, and, in the shape of the Great Mother, the archetypal—may lead.

4. Robert Duncan and the Opening of the Field in "Often I Am Permitted to Return to a Meadow"

Robert Duncan (1919-1988) may have been the most powerful poet (besides Olson) associated with Black Mountain College where he had briefly studied in 1938. As a published poet, Olson invited him to teach at Black Mountain College in 1956/57. Duncan was also a central figure in the group usually called the San Francisco Renaissance, a term popularized by Allen's anthology, *The New American Poetry*, cited above. Among the other poets of this very loosely connected group are Jack Spicer, David Meltzer, Michael McClure, and Gary Snyder. Some were closely associated with the Beat movement, and therefore Allen Ginsberg was an important figure for the San Francisco group. They were, in many ways, part of the West Coast counterculture emerging in the late 1940s

and early 1950s and found a focal point in Lawrence Ferlinghetti's San Francisco City Lights Bookstore, founded in 1953, and the famous publishing press
resulting from it. As an openly gay man (see his 1944 landmark essay "The
Homosexual in Society"), Duncan enjoyed being part of this bohemian lifestyle.
For many years he lived with the painter Jess Collins and was thus also on in-
timate terms with the contemporary art scene. The three volumes that brought
him wider recognition, and are commonly regarded as his pinnacle work, are
The Opening of the Field (1960), *Roots and Branches* (1964), and *Bending the
Bow* (1968). In addition to shorter lyrical pieces, they also contain series of
poems like "The Structure of Rime" whose individual parts include prose poems.
This series, like the programmatically open "Passages," extend over several of
Duncan's volumes of poetry.

Duncan was impressed by Olson's *The Maximus Poems* and "Projective Verse,"
and some of his self-comments mark his adherence to the Projectivist project:

> The poem is not a stream of consciousness, but an area of composition in which I
> work with whatever comes into it. Only words come into it. Sounds and ideas.
> The tone leading of vowels, the various percussions of consonants. The play of
> numbers in stresses and syllables. In which meanings and ideas, themes and
> things seen, arise. So that there is not only a melody of sounds but of images.
> Rimes, the reiteration of formations in the design, even puns, lead into complexi-
> ties of the field. But now the poet works with a sense of parts fitting in relation to
> a design that is larger than the poem. The commune of Poetry becomes so real
> that he sounds each particle in relation to parts of a great story that he knows
> will never be completed. A word has the weight of an actual stone in his hand.
> The tone of a vowel has the color of a wing. ("Introduction," 1968: vi)

Duncan's pervasive intertextuality thus does not stop with other texts but grows
into an interconnection with the (outer and inner) 'real.' Much more often than
Creeley and even Olson he will quote from all kinds of sources. Moreover, he
links his work with the divine, quoting Olson's comment on the connection of
breath and line, then adding: "But there is the third: the inspiration, the breath
of Creation, Spiritus Sanctus, moving between the creator breathing and the
breath of his creature" (1968: viii). Duncan believes in myth as the original embodiment of eternal truths about humans and world order, something he points
out in his long essay "The Truth and Life of Myth: An Essay in Essential Autobiography" (accessible in *Fictive Certainties*, 1985: 1-59). He compiled essay upon essay of what was intended to become *The H.D. Book* (finally published in
2012), an intellectual exchange with the great modernist poet Hilda Doolittle
who was also a mythopoetic writer.

More strongly than others, Duncan believed in the self-writing of the text, in
his/the inspiration that makes him 'receive' his poems and demands that he
should remain true to inspiration even where it appears faulty. Unmistakably,
he follows Freud's notion that what is said is meaningful as an expression of the
sub- and pre-conscious. Consequently, after having struggled repeatedly with
his crucial poem "Often I Am Permitted to Return to a Meadow" (1960), he decided to stop revising his texts, and when he found revision necessary, he would
write another version, that is, another poem. He believed in a trans-personal
community of writers, all intuitively following the law of the cosmos. Thus, the
poem does not impose order on its material but discovers its order.

The esotericism of some of Duncan's writing notwithstanding, he participated actively in the socio-political debate and wrote some of the most impres-

sive poems against the Vietnam War. One of them is "The Fire" in *Bending the Bow*, which is number 13 in the "Passages" series, "a series that extends in an area larger than my work in them. I enter the poem as I entered my own life, moving between an initiation and a terminus I cannot name" (1968: v). The poem consists of three main parts; I and III are formed by hexagrams of six times six words. The concluding hexagram places the words from part I in a different arrangement, having turned the hexagram by 90 degrees. These textual blocks offer the verbal material—mainly monosyllabic words associated with nature, particularly water—that might be used in varied combinations like those found in the old Chinese *Yi Jing*, the Daoist *Book of Changes*.

jump	stone	hand	leaf	shadow	sun
day	plash	coin	light	downstream	fish
first	loosen	under	boat	harbor	circle

(1968: 40, ll. 1-3)

and so forth. The words can be read in any order and, particularly through the 90 degree turn at the end, indicate the permanent change of the forces of origin: heaven/earth, light/dark, soft/firm, giving/receiving. The main part consists of ekphrastic passages: the description of Piero di Cosimo's painting *A Forest Fire*, ending in a vision of peace, "a charmd field" (l. 48) that is contrasted with the description of an unnamed painting by Hieronymus Bosch with its vision of hell and leering faces, which are then identified with those of twentieth-century politicians from Roosevelt and Mussolini through Eisenhower and Nixon and associated with the nightmare these men have brought on earth and that is continued in the Vietnam War that Duncan refers to in his introduction.

The poem is thus a collage of diverse elements, quotations, and references. It is open field poetry by its use of the space of the page and its composition by breath and sound sequences. It is modernist in the use of cultural tradition and its reference to a *Weltgeist*, "Anima Mundi" (l. 53), connecting soul and outer reality. It is postmodern in its radical formal openness—in the aleatoric component of sheer chance that is introduced by the use of the hexagrams that form, in a sense, a multi-component metaphoric field and are also two pieces of concrete poetry, because the lines neo-impressionist-like form the picture of nature, notably the water surface they evoke. It presents two models of dealing with destruction, one where the fire ends in a harmony where the boundaries grow indistinct: "featherd, furrd, leafy / boundaries where even the Furies are birds / and blur" (ll. 45-7), and the other derived from the history of the twentieth century as a success story of the Satanic with its scientific rationality, from which only further destruction can come, unless the universal, the poetic, comes to the rescue.

"Often I Am Permitted to Return to a Meadow," the opening poem of Duncan's volume *The Opening of the Field*, was one of Creeley's favorites, and rightly so because it sets the tone for Duncan's whole endeavor. The title is also the first line as we discover when we read on. This is not a poem without a title, but the double function of its first line as title and beginning of the text serves to pique our curiosity. The line immediately raises expectations and makes us ask: which meadow? And who gives permission? These questions remain open; they could be answered in many ways and thus necessitate the engagement of the reader, requiring his or her meditation. We are asked to follow the text's suggestions, but in the final analysis we are required to bear its fundamental openness.

"Often I Am Permitted to Return to a Meadow" consists of 9 stanzas of 2 or 3 lines and appears to be symmetrically built: 2-3-2-3-3-3-2-3-2; however, since the title is also the first line, we have to prefix a one-line stanza, or else count the title with stanza one—structural ambiguities that correspond to those on any other level of the text. The first stanzas complete the sentence begun in the title:

OFTEN I AM PERMITTED TO RETURN TO A MEADOW

as if it were a scene made-up by the mind,
that is not mine, but is a made place,

that is mine, it is so near to the heart,
an eternal pasture folded in all thought
so that there is a hall therein

that is a made place, created by light
wherefrom the shadows that are forms fall. (1960: 7, ll. 1-8)

The primal place, and hence the primal scene alluded to, might be the speaker's childhood, the mother's womb, paradise, or any other mythic place with positive connotations. It might be a dream scene, or perhaps the field of language and poetry. In the course of the text it must also be seen as the field of the poem as defined by Olson and by Duncan himself. The stunning musicality of Duncan's text, the play of alliteration and of assonance ("made place"), the half rhyme of "mind" and "mine," the internal rhyme of "hall" and "fall" and so forth, which continues through the whole poem, also creates a field of sound that surrounds the reader/listener and carries him or her through the meandering sentence beginning again and again in many (mainly subordinate) clauses that make us wonder what the specific term of reference might be. Does "that is not mine" refer to "a meadow," "a scene," or "the mind" (ll. 3, 1, 2)? An "eternal pasture folded" reminds us of the Christian simile of the Good Shepherd herding his fold, but from the vantage point of "all thought" (l. 5), individual myths are only extracts from and examples of a greater truth, as Duncan pointed out in "The Truth and Life of Myth" (see 1985). In any case we get the idea of a field of reference that may be imaginative, "made up by the mind" (l. 2), that is not simply a natural given but a (divine? human? imaginative?) construction and thus contains an even more strongly enclosed and shielded space: "a hall . . . created by light" (ll. 6-7) that reminds us of Plato's allegory of the cave where the shadows are all that the imprisoned onlookers see of true reality, of true ideas, of "forms" (l. 8). Duncan suspends Plato's distinction between the ideas or "forms" and their shadows, between truth and illusion, thus elevating human comprehension to the level of adequate, albeit pictorial and imaginative, not rational, cognition.

The next stanza names the central mythic content of this imaginative journey:

Wherefrom fall all architectures I am
I say are likenesses of the First Beloved
whose flowers are flames lit to the Lady. (ll. 9-11)

That the constituents of the "I," his "architectures," which must include his creations, should not simply *come* from that "made place" but "fall" like shadows creates a contradictory impression of constructive activity and collapse, a kind of suspension of rational meaning that is well expressed also by the ambiguous syntax, the double (*apokoinu*) construction of "all architectures": "a made place . . . / Wherefrom fall all architectures I am" (ll. 7, 9), versus "all architectures I am / I say are likenesses" (ll. 9-10). The speaker's "architectures," his appear-ance and gifts, are made in the likeness of the "First Beloved" who is, perhaps, his mother or some other longed-for figure. Her external floral ornaments, or the flowers on the meadow, further refer to the dominant female principle, "the Lady." We cannot exclude the possibility, though, that the "First Beloved" might also be a religious reference to Jesus, the beloved Son of God, in whose like-ness the speaker sees himself. The "Lady" then would be the Mother of God.

The confluence and constant reshaping of meaning applies to the mythic core of the text as well. The central stanza 5 appears to contain a revelation and iden-tification of the Lady: "She it is Queen Under The Hill / whose hosts are a dis-turbance of words within words / that is a field folded" (ll. 12-4). However, the apparent symbolic subordination of the "First Beloved" to the "Lady," that is, the "Queen" in the field of myth and religion, may also be just part of an open series of semantic references: meadow—scene—mind—heart—eternal pasture—all thought—hall—all architectures I am—likenesses of the First Beloved—the Lady—Queen Under The Hill. Possible hierarchies/distinctions and similarities/ identities are developed simultaneously through a constant "disturbance of words within words." The "Queen Under The Hill" can be identified as some maternal fertility goddess personifying life and death—Demeter/Kore, like in Creeley's "The Door." She might be the Irish Queen Medb, who is said to have been buried un-der a giant cairn, but also her avatar in literature—the Queen Mab of Shake-speare's *Romeo and Juliet* and of chapter 31 in Melville's *Moby-Dick*—that is, a fairy or other mythological figure having the power to induce and influence dreams. Her "hosts" continue the chain of references by possibly meaning (a) the wafers used in Holy Communion and thus referring to the body of Christ (the First Beloved), (b) her army or multitudes (perhaps army of angels as in the bibli-cal "heavenly hosts"), or (c) some persons inviting guests. What they invite us to do is partake in a game of proliferating meanings, a chain of semantic and acous-tic (note, for instance, the ablaut in "field folded") metamorphoses.

The last line of stanza 5, "that is a field folded" (l. 14), initiates a counter-movement and hints at the possibility of closure, with "folded" referring both to the sheltered herd of the "pasture" and to the folding of paper, a closing of a text. In tune with the Queen Mab allusion, stanza 6 brings the almost sad in-sight: "It is only a dream of the grass blowing / east against the source of the sun / in an hour before the sun's going down" (ll. 15-7), a reference to the inevit-able circularity of day and night, life and death, confirmed by stanza 7: "whose secret we see in a children's game / of ring a round of roses told" (ll. 18-9). Ac-cording to popular theory, the game arose during the plague in England as ei-ther a playful imitation of the behavior of people during the pestilence or else as a charm to ward it off. In any case, at this point the speaker has come full circle and repeats the title line, but this time with more decisive and even defensive connotations: "to return to a meadow / as if it were a given property of the mind / that certain bounds hold against chaos" (ll. 20-2), as if order were possible. But the referential uncertainty of the beginning reappears, and "that is a place of first permission" (l. 23) in stanza 9 may refer to "meadow," as order, namely "a given property of the mind," or else to "chaos." And the final line, "everlasting omen of what is" (l. 24), not only shares this referential uncertainty but is am-biguous in itself. Omens refer to the future. If the meadow, the place of first permission or the mental act associating the speaker with it, is an omen but refers to the present "what is," this means that future and present collapse into one, that the meadow as the place of creativity and emotion is also a reminder of the inevitability of the end out of which fresh beginnings may come. Not accidentally this text about the "field folded" opens the volume *The Opening of the Field*. In its evocation of a mythic center and place or figure of origin it suggests both a deeper structure and the possibility of an endless unfolding of meaning and sounds, "a disturbance of words within words."

Compared to Creeley's "The Door," Duncan's poem, though related in theme and allusions, is much less hesitant and uncertain. Its language is more pervasively musical and literary, its openness more affirmative. While the speaker acknowledges circularity and mortality, he gives his text a richness that is less a testimony of desperate searching than of confident achievement.

5. Denise Levertov, Edward Dorn,
and the Legacy of the Black Mountain School

Among the other significant poets connected with the Black Mountain School, Denise Levertov and Ed Dorn should not go unmentioned. Levertov (1923-1997) is associated with the Black Mountain group primarily through her contributions to the *Black Mountain Review*, as she disclaimed any formal adherence to any school. The British-born poet of Welsh and Russian Jewish ancestry became an American citizen only after her marriage to writer Mitchell Goodman, but this biographical move entailed a turn away from her more conventional English beginnings toward the formal freedom of American modernism and postmodernism. She saw herself as under the influence of William Carlos Williams and of Olson's "Projective Verse," and she formed friendships with Creeley, Duncan, and other American poets. Levertov followed Williams with her idea of "organic form," "the concept that there is a form in all things (and in our experience) which the poet can discover and reveal" (1973: 7). She differs from Olson in seeing his notion of breath as a shaping unit often not realizable in practice, and prefers to relate the poem's organic form to the poet's "*inner* voice" (ibid.: 23; original emphasis). Organic poetry then, is the exploratory "method of apperception, i.e., of recognizing what we perceive, and is based on an intuition of an order, a form beyond forms, in which forms partake, and of which man's creative works are analogies . . ." (ibid.: 7). Levertov modifies Creeley's and Olson's dictum into "Form is never more than a *revelation* of content" (ibid.: 13; original emphasis). In her poetic practice this results in a lovely play of formal elements like line breaks and stanza length or sound patterns on the one hand, and the sentence—the development of an argument—on the other, as in the speaker's self-definition as a woman toying with traditional and stereotypical ideas in "Stepping Westward" (1967):

> What is green in me
> darkens, muscadine.
>
> If woman is inconstant,
> good, I am faithful to
>
> ebb and flow, I fall
> in season and now
>
> is a time of ripening. (1983: 165, ll. 1-7)

The imagery and the amazing aural quality of Levertov's poetry here deconstruct rigid patterns of thought and perception. For example, the half rhyme of "green" and "muscadine" creates an intensification toward the end of the stanza, with the second term (referring to a kind of grape) bringing in the notion of something choice and delicious, foreshadowing the "ripening" in stanza 4 that calls into question a rigid, conventional notion of constancy. As in many of her poems, it is the concrete physical detail that carries the poem forward, step by step, as in the final lines:

> If I bear burdens
>
> they begin to be remembered
> as gifts, goods, a basket
>
> of bread that hurts
> my shoulders but closes me
>
> in fragrance. I can
> eat as I go. (ll. 26-32)

More than her late religious poetry, Levertov's angry Vietnam War poems and other political poetry will be remembered even though they may be less formally pleasing.

Edward (Ed) Dorn (1929-1999) did indeed study at Black Mountain College. He was strongly influenced by Charles Olson's poetics but managed to develop a highly individual way of writing. Although he traveled widely and taught some years in England, he is primarily a poet of the American West in a broad sense that includes the Native Americans honored in many of his texts. Dorn is the most political poet of the group, a modern-day satirist and social critic. He is most famous for his long narrative poem *Slinger* (1975), consisting of four books and a section titled "The Cycle" that were published individually over several years. The term *Slinger* derives from the original title and hero, *Gunslinger.*

> I met in Mesilla
> The Cautious Gunslinger
> of impeccable personal smoothness
> and slender leather encased hands
> folded casually
> to make his knock. (1975: n.p., ll. 1-6)

In addition to the narrator and the mythic eponymous protagonist, there is the gunslinger's drug-addicted, talking horse by the name of Claude Lévi-Strauss; they are on a quest for Howard Hughes, the celebrated, mysterious millionaire, aviator, film-maker, and philanthropist who symbolizes the negative developments taken by modern mankind. The mixture of Western slang, elements from pop music, drug jargon and scholarly speech, wordplay, and numerous intertextual quotes and allusions make this long poem a unique reading experience.

Place and history are at the center of Dorn's writing, and he therefore engaged with Olson's Gloucester both in his long essay "What I See in the Maximus Poems" (1960) and in the poem "From Gloucester Out" (1964). But in the travel poem "Idaho Out" (1965) Dorn finds his own, more critical voice. He draws a grim picture of the Midwest—

> So black & red simplot fertilizer smoke
>
> drifts its excremental way
> down the bottle of our
> valley (1978: 34, ll. 5-9)

—and its Mormon past, but also illustrates the beauty of people and land-scapes. The limitations of Idaho are not only geographical but ideological, and it serves as an epitome of what went wrong with America and what is also a heavy mortgage on its literature: "it is truly the West / as no other place, / ruined by an ambition and religion / cut, by a cowboy use of her nearly virgin self / . . . this / is the birthplace / of Mr. Pound / and Hemingway in his own mouth / chose to put a shotgun" (49, ll. 518-29).

After the closing of Black Mountain College, Olson, Creeley, Duncan, Lever-tov, Dorn, and the other Black Mountain poets continued to write open form poetry wherever they settled, and they exchanged their ideas with other lyrical groups and individuals, notably in New York and San Francisco. The efforts of Creeley and others to resuscitate Black Mountain College at the State University of New York, Buffalo, as "Black Mountain II" resulted in an interdisciplinary studies program and a journal. The influence of the Black Mountain Group is also acknowledged by the later LANGUAGE poets who radicalized some of its linguistic explorative experiments. In 2010, The Black Mountain North Symposi-um—a conference and arts festival in Rochester, New York—commemorated the centenary of Olson's birth. The symposium brochure summed up the spread of Black Mountain ideas in the various arts and, in particular, concerning poetry:

> When Black Mountain closed its doors, the exodus of students and faculty to San Francisco and New York City helped precipitate tremendous explosions of radical creativity. Closer to home, Charles Olson, Eric Bentley, John Wieners, and Robert Creeley helped transform the University of Buffalo into what has been labeled "Black Mountain II." Ed Sanders in Woodstock, Albert Glover at St. Lawrence University, Don Byrd and Pierre Joris at SUNY/Albany, and Jack Clarke at Buffalo helped continue the Black Mountain poetry tradition, along with frequent visitors to WNY like Joel Oppenheimer, Jonathan Williams and Robert Duncan. Literary centers like Rochester's Writers & Books and NY State Literary Center and Buffalo's Just Buffalo and Hallwalls Gallery, as well as poetry societies like Rochester's Just Poets and Poetry Society of Rochester and Alba-ny's Rootdrinker Institute, did much to find an audience for innovative poetry beyond the academy. Writers & Books also helped showcase the ASL Poetry Re-naissance in the 1980s, a deaf poetry movement influenced by the Beat and Black Mountain traditions (Cornell 2010).

The participation—not only of historians, but of active writers and artists—shows how Black Mountain College's legacy has continued to influence the in-tellectual scene to this day.

Bibliography

Selected Primary Literature

Allen, Donald (ed.). 1960. *The New American Poetry 1945-1960*. New York: Grove P.

Creeley, Robert. 1970. *A Quick Graph: Collected Notes and Essays*. Ed. Donald Allen. San Francisco: Four Seasons Foundation.

——. 1982. *The Collected Poems of Robert Creeley, 1945-1975*. Berkeley and Los Angeles: U of California P.

——. 2008. *The Collected Poems of Robert Creeley, 1975-2005*. Berkeley and Los Angeles: U of California P.

Dorn, Edward. 1975. *Slinger*. Berkeley: Wingbow P.

——. 1978. *Selected Poems*. Bolinas: Grey Fox P.

——. 2012. *Collected Poems*. Manchester: Carcanet P.

Duncan, Robert. 1944. "The Homosexual in Society." In: *Politics: A Monthly Review* (Aug.): 209-11.

——. 1960. "Often I Am Permitted to Return to a Meadow." <http://www.poets.org/viewmedia.php/prmMID/15708>. Web. 14 Oct. 2014.

——. 1960. *The Opening of the Field*. New York: New Directions.

——. 1964. *Roots and Branches*. New York: New Directions.

——. 1968. *Bending the Bow*. New York: New Directions.

——. 1985. *Fictive Certainties: Essays*. New York: New Directions.

——. 2012. *The H.D. Book*. Ed. Michael Boughn and Victor Coleman. Berkeley and Los Angeles: U of California P.

Levertov, Denise. 1973. *The Poet in the World*. New York: New Directions.

——. 1983. *Poems 1960-1967*. New York: New Directions.

—— and Robert Creeley. 1980-1996. *The Complete Correspondence*. Ed. George F. Butterick. Santa Barbara, CA: Black Sparrow.

Olson, Charles. 1947. *Call Me Ishmael*. New York: Reynal & Hitchcock.

——. 1966. *Selected Writings*. Ed. Robert Creeley. New York: New Directions.

——. 1950. "I, Maximus of Gloucester, to You." <http://www.poetryfoundation.org/poem/176950>. Web. 14 Oct. 2014.

——. 1974. *Additional Prose: A Bibliography on America, Proprioception and Other Notes and Essays*. Ed. George F. Butterick. Bolinas: Four Seasons Foundation.

——. 1983. *The Maximus Poems*. Ed. George F. Butterick. Berkeley and Los Angeles: U of California P.

——. 1987. *The Collected Poems of Charles Olson. Excluding the Maximus poems*. Ed. George F. Butterick. Berkeley and Los Angeles et al.: U of California P.

Pound, Ezra. 1968. *Literary Essays of Ezra Pound*. New York: New Directions.

Selected Secondary Literature

Butterick, George F. 1978. *A Guide to the* Maximus Poems *of Charles Olson*. Berkeley and Los Angeles: U of California P.

Indispensable tool offering numberless helpful references.

Christensen, Paul. 1979. *Charles Olson: Call Him Ishmael*. Austin: U of Texas P.

Contains a section on Olson's role for other Black Mountain poets.

Cooley, Dennis. 1980. "The Poetics of Robert Duncan." In: *Boundary 2* 8.2: 45-73.

Good and compact overview.

Dewey, Anne. 2007. *Beyond Maximus: The Construction of Public Voice in Black Mountain Poetry*. Palo Alto, CA: Stanford UP.

Important study of the development of the group and its use of field poetics for a combination of avant-garde poetry and public voice.

Duberman, Martin. 2009. *Black Mountain: An Exploration in Community*. Evanston, IL: Northwestern UP.

Reissue of the classic history of Black Mountain College of 1972.

Foster, Edward Halsey. 1994. *Understanding the Black Mountain Poets*. Pembroke, NC: U of North Carolina P.

Foster's study offers a general introduction to major aspects of the Black Mountain poets.

Fredman, Stephen and Steve McCaffery (eds.). 2010. *Form, Power, and Person in Robert Creeley's Life and Work*. Iowa City: U of Iowa P.

Jarnot, Lisa. 2012. *Robert Duncan, The Ambassador from Venus: A Biography*. Berkeley and Los Angeles: U of California P.

This is a definitive biography and analysis of Duncan's literary development.

Katz, Vincent (ed.). 2013. *Black Mountain College: Experiment in Art*. Cambridge, MA: MIT P.

Focuses on the fine arts but contains relevant material about some of the poets.

Merrill, Thomas F. 1982. *The Poetry of Charles Olson: A Primer*. Newark: U of Delaware P.

Merrill's book is a most useful and reliable introduction.

Paul, Sherman. 1978. *Olson's Push: Origin, Black Mountain and Recent American Poetry*. Baton Rouge: Louisiana State UP.

Paul's volume is a groundbreaking study.

Schiffer, Reinhold. 1972. "Vers, Energie und Realität. Bemerkungen zur Poetik Charles Olsons." In: *Poetica* 2: 212-32.

This essay contains one of the best short introductions into Olson's poetics.

Further References

Bertholf, Robert J. and Ian W. Reid (eds.). 1980. *Robert Duncan: Scales of the Marvelous*. New York: Norton.

Butterick, George F. 1980. "Charles Olson and the Postmodern Advance." In: *Iowa Review* 11: 4-27.

Byrd, Don. 1980. *Charles Olson's Maximus*. Urbana: U of Illinois P.

Cornell, Tom. 2010. "A Symposium in Rochester, New York." *Black Mountain Symposium*. <http://www.blackmountainnorth.org/>. Web. 14 Oct. 2014.

Corrigan, Matthew (ed.). 1974. *Charles Olson: Essays, Reminiscences, Reviews*. In: *Boundary 2* 2.1/2 (special issue).

Davidson, Michael. 1989. *The San Francisco Renaissance: Poetics and Community at Mid-century*. New York: Cambridge UP.

Davies, Alice Susanna. 1996. "Creeley Among Others: An American Poetics in Context." Diss. U of Durham, 1996. <http://etheses.dur.ac.uk/6192/1/6192_3546.PDF>. Web. 14 Oct. 2014.

Edelberg, Cynthia. 1978. *Robert Creeley's Poetry: A Critical Introduction*. Albuquerque: U of New Mexico P.

Faas, Ekbert. 2001. *Robert Creeley: A Biography*. Hanover, MA: McGill-Queen's UP.

Ford, Arthur L. 1978. *Robert Creeley*. Boston: Twayne.

Gelpi, Albert and Robert Bertholf (eds.). 2006. *Robert Duncan and Denise Levertov: The Poetry of Politics, the Politics of Poetry*. Palo Alto, CA: Stanford UP.

Maynard, James (ed.). 2011. *(Re:)Working the Ground: Essays on the Late Writings of Robert Duncan*. New York: Palgrave Macmillan.

Mersman, James E. 1974. *Out of the Vietnam Vortex: A Study of Poets and Poetry against the War*. Lawrence: UP of Kansas.

Mesch, Harald. 1982. "Robert Creeley's Epistemopathic Path." In: *Sagetrieb* 1.3 (Special issue Robert Creeley): 57-85.

Nelson, Cary. 1981. *Our Last First Poets: Vision and History in Contemporary American Poetry*. Champaign, IL: U of Illinois P.

Paul, Sherman. 1981. *The Lost America of Love: Rereading Robert Creeley, Edward Dorn and Robert Duncan*. Baton Rouge: Louisiana State UP.

Spanos, William (ed.). 1978. *Robert Creeley: A Gathering*. In: *Boundary 2* 6.3/7.1 (special issue).

von Hallberg, Robert. 1978. *Charles Olson: The Scholar's Art*. Cambridge, MA: Harvard UP.

Wilson, John (ed.). 1987. *Robert Creeley's Life and Work: A Sense of Increment*. Ann Arbor, MI: U of Michigan P.

20.

Beat Poetry and the Cold War

Lawrence Ferlinghetti's "In Goya's Greatest Scenes"
and Allen Ginsberg's "Howl"

Philipp Löffler

1. The Formation of the Beat Generation

The Beat Generation emerged in the United States as a central literary and cultural movement located primarily in and around greater New York and San
Francisco during the immediate postwar years. Writers generally associated
with the core of the Beat Generation include Allen Ginsberg, Jack Kerouac,
Lawrence Ferlinghetti, Gregory Corso, Michael McClure, William S. Burroughs,
and Gary Snyder. But depending on the anthology students pick up, there are a
good dozen other figures who also count as Beat writers, who purportedly col-
laborated with Beat writers, and who influenced the evolution of the movement
in some way or another (cf. Charters 1992: xv-xxxvi; Johnson 2013: 80-94). As
with so many literary movements, there is no exact starting point of the Beat
Generation as a collective artistic project. John Clellon Holmes's landmark
essay "This is the Beat Generation," published in 1952 in the *New York Times
Magazine*, is one of the first programmatic statements. Many scholars believe,
however, that Ginsberg's Six Gallery reading of "Howl" on October 13, 1955—
legendarily portrayed in Kerouac's *The Dharma Bums*—marks the most significant formative event in the development of the Beats as a group. The centrality
of "Howl" has persisted ever since, not least because of Lawrence Ferlinghetti's
publishing initiative and the ensuing obscenity case that subsequently boosted
Ferlinghetti's own popularity and his career as a poet during the early Cold War
years.

The popular, non-academic reception of the Beat Generation and their legacy
still seems to depend primarily on a few canonical works, such as Allen Ginsberg's "Howl," Jack Kerouac's *On the Road*, or William S. Burroughs's *Naked
Lunch*. These canonical works have come to represent the very essence of Beat
poetics and Beat life, featuring homelessness, mobility, drug abuse, and ethnic,
sexual, or religious border crossings in provocative, non-conventional poetic
language. In the broadest sense, the idea of Beat literature was to challenge the
stability and social cohesiveness of postwar American culture and society and to
advertise collectively a viable life alternative to suburban middle class homes
and the corporate liberalism of the Cold War era.

Such homogenized images of the Beat Generation are not completely inaccu-
rate, but they belie the fact that the movement did not consist exclusively of
like-minded individuals rejecting Cold War America in the pursuit of a shared
political or aesthetic agenda. The main roster of the group resists easy categorization, and a shared agenda never existed, although there are a couple of programmatic theoretical statements about Beat writing and Beat life that are frequently used by scholars to outline the broader aesthetic and political concerns
of the group. Now commemorated and studied as a relatively cohesive artistic
formation, the movement originally consisted of a rather loosely connected

group of individuals with diverse and often contradictory literary influences and interests. Even the term "Beat" has remained rather ambivalent, oscillating between notions of desolation and exhilaration, despair and optimism (cf. Kerouac 1993: 55-65, 69-74; Ginsberg 2000 [1981]: 236-9; Holmes 1952: 10; Kupferberg 1992 [1960]: 385-7).

The literature of the Beat Generation comprises a startling variety of literary styles, genres, and performative practices that jeopardize traditional forms of periodization. Writers such as Allen Ginsberg and Gary Snyder appropriated Romantic poetic traditions, notably William Blake and Walt Whitman, as they reflected lyrically on their political and social environments. Other texts were produced in the vein of Modernist avant-garde poetics. First propagated by the Black Mountain School, the idea of the poem as an "open field" was a major influence on the Beat's experimentation with voice and breath. A similar focus on the somatic dimension of poetry can be found in various cross-disciplinary art projects that sought to combine the experimental writing of the Beats with both the music of the postwar jazz scene and the techniques of abstract expressionism in painting (cf. Belgrad 1998: 179-220). A quite different sense of poetic fusion can be found in the works of authors like Gary Snyder and Philip Whalen, who feature romantic explorations of natural landscapes on the basis of Chinese and Japanese models of poetry and religious song. Other authors, such as Lawrence Ferlinghetti, Bob Kaufman, and Jack Kerouac, used their texts to inquire into contemporary American popular culture, openly rejecting the New Critical branch of elite Modernist writing. Finally, French surrealism represents another, particularly fruitful, artistic influence on the Beat community, as it is reflected in the works of Jack Spicer, Michael McClure, and Philip Lamantia.

Given this vast spectrum of styles and performative practices, the term 'Beat Generation' seems deceptively organic. For the purpose of this article, I will use it as an umbrella term for a number of conceptually related literary experiments that occurred simultaneously in a few geographically limited regions and cities on both the East Coast and the West Coast of the U.S. between the early 1950s and the late 1960s. What provides for the sense of group coherence that we still associate with the Beat Generation can then be explained by three overlapping historical and conceptual frameworks:

a. The postwar years saw the creation of new sites and venues of artistic production that fused the prestige of traditional institutions and schools with the lure of improvised coffee house and jazz bar gatherings in which many Beat writers performed their works. After World War II, New York and San Francisco became ideal urban contact zones in which the cultural and intellectual mainstream—prominently represented by the big universities and art institutes—was absorbed and gradually transformed by a growing countercultural avant-garde. Many Beat writers originally led a double life. While fashioning themselves as independent, creative bohemians, they were also closely affiliated with the institutional structures of or even enrolled at Columbia University, NYU, UC Berkeley, or at one of the newly founded art schools and galleries in New York City and in the Bay Area, such as the California School of Fine Arts or the King UBU Gallery, which later became the iconic Six Gallery that featured Ginsberg's first "Howl" performance.

b. The conceptual backbone of many Beat projects—as diverse as they were —was a shared "performative attitude toward language" (Davidson 2013: 70; cf.

also 1989: 3-60). Beat writers took the Modernist obsession with literary form seriously, but they transgressed the legacy of their heroes—Ezra Pound and William Carlos Williams are constant figures of reference—by staging the very emergence of form as a collective and often improvised public event. In a well-known prefatory note, Jack Kerouac compared the underlying idea of his *Mexico City Blues* to "an afternoon Jazz session on Sunday" (1959: i). And the individual poems are described as "choruses" that need to be performed musically (ibid.). Hence, while the surrounding fields of artistic production were gradually transformed into public platforms of social, political, and aesthetic exchange, the Beats simultaneously crafted a poetics that was bound to transcend the limits of the written word.

c. A more general and fundamental dimension of the Beats' self-understanding as a group can be explained by the shared experience of the Cold War period. In 1958, Herb Caen, Pulitzer Prize winner and longtime editorialist at the *San Francisco Chronicle*, fittingly referenced the launching of the Soviet satellite Sputnik in one of his pieces on the Bay poets as he added the suffix "nik" to the term "Beat," thus underlining the close proximity between the rise of the American Beatnik and the centrality of global Cold War politics during the 1950s and 1960s. Beat poetics and the non-conventional lifestyle of many Beat writers evolved independently as unique forms of literary self-fashioning in the postwar decades. But the movement as a whole must still be read in direct relation to such events as the Korean War, the political persecution of the American Left under McCarthy, the Rosenberg case, and growing racial tensions in American higher education. If the Beats never stood for just one coherent poetic or political program, their poetics were nonetheless crucially defined by the ways the Cold War shaped American cultural life.

2. Writing in the Shadows of the Cold War:
Lawrence Ferlinghetti's "In Goya's Greatest Scenes"

Lawrence Ferlinghetti published Ginsberg's *Howl and Other Poems* shortly after Ginsberg's Six Gallery reading as volume four in his Pocket Poets Series at San Francisco City Lights Books in 1956. Two years later, Ferlinghetti's *A Coney Island of the Mind* appeared. The historical proximity of both publications, and the fact that *Howl and Other Poems* was banned on charges of obscene language a year after it came out, provides reasons enough to discuss Ginsberg and Ferlinghetti as two central and likeminded members of the Beat Generation. It seems even more plausible, however, to discuss Allen Ginsberg's and Lawrence Ferlinghetti's poetry to illustrate the extent to which the Cold War world became an integral reference frame for larger parts of Beat poetry and Beat performance. Both politically and poetically, "Howl" and "In Goya's Greatest Scenes" convey a pervasive anxiety about the pathologies of American Cold War society, about the limits of individuality, and about the threat of psychological and emotional alienation. Both poems center on descriptions of sickness, dying, and despair, scrutinizing contemporary America in a combination of lament and aggressive accusation as if the country was deliberately turned into a massive site of mental and physical pain.

"In Goya's Greatest Scenes" imparts this sense of sickness and despair through juxtaposed readings of Francisco Goya's "greatest scenes" (presumably based on his later war paintings) and postwar American urban industrial land-scapes. Both parts are featured in two individual sections of almost equal length connected through a hyperbolic blending, in which Goya's works are declared to be "so bloody real / it is as if they really still existed / And they do" (Ferlinghetti 1993 [1958]: 79, ll. 19-21). The paintings described in the first part of the poem (ll. 1-20) are never clearly identified, but based on the imagery and the domi-nant tone readers can assume they are part of Goya's "The Disasters of War" series (1810-1814). The poem begins with a lengthy characterization of "the people of the world" (l. 2) at the very moment at which they became what the poem suggests is a "'suffering humanity'" (l. 5). The impression of suffering is intensified and further detailed in the poem's first section when the speaker ob-serves that "the people of the world" are captured in a "veritable rage / of adver-sity" (ll. 7-8); they are placed "under cement skies" (l. 11) with all that is part "of the / 'imagination of disaster'" (ll. 17-8). The imagination of disaster is further specified in a post-apocalyptic setting of death and dying: the natural world no longer exists in its original form; there are only "blasted trees" and "slippery gib-bets" amongst "cadavers" that are eaten up by "carnivorous cocks" (ll. 12-5).

In spite of such devastating imagery, however, the struggle Goya depicts—that of the Spanish people against Napoleonic usurpation—is motivated by laudable political ideals. Ferlinghetti's implementation of Goya's paintings as the visual and political backdrop against which his poem develops exceeds the purpose of mere lamentation, protest, or shock. His poetics of disaster convey a liberationist program that ultimately inspires the poem as a whole. Although this may only be of biographical interest, it should be noted that Ferlinghetti was a committed left-wing thinker. He visited Fidel Castro in the wake of the Cuban revolution and never stopped believing that the Capitalist system was inevitably going to collapse. In that sense, the suffering depicted in Goya can be read as an anticipatory allegory in the poem for the suffering of the American nation as it awaits the coming of the revolution. And still, "In Goya's Greatest Scenes" never fully articulates this idea of liberation. If there is a more detailed political agenda the speaker wants to raise, it remains coated at first sight by bitterness and despair. As we will see later, the poem's lack of a clear and posi-tive political vision is compensated for on the level of style and composition.

The bleak atmosphere created in this first section is continued in the sec-ond. Structurally linked by the single line "And they do" (l. 21), both sections are additionally bridged by the use of similar imagery. The "cement skies" are connected semantically to the "concrete continent" (l. 29), and Goya's people of the world "are the same people" (l. 26) today; "only the landscape is changed" (l. 22). Whereas in part I there are "carnivorous cocks" that live on cadavers, in part II there are "engines . . . that devour America" (l. 37). Though the poem it-self never explicitly suggests this comparison, the speaker's fear or abhorrence of the machine world that dominates and ultimately cripples America may be viewed in direct relation to the technological achievements of the postwar world: the American nuclear weapons program, the Soviet-American space race, the breakthrough of the American car as a standard middle-class commodity. These supposed achievements drive people away from their true identity; they are blinded by a world of "false windmills" (l. 25), and as they begin to follow the homogenizing logic of postwar America, they reproduce mechanically and with-out a sense of direction the very system that oppresses them, just like "de-mented roosters" (l. 25) walking back and forth in their cages.

The context of the poem's lament is very concrete and yet, in its first section, the poem defies exact geographical locations and instead presents its bleak scenery "in an abstract landscape" (l. 12), thereby additionally emphasizing the universality of its message and its assumed readership. The second part, however, counters this sense of universality by referencing "a concrete continent" (l. 29) with freeways that are "fifty lanes wide" (l. 28) and with "bland billboards" (l. 30) that no longer advertise the individual's pursuit of happiness but instead reveal "imbecile illusions of happiness" (l. 31). Hence, although "American" is not mentioned before the poem's final line (l. 37), the beginning of the second section helps readers identify the specifically national setting, as the speaker (and possible alter ego of Ferlinghetti) uses the inclusive "we" to project Goya's vision onto a present day context (l. 23). The abstract landscape under "cement skies" described in part I is thus turned into a very specific dystopian image of America as it is "devour[ed]" (l. 37) by the very engines the country has helped to create.

The same shift from universality to particularity can be observed in the poem's temporal and historical dimension. Though readers learn in the first section that, in Goya, "the people of the world" are shown "exactly at the moment when / they first attained the title of / 'suffering humanity'" (ll. 3-5), the poem never fully discloses when this moment took place or exactly what triggered it. Two readings seem possible here. One option would be that the poem's historical dimension must be interpreted as part of a larger critique of the emergence of the modern world with all the supposed achievements that are nowadays attributed to the rise of American consumer capitalism. Such a reading makes sense particularly in light of the poem's second section in which the speaker explicitly links Goya's visionary insight into the suffering of the world to the ills of contemporary urban America: the people of the world "are so bloody real / it is as if they really still existed" (ll. 19-20). The evocative "people of the world" in the second line of the poem may or may not be a deliberate reference to the proletarian internationalism proclaimed in the *Communist Manifesto* ('Proletarians of the World, Unite!'). But such speculations are irrelevant for a reading of Ferlinghetti's text in which the exposure of America's spiritual and social hollowness is understood within the context of a more general critique of the constraints of global modernity. A second, equally suggestive reading would be to interpret the speaker's use of "Goya's greatest scenes" in the first part of the poem as a Christian allegory implemented to illustrate the shift from a prelapsarian to a postlapsarian world. The biblical fall of humanity thus imagined would then figure structurally and thematically as the pretext for a decidedly secular critique of contemporary American culture and politics in part II of the poem. As in the secular political reading, the religious allegory provides for an immediately generalizing argument that translates the specific American context described by the poem into the spheres of a more global, universal history of mankind.

Whichever route readers take to solve this puzzle, "In Goya's Greatest Scenes" remains a text that—precisely because it oscillates between the universal and the particular, the global and the national—conveys the heated political atmosphere that pervaded American Cold War culture. The poem captures the idea of a homogenized, oppressive national identity as it was reflected by the political, social, and infrastructural transformations in the United States of the late 1940s and 1950s: the invention of the U.S. as a legitimate ideological counterforce to the Soviet Union and the massive privacy violations of the House Un-American Activities Committee, the Cold War celebration of the nuclear family and the parallel rise of a streamlined middle-class consumerism, and the creation of a "concrete continent" with "freeways fifty lanes wide" that gradually absorbed romanticized images of the old highway system as it was still celebrated in many Beat novels. Moreover, "the imagination of disaster" invoked by the poem expresses the constant fear of nuclear destruction, which was a concrete reality of ordinary Cold War life and simultaneously reinforced and transcended the confines of American domestic life during these years (cf. May 1988: 10-29). Openly addressing these haunting visions, "In Goya's Greatest Scenes" not only provides for a desperate and thus critical outlook on contemporary American culture, the poem also makes political intervention imperative for the improvement of life, as if maintaining that resistance to social and political coercion is possible at any given moment. This message, however, is never spelled out explicitly and is instead incorporated into the form of the poem itself.

The formal structure of "In Goya's Greatest Scenes" seems to reflect the implicit plea for resistance on several levels as it defies generic models of poetic form. We do not find a regular meter, there is no detectable rhyme scheme, and the organization of the poem as a whole appears to result from the intuitive coupling of images rather than from a preconceived series of stanzas or a specific number of verses. Despite the apparent structural openness of the text, however, Ferlinghetti's poem is a deliberate rhetorical artifact. Its clusters of images are carefully placed next to or against one another, and there are several verses that alliterate internally or feature assonant vowel chains, thus creating a sense of momentum or flow of voice that underlines crucial elements of the poem's general argumentative frame ("veritable rage / of adversity," "babies and bayonets," "bent statues bats wings and beaks," "slippery gibbets," "cadavers and carnivorous cocks," "concrete continent," "bland billboards / illustrating imbecile illusions of happiness," (ll. 7-31). Likewise, the line breaks are used strategically to delay or accelerate the reading pace and thus emphasize certain key phrases or argumentative turning points throughout the poem, as in lines 2, 5, 18, 21, 26, and 37. Especially when the poem is read aloud, its formal structure seems to correspond almost naturally to the rhythm of the verbal performance. The prose-like character of "In Goya's Greatest Scenes" is thus underwritten by the rhythmicality of reading and a corresponding textual format that breaks open the linearity of prose discourse and installs a tonal and thematic hierarchy that crucially highlights the poem's underlying political agenda.

The overt rejection of traditional poetic structures in Ferlinghetti's text may in itself be read as a proclamation of individual freedom and the non-conformist poetics with which the Beat Generation is traditionally associated. The formal structure of "In Goya's Greatest Scenes" would then reenact exactly that which the poem bemoans as a mere impossibility: the autonomy of the individual poetic mind and a powerful refutation of the very ideological apparatus the speaker finds responsible for the death of the individual subject. On a more strictly poetic note, the formal composition of "In Goya's Greatest Scenes" must be contextualized as a salient example of the Beats' commitment to spontaneous writing as it is outlined in several key essays. Although there is a variety of equally important texts, the most popular manifestations of the spontaneity idea may be found in Jack Kerouac's "Essentials of Spontaneous Prose," in his "Belief and Technique for Modern Prose," and in Allen Ginsberg's "Notes Written on Finally

Recording *Howl.*" What conjoins these rather theoretical accounts of Beat writing is the assumption that written and spoken words must no longer be neatly distinguished from one another. Rather, the writing process should resemble the very working of the mind as it translates into words or verbal images. In Kerouac's "Essentials" then, readers are encouraged to follow the "free deviation (association) of mind into limitless blow-on-subject seas of thought, swimming in sea of English with no discipline other than rhythms of rhetorical exaltation" (1993 [1957]: 69). And Ginsberg recalls how, in the process of writing "Howl," he discovered the "single breath unit" (2000 [1959]: 230) as the central device for determining poetic structure.

The perpetual emphasis on the centrality of voice and breath echoes the continued influence of the Black Mountain poets who insisted on abandoning the controlling authority of the lyrical subject in favor of an unconstrained bodily expression of poetic truth through life itself (cf. Olson 1967 [1950]: 15-31; Creeley 1988 [1951]: 464). Ferlinghetti's "In Goya's Greatest Scenes" acknowledges the physicality and bodily force of poetic language in similar ways. But whereas many Black Mountain poets and, in fact, many Beat writers used the idea of the body in the creation of the poem as a novel form of spiritual self-introspection, in Ferlinghetti's text poetic form serves a more concretely political purpose. The formal organization of the poem counteracts as well as underlines the dystopian image of an American nation suffering from the very world of engines it deliberately helped to create and sustain. And this is exactly the point at which "In Goya's Greatest Scenes" connects with Ginsberg's "Howl" as a political statement about the Cold War world.

3. Singing the American Body Electric: Allen Ginsberg's "Howl"

Almost immediately after its first performance on October 13, 1955, Allen Ginsberg's "Howl" attained the status of a literary classic, not least because it was banned on the basis of obscenity charges for a brief period of time between 1956 and 1957. Early on, critics and fans alike considered the poem to be an iconic document recording both the collective mindset of the postwar American counterculture and the onset of a new wave of experimental poetry that would translate the legacies of the Modernist avant-gardes into the realm of contemporary American popular culture. The events that lead up to the obscenity trial and the several responses to its outcome are described comprehensively in Ferlinghetti's "Horn on Howl," where he calls Ginsberg's text "the most significant single long poem to be published in this country since World War II, perhaps since T.S. Eliot's *Four Quartets*" (1992 [1959]: 255). However one understands the poem, "Howl" is first and foremost a very astute poetic response to the predominance of American Cold War paranoia. Similarly to Ferlinghetti's "In Goya's Greatest Scenes," Ginsberg's "Howl" opens in the form of a lament in which the speaker bemoans the suppression of the individual and its creative capacities through social and political coercion:

> I saw the best minds of my generation destroyed by madness, starving
> hysterical naked,
> dragging themselves through the negro streets at dawn looking for an angry fix,
> angelheaded hipsters burning for the ancient heavenly connection to the starry
> dynamo in the machinery of night, (1988 [1956]: 126-33, ll. 1-3)

Over the course of three lengthy sections and an additional forth section titled "Footnote on Howl," the poem catalogues in minute detail the fate and suffering of what the speaker asserts is "my generation" (part I); in part II the poem shifts its focus to the oppressive forces to which the speaker and his fellow poets are exposed—prominently outlined in the concept of "Moloch"—in order to conclude, in part III, with an overt and in many ways more hopeful address to Ginsberg's friend and alleged lover Carl Solomon. Ginsberg met Solomon during a brief period at a psychiatric institution that is referenced to in the poem as "Rockland"; the poem uses Rockland as a manifest version of the suppressive political and metaphysical energies that we find described in detail as "Moloch" in section II. "Howl" ends with an ecstatic vision of the speaker, or Ginsberg's alter ego, in which the walls of "Rockland" fall apart and Carl Solomon returns to Ginsberg's home in Berkeley, California.

The idea of a "suffering humanity" in Ferlinghetti's poem is also central to Ginsberg's notion of the "best minds of my generation" (l. 1). But unlike "In Goya's Greatest Scenes," "Howl" begins with a very personal, subjective account of the postwar years, listing a multiplicity of personal events, memories, and mere thought associations taken directly out of Ginsberg's own biography. Readers will notice immediately how consciously the poem's speaker locates himself as the lyric persona within the domain of the everyday. Against earlier conceptions of the poet as professionalized aestheticist, Ginsberg's speaker presents himself as a different type of outcast: a street-life man without attachments to home or family, crossing the country from east to west, striving for the new and the unknown, all the while realizing how hard such a life can be in a society that treats the hipster in madhouses with "Metrazol electricity hydrotherapy psychotherapy occupational therapy pingpong & amnesia" (l. 65). The descriptions and memories are firmly embedded within recognizable urban environments, and so part I of "Howl" may be understood as a wide panorama of Beat life, reiterating some of the most popular ideas and images typically linked with the Beats' countercultural poetic agenda: drug use and drug-induced writing (cf. ll. 2, 9, 11, 14, 33, 44), jazz music (cf. ll. 4, 27, 57-8, 75), life on the road—both within and outside the U.S. (cf. ll. 9, 20-9, 42, 58-9)—, the centrality of big coastal cities (New York in the case of "Howl" (cf. ll. 14-7, 43-6, 55-6)), anticapitalism (cf. ll. 30-1), open sexuality (cf. ll. 32-42), and the search for spiritual transcendence (cf. l. 72). Part I consists of a single sequence of syntactically linked exclamations, complaints, and angry demands. The recurring "who" provides the base pattern in the reading process, while the intermediate lines present improvised images, associations, and memories that the speaker uses to identify more concretely "my generation" (l. 1). The vocabulary used throughout the poem is drastic, replete with vulgarities and explicit imagery.

"Howl" is, of course, more than an accumulation of clichés presented in drastic language. Despite its aggressive performative tone, the poem as a whole follows a rather traditional argumentative structure in that it stages the "best minds of my generation" of section I in opposition to an antagonizing system or power structure that the speaker addresses as "Moloch" in section II (ll. 78-87). Both parts are linked in the opening lines of the second part as the reader is asked rhetorically to speculate about those forces responsible for the death of the "best minds": "What sphinx of cement and aluminum bashed open their skulls and ate up their brains and imagination?" (l. 77). Section III, then, functions much like a resolution of the conflict between the best minds and Moloch, which has been established through sections I and II, indicating a future possible state of freedom "where we wake up electrified out of the coma by our own souls' airplanes roaring over the roof" (l. 127). In the final lines of the poem, the "coma" connotes a severe moment of alienation caused by "Solitude! Filth! Ugliness!" (l. 78). This state of alienation is further specified as a non-identity between body and soul ("Moloch in whom I am a consciousness without a body," (l. 85) and thus presented as a condition of not only spiritual but also political stasis or paralysis.

In its original religious sense, "Moloch" derives from the Judeo-Christian tradition where it signifies both an idolatry and a particular form of child sacrifice in the name of the god Moloch. The term is employed in "Howl" to highlight a number of other, more specifically political issues in 1950s America with which the speaker must cope. "Moloch" is described as the modern American metropolis "whose factories dream and croak in the fog! . . . whose smokestacks and antennae crown the cities!" (l. 82), and "whose soul is electricity and banks" (l. 83). As if yelling in staccato, the speaker then lists all that which "Moloch" stands for: "Moloch! Moloch! Robot apartments! invisible suburbs! skeleton treasuries! blind capitals! demonic industries! spectral nations! invincible mad houses granite cocks! monstrous bombs!" (l. 86). But "Moloch" also attains a more spectral, metaphysical quality when the term is equated with the "mind," the "mental," and "the heavy judger of men" (ll. 83, 79). The term is thus understood in reference to a concrete political wasteland as well as to a state of spiritual crisis or instability, underscoring the broader existential predicament in which the speaker finds himself and his "comrades" (l. 300) captured. The gravity of lament and anger expressed in section II is amplified additionally in the repeated exclamatory address of "Moloch!" which occurs in nine lines and combines both a demanding and accusatory tone. The form of section II at once relates to and differs from section I. It also implements structures of repetition, but it notably differs from the previous part of the poem in its continued staccato rhythm that results from the asyndetic linking of screams or yells that are employed all along, yet with increased intensity towards the end of section II; "Visions! omens! hallucinations! miracles! ecstasies! gone down the American river! Dreams! adorations! illuminations! religions! The whole boatload of sensitive bullshit!" (ll. 88-9).

While part II of "Howl" ends on a rather depressing note—everything one has ever hoped for has "gone down the flood" (l. 90) or "down the American river" (l. 88)—part III inverts this sense of desolation in a hymn of solidarity and hope. The speaker addresses Carl Solomon directly, repeating the affirmative "I'm with you in Rockland" a total of 18 times (ll. 92-128), each time adding either a personal anecdote or a new spiritual or political vision to the foregoing proclamation of solidarity. Whereas part I depicts a suffering humanity bereft of any hope for redemption or the possibility to escape, part III celebrates a new age in which "you will . . . resurrect your living Jesus from the superhuman tomb" (l. 121) with "twentyfive thousand mad comrades all together singing the final stanzas of the Internationale" (l. 123). Religious and social-political claims for a brighter future are fused and projected into the exemplary figure of Carl Solomon, who is used throughout the poem as a constant reference figure to symbolize a whole generation of seekers struggling to define their individuality against the mainstream standards of postwar American culture. Taken as a whole, then, "Howl" must be read as a huge chant against the psychopathologies of postwar America and as a celebration of a future possible revolution in which ideas of spiritual self-renewal and social-political equality go hand in hand.

The poem's hopeful concluding lines separate "Howl" from "In Goya's Greatest Scenes" on a mere thematic level. "In Goya's Greatest Scenes" refuses to spell out the hope for a better future; instead it banks on the reader's individual motivation to fight the very machines that are about to "devour" America. Hence, Ferlinghetti's ending is best understood as the expression of a "super realist," a term introduced in his popular "Constantly Risking Absurdity." The "super realist" (1993: 96, 19) can never just give away beauty or the hope for beauty, but must first "perforce perceive / taut truth" (ll. 20-1). By contrast, Ginsberg's speaker does not seem to be able to remain in the realms of realism, but must resort to the shelter of religious self-empowerment to overcome the dire reality that so depresses him. This prospective religious-political vision is additionally emphasized in the "Footnote to Howl," published the same year, that catalogues fellow writers and friends: "Lucien," "Kerouac," "Huncke," "Burroughs," "Cassady" (1988 [1956]: 137, 11-2) and material objects—both manufactured and natural—as "holy." The gesture of an all-embracing sanctification in the "Footnote to Howl" can thus be interpreted as a renewed confirmation of the text's optimistic final lines. The structure of the "Footnote" additionally confirms such a reading, as it centers on the same combinations of anaphoric repetition and subsequent improvisation as the main parts of the text.

It thus becomes clear that "Howl"'s success as a poem, with its vigorous critique of American Cold War culture, cannot be explained independently of its deliberate performative poetic form. Like Ferlinghetti's "In Goya's Greatest Scenes," "Howl" is structured mainly by the rhythm of the voice as the poet or imagined reader reads the text. Line breaks and syntactical structures in the text are modeled after individual breath intervals. And yet there are notable differences in the use of the line break and the breath interval in both poems. In "Howl," the pronoun "who" in section I, "Moloch" in section II, and the phrase "I am with you" in section III all provide "a base to keep measure, return to and take off again onto another streak of invention" (2000 [1959]: 229), as Ginsberg himself explains about the writing process of "Howl." This sense of a base pattern, which rhythmizes the poem on the level of the line sequence, is not used in "In Goya's Greatest Scenes." In Ferlinghetti, the text remains structurally open, and the lyrical I's attitude much resembles that of a speaking or arguing person. Ginsberg's "Howl" employs more repetitive, musical elements, and in that way underlines the performative character of the poem as a song or religious hymn. In "purpose, in language and in subject matter," "Howl" "covers the field of typically prophetic poetry," as Kenneth Rexroth is fittingly quoted in Ferlinghetti's "Horn on Howl" (in Ferlinghetti 1992 [1959]: 260). "The theme is the denunciation of evil and a pointing out of the way out, so to speak. That is prophetic literature. 'Woe! Woe! Woe! The City of Jerusalem! . . .'" (ibid.).

At the same time, the repeated "streak of invention" suggested by Ginsberg points to the important role of improvisation and the idea of freedom in poetic composition that seems to be endorsed by the loose overall structure of the poem. Understood in that sense, "Howl" repeats the call and response pattern typical of traditional jazz improvisation, in which one or several soloists interact freely on the basis of a few recurring rhythmical, melodic, or harmonic elements. If we take the three sections of the poem as "choruses" of a jazz tune, which is what Ginsberg himself repeatedly claimed (cf. 2000 [1959]: 230; 2000

[1957]: 239-43), then the analogy becomes even clearer. Each section functions much like an individual solo part, evolving through a series of intuitive and yet related associations and images towards a climax of expressive intensity. In each section of "Howl," the increased rhetorical-performative energy is indicated by the text's break from or alteration of the call-and-response pattern that it initially installs (cf. ll. 70-6, 86-9, 127). The three parts are connected through overlapping themes or the logic of the poem's argument rather than by rigid formal devices. Striking examples are the question at the beginning of part II (l. 77) that refers back to the previous part I, or the juxtaposition of despondency and hope that connects part II with part III (91-2). The poem addresses this dimension of improvised interaction several times in a self-reflexive manner by referencing the jazz club as the very site of communal artistic performance.

The fact that "Howl" was originally performed—and not first published as a book—confirms this notion of performativity and once again stresses how intimately written *and* spoken poetic discourse were intertwined in many popular Beat texts. The title itself may be the best illustration of the poem's overall message: a howling expression of collective political and cultural unrest and tension during the early Cold War years. To make this message heard, Ginsberg wanted what Michael Davidson describes as "a fusion of romantic expression, community, and politics that had been sidetracked by Cold War consensus" (2013: 77). To achieve this sense of fusion, Ginsberg did not focus his address on dedicated readers studying his text as scholars. What he really wanted was to incite people, to get them angrily shouting—literally "howling" in "protest against the dehumanizing mechanization of American culture—and demanding an affirmation of individual particular compassion in the midst of a great chant" (2000 [1957]: 241). However successful Ginsberg's poem was in terms of its political impact, "Howl" was an immediate success when it was published as a book in Ferlinghetti's poetry series. And ever since, scholars, critics, and fans have followed his "Howl" as a testament of countercultural energies during the early Cold War years.

4. Conclusion

By the mid-1960s the Beat Generation began to dissolve as a community and to branch out into other fields of poetic practice. The political dimension of many Beat texts was carried over into various popular political movements that began to shape American cultural life during the 1960s—the Free Speech movement and Second Wave Feminism, for example—and in the political and artistic formation of many minority communities that were very receptive to and indeed directly profited from the Beats' commitment to poetic and political freedom. It is no coincidence that Allen Ginsberg and others actively supported student protests in Berkeley in 1965. Two different but equally intense poetic continuations of the Beats' political convictions can be found in Amiri Baraka's and Denise Levertov's work of the late 1960s and 1970s (see Baraka 1964, 1970; Levertov 1971, 1975). The formal experimentation of Beat poetry and the sense of communal improvisation were continued more specifically, however, in several works of the Language school. While also denouncing the Beats' commitment to expressive subjectivity, writers such as Bob Perelman, Barrett Watten, Ron Silliman, Lyn Hejinian, and Carla Harryman radicalized the Beats' interest in the limits of poetic form and their belief in communal forms of poetic practice in a number of individual and collaborative writing projects exploring the materiality of language, i.e., sound and written word, as the foundation of contemporary political life (cf. Hejinian 2000: 40-58; see Perelman 1993; Watten 2002). Finally, the public performative aspect of many Beat projects has remained a central element in the evolution of open-mike poetry slams, standup comedy, and the institutionalization of the open jam sessions in jazz clubs. The emergence of avant-garde theater in the Bay Area during the late 1970s is one specific variation of this evolution.

Apart from these immediate historical continuities, the literature of the Beat Generation has developed into a canonical segment of postwar American literature classes in high schools, colleges, and universities. Allen Ginsberg and Lawrence Ferlinghetti, though originally branded as countercultural rabble-rousers, are now anthologized as poets of a consecrated avant-garde that has become an integral part of American intellectual mainstream culture. This may not be what the Beats originally aspired to, but it is the best indication of how powerfully their works have influenced postwar American culture. The Beats' belated mainstream success is the necessary precondition for a broader acknowledgement of their literary and political achievements: both "Howl" and "In Goya's Greatest Scenes" reflect the oppressive nature of American Cold War ideology while speculating—poetically—about potential life forms beyond the confines of these ideological prescripts.

Bibliography

Selected Primary Literature

Baraka, Amiri. 1964. *The Dead Lecturer: Poems*. New York: Grove Press.
——. 1970. *It's Nation Time*. Chicago: Third World Press.
Creeley, Robert. 1989 [1951]. "A Note on the Objective." In: *The Collected Essays of Robert Creeley*. Berkeley: U of California P. 464-5.
Ferlinghetti, Lawrence. 1992 [1959]. "Horn on Howl." In: Ann Charters (ed.), *The Portable Beat Reader*. New York and London: Penguin Books. 254-63.
——. 1993. *These Are My Rivers. New and Selected Poems 1955-1993*. New York: New Directions Books.
Ginsberg, Allen. 1988. *Collected Poems 1947-1980*. New York: Harper Perennial.
——. 2000. *Deliberate Prose. Selected Essays 1952-1995*. New York: Harper Perennial.
——. 2000 [1957]. "The Six Gallery Reading." In: Ginsberg 2000. 239-43.
——. 2000 [1959]. "Notes Written on Finally Recording *Howl*." In: Ginsberg 2000. 229-32.
——. 2000 [1981]. "A Definition of the Beat Generation." In: Ginsberg 2000. 236-9.
Holmes, John Clellon. 1952. "This is the Beat Generation." *New York Times Magazine* November 16: 10.
Johnson, Ronna C. 2013. "Three Generations of Beat Poetics." In: Ashton 2013. 80-94.
Kerouac, Jack. 1959. *Mexico City Blues*. New York: Grove Press.
——. 1993. *Good Blonde and Others*. San Francisco: Grey Fox Press.
——. 1993 [1957]. "Essentials of Spontaneous Prose." In: Kerouac 1993. 69-72.

——. 1993 [1959]. "The Origins of the Beat Generation." In: Kerouac 1993. 55-65.

——. 1993 [1959]. "Belief and Technique for Modern Prose." In: Kerouac 1993. 72-4.

Kupferberg, Tuli. 1992 [1960]. "Greenwich Village of My Dreams." In: Charters 1992. 385-7.

Levertov, Denise. 1971. *To Stay Alive*. New York: New Directions.

——. 1975. *The Freeing of the Dust*. New York: New Directions.

Olson, Charles. 1967 [1950]. "Projective Verse." In: *Selected Writings*. Ed. Robert Creeley. New York: New Directions. 15-31.

Selected Secondary Literature

Ashton, Jennifer (ed.). 2013. *The Cambridge Companion to American Poetry since 1945*. Cambridge and New York: Cambridge UP.

A very useful selection of essays on major poetry movements after World War II that help to contextualize the Beat Generation within postwar American literature.

Burns, Glen. 1983. *Great Poets Howl. A Study of Allen Ginsberg's Poetry, 1943-1955*. New York et al.: Peter Lang.

One of the most attentive close-reading studies of Ginsberg's early poetry.

Cherkowsky, Neeli. 1979. *Ferlinghetti. A Biography*. New York: Doubleday.

The only biography on Ferlinghetti to this date. Lots of rare background information on Ferlinghetti's political activism.

Davidson, Michael. 2013. "The San Francisco Renaissance." In: Ashton 2013. 66-79.

A condensed and still very useful version of Davidson's longer work on the Bay poets.

Nelson, Deborah. 2002. *Pursuing Privacy in Cold War America*. New York: Columbia UP.

A brilliant account of the connections between selfhood, individuality, and power politics during the Cold War years.

Raskin, Jonah. 2004. *American Scream. Allen Ginsberg's Howl and the Making of the Beat Generation*. Berkeley: U of California P.

This is a very interesting book on Ginsberg as one of the founding fathers of the Beats. Not a real scholarly book, but full of intriguing anecdotes and hard to find background information about the evolution of the Beat Generation as a movement.

Skerl, Jennie (ed.). 2004. *Reconstructing the Beats*. New York: Palgrave/St. Martin's Press.

One of the best essay collections on the Beat Generation. Very student friendly.

Smith, Richard Candida. 1995. *Utopia and Dissent: Art, Poetry, and Politics in California*. Berkeley: U of California P.

A diverse and historiographically nuanced study of California as the birth place of cultural revolutions.

Trigilio, Tony. 2007. *Allen Ginsberg's Buddhist Poetics*. Carbondale: Southern Illinois UP.

The first book-length study on the role and development of Buddhist religion in the poetry of Ginsberg.

Further References

Belgrad, Daniel. 1998. *The Culture of Spontaneity. Improvisation and the Arts in Postwar America*. Chicago: U of Chicago P.

Charters, Ann. 1992. *The Portable Beat Reader*. New York and London: Penguin.

Davidson, Michael. 1989. *The San Francisco Renaissance. Poetics and Community at Mid-Century*. Cambridge et al.: Cambridge UP.

Hejinian, Lyn. 2000. *The Language of Inquiry*. Berkeley: U of California P.

May, Elaine Tyler. 1988. *Homeward Bound: American Families in the Cold War Era*. New York: Basic Books.

Perelman, Bob. 1993. "Parataxis and Narrative. The New Sentence in Theory and Practice." In: *American Literature* 65.2: 313-24.

Watten, Barrett. 2002. "The Turn to Language and the 1960s." In: *Critical Inquiry* 29.1: 139-83.

21.

Confessional Poetry and the 1960s

Robert Lowell's "Skunk Hour" and Sylvia Plath's "Lady Lazarus"

Carsten Albers

1. Confessional Poetry as Provocation and Liberation:
A Poetic Movement and Its Socio-Cultural Background

With the publication of "Poetry as Confession"—M. L. Rosenthal's highly influential review of Robert Lowell's *Life Studies*—in the November 19, 1959 issue of the liberal magazine *The Nation*, the era of confessional poetry made its official debut. The article, which became the basis of Rosenthal's *The Modern Poets: A Critical Introduction* (1960), caught the attention of many contemporary readers because its author identified something in American poetry that was not necessarily new, but had never been so open and honest: the poignant admissions of personal failure, human inadequacy, and serious disorders. What, one might ask, would poets divulge that could be considered 'a confession'? In the original context of the word (Catholicism), the term denotes the acknowledgement of sins and repentance to a priest, who may then grant God's forgiveness. "Confessional writing," says Deborah Nelson in her article "Confessional Poetry,"

> is part of a religious tradition that dates back to Augustine and became part of a therapeutic tradition even before the advent of psychotherapy, which certainly shaped and accelerated the outpouring of personal self-revelation in the twentieth century. Moreover, in confessional poetry, both religious belief and Freudian psychotherapy play very important roles. Confession, with or without the motivation of penance or psychic pain relief, also represents one of the most varied and intense forms of artistic experimentation in the latter half of the twentieth century. (2013: 33)

One can only confess to something that would be considered a *trespass* against (mostly society- or church-given) moral rules, regardless of one's intention behind a confession. The term "confessional poetry" as poetic genre or movement thus connotes a cultural and moral climate in which there are rules, mostly unwritten, that declare what is proper and decent to say in public or write in poems. Among the topics considered taboo were such things as divorce, mental illness, homosexuality, alcoholism, and drug abuse (see Nelson 2013, Middlebrook 1993, and Lerner 1987). Among the writers who would breach these taboos in their poems were John Berryman (1914-1972), Robert Lowell (1917-1977), Anne Sexton (1928-1974), and Sylvia Plath (1932-1963)—as suggested by Rosenthal—but also W.D. Snodgrass (1926-2009), and, to a large degree, Beat poet Allen Ginsberg (1926-1997), and New York School poet Frank O'Hara (1926-1966). These poets confessed with honesty and directness to each of the issues mentioned above. In his volume *Heart's Needle* (1959) Snodgrass displayed, with painful openness, the disintegration of his marriage and his heart-rending longing for his daughter; Berryman wrote of his failing relationships and alcohol excesses, Sexton of her struggles in and outside mental institutions, Plath of her clinical depression and self-destructive impulses, Ginsberg and

O'Hara of their homosexuality. But not all confessions were authentic. The speaker of Sexton's poem "The Abortion" confesses to an abortion that, according to her biographers, the author did not even have (cf. Albers 2001: 360).

To understand the possible motifs of the poets for their confessions, their work needs to be read against the historical, political, and cultural backgrounds of the 1950s. The late 1950s and early 1960s in the United States could be characterized (in an extremely simplified manner) as an era of political and cultural conservatism, particularly in the South. The civil rights movement had just about reached full stride, the feminist movement was making slow progress, gay liberation was only beginning to coalesce into a movement, and forms of cultural expression still moved in the tradition of High Modernism. New forms of poetry were tried out in what later would become known as the Black Mountain School poetry from North Carolina and the Beat Poetry associated with the San Francisco Renaissance. Confessional poetry, however, had its origins in the conservative, academic traditions of New England, particularly in Cambridge, Massachusetts. This is where the most renowned and respected poet of his time, Robert Lowell, had grown up and would later become a professor at Harvard University where he taught creative writing; poets Anne Sexton and Sylvia Plath were among his students.

New England's traditional values included, next to those of a Protestant ethics, the appreciation of family traditions and history, a sense of decency and propriety. Religion, politics, and sexuality were topics to avoid at dinner parties in conservative circles. Privacy was a realm defined in terms of social *roles*, not in terms of individual *needs*. All these factors led to a climate of complacency in which the private was not yet considered political and individuals needed to conceal that which was not considered relevant for (mainstream) society. As much of a provocation as it was to question old traditions and values, or to reveal family secrets, illicit longings, or mental illnesses, the mere act of doing so could, in retrospect, be considered a form of liberation for readers who had not been granted free discourse of these issues in society. Disclosing secrets that existed everywhere behind a façade of decency could thus help renew a society, much of which had become too self-assured and complacent to face changing attitudes and opinions.

Robert Lowell was a typical representative of this kind of liberation. In his three earlier volumes of poetry (*Land of Unlikeness*, 1944; *Lord Weary's Castle*, 1946; and *The Mills of the Kavanaughs*, 1951), Lowell had dealt with topics related to his conversion to Catholicism, spiritual doubt, family traditions, and New England's cultural history in a fairly conventional diction. His fourth volume, *Life Studies* (1959), marked a shift in his artistic development: a change of subject matters or their treatment, a more informal diction and tone, and an experimental handling of metric and stanzaic forms. The last poem of *Life Studies*, titled "Skunk Hour," remains one of his most anthologized and best-known poems and can be used as an example of these characteristics.

2. Robert Lowell's "Skunk Hour" (1959) and Old New England Traditions

"Skunk Hour," dedicated to Lowell's close friend and fellow poet Elizabeth Bishop, consists of eight six-line stanzas (sestets) of varying line lengths and an equally varying number of rhymes per stanza. Yet no stanza is completely without rhyme; each contains at least one perfect rhyme and some have as many as three. Thus, Lowell makes it clear that his stanzas are intended to be read as separate and distinguishable units, the length of which is all but arbitrary. This impression is underlined by the fact that all stanzas but one close with the end of a sentence—a characteristic that encourages individual consideration of each stanza. The rhyme scheme of stanzas 3, 4, 5, and 7 establishes a correspondence between the first and last lines of each stanza; the middle lines of stanzas 4 and 5 show a cross rhyme; and in stanza 7 they are grouped in pairs. The rhyme scheme gives the stanzas an underlying poetic structure that stays unobtrusively in the background and never becomes dominant. This characteristic places the poem stylistically between traditional formalism and a modern strand of free-verse poetry in a more casual diction, perfectly reflecting the poem's concern with change and renewal versus history and tradition.

The first stanza is devoted to "Nautilus Island's hermit / heiress" (ll. 1-2). With the "hermit heiress" as subject, Lowell marks the setting of his poem: Nautilus Island, a privately owned, 38-acre island in Penobscot Bay, Maine, half a mile south of Castine. Not only do these lines identify the poem's place, they also comment on the inhabitants who live there: one is a wealthy lady of old money who has noticeably aged both physically and mentally: "she's in her dotage" (l. 6), a formulation that suggests senility. Although she must be very rich, she lives "through winter in her Spartan cottage" (l. 2), which makes one wonder whether she is extremely modest or miserly. Two men are mentioned in connection with the wealthy old lady: her son, who is a bishop (cf. l. 4), and her farmer, the "first selectman in our village" (l. 5). These men are representatives of a conservative society with patriarchal structures based on religion and tradition, and they occupy important positions in village administration and the church. That this kind of structure seems to be in decline or is already obsolete is alluded to by the fact that the woman's residence ("cottage," l. 2) only forms a half rhyme with "village" (l. 5), but a full rhyme with "dotage" (l. 6).

The speaker does not refer to any other members of the island's population; the only other living beings named are the heiress's sheep, which "still graze above the sea" (l. 3). The second stanza describes the lady's actions ("she buys up all / the eyesores facing her shore, and lets them fall," ll. 10-2) and their underlying motifs ("Thirsting for / the hierarchic privacy / of Queen Victoria's century," ll. 7-9). Her acquisition of run-down buildings (metaphorically called "eyesores" in line 11) would not be cause for criticism except that she lets them further deteriorate and eventually tears them down, illustrating the traits of an absolutist society that is also evident in her longing ("thirsting") for "the hierarchic privacy / of Queen Victoria's century" (ll. 8-9). Privacy, it seems, exists in different forms; a *hierarchic* privacy might be that of monarchs who can afford to distance themselves from their subordinates thanks to their power. That this kind of privacy, for which the heiress seems to thirst, has become somewhat outdated in 1959 (and maybe also out of place in the United States) is indicated by the allusion to Great Britain in the nineteenth century ("Queen Victoria's century," l. 9).

The first two stanzas of "Skunk Hour" can be interpreted as an oblique criticism of New England's outdated social structures (symbolically represented by the heiress and her small island dominion), which give a few affluent people too much influence. The old lady's conception of privacy also stands in contrast to a modern-day notion of what privacy entails (in stanza five, a sphere of privacy is invaded by the speaker of the poem).

In the third stanza the speaker uses the first-person plural pronoun "we" to indicate that he is one of the island's community and speaks as part of a collective. The judgmental statement "The season's ill—" (l. 13) finds its purely material explanation in the loss of a source of income, personified as "our summer millionaire" (l. 14). This character is described as one "who seemed to leap from an L.L. Bean / catalogue." L.L. Bean is the name of a clothing brand specializing in casual, sporty-but-conservative clothing and outerwear. In the context of late 1950s New England, that kind of clothing was fairly new and must have been deemed to traditional New England islanders as unsuitable attire for a millionaire. The remains of his luxury belongings ("His nine-knot yawl," l. 16) are taken over by traditional fishermen ("lobstermen," l. 17) to whom the boat was "auctioned off" (l. 17). This fact seems to exemplify a development that could be called regressive; contemporary influences diminish (as indicated by the comparison to a model from an L.L. Bean catalogue), while old traditions (re-)claim their place. As if to comment ironically on this, the stanza ends with the sentence "A red fox stain covers Blue Hill" (l. 18). Apparently a red fox has left his droppings in a highly representative place that showcases the island's beauty and attracts visitors. The innocent fox, whose red color strongly contrasts with the blue in "Blue Hill," did not realize that this was an inappropriate place to deposit his feces— and simply did not care. The stain that covers Blue Hill can be interpreted as a scornful statement about the importance of places that thrive on money and appearance. That this seemingly nonsequitur sentence forms the end of the stanza is not arbitrary because it brings closure to it, establishing the stanza's only rhyme that connects this last line with the stanza's first line.

The fourth stanza is also devoted to an individual character: "our fairy / decorator" (ll. 19-20). The possessive pronoun "our" indicates that the speaker considers him part of the close-knit small community of islanders who may or may not be comfortable with the fact that he is (allegedly) gay. That he "brightens his shop for fall" accentuates the apparent need to light up the upcoming season of an increasingly colder and more hostile climate (possibly so in social terms as well). In order to achieve the desired effect, he colors all items of his decoration orange, the traditional color of fall ("his fishnet's filled with orange cork, / orange, his cobbler's bench and awl," ll. 21-2); an idea the simplicity of which seems rather dull or uninspired.

The last two lines of the stanza ("there is no money in his work, / he'd rather marry," ll. 23-4) can be interpreted in different ways. They could be read as an indication of his more feminine side—that he'd rather marry and take care of the house than earn a living working outside the home—or as a rather cynical remark concerning his difficult economic situation. In the late 1950s, marriage was a way to find economic safety for many women financially supported by their husbands who—as sole breadwinners—did not expect their wives to contribute to the family income. This 'solution,' however, is not really feasible for the decorator because marrying a wealthy woman for mere financial reasons would have been a form of deception and self-denial; gay marriage did not exist yet and was still far from even being an option. It is interesting though that the rhyme-word Lowell uses for "fairy" is "marry"—maybe the slight imperfection of the rhyme, likewise, reflects Lowell's view of the supposed incongruity of the two concepts (homosexuality and marriage). The rhyme embraces a cross rhyme in the stanza's middle ("fall" / "cork" / "awl" / "work," ll. 20-3), which consists of a perfect rhyme and an eye rhyme. In the context of the statement that is formed in the stanza (a not very creative gay decorator prefers marriage to his job and moderate income) the eye rhyme perfectly mirrors a desired congruence or euphony which (at closer inspection) is not really there.

At this point—right in the middle of the poem—a major shift occurs with a change in subject, perspective, tense, and tone. The fact that the second half of the stanza was composed before the first half (cf. Kalstone 1977: 88) might explain the abruptness of the shift and why the two halves initially seem incongruent. The first line of the fifth stanza ("One dark night," l. 25) is a direct reference to the first words of mystic Saint John of the Cross's poem "The Dark Night" (San Juan de la Cruz, "Noche oscura" 1577/8), to which it forms a sort of counter-version because, unlike St. John's speaker, Lowell's does not find spiritual solace in the night. The words rather sound like the introduction to a Gothic tale and raise the reader's expectation for something extraordinary to happen. The two-clause compound sentence reads: "One dark night / my Tudor Ford climbed the hill's skull; / I watched for love-cars" with only the (remotely metaphorical) expression "the hill's skull" as another Gothic or biblical reference ('Golgotha' of the Bible literally means 'place of the skull'). Here, for the first time in the poem, the speaker refers to himself as "I" (prominently placed at the beginning of line 27), and confesses to his secret voyeurism: searching for cars in which there are couples engaged in lovemaking ("love-cars," l. 27). It is interesting to observe how the subject in the two clauses changes from an old, almost anachronistic "Tudor Ford" (an allusion to British history in its connection to New England traditions, similar to "Queen Victoria's century" in the second stanza) to the speaker himself ("I"). The personification of the car ("my Tudor Ford *climbed*," l. 26, emphasis added) at first seems to avert the aspect of agency and responsibility from the speaker (it is, after all, the speaker who steers the vehicle) who then admits to his inappropriate behavior. What he sees forms the core of the stanza: "Lights turned down, / they lay together, hull to hull, / where the graveyard shelves on the town . . ." (ll. 27-9; ellipses in original). With their dimmed lights, the cars are compared indirectly to the boats typical of coastal New England and, when the speaker uses the expression "hull to hull" in line 28, are a reminder of Nautilus Island's harbor; this disambiguates the phrase "they lay together," which otherwise could have also referred to the lovers in the cars. The setting for their nightly trysts (next to the graveyard) seems odd, but ties in with the Gothic atmosphere of the entire stanza and alludes to the connection of *eros* and *thanatos*. The ellipses at the end of the line allude to something unsaid or mark the wandering imagination of the speaker.

The stanza ends with a statement that is fundamentally confessional: "My mind's not right" (l. 30), as the speaker acknowledges a mental disorder or disturbance into which the sixth stanza provides a closer look. Whereas the former consisted of three perfect rhymes, this stanza contains only one ("cell," "hell," ll. 33, 35), since lines 32 and 36 form an identical rhyme ("hear," "here") and lines 31 and 34 are not rhymed at all ("bleats," "throat"). In terms of poetic form, the stanza gives the impression of less order or formal closure, which corresponds with its topics: loneliness, self-loathing, and self-destructive thoughts. The stanza begins with two strong sound impressions: music from a car-radio ("A car radio bleats, / 'Love, O Careless Love . . .'," ll. 31-2), and a sound that only the speaker can detect: "I hear / my ill-spirit sob in each blood cell," ll. 32-3).

The contrast of the melodramatic blues song "Careless Love," known in versions by Bessie Smith and by Pete Seeger, and the sobbing of the speaker's "ill-spirit" highlights the speaker's inner turmoil; whereas the song's singer threatens to kill his or her obstinate lover, the sobbing of the "ill-spirit" is caused by the speaker of Lowell's poem threatening to kill it: "as if my hand were at its throat . . ." (l. 34; ellipses in original). The image that Lowell uses here symbolizes the state of mind of someone struggling against a demon that has gotten hold of him; the image reminds the reader of an obsession of supernatural, almost religious, dimensions—a scene from Milton or Dante. It thus befits the poem that the speaker contrasts his feeling of loneliness (l. 36) with a quote from Satan in Milton's *Paradise Lost* (Book 4, line 75): "I myself am hell; / nobody's here—" (ll. 35-6). Lowell's speaker confesses his lack of sanity and illustrates it as a struggle with an enemy inside himself. The recognition that it is the *self* that causes this most undesirable state ("hell"), possibly caused or bolstered by loneliness and desire, stands in contrast to Sartre's dictum "l'enfer, c'est les autres" (hell is other people). In his state of anguish and confusion the speaker becomes his own personal enemy. David Kalstone points out that Lowell uses several "monosyllables with final and emphatic rhymes" (1987 [1977]: 89), which he interprets as "the diseased speaker's own obsessive sounds" (ibid.). The word "hell" is only the last in a chain of words that make use of this final l-sound: "still" (twice) in the first stanza; "all" and "fall" in the second stanza; "ill," "yawl," and "Hill" in the third stanza; "fall" and "awl" in the fourth stanza; "hill's skull" and "hull to hull" in the fifth stanza; "ill-spirit," "cell," and "hell" in the sixth stanza. The sound also appears inside words such as "village" (first stanza), "millionaire" (third stanza), and "filled" (fourth stanza). After his confessional statement in the sixth stanza, the sound disappears for one single stanza.

In the seventh stanza, the poem's penultimate unit, the title "Skunk Hour" finally becomes clear, when the sentence of the stanza ("Nobody's here—") continues with the words "only skunks, that search / in the moonlight for a bite to eat" (ll. 37-8). The entire stanza is devoted to the animals and the setting, a New England village with its Main Street and Trinitarian Church:

> They march on their soles up Main Street:
> white stripes, moonstruck eyes' red fire
> under the chalk-dry and spar spire
> of the Trinitarian Church. (ll. 39-42)

The use of the words "They *march*" (l. 39) and "*column* of kittens" (l. 45; both emphases added) makes the skunks seem like protesters in a demonstration. The colors of the image Lowell creates are mostly black and white; not only the skunks' black fur with "white stripes" (l. 40), but also the church steeple which is "chalk-dry" (l. 41). Surprisingly, the speaker accentuates the image with some splashes of red ("eyes' red fire"), which raises a question: Since skunks do not have red eyes, and even if they did, the color would not be visible in the dim light of the moon, what function might these splashes of red have? Linking the skunks' red eyes with the adjective "moonstruck" (l. 40) illustrates, on the one hand, the speaker's imagination in attributing an almost mystic quality to the skunks; or it could be read as the 'red-eyed determination' of their silent protest. On the other hand, it makes them part of the Miltonic drama of hell and fire in which the speaker sees himself. In this image of skunks and church, "soles" (l. 39) might even be read as a pun on "souls."

In the last stanza the speaker positions himself within his own verbal tableau: "I stand on top / of our back steps and breathe the rich air—" (ll. 43-4);
apparently he lives in a house not far from Main Street with a front and back
entrance, from where he can watch the scene in a contemplative and peaceful
mood. Line 45, with its sixteen syllables, is by far the longest line of the entire
poem: "a mother skunk with her column of kittens swills the garbage pail." The
image is touching and somewhat repulsive at the same time; the mother skunk
with her kittens evokes feelings of sympathy in the reader, but rummaging
through a garbage pail in search of food is rather disgusting. The last three lines
of the poem have the same contrary quality:

> She jabs her wedge-head in a cup
> of sour cream, drops her ostrich tail,
> and will not scare. (ll. 46-8)

The "cup / of sour cream" (ll. 46-7) in the garbage into which the mother skunk
"jabs her wedge-head" (l. 46) evokes associations of disgust, but her lowered "os-
trich tail" and the fact that she "will not scare" (l. 48) gives the scene an atmosphere of comfort and safety: she is comfortable in the trash, does not anticipate
having to defend herself or her kittens, and since her tail is down, will not spray
anyone. In the last four lines of the poem the 'l-sound' that had been absent for
six lines reemerges in the words "swills," "garbage pail," "tail," and "will." This
may indicate that the speaker's obsession and distress, which had found only a
brief, temporary relief, have now returned.

On this note the speaker lets the poem end. Does he find solace in the sight
of an animal in search of food, caring for her young with a natural vitality that he
apparently lacks? Does he even feel empathy for a wild creature that depends
upon human civilization's rubbish? Is this a metaphor for how Lowell sees himself as a poet? Or does the poem's speaker feel simply like someone who has
come down so far in the world that he identifies with an animal that rummages
through garbage just to stay alive? All of these questions are left open. The vividness, evocative quality, and ambiguity of the poem's final image—all characteristic of confessional poetry—contribute to its poetic quality and force the reader
to make sense of the image. In this respect the poem is markedly comparable to
Elizabeth Bishop's "The Moose" (1979) and to her poem, "The Armadillo," which
was published in 1965 and dedicated reciprocally to Robert Lowell.

The poem's entire structure and development of ideas is a progression that
moves from history and civilization (stanzas 1-2) via economic decline (stanzas
3-4) to mental and emotional disorder (stanzas 5 and 6) and, finally, to a regres-
sion into the natural sphere with its non-human creatures whose sole focus is
survival. The poem combines local and personal issues with social and universal
questions. "Lowell's accomplishment in 'Skunk Hour,'" Kalstone points out, "is
to have found a tone which at once gestures toward larger meanings and yet
allows for the speaker's own crippling nightmare" (1987 [1977]: 90).

3. Sylvia Plath's "Lady Lazarus" (1962) and Female Self-Assertion

"Lady Lazarus" is probably Sylvia Plath's most famous poem; after her suicide in
1963 it has been read as an open confession of depression and her repeated attempts to kill herself. Although the parallels between the poem's speaker and

the author are undeniable, an equation of speaker and author misses the point that poems, self-revelatory as they may be, are not diary entries to be taken at face value. Confessional poetry is, after all, a *literary* genre, and as such it demands to be read as an *artistic* achievement and not as biographical documents. The following interpretation of "Lady Lazarus" approaches the poem from a predominantly rhetorical and stylistic perspective.

It makes sense to first observe how Plath uses the title of her poem to create a persona that correlates with the biblical character Lazarus, a man who was raised from the dead. It is clear from the title that Plath has a female version of this character in mind, one who is not raised from the dead by Christ but by physicians and modern medicine. While the biblical Lazarus's re-animation is an act of God's grace, in Plath's poem, being raised from the dead seems to go against the speaker's volition, and she expresses her feelings in a variety of ways. Rather than quoting from or summarizing the many different interpretations of "Lady Lazarus" (which my contribution does not intend to replace), the following close reading of the poem will concentrate on a number of central aspects that prominently figure in this long and dramatic monologue of 84 lines in 28 tercets to explain the use of formal elements and rhetoric devices that create different modes of expression and tone.

The speaker, who identifies herself as a thirty-year-old woman ("I am only thirty," l. 20), confesses: "I have done it again. / One year in every ten / I manage it—" (ll. 1-3). Although exactly what the speaker has done is deliberately left unsaid at the beginning of the poem, her actions become clear at the end of the seventh and the beginning of the eighth stanza when she says: "And like the cat I have nine times to die. / This is Number Three" (ll. 21-2). It should be noted that the speaker confesses not to committing suicide or rather attempting to, but to "dying." Her tone is partly cynical and partly disillusioned when she says: "Dying / Is an art, like everything else. / I do it exceptionally well" (ll. 43-5). The capitalization of the words "Number Three" (l. 22) makes it seem like a show-act, a number in a revue show. The speaker then explains her two previous 'deaths'/ incidents: "The first time it happened I was ten. / It was an accident" (ll. 35-6). Here it seems that she talks about *surviving* rather than dying. But the next incident is a different story: "The second time I meant / To last it out and not come back at all" (ll. 37-8). In this sentence the confessional element is obvious: "To last it out," in this context, can only mean death, and the words "I meant" is proof of the speaker's self-annihilating intention.

Both instances have a biographical background in Plath's life: her father died when she was ten years old, and the lines about the "second time," Whitney Naylor-Smith explains, "describe the incident of Plath's early attempt at suicide, during which she overdosed on sleeping pills, climbed into a crawl space in her mother's cellar, and was not found for several days (as is widely publicized and described in Plath's semi-autobiographical novel *The Bell Jar*)" (2013: 324). Readers of the poem may wonder whether this third attempt occurred before her actual suicide on February 11, 1963, or whether at the time of writing "Lady Lazarus" (October 23-9, 1962) it was still a sort of prophecy that the author fulfilled four months later. The simile "I rocked shut / As a seashell" (ll. 39-40) and the additional comment about her re-animation "They had to call and call" (l. 41) indicates the stubbornness with which the speaker intends to "not come back at all."

On the visual level, Plath employs images of bodily decay and decomposition to illustrate that the re-animated body, called back to life like Lazarus in the Bible, has already putrefied: Not only did the physicians have to "call" her repeatedly, they also had to "pick the worms off me like sticky pearls" (l. 42). The simile that compares worms to "sticky pearls" is ambiguous; whereas "pearls" has positive connotations of wealth and beauty, the adjective "sticky" devaluates it and turns the image into something disgusting. Earlier in the poem the speaker claims: "Soon, soon the flesh / The grave cave ate will be / At home on me / And I a smiling woman" (ll. 16-9). The flesh of her body has been eaten by the personified "grave cave"—an internal rhyme that carries another allusion to the biblical Lazarus who was buried in a cave. What, one wonders, does she mean when she says that this flesh will be "at home" on her? Can the claim that she will be "a smiling woman" be anything but cynical? In the fourth stanza, when it is not yet clear whom the speaker is addressing with the words "O my enemy," one might get the impression that this provocative tone and vexing address is vented right at the reader when the speaker says:

> Peel off the napkin
> O my enemy.
> Do I terrify?—
>
> The nose, the eye pits, the full set of teeth?
> The sour breath
> Will vanish in a day. (ll. 10-5)

Only later do we learn that the "enemy" is apparently the physician on duty. In lines 65 and 66 she calls him "Herr Doktor" and "Herr Enemy." The German address "Herr," the use of capital letters and the German spelling of "Doktor" is an allusion to Nazi Germany and the Holocaust; imagery she uses elsewhere in the poem as well (a characteristic that will be discussed later). The speaker goes on to say:

> I am your opus,
> I am your valuable,
> The pure gold baby
>
> That melts to a shriek.
> I turn and burn.
> Do not think I underestimate your great concern. (ll. 67-72)

Here, the speaker is contemptuous of the one who has apparently brought her back to life—against her wish—and sees herself now as his creation, his "opus," a commodity, a "valuable," a "pure gold baby." Unlike a real newborn child, she does not start living but "*melts* to a shriek" (l. 70, emphasis added) and finally burns up. The cynicism of the statements, which can ultimately be interpreted as a provocation of the readers who are accustomed to feeling appreciation for doctors who serve as life-savers, is made even more effective by the use of several stylistic devices such as anaphora in lines 67 and 68, onomatopoeia in line 70, internal rhyme in line 71, and a striking contrast in the length of lines 71 and 72.

The speaker's disillusionment concerning the decades through which she has lived, namely the 1930s, '40s, and '50s, is expressed when she says: "What a trash / To annihilate each decade. / What a million filaments" (ll. 23-5). The word filaments can be understood both in the biological sense as bodily tissue (in other words, the muscles and fibers of her own body) and in a more general way in the sense of 'threads,' which could be interpreted as a metaphor of life's thin but interwoven texture. 'Threads' also reminds the reader of an image used earlier in the poem—that of "Jew linen" (l. 9), an expression that will be discussed later in connection with Holocaust imagery.

The speaker's emotion turns into anger when she describes the people—who want to watch as she comes back to life—as a voyeuristic crowd at a strip-tease show; the only difference is that she does not undress herself, but is "unwrapped" by medical doctors and health-care people:

> The peanut-crunching crowd
> Shoves in to see
>
> Them unwrap me hand and foot—
> The big strip tease. (ll. 26-9)

She then directly addresses this audience: "Gentlemen, ladies . . ." (l. 30), an address which in the communicative situation of the poem could also be read as an address to the poem's readers. What she has to present—the parts of her body—is a sight both banal and spectacular; banal because there is nothing extraordinary about it, and spectacular because it has the status of a corpse resurrected:

> These are my hands
> My knees.
> I may be skin and bone,
>
> Nevertheless, I am the same, identical woman. (ll. 31-4)

With the last line the speaker maintains that she has not changed at all despite the visible alterations in her cave-eaten body. Regardless of the outward changes, her inner self is still the same; the speaker's personality, she claims, is not affected (neither for better nor for worse) by the re-animation of her body. This reading is ambiguous, since it suggests a duality of body and mind that denies a mutual influence of the two, and in the case of someone who has survived a suicide attempt, a personality change could also be beneficial for the survivor's future life. The speaker feels offended by the visitors' exclamations of thankfulness and wonder ("'A miracle!'") at the sight of her resurrection. About her coming back to life she says:

> It's the theatrical
>
> Comeback in broad day
> To the same place, the same face, the same brute
> Amused shout:
>
> 'A miracle!'
> That knocks me out. (ll. 51-6)

The fact that she calls her comeback "theatrical" indicates how uncomfortable and self-conscious she feels about her situation. The repetition of "the same" in line 53 expresses annoyance and disgust, further stressed by the length of the line. In her view, the expression of wonder and relief, which 'A miracle!' could also be, is a "brute / Amused shout"—this reflects a subjective, cynical and partly distorted view of the situation; a view which may evoke empathy and opposition in the reader at the same time. To claim that the visitors' amazement is what "knocks [her] out" expresses an indirect form of accusation and reproach. The tone changes in the next eight lines to an almost hysterical desperation that is marked by the insisting repetition "There is a charge" (l. 57), "there is a charge" (l. 58), "And there is a charge, a very large charge" (l. 61):

> There is a charge
>
> For the eyeing of my scars, there is a charge
> For the hearing of my heart—
> It really goes.
>
> And there is a charge, a very large charge
> For a word or a touch
> Or a bit of blood
>
> Or a piece of my hair or my clothes. (ll. 57-64)

The speaker is offended by the curiosity and voyeurism of her visitors, against which she helplessly defends herself by demanding to be paid a fee in return, highlighted by the internal rhyme "large charge" (l. 61), the anaphora "For the . . ." (ll. 58-9), and the alliterations "hearing of my heart" (l. 59) and "bit of blood" (l. 63; emphasis added). Her helplessness or outright desperation find verbal expression in a list of minuscule items added in a long polysyndeton connected by "or" (ll. 62-4). No matter how out of control the speaker's emotions may be, Plath finds a perfectly controlled verbalization for them. This contrast—a state of emotional disintegration expressed in a poetic idiom marked by precision and carefully planned lyrical structures—contributes to the poem's intensity and shows that confessional poetry is not simply emotional outpouring, but controlled artistic expression.

Plath uses Holocaust imagery and allusions to Nazi atrocities, making parts of this poem particularly hard to bear. The German address "Herr" (with "Herr Doktor," "Herr Enemy," "Herr God," and "Herr Luzifer" in a carefully chosen gradation) could be interpreted as an allusion to KZ physician Josef Mengele and his experiments. The simile and metaphors "my skin / Bright as a Nazi lampshade, / My right foot // A paperweight, / My face a featureless, fine / Jew linen" (ll. 4-8) even more explicitly establish the connection of the speaker's physiognomy to that of Auschwitz victims. At the end of the poem, the speaker is literally burned ("I turn and burn," l. 71), reminiscent of the ovens in the concentration camps from which only ashes emerged that were poked through in search of gold dental fillings. This image is taken up again when the speaker addresses her physician with the words:

> Ash, ash—
> You poke and stir.
> Flesh, bone, there is nothing there—
>
> A cake of soap,
> A wedding ring,
> A gold filling. (ll. 73-78)

The use of these images provoked a controversy among critics with regard to the allusions' appropriateness and lack of piety. Some critics argued that the imagery was inaccurately motivated, out of context, and thus inappropriate. Others thought the images belittled the Holocaust by applying them to the personal problems of an individual, showing little respect for the genocide of millions of innocent people. The debate came to a halt with James Young's influential study *Writing and Rewriting the Holocaust* (1988) in which he devoted an entire chapter to Sylvia Plath's poetry. He says:

> In Plath's case, rather than disputing the authenticity of her figures, we might look to her poetry for the ways the Holocaust has entered public consciousness as a trope, and how it then informs both the poet's view of the world and her representation of it in verse. (1988: 132)

The traumatic experiences of the speaker in Plath's poem, and the troubled mind of Plath herself, may be interpreted as her own personal hell, her own 'personal Holocaust'—an ordeal she eventually did not survive. In a more recent article on Plath's confessional poetry, Naylor-Smith defends Plath's imagery and claims:

> The criticisms on Plath's Holocaust imagery rest in an inability to understand the Holocaust as an appropriate metaphor for women's struggles with self-effacement and domestic erasure. Irving Howe stated that "it is decidedly unlikely that [the experience of Holocaust victims] was duplicated in a middleclass family living in Wellesley, Massachusetts" (qtd. in Boswell 53) . . . Howe's narrow view of Plath's poetry as exclusively confessional offensively attempts to compare degrees of oppression among subjugated groups. He is acknowledging the public, historical Holocaust while dismissing the domestic holocaust women have experienced personally and privately. (2013: 319-20)

Naylor-Smith's article shows that the debate about Plath's Holocaust imagery is far from over and suggests that her work is considered to be more than merely confessional or personal. Moreover, the fact that Plath's perspective is influenced by her paternal German heritage should be acknowledged; this additional dimension and her personal reflection of the Holocaust connect public and private history (see Kalaidjian 2006).

The speaker's comments on suicide, dying, and the 'theater of resurrection' in "Lady Lazarus" can be read with irony while sounding both cynical and morbid at the same time. At one point she calls dying "an art" and says:

> Dying
> Is an art, like everything else.
> I do it exceptionally well. (ll. 43-5)

Whereas writing poetry is considered an art—and Plath was in fact said to "do it exceptionally well" (l. 45)—the equation of dying and art makes the reader wonder about the speaker's concept of art, particularly when she claims that it is an art "like everything else" (l. 44). In fact, this use of the word makes "art" sound rather banal. If everything is an art, the word art loses its quality of being something special that can be created only by specifically talented or trained artists. Dying is not something limited to the talented or trained, it cannot be exercised or rehearsed, nor can it—in the strict sense of the word—be repeated; thus "I do it exceptionally well" sounds like a paradox. What the speaker implies is that her kind of dying is a self-induced and autonomous process that may be reversed. In that sense, "dying" acquires the meaning here of 'killing yourself' or 'attempting to commit suicide.' With this definition in mind, the following lines have exactly the confessional quality that gave confessional poetry its name:

> I do it so it feels like hell.
> I do it so it feels real.
> I guess you could say I've a call.

It's easy enough to do it in a cell.
It's easy enough to do it and stay put. (ll. 46-9)

The anaphora and repetition of almost the entire line ("I do it so it feels . . .,"
ll. 46-7) endows the action with the quality of first-hand experience and proud
avowal. What the actual experience is, however, if it only *feels* real, remains unsaid: a magic trick? a mere illusion? The same stylistic device (anaphora and
repetition) is used in the following stanza: "It's easy enough to do it . . .," ll. 48-9).
Whereas the first of these two sentences ends in "in a cell" (an obvious allusion
to killing oneself in prison or a mental hospital), the second sentence finishes
with the words "and stay put" (l. 49). Apparently what makes her "dying" different from that of other suicides is the deliberate will not to "stay put." These two
different but analogously repeated sentences are connected by the sarcastic remark "I guess you could say I've a call" (l. 47), with a notable typographic correspondence in the words "call" (l. 48) and "cell" (l. 49). What makes this statement so sarcastic is the fact that "call" can be read in the meaning of 'call to a
profession,' 'a demand to oneself,' or even as the call, in the biblical context,
that summoned Lazarus from the dead.

The speaker's monologue can be read as an allusion to Samuel Taylor Coleridge's "Kubla Khan" ("And all should cry, Beware! Beware! / His flashing eyes,
his floating hair!"), the prophet poet that Plath uses as a contrast to her own
female version. At the same time her exclamation gains a biblical dimension,
too, when she says:

Herr God, Herr Lucifer
Beware
Beware. (ll. 79-81)

This apostrophe to god and the devil is meant as a warning, and it should be
noted that it is the speaker who gives the warning and not vice versa. What at
first looks like hubris can also be read as an act of female empowerment because Herr God and Herr Lucifer—as male figures—have in some respect (like
Plath's father and her husband, or the speaker's physician) become her adver-
saries against whom she needs to assert herself. The warning ultimately turns
into prophecy and threat:

Out of the ash
I rise with my red hair
And I eat men like air. (ll. 82-4)

Here the speaker presents herself in the image of the phoenix, who rises from its
own ashes. Thus, the poem does not end on a note of death and ultimate destruction, but rather in a form of resurrection that works as an alternative version to that of the biblical Lazarus who is revived by the grace of the (Judeo-
Christian) male god. Lady Lazarus, however, rises in her own right (cf. l. 83),
equipped with the power to destroy men who are without substance (air) and
helpless in comparison: "And I eat men like air" (l. 84). These lines can be read
not only as a kind of gendered retribution, but also as the desperate wish for
female self-assertion. For this, the genre of confessional poetry with its new possibilities offered an ample realm to a poet whose provocative lyrical voice and
intellectual brilliance have long survived her premature death at the age of thir-
ty-one. "The mixed ferocity and coldness of Plath's work in poems such as 'Lady

Lazarus' or 'Lesbos,'" Nelson astutely remarks, "is the aspect of her work least dulled by time and the conventionalization of confession" (2013: 34).

4. The 'End' of Confessional Poetry and Its Aftermath

As a poetic movement of the 1960s, confessional poetry opened up the range of topics for poems toward the highly personal and intimate. Its self-revelatory nature ended High Modernism's claim for depersonalization and self-restraint and introduced a new kind of subjectivity to American poetry. It should thus be understood as both a reaction to traditional poetics and to socio-cultural and even political developments. Nelson (ibid.: 32) asserts:

> To the extent that we want to consider it a movement, confessional poetry ends in the mid-1970s. In 1973, Lowell published the last and most controversial of his confessional works, *The Dolphin* . . . By 1975, when Sexton's last collection, *The Awful Rowing Toward God*, was published posthumously, she, Berryman, and Plath were all dead and by their own hand.

With the death of some of major "confessional" poets, the movement thus labeled came to a standstill; what endured, however, was the strong impact that confessional poetry had exerted on public and poetic discourses. One of the major values in the 'public consciousness' of American society of the 1950s had been privacy. With their candid, direct, and transgressive poems—which at the time of publication were read as an almost exhibitionist kind of self-exposure—the confessional poets violated a cultural code of decency and breached a social consensus. In this respect, confessional poetry "represents a counter-discourse on privacy, one that undermined the sanctity of the home and deflated the value of privacy by attending to its deprivations" (ibid.: 38). By making the private public through poetry, the confessional poets had a lasting influence on what was considered politically relevant. With the civil rights movement, the debate on women's rights and abortion, and the gay liberation movement, the 'private' had become political, and speaking out in public became accepted as an act of resistance and self-empowerment. By the late 1970s and early 1980s, confessing to marital problems and infidelity, dysfunctional families, alcoholism, depression, or sexual difference was no longer new or shocking.

The aftermath of confessional poetry has led to two developments: "post-confessional poetry" grew out of the insistence on self-expression and is represented by poets such as Frank Bidart (b. 1939) and Sharon Olds (b. 1942); the second development is evidenced by the current discourse on privacy (cf. ibid.: 33-43). In talk shows and talk radio, TV formats, and more recently on social networks and blogs, the act of confession in writing is no longer the domain of fiction writers and poets, but is available to anyone with the desire to publicly confess. The initial criticism that confessional poetry lacked artistry—a critique that was quickly revised—can now be leveled against many of the blogs that are sometimes intended to be literary but mostly lack the artistic sophistication, formal control, idiomatic refinement, and emotional strength that characterize the work of Sexton, Berryman, Snodgrass, Lowell, and Plath.

Bibliography

Selected Primary Literature

Bishop, Elizabeth. 1995 [1965]. "The Armadillo." In: *The Complete Poems 1927-1979*. New York: Farrar, Straus & Giroux. 103-4.
——. 1995 [1979]. "The Moose." In: *The Complete Poems 1927-1979*. New York: Farrar, Straus & Giroux. 169-73.
Ginsberg, Allen. 2001 [1956]. *Howl and Other Poems*. San Francisco: City Lights.
Lowell, Robert. 2007 [1973]. *The Dolphin*. In: *Collected Poems*. Ed. Frank Bidart and David Gewanter. New York: Farrar, Straus & Giroux.
——. 2006 [1959]. "Skunk Hour." In: *Selected Poems: Expanded Edition*. New York: Farrar, Straus & Giroux. 177.
——. 2006 [1964]. "Night Sweat." In: *Selected Poems: Expanded Edition*. New York: Farrar, Straus & Giroux. 133.
O'Hara, Frank. 2001 [1964]. *Lunch Poems*. San Francisco: City Lights.
Plath, Sylvia. 2004 [1965]. *Ariel: The Restored Edition. A Facsimile of Plath's Manuscript, Reinstating Her Original Selection and Arrangement*. New York: Harper Collins.
——. 1992 [1962]. "Lady Lazarus." In: *The Collected Poems*. Ed. Ted Hughes. New York and Cambridge, MA: Harper Perennial. 244-7.
——. 2005 [1971]. *The Bell Jar*. New York: Harper Perennial.
Sexton, Anne. 1981. *The Complete Poems*. Boston and New York: Houghton Mifflin.
Snodgrass, W.D. 1983 [1960]. *Heart's Needle*. New York: Knopf.

Selected Secondary Literature

Bassnett, Susan. 2005. *Sylvia Plath: An Introduction to the Poetry*. 2nd ed. Houndmills, Basingstoke and New York: Palgrave Macmillan.

   Unlike Gill, who approaches Plath's poetry chronologically, Bassnett's introduction chooses a thematically-ordered structure and bases her interpretation on close-reading analysis.

Gill, Jo. 2008. *The Cambridge Introduction to Sylvia Plath*. Cambridge and New York: Cambridge UP.

   This study serves as a good starting point for students who want to get an overview of Plath's poetry and brief information on Plath's life.

Middlebrook, Diane Wood. 1993. "What Was Confessional Poetry?" In: Jay Parini and Brett C. Millier (eds.), *The Columbia History of American Poetry*. New York: Columbia UP. 632-49.

   This article is a good start to get a general idea concerning the characteristics and topics of confessional poetry.

Nelson, Deborah. 2013. "Confessional Poetry." In: Jennifer Ashton (ed.), *The Cambridge Companion to American Poetry since 1945*. Cambridge and New York: Cambridge UP. 31-45.

   Like Middlebrook's article, this one gives a concise overview of confessional poetry.

Witek, Terri. 1993. *Robert Lowell and Life Studies: Revising the Self.* Columbia, MO: U of Missouri P.

This provocative and controversial study explores Robert Lowell's fourth volume of poetry in detail, focusing on crisis and identity formation.

Young, James E. 1998. *Writing and Rewriting the Holocaust: Narrative and the Consequences of Interpretation.* Bloomington and Indianapolis: Indiana UP.

This book is considered a landmark in literary studies of the Holocaust and devotes one chapter to the poetry of Sylvia Plath.

Further References

Albers, Carsten. 2001. "Confessional Poetry Revisited: Sexton, Plath, Lowell, and Snodgrass from a 90s Perspective." In: Jürgen Heideking, Jörg Helbig and Anke Ortlepp (eds.), *The Sixties Revisited: Culture—Society—Politics.* Heidelberg: Winter. 357-79.

Bawer, Bruce. 1991. "Sylvia Plath and the Poetry of Confession." In: *The New Criterion.* 9.6: 18-27.

Britzolakis, Christina. 1999. *Sylvia Plath and the Theatre of Mourning.* Oxford and New York: Clarendon Press.

Brunner, Eva. "Confessional Poetry: A Poetic Perspective on Narrative Identity." In: Claudia Holler and Martin Klepper (eds.), *Rethinking Narrative Identity: Persona and Perspective.* Amsterdam and Philadelphia: Benjamins. 187-202.

Bundtzen, Lynda K. 1983. *Plath's Incarnations: Women and the Creative Process.* Ann Arbor: The U of Michigan P.

Collins, Theresa. 1998. "Plath's 'Lady Lazarus.'" In: *The Explicator* 56.3: 156-8.

Kalaidjian, Walter. 2006. *The Edge of Modernism: American Poetry and the Traumatic Past.* Baltimore, MD: Johns Hopkins University Press.

Kalstone, David. 1987 [1977]. "The Uses of History." In: David Kalstone. *Five Temperaments.* Repr. in: Harold Bloom (ed.), *Robert Lowell: Modern Critical Views.* New York and Philadelphia: Chelsea House. 81-100.

Kendall, Tim. 2001. *Sylvia Plath: A Critical Study.* London: Faber and Faber.

Kirsch, Adam. 2005. *The Wounded Surgeon: Confession and Transformation in Six American Poets. The Poetry of Lowell, Bishop, Berryman, Jarrell, Schwartz, and Plath.* New York: Norton.

Lerner, Laurence. 1987. "What Is Confessional Poetry?" In: *Critical Quarterly* 29.2: 44-66.

Naylor-Smith, Whitney. 2013. "Refiguring Women: Metaphor, Metonymy, and Identity in Plath's Confessional Poetry." In: *Plath Profiles* 6: 319-27.

Wagner, Linda W. (ed.) 1984. *Critical Essays on Sylvia Plath.* New York: G.K. Hall.

Wagner-Martin, Linda. 1999. *Sylvia Plath: A Literary Life.* Houndmills, Basingstoke and London: Macmillan.

Yezzi, David. 1998. "Confessional Poetry and the Artifice of Honesty." In: *The New Criterion* 16.10: 14-21.

22.

New Formal Languages

Frank O'Hara's "The Day Lady Died" and
John Ashbery's "Self-Portrait in a Convex Mirror"

Ulfried Reichardt

1. Postmodern American Poetry and the New York School of Poetry

With the center of painting moving from Paris to New York in the wake of the German occupation of the French capital in 1940, New York became the new global center of the arts. Of course, modern art did not remain unaffected by this transatlantic shift of milieu. While the new developments in American art remained strongly linked to European modernist ideas and avant-gardes, post-modernism can be seen not only as a development beyond modernism (in the sense of a further development and radicalization of modernist ideas) but also as an Americanization of many elements found in the earlier European versions of modernist art. Some significant features can be summed up as modularity: taking aesthetic forms apart and recombining the elements in new ways, de-hierarchization and democratization, a relaxed attitude with regard to the distinction between highbrow and lowbrow culture, and a strong focus on colloquial and vernacular languages and forms (cf. van Elteren 1996: 61). Popular and mass culture have often been appropriated by so-called 'high culture,' and new hybrids between 'high' and 'low' have almost become the norm. Additionally, the emphasis on the surface of phenomena and objects, implying the absence of an essence lying beneath the signs, has been named as an important postmodern-ist characteristic.

In post-World War II American poetry, the New York School in particular developed new formal languages that exemplify several of these modular characteristics. Frank O'Hara and John Ashbery, along with Kenneth Koch, Barbara Guest, and James Schuyler, belong to what became known as the New York School of Poetry, a loose group of poets that formed in the early 1950s. The term is modeled on the more famous and already established New York School of Painting, including such illustrious names as Jackson Pollock, Willem de Kooning, and Franz Kline, better known as painters of Abstract Expressionism. This school is regarded as the first genuine American movement in painting and the first to be recognized worldwide. Not only was it championed by influential art critics such as Clement Greenberg and Harold Rosenberg, it was advertised as a prototypical product of the free world, signaling the freedom of expression of the supposedly unencumbered Western individual in the Cold War of words. The proximity to these painters in Manhattan was important for the formal development of the New York School poets. Harold Rosenberg describes the attitude of the Abstract Expressionists: "[they] appropriated modern painting . . . to what is basically an individual, sensual, psychic, and intellectual effort to live actively in the present" (in Ashton 1973: 184). And as painter Robert Motherwell explained: "The process of painting then is conceived of as an adventure, without preconceived ideas . . . Fidelity to what occurs between oneself and the canvas . . . becomes central" (in Sandler 1970: 96). In a book significantly called *The Triumph of American Painting*, Irving Sandler suggests that this approach has been characterized as painting in "an open field of free gestures" (ibid.: 92). What is most important to these painters is the creative engagement with their own experience through the process of painting.

Two features of the new American painting had a particularly strong influence on the poets of the New York School. First, the two-dimensional surface of the canvas is emphasized and the Renaissance perspective, which creates the illusion of three-dimensionality, is cast aside. For the observer, this central perspective entails the belief that s/he controls the picture in and by the act of looking. Second, the canvas is reconceived as a field of action, and painting is staged as an event in which artists express themselves spontaneously. A final extra-temporal meaning thus cannot be produced or extracted. Moreover, foreground and background, figure and ground, can no longer be separated. As Frank O'Hara quotes Jackson Pollock characterizing his painterly approach, the artist is "in the painting"—a dynamic process (1959: 32). Similar to the act of painting, the poem is no longer conceived of as the recording of a temporally and spatially distanced act of observation; rather, it is understood as the ongoing observation of what is going on both outside and inside the poet's mind. It is the distance of the observing 'eye' as an individual 'I'—a conceptional attitude which can be traced back to René Descartes—that has been put into question in the new American art since the 1950s; and this, I want to claim, is one of the crucial moments that distinguishes it from modernist art.

Both Ashbery and O'Hara wrote about art and were otherwise involved in the world of the visual arts: O'Hara as a curator at the Museum of Modern Art and as a reviewer for *Artnews*, and Ashbery as an art critic for *New York* and *Newsweek* magazines. Both poets also have strong links to the newly composed music of the period; for example, Ashbery is well versed in modern and contemporary music, O'Hara wrote a poem for Morton Feldman, and Feldman posthumously composed a piece for O'Hara. Thus we must also consider the aesthetic exchange of the poets with avant-garde music, for instance, the refusal to strictly separate sound and music in John Cage's compositional acts. This exchange is important, as the temporal arrangement of their poetry cannot be attributed exclusively to similarities with painting.

More generally, both Ashbery and O'Hara are distinguished as New York Poets by their proximity to the American post-World War II avant-garde—an aesthetic rather than a political or social avant-garde. They distrust any form of doxa or dogmatism, an attitude that can be explained in the context of the Cold War, McCarthyism, and an atmosphere that Robert Lowell called the "tranquilized *Fifties*" ("Memories of West Street and Lepke," 1959; original emphasis). Central to their concerns is the experimental use of language—analogous to handling sounds and paint—and also the exploration of new ways of (re-)presenting the self, while identity politics is of no concern. Their poetry, strongly influenced by the other arts, negotiates their aesthetic strategies. They were among the avant-garde—the bohemian coterie situated in Manhattan—and thus associated with an idea of the metropolis that emerged in the nineteenth century. In the title of his 1998 book, David Lehman even calls the New York School of Poets "the Last Avantgarde."

2. Frank O'Hara, "The Day Lady Died" (1959):
Self-Surfing on the City's Surfaces

Frank O'Hara was born in Baltimore in 1926, spent two years in the U.S. Navy, and studied first music and then English at Harvard where he met Ashbery and Koch. In 1951 he went to New York City and worked as a curator at the Museum of Modern Art (MOMA) until his untimely death on July 27, 1966 after being struck by a beach buggy on Fire Island in the early morning of July 26. Like Ashbery, O'Hara was gay—a focus of recent criticism; at the time, homosexuality could not be spoken about openly. It often involved certain codes of behavior and aesthetic forms such as "camp," a term that connotes a form of playfulness and connoisseurship which toys with ornaments and does not shy away from kitsch (see Susan Sontag's "Notes on Camp," 1964). Elements of such an aesthetic can be found in O'Hara's poems. His social nature led to O'Hara being called a 'coterie' poet—one who writes and acts within a group of like-minded artists and whose texts must be decoded with reference to these people. He knew many painters, composers, and poets, and curated several shows of Abstract Expressionist painters while at the MOMA.

"The Day Lady Died" is O'Hara's most famous poem and is symptomatic of his approach to poetry (1974 [1959]: 146). It belongs to his "I do this I do that" poems and also to his "lunch poems" (see *Lunch Poems* 1964), which were often written during his lunch hour at the MOMA. While these terms imply a nonchalant and off-hand approach to writing, even the title is composed in a complex manner. "Lady Day" is the stage name of Billie Holiday, a brilliant jazz singer who died on July 17, 1959. It is the only time Holiday is indirectly mentioned in a postmodernist poetic version of an elegy. The title tells us that the poem will not speak directly about the jazz singer but rather stages the context in which the speaker learned of her death. The poem presents the day Billie Holiday died from within the experience of the poet and focuses on the ways in which the speaking 'I' contextualizes the news of her death, how he remembers her, and what he associates her with: a beautiful woman, the tragic life of an African American artist, her music and singing.

The poem begins with a precise statement of time and place: "It is 12:20 in New York a Friday / three days after Bastille day, yes / it is 1959 and I go get a shoeshine / because I will get off the 4:19 in Easthampton at 7:15 and then go straight to dinner / and I don't know the people who will feed me" (ll. 1-6). While the time and place is a significant moment in Billie Holiday's life, it is not yet so for O'Hara's. The poet is simply going about his daily routine, and it is this routine that makes up most of the poem—a sequential list of places he goes, things he does, objects he buys, thoughts he has, and people he sees. There are at least two ways of looking at the routine character of his lunch hour activities however, two perspectives that do not exclude each other. One is to stress the arbitrariness of the items described and things he does; the other is to read these items and actions as significant for the context in which the memory of Billie Holiday occurs. Both approaches have been defended by critics. The first emphasizes the horizontal and sequential extension with the juxtaposition of names, places, people, and activities, and focuses on the paratactical form, a logic of the "and . . . and . . . and." The other attempts to extract meaning from the individual items selected by the poet—a vertical focus that uses associations connected with words to posit lines of connections such as selection based on

Francophilia, exoticism, homosexuality, black culture and Africa, rebellious writers and bohemianism, and consumerist pleasure, among other things: "in the GOLDEN GRIFFIN I get a little Verlaine / for Patsy with drawings by Bonnard although I do / think of Hesiod, trans. Richard Lattimore or / Brendan Behan's new play or *Le Balcon* or *Les Nègres* / of Genet" (ll. 14-8; original emphasis). Yet the basic structure of the poem is a long deferment, as the title indicates an event that is mentioned only in the last section.

The narration of some accidentals of this particular lunch hour can be seen as a frame for the subject of the elegy; yet frame and picture, or figure and ground, do not differ in any explicit manner. Rather, the poet is 'in the picture' in the same way that representation as presentation is understood in Jackson Pollock's drip paintings. Surface and depth can no longer be distinguished. No symbols are used because usually the link between symbol and meaning has been conventionally structured, is predictable, and thus carries—in the diction of information theory—no information. If life is made up, to a considerable degree, of the everyday, then shouldn't the everyday itself carry significance and produce meaning? In another poem O'Hara writes that "the surface and the meaning . . . the one is the other" (1971 [1953]: 497). And philosopher Stanley Cavell argues that it is the everyday experience and ordinary language which are the sites where meaning is created (see *In Quest of the Ordinary* 1994). Therefore, the poem's enumeration of ordinary places, objects, and people can be read as being meaningful in itself as well as creating a specific field of forces in which the news of Billie Holiday's death is experienced.

However, the poet does not merely register events. What is important is his attention to even the minute details, the intensity of his perception, his openness to impressions. One could speak of 'hyperrealism' in the sense that he mentions, for example, the train's departure and arrival times, information that is plainly irrelevant, then as now. Yet even while consumption is his aim, the speaker's movements are not directed but rather meandering as they convey the fast, pulsating rhythm of the city at noon. He notes the irregularity when the bank teller—for once in her life—does not look up his balance, yet this variation in routine does not constitute a special moment. He knows her first name and she becomes individualized, but only for a passing moment. The course of his day is accidental, singular; every day is different. Yet it is situated within a personal network of horizontal correspondences created by the names of the friends and places he mentions.

In the fourth section the flow of images accelerates, achieved by O'Hara's listing and juxtaposing snapshots. Here the conjunction "and" occurs seven times; the text 'swings' and is highly dynamic. It is in the middle of this movement that the vibrant flow suddenly comes to a momentary standstill. When the poet stops to buy cigarettes, he sees Billie Holiday's face on the title page of the *New York Post*, and this hits him like a shock. As Walter Benjamin writes: "Perhaps we can see the peculiar workings [*Leistung*] of the defense against shocks in giving the event an exact position in time at the expense of its content" (1977 [1955]: 193; my translation). The impression becomes an event, and for a moment the poet is catapulted out of time. Yet he immediately reenters the present by stressing that he is sweating by now. Only his subjective experience, his response to the news of her death are reported. Yet he is not drawn into the past; no modernist *mémoire involuntaire* for him:

and for Mike I just stroll into the PARK LANE
Liquor Store and ask for a bottle of Strega and
then I go back where I came from to 6th Avenue
and the tobacconist in the Ziegfeld Theatre and
casually ask for a carton of Gauloises and a carton
of Picayunes, and a NEW YORK POST with her face on it

and I am sweating a lot by now and thinking of
leaning on the john door in the 5 SPOT
while she whispered a song along the keyboard
to Mal Waldron and everyone and I stopped breathing
(ll. 20-9; original emphasis)

The memory captures only one single moment, and its intensity is based on its position within the ongoing sequence of the poet's undirected wanderings. This moment is, paradoxically, as much part of this sequence—and thus one event or impression among others—as it is a moment beyond it, and can be understood on two levels. First, the poet's remembrance of Billie Holiday appears as yet another event in his day, and second, he remembers her by quoting a special moment when he heard her sing. While the greater part of the poem is an autobiographical narrative, the poet's memory of Billie Holiday is impressionistic, evocative, allusive. In the course of his stroll on a hot and humid July midday in mid-Manhattan, a man in his mid-life is beginning to sweat; when he sees her picture on the paper's front page, he thinks of her singing and how he had been casually leaning on the toilet door, maybe having just strolled into the then famous jazz club 5 Spot. As critics have pointed out, at the time Holiday had almost entirely lost her voice and did, in fact, whisper, which can be interpreted here as a sound so weak that it seems to come from somewhere beyond, a shadow of her real voice. As "she whispered a song along the keyboard"—for O'Hara, an intimate act—everyone stopped breathing. The syntactic position of "everyone" in the last line is, as has often been remarked, ambivalent: it could imply that Holiday whispered to Mal Waldron and everyone, and I stopped breathing; or it could mean that she whispered only to Mal Waldron, and everyone and I stopped breathing; it certainly implies both. The shifting syntactic place of the word is (probably) not accidental, but rather functions as a link between Holiday and her singing, the pianist, the whole room full of people, and O'Hara himself, who records the feeling. She breathes vicariously for everybody in the room—a moment of the highest intensity. We remain in the paratactical universe of juxtaposition and sequence until the simultaneity of his and her presence is punctuated by the conjunction "while," emphasizing co-presence and simultaneity.

And then the poem abruptly ends, suspended in the stopped breath. Breath, of course, is the medium of singing, and Billie Holiday's breathing had stopped three days before. Yet this unpunctuated ending also leaves the poem open-ended. There is no period; the hiatus is prolonged; the moment extended into the present as memory. The sound continues and reverberates, as in an empty hall. The sequence has been, at least temporarily, broken or suspended. Yet the sound of her voice continues, stressing the sensual, experiential dimension of her singing that the poem evokes, the relationship momentarily established between her and him (and everyone else in the room, and perhaps, even beyond the room). The poem focuses on the physical dimension, the corporality of her voice, her presence as voice. As O'Hara emphasizes in another poem, "the mere presence / changes everything like a chemical dropped on a paper / and all thoughts disappear in a strange quiet excitement / I am sure of nothing but this, intensified by breathing" (1971 [1959]: 350).

Frank O'Hara's poetry is closely linked to New York City. At the fence of Battery Park in downtown Manhattan, a few lines of his on the city are quoted: "I have never clogged myself with the praises of pastoral life, nor with nostalgia for an innocent past of perverted acts in pastures. No. One need never leave the confines of New York to get all the greenery one wishes—I can't even enjoy a blade of grass unless I know there's a subway handy, or a record store or some other sign that people do not totally *regret* life" (1974 [1957]: 87; original emphasis). For O'Hara, the city is a stage, a forum, a place of freedom and expression, of swiftly changing surfaces and ever new encounters, a network of friends and fellow artists, of cultural events, diversity and variety, interesting and non-conventional people, of amplitude as opposed to the narrowness of 1950s suburban America. It is the opposition of suburbia and emphatically not a place where Tupperware parties count as cultural events. "The Day Lady Died" therefore can also be seen as a sequence of personal snapshots of mid-twentieth-century life in Manhattan.

3. John Ashbery, "Self-Portrait in a Convex Mirror" (1975): An Interior Dialogue with a Renaissance Painter

Following the publication of *Self-Portrait in a Convex Mirror* in 1975, John Ashbery received all three important American literary prizes: the Pulitzer, the National Book Award, and the National Book Critics Circle Award. While before this date he had been a rather unknown poet of complex avant-garde poetry, this publication catapulted him into the center of interest for both the literary establishment and the media. He is now one of the most famous American poets of the second half of the twentieth century: in 2008 The Library of America published *John Ashbery: Collected Poems, 1956-1987*, "the first collection of a living poet ever published by that series" (Hennessy: 39). Yet many readers note that they do not understand his poems. Ashbery was born in 1927 in Rochester, New York and grew up on his father's farm. He studied at Harvard and Columbia, spent ten years in Paris, and returned in 1965 to New York City. Ashbery currently lives in Hudson, about two hours north of the City. For many years he wrote art reviews and taught poetry at colleges in New York. His first collection of poems, *Some Trees*, was selected by W.H. Auden for the Yale Younger Poets prize in 1956.

"Self-Portrait" (1975) is Ashbery's most frequently anthologized poem. It is also among his most accessible poems, as it refers to a painting we can hold in front of us and thus easily visualize. The poem is an extended meditation on the Italian painter Francesco Parmigianino's very small (24.4 cm in diameter) "Self-Portrait in A Convex Mirror," which he painted in 1524. It can be seen today at the Kunsthistorisches Museum in Vienna, Austria, and is symptomatic of Mannerism in the arts. Mannerism is a development within Italian Renaissance art in which the period's characteristic emphasis on harmony is distorted and broken up. Ashbery's poem is also an example of *ekphrasis*—a text that focuses on an image, most often a painting or a sculpture, and describes or translates it in(to) words. The term goes back to ancient rhetoric, yet it recently has become current in the context of research on intermediality. James Heffernan remarks that "Parmigianino's 'Self-Portrait' is . . . the first mirror portrait that *openly reveals itself as such* . . . Ashbery's poem simply makes explicit what all *ekphrasis* entails and implies: the experience of the viewer, and the pressure of that experience on his or her interpretation of the work of art" (1998: 201-2; original emphasis).

While the distance in time, place, and social development between Parmigianino and Ashbery is immense, there are, nevertheless, important similarities. Mannerism distorts Renaissance harmony, while Postmodernism distorts the 'Tradition of the New,' which is what Modernism had become by the 1950s. More importantly, Parmigianino's portrait is a consciously contorted image of himself; it therefore explicitly involved acts of self-reflection on visual as well as cognitive levels, which is also an aspect of postmodernism. An important historical context to mention here is that in 1436 Leon Battista Alberti first proposed the method of constructing a painting following the principle of central perspective, in which the observer is able to control visually the whole picture and see it at once in its entirety, offering a fore-, middle- and background that simulates three-dimensionality on a two-dimensional canvas (cf. Belting 2008: 10, 31-6). Several scholars have argued that this innovation is linked with the emergence of the subject as individual, an 'I' conceived of as an observing 'eye' (cf. Walter Ong in Jay 1993: 67). However, early on—as Parmigianino's painting foregrounds—these important developments were thwarted by the counter-tendency to 'deconstruct' the newly won stability and unity of the subject. Parmigianino portrays his 'self' in a 'mannered' fashion, thus disrupting the very harmony the Renaissance had just inaugurated. It is precisely this moment in art history that interests John Ashbery. Reflecting on this self-portrait allows him to speak about the history of representation and of the subject with reference to a concrete image.

The poem, in Penguin's 1975 edition, is 16 pages long and divided into six sections (68-83). Many statements essential to the argument and development of the poem as a whole can be found in the first part. In addition to the portrait itself, Ashbery uses both Giorgio Vasari's book on the life of Parmigianino (1568) and Sidney Freedman's 1950 study of the painter. Art and art history, then, are intricately entwined in the poem:

> The first three [parts] consider the self in the present, past, and future; the second three confront the otherness of the painting of one's environment and history, and of one's actions. The language of art criticism, predominant only in the first globe, disappears along with Parmigianino's painting for long stretches, but both the painting and the critical discourse return periodically to provide Ashbery with fresh points of departure. (Shoptaw 1995: 174-5)

The poem begins with a gesture that compares Parmigianino's painterly and Ashbery's poetic acts, intricately linking the two moments in time as a performative act:

> As Parmigianino did it, the right hand
> Bigger than the head, thrust at the viewer
> And swerving easily away, as though to protect
> What it advertises. A few leaded panes, old beams,
> Fur, pleated muslin, a coral ring run together
> In a movement supporting the face, which swims
> Toward and away like the hand
> Except that it is in repose. It is what is
> Sequestered. (ll. 1-9; first section)

The hand's gesture can be understood as an invitation, whereas the face is shielded by the hand and the convex form. The poem, then, starts with a paradoxical statement—the self-portrait invites, greets, and distances the viewer all at the same time. Moreover, this beginning is a straightforward description of the painting, an explicit act of *ekphrasis*. The unusual forms inevitably focus the viewer's attention on the fact of representation itself. Francesco copied what he saw in a convex mirror: "Chiefly his reflection, of which the portrait / Is the reflection once removed. / The glass chose to reflect only what he saw / Which was enough for his purpose." His face is described as "a recurring wave / Of arrival" (ll. 16-9, 23-4; first section). The relationship between the portrayed self and the poet registering his own responses sets the tone of the poem; it will not be a merely formal description. The following lines contain some of the central statements of the poem:

> . . . The soul establishes itself.
> But how far can it swim out through the eyes
> And still return safely to its nest? . . .
> . . . to make the point
> That the soul is a captive, . . .
> The soul has to stay where it is . . .
> This is what the portrait says . . .
> . . . that the soul is not a soul,
> Has no secret, is small, and it fits
> Its hollow perfectly: Its room, our moment of attention.
> That is the tune but there are no words.
> The words are only speculation . . .
> But it is life englobed.
> One would like to stick one's hand
> Out of the globe, but its dimension,
> What carries it, will not allow it. (ll. 24-6, 28-9, 34, 39, 44-8, 55-8; first section)

The poem maintains that the soul, mind, or person is encapsulated in the skull and also in its representation. Only when we pay attention does it come alive, as works of art are always co-productions between the observer and the observed. But there are no words to articulate exactly or to clearly communicate to another person what the soul is. Words are only speculation, the poem claims, in several senses of the word—as mirror reflection and as speculation in the sense of ungrounded reasoning. It is one of Ashbery's signature traits to make abstract statements that seem to be straightforward in their meaning but then to undercut their claim, to immediately contradict them, or, as in this instance, to render the claim ambivalent so that it is put into doubt. The hand's gesture shields and invites, yet the globe's surface constitutes the boundary for the represented self; this has much to do with the limitations of the medium of language as well.

The poet concludes: "But your eyes proclaim / that everything is surface. The surface is what is there / And nothing can exist except what's there" (ll. 79-81; first section). The speaking 'I' cannot reach the painter; in a somewhat old-fashioned manner he refers to Parmigianino's inner core as his soul. While Francesco's face is beautiful and expressive, it remains paint on the canvas, a representation of somebody long gone. (Note that "surface" here has a meaning quite different from the glittery surfaces of O'Hara's New York City.) Yet the thrust of Ashbery's argument extends further; we can never reach anybody's real self, only the exterior surface, her or his consciousness being a 'black box.'

The argument is known in philosophy as the problem of 'other minds': How can we know another's thoughts and feelings if we have to rely on words, gestures, and other external signs? Yet while Ashbery propagates a postmodern aesthetic of the surface, at the same time he laments its emptiness; a certain nostalgic tone can be felt in this poem.

A second important observation is that the spherical representation freezes the painter into an ideal yet unchanging position. As John Shoptaw comments: "The sphere is a geometrically perfect but rhetorically imperfect figure, granting central, synecdochal power but prohibiting linear movement. Parmigianino's spherical poetics thus rules out change as a topic within his poem. Ashbery warps the sphere into an hourglass or a vase and temporalizes it by continually shifting our vantage point" (1995: 177). An implicit reference to John Keats's "Ode to a Grecian Urn" cannot be overlooked: "Thou still unravish'd bride of quietness / Thou foster-child of Silence and slow Time" (Keats 1970 [1819]: 533). The portrait's temporal stasis, and also its perfection and beauty, constitute a further starting point for the poet's meditations. He misses the temporal dimension, the flux and shifting moments, which necessarily make perfection impossible but render a face real.

Yet the moment of creation of every work of art is situated in a particular time and place, a concrete situation. In order to trace this atmosphere, the poem swerves away from its focus and imagines the context of the portrait's painting, its everyday surroundings, the people who came and went, the changing light and weather, "until no part / Remains that is surely you" (ll. 13-4; second section). Not only is the soul inaccessible to another person, but the person itself is made up of fragments of the exterior, of communication, of others, and is thus not completely identical to him- or herself.

Nevertheless, the portrait signifies an attempt to render the features "So as to be perfect and rule out the extraneous / Forever" (ll. 45-6; second section). The perfect beauty of the painting is based on the exclusion of time's and the environment's contingency and thus appears 'untrue.' Read within the history of the emergence of the modern individual, the portrait—the distorted yet also self-enclosed 'sphere' which in Ashbery's reading is self-referential—can be interpreted as a sign of the withdrawal of the self from its entanglements with the world as well as with transcendence. Individuals in the modern sense neither existed nor could they be thought of before the Renaissance. Since then, however, philosophy has been focused on the subject and its capabilities, separating humans from their surroundings and opposing them to the outside world. Yet as Shoptaw argues, narcissism in "Self-Portrait" "involves seeking the self in another and finding the other in oneself" (1995: 181-2). The poem, then, can be seen as an internal dialogue between the poet and the portrait, the poet seeking out the painter, yet in the act of searching being confronted only with himself. The represented person's strangeness, and the poet's failure to grasp the otherness of the other person, return the observer to himself. By reflecting on the painter's self-portrait, the poem emphasizes the multiple entangled relations between the portrait, the painter's reflection in the mirror, and the poet's self-reflection.

A further association brings us to the city: to the Sack of Rome in 1527, to Vienna in 1959 where the poet (actually) saw the painting with his French friend Pierre, and to New York in the poem's present, which he calls "a logarithm / Of other cities" (ll. 8-9; fifth section). Yet these cities are only indirectly present in the painting and in the poem, as injected urgency ("the city injects its own / Ur-

gency," ll. 1-2, fifth section), as the poem puts it. But the strong contrast between the hardly perceivable background of Parmigianino's face and the real city
outside is stressed: "the backing of the looking glass of the / Unidentified but
precisely sketched studio" (ll. 23-4; fifth section). Ashbery calls that which is
happening inside "a magma of interiors" (l. 32; second section). Now the speaker
directly addresses Francesco, pointing out newness and change, and suggests:
"What we need now is this unlikely / Challenger pounding on the gates of an
amazed / Castle" (ll. 39-40; fifth section). The internal dialogue between speaker
and painter again addresses the question of the portrait's seeming extra-
temporality and stresses the process of change.

At this point we have to suspend our efforts to make sense of Ashbery's ru-
minations and step back to take a more analytical look at the structure of his
poetry. Often we cannot find a direct reference, and the continuity of a sustained argument, narrative, or image seems to be broken. Other principles must
therefore be in place to organize how words and sequences of words are linked.
Frequently, the motivations for the movement are not directly visible and thus
must be located beneath the surface. We have already seen that the poem is as
much interested in the painting itself as in what happens within the process of
looking and reflecting about it. The perceptive, cognitive, and emotional processes of association are in the foreground. While being interviewed, Ashbery
spoke of attempting to present "the experience of experience. . . . The particular
occasion is of lesser interest to me than the way a happening or experience fil-
ters through to me. I believe this is the way it happens with most people. I'm
trying to set down a generalized transcript of what's really going on in our minds
all day long" (in Molesworth 1979: 177). Moreover, in a useful statement Ashbery compares his poetry to music, as music does not signify referentially nor
present arguments, yet still conveys meaning and signifies in a complex and
abstract manner: "What I like about music is its ability of being convincing, of
carrying an argument through successfully to the finish, though the terms of
this argument remain unknown quantities. What remains is the structure, the
architecture of the argument, scene or story. I would like to do this in poetry"
(Ashbery 1965: 523). If we take these statements seriously, our attempt at decoding the poem has to explain the hidden dynamics of the text. The 'argument' of
such a poem will be abstract, structural. The two main strategies employed are
based on the trope of metonymy and the confusingly floating use of pronouns.

Metonymy refers to tropes which, according to Roman Jakobson, are linked
to their reference by proximity—that is, contiguity, not similarity. The terms are
next to each other, as when I say Washington and mean the U.S. government.
Ashbery's poetry, however, contains sequences of associations which are connected metonymically to what is going on in the poet's mind. If one wants to
represent thinking as an ongoing process, one could use natural metaphors. As
such images would be worn out quickly, however, a different approach is necessary. Moreover, metaphors point to thought as finished entities rather than to
thinking as process. Images, fragments of memories, motivated and unmotivated associations, simply appear in the stream of consciousness. Associations
are motivated, yet we often do not consciously think of the reasons and links or
we forget them. Ashbery tends to leave out the concrete information, does not
mention the concrete reason for a mental image, thereby implying it is not interesting to the reader, and thus only records the fragments which come to the surface. The 'flow' of experience, of associations, superimposes the concrete and

specific experiences; images are metonymically related to memories or feelings which are not named, and only the effects of these are mentioned. Ashbery himself speaks of "a loosening of syntactical connections that allows experience to happen rather than to make sense" (in Nicholls 2000: 158). Another typical device is the peculiar floating use of personal pronouns, rendering it difficult to ascribe to a particular subject what is going on. While both devices make his poetry difficult, they allow Ashbery to undercut the conventionality of referential language and to use language in a quasi-musical, abstract fashion which, nevertheless, does not sever entirely the ties to signification and communication (cf. Reichardt 1991: 59-84).

To return to the poem, the following passage exemplifies Ashbery's approach to poetry as a recording of his thought process:

> It seems like a very hostile universe
> But as the principle of each individual thing is
> Hostile to, exists at the expense of all others
> As philosophers have often pointed out, at least
> *This* thing, the mute, undivided present
> Has the justification of logic, which
> In this instance isn't a bad thing
> Or wouldn't be, if the way of telling
> Didn't somehow intrude, twisting the end result
> Into a caricature of itself. (ll. 126-35; sixth section, original emphasis)

The thing or the person is exclusive of everything else in order to be an individual and thus exists in an unquestionable present, creating its meaning self-referentially by way of its existence. Yet Ashbery retraces his steps, skeptical of any affirmative statement that would fixate the "loose meaning" (cf. Ashbery's poem "Soonest Mended": "underneath the talk lies / The moving and not wanting to be moved, the loose / meaning, untidy and simple like a threshing floor," 1970 [1966]: 18). Such a presence would be irrefutable, as O'Hara insists, if language did not intervene, distorting the intended meaning. Representation, as Jacques Derrida has argued, implies repetition and copying, and thus the loss of originality and individuality. Entering into language per se involves partaking in a medium of communication that everybody can use, thereby de-individualizing what one wants to say. The poem reflects on representation, both in language and in painting, as a process of mediation that sets up a 'screen' between subject and expression, yet without which no communication were possible.

The poem ends on a melancholic note of farewell: "This otherness, this / 'Not-being-us' is all there is to look at / In the mirror" (ll. 156-8; sixth section). The poet's attention drifts. The portrait's gesture appears merely as a rhetorical convention. Francesco is lost in time and space, only present "Here and there, in cold pockets / Of remembrance, whispers out of time" (ll. 232-3; sixth section). Nostalgia for a lost past or another person cannot be satisfied, yet continues nevertheless. Memories are contingent; another person cannot be willed into presence. Traces linger only in hidden and unexpected places.

In summary, we can say that "Self-Portrait" is an *ekphrastic* poem about a sixteenth-century visual self-portrait, and its structure has affinities to the abstract logic of music. At the same time, it is a poetological poem focusing on the question of representation in art and in poetry, improvising on the relationship between reflection and self-reflection. The distortion of the central perspective in

Parmigianino's painting, recently introduced at that time, is further dissolved by temporalizing the portrait itself and staging the imagined one-sided dialogue between observer and observed and, moreover, the observer observing himself in the act of observing the painting. The multiple interconnected relations and movements are more important than the focus. The poem's use of language tests the limits of communicative language, exploring the potential of significa-tion beyond codified semantics and reference. Other, more structural forms of coherence are therefore tested. Charles Altieri usefully speaks of "tonal perspec-tives," of "variations amid repetition" and of "permutations of idea and tone" (1984: 155). Yet the reference of this new form of language remains the world of everyday experience. Susan Schultz concludes that "Ashbery's real importance may lie in the fact that we cannot separate his work from the language we use each time we think about the world" (1995: 9-10).

4. Conclusion

John Shoptaw claims that although "the aims of Ashbery's 'Self-Portrait' are lim-ited, it rivals Eliot's *Four Quartets* and Stevens's *Notes Towards a Supreme Fiction* in the perfection of its design" (1995: 174-5). Altieri writes that "[David] Carroll is correct in insisting that "The Day Lady Died" is a crucial touchstone for postmod-ern poetry" (1979: 122). While both poets' legacies are strong, their work, never-theless, belongs to a specific era and is symptomatic of that era. In different ways they convey the atmosphere of and ask urgent questions concerning the post-World War II period in America. Their work is part of the specifically American avant-garde of artists such as Jackson Pollock, Franz Kline, Willem de Kooning, Robert Motherwell, and Andy Warhol, composers such as John Cage and Morton Feldman, choreographers such as Merce Cunningham, and novelists like John Barth. In the work of these postmodernist artists, earlier forms of representation are experimentally explored and new formal languages are investigated.

Although several new movements have emerged in the meantime, the influ-ence of both O'Hara and Ashbery can still be detected in today's poetry. Because of O'Hara's early death in 1966, his direct influence on other poets is limited even while his poetry continues to be widely read and studied. In Germany, for instance, Rolf Dieter Brinkmann took O'Hara's poetry as a model for his own poetic improvisations. Ashbery, however, is still regarded as a major force on the poetry scene in America. Langdon Hammer, in *The New York Times* in 2008, even goes as far as to claim: "No figure looms so large in American poetry over the past 50 years as John Ashbery" (2008: n.p.). Language poetry, a movement within American poetry since the 1980s, has affinities not only to Ashbery's early phase of writing (*The Tennis Court Oath*, 1962) but also to his prose po-ems. As Language poets are interested in the ways in which the use of language and the meanings conveyed by language are always socially constructed and ideologically charged, Ashbery's poetry serves as a model for their using every-day language in a playful and ironic manner, yet at the same time for exploring its saturation with clichéd ways of thinking and speaking. Ashbery himself has been extremely prolific and continues to publish up to the present.

Bibliography

Selected Primary Literature

Ashbery, John. 1970. *The Double Dream of Spring.* New York: E. P. Dutton & Co.
——. 1972. *Three Poems.* New York: Penguin.
——. 1975. "Self-Portrait in a Convex Mirror." In: John Ashbery, *Self-Portrait in a Convex Mirror.* New York: Penguin. 68-83.
O'Hara, Frank. 1974. *The Selected Poems of Frank O'Hara.* Ed. Donald Allen. New York: Vintage.
——. 1974 [1959]. "The Day Lady Died." In: O'Hara 1974. 146.
——. 1971. *The Collected Poems of Frank O'Hara.* Ed. Donald Allen. Berkeley: U of California P.
——. 1959. *Jackson Pollock.* New York: George Braziller.
——. 1964. *Lunch Poems.* San Francisco: City Lights.

Selected Secondary Literature

Altieri, Charles. 2006. *The Art of Twentieth-Century Poetry: Modernism and After.* Oxford: Blackwell.

Introduction to and overview of American poetry in the twentieth century, with a final subchapter on John Ashbery's poetry.

Hampson, Robert and Will Montgomery (eds.). 2010. *Frank O'Hara Now: New Essays on the New York Poet.* Liverpool: Liverpool UP.

Recent collection of essays looking at O'Hara's poetry and life from today's perspective, focusing on current aesthetic and cultural concerns.

Lehman, David. 1998. *The Last Avantgarde: The Making of the New York School of Poets.* New York: Doubleday.

A cultural history that situates the poets of the New York School in the context and artistic atmosphere of the city in the years 1948-1966, with chapters on Frank O'Hara and John Ashbery.

—— (ed.). 1980. *Beyond Amazement: New Essays on John Ashbery.* Ithaca: Cornell UP.

Important collection of essays on Ashbery's earlier poetry from several critical perspectives and with a look at different media like painting and music.

Perloff, Marjorie. 1997 [1977]. *Frank O'Hara: Poet Among Painters.* 2nd ed. Chicago: U of Chicago P.

This early major study of O'Hara's poetry stresses his relationship with Abstract Expressionist painting and offers close readings; the 1997 introduction adds a new focus on O'Hara's sexual orientation's influence on his style.

Reichardt, Ulfried. 1991. *Innenansichten der Postmoderne: Zur Dichtung John Ashberys, A. R. Ammons', Denise Levertovs und Adrienne Richs.* Würzburg: Königshausen & Neumann.

The study analyzes Ashbery's poetry and poetics in the context of postmodernism, focusing on theoretical as well as formal dimensions.

Schultz, Susan M. (ed.). 1995. *The Tribe of John: Ashbery and Contemporary Poetry.* Tuscaloosa: The U of Alabama P.

A collection of essays reconsidering Ashbery's poetry and investigating his immense influence on contemporary poets.

Shoptaw, John. 1995. *On the Outside Looking Out: John Ashbery's Poetry*. Cambridge, MA: Harvard UP.

Detailed study of Ashbery's complete work (up to the early 1990s); the author had access to Ashbery's manuscripts.

Further References

Altieri, Charles. 1979. *Enlarging the Temple: New Directions in American Poetry during the 1960s*. Lewisburg: Bucknell UP.

——. 1984. *Self and Sensibility in Contemporary American Poetry*. Cambridge. Cambridge UP.

Ashbery, John. 1965. "John Ashbery." In: Paris Leary and Robert Kelly (eds.), *A Controversy of Poets: An Anthology of Contemporary American Poetry*. New York: Doubleday. 523-4.

Ashton, Dore. 1973. *The New York School: A Cultural Reckoning*. New York: Vintage.

Belting, Hans. 2008. *Florenz und Bagdad: Eine westöstliche Geschichte des Blicks*. München: C. H. Beck.

Benjamin, Walter. 1977 [1955]. "Über einige Motive bei Baudelaire." *Illuminationen*. 2nd. ed. Frankfurt am Main: Suhrkamp. 185-229.

Cavell, Stanley. 1994. *In Quest of the Ordinary: Lines of Skepticism and Romanticism*. Chicago: U of Chicago P.

Hammer, Langdon. 2008. "But I Digress." In: *The New York Times*, Web. 1 Nov. 2014. <http://www.nytimes.com/2008/04/20/books/review/Hammer-t.html?_r=0>.

Heffernan, James A.W. 1998. "Entering the Museum of Words: Ashbery's 'Self-Portrait in a Convex Mirror'." In: Valerie Robillard and Els Jongeneel (eds.), *Pictures into Words: Theoretical and Descriptive Approaches to Ekphrasis*. Amsterdam: VU UP. 189-211.

Hennessy, Christopher. 2011. "John Ashbery: An Interview with Christopher Hennessy." In: *The American Poetry Review* (July/August): 39-44.

Herd, David. 2001. "John Ashbery: *Self-Portrait in a Convex Mirror*. In: Neil Roberts (ed.), *A Companion to Twentieth-Century Poetry*. Oxford: Blackwell. 536-46.

Jay, Martin. 1993. *Downcast Eyes: The Denigration of Vision in Twentieth-Century French Thought*. Berkeley: U of California P.

Keats, John. 1970. *The Poems of John Keats*. Ed. Miriam Allott. London: Longman.

Looper, Travis. 1992. "Ashbery's 'Self-Portrait'." In: *Papers on Language and Literature* 28.4 (Fall): 451-6.

Molesworth, Charles. 1979. *The Fierce Embrace: A Study of Contemporary American Poetry*. Columbia: U of Missouri P.

Nicholls, Peter. 2000. "John Ashbery and Language Poetry." In: Lionel Kelly (ed.), *Poetry and the Sense of Panic: Critical Essays on Elizabeth Bishop and John Ashbery*. Amsterdam: Rodopi. 155-67.

Ross, Andrew. 1989. "The Death of Lady Day." In: *Poetics Journal* 8 (June): 68-77.

Sandler, Irving. 1970. *The Triumph of American Painting: A History of Abstract Expressionism*. New York: Harper & Row.

Sontag, Susan. 1964. "Notes on Camp." In: *Partisan Review* 31: 515-30.

van Elteren, Mel. 1996. "Conceptualizing the Impact of US Popular Culture Globally." In: *Journal of Popular Culture* 30.1: 47-89.

23.

Performance Poetry

Anne Waldman's "skin Meat BONES (chant)" and Saul Williams's "Amethyst Rocks"

Harald Zapf

1. Performance Poetry and the Performance of Poetry

Poetry, Edward Hirsch says, is an "inexplicable (though not incomprehensible) event in language; an experience through words . . . a human fundamental, like music" (2014: 473). "Poetry atrophies when it gets too far from music," Ezra Pound aphoristically claimed in his indispensable primer on literature, *ABC of Reading*, where he distinguishes "three kinds of melopoeia, that is, verse made to sing; to chant or intone; and to speak" (1960 [1934]: 61). By foregrounding melopoeia—singing, chanting, and speaking—performance poetry remains closer to music than many other sorts of Western poetry, which "originated in orality, but has moved away from it" (2013: ix), write B. Eugene McCarthy and Fran Quinn in *Sound Ideas*, their book on *Hearing and Speaking Poetry*.

Different kinds of poetry demand different ways of perception. Performance poetry is meant to be spoken aloud and heard with physical ears, not primarily with mental ones. The physical/mental distinction, with its implied hierarchy and its connotations, shows why performance poetry is often considered a lesser type, but it also makes clear why performance poetry can be seen as being closer to the oral roots of poetry, for example non-academic and anti-elitist slam poetry, which Yale critic Harold Bloom called "the death of art" (in Rohter 2009). In this kind of poetry, textuality is inextricably linked to theatricality. Performance poetry revolves around the physicality and presence of the word, and the performed poetic word is endowed with the physical power to achieve immediate effects. In the modern Western institution of literature, performance poets are probably the ones who most ambitiously aim at immediacy.

Bob Holman—performance poet, poetry slam host, and poetry activist—thinks that "poetry is a contact sport" (Algarín/Holman 1994: 1) and speaks of the "poem's direct flight from mouth to ear" (ibid.). This direct flight is short-lived: "Perf is evanescent," Holman writes in his article on performance poetry, which "makes the lineage impossible to trace" (2002: 342). He then portrays today's performance poetry in a positive light by sketching its multicultural and global ancestry from Homer ("great oral poet"), Confucius, the African griots, and American Indian shamans via the troubadours of the Middle Ages and early 20th-century avant-gardes (e.g., dada, surrealist, and futurist performer poets of Russia and Italy) to contemporary strands of performance poetry in the United States: Music and Poetry (e.g., Gil Scott-Heron, Patti Smith), Sound poetry/multivoice (e.g., John Giorno, Jerome Rothenberg), Dub poetry (e.g., Linton Kwesi Johnson, Jean Binta Breeze), Slam (e.g., Marc Smith, Beth Lisick), Cowboy poetry (e.g., Baxter Black, Sue Wallis), Audio, film, and video poetry (e.g., Kurt Heintz, Jean Howard), Political Heart (e.g., Sonia Sanchez, Sherman Alexie), ASL (e.g., Peter Cook, Kenny Lerner), Trance (e.g., Janet Hamill, and also

Saul Williams, "who orbits hip-hop to land on his own turntable globe"), Personae (e.g., Patricia Smith, Dael Orlandersmith), and Web poetry (ibid.: 342-5).

Holman gives performance universal significance by depicting it as part of
the human condition. Sometimes he seems to use 'performance' and 'oral' interchangeably, for example when he opens up the oral/written dichotomy: "Anthropologists count as oral literature only that which has never been written
down, when in fact, any time a poem is read aloud it is oral literature" (ibid.).
Does it make sense to speak of 'oral literature'? And what is 'orality'? In *Orality
and Literacy*, Walter Ong deals with these questions in a lucid way. He distinguishes between "primary" and "secondary orality":

> I style the orality of a culture totally untouched by any knowledge of writing or
> print, 'primary orality'. It is 'primary' by contrast with the 'secondary orality' of
> present-day high-technology culture . . . Today primary oral culture in the strict
> sense hardly exists, since every culture knows of writing and has some experi-
> ence of its effects. Still, to varying degrees many cultures and subcultures, even
> in a high-technology ambiance, preserve much of the mind-set of primary
> orality. (1982: 11)

What is called 'performance poetry' today belongs, of course, in the category of
secondary orality; it is oral poetry within a culture of writing and print, but it
often tries to "preserve" or go back to the "mind-set of primary orality," which is
impossible, should one follow Ong. For him, 'oral literature,' which has increased in popularity in contemporary performance poetry contexts, is not only
a contradiction in terms, it is a "monstrous concept": "[I]t appears quite impossible to use the term 'literature' to include oral tradition and performance without subtly but irremediably reducing these somehow to variants of writing.
Thinking of oral tradition or a heritage of oral performance, genres and styles as
'oral literature' is rather like thinking of horses as automobiles without wheels"
(ibid.: 12). Holman's use of the term 'oral literature' in 2002 shows that Ong's
"battle to eliminate it totally" has, so far, failed (ibid.: 14). The term has survived, perhaps simply because "[w]e don't have a better term," writes John
Sutherland in his *Little History of Literature* (2013: 7).

It might not be sensible to adopt Ong's rigorous attitude toward 'oral literature,' but with Ong one can clearly see the current situation everybody has to
deal with, one can see the dilemma but also the particular appeal of contemporary performance poetry in a writing and print culture: everything said about
this type of oral poetry today—by opponents, advocates, representatives, protagonists, practitioners, scholars, critics—is uttered from a perspective of literacy,
approaching "a primary phenomenon by starting with a subsequent secondary
phenomenon" (Ong 1982: 13), which often makes performance poetry look defi-
cient, even when proponents try to show its positive features, as Holman does in
his unsystematic way.

Holman blurs the distinctions between performance poetry and other genres,
and questions the somewhat arbitrary categories. He refuses to accept a narrow
definition of 'performance poetry':

> A performance poem is a poem written to be performed before an audience,
> Anne Waldman once told me, and I believe her. But as a poets' theater director
> . . . I must add: any poem deemed unperformable simply awaits the poet/per-
> former with appropriate vision. And most of the poets who write what I would
> call performance poetry do not write exclusively for the stage, but do acknow-

ledge the multitasking possibilities of a poem. As text, as performed live, as re-corded on film or audio- or videotape, via HTML on the Net, it's still a poem, the poem. (2002: 341)

Holman quotes Waldman with a common, clear definition of 'performance poem' that illustrates the link between textuality and theatricality, between page and stage, and that turns poetry into one of the performing arts (such as dance, drama, and music). But this definition is not broad enough for Holman, for whom fuzzi-ness seems to be part of a discourse strategy to enhance performance poetry's reputation: "Those who scoff at performance poetry as simply using live perfor-mance skills to hide a poorly written poem haven't learned to trust their ears as much as their eyes" (ibid.). Holman may play the role of a sassy and self-con-fident performance poetry salesman, but his advertisement cannot obliterate the undertone of resentment and the underlying sense of inferiority.

Disregarding the tendentious and defensive tone of its author, who is strategi-cally championing a cause, one can find key aspects of performance poetry in Holman's article or infer them from it: On the extra-textual level of performance poetry's model of communication are poet, performer, and audience (even a soli-tary reader can become a performer performing to him- or herself as an audience of one). Since poet and (professional or non-professional) performer can (but do not necessarily have to) be the same person, poetry production must be distin-guished from poetry performance. Performances can be immediate or mediate, live or recorded; performance poems can appear in print, in other media, or in multimedia contexts. Performance poets and performers work in various settings and present their art in a variety of media (not only on stage), and they have indi-vidual performance styles: "How you decide to perform is up to you" (ibid.: 345).

It is important to remember the difference in meaning of 'perform' and 'per-formance' and also to consider the different contexts in which they appear. 'Per-form' and 'performance' are not only used in the narrow context of performance poetry. We hear of a poet 'performing' his page-poetry in a poetry reading, or a professional actor 'performing' the written and published work of a print-poet on stage; there is the "public performance of printed poems," and there are "contem-porary poems composed for public performance" (Abrams/Harpham 2015: 271). 'Performance poetry' and 'poetry performance' are not the same: Any poem can be 'performed'—read or presented orally in public before an audience—but not every poem is a 'performance poem.' Someone's recitation of a poem in front of an audience does not turn it into a performance poem. The more theatrical poetry is as an art form, the more appropriate are the words 'perform' and 'per-formance.' The performance poems I will deal with in the following pages—Anne Waldman's "skin Meat BONES (chant)" and Saul Williams's "Amethyst Rocks"—are two cases in point.

2. Performance Poetry as Post-Avant Art:
Anne Waldman's "skin Meat BONES (chant)" (1985)

In "skin Meat BONES (chant)," the postmodern poet Anne Waldman places her poem's speaker self-confidently and (mock-)studiously in literary history by re-ferring to American vernacular and expatriate modernists/avant-gardists who stress the materiality, the eventfulness, and the act of the experiencing of lan-guage (William Carlos Williams and Gertrude Stein) and to innovative European masters of the chant and the poem to be sung (Dante Alighieri and Thomas Campion): "I'm BONING up on my Dante, William Carlos Williams, / Campion and Gertrude Stein" (Waldman 1994 [1985]: 458, ll. 68-9). By employing the first-person voice in "skin Meat BONES (chant)," e.g., for double-entendre and sex talk, Waldman also plays with conventions—"'naked,' honest expression"; "spontaneity, immediacy, and a conversational style"; privileging "process over product"; "conjoining poetry and everyday life"—conventions of postwar American neo-romantic, autobiographical, and confessional poetry, which has sometimes been thought of as "an important influence on . . . performance art" (Rosenbaum 2012: 296).

"skin Meat BONES (chant)" was published in 1985, before the slam/spoken-word craze and before rap's rise to global popularity. This paradigmatic performance poem is a hybrid in which both textuality and theatricality are of the utmost importance. It features primary and secondary text, which is typical for the genre of drama and its hybrid nature but unusual in poetry. The verb "chant" in the imperative (Waldman 1994 [1985]: 456), referring in brackets to the poem's title nouns and to the following text, should be understood as secondary text relevant for the performer/s who is/are supposed to enact the text, to take it off the page and onto the stage. The stage directions in the secondary text that follows the primary poetic text also show that "skin Meat BONES (chant)" was composed as a score for performance before an audience physically listening with their ears. As they are in dramatic texts, the stage directions are printed in italics to set them off from the primary text: "*This piece is intended to be read aloud, singing the words 'skin,' 'Meat,' 'BONES' as notes: 'skin,' high soprano register, 'Meat,' tenor, 'BONES,' basso profundo. The 3 notes may vary, but the different registers should be markedly distinguishable*" (ibid.: 458, ll. 85-8). Providing various staging options, the secondary text clearly indicates that the primary text is intended to be treated as a score, "the written form of a composition for . . . vocal parts" (*American Heritage Dictionary* 2011: 1572). It is meant to be performed (collaboratively) in public. The primary text could be presented by one or several speakers and singers of different sexes and with different bodies.

Solitary, silent reading, as with non-embodied poetic texts, is not applicable here. Waldman's poem exemplifies that "[p]leasure in poetry, like speech itself, is both intellectual and bodily. Spoken language, an elaborate code of articulated grunts, provides a satisfaction central to life, with all the immediacy of our senses" (Pinsky 2009: 1). But here, speaking or reading language aloud is not enough. Waldman moves poetry closer to music by adding another dimension to her poem: singing. And thus, all three kinds of Pound's melopoeia are here: singing, chanting, and speaking. The suggested vocal registers correspond semantically and visually with the title words and the way in which they are printed. The deepest register, for example, basso profundo, corresponds with the word denoting the hardest physical element on the deepest level of the body: bones, written in capital letters. The human body has bones at its base (basso profundo), skin on the highest, outermost level (soprano), and meat in-between (tenor). With these three registers (soprano, tenor, basso profundo) and the three words of the title (skin, Meat, BONES) printed in a particular way, Waldman sonically, semantically, and visually represents and integrates the three elements of poetry that Pound termed melopoeia, logopoeia, and phanopoeia; she makes something with music, meaning, and image.

Waldman's partly "speech-like," associative, disjointed, stylistically incon-
sistent, and somewhat "messy" poem is a visual, semantic, and aural/oral
event, an aesthetic event in space and time (Bernstein 2006: 279). The poem as
a whole enhances eventfulness with its "fast paced," "jerky," and "kinetic" disposition, its "found or quoted material," and its divergent phrases, clauses, and
sentences moving "from one thing to another" (ibid.: 279-80). With "textual particulars that refuse to be subdued to an encompassing whole" (Bogel 2013: 13),
the poem is chiefly held together by iteration and frequency: visual, lexical-
thematic, and rhythmic-acoustic repetitions of its title words (in variations) occurring at certain intervals. The words "skin," "Meat," and "BONES" recur
throughout the poem in various forms: sometimes printed differently, sometimes in different grammatical form, sometimes in compounds or as part of an
adjective. After the first third of the poem, in which "skin," "Meat," and
"BONES"/"BONE" alternate irregularly, there are individual skin-, meat-, and
bone-pieces (featuring, for example, figurative language and idiomatic expressions) in which the other two words and their variations do not appear. The individual subdivisions are loosely held together by the semantic common denominator 'physicality.'

Performance poetry foregrounds physicality, which manifests itself on different levels here. Looking at the poem's shape and typography (phanopoeia), the
arrangement, composition, and appearance of its printed matter and material in
different type-size, at how its elements are spread over the page, the reader immediately sees that some of the printed words (mostly "skin," "Meat," "BONES,"
but occasionally a variation or a substitute of these words and their print-
image) are indented or reach out into the white space of the page. Not everything is aligned evenly along the left edge of the typeset page. The 'body' of the
poem, which occupies quite a lot of space, is not a solid, immobile block of text
with every line having the same length but rather an agile 'being' swiftly stretching and extending its 'limbs' as it pleases. There are different extensions of white
space between words, phrases, and lines, which sometimes look like visualiza-
tions of temporal pauses, hints for performers using the printed text as a score.
The title words are sometimes arranged like notes on a sheet of music. The surprising replacement of "Meat" and "BONES" with "head" and "haircut" in this
arrangement occurs only once, which means that the sequence "skin head haircut" is a semantic event in an emphatic sense (Waldman 1994 [1985]: 457,
ll. 38-40). On the lexical-thematic level (logopoeia), physicality rules throughout
the poem. "skin Meat BONES" denotes and connotes different dimensions of
physicality: it refers to real objects that we can touch, see, and feel, and it
synecdochically relates to our body rather than to our mind or emotions, for example—in lower, informal registers of language, in slang and vulgar slang—to
carnality and sex (pornography, the genitals, the human body as object of sexual desire, sexual intercourse, penises). It is also a 'physical' poem that 'touches'
people aurally, maybe even in a rough or violent way (melopoeia). One thing that
a poem like "skin Meat BONES" says about poetry in general and about performance poetry in particular is that—in the words of Robert Pinsky—"poetry penetrates to where the body recognizes the stirring of meaning" (2002: 46).

Here, I will briefly consider an audio-visual recording of the poem by the au-
thor herself, which can be found on her website. It is part of the 1978 movie
Fried Shoes, Cooked Diamonds, an hour-long color film produced at the Jack
Kerouac School of Disembodied Poetics, Naropa University, Boulder, Colorado.

"skin Meat BONES" can also be heard on the Waldman author page at *PennSound*, an invaluable website for poetry readings and performances. *PennSound* gives listeners the opportunity to compare different performance styles, for example those of Anne Waldman and John Ashbery, which I will cursorily examine in the following.

What is a felicitous performance style? When do we say that a poem is performed well? In his introduction to the anthology *Committed to Memory*, in which he also deals with poetry reading, John Hollander clearly distinguishes between poets who read aloud very well and those who do not. Those who perform well

> read the poems for their meaning, rather than to express their personal presences: the 'performance' in this case is more like that of a musician playing—and thereby interpreting—a solo piano piece, say, than it is like what has gotten to be called 'performance art' (a sword-swallower or fire-eater or stand-up comic). In reciting a poem aloud, you are not like an actor, coming to understand, and then to feel yourself in a dramatic part, a fictional person. It's rather that you come to understand, and then to be, the voice of the poem itself. (1996: 5-6)

There are two different dimensions—the performance potential of the poem itself and the performance mode of the person presenting the poem (e.g., an actor on stage, a poet during a poetry reading, etc.)—that do not necessarily (have to) correspond; they can also be in a conflicting relationship with each other, which might be considered fascinating, especially if one thinks that Hollander is too fixed-thing focused. "One of the most interesting things about oral literature," John Sutherland writes in his *Little History of Literature*, "is its fluidity. Like conversation it is flexible and changeable; it takes on the personality of whoever is then in charge of it" (2013: 265). Seen this way, there is no such thing as Hollander's "voice of the poem itself"; there are as many voices as there are performers with individual styles. Comparing the performance styles of Anne Waldman and John Ashbery (reading, for example, his "They Dream Only of America," 1962), one could say that neither of the two performs the poem as if it was speaking with its own voice: Ashbery undertreats his poem, and Waldman overtreats hers. Neither of these performance styles necessarily has to be considered either good or bad, but each of them represents a fundamentally different way of performing poetry. One could be called 'subtractive style' (Ashbery), the other 'additive style' (Waldman).

Sometimes performers not only serve the interests of a poem, e.g., by helping the work foreground the musical dimension of its textuality, they also add theatricality to it, which Anne Waldman does. Her performance seems to be superimposed on the poem, which can be seen and heard very well in the aforementioned audio-visual document of "skin Meat BONES." Waldman speaks and chants with high intensity from beginning to end. With her ecstatic way of presenting the poem she seems to throw "Words in Your Face" (Holman 1996: 12). The aesthetic effect of event-oriented performance poetry like this is not indirect, as is that of some other forms of poetry. It is more like Amiri Baraka imagined in his poem "Black Art": Poems shoot words at you and words become bullets that hit you directly. In her performance Waldman adds a considerable amount of theatricality to the poem, but it is debatable whether the text itself requires it or can bear it. Ashbery does the exact opposite when he reads his poems aloud at poetry readings. He shuns exaggeration and almost shyly presents his texts with understatement and *sprezzatura*, an effortless ease and (deliberate?) lack of emphasis in expression, with the effect of augmenting the "wackiness quotient" of his poetry (Bernstein 2006: 279). Ashbery achieves this by means of contrast between textual weirdness and vocal dullness. Waldman, however, who most definitely does not lack liveliness, arouses interest for her text via an uninhibited performance. Perhaps Ashbery does less and Waldman more than what their texts allow; whereas Ashbery, who is not a performance poet, humbly retreats from his, Waldman may assume too much control over hers.

3. Performance Poetry as Popular Art: Saul Williams's "Amethyst Rocks" (2006)

In performance poetry, texts sometimes disappear behind their performers and performances; this becomes apparent in the central prison scene of the 1998 film *Slam*. As well-built musclemen are engaged in workout and weight training, the imprisoned Raymond Joshua, played by performance poet, alternative hiphopper, and Nuyorican Poets Cafe's Grand Slam Champion Saul Williams, finds himself between rivaling gangs and is about to be physically beaten by China, one of the gang leaders, who has big powerful shoulders and well-developed muscles with very good definition. We read in the screenplay's secondary text that Ray, a thin, gangling, not very strong man "is like a cornered animal" when "he sees China coming for him. He's surrounded. He stands suddenly and forcefully. As China moves in for the kill, Ray faces him and explodes into verse. They all stop, shocked, mesmerized, as Ray lets loose the passion and heart of his verse" (Stratton/Wozencraft 1998: 216). With his unforeseen and unexpected outbreak, Ray immediately creates an interruption. All of a sudden, he meets his opponents with dense acoustic force and starts to beat China and the other gang members with his strong, powerful voice and his dumbfounding words, "BELLOWING the poem at them, for them, about them" (ibid.: 217). He is—metaphorically speaking—smashing in their faces and heads with a spoken-word poem written in prison, an original composition of his, a non-metrical piece of oral textual poetry, a black awareness text that ends with the words "and we are public enemies number one! / one one one! / one one one!" (ibid.: 218, ll. 56-8), intertextually referring to a classic from militant black cultural nationalist rap group Public Enemy's first album *Yo! Bum Rush the Show* (1987).

For the (mainly black) inmates who are present in the prison yard during Ray's live enactment of the poem, his angry outburst and aggressive delivery style, wild gesticulations, dramatic facial expressions, and loud words, which hit and overwhelm them at once, contribute to an awe-inspiring, non-repeatable event after which they stand in stunned silence. The impressive embodied text makes them forget instantly that only a moment ago they wanted to engage in interpersonal violence. The end of this scene illustrates what Cicely Berry in *The Actor and the Text* considers "one of the most important points to keep in mind: that words change both the situation, the speaker and the listener. After words are spoken, nothing is quite the same again" (2000: 20). This scene from *Slam* creates the impression that performed words really have the physical power to achieve immediate effects. The scene may convince viewers that performance poetry revolves around the physicality and presence of words in action, words doing something, but it might make them question whether it actually matters what exactly the words are saying. It is obvious that "Ray has won the battle" by "using the word as his sword," as a weapon (Stratton/Wozencraft 1998: 218). But is the meaning of the word as significant as its function? Is the mode of utterance (here: "BELLOWING") in performance poetry more important than the sense of the uttered word? Could Raymond Joshua, an awesome performer, have achieved the same effect without the particular ethnic, racial, social, and gendered content of his critical poem, without referring to the "endangered species" (see Ice Cube 1990) of the black male in the crime- and drug-infested inner cities of the U.S.?

Saul Williams's "Amethyst Rocks" is full of words, phrases, images, and topoi evoking gangsta rap, Afrocentric or black political rap, and conscious rap, each a different style of the most popular genre of performance poetry today. The poem is also reminiscent of (P-)Funk and Afrofuturism. It combines 'street knowledge' with galactic imagery. The beginning of the text unfolds the common urban ghetto setting that is evocative of gangsta rap, with stereotypical activities and a pusher-persona speaking: "I stand on the corner of the block slinging / . . . rocks / drinking 40's . . . / dodging cops / 'cause five-oh be the 666" (Williams in Stratton/Wozencraft 1998: 216, ll. 1-6). Listeners of rap songs and rhymes have heard these or similar words many times, but Williams also counters the stereotype with a suggestive, Afrofuturistic Funkadelic-like line: The gangsta figure is not drinking cheap malt liquor beer of low quality, but "40's of Mother Earth's private nectar / stock" (ibid., ll. 3-4). The poem features many semantic events like that and like the following: The speaker is "snorting . . . candy yams" (ibid., l. 10), not cocaine or heroin. With this line, Williams instantly moves the setting to the Deep South and immediately gets a new chain of associations going. There is not only gangsta intertextuality here, but also Afrocentric mythology ("horus," "isis," "osiris"), neo-Black Power rap criticism of the United States ("the Feds are also plottin' me / they're tryin' to imprison my astrology / to put my stars behind bars / my stars in stripes / using blood splattered banners / as nationalist kites" or "stealing us was the smartest thing they ever did / too bad they don't teach the truth to their kids / . . . their existence is that of a schizophrenic vulture"), and consciousness-raising rap mixed with Afrofuturism: "so what are you bound to live, nigga / so while you're out there serving your time / i'll be in sync with the moon / while you run from the sun / life of the womb / reflected by guns / worshipper of moons / i am the sun" (ibid.: 216-8, ll. 28-30, 20-5, 39-44, 48-55).

Just as in the film *Slam*, Williams conveys the idea of rap and spoken-word poetry as manifestations of popular culture, understood as "the expression of the people," and as popular forms giving "voice to the culture of marginalized groups," e.g., African American men (Culler 2011 [1997]: 45-6). In "A Confession," a kind of (pseudo-)personal, partly fictional introduction to *The Dead Emcee Scrolls*, in which he transfers the literary convention of the editor-, translator-, decipherer-, and copyist-fiction to hip-hop culture and contemporary performance poetry (2006: xi), Williams recounts the imaginary genesis of his poem "Amethyst Rocks" as being derived from an ancient manuscript ("Pyramid old. But it still felt graffiti connected," ibid.: xix) that he allegedly found in a spray paint can on an "underground graffiti tour" (ibid.: xvi). In this fictional story, the performance poem is not an aesthetic elite product created by an autonomous individual or artistic genius but emerges from and is inscribed in the cultural matrix of a community—with the author-subject functioning as medium, con-servator, and renewer of the matrix.

As a performance poet, Williams, who was once promoted with the title 'hip-hop's poet laureate,' seems to aim at the immediacy of music, especially of hip-hop: "Music speaks directly to the subconscious. The consciously simplified beat of the hip-hop drum speaks directly to the heart . . . There is no music more powerful than hip-hop. No other music so purely demands an instant af-firmative on such a global scale. When the beat drops, people nod their heads, 'yes,'" Williams writes in *The Dead Emcee Scrolls* (ibid.: xi).

Like in many forms of (contemporary) popular poetry, primarily in rap, the fundamental and predominant characteristics of Williams's performance poem are non-semantic features, mainly rhythm and rhyme. Both can be described as "repetition with a difference," which the poet Edward Hirsch does in his splen-did *Poet's Glossary* (2014: 528, 534). "The word *rhythm*," Hirsch writes, "comes from the Greek word *rhythmos*, 'measured motion,' which in turn derives from a Greek verb meaning 'to flow.' Rhythm is sound in motion. It is related to the pulse, the heartbeat, the way we breathe. It rises and falls" (ibid.: 534). Listening to "Amethyst Rocks" with mental or physical ears, one hears a steady, driving pulse with impressive irregularities, a turbulent flow. Speaking it aloud can be a physical pleasure: we can feel the motive power of the poem and sense the aes-thetic quality of the strong beats. The definition of rap as "percussive speaking" then becomes manifest (DJ Renegade 2002: 272). Williams makes loose use of popular sound and verse structures, which are defined in "The Metrics of Rap" by performance poet DJ Renegade: Among the "strongest poetic influences on rap are popular poems with four beats per line (Eenie meenie, mynie moe / Catch a tiger by the toe) . . . In the most common [rap] form (95 to 120 bpm), one line has four to sixteen syllables, and four beats" (ibid.: 272-3; original em-phasis). Rhythmically anchored by the four-stress pattern of pure accentual meter, the text of "Amethyst Rocks" exists in various print and online versions, with enjambed and end-stopped lines of varying length, sometimes with more than four stressed syllables per (syncopated) line, and sometimes with fewer. There are rhythmic changes and multiplicities in Williams's poem more akin to Gerard Manley Hopkins's orally driven counterpoint and sprung rhythm than to rap's often-used symmetrical four-beat rhythm. Sprung rhythm, Hopkins said,

> is the nearest to the rhythm of prose, that is the native and natural rhythm of speech, the least forced, the most rhetorical and emphatic of all possible rhythm . . . combining . . . opposite and . . . incompatible excellences, markedness of rhythm—that is rhythm's self—and, naturalness of expression . . . My verse is less to be read than heard. (Hopkins in Hirsch 2014: 607-8)

Hopkins's explanation of his method of timing could have been written by Wil-liams, who would probably subscribe to Hopkins's view (presented here by Hirsch) that a stressed syllable "accompanied by a uniform number of un-stressed ones" is "musically deadening" (2014: 607). "Rhythm is the combina-tion in English of stressed and unstressed syllables that creates a feeling of fixi-ty and flux, of surprise and inevitability. Rhythm creates a pattern of yearning and expectation, of recurrence and change" (ibid.: 534). What Hirsch says here is particularly relevant for a live audience's aesthetic experience of performance poems such as "Amethyst Rocks," especially if listeners do not know the text or do not have it in front of them to read along, which is most often the case in live contexts. In situations like these, rhythm and rhyme provide orientation while also making room for unexpected events. They contribute substantially to the sensual delight the audience gets from the materiality of language. "Rhyme," Hirsch points out, "foregrounds the sounds of words as words . . . There is a pleasure in the sound of words coming together, in the pulse and beat, the rhythm of their conjoining" (ibid.: 528). Rhythm and rhyme are part of what Canadian literary critic Northrop Frye called "babble," the element "of subconscious association" forming "the basis for lyrical *melos*" (1990 [1957]: 275): "In babble, rhyme, assonance, alliteration, and puns develop out of sound-associations. The thing that gives shape to the associating is what we have been calling the rhythmical initiative" (ibid.). "Poems babble, foregrounding non-semantic features of language—sound, rhythm, repetition of letters—to produce charm or incantation," says Jonathan Culler (2011 [1997]: 79), especially popular performance poems like "Amethyst Rocks," one could add with regard to Frye: "An obvious priority of rhythm to sense is a regular feature of popular poetry" (1990 [1957]: 276).

We can easily perceive that "the sound of words coming together" is a main source of the aural/oral enjoyment we get out of speaking/listening to Williams's poem (Hirsch 2014: 528), when we read or hear lines like these: "resurrected like lazarus / but you can call me lazzie / lazy / yeah, i'm lazy . . ." (Williams in Stratton/Wozencraft 1998: 217, ll. 32-5). Here, the poem "babbles" (see Frye 1990 [1957]), foregrounding the non-semantic feature of alliteration that, as Hirsch explains, "predates rhyme and takes us back to the oldest English and Celtic poetries. It is known as *Stabreim* in the ancient Germanic languages" (2014: 19). Alliteration, therefore, takes us from ancient Germanic to contemporary North American vernacular poetries such as rap-based performance poetry with a *Stabreim* such as lazarus-lazzie-lazy. The conjoining of these words in this part of the poem demonstrates how meaning often develops out of "sound-associations" (see Frye 1990 [1957]) in "Amethyst Rocks." Non-semantic features are arguably Williams's first priority here. In addition to alliteration, there are, for example, assonance ("stock/dodging cops"), consonance ("Dogon niggas"), assonance and consonance together ("blood splattered banners"), and there is an abundance of rhyme, as in rap, but not as monotonous as it is sometimes in rap (Williams in Stratton/Wozencraft 1998: 216, ll. 4-5, 19, 24). Rhyming in "Amethyst Rocks" is not tediously repetitious; it does not follow a certain pattern. The poem breaks expectation with irregular rhyme and features a variety of different rhymes: perfect end rhyme (rain-insane-lane); imperfect rhyme (rock-cops); internal, leonine rhyme ("to put my stars behind bars"); masculine rhyme (sun-one); feminine rhyme (culture-vulture); and triple rhyme (consecutive-executive) (ibid.: 216-8, ll. 7-9, 2-5, 22, 55-8, 43-4). Unlike the post-Beat poet Anne Waldman in her unrhymed performance poem "skin Meat BONES," rap-influenced spoken-word artist Saul Williams uses the non-semantic feature rhyme (but no rhyme scheme). Williams's boisterous, profusely rhymed poem somewhat confirms Allen Ginsberg's dictum that "[t]he spoken-word movement comes out of the Beats, but with rhyme added" (in Hirsch 2014: 606). "Spoken-word movement" could be replaced by other terms here, even by 'rap,' and the Ginsberg quotation would still be true to some extent, because the Beats can be considered the paradigmatic countercultural movement of postwar poetic rebelliousness. Contemporary popular performance poetry can therefore be considered a new branch on the postmodern Beat family tree.

4. Performance Poetry in American Literary History

The history of poetry is partly written with anthologies, particularly in the United States. To conclude, I will compare the two editions of Paul Hoover's *Postmodern American Poetry: A Norton Anthology* with regard to the representation of performance poetry and the status given to it as a subgenre within the social system of American poetry. The first edition of this collection came out in 1994; the second, heavily revised and expanded edition was published in 2013, almost twenty years later. Comparing the ways in which these two editions depict performance poetry in general, its major poets, important pioneers such as Jerome Rothenberg, and the authors and poems discussed above, one notices major differences. Rothenberg in particular can be considered a symbol of the marked changes and transformations that happen over time in canon formation and literary history, even in a relatively short period of 'only' twenty years.

In the first edition of Hoover's anthology, both Rothenberg and Waldman are included: Waldman with three poems, "skin Meat BONES (chant)" among them; Rothenberg with "Cokboy" (1974) and, in the comparatively small poetics section consisting of only 18 authors, with "Notes Toward a Poetics of Performance" (1977). In the second edition, Rothenberg's texts have been left out. Even his "Notes" have been omitted from the poetics section, which no longer includes a text on performance poetry. Does Hoover now consider Rothenberg an unimportant representative of postmodern American poetry? What about Rothenberg's role as a forerunner and pioneer of performance poetry (e.g., of Waldman's "use of the chant"), which Hoover drew attention to in the first edition (1994: xxxviii)? Waldman is present in the 2013 edition, but not her "skin Meat BONES (chant)." In both editions Hoover calls Waldman "a leading advocate of oral poetics and performance-related poetry" (1994: 452; 2013: 407). In his introduction to the second edition he stresses her institutional importance: "Anne Waldman, with her extraordinary skills as a poet, performer, and organizer, provided much of the energy that made the Poetry Project at St. Mark's Church and later Naropa University in Boulder, Colorado, powerful literary centers" (2013: xl). Whereas Waldman more or less keeps her prestige in the 2013 edition, Rothenberg completely lost his—relatively high—canonical status by exclusion.

What about other writers linked to performance poetry in the two editions? In his introduction to the first edition, Hoover presents forefathers, such as Allen Ginsberg and Amiri Baraka, pioneers in addition to Rothenberg, namely David Antin and John Giorno, and "[o]ther leading performance poets" besides Anne Waldman (1994: xxxviii): Jayne Cortez, Kenward Elmslie, Ed Sanders, Miguel Algarín, Jimmy Santiago Baca, Victor Hernández Cruz, and Wanda Coleman. Of these thirteen poets (including Rothenberg and Waldman), only five made it into the second edition: the two forefathers, Ginsberg and Baraka, none of the pioneers, and only three of the eight so-called leading performance poets, Elmslie, Coleman, and Waldman. It is especially surprising that the improvisatory talk poems of David Antin are not represented in the 2013 anthology even though in the first edition Hoover wrote that Antin was "at the foreground of performance poetry internationally" (ibid.: 229). In his introduction to the second edition, Hoover writes: "Among the poets here represented, Anne Waldman, Wanda Coleman, Christian Bök, and Edwin Torres have the largest commitment to performance" (2013: xliii). This list is significantly shorter than the one in the first edition, and there are only two names found on both lists:

Waldman and Coleman. Hoover even seems to have lost interest in what poet and performer Tony Lopez calls "the performance element of avant-garde practice," "a poetry performance practice that is not reducible . . . to empty gestures of pop-imitation," to say nothing of performance poetry that "wishes to impersonate" pop music (2006: 74). Hoover's new collection does not feature authors such as Steve Benson or performance artists such as Laurie Anderson, nor does it include popular rap-related performance poets such as Saul Williams. Even Marc Kelly Smith, the so-called father of the poetry slam and co-editor of *The Spoken Word Revolution,* is not included in the second edition.

It appears that Hoover does not believe in the revolutionary potential of performance poetry. In both editions of his anthology, performance poetry is portrayed as a reactionary guard rather than an avant-garde, which becomes evident in sentences such as: "If language poetry seeks to invent a future through the written text, performance poetry bears nostalgia for a more perfect past when orality was primary" (1994: xxxviii). Hoover speaks of "difficulty" when referring to Language poetry in 1994 (xxxv), and even of "intellectual difficulty" in 2013 (xliii); in the second edition he also considers the "complexity and literariness" of Language poetry as well as performance poetry's "popular audience of noninitiates" (ibid.). In the social systems of literature and academia (the target audience of such an anthology), these words have clear connotations. "Intellectual" and "complexity" are positive terms, whereas "nostalgia" and "noninitiates" are negative ones. "Noninitiates" evokes a deficiency, the association of ordinary people lacking the literary competence needed to decode complex and intellectually demanding texts of serious literature.

What will performance poetry look like in an increasingly post-print, electronic writing culture? Perhaps literature will "be seen less as the fixed text . . . and more as an event," as Jonathan Culler writes in his introduction to *PMLA*'s special issue on literary criticism for the twenty-first century (2010: 907). Culler asks how this might affect criticism: "Will performance studies . . . take on a new centrality in literary studies, as it comes to treat texts less as signs to be interpreted than as performances whose conditions of possibility and of success can be interrogated?" (ibid.). In the realm of contemporary poetry, Culler says, the rise of rap "suggests the possibility of reverting to a notion of the work as act of language" (ibid.: 907-8). Maybe in the future, contemporary performance poetry will have gained a reputation as *the* literary avant-garde.

Bibliography

Selected Primary Literature

Algarín, Miguel and Bob Holman (eds.). 1994. *ALOUD: Voices from the Nuyorican Poets Cafe.* New York: Henry Holt.

Bradley, Adam and Andrew DuBois (eds.). 2010. *The Anthology of Rap.* New Haven and London: Yale UP.

Eleveld, Mark and Marc Smith (eds.). 2003. *The Spoken Word Revolution: Slam, Hip Hop and the Poetry of a New Generation.* Naperville, IL: Sourcebooks.

Hoover, Paul (ed.). 1994. *Postmodern American Poetry: A Norton Anthology.* 1st ed. New York: Norton.

——. 2013. *Postmodern American Poetry: A Norton Anthology.* 2nd ed. New York: Norton.

PennSound. Center for Programs in Contemporary Writing at the University of Pennsylvania. Web. 03 Aug. 2014. <http://writing.upenn.edu/pennsound/>.

Pinsky, Robert (ed.). 2009. *Essential Pleasures: A New Anthology of Poems to Read Aloud*. New York: Norton.

Stratton, Richard and Kim Wozencraft (eds.). 1998. *Slam*. New York: Grove P.

Waldman, Anne. 1994 [1985]. "skin Meat BONES (chant)." In: Hoover 1994. 456-8.

——. The Official Website. Web. 03 Aug. 2014. <http://www.annewaldman.org/>.

Williams, Saul. 2006. *The Dead Emcee Scrolls: The Lost Teachings of Hip-Hop and Connected Writings*. New York: Pocket Books.

Selected Secondary Literature

Abrams, M.H. and Geoffrey Galt Harpham. 2015. *A Glossary of Literary Terms*. Stamford, CT: Cengage Learning.

An immensely useful handbook, now in its eleventh edition. The entry on "performance poetry" has a comparatively large section on rap.

Bernstein, Charles (ed.). 1998. *Close Listening: Poetry and the Performed Word*. New York: Oxford UP.

A seminal collection of essays by scholars and poets related to the postavant tradition of American poetry, protagonists of Language poetry among them, who discuss many different aspects of performance, "the sounded and visualized word."

Brogan, T.V.F., Wolfgang Bernhard Fleischmann, Tyler Hoffman and Thomas Carper. 2012. "Performance." In: Roland Greene et al. (eds.), *The Princeton Encyclopedia of Poetry and Poetics*. Princeton and Oxford: Princeton UP. 1016-20.

A thorough entry, with extensive bibliography, in the best one-volume reference book about poetry and poetics.

Holman, Bob. 2002. "Performance Poetry." In: Annie Finch and Kathrine Varnes (eds.), *An Exaltation of Forms: Contemporary Poets Celebrate the Diversity of Their Art*. Ann Arbor, MI: The U of Michigan P. 341-51.

A non-scholarly depiction of performance poetry by a major proponent, biased representative, and slam movement activist who makes definitions less clean—or does he productively trouble them?

McCarthy, B. Eugene and Fran Quinn. 2013. *Sound Ideas: Hearing and Speaking Poetry*. Brookline, NH: Hobblebush.

The authors show ways of taking poems off the page by moving "forward step by step in the process of learning how to listen to and speak" them. For those who think that internal ears do not hear enough.

Rothenberg, Jerome. 1994 [1977]. "New Models, New Visions: Some Notes Toward a Poetics of Performance." In: Hoover 1994. 640-4.

A pioneering piece on performance poetics.

Somers-Willett, Susan B.A. 2009. *The Cultural Politics of Slam Poetry: Race, Identity, and the Performance of Popular Verse in America*. Ann Arbor, MI: The U of Michigan P.

*A comprehensive account, with chapters on the genre, its socio-political as-
pects, related genres such as rap and spoken-word poetry, and an epilogue on
the future of slam poetry, including an appendix with national poetry slam
rules and instructions for judges.*

Further References

American Heritage Dictionary of the English Language. 2011. 5th ed. Boston:
Houghton Mifflin Harcourt.

Bernstein, Charles. 2006. "Creative Wreading: A Primer." In: Joan Retallack and
Juliana Spahr (eds.), *Poetry and Pedagogy: The Challenge of the Contemporary*. New York: Palgrave. 275-81.

Berry, Cicely. 2000. *The Actor and the Text*. London: Virgin.

Bogel, Fredric V. 2013. *New Formalist Criticism: Theory and Practice*. New York:
Palgrave Macmillan.

Culler, Jonathan. 2010. "Introduction: Critical Paradigms." In: *PMLA* 125.4:
905-15.

——. 2011 [1997]. *Literary Theory: A Very Short Introduction*. Oxford: Oxford UP.

DJ Renegade. 2002. "The Metrics of Rap." In: Annie Finch and Kathrine Varnes
(eds.), *An Exaltation of Forms: Contemporary Poets Celebrate the Diversity of
Their Art*. Ann Arbor, MI: The U of Michigan P. 272-8.

Frye, Northrop. 1990 [1957]. *Anatomy of Criticism: Four Essays*. Princeton, NJ:
Princeton UP.

Hirsch, Edward. 2014. *A Poet's Glossary*. Boston and New York: Houghton Mifflin Harcourt.

Hollander, John (ed.). 1996. *Committed to Memory: 100 Best Poems to Memorize*.
New York: Books & Co./Turtle Point.

Holman, Bob. 1996. "Welcome to the United States of Poetry!" In: Joshua Blum
et al. (eds.), *The United States of Poetry*. New York: Harry N. Abrams. 6-15.

Ice Cube. 1990. "Endangered Species (Tales from the Darkside)." *AmeriKKKa's
Most Wanted*. Hollywood, CA: Priority Records. CD.

Lopez, Tony. 2006. *Meaning Performance: Essays on Poetry*. Cambridge: Salt.

Ong, Walter J. 1982. *Orality and Literacy: The Technologizing of the Word*. London and New York: Routledge.

Pinsky, Robert. 2002. *Democracy, Culture and the Voice of Poetry*. Princeton, NJ
and Oxford: Princeton UP.

Pound, Ezra. 1960 [1934]. *ABC of Reading*. New York: New Directions.

Rohter, Larry. 2009. "Is Slam in Danger of Going Soft?" *New York Times*. Web.
24 Sept. 2013. n. pag. <http://www.nytimes.com/2009/06/03/books/
03slam.html?_r=0>.

Rosenbaum, Susan. 2012. "Confessional Poetry." In: Roland Greene et al. (eds.),
The Princeton Encyclopedia of Poetry and Poetics. Princeton and Oxford:
Princeton UP. 296-7.

Sutherland, John. 2013. *A Little History of Literature*. New Haven and London:
Yale UP.

24.

Language Poetry

Lyn Hejinian's "As for we who 'love to be astonished'" and Charles Bernstein's "The Klupzy Girl"

Kathy-Ann Tan

1. Linguistically Experimental Poetry and the Language School of Writing

Ludwig Wittgenstein's famous aphorism in *Tractatus Logico-Philosophicus* (1921, English translation 1922) that "the limits of my language mean the limits of my world" (trans. Kegan 2013: 68) expressed his personal belief in linguistic determinism, an ethos that language determines thought. Since its articulation, this well-known phrase has motivated literary attempts to explore, but also to challenge, the limits of representation via modes of linguistic experimentation. These endeavors have found particular resonance in the works of the Language School of writing. The latter emerged in the late 1960s and early 1970s in San Francisco and New York in critical response to traditional forms of American poetry and its poetic institutions. Opposing conventional forms of the lyric and its common expression of personal feeling—"breaking the automatism of the 'I' and its naturalized voice" (Perelman 1996: 13)—, Language poetry sought to investigate the limits of language and expression while engaging in a radical cultural poetics that contested the status quo in the U.S. The work of the Language School has therefore challenged conventional notions of lyric subjectivity and poetic agency via methods of defamiliarization as well as syntactic fragmentation and formal disjunction.

Despite the flourishing of linguistically-experimental writing in the second half of the twentieth century, therefore, the urge to experiment with language in literature should not be regarded as a postmodern phenomenon but one that dates back to the early twentieth century. This is evinced in the literary precursors and influences on the avant-garde poetries that emerged in the late 1960s and early 1970s in the United States, including that of the Language School. The works of the Russian formalists, in particular the writings of Viktor Shklovsky and other members of the OPOJAZ (Obščestvo izučenija POėtičeskogo JAZyka, "Society for the Study of Poetic Language") group from 1916 to the early 1930s, were particularly significant to the development of language-centered writing. For instance, Viktor Shklovsky's notion of "estrangement" (*ostranenie*) has influenced the writings of Lyn Hejinian, in particular *The Guard* (1984), *Oxota: A Short Russian Novel* (1991), and *Leningrad* (1991). In these works, Hejinian "extends her poetics of estrangement beyond the textual, connecting the radical artifice of poetic language with the act of seeing the world anew" (Edmond 2006: 98). This entreaty to "make it [the old, the familiar] new" clearly references the injunction of American Modernist poet Ezra Pound who published his eponymous volume of literary criticism *Make It New: Essays* in 1934. Another strong influence on the Language School were the Objectivist poets, a group of second-generation American Modernists who were writing in the 1930s that included George Oppen, Charles Reznikoff, Carl Rakosi and Louis Zukofsky. The Language School adopted the Objectivist aesthetic that was attentive to, and reflected, "the material world, politics, society, and history [in] readings

concerned with the production, dissemination, and reception of poetic texts"
(ibid.). Additionally, the procedural nature, as well as the musical and aleatory
quality, of much Objectivist verse found particular resonance among the Language poets. Indeed, much Language writing develops and extends the two defining characteristics of Objectivist poetry according to Zukofsky—"sincerity"
and "objectification" (1931: 272)—, treating the poem itself as an object and
calling attention to the materiality of the text and its signifier. Consequently, the
onset of poststructuralist thought across the Atlantic into the American academy
in the late 1970s prompted poets affiliated with the Language School to interrogate linguistic structures and find new import in the earlier experimental writings of poets such as Gertrude Stein, works that had already disrupted the conventional unity of sign and signifier.

The role of small poetry presses should not be understated in terms of their
dissemination of the work of the Language School. In fact, the name of the
group originated from a poetics journal, $L=A=N=G=U=A=G=E$, that was published between 1978 to 1981 under the editorship of Charles Bernstein and
Bruce Andrews. Many of the Language poets were directly involved in these
presses and the independent magazines they issued. The poetry journal *This*,
for example, whose first three issues were edited between 1971 and 1973 by
Robert Grenier and Barrett Watten, showcased the work of Lyn Hejinian,
Michael Palmer, Kit Robinson, Steve Benson and Bernadette Mayer, among
others. The first issue of the journal famously contained Robert Grenier's ad-
monition "I HATE SPEECH," which became the maxim that, according to Ron
Silliman, "announced a breach [with tradition]—and a new moment in American
writing" (2001 [1986]: xvii). Under the imprint of This Press, the works of Carla
Harryman, Clark Coolidge, Ron Silliman, Bruce Andrews, and Larry Eigner were
also published in the 1970s and 1980s. The poetry magazine $L=A=N=G=U=A=G=E$
was, moreover, highly influential for circulating the early 'manifestos' of the
loosely collected group of Language poets. These included the opinions of Ron
Silliman, the editor of *In the American Tree* (1986), an anthology of linguistically
and formally experimental work by younger poets at the time whose style
marked a turning away from the confessional poetics of the Black Mountain and
Beat generation of poets, although Charles Olson's concept of "open field" composition remained highly influential to Language writing.

The emergence and 'flourishing' of the independent poetry journals *This* and
$L=A=N=G=U=A=G=E$, as well as small presses such as Burning Deck Press
(founded by Rosmarie and Keith Waldrop in 1961), Tuuma Press (founded in
1976 by Lyn Hejinian) and Sun and Moon Press (founded by Douglas Messerli
in 1976), clearly did not exist in a vacuum, and it is imperative to contextualize
their existence and development against the socio-political backdrop of the Civil
Rights movement, second-wave feminism, counterculture and the student protests of the 1960s. Chief among the latter were the Berkeley Riots, a series of
demonstrations that were part of three larger political movements—the Civil
Rights movement, the Free Speech movement, and the anti-Vietnam war movement. The recently-published series *The Grand Piano* (2006-2010), a ten-volume
collaborative autobiography by ten poets associated with the Language School
during its advent in the 1960s—Rae Armantrout, Steve Benson, Carla Harryman, Lyn Hejinian, Tom Mandel, Ted Pearson, Bob Perelman, Kit Robinson, Ron
Silliman, and Barrett Watten—revisits and critically reflects on some of these
historical moments and their significance in fashioning a communal, if at times

divergent, poetics of linguistic and formal experimentation, resistance, and radical cultural inquiry.

While much of Language writing in the late 1960s and early 1970s displayed a historical situatedness and contextualization by engaging with the socio-political issues mentioned above, a concurrent impulse in the writings of the group was also the exploration of modes of perception and expression that were dialogic, playfully paratactic and digressive. Interestingly, the latter combines an avant-garde poetics of experimentation with a revisiting of more 'traditional' notions of narrative trajectory, the unified and coherent poetic subject and lyric voice, as well as modes of perception, reflection and self-introspection. This is manifested in the early works of Lyn Hejinian, especially *A Thought Is the Bride of What Thinking* (1976), *Writing is an Aid to Memory* (1978) and *My Life* (1980), via the use of what Ron Silliman has termed the "new sentence" in which "sentence structure is altered for torque, or increased polysemy/ambiguity" (1987: 91). The lack of clear or comprehensible transitions between sentences demonstrates what Bob Perelman has described as an experiential mode of "parataxis," wherein "the internal, autonomous meaning of a new sentence is heightened, questioned, and changed by the degree of separation or connection that the reader perceives with regard to the surrounding sentences" (1993: 313). The following paired reading of two poems by Lyn Hejinian and Charles Bernstein will serve to illustrate some of these devices of formal and linguistic experimentation.

2. "As for we who 'love to be astonished'": Lyn Hejinian's *My Life* and Experimental Autobiography

An influential figure associated with the Language School, and one of the foremost practitioners of experimental and avant-garde poetics and performance, Lyn Hejinian, born 1941 in the San Francisco Bay Area, is also an essayist, translator and small-press publisher. Her linguistically experimental poetry is characterized by an attention to alternative or multiple ways of perception and telling. It is also exemplified by an engagement with the everyday and the autobiographical, even as it simultaneously pushes at the boundaries of subjectivity and is deliberately anti-confessional and anti-realist, fostering, instead, an act of resistant reading. In her theoretical essay, "The Rejection of Closure," Hejinian develops her concept of the "open text," one that "is open to the world and particularly to the reader . . . invites participation, rejects the authority of the writer over the reader and thus, by analogy, the authority implicit in other (social, economic, cultural) hierarchies" (2000: 43). This poetic ethos is reflected in her oeuvre of works from the earliest *A Thought Is the Bride of What Thinking* (1976) to the most recent *The Book of a Thousand Eyes* (2012). She remains most well-known for her experimental 'autobiography,' *My Life*, a procedural work first published in 1980 and subsequently revised and re-issued twice: first as the 1987 edition that expanded the original work of thirty-seven sections comprising thirty-seven lines each (reflecting Hejinian's age in 1978) to forty-five sections comprising forty-five sentences each and, second, as the separate, though related, ten-part work *My Life in the Nineties* in 2003 (with each of the ten sections consisting of a sixty-sentence paragraph, reflecting Hejinian's turning sixty in 2001). Both these revisions were collectively reissued in one volume as *My Life and My Life in the Nineties* (2013).

Lyn Hejinian's "As for we who 'love to be astonished'" is a sequence taken from
My Life. As a semi-autobiographical prose poem that complicates conventional
models of subjectivity and self- or life-writing, the poem refuses to adopt a stable
subject position and undermines the notion of a coherent self or author whose life
is recounted in a series of narrative events. Instead, the text resists linear
chronology, splices temporal moments, revels in syntactic disruption and defies
closure. As the speaker asserts, "[w]hat follows a strict chronology has no memory.
For me, they must exist, the contents of that absent reality, the objects and occasions which I now reconsidered" (Hejinian 1980: 13). Breaking with established
precepts of autobiographical writing such as Philippe Lejeune's truth-telling "autobiographical pact" (1989: 19) between the author and reader, Hejinian's *My Life*
can be read instead as an experiment in non-Cartesian formations of the self that
challenges the formal dualism of material body vs. immaterial mind, indulging in a
playful refusal to adopt any stable or singular subject position.

The linear trajectory of conventional autobiographical writing from beginning
to end is therefore disrupted in the poem in favor of repetition, digression and
paratactical narration. The following excerpt—taken from the 'original' 1980 edition—will illustrate this claim.

As for we who   You spill the sugar when you lift the spoon. My father
"love to be astonished"   who had filled an old apothecary jar with what he
                           called "sea glass," bits of old bottles rounded and tex-
                           tured by the sea, so abundant on beaches. There is
                           no solitude. It buries itself in veracity. It is as if one
                           splashed in the water washed by one's tears. My
mother had climbed into the garbage can in order to stamp down the accumu-
lated trash, but the can was knocked off balance, and when she fell she broke
her arm. She could only give a little shrug. (1980: 10)

The phrase "As for we who 'love to be astonished'" is one of thirty-seven phrases
set in a square tile in the top left-hand corner of each of the sections of the
work. This phrase is then repeated throughout the entire text, each time occurring in a different context, thus revising the meaning of the phrase in its different permutations. This recalls Gertrude Stein's claim in her essay "Portraits and
Repetition" that "there is no such thing as repetition" (1935: 174) because each
time the phrase is used, it acquires a different significance. The phrase "As for
we who 'love to be astonished'," for instance, occurs not only in the excerpt
above but also reappears subsequently in the text in the variants "As for we who
'love to be astonished', we might go to the zoo and see the famous hippo named
'Bubbles'" (1980: 18) and "As for we 'who love to be astonished', my heartbeats
shook the bed" (ibid.: 22). This pattern of repetition-as-variation in *My Life* not
only invites the reader to create multiple narratives, but also alludes to the
composite natures of perception and memory.

My Life is, therefore, less a chronological account of Lyn Hejinian's childhood
and life up until the age of thirty-seven, than a contemplation of the tropes of
memory/recollection, time, perception and expression through language. Events
are not retold according to the sequence in which they occurred, but in the
order that they are recollected by the speaker, who moves freely between memories in an associative and contingent manner. The next three sentences of "As
for we who 'love to be astonished'" will illustrate this point:

The family had little money but plenty of food. At the circus only the elephants
were greater than anything I could have imagined. The egg of Columbus, land-

scape and grammar. She wanted one where the playground was dirt, with grass, shaded by a tree, from which would hang a rubber tire as a swing, and when she found it she sent me. (ibid.: 10)

The use of the unmarked, definite article "the" in reference to the family makes it unclear whether the speaker is referring to her own family or another (her neighbor's?) with whom she is familiar. The impersonal and objective commentary about the family who is poor but well-stocked with food shifts, in the next sentence, to the speaker's personal reminiscence about her trip to the circus. Nevertheless, this is not a straightforward narrative recollection of the event, but one that is semantically ambiguous. The sentence "[a]t the circus only the elephants were greater than anything I could have imagined" could mean, for instance: a) *only* the elephants were larger than anything the speaker could have imagined; all the other zoo animals were not, or b) only the *elephants* (as opposed to the giraffes, rhinoceroses or polar bears) were larger than anything the speaker could have imagined. In the last two sentences, semantic ambiguity is coupled with paratactic association. "The egg of Columbus, landscape and grammar" reads like an unlikely list of objects, hence inviting the reader's interpretation at this point—one possible explanation is that all three can be 'flattened'—and it is unclear what "one" in the subsequent sentence refers to—a house, a school, a kindergarten?

These excerpts from "As for we 'who love to be astonished'" thus exemplify Silliman's "new sentence" in their polysemy and semantic ambiguity. They also illustrate a poetics of parataxis whereby the meaning and significance of each sentence is altered by its surrounding ones. The text of *My Life*, as illustrated by the section titled "As for we who 'love to be astonished,'" exhibits a logic of non-sequentiality that allows for divergent and tangential ideas to be introduced and interlinked. Expressing an affinity for the "hopelessly frayed" nature of "loose ends" (ibid.: 18), "shard[s]" (ibid.: 71) and "separate fragment[s]" (ibid.) rather than a coherent, seamless flow of first-person narrative, Hejinian's experimental autobiography challenges the reader to abandon conventional understandings of life-writing and, rather, "[t]o follow the progress of ideas, or that particular line of reasoning, so full of surprises and unexpected correlations" (ibid.: 12).

My Life's formal experimentation—its poetics of parataxis and association, its rejection of traditional linear modes of autobiographical writing in favor of digression, repetition and ambiguity—constitutes an example of the avant-garde's critical reflections on American society in the 1970s. Emerging out of a decade of political disillusionment and cynicism after the Vietnam War and the Watergate scandal—a decade of a "crisis of confidence," as President Jimmy Carter described it in his famous speech of July 15, 1979,—*My Life* is at once a critical commentary on the social climate of anger, yet malaise, of transition, yet uncertainty and loss of direction, in America. Interestingly, rather than locate her speaker in the turbulent political present, Hejinian situates her in the past of childhood memories and a familial environment; it is out of that setting that the speaker's feminist 'self' emerges. In other words, the speaker's mediation of these recollections from the past form the basis of her self-invention—as a woman, as an avant-garde poet, as a female avant-garde poet—in a social, historical and cultural present (the 1970s) that was witnessing second-wave feminism's challenging of traditional gender roles. The second version of *My Life* published in 1987 and the third 'version', published as *My Life in the Nineties* in 2003, can both be read as reiterations of the poet's conviction that her work re-

mains an "open text," one that "resists the cultural tendencies that seek to identify and fix material and turn it into a product" (Hejinian 2000: 43). As a continuous poetic project that resists the ideologies of "reduction and commodification"
(ibid.) in contemporary America's consumerist society, Hejinian's *My Life* remains
an important and highly relevant example of contemporary American poetry.

3. Swooning, Swooping and Re-ascending: Charles Bernstein's "The Klupzy Girl" and the Poetry of Motion

A founding member of the Language School and prominent practitioner of lan-
guage-oriented writing, poet, essayist, and scholar Charles Bernstein was born
in 1950 in New York City. The influence of Ludwig Wittgenstein's and Gertrude
Stein's writings on his own work are evident from his senior thesis while studying philosophy at Harvard University, later published as *Three Compositions on
Philosophy and Literature: A Reading of Gertrude Stein's 'The Making of Americans' through Ludwig Wittgenstein's 'Philosophical Investigations'* (1972). A central preoccupation in this book and, more broadly, throughout Bernstein's poetry, is an inquiry into how words refer to objects in the external world. To this
end, his writings engage with the different registers of language in various contexts such as politics, popular culture, literary and critical jargon. Between
1978 to 1981, Bernstein published, with fellow Language poet Bruce Andrews,
the seminal *L=A=N=G=U=A=G=E* magazine (now available in full online) which
became a forum for experimental and avant-garde writing about poetry and
poetics. A professor of English at the University of Pennsylvania and ex-Director
of the Poetics Program at the State University of New York at Buffalo, which he
co-founded with poet Robert Creeley, Susan Howe and others, Bernstein continues to be highly active on the contemporary American poetry circuit, largely
through the *Electronic Poetry Center* (epc), an initiative he co-established with
professor of Media Studies and digital poetics scholar Loss Glazier, and through
the poetry audio archive *PennSound*, which he co-directs with Al Filreis.

  "The Klupzy Girl" is one of Charles Bernstein's most anthologized poems.
Originally published in *Islets/Irritations* (1983), a volume of poems that critically
engages with the nature of language and communication, "The Klupzy Girl" centrally explores the relationship between form and content/expression, art and
mimesis/representation, and the possibilities of the latter via modes of repetition, variation, refraction and alteration. It is also a poetic meditation on the
material conditions of poetic (re-)production and consumption via an exegesis of
Walter Benjamin's writings on historical materialism. In comparison to the
prose format of Hejinian's "As for we who 'love to be astonished'," Bernstein's
"The Klupzy Girl" is written in free verse and replete with enjambments that set
the poem into dizzying motion. As the opening lines affirm, "Poetry is like a
swoon, with this difference: / it brings you to your senses" (Bernstein 2010: 84).
The poem abounds with images of swooning, "stoop[ing]" (ibid.: 84), "swoop[ing],
and reascend[ing]" (ibid.: 88) and the speaker/persona (presumably the eponymous "Klupzy Girl," "klupzy" being a corruption of "klutzy", a colloquial American
term for "clumsy" or "awkward") moves and dances to a logic that is all her own
("I'm on a different / scale of jags," ibid.: 87) in "a maniac / state of careless
grace" (ibid.: 89). "Fumbling clumsily / with the others" (ibid.: 85), the speaker
confronts "the evocations, explanations, / glossings of 'reality'" (ibid.) but be-

comes increasingly "perplexed" (ibid.: 88) at the cruelty of the 'real' world with its vicious circle of class-struggle and consumerism, where cars are smashed into; cameras stolen, where one runs out of money and writes to a family member for more, but it does not come (ibid.: 89).

In this respect, it is apt that Bernstein's poem includes several references to Walter Benjamin's *Thesis on the Philosophy of History* (1940), wherein the latter famously wrote that "[t]here is no document of civilization which is not at the same time a document of barbarism" (1968: 248). Expressing a critique of Karl Marx's version of historical materialism, whereby the past is regarded as a continuum of progress, Benjamin adopted the view that history comprises different folds in time that do not stretch out into a linear continuity. Rather, he posited that each singular historical event could be perceived simultaneously as one of civilization/modernity or barbarism/imperialism, depending on which perspective is espoused—that of the victor or the 'oppressed'. In "The Klupzy Girl," the speaker first references Benjamin's version of historical materialism in the following passage:

> To stroll on the beach is to be in
> the company of the wage-earner
> and the unemployed on the public way, but
> to command a view of it from a vantage
> both recessed and elevated is to enter
> the bourgeois space; here vantage and view
> become consumable. (Bernstein 2010: 87)

In this excerpt above, a walk on the beach can thus be perceived as a leisurely, non-hierarchical activity in the company of other working class or unemployed people. Yet, if perceived from the "recessed and elevated" position of the bourgeoisie who symbolically and literally look down upon the less privileged classes, then the latter's inferiority in terms of social status and standing is brought into sharp relief. A dialectic is drawn between the bourgeois space (with its elevated view of the beach) and that of the working class and unemployed (the beach), yet Bernstein ironically points out that this is an opposition that is not only sustained by, but also tied to and inscribed in, the logics of capitalism and its consumerist cultures. The elevated viewing point of the bourgeoisie does not exist outside of, and hence is also entangled in, the workings of materialism. Hence, both "vantage and view / become consumable." Here, Bernstein is extending Benjamin's reflections on how, as the latter expressed in his 1936 essay "The Work of Art in the Age of Mechanical Reproduction," the material conditions of production influence political and economic society. In the age of late capitalism, Bernstein suggests, it is not only the means of production, distribution and exchange, but also the dynamics of consumption or, more specifically, consumerism, that play a major role in configuring society and its status quo. The intertextual references to Benjamin's theories of the material conditions of poetic/artistic creation and reception in the poem can therefore be read as a larger critical social commentary on the workings of a consumerist American society, where forms of (high and popular) art and mainstream poetry are commoditized.

Using various techniques such as disjunction, unexpected truncation, shifts in focus, exaggeration, contradiction and interruption, Bernstein's poem thus foregrounds its own artifice and the material conditions of its production and consumption. This is done differently than in Hejinian's "As for we 'who love to be astonished'" sequence, however, which also calls attention to the constructedness of its own narrative, but as part of an extended meditation on the multiple nature of perception, experience and memory. In Bernstein's poem, it is not only the nature of perception and experience that is contemplated, but their commodification and consumption in contemporary American society that is critiqued. The speaker's observations in Bernstein's "The Klupzy Girl" are therefore comparable, yet dissimilar, to those of the speaker in Hejinian's poem. In "As for we 'who love to be astonished,'" the opening lines of the poem establish a materially familiar environment (sugar bowls, spoons, the speaker's father's old glass collection) that is sustained throughout the work, supplemented by memories of the speaker's childhood. In contrast, in Bernstein's "The Klupzy Girl," the speaker attempts to remain distant, at one remove; personal statements such as "I can't describe / how insulted I felt . . . / I didn't think you'd turn / on me" (ibid.: 87) transform into more impersonal fragments of office memorandums and more 'standard' forms of workplace communication. In this respect, although both poems foreground the process of textual or literary creation as artifice, the speaker of Hejinian's "As for we 'who love to be astonished'" engages the reader on a very personal level that the speaker of Bernstein's poem, perhaps deliberately, does not.

It is useful here to adopt the terms "absorptive" and "antiabsorptive" which Bernstein coins in one of his formative essays on poetry, "Artifice of Absorption," itself written in verse and published in the collection of essays *A Poetics* (1992). In this essay, he draws a distinction between what he terms "absorptive" (ibid.: 30) characteristics and "antiabsorptive" (ibid.: 30), "impermeable" (ibid.: 22) characteristics in writing. Bernstein defines "absorptive" writing as realistic, transparent ("conjuring the thing seen / before our eyes, the page dissolved"; ibid.: 26) and "antiabsorptive" writing as that characterized by digression, discontinuity, exaggeration, artifice and metafictional self-reflexivity while "acknowledging, calling attention / to, the reader/writer relationship" (ibid.: 34). Crucially, he emphasizes that the "absorptive" and the "antiabsorptive" techniques of writing "should not be understood as mutually exclusive, / . . . or even conceptually separable" (ibid.: 22); indeed, they can also exist side by side in any given poetic text.

The textual dynamics of "The Klupzy Girl," as generated by the juxtaposition and the interplay of absorptive and antiabsorptive sequences in the text, supplement the motion in the poem that is created by its vocabulary ("swoon," "stoop," "bend," "push," "slump," "enter," "swoop," "reascend" and "zig-zag"). Highly absorptive, personal and emotional sequences in the poem are interspersed with antiabsorptive, impersonal observations, quotations from literary and philosophical works, political pamphlets and office memorandums. In contrast to Hejinian's minute observations and attention to detail in her recollections of her childhood in "As we who 'love to be astonished',," Bernstein's "The Klupzy Girl" encompasses—in a nod to Walter Benjamin's "Thesis IX" of "Theses on the Philosophy of History"—the past and present in one grand sweeping motion:

> History and civilization
> represented as aura—piles
> of debris founded on a law and mythology
> whose bases are in violence, the release
> from which a Messianic moment
> in which history itself is vanquished. (2010: 88)

The allusion to Walter Benjamin's famous figure of the "Angel of History," based on Paul Klee's painting "Angelus Novus," is evident. Yet, Bernstein simultaneously takes up and expands Benjamin's call to "brush history against the grain" (1968: 248). He does this by engaging with Benjamin's central concept of the "aura" of a work of art which, the latter famously advanced, "withers in the age of mechanical reproduction" (ibid.: 216).

Specifically, in "The Work of Art in the Age of Mechanical Reproduction," Benjamin argued that the decline of the "aura" of great artworks in an age of technological reproducibility constituted a democratizing gesture that engendered "the formulation of revolutionary demands in the politics of art" (ibid.: 218). While the speaker of Bernstein's poem seems to agree with Benjamin that historical events, particularly the metanarratives (Lyotard 1979) of civilization and modernity, need to be uncoupled, or "released," from their "aura" (as the excerpt from "The Klupzy Girl" above illustrates), he also attempts to develop an alternative sense of "aura" that critiques the "non-auratic" forms of mass reproduction that he associates with the culture of commoditization and consumerism in America. One could therefore argue that Bernstein seeks to reinscribe poetry with an different sense of the "auratic", one that acknowledges not only the conditions of material production (the poetic text as material artifact) but also the avenues of poetic consumption and distribution. In line with the ethos of the Language School, therefore, Bernstein stresses the central role of readerly participation, inviting the reader to become the co-creator of the text, an act that challenges a passive 'consumption' (the mode that accompanies "non-auratic" art forms such as mainstream or popular film) of the poetic text.

To return to the opening sentence of Bernstein's poem, therefore, "Poetry is like a swoon, with this difference: / it brings you to your senses" (2010: 84). To swoon means to faint, to lose consciousness, to lose one's senses for a moment; one swoons when one is overcome by extreme emotion, or overcome with awe by the "aura" of the encounter with the artwork. The difference with contemporary linguistically-oriented and avant-garde poetry as an "auratic" art form, "The Klupzy Girl" suggests, is in its potential to challenge passive consumption in a commodity culture, and hence to beget social and political change. Characteristically, this claim is tinged with a note of irony that acknowledges how language itself does not and cannot exist outside of its socio-political context—in this instance, the neoliberal framework of American capitalism and its mechanics of mass (re-)production, commoditization, and consumption: "The Ideal / swoops, and reascends. 'With real / struggle, genuine tax relief / can be won'" (Bernstein 2010: 88).

4. Conclusion

Charles Bernstein's "The Klupzy Girl" and Lyn Hejinian's "As for we 'who love to be astonished'" are well-known poems that are often included in linguistically-experimental verse anthologies; yet, they remain non-canonical examples of contemporary American poetry. In terms of their experimentation with language and their emphasis on the materiality of the signifier, they elicit associations with earlier traditions of avant-garde poetry rather than contemporary mainstream American poetry. The poems should therefore not be read as stand-alone pieces. They demand contextualization (even if they themselves include sentences and fragments that have been taken out of their original contexts) and necessitate reference to other works of literary theory and criticism (even if they themselves advance a poetics of non-referentiality at the level of the sentence). Lyn Hejinian's "As for we 'who love to be astonished'" must be read as part of her larger compositional experiment in autobiography, *My Life*, which itself bears fruitful analysis and interpretation if placed in conversation with the other works in her oeuvre. Similarly, it would be beneficial to read Charles Bernstein's "The Klupzy Girl" alongside the other poems in his collection *Islets/Irritations*, which itself offers productive comparison with his other volumes of poetry from the 1980s that all variously explore the nature of language and experience, 'truth' and reason—*Controlling Interests* (1980), *Stigma* (1981), *Resistance* (1983) and *The Sophist* (1987).

The two poems aptly illustrate some of the defining formal characteristics of Language poetry: attention to the opacity of language, the materiality of the signifier and the poem as object; a challenging of conventional notions of poetic agency and lyric subjectivity; linguistic experimentation, syntactic and formal disjunction through the use of parataxis and the new sentence. While Hejinian's poem playfully indulges in the slipperiness of language, memory and representation and hence questions the efficacy of traditional lyric subjectivity, Bernstein's brings to the fore the genre's potentiality as an indirect means of political intervention, critical commentary and social change, even as it also acknowledges the increasing institutionalization of the arts and the humanities.

Given that both poems were published in the 1980s, further investigations might wish to explore the trajectories of linguistically innovative or language-centered writing at the turn of the new millennium and thereafter. Some potential avenues of critical study in this respect might include the following topics: first, the turn to collaborative forms of authorship as evinced by the ten-volume collection of writings *The Grand Piano* project by ten members closely associated with the Language School in the 1970s (Hejinian is one of the ten, Bernstein is not). Second, students seeking to ride the crest of the wave in digital humanities might want to explore the ways in which computer and information technology re-shape existing paradigms of literary scholarship by, for instance, making out-of-print small press poetry chapbooks more accessible. The full catalogue of the *L=A=N=G=U=A=G=E* and *This* poetry journals, for example, are available online as electronic texts. Third, future scholarly work might explore the poetics of post-language poetry, as exemplified by the works of Juliana Spahr, Mark Wallace, Peter Gizzi, Jennifer Moxley, Tan Lin, Susan Schultz, Rodrigo Toscano, Myung Mi Kim and Lisa Jarnot, to name but a few practitioners, that are characteristically defined by a heightened use of intermediality (often combining visual and word-based arts with music), a sense of cultural diversity and hybridity, as well as a re-inscription of traditional poetic forms (such as the lyric) that were largely eschewed by the Language School. Last but not least, further research might want to focus on the issue of race, which has been marginalized in academic work on contemporary linguistically-experimental writing in the U.S. One could, for instance, examine the poetics of Black experimental writing as represented by the works of Russell Atkins, Nathaniel Mackey, Will Alexander, Harryette Mullen, Claudia Rankine, Erica Hunt, Tracie Morris and Ed Roberson, and the impact of the Black Arts Movement. These recommended avenues of exploration will certainly generate new approaches to the study of linguistically-experimental poetry and provide useful critical assessments of not only the histories, but also the futures, of American poetry.

Bibliography

Selected Primary Literature

Benson, Steve. 1988. *Blue Book*. Great Barrington, MA: The Figures.
Bernstein, Charles. 2010. "The Klupzy Girl." In: *All the Whisky in Heaven: Selected Poems*. New York: Farrar, Straus and Giroux. 84-9.

Eigner, Larry. 1986. *Air the Trees*. Boston: Black Sparrow P.

The Grand Piano: An Experiment in Collective Autobiography 1-10. Rae Arman-trout et al. Detroit: Mode A/This Press.

Grenier, Robert. 1978. *Sentences*. Cambridge, MA: Whale Cloth P.

Harryman, Carla. 1995. *There Never Was a Rose Without a Thorn*. San Francisco: City Lights.

Hejinian, Lyn. 1980. *My Life*. Los Angeles: Sun and Moon P.

Mayer, Bernadette. 1975. *Studying Hunger*. New York: Adventures in Poetry.

Perelman, Bob. 1979. *a.k.a.* Berkeley: Tuumba P.

Robinson, Kit. 1991. *The Champagne of Concrete*. Elmwood, CT: Potes & Poets P.

Silliman, Ron (ed.). 2001 [1986]. *In the American Tree*. Maine: National Poetry Foundation.

Watten, Barrett. 1998. *Bad History*. Berkeley: Atelos.

Selected Secondary Literature

Andrews, Bruce. 1996. *Paradise and Method*. Evanston: Northwestern UP.

A pivotal collection of essays by a pioneering Language poet that reflect "a desire to explore language, as up close as possible, as a material and social medium for restagings of meaning and power" (vii).

Bernstein, Charles. 1986. *Content's Dream: Essays 1975-1984*. Los Angeles: Sun and Moon P.

——. 1992. *A Poetics*. Cambridge: Harvard UP.

Bernstein explores the relation of art and culture to the politics of poetic form, and investigates the role that poetics should play in contemporary American culture.

Edmond, Jacob. 2006. "Lyn Hejinian and Russian Estrangement." In: *Poetics Today* 27: 97-124.

This essay sheds critical insight on the connections between Viktor Shklovs-ky's concept of estrangement (ostranenie) and Hejinian's poetics of the "person," which she develops in her writings on Russia.

Hejinian, Lyn. 2000. *The Language of Inquiry*. Berkeley: U of California P.

This collection of essays on poetry and poetics covers a wide range of topics from the influence of Viktor Shklovsky and Russian Formalism to the writings of Hannah Arendt.

Perelman, Bob. 1993. "Parataxis and Narrative: The New Sentence in Theory and Practice." In: *American Literature* 65: 313-24.

——. 1996. *The Marginalization of Poetry: Language Writing and Literary History*. Princeton: Princeton UP.

In these works, Perelman elaborates on his concept of "parataxis," which has become central to scholarly discussions of Language-centered/Language-oriented poetries.

Perloff, Marjorie. 1984. "The Word as Such: LANGUAGE: Poetry in the Eighties." In: *American Poetry Review* 13: 15-22.

This essay on avant-garde American poetry in the 1980s has become a standard inclusion in the syllabi of university classes on contemporary American poetry.

Silliman, Ron. 1987. *The New Sentence*. New York: Roof Books.

Expounds Silliman's concept of the "new sentence" which, together with Perelman's notion of "parataxis," has become foundational in critical discussions of the formal and linguistic aspects of Language and avant-garde poetries.

Watten, Barrett. 2003. *The Constructivist Moment: From Material Text to Cultural Poetics*. Middletown: Wesleyan UP.

A collection of theoretically-informed essays and close readings that advance a revisionist account of the avant-garde through the methodologies and cultural politics of cultural studies.

Further References

Altieri, Charles. 1989. *Painterly Abstraction in Modernist American Poetry.* New York: Cambridge UP.

—. 2006. *The Art of 20th Century American Poetry: Modernism and After.* London: Blackwell.

Bartlett, Lee. 1986. "What is 'Language Poetry'?" In: *Critical Inquiry* 12.4. 741-52.

Benjamin, Walter. 1968. "Theses on the Philosophy of History." In: *Illuminations: Essays and Reflections.* New York: Schocken. 253-64.

Davidson, Michael. 1989. *The San Francisco Renaissance: Poetics and Community at Mid-Century.* Cambridge: Cambridge UP.

—. 1997. *Ghostlier Demarcations: Modern Poetry and the Material Word.* Berkeley: U of California P.

DuPlessis, Rachel Blau. 1990. *The Pink Guitar: Writing as Feminist Practice.* New York and London: Routledge.

— and Peter Quartermain (eds.). 1999. *The Objectivist Nexus: Essays in Cultural Poetics.* Tuscaloosa: U of Alabama P.

Golding, Alan. 1995. *From Outlaw to Classic: Canons in American Poetry.* Madison: U of Wisconsin P.

Hartley, George. 1989. *Textual Politics and the Language Poets.* Bloomington: Indiana UP.

Lejeune, Philippe. 1989. *On Autobiography.* Minneapolis: U of Minnesota P.

Lyotard, Jean-François. 1984 [1979]. *The Postmodern Condition: A Report on Knowledge.* Trans. Geoff Bennington and Brian Massumi. Minneapolis: U of Minnesota P.

McCaffery, Steve. 1986. *North of Intention: Critical Writings 1973-1986.* New York: Roof Books.

—. 2001. *Prior to Meaning: The Protosemantic and Poetics.* Evanston: Northwestern UP.

McGann, Jerome. 1987. "Contemporary Poetry, Alternative Routes." In: von Hallberg 1987. 253-76.

Middleton, Peter. 1990. "Language Poetry and Linguistic Activism." *Social Text* 25-26: 242-53.

Pound, Ezra. 1934. *Make it New: Essays.* London: Faber and Faber.

Reinfeld, Linda. 1992. *Language Poetry: Writing as Rescue.* Baton Rouge: Louisiana State UP.

Rodefer, Stephen. 1982. *Four Lectures.* Berkeley: The Figures.

Ross, Andrew. 1988. "The New Sentence and the Commodity Form." In: Cary Nelson and Larry Goldberg (eds.), *Marxism and the Interpretation of Culture.* Urbana: U of Illinois P. 361-80.

Stein, Gertrude. 1935. "Portraits and Repetition." In: *Lectures in America.* Boston: Beacon. 165-206.

Vickery, Ann. 2000. *Leaving Lines of Gender: A Feminist Genealogy of Language Writing.* Middletown: Wesleyan UP.

von Hallberg, Robert (ed.). 1987. *Politics and Poetic Value.* Chicago: U of Chicago P.

Ward, Geoff. 1993. *Language Poetry and the American Avant-Garde.* Keele: British Association for American Studies.

Wittgenstein, Ludwig. 2013/1989 [1921]. *Tractatus Logico-Philosophicus.* Trans. Paul Kegan. New York: Routledge, 1981; 2013.

Zukofsky, Louis. 1931. "Sincerity and Objectification: With Special Reference to the Work of Charles Reznikoff." *Poetry* 37: 272-85.

V Contemporary
American Poetries

25.

Poetry of the Native American Renaissance and Beyond

Louise Erdrich's "Jacklight" and Joy Harjo's "Deer Dancer"

Helmbrecht Breinig

1. Authors, Themes, and Forms

When Kenneth Lincoln published his groundbreaking study *Native American Renaissance* in 1983, he provided a name for what was neither a literary movement, nor a school, nor a period, but simply an astonishing number of significant literary publications by Native authors that were triggered, one may assume, by the unexpected success of Kiowa writer N. Scott Momaday's first novel, *House Made of Dawn* (1968), which won the Pulitzer Prize for Fiction in 1969. There had been important Native American novels and short stories published earlier in the century, notably those by D'Arcy McNickle and Zitkala-Sa, just as there had been significant poetry written by authors including Creek writer Louis Oliver and Frank James Prewett, a Canadian who may have had Indian ancestors. Typically though, most indigenous writers gained a wider readership (sometimes posthumously) as representatives of Native American literature only after this literature began to receive a wider recognition in the late 1960s and the 1970s. This development was fostered by the Civil Rights Movement of that period and its Native American branch—the American Indian Movement—that opposed the continuing discrimination and post-war governmental attempts to terminate the special status of tribes and reservations and to relocate Indians to the big cities in order to speed up assimilation into the social mainstream. Indian literature also gained impetus by the steep rise in the number of Natives with higher education. It was produced by authors who could handle the English language as masterfully as any non-Indian although the flip side of this competency was often their loss of their tribal language, in case it was still spoken.

The term Native American Renaissance (subsequently NAR) is problematic not only because "Native American" is hardly less confusing than the colonialist, yet, in the context of treaty rights, indispensable terms "Indian" or "American Indian" (for lack of a convincing alternative all these terms are used here interchangeably). And in using "Renaissance" we must ask what should be considered the original 'birth' and whether what was to be reborn had ever truly died. The oral text tradition had survived conquest, genocide, and ethnocide in most tribes (cf. Lincoln 1983: ch. 3), yet the term "Renaissance" denotes a fresh beginning after a period of great difficulty. In this respect it is fitting, as it signalizes Native "survivance," a term introduced by Gerald Vizenor (Anishinaabe/French-American) to denote a more active, dynamic sense of presence and a tribal and cultural vitality that far exceeds mere "survival" (2008: 1-23).

Good luck and personal connections made it possible for Momaday to publish *House Made of Dawn* with Harper & Row, one of the leading trade publishers, with whom he then also published his poetry volume *The Gourd Dancer* (1976) and several other books. Harper used the success of Momaday's first novel and the spirit of the times to start a "Native American Publishing Program" in 1972 that existed for a number of years and was, for a time, edited by Duane

Niatum (Klallam), who also edited one of the most important anthologies of Native poetry, *Carriers of the Dream Wheel* (1975), the fifth volume in the Native American series. Most Indian poetry was published in small press houses or in Native owned publication organs like the leading (Mohawk) Indian political newspaper, *Akwesasne Notes*, founded in 1969.

While most of the collections of traditional Native literature have come out in English translation, there are some efforts to present such material bilingually, as in parts of *The South Corner of Time: Hopi Navajo Papago Yaqui Tribal Literature*, edited by Larry Evers (1980). A few contemporary poets produce work in their tribal language, for example Luci Tapahonso (Navajo), who integrates tribal phrases into her poetry, or Simon Ortiz (Acoma) who, in his "Acoma Poems" in *Out There Somewhere*, published his poems in both languages. The poets and other writers in *The Remembered Earth* (1979), edited by Cherokee/Chickasaw writer Geary Hobson, represent 38 of the hundreds of tribes in North America. Specific tribal affiliation may be of minor importance in not a few cases, because these writers see themselves as spokespersons of pan-tribal and often urban Native America or as mixed Native and Euro-Americans. Tribal issues matter in many works, however, and must not be ignored even where they do not show on the linguistic level and are not addressed specifically in the text.

There is no established list of poets associated with the NAR. While there were significant authors born earlier in the century—Marnie Walsh (Lakota) in 1916, Mary TallMountain (Athabascan) in 1918, Maurice Kenny (Mohawk) in 1929, Carter Revard (Osage) in 1931, and Peter Blue Cloud (Mohawk) in 1935—whose works became more widely known after the 1968 publication of Momaday's *House Made of Dawn*, most of the poets associated with the NAR were born in the twenty years between 1938 and 1958: Duane Niatum (Klallam), Paula Gunn Allen (Laguna/Lakota), James Welch (Blackfoot), Simon Ortiz (Acoma Pueblo), Diane Glancy (Cherokee), Joseph Bruchac (Abenaki/Slovak), Lance Henson (Cheyenne), Phil George (Nez Perce), Adrian C. Louis (Paiute), Chrystos (Menominee), Linda Hogan (Chickasaw), Wendy Rose (Hopi/Miwok), Leslie M. Silko (Laguna), Ray A. Young Bear (Meskwaki), Joy Harjo (Muscogee), Luci Tapahonso (Navajo), Louise Erdrich, Kimberly Blaeser, and Gordon Henry, Jr. (Anishinaabe), Allison Hedge Coke (multitribal), to name, in ascending age sequence, only the most often quoted. Sherman Alexie (Spokane/Coeur d'Alene), who was not born until 1966, is often called a member of the second generation of NAR writers. It is here that the term loses its usefulness. The "Four American Indian Literary Masters" that Alan Velie (1982) discusses in his pioneer study by that title—Momaday, Welch, Silko, and Vizenor—form the core group of most critical studies. Velie's emphasis is on Native American novels, although he does devote some chapters to poetry. (The predominance of fiction and other prose writing in Native American literature, both as far as the production and the critical reception is concerned, has continued to this day.) Silko, born in 1948, is the youngest of the group; Welch was born in 1940, and both Momaday and Vizenor were born in 1934.

Of this list, Momaday deserves to be mentioned first, but not just because of the impact of *House Made of Dawn*. Of mixed Kiowa and Euro-American/Cherokee descent, with college-educated parents, he studied at Stanford on a grant and earned his Ph.D. there, enabling him to pursue a brilliant teaching career at first-rate universities—hardly an example of racial deprivation. The first thing one must know about the NAR, then, is that it is part of American literature in general even though it pursues a specific cultural and political agenda (cf. also

Lincoln 2000). To regard it by different standards would mean another form of discrimination, although there are quite a few Native separatists who insist on a radical difference from the cultural and social mainstream.

Surely, in its thematic range and modernist form, *House Made of Dawn* was the groundbreaking Native book of the times. However, Momaday had been an accomplished modernist poet before writing this novel. The poetry he wrote while at Stanford was particularly influenced by his mentor, the poet and critic Yvor Winters, and by his reading of Emily Dickinson, Paul Valéry, and Wallace Stevens, just as his fictional model was Faulkner rather than the Navajo *Night Chant* which he quotes in his book. Momaday—the man who stands at the beginning of this boom of Native writing—was capable (as were many later writers, as well) of using the whole range of modern Western forms of literature. For example, his early poem "Before an Old Painting of the Crucifixion" (1960) resembles Stevens's "Sunday Morning" in tone and through the theme of the loss of belief (Schubnell 1985: 205-6, 209-12). Yet the musical quality, the iambic pentameters, alliterations and assonances, as well as the imagery and choice vocabulary indicate that here is a poetic talent of the highest order:

> I ponder how He died, despairing once.
> I've heard the cry subside in vacant skies,
> In clearings where no other was. Despair,
> Which, in the vibrant wake of utterance,
> Resides in desolate calm, preoccupies,
> Though it is still. There is no solace there. (1976: 28, ll. 1-6)

There is nothing even faintly suggesting that this author is a Native American. The same is true for "The Bear" (1960), a poem that stems not from a closeness to the totemic animal but from an observation of nature colored by the reading of Faulkner's masterful novella *The Bear*. Momaday later gave the subject a tribal turn when he identified with the bear as a mythic animal; one of his Kiowa names, Tsoai-talee, is derived from a Kiowa myth involving a boy turning into a bear. "The Delight Song of Tsoai-talee" (1975) is a kind of prayer or incantation of life, echoing patterns of traditional Native songs, myths, and ceremonial texts. In contrast to his earlier work, many of his 'Native' poems are written in more open forms and in varieties of free verse, or even prose poetry as in the marvelous sequence "The Colors of Night." It was not only the sheer literary excellence of his works but his ability and readiness to integrate traditional patterns and thematic elements into his texts in a great variety of genres as well as into his paintings and drawings—Momaday is also a celebrated artist—that made him a model for other writers and a spokesman for Native America.

With regard to the writers in the list above, one might start grouping them by form, by the way they—like Momaday—adapt and combine Native or European genre traditions to create forms like the prayer, or by theme, the focus on nature, the spiritual world, family and clan, Native American myths, the plight of Indians in the big city, and historical trauma. Sometimes the intercultural connections reach even farther as with Gerald Vizenor, known mainly for his postmodern, satiric novels. His verse is strongly influenced by Japanese haiku, whose similarities to the quasi-Imagist condensation of traditional Anishinaabe dream songs are obvious:

> cedar cones
> tumble in a mountain stream
> letters from home (1984: 23, ll. 4-6)

Vizenor has even made the short, two-stress line the medium for a booklength narrative poem, *Bear Island: The War at Sugar Point* (2006). Bold formal experiments have been made by other Native American poets as well, but given the large number of these authors, a short overview is best organized by theme or a combination of theme and form, where the latter follows traditional models.

One of these forms is the prayer, and a good example is Simon Ortiz's "Smoking My Prayers." Ortiz, who is a member of the Acoma Pueblo nation, often refers to the very long cultural tradition of this Southwestern agricultural tribe, and "Smoking My Prayers" highlights the performative quality of traditional Native literature, as body movements accompany the text in the ritual of smoking as paying homage to the powers of the universe: "now that i have lighted my smoke / i am motioning to the east" (Dodge/McCullough 1974: 81, ll. 1-2). Songs and prayers are related forms, and so Linda Hogan's "Elk Song" starts out as a poem of thanksgiving: "We give thanks / to deer, otter, / the great fish / and birds that fly over / and are our bones and skin" (Purdy/Ruppert 2001 [1988]: 493-4, ll. 1-5). This Chickasaw poet is also a great ecologist, and she adroitly turns the text into both an accusation—"The earth / is . . . / a slaughterhouse / for humans as well" (ll. 10-3)—and an invocation of the healing powers of nature: "out there / . . . the gone elk . . . / are drumming / back the woodland, / tall grass and days we were equal / and strong" (ll. 40-6). Many poems point out the beauty of nature and a harmonious relation with animals, but anger and despair over the destruction of the traditional Native land, its plants and wildlife, is a recurrent theme found also, for example, in Mary TallMountain's "The Last Wolf" (ibid. [1981]: 554).

Nature cannot be separated from the spiritual world. Indeed, in what has often been called the magic realism of the powerful nature poems by Ray Young Bear, a Meskwaki from Iowa who is steeped in the tradition of the Woodland Indians, there is a constant transformational process involving people and animal people, living and dead, the factual and the spiritual (see for example "The First Dimension of Skunk," ibid. [1990]: 578-81). Although Young Bear no longer conceives his poems in Meskwaki and then translates them into English as he did in his early poetry, much cultural knowledge is hidden under the surface of the sometimes ordinary and sometimes surreal observations that make up his writing. He consistently avoids using sacred material in any explicit way. Indeed, the use of myth has been a hotly debated issue among Native American writers, with positions varying from total avoidance to playful and even parodistic use. One semi-divine figure in almost every culture who invites such flippancy is the trickster, appearing in some cultures as Coyote, whose role fluctuates between creator and irresponsible egotist. In Simon Ortiz's retelling of the Acoma creation myth, "The Creation, According to Coyote," it is Coyote who assumes the role of storyteller and provides the speaker with essential, though completely fragmentary, elements of the myth. Yet after all this debunking, the final line of the poem—the punch line—reaffirms exactly the truth and life of the tribal belief system: "And you know, I believe him" (1992: 42, l. 38).

Another way of approaching myth is by transferring its narrative content into a contemporary setting as Leslie Silko has done in her brilliant combination of myth and short story "Yellow Woman," and also in "Storytelling," the poetic version of that material in which a woman either elopes or is abducted by a man who may be a supernatural being. "My husband / left / after he heard the story / and moved back in with his mother. / It was my fault . . . / I could have told / the story / better than I did" (1981: 98, ll. 96-104). Many Native writers have composed such meta-narrative texts where the nature of storytelling is demonstrated and problematized, a kind of meta-cultural commentary on the simultaneous distance from and closeness to the tribal tradition. Such poetological meta-texts also address the problem of writing 'in the enemy's language' (see Bird/Harjo) or of belonging to two cultural traditions. Linda Hogan's "The Truth Is" puts this nicely: "In my left pocket a Chickasaw hand / rests on the bone of the pelvis. / In my right pocket / a white hand . . . The truth is / we are crowded together / and knock against each other at night" (Purdy/Ruppert 2001 [1985]: 492-3, ll. 1-4, 16-8).

Not every text will achieve some kind of bi-cultural reconciliation or thrive on the tension of transdifference—in this case, the co-presence of different socio-cultural affiliations in texts by what Vizenor has called "Postindian crossbloods," a status he openly accepts for himself (see Vizenor/Lee 1999). Much Indian writing is political, with conflict and resistance forming the themes of a vast body of poetry. In Oneida poet Roberta Hill Whiteman's "Dream of Rebirth," anger and grief find powerful metaphoric expression: "We stand on the edge of wounds, hugging canned meat, / . . . Our luxuries are hatred. Grief. Worn-out hands / carry the pale remains of forgotten murders. / If I could only lull or change this slow hunger, / this midnight swollen four hundred years" (1984: 282, ll. 1, 5-8). Rebirth is envisioned in terms of a purification ritual: "We need to be purified by fury. / Once more eagles will restore our prayers. / We'll forget the strangeness of your pity" (ll. 19-21). In the context of the lives of urban Indians, such hope of healing is often absent, and texts addressing the grim social conditions on the reservations or in big city environments, such as Harjo's representative suicidal "Woman Hanging from the Thirteenth Floor Window" (1983) can be quite drastic. The horrible effects of the Indian Relocation Act on the Native persons finding themselves alienated and stranded in the cities are expressed in poems like Ortiz's "Relocation": "The lights, / the cars, / the deadened glares / tear my heart / and close my mind" (1992: 76, ll. 4-8). Again and again these texts are a reckoning, a getting-even with persons and institutions that have destroyed tribal life and natural environments as in Hopi poet and anthropologist Wendy Rose's "Subway Graffiti: An Anthropologist's Impressions" (1994).

If a good deal of Native American poetry is thus concerned with contemporary marginalization, victimization, and the dissolution of family and community order, and as a consequence of the latter presents also quite a few texts of self-accusation (on the individual and on the group level), the most profound and encompassing traumata pointed out are those of the past. Many writers have found words for what lies even beyond the range of language to represent: genocide and ethnocide. Historical trauma can be evoked in heart-rending detail as in Wendy Rose's "I expected my skin and my blood to ripen" (1980), a poem that cries out against the added injustice of the sale of the clothes and ornaments of those slain at the Wounded Knee Massacre of 1890. Some poems are nostalgic, such as Osage poet and scholar Carter Revard's moving open-form "Wazhazhe Grandmother," which mourns the repeated loss of land—even that which was given to his grandparents under the General Allotment Act, including the homestead in its idyllic surroundings—when the whole area is drowned in a water reservoir. The bitter line "blessed with a dam" (Purdy/Ruppert 2001 [1993]: 529, l. 55) homophonetically (dam/damn) expresses the clash of values.

As in any literature worldwide, Native American poets have written many poems on love, sex, and gender relations, with some of them addressing the double marginalization as Indians/mixed-bloods and gays/lesbians. What strikes the non-Native reader as specific, though, is the role played by the family, here understood in the extended sense, with grandparents or uncles and aunts taking significant positions, as is often the rule in the tribal order, or by the clan when defining the marriage rules. In Luci Tapahonso's often anthologized "Hills Brothers Coffee" (1978), for example, family relations have a healing function, and in the poem for her granddaughter's birth, "Blue Horses Rush In" (1997), the family event is linked with the belief system and the symbolic order of their culture. Profoundly disturbing consequences for the individual can arise when family and tribal order are broken or conflicted. Wendy Rose, for instance, was not accepted as a member of the Hopi nation because it was her father who was a full-blood Hopi and not her mother, as required by this matrilinear culture. Many of Rose's poems are echoes of her identity problems—a topic that American Indian literature shares with that of any other ethnicity or minority.

It would be a serious mistake to see modern Native American poetry as dominated only by the past, tribal traditions and practices, and a value system based on a land ethic and a reverence for nature. There is also resistance against tribal authority, as in Phil George's "Battle Won Is Lost," which ends a series of calls for heroism by the elders with "They said, 'To die is glorious.' / They lied" (Dodge/McCullough 1974: 46, ll. 17-8). There is continuous cultural change that defies the stereotypical notions that tend to freeze American Indians in their tradition. There is also much humor and satire, notably in the poetry of Sherman Alexie, who not only describes new cultural forms like the powwow circuit but also modern Indian ways of tricking those who try to enforce tribal or Bureau of Indian Affairs regulations, for instance in "No Drugs or Alcohol Allowed" (1992). And there is the inter-Indian debate regarding the preference for a "Postindian," interactional position vis-à-vis the dominant culture and society, for versions of hybridity (represented, for instance, by Gerald Vizenor) and a separatist, nationalist counter-position (formulated by Simon Ortiz and others) that prioritizes Native political and cultural sovereignty and separateness (cf. Weaver/Womack/Warrior 2006).

2. The Reversal of Power in Louise Erdrich's "Jacklight"

Louise Erdrich (born in 1954) is of Ojibwa (Anishinaabe) and German-American descent. Perhaps more than any other contemporary Native American author she has managed to bridge the gap between tribal, highbrow, and popular literatures; she has become an internationally known figure. Although her fame rests on her many novels—most of them located around the town Argus near an Ojibwa reservation in North Dakota and featuring a locale and a group of Native and Euro-American characters first introduced in her highly successful novel *Love Medicine* (1984), as well as on her many short stories that often form the nucleus of the novels to come—she started out as a poet and has occasionally returned to the genre. *Jacklight* (1984) was Erdrich's first literary book publication. The poems that went into this volume were part of her master's thesis at Johns Hopkins University. The book contains poems that reflect the contemporary or historical situation of Native Americans, such as "Indian Boarding School: The Runaways," commemorating the Indian children who ran away from the forced assimilation practices at the boarding schools and tried to get back to their families; love poems like "The Woods"; a series of modern Ojibwa prose myths about the central character Potchikoo, and also a section of poems on "The Butcher's Wife" featuring German immigrants. In her poetry, as in her fiction, Erdrich gives credit not only to her Ojibwa heritage but also to her German-American roots. In her bitter review of *The Beet Queen*, Erdrich's second novel in her Argus cycle, Leslie Silko accused her Ojibwa colleague of writing in a postmodern, self-referential manner, albeit in "dazzling and sleek" poetic prose (Silko 1986: 178), that did not sufficiently address the reality of reservation and off-reservation Indian life. Silko's critique has created quite a controversy among Native and non-Native writers and critics, but it may have resulted from a misunderstanding of Erdrich's intentions and an essentialist point of view that reduces Indian writing to a separatist, accusative mode based on a stable concept of ethnicity and a necessity of referring to the respective tribal tradition (see Pérez-Castillo 2001). Erdrich, however, never denied her bi-cultural background and will not restrict herself to contributing to 'American Indian Literature' exclusively. This is true of her thematic range in *Jacklight*, and also of individual poems that are multi-voiced, complex, and ambiguous.

The opening poem, "Jacklight," is to be seen as programmatic for the book. The poem is in free verse and consists of seven stanzas varying from four to nine lines, each between four and thirteen syllables long. The language is melodic and rhythmic, with passages approaching metric regularity, like the first line with its three anapests that then dissolve in more irregular but strongly musical rhythms in the next three lines of the first stanza:

> We have come to the edge of the woods,
> out of brown grass where we slept, unseen,
> out of knotted twigs, out of leaves creaked shut,
> out of hiding. (1984a: 3, ll. 1-4)

The half rhyme of "leaves creaked" and the four anaphoric "out of" give the impression of a soft, musical voice presenting a decidedly rhetorical text. This is good modern poetry, and it is good Native poetry although it is in no way marked as such. Nor is there any explicit mention of Indianicity in the whole text. The only clue to its Native thematics and, possibly, authorship, is the epigraph, a quotation from R.W. Dunning's 1959 study *Social and Economic Change Among the Northern Ojibwa*: "*The same Chippewa word is used both for flirting and hunting game, while another Chippewa word connotes both using force in intercourse and also killing a bear with one's bare hands*" (ibid.; original italics). From this hint we may deduce that this is an American Indian poem having to do with love and sex, but also with hunting. But there is much more to this poem, as we shall see.

The title, "Jacklight," refers to a lantern or flashlight used (mostly illegally and, it seems, unfairly) as a ruse to lure game while hunting at night. The text explores the relationship between the lured and those using this device: the hunted and the hunters. There is no lyrical "I"; the speaker is part of a "we" whose nature it is essential to explore. At first the "we" appears to be the animals that are made to come to the edge of the forest by the jacklight. As James Ruppert has argued, the "we" might also "engage a discourse about the natural world versus civilization and the animal nature that is on occasion hidden within us" (2004: 171). The second stanza already imbues the "we" with a degree of self-reflexivity, which indicates that the deer of the forest are also a metaphor for a group of humans. Both the light, anthropomorphized by being "clenched to a fist of light" (l. 6) as well as by its capacity to "glance" and "point," and the answering individuals represent humans engaging in some kind of relationship:

> At first the light wavered, glancing over us.
> Then it clenched to a fist of light that pointed,
> searched out, divided us.
> Each took the beams like direct blows the heart answers.
> Each of us moved forward alone. (ll. 5-9)

Is the emotion ("heart") fear or a feeling of attraction? The situation resembles that of a casting call, and it seems that here women are singled out by a male, phallic ("beam") power or authority. Not only are these females made to leave the security of their group, but in stanza three "we" are even "drawn out of ourselves" (l. 11). Their natural identity is called into question by the other side, which is seen as technological, unnatural ("this night sun," ibid.), and divisive, polarizing by the "battery of polarized acids" (l. 12) of the flashlight.

The confrontation of deer vs. hunters, nature vs. civilization, women vs. men, that until now looked like a contemporary situation, is given a historic dimension in stanzas four and five where anonymous strangers ("they are faceless, invisible" behind the light, l. 15) can nonetheless be identified by their smell, as shown by a long series of anaphoras:

> We smell the raw steel of their gun barrels,
> mink oil on leather, their tongues of sour barley.
> We smell their mothers buried chin-deep in wet dirt.
> We smell their fathers with scoured knuckles,
> teeth cracked from hot marrow.
> . . .
> We smell the itch underneath the caked guts on their clothes. (ll. 16-20, 24)

Here, clearly, are references to a historic pioneer society, its technology, its eating and drinking habits, its insufficient hygiene and its primitive sod-houses where the "mothers" are virtually "buried." For them, the Other is not simply the animals but the wilderness they are trying to overcome (or emerge from) and, specifically, "the Indians."

The confrontation of Self vs. Other that is being played out on the metaphorically linked levels of hunt, nature/civilization, gender relations, and ethnic conflict takes a different turn from stanza five on. While the aggressors remain dangerous and violent—"We smell their minds like silver hammers / cocked back, held in readiness / for the first of us to step into the open" (ll. 25-7)—the superior ability to "smell their minds" indicates a shift in power. The sixth stanza repeats the first but with variations in the last two lines: "out of leaves creaked shut, out of *our* hiding. / *We have come here too long*" (ll. 30-1; emphasis added). The passive side reveals a power of agency, from now on setting the terms:

> It is their turn now,
> their turn to follow us. Listen,
> they put down their equipment.
> It is useless in the tall brush.
> And now they take the first steps, not knowing
> how deep the woods are and lightless.
> How deep the woods are. (ll. 32-8)

This reversal of power indicates that any relationship of Self and Other is two-sided: where there is power there is also some element of counter-power (see Giddens 1984). Like in the concluding lines of Denise Levertov's beautiful poem "Ways of Conquest": "What I invaded has / invaded me" (1975: 19), there is mutuality found even in asymmetrical power relations. Tribal Native Americans pacify, to this day, the spirit of animals killed in hunting by prayers and offerings so that their reincarnations or the animals' offspring may offer themselves for food in the future. To ignore such mutuality is dangerous for the perpetrators; to use only violence will denature them and turn them into unfeeling monsters.

What the hunters/men/pioneers can learn by entering the world of their respective Other is mysterious and possibly dangerous, too. Native mythology of various tribes abounds in stories of the sexual attractiveness of the Deer Woman or Antelope Woman, her powers of seduction leading to a loss of both control and social responsibility (see Van Dyke 2003/2004). Thus, if the "we" of the beginning of the poem are involuntarily drawn to the light or attracted by the gifts and benefits offered by men/European civilization, there is a reverse allurement indicated at the end. To what extent those entering "the woods" are aware of the risk involved remains open; curiously the version of the poem in Erdrich's volume Original Fire has "now knowing" rather than "not knowing" in line 36. In any case, this programmatic text is both a love poem and a nature poem, with a hint of the traditional, mythological level added. It is a poem about the conflict of cultures that reveals the interrelatedness of the natural and the cultural, the personal and the societal. In this it is an excellent example of Native American as part of American poetry.

3. Myth and Imagination in Joy Harjo's "Deer Dancer"

Joy Harjo, born in Tulsa, Oklahoma in 1951, is an enrolled member of the Muskogee (Creek) Nation and of Creek and Cherokee/French descent. She carries the communal burden of the historic trauma of the forced removal of both her tribes in the 1830s from their homeland in the Southeast to the so-called "Indian Territory" in what is today Oklahoma, and the subsequent loss of even their new lands by measures like the General Allotment Act, which disrupted both the traditional forms of land use and the tribal cultures. Further traumatized by a family breakup, Harjo found renewed energy in her creative work which includes not only writing but also fine art and, especially, music: with her band, Poetic Justice, she has managed to combine elements of Jazz, Rock and traditional Native music; she also sings her poetry. In addition to her teaching career, she has pursued literary and musical careers that have gained her a reputation as one of the leading Native American and feminist artists of her time: "Loss of identity, dissolution of cultural roots, disintegration of the community and the family unit, alcoholism, violence, the tenacious will to survive and breathe new life into one's group . . . represent [her] main themes" (Coltelli 2005: 284). Harjo's third volume of poetry, She Had Some Horses (1983), made her famous. It deals not only with the problems listed by Coltelli and with the resulting fear that threatens to overwhelm the speaker, but also with ways of overcoming this fear, for instance by evoking the power and beauty of horses that, in the eponymous poem "She Had Some Horses," turn out to be the em-

bodiment of natural forces, of people the speaker has known, of types of characters and relationships, horses that finally also symbolize her own multifaceted
being and identity.

Harjo's next important volume of poetry, *In Mad Love and War* (1990), further develops possibilities of exploring but also overcoming such conflicts and
contradictions. "Deer Dancer" (ibid.: 5-6) is an excellent example. It is a prose
poem, a form Harjo used more and more frequently. This prose form is also
popular with many other Native American poets whose sense of the prosaic reality principle is strong enough to make them distrust the elegance of modernist
poetic forms. And yet "Deer Dancer" is not pure prose, as is, for instance, "Day
of the Dead" in the same volume, where the right-hand margin is aligned. "Deer
Dancer" consists of lines taking almost the whole width of the page, creating the
impression of ragged right printing, but in one case (l. 28) the next line is indented, indicating that it belongs to the one above and thus forms a regular
verse line. Also, the first word of the lines often carries particular weight like in
much modernist free verse. In other words, Harjo plays with the respective qualities of verse and prose and achieves an ambivalence that the reader has to accept, endure, and turn into a creative engagement with the issues presented by
the text. The poem consists of 13 stanzas (assuming that line 30 is part of stanza five and not a separate stanza), the first five looking fairly regular, each having five to seven lines. The second half is more broken, with stanzas varying
from one to four lines in length. Stanza six, the single line 31, marks the center
and turning point and is therefore followed by a slightly larger space (see below).

The scene described in stanza one is an urban bar during "the coldest night
of the year" (l. 2) after everybody has left except the "hardcore" (ibid.) Indian
drinkers—"We were Indian ruins" (l. 3). Enter the incredible: a woman, a
stranger who "was the end of beauty" (l. 4); her unsurpassable beauty is also
the suspension—"the end"—of such ordinary criteria. She can perhaps be culturally located: "the stranger whose tribe we / recognized, her family related to
deer, if that's who she was, a people / accustomed to hearing songs in pine
trees, and making them hearts" (ll. 4-6). These people live close to nature—quite
different from the persons in the bar—and are obviously gifted in transcending
the boundaries of their reality and in transforming its elements, "making them
hearts." But there is also a suspicion that the stranger may be from beyond
such a boundary, that she is Deer Woman herself, a mythic being.

Deer Woman is a spirit whose role in tribal mythology (Cherokee, Muskogee,
Choctaw, Seminole, and other tribes) is to provide young persons with sexual
temptations that will indirectly remind them of their responsibility to choose
good, socially acceptable partners and enter into stable relationships that will
ensure the continuity of fertility and life (see Dunn 2003). We don't know if the
stranger is, indeed, Deer Woman in modern disguise, but she has an inner
strength that works miracles in the indicated manner, made clear in stanza two:
"The woman inside the woman . . . / blew deer magic. Henry Jack, who could
not survive a sober day . . . [a]ll / night . . . dreamed a dream he could not say.
The next day he borrowed / money, went home, and sent back the money I lent.
Now that's a miracle" (ll. 7-11). The humorous, even sardonic tone that characterizes much of the poem only superficially conceals the deep impression the
event has made on the speaker. Words like "dream" or "vision" (l. 12) evoke the
spiritual sphere behind the ordinary that will be found more easily at "home,"

on the reservation, but can miraculously appear even in this "bar of broken survivors" (l. 13).

The third stanza presents versions of coping with the incredible: "We who
were taught not to stare drank our beer" (l. 14). Is 'not staring' just a rule of ordinary politeness, or does it refer to a religious taboo, as in 'you do not stare at
spirits'? Such uncertainties continue to characterize the descriptive language.
Yet when the dramatic does happen—Richard's jealous wife "dove to kill her"
(l. 16)—the solution is banal and ludicrous: "We had to hold her back, / empty
her pockets of knives and diaper pins" (ll. 16-7). Consequently, in stanza four
the speaker addresses the question of how to deal with the inroad of the mysterious in language: "How do I say it? In this language there are no words for how
the real world / collapses. I could say it in my own and the sacred mounds
would come into / focus, but I couldn't take it in this dingy envelope" (ll. 19-21).
Colloquial English is hardly adequate to express the unreal, but using the Native tongue and thus evoking the image of the cultural tradition appears as sac-
rilege in an ordinary text, an ordinary, (seemingly) prosaic piece of literature.
The speaker therefore continues to approach her subject indirectly by mentioning her brother-in-law who gave up a law career in the white world and "practiced law on the streets with his hands" (l. 26). Is he a street fighter? A police-
man? His previous love experiences merge into the current encounter with her
who may be Deer Woman: "He jimmied to the proverbial / dream girl, the face of
the moon . . . / He bragged to us, he told her magic words and that's when she
broke, became human" (ll. 26-8). Is this the momentary situation or an analep-
tic glance at a previous conquest? After all, "the proverbial dream girl" sounds
too trite for the strange woman. The collapse of two situations into one becomes
apparent when "we all heard his bar voice crack: / *What's a girl like you doing in
a place like this?*" (ll. 29-30; original emphasis), a question the speaker tries to
connect with the common Native experience of cultural dislocation: "That's what
I'd like to know, what are we all doing in a place like this?" (l. 31), which is the
central line of the poem, forming a stanza (six) by itself.

The second half of the poem, beginning with stanza seven, intensifies the
impression of confusion. There is the drab reality of the bar and the woman in
cheap clothes who will finally dance naked on a table like a hooker and whose
motives are unclear—"What was she on?" (l. 33)—the person who has become
the focus of everybody's desire; and yet there is also a dream of reconciliation
with the world of spirits and fertility, for which language must transcend
speech-act logic, must become a series of poetic associations hardly translatable
into common understanding: "This is not a rooming house, but / a dream of
winter falls and the deer who portrayed the relatives of / strangers. The way
back is deer breath on icy windows" (ll. 37-9). The woman is or is imagined to be
pregnant, and it is for the sake of the baby "inside the girl sealed up with a lick
of / hope and swimming into the praise of nations" (ll. 36-7), of continued life
and future glory, that the speaker must try to evoke the 'pregnant' atmosphere
beyond the associations raised by the music from the juke box, the well-known
Kenny Rogers song "*You picked a fine time to leave me, Lucille. / With four hungry children and a crop in the field*" (ll. 43-4; original emphasis). Chances are
that the woman is another Lucille—the sentence immediately following is "And
then she took off her clothes" (l. 45)—but she is imagined by the onlookers as
"the myth slipped down through dreamtime . . . / The deer who crossed through
knots of a curse to find / us" (ll. 47-9).

The world is what we imagine it to be, and language has a creative power: this common Native American view, superbly expressed in Momaday's phrase, the "man made of words" (1997: 9-12), is emphasized by stanza 13, the ending of the poem. The speaker acknowledges the imaginative quality of the event described in her "story" (l. 50) when she confesses: "I wasn't there. But I imagined her / like this, not a stained red dress with tape on her heels but the deer who / entered our dream in white dawn, breathed mist into pine trees, her fawn a / blessing of meat, the ancestors who never left" (ll. 50-3). As a factual eye-witness account her story collapses at his point, only to be transferred onto the plane of the deeper truth of stories that render essential beliefs of a society, as myths, as lyrical fantasies, even as erotic dreams. The heightened poetic language of the last sentence, the rhyme of "dawn" and "fawn," the alliterations ("dress," deer," "dream," "dawn"), the assonances ("heels," "deer," "dream," "meat"), and the rich imagery all contribute to our feeling that, indeed, the ancestors have never left, that there will be continuation of value-determined life. It does not matter, therefore, that the speaker's lending money to one of her fellow "survivors" and the "miracle" of his sending it back may never have happened this way. What counts is that the inroad of the incredible makes survivance possible even for those "poison[ed] by culture" (l. 14).

4. Outlook

A list published by the Poetry Foundation (see www.poetryfoundation.org/article/ 245706) contains the names of 50 current Native American poets, among them a number of writers born in the 1970s—Cedar Sigo (Suquamish), Stuart Youngman "Sy" Hoawah (Comanche), Sherwin Bitsui (Navajo), and Santee Frazier (Cherokee)—poets who represent a younger generation and are decidedly not counted among those of the NAR. Considering that some of the founding figures of the NAR, like Momaday and Vizenor, are still active, there is an enormous range of biographies and experiences, of styles and themes. As early as 1995 the Paiute poet Adrian Louis published his "Electric Genocide Rap," which begins: "No sense crying. America is dying. We huddle in the most violent nation in the history of human constipation" (1995: 55), and hip-hop has become an important genre of dealing with Native issues (see Sheffield 2011). Native writers use forms of online poetry or appear at poetry slams, sometimes with improvised texts. It may be well, therefore, to conclude with some lines from Anishinaabe Gordon Henry's witty, self-positioning prose-poem "The First Door: I As Not I":

> I am not:
>
>   postmodern or modern; a sign, or a signifier, between
> signifieds; surreal or existential; neo-traditional or beat;
> transcendental or metaphysical; confessional, shaman, warrior,
> or sun priest; trickster, nationalist, exile or anthropocentric;
> psycho-dramatizer, or dishwasher safe, microwaveable . . . (2007: 22, ll. 1-6)

and so on, for more than two pages, up to the confession: "These are just some of my relatives" (l. 71). Native American poets belong to a network of identity positions and inter-cultural ascriptions that make them take part in the dissolution of a nation as defined by a coherent mainstream and, as such, make them members of a multiethnic American literature.

Bibliography

Selected Primary Literature

Alexie, Sherman. 1992. *The Business of Fancydancing: Stories and Poems*. Brooklyn, NY: Hanging Loose Press.

Bird, Gloria and Joy Harjo (eds.). 1998. *Reinventing the Enemy's Language: Contemporary Native Women's Writings of North America*. New York: W. W. Norton.

Dodge, Robert K. and Joseph B. McCullough (eds.). 1974. *Voices from Wah'Kon-Tah: Contemporary Poetry of Native Americans*. New York: International Publishers.

Erdrich, Louise. 1984a. *Jacklight*. New York: Henry Holt.

—. 1984b. "Jacklight." Web. 10 Aug 2014. <http://foreveronalilo.wordpress.com/2013/02/25/poem-of-the-week-jacklight-by-louise-erdrich>.

—. 2003. *Original Fire: Selected and New Poems*. New York: Harper Collins.

Evers, Larry (ed.). 1980. *The South Corner of Time: Hopi Navajo Papago Yaqui Tribal Literature*. Tucson: Sun Tracks.

Harjo, Joy. 1983. *She Had Some Horses*. New York: Thunder's Mouth Press.

—. 1990. *In Mad Love and War*. Middletown: Wesleyan UP.

Henry, Gordon, Jr. 2007. *The Failure of Certain Charms and Other Disparate Signs of Life*. Cambridge, UK: Salt Publishing.

Hobson, Geary (ed.). 1979. *The Remembered Earth: An Anthology of Contemporary Native American Literature*. Albuquerque: U of New Mexico P.

Hogan, Linda. 1993. *The Book of Medicines*. Minneapolis: Coffee House Press.

Levertov, Denise. 1975. *The Freeing of the Dust*. New York: New Directions.

Louis, Adrian C. 1995. *Vortex of Indian Fevers*. Evanston: TriQuarterly Books/ Northwestern UP.

Momaday, N. Scott. 1968. *House Made of Dawn*. New York: Harper & Row.

—. 1976. *The Gourd Dancer*. New York: Harper & Row.

—. 1997. *The Man Made of Words: Essays, Stories, Passages*. New York: St. Martin's P.

Niatum, Duane (ed.). 1975. *Carriers of the Dream Wheel: Contemporary Native American Poetry*. New York: Harper & Row.

— (ed.). 1988. *Harper's Anthology of Twentieth Century Native American Poetry*. San Francisco: Harper.

Ortiz, Simon J. 1992. *Woven Stone*. Tucson: U of Arizona P.

—. 2002. *Out There Somewhere*. Tucson: U of Arizona P.

Purdy, John L. and James Ruppert (eds.). 2001. *Nothing But the Truth: An Anthology of Native American Literature*. Upper Saddle River, NJ: Prentice Hall.

Revard, Carter. 1993. *An Eagle Nation*. Tucson and London: U of Arizona P.

Rose, Wendy. 1980. *Lost Copper*. Banning, CA: Malki Museum Press.

—. 1994. *Bone Dance: New and Selected Poems 1965-1993*. Tucson and London: U of Arizona P.

Silko, Leslie Marmon. 1981. *Storyteller*. New York: Seaver Books.

TallMountain, Mary. 1981. *There Is No Word for Goodbye*. Marvin, SD: Blue Cloud Quarterly.

Tapahonso, Luci. 1993. *Sáanii Dahataał—The Women Are Singing: Poems and Stories*. Tucson and London: U of Arizona P.

—. 1997. *Blue Horses Rush In: Poems and Stories*. Tucson: U of Arizona P.

Vizenor, Gerald (ed.). 1965. *Summer in the Spring: Lyric Poems of the Ojibway*. Minneapolis: Nodin P.

—. 1984. *Matsushima: Pine Islands*. Minneapolis: Nodin P.

— and A. Robert Lee. 1999. *Postindian Conversations*. Lincoln: U of Nebraska P.

——. 2006. *Bear Island: The War at Sugar Point*. Minneapolis and London: U of Minnesota P.

——. 2006. *Almost Ashore: Selected Poems*. Cambridge, UK: Salt Publishing.

Welch, James. 1976 [1971]. *Riding the Earthboy 40*. New York: Harper & Row.

Whiteman, Roberta Hill. 1984. "Dream of Rebirth." In: Rayna Green (ed.), *That's What She Said: Contemporary Poetry and Fiction by Native American Women*. Bloomington: Indiana UP. 282.

——. 1994. *Star Quilt*. Duluth, MN: Holy Cow! Press.

Young Bear, Ray. 1980. *Winter of the Salamander: The Keeper of Importance*. New York: Harper Row.

Selected Secondary Literature

Bruchac, Joseph. 1996. "Contemporary Native American Writing: An Overview." In: Andrew Wiget (ed.), *Handbook of Native American Literature*. New York and London: Garland. 311-28.

Bruchac's essay is a basic source of information on Native American writers; Wiget's handbook offers an excellent survey of a wide range of literary topics.

Coltelli, Laura. 2005. "Joy Harjo's Poetry." In: Joy Porter and Kenneth M. Roemer (eds.). *The Cambridge Companion to Native American Literature*. Cambridge: Cambridge UP. 283-95.

Coltelli provides an astute introduction to Harjo's work and ideas.

Fast, Robin Riley. 1999. *The Heart as a Drum: Continuance and Resistance in American Indian Poetry*. Ann Arbor: U of Michigan P.

Most sophisticated study to date, using Bakhtin's theory and terminology for a discussion of Native American texts as a poetry of contested spaces between a variety of commitments.

Jacobs, Connie A. and Greg Sarris (eds.). 2004. *Approaches to Teaching the Works of Louise Erdrich*. New York: MLA.

The collection of essays focuses on Erdrich's fiction, but contains some valid discussion of her poetry.

Lincoln, Kenneth. 1983. *Native American Renaissance*. Berkeley and Los Angeles: U of California P.

One of the groundbreaking works on the Native American Renaissance.

——. 2000. *Sing with the Heart of a Bear: Fusions of Native and American Poetry 1890-1999*. Berkeley and Los Angeles: U of California P.

Only extended study to show the place of Native American poetry in the context of American poetry in general.

Rader, Dean and Janice Gould (eds.). 2003. *Speak to Me Words: Essays on Contemporary American Indian Poetry*. Tucson: U of Arizona P.

Contains articles on a fairly wide range of themes, including essays by some Native writers.

Schubnell, Matthias. 1985. *N. Scott Momaday: The Cultural and Literary Background*. Norman: U of Oklahoma P.

An essential study of Momaday's earlier work.

Wilson, Norma C. 2001. *The Nature of Native American Poetry*. Albuquerque: U of New Mexico P.

Short introductory monograph, containing chapters on eight individual poets.

Further References

Dunn, Carolyn. 2003. "Deer Woman and the Living Myth of the Dreamtime." *Journal of Mythic Arts*, Endicott Studio. Web. 10 Aug 2014. <www.endicott-studio.com/rdrm/rrwoman.html.>

Giddens, Anthony. 1984. *The Constitution of Society: Outline of the Theory of Structuration*. Cambridge, UK: Polity Press.

Pérez-Castillo, Susan. 2001. "Postmodernism, Native American Literature and the Real: The Silko-Erdrich Controversy." In: Purdy/Ruppert 1996: 15-22.

Poetry Foundation. "Native American Poetry and Culture: A Selection of Poets, Poems, and Articles Exploring the Native American Experience." Web. 10 Aug 2014. <www.poetryfoundation.org/article/245706>.

Ruppert, James. 2004. "Identity Indexes in *Love Medicine* and 'Jacklight'." In: Jacobs/Sarris 2004. 170-4.

Sheffield, Carrie Louise. 2011. "Native American Hip-Hop and Historical Trauma: Surviving and Healing Trauma on the 'Rez'." In: *Studies in American Indian Literatures* 23.3: 94-110.

Silko, Leslie Marmon. 1986. "Here's an Odd Artifact for the Fairy-Tale Shelf." In: *Studies in American Indian Literatures* (1st series) 10.4: 178-84.

Van Dyke, Annette. 2003/2004. "Encounters with Deer Woman: Sexual Relations in Susan Power's *The Grass Dancer* and Louise Erdrich's *The Antelope Wife*." In: *Studies in American Indian Literatures* 15.3-4: 168-88.

Velie, Alan R. 1982. *Four American Indian Literary Masters: N. Scott Momaday, James Welch, Leslie Marmon Silko, and Gerald Vizenor*. Norman: U of Oklahoma P.

Vizenor, Gerald (ed.). 2008. *Survivance: Narratives of Native Presence*. Lincoln and London: U of Nebraska P.

Weaver, Jace, Craig S. Womack and Robert Warrior. 2006. *American Indian Literary Nationalism*. Albuquerque: U of New Mexico P.

26.

African American Poetry

Amiri Baraka's "Leadbelly Gives an Autograph" and Rita Dove's "Claudette Colvin Goes to Work"

Erik Redling

1. "Is It Because I Am Black?": African American Poetry from the Black Arts Movement to Contemporary Cosmopolitanism

Amiri Baraka (1934-2014) and Rita Dove (1952-) are towering giants in African American poetry who represent two different periods and attitudes. The former is commonly regarded as the founder of and perhaps the most talented driving force behind the Black Arts Movement, which promoted the spirit of rebellion and a black nationalist agenda; the latter, in the words of the critic Henry Louis Gates, Jr. "rejected what she perceived to be the narrowness of the 1960s Black Arts movement in favor of a more inclusive sensibility" (2004: 2611). Other critics such as Arnold Rampersad (especially in his essay "The Poems of Rita Dove") and Malin Pereira also place Dove's work squarely in opposition to the Black Arts Movement and characterize her poetry as a combination of black themes with a more cosmopolitan outlook. Indeed, the selected poems for this paired reading—Baraka's "Leadbelly Gives an Autograph" (1969) and Dove's "Claudette Colvin Goes to Work" (1999)—are ideally suited to illustrate the deep chasm between the two African American poets.

Baraka composed a poem that works on two levels: first, it replicates a rebellious bebop solo, and second, it features an unnamed, presumably male speaker who notes the decline of Western culture and civilization. As the spokesperson for all African Americans, and with the help of black music and black speech, he calls for the creation of a new black world. He then dons the roles of a godlike creator who will provide for the denizens of this new world, and of a prophet who divines an apocalyptic black revolution in the cities. Dove's poem also displays influences of music, especially the blues, and puts the spotlight on a lesser known but historically significant black woman, Claudette Colvin, whose refusal to give up her seat to a white person on a bus in 1955 preceded Rosa Parks's famous bus boycott by nine months. Rather than portraying Colvin's defiant act against segregation, the poem focuses on the bleak situation, the quiet suffering, and the determined resilience of the aged protagonist who works the night shift at an elderly care facility. Thus, the two poems are diametrically opposed even though they share the context of the Civil Rights era. The following discussion will first sketch the development of African American poetry from the black nationalism of the Black Arts Movement to the cosmopolitanism of contemporary poets and, in a next step, provide close readings and a contrastive analysis of Baraka's and Dove's poetic texts before it concludes with a brief overview of recent trends in contemporary African American poetry.

Although the roots of the Black Arts Movement and black nationalism can be traced back at least to W.E.B. Du Bois's celebration of "blackness" in his poem "The Song of the Smoke" (1907), the expressions "Black Arts," "the Black Arts Movement," and "Black Aesthetic" first appeared in the mid- to late 1960s (cf. Smethurst/Rambsy 2011: 406-7). Following the 1965 assassination of Malcolm X, many black artists and intellectuals radically reevaluated and questioned their positions in American society and abandoned the moderately successful nonviolent attitudes and strategies of the Civil Rights Movement (e.g., sit-ins) in favor of a philosophy of black nationalism, self-reliance, and militancy promoted most forcefully by the Black Power Movement. Shocked by the murder of Malcolm X, LeRoi Jones (who later renamed himself 'Amiri Baraka') and other African American writers and artists such as Charles and William Patterson, Larry Neal, Clarence Reed, and Rolland Snellings (Askia Touré) established the Black Arts Repertory Theatre/School (BARTS) in Harlem that "would, in part, extend the slain leader's black radical vision" (ibid.: 407). They wrote plays and poetry to reach and galvanize the masses, and even though the arts school was closed only a few months after its opening, it managed to "generate attention based on its militant, grassroots determination" and popularize the term "Black Arts" (ibid.). The Black Arts Movement was born.

In the frequently anthologized essay "The Black Arts Movement" (1968), Larry Neal explains the central aims and objectives of the movement as follows:

> The Black Arts Movement is radically opposed to any concept of the artist that alienates him from his community. Black Art is the aesthetic and spiritual sister of the Black Power concept. As such, it envisions an art that speaks directly to the needs and aspirations of Black America. In order to perform this task, the Black Arts Movement proposes a radical reordering of the western cultural aesthetic. It proposes a separate symbolism, mythology, critique, and iconology. The Black Arts and the Black Power concept both relate broadly to the Afro-American's desire for self-determination and nationhood. Both concepts are nationalistic. (1968: 29)

Baraka and the other members of the Black Arts Movement viewed "the Western aesthetic" as a "decaying structure" that needed to be radicalized if not destroyed and encouraged the development of a "black aesthetic" with an entirely separate set of symbols and myths (ibid.): "We advocate a cultural revolution in art and ideas" (ibid.). Adopting the rhetoric of violence and revolution, Baraka expressed the opinions and feelings of black artists in his poem "Black Art" (1965), which is commonly regarded as the poetic manifesto of the Black Arts Movement. It begins with the legendary statement that "poems are bullshit" unless they are antagonistic and attack (Baraka 1995b: 142, l. 1); it then proclaims that "We want 'poems that kill'" (l. 19) before concluding with the 'loud' demand:

> We want a black poem. And a
> Black World.
> Let the world be a Black Poem
> And Let All Black People Speak This Poem
> Silently
> or LOUD (ll. 50-5; original emphasis)

Baraka and several other members of the movement, including Don Lee (later Haki Madhubuti), Sonia Sanchez, Etheridge Knight, Mari Evans, Nikki Giovanni, and Henry Dumas, agreed that black expressive culture—in particular African American music and black speech—should serve as the inspirational, authentic source for black nationalist art. Consequently they "sought to combine the African American vernacular resonances of sermons, popular music, and black mass 'speech' into a rousing new form of poetry" (Gates 2004: 1838).

They privileged free verse and produced what Gates calls "jazzy" and "bluesy" verse (ibid.). Some of the best works that show the immense creative energy unleashed by the Black Arts Movement are the anthologies *Black Fire: An Anthology of Afro-American Writing* (1968) and *The Black Aesthetic* (1971) as well as Don Lee's slender volume *Don't Cry, Scream* (1969) and, most notably, Baraka's collection of poems *Black Magic: Collected Poetry 1961-1967* (1969).

The high level of literary activity and poetic output that characterized the Black Arts Movement radically declined after the movement broke up in the mid-1970s. Some of the members continued to write poetry, but it was "often with altered sensibilities that reflected the arrival of a more sober, perhaps more chastened sense of American political reality" (Rampersad 2006: xxviii). Fresh impulses came from younger poets such as Michael Harper, who, in his volume *Nightmare Begins Responsibility* (1975), "fused the passion and rebellious creativity of an earlier time with a broadening vision of the human experience and a more cosmopolitan sense of the literary tradition" (ibid.). However, the emerging "cosmopolitan" sensibility found in Harper's poetry, for example, was far from being a novel phenomenon. In the groundbreaking study *Color and Culture: Black Writers and the Making of the Modern Intellectual* (1998), Ross Posnock identifies a "cosmopolitan" strand in black intellectual history and claims that for black intellectuals such as Du Bois and Locke, "cosmopolitanism" meant that "'culture has no color'" (1998: 10; cf. Pereira 2003: 3). According to Posnock, the writings of African American authors such as W.E.B. Du Bois, Alain Locke, Charles Chesnutt, Zora Neale Hurston, Ralph Ellison, and James Baldwin manifest cosmopolitan ideas such as the belief in being a "world citizen" and the notion that, quoting Locke, "cultural goods" belong to everyone (ibid.: 11; cf. Pereira 2003: 3). From this point of view, the rise of a more cosmopolitan attitude among younger African American poets in the mid-1970s until the present is grounded in a black intellectual tradition that began in the early twentieth century.

Thus it was the decline of radicalism which permitted a new group of black poets to come forward and opt for a worldwide humanism and equality. Although they are still committed to black causes, they simultaneously regard themselves as citizens in a global world and demonstrate an aspiration to human dignity which contrasts with the nationalistic and destructive fervor of black and white extremists of the 1960s. In the wake of the recent interest in transnational and global issues, critics began using the term "cosmopolitanism" (or "black cosmopolitanism") to foreground the concept of a black "world citizen" as well as the view of human interconnectedness and mutual obligations that more and more black artists seemingly embraced after the period of black nationalism.

Indeed, critics have noted a cosmopolitan sensibility in the works of a number of contemporary African American poets, including the poetry of the Pulitzer Prize-winner and former Poet Laureate of the United States Rita Dove. In *Rita Dove's Cosmopolitanism* (2003), for instance, Pereira traces the ways in which Dove combines African American elements with cosmopolitanism in her poetic œuvre. However, not all of Dove's poems exhibit a cosmopolitan stance. A case in point is Dove's poem "Claudette Colvin Goes to Work" (1999), which revisits a less well-known incident in the history of the Civil Rights Movement and focuses on the thoughts and individual human fate of a black woman in the 1990s. The following paired readings of Baraka's "Leadbelly Gives an Autograph" (1969) and Dove's "Claudette Colvin Goes to Work" will begin with a close analysis of Baraka's poem in order to illustrate the major aspects of his black nationalist aesthetics.

2. "We Want 'Poems That Kill'": Amiri Baraka, Bebop, and the Black Spirit of Rebellion

Baraka's poem "Leadbelly Gives an Autograph" (1999 [1969]: 213-4) not only embodies the militant ethos that characterized the Black Arts Movement in the 1960s, it also serves as a perfect example to show how the philosophy of black aesthetics shaped Baraka's poetic art. The overall theme that guides the poem is rebellion: on the one hand, Baraka draws on bebop jazz that revolutionized jazz music in the 1940s and 50s with its rebellious character to create a poem that emulates a bebop solo in the line of the famous jazz saxophonist Charlie Parker. On the other hand, he also employs the typical features of the black aesthetics: the militant tone, the call for a black world, the need for new myths, and the vision of a black urban revolution. At the end of the poem, Baraka literally follows his own dictum "We want 'poems that kill'" when the speaker murders a Southern white lady in order to denote the end of a white-dominated history and world. The poem, then, has two levels: a literal level (the linguistic meaning of the text) and a 'musical' level in which the reader is invited to create correspondences between the text and bebop jazz.

Adhering to the view that only black music can serve as an inspiration and model for a new black aesthetics, Baraka uses bebop jazz—characterized by a fast tempo, sudden changes, irregular phrase-length, short pauses, syncopated rhythms, repetition of musical phrases and notes, and melodic breaks—to deconstruct Western poetic conventions and create the rebellious bebop poem "Leadbelly Gives an Autograph." The following close reading of two sections of the poem illustrates the way readers can conceptualize the poem in terms of bebop music.

The title of the poem is deliberately misleading: it refers to the famous folk and blues musician Huddie William Ledbetter (1888-1949), who is commonly known as "Lead Belly" or "Leadbelly," and generates the expectation that the poem will elaborate on the initial theme and describe, for instance, the context of Leadbelly's act of giving an autograph to an adoring fan of his music and live performance. Yet the poem never addresses this topic. Instead, it begins with an unnamed speaker instructing Leadbelly (or, more likely, himself) to "Pat your foot" (l. 1) and then, in another abrupt shift, veers off into a completely different subject: "and turn / the corner" (ll. 2-3). Such sudden changes represent a hallmark of bebop jazz solos and occur throughout the poem. Another example from the first stanza will illustrate this technique:

> Pat your foot
> and turn
>   the corner. Nat Turner, dying wood
> of the church. Our lot
> is vacant. *Bring the twisted myth*
> *of speech. The boards brown and falling*
> *away. The metal bannisters cheap*
> *and rattly.* Clean new Sundays. We thought
> it possible to enter
> the way of the strongest. (ll. 1-10; emphasis added)

Due to the proximity of the noun "church," we first identify the meaning of "lot" as "fate" and then revise the meaning to "a small piece of land" after we have jumped to the next line and read that it "is vacant" (ll. 4-5). The above-quoted

stanza also exhibits additional features of the bebop style: e.g., arrhythmic phrasing or syncopation ("and turn"—short pause—"the corner," ll. 2-3); improvisation
on the melody as the speaker/musician plays a melodic phrase "and turn / the
corner" and then plays the two separate notes "turn" and "corner" together,
blending them smoothly to produce "Turner" (ll. 2-3); and a versatile variation of
symmetrical and asymmetrical, short and long phrases or musical statements
with three nearly symmetrical statements (italicized above) having rhythmic emphasis on the last two notes placed at the beginning of the next verse, followed by
a short, fresh phrase—"Clean new Sundays"—and a longer, more convoluted one:
"We thought / it possible to enter / the way of the strongest" (ll. 8-10).

A solo break ensues just a few lines afterwards when the speaker's pronounce-
ments are interrupted by an interlude that introduces an unrelated theme:

> But it is rite that the world's ills
> erupt as our own. Right that we take
> our own specific look into the shapely
> blood of the heart.
>   Looking thru trees
> the wicker statues blowing softly against
> the dusk.
> Looking thru dusk
> thru dark
> ness. A clearing of stars
> and half-soft mud. (ll. 11-21)

Both the typographical arrangement of the two verses "blood of the heart" (l. 14)
and "Looking thru trees" (l. 15), as well as the meaning of the latter phrase that
bears no connection to the previous text, indicate a break within the bebop solo:
the speaker/musician shifts from one theme to another, improvising on a
romantic melody that is not tied to the earlier sober reflections. The vocabulary
(trees, wicker statues, dusk, darkness, and stars), the personification of "the
wicker statues" (l. 16) that blow "softly against / the dusk" (ll. 16-7), and the
metaphor "A clearing of stars" (l. 20) point to a dreamlike solo that floats freely
in a romantic sphere and stands in contrast to the forceful statements in the
first ten lines (note also the end focus of "strongest" which gives it special emphasis). Several clues in the text give further hints at the way the jazz musician
plays the solo break: the phrase "blowing softly" refers to the soft phrasing of
the melody and to a wind instrument that is, most likely, an alto saxophone, the
preferred instrument played by Baraka's favorite bebop musician Charlie
Parker; the solo repeats a phrase with a slightly different ending: "Looking thru
trees" and "Looking thru dusk" (ll. 15, 18), whereby the noun/note "dusk" of the
latter phrase has been picked up from the previous line; the play with the words
"dusk" and "darkness" and the slight difference between "dusk" and "dark /
ness" (ll. 18-20) correspond to tonal play with two adjoining notes in a low pitch
(with an emphasis on "-ness") and notes in a high pitch ("A clearing of stars");
and the final phrase—"half-soft mud" (l. 21)—that denotes the half-soft mood of
the last phrase in this break.

Apart from the rebellious bebop form with its improvisational, jagged, free verse
lines, the content of Baraka's poem specifically addresses the topic of a black rebellion. At the beginning of the poem, the speaker spontaneously invokes the name of
"Nat Turner," a slave who led an insurrection in Virginia during August 1831 that
left more than 55 white men and women dead. Unlike other poetic texts from the

Black Arts era, such as Samuel Allen's "Nat Turner" (1972), which celebrate Nat Turner's slave rebellion because it struck fear in the hearts of white people in the antebellum South, Baraka's speaker only mentions the name to introduce—like an instant flash—the major theme of black rebellion. In musical terms, the name "Nat Turner" can be regarded as the tonality that underlies the bebop solo and determines the intimidating and foreboding tone of the whole piece.

The poem progresses in three steps: first, the speaker argues that crumbling Western systems are futile and should be discarded; second, the speaker wants to make African Americans aware of their own cultural resources and points out the possibilities of music and language which allow for the expression of black issues and the use of formerly suppressed statements; third, the speaker takes on the role of a creator when he announces that he will provide the new black world with "beasts / and myths" (ll. 40-1) and then becomes a prophet who foresees a black insurrection in the cities (which probably refers to the black demonstrations in cities like Chicago and New York that occurred throughout the U.S. in the mid-1960s), and subsequently paves the way for a black history by 'killing' the history of the white South.

In the first part of the poem, the speaker declares that Western spirituality and the belief in a Christian God should be abandoned since both have utterly failed to advance the cause of African Americans. He describes Christian religion metaphorically as a decaying church building ("dying wood / of the church," ll. 3-4, "The boards brown and falling / away. The metal bannisters cheap / and rattly," ll. 6-8) and suggests the necessity of erecting a new church, that is, a new kind of spirituality, on a vacant lot (ll. 4-5). Assuming the tone of a priest, the speaker asks for the "twisted myth / of speech" (ll. 5-6) before he changes into the spokesperson of the black people ("We") and proclaims that they have put their hopes in the Christian religion and a powerful God for a better life in America: "We thought / it possible to enter / the way of the strongest" (ll. 8-10). But their hopes were disappointed: the Christian religion turned out to be a useless myth. The God was weak, and thus, the old Christian myth must be left behind ("Clean new Sundays," l. 8) in favor of new myths.

In a second step the speaker argues that African Americans should rely on their own expressive culture as a source of black spirituality ("Right that we take / our own specific look into the shapely / blood of the heart," ll. 12-4) and singles out two elements of black expressive culture—black music and black language—from which new possibilities of black expression and art arise:

The possibilities of music. First
that it does exist. And that we do,
in that scripture of rhythms. The earth,
I mean the soil, as melody. The fit you need,
the throes. To pick it up and cut
away what does not singularly express.
. . .
The possibilities of statement. I am saying, now,
what my father could not remember
to say. What my grandfather
was killed
for believing.
            Pay me off, savages.
            Build me an equitable human assertion. (ll. 22-7, 32-8)

First, the speaker is grateful that the "possibilities of music" (l. 22) exist and that African Americans live 'in music' which, as the metaphor "scripture of rhythms" (l. 24) indicates, has a spiritual dimension as well. He conceptualizes the "earth" or "soil" in terms of a "melody" (ll. 24-5; probably a reference to spirituals and blues which originated on the plantations in the South) and then elaborates the metaphor: the music is suitable for expressing the pain African Americans have experienced in the past and present ("The fit you need, / the throes," ll. 25-6), and it can be stripped of anything that detracts from its black expressive force. Second, he praises the "possibilities of statement" because, unlike his father and grandfather, he can freely demand reparations from the white "savages" for the immeasurable injustices suffered by slaves and their families: "Pay me off, savages. / Build me an equitable human assertion" (ll. 37-8). Instead of demanding money, he metaphorically asks white America to build a mighty edifice for African Americans on the vacant lot that will powerfully demonstrate their total equality as human beings in the American society.

In the final part of the poem, the speaker picks up the metaphor from the last section and specifies how the building should look before he takes on the role of the creator who will provide the 'tenants' of the edifice:

> One that looks like a jungle, or one that looks like the cities
> of the West.   But I provide the stock. The beasts
> and myths.
>   The City's Rise!
>   (And what is history, then? An old deaf lady)
>   burned to death
>   in South Carolina. (ll. 39-45)

Apparently it does not matter to the speaker whether the building will look "like a jungle" (l. 39) in Africa or "like the cities / of the West" (ll. 39-40) as long as he can provide the material for a new kind of civilization: "the stock. The beasts / and myths" (ll. 40-1). He then assumes the role of a prophet, a seer who has an apocalyptic vision of a black urban rebellion ("The City's Rise!," l. 42), and subsequently becomes a revolutionary when, in an aside, he equates history with an old deaf lady who, like lynched African Americans in the South, is "burned to death / in South Carolina" (ll. 44-5). The murder of an old deaf lady, who is obviously unable to hear the black music (the "possibilities of music," l. 22) and his prophecy (the "possibilities of statement," l. 32), not only refers back to Nat Turner, the leader of a slave insurrection, it also divorces African Americans from the old mythology and white-dominated history and paves the way for a new history of a black civilization.

Baraka's poem "Leadbelly Gives an Autograph" is utterly characteristic of his poetic output during his black nationalist period (cf. the poem "AM / TRAK," 1979). As Kimberly Benston states, Baraka promotes

> the idea that man (of course, the black man) is an infinite reservoir of possibilities, and that if one can rearrange society by the reconstruction of oppressive order or the imposition of a new structure upon the withering old, then these possibilities will reap infinite progress. (1976: 132)

Indeed, his poem celebrates the possibilities of black expressive culture which not only permit the creation of a new black world, but also serve as the vital source for a new black aesthetics. But whereas critics such as Benston maintain that for Baraka and the Black Arts Movement, "music has become not only the model but the actual goal of black poetry" (ibid.: 73), the close analysis above shows that Baraka's poem does not strive towards blues and jazz music, but *is*, in fact, jazz music. And it really is, metaphorically speaking, a bebop solo which concurrently conveys linguistic meaning. It is free verse and jazz music at the same time.

3. "We Do Need Fire, But We Need More Than Fire, Too": Revisiting the Civil Rights Movement with Rita Dove

The last section of Rita Dove's volume *On the Bus with Rosa Parks* (1999: 79-80) carries the same title as the volume and consists of ten poems, eight of which "affirm the historical significance of the ordinary black women whose resistance to segregation embodied the civil rights movement" (Righelato 2006: 201). An excellent example is the poem entitled "Claudette Colvin Goes to Work," which draws attention to the little known fact that Claudette Colvin's brave act of refusing to give up her seat to a white person on a city bus in Montgomery, Alabama happened nine months before Rosa Parks challenged the same segregation laws, in the same city, within the same bus system, and with a similar act of defiance. In fact, the epigraph to the poem is taken from a boycott flyer that was distributed four days after Rosa Parks was arrested on December 1, 1955, and thus links the two cases together (cf. ibid.: 203). However, Dove's poem neither relates Colvin's act of resistance at the age of fifteen nor her subsequent arrest by two white police officers, but focuses on Colvin's thoughts thirty-five years later as she walks to her job at an elderly care facility (cf. ibid.). In her work *Rita Dove's Cosmopolitanism*, Pereira concludes that Dove's return to the Civil Rights Movement represents a departure from her earlier cosmopolitanism: "*On the Bus with Rosa Parks* lacks the focus and cosmopolitan tensions characteristic of Dove's earlier work" (2003: 154). Yet Dove maintains her resistance at being typecast as an angry black poet who writes more or less predictable poems along the lines of the Black Arts Movement. Instead, her poem "Claudette Colvin Goes to Work" differs from Baraka's poem "Leadbelly Gives an Autograph" in both fervor and mood. Her poem exhibits a softer, blues-like tone that reflects Claudette Colvin's thoughts, her bleak surroundings, and her determined resilience in her daily struggle to survive in a godforsaken world.

In contrast to Baraka's 'loud' bebop poem that calls for the creation of a new black world and envisions an urban black rebellion, Dove's poem manifests a sad, melancholic tone and focuses on the loneliness of the protagonist and her desolate surroundings:

> Menial twilight sweeps the storefronts along Lexington
> as the shadows arrive to take their places
> among the scourge of the earth. Here and there
> a fickle brilliance—lightbulbs coming on
> in each narrow residence, the golden wattage
> of bleak interiors announcing *Anyone home?*
> or *I'm beat, bring me a beer.* (ll. 1-7; original emphasis)

The position of "Menial" (l. 1) as the first word of the poem gives special emphasis to Claudette Colvin's unskilled job and highlights the dreariness of her black neighborhood that she, alluding to the Bible, perceives as "the scourge of the earth" (l. 3). Although she uses the term "brilliance" (l. 4) to describe the flickering lights that are turned on as darkness approaches, she does not associate the lights with hope but imagines situations that express loneliness: "*Anyone home?*" (l. 6) and resignation: "*I'm beat, bring me a beer*" (l. 7).

At times, Claudette Colvin wants to give up and vanish from the face of the earth, but she stands up every single day and, taking on her responsibilities, continues her struggle to live:

> Mostly I say to myself *Still here.* Lay
> my keys on the table, pack the perishables away
> before flipping the switch. I like the sugary
> look of things in bad light—one drop of sweat
> is all it would take to dissolve an armchair pillow
> into brocade residue. Sometimes I wait until
> it's dark enough for my body to disappear; (ll. 8-14; original emphasis)

Her auto-suggestive, affirmative "*Still here*" (l. 8) in the first line of the second stanza underscores her willpower and the great strength that is needed to get up and go to work. After switching off the light, Claudette Colvin pays careful attention to sensory details and fantasizes about how one drop of sweat could turn "an armchair pillow / into brocade residue" (ll. 12-3). Her on-and-off ritual of waiting for her body to disappear in the dark (together with the rhyme of the last syllable in "*Still here*" with the last syllable in "disappear") points to an inner struggle between her will to survive and easy defeat, in which her self-chosen moral obligation to help others always wins the upper hand.

In addition to the difficult struggle to survive another day, Claudette Colvin's sense of self-worth takes a severe blow. On her way to the bus stop she passes a few young black men who think they are cool, and when she ignores their initial insinuating remarks, the comments escalate to harassment:

> then I know it's time to start out for work.
> Along the Avenue, the cabs start up, heading
> toward midtown; neon stutters into ecstasy
> as the male integers light up their smokes and let loose
> a stream of brave talk: "Hey Mama" souring quickly to
> "Your Mama" when there's no answer—as if
> the most injury they can do is insult the reason
>
> you're here at all, walking in your whites
> down to the stop so you can make a living.
> *So ugly, so fat, so dumb, so greasy—*
> What do we have to do to make God love us?
> Mama was a maid; my daddy mowed lawns like a boy,
> and I'm the crazy girl off the bus, the one
> who wrote in class she was going to be President. (ll. 15-28; original emphasis)

Her first reaction is to ignore the insults ("Your Mama," l. 21), but when she thinks of the demeaning invectives she has heard and endured over time ("*So ugly, so fat, so dumb, so greasy—*," l. 24), she gives way to despair and, putting her suffering in a larger perspective, asks herself what African Americans "have to do to make God love us" (l. 25). She believes that God, seemingly unaware of the fate of blacks, has forsaken her and the African American people. Her mind wanders to her mother and father who, like slaves, worked for white people in demeaning jobs, and then turns back to herself, "the crazy girl off the bus" (l. 27) who dreamed of becoming the U.S. president and who resisted segregation on the bus system in Montgomery. It is this moment of despair and pain that makes her recall a long history of African American misery. She remembers her parents' suffering and hard work, and considers the stark contrast between her long ago dream of becoming the president and the reality of her menial job at an elderly care facility; she also recognizes that her rebellious act of resisting segregation on the bus system in Montgomery has not changed her life at all—she is still riding the bus to work and she still lives in a bleak and lonely world. Like her parents, she tried to win God's love and help, but to no avail.

Yet Claudette Colvin's despair is only short-lived, as her deeply ingrained moral belief in helping those "who can't help themselves" (l. 33) reasserts itself in the final stanza of the poem:

> I take the Number 6 bus to the Lex Ave train
> and then I'm there all night, adjusting the sheets,
> emptying the pans. And I don't curse or spit
> or kick or scratch like they say I did then.
> I help those who can't help themselves,
> I do what needs to be done . . . and I sleep
> whenever sleep comes down on me. (ll. 29-35)

Contrary to the fervor and anger that accompanied her teenage act of resistance, now that she is older she has lost the rebellious spirit of her younger days. She cannot expect praise or public attention for her menial work, so she can draw satisfaction only from helping old people at an elderly care facility. Her disparate activities of rebellion and menial labor are based on her firm commitment to "do what needs to be done"; as Pat Righelato puts it: "Her job, emptying bedpans, contrasts with her youthful fieriness, but the two so different kinds of actions are both part of her life's dedication to doing what is needed" (2006: 204). In fact, Claudette Colvin's great strength and willpower stem from her belief in universal human values such as the notion of a common humanity. The closing lines of the poem show that she does not go to bed angry, but falls asleep when sleep arrives. These lines probably allude to W.C. Handy's blues tune "St. Louis Blues" (1914, see the first line: "I hate to see that evening sun go down") which, in turn, relies on a quotation from the Bible: "'In your anger do not sin': Do not let the sun go down while you are still angry" (Ephesians 4:26). Unlike the speaker's voice in Baraka's poem, Claudette Colvin's voice is neither indignant nor rebellious but—like the blues—rather quiet and dignified.

A deep chasm between the two poets opens up when we compare Dove's protagonist Claudette Colvin with Baraka's unnamed speaker. Baraka's angry and (most likely) male black speaker expresses a militant attitude towards an old, decaying white America, celebrates the possibilities of black music and vernacular speech, and at the end of the poem sees himself as a godlike creator and prophet of revolution; Dove's black female protagonist is an ordinary woman who has a regular job caring for elderly people. Her daily ritual of getting ready for the night shift, walking to the bus station, and then working at the facility is highlighted by the 'regular' shape of the lines (no jagged lines or typographic experiments) and the seven-line stanzas that may point to the seven days of a week.

Dove refrains from portraying Claudette Colvin as a black revolutionary who belts out her speech and mythic visions. Rather, she describes Colvin as a contemplative person who sees the desolation that surrounds her and sometimes even thinks about giving up, but whose belief in universal human values provides her with the necessary strength to continue with her life and work. Indirectly, Dove points her finger at the stark contrast between the dreams that governed the Civil Rights Movement and the desolate reality of the 1990s. While Claudette

Colvin's act of refusing to give up her seat to a white person on a bus in Montgomery helped start the Civil Rights Movement, it failed to improve her life. She is still riding on a bus and her situation—metaphorically the situation of all African Americans in American society—is bleak. Instead of becoming president of the United States, she has a menial job emptying bedpans and changing sheets. However, Dove gives credit to people like Claudette Colvin who muster their inner strength in their struggles for survival and, adhering to fundamental human and moral values, help other people in need. It is the deep commitment to universal human values that perhaps most exhibits a cosmopolitan sensibility.

Dove's statement "Yes, we do need fire, but we need more than fire, too" (Ratiner 2003: 117) nicely sums up her response to the Black Arts Movement. She sees the need for the angry black poetry of the 1960s, a time of black protest and upheaval, but she refuses to limit herself to this type of verse. African American poetry, for her, is "more than fire," and her poem "Claudette Colvin Goes to Work" perfectly illustrates her diametrically opposed reaction toward the Black Arts Movement exemplified by Baraka's poem "Leadbelly Gives an Autograph." In fact, a series of oppositional pairs can help to describe the radical differences between Baraka's and Dove's respective poetry: loud vs. quiet/contemplative, hot vs. cool, revolution vs. routine, male vs. female, spokesperson of the African American people ("we") vs. individual black person, big issues vs. small details, and so on. However, Dove maintains that both kinds of poetry complement each other, and she favors the 'both/and' view to an 'either/or' relationship between them. As a matter of fact, her poem "Claudette Colvin Goes to Work" provides a glimpse of the human dignity of a courageous black woman in a bleak situation and thereby adds a sparkling facet to the rich African American poetic tradition.

4. "Fired Up!!": African American Poetry in the 21st Century

Rita Dove may be one of the most prominent voices in contemporary African American poetry at the moment, but various other African American poets such as Elizabeth Alexander, Cornelius Eady, Yusef Komunyakaa, Nathaniel Mackey, and Tracy Smith have received much public acclaim as well, which suggests "the arrival of African American poetry on the national scene" (Rampersad 2006: xxviii). What is most striking about the work of present-day African American poets is the fascinating diversity of their respective œuvre which typically displays a broad spectrum of topics and styles. Their poetry seems to have abandoned the angry "in your face" attitude that characterized the Black Arts poems of the 1960s and early 70s in favor of a more cosmopolitan sensibility that allows for experiments with different kinds of material. The subjects covered in Alexander's *American Blue: Selected Poems* (2006), for example, range from a slave-ship rebellion to the lives of jazz musicians and personal experiences. But perhaps an even better indicator of this phenomenon is Rampersad's highly praised anthology, *The Oxford Anthology of African-American Poetry* (2006), which is divided into fifteen major themes with titles taken from well-known poems (e.g., "1. To Make a Poet Black," "5. If We Must Die," "8. Is She Our Sister," and "15. I Dream a World") that demonstrates the incredible versatility of past and present African American poets. In recent years, an avalanche of jazz poems and the rise of performance poetry, rap poems, and hip-hop poetry have added a new vibrancy to an ever-evolving experimental field. It is poetry, to use the title of a poem by Everett Hoagland, all "Fired Up!!"

Bibliography

Selected Primary Literature

Baraka, Amiri. 1995a [1979]. "AM / TRACK." In: Vangelisti 1995. 187-95.
——. 1995b [1965]. "Black Art." In: Vangelisti 1995. 142.
——. 1999 [1969]. "Leadbelly Gives an Autograph." In: *The LeRoi Jones/Amiri Baraka Reader by Amiri Baraka*. Ed. William J. Harris. New York: Basic Books. 213-4.
Dove, Rita. 1999. "Claudette Colvin Goes to Work." In: *On the Bus with Rosa Parks*. New York and London: Norton. 79-80.
Rampersad, Arnold (ed.). 2006. *The Oxford Anthology of African-American Poetry*. New York: Oxford UP.
Vangelisti, Paul (ed.). 1995. *Transbluesency: The Selected Poems of Amiri Baraka/LeRoi Jones (1961-1995)*. New York: Marsilio.

Selected Secondary Literature

Benston, Kimberly W. 1976. *Baraka: The Renegade and the Mask*. New Haven and London: Yale UP.
Focuses on Baraka's early poetry and prose written during the Black Arts period.

Pereira, Malin. 2003. *Rita Dove's Cosmopolitanism*. Urbana and Chicago: U of Illinois P.
The study traces the combination of black issues and a cosmopolitan outlook in Dove's poetic work.

Ratiner, Steven. 2003. "A Chorus of Voices." Interview. In: Earl G. Ingersoll (ed.), *Conversations with Rita Dove*. Jackson, MS: UP of Mississippi. 103-20.
A collection of interviews that provides valuable insights into Dove's life, views, and work.

Righelato, Pat. 2006. *Understanding Rita Dove*. Columbia: U of South Carolina P.
A good starting point for students who want to get a first impression of the topics covered in Rita Dove's poetic work.

Further References

Alexander, Elisabeth. 2006 [1990]. "Robeson at Rutgers." In: Rampersad 2006. 121.
Dove, Rita. 2006 [1952]. "Canary *(for Michael S. Harper)*." In: Rampersad 2006. 175.
Eady, Cornelius. 2006 [1995]. "Paradiso." In: Rampersad 2006. 351.
Gates, Henry Louis, Jr. 2004. "The Black Arts Era 1960-1975." In: Henry Louis Gates, Jr. and Nellie Y. McKay (eds.), *The Norton Anthology of African American Literature*. New York: Norton. 1831-50.
——. 2004. "Rita Dove." Henry Louis Gates, Jr. and Nellie Y. McKay (eds.), *The Norton Anthology of African American Literature*. New York: Norton. 2611-3.
Holy Bible: New International Version. 2011. Colorado Springs: Biblica.
Madhubuti, Haki (Don L. Lee). 2006 [1969]. "Don't Cry, Scream *(for John Coltrane / from a black poet / in a basement apt. crying dry tears of "you ain't gone.")*." In: Kevin Young (ed.), *Jazz Poems*. New York and London: Alfred A. Knopf. 156-61.
Neal, Larry. 1968. "The Black Arts Movement." In: *The Drama Review* 12.4: 29-39.
Posnock, Ross. 1998. *Color and Culture: Black Writers and the Making of the Modern Intellectual*. Cambridge, MA and London: Harvard UP.
Rampersad, Arnold. 1986. "The Poems of Rita Dove." In: *Callaloo* 9.1: 52-60.
——. 2006. "Introduction." In: Rampersad 2006. xix-xxix.
Smethurst, James E. and Howard Rambsy II. 2011. "Reform and Revolution, 1965-1976: The Black Aesthetic at Work." In: Maryemma Graham and Jerry W. Ward, Jr. (eds.), *The Cambridge History of African American Literature*. Cambridge and New York: Cambridge UP. 405-51.

27.

Contemporary Women's Poetry

Adrienne Rich's "Diving into the Wreck" and
Harryette Mullen's "She Swam On from Sea to Shine"

Christian Kloeckner

1. Introduction

Well into the second half of the 20th century, U.S. poetry had remained a fundamentally male domain. As this volume clearly demonstrates, this male dominance was certainly not due to a dearth of American women writing important and innovative poetry. The 'slave poet' Phillis Wheatley became somewhat of a literary sensation in the 18th century, Emily Dickinson stands alongside Walt Whitman as the most important poet of the 19th century, and modernists such as Gertrude Stein and Amy Lowell were (in)famous figures in their lifetimes. In New York and in Chicago, modernism blossomed in the context of feminist and socialist activism, and women founded magazines such as *Poetry* and the *Little Review* for experimental writing. Yet, these examples also highlight the obstacles women poets faced in negotiating the policed borders of the poetic tradition: for a long time, women's poetry was met with little more than bewilderment and belittlement, particularly if it set out to take a specifically female perspective and speak of women's experience. These strictures certainly pertained to all of women's writing, yet in light of poetry's traditional association with divine inspiration, bardic ritual, classical education, and an assertive individuality, the stakes were even higher (cf. Gilbert/Gubar xx-xxii). Often pathologized as madwomen, female poets all too often went into inner or outer exile or were actively relegated to the margins of the literary world. Much of their writing—typically judged as minor, lacking in quality, or as too eccentric—either remained unpublished or was soon forgotten.

One case of well-meaning poetic patronage clearly illustrates the space that had been carved out and reserved for American women poets in the mid-twentieth century. When in 1951, a 21-year-old woman poet's debut book entitled *A Change of World* was chosen to appear in the *Yale Series of Younger Poets*, the *Series* editor and renowned poet W. H. Auden penned a preface that praised the poet's display of "a modesty not so common at that age, which disclaims any extraordinary vision, and a love for her medium." The poems, he continued, "are neatly and modestly dressed, speak quietly but do not mumble, respect their elders but are not cowed by them, and do not tell fibs" (in Gelpi/Gelpi 1993: 278-9). In the conservative post-war cultural climate, such respect for the traditional (poetic) order was suitable because Auden did not believe society to have fundamentally changed since the modernists had broken away from the Victorians:

> Before a similar crop of revolutionary artists can appear again, there will have to be just such another cultural revolution replacing these attitudes with others. So long as the way in which we regard the world and feel about our existence remains in all essentials the same as that of our predecessors we must follow in their tradition. (ibid.: 278)

Little did Auden know that the seemingly modest, decorous, and respectful poet whose book he introduced would later contribute significantly to a "cultural revolution" that changed the world of poetry. By the end of the twentieth century, scholars writing about this female poet could legitimately declare: "Few women writers have had such a wide impact on contemporary feminist thought as Adrienne Rich" (Yorke 1997: 1).

An explication of the evolution of feminist thought in the latter half of the 20th century is, of course, well beyond the scope of this article. By focusing this chapter on Adrienne Rich and Harryette Mullen, an African American poet of the generation that followed Rich, I hope to sketch at least a few contours of the vast field of contemporary women's poetry and feminist thought about gender, sexuality, and race. In their politics and poetics, these two feminist writers often seem to be oceans apart. Yet the ways in which both Rich and Mullen make use of the trope of the shipwreck will let us explore not only their intellectual and poetic differences but also their convergence in raising ethical questions of (female) agency, power, and survival. Both poets' efforts to recover and "re-vision" marginalized traditions, to give voice to structures of injustice and histories of violence, and to create new coalitions and communities are, in fact, principles at the heart of the feminist movement and women's writing in the past few decades.

During the first wave of 20th-century feminism, modernist women's poetry celebrated female independence by alternatively disavowing and highlighting gender differences. Marianne Moore's belief in the equality of the sexes in all aspects of life motivated her choice of a largely gender-neutral, "hard" poetry while poets like H.D. or Amy Lowell explored material and mythical female spaces, codified alternative sexualities in allusive language, and defined the feminine as a universal resource for human development (cf. Keller/Miller 2005: 76-81). By mid-century, however, a conservative backlash and a reinvigorated ideal of female domesticity in the post-war suburban consumer culture had erased much of the previous social progress and marginalized feminist poetry anew. It took the 1960s women's movement—inspired by Simone de Beauvoir's work on the social construction of gender in *The Second Sex* (1949) and Betty Friedan's ironic presentation of the female condition in *The Feminine Mystique* (1963)—to bring about increasingly vocal and radical women poets. In this second wave, feminist poetry explored women's position in relation to a society that was patriarchal, sexist, militarist, and racist; it sought to raise consciousness about women's issues, present positive role models, and promote solidarity and sisterhood. And because the personal was understood to be political, as the famous feminist slogan had it, lyric poetry's traditional authority over matters of the self enabled it to attain a particularly popular status in the fight for equality.

In order to reveal the historical oppression of woman and to create an alternative lineage of literary history, feminist scholars and poets such as Rich, Alicia Ostriker, and Lucille Clifton began to unearth previously unknown women's texts and to rewrite from a feminist perspective genres traditionally associated with male speakers. Elaine Showalter's "Toward a Feminist Poetics" (1979) became an important essay in feminist literary criticism, pleading for a project of "gynocritics" whose purpose was to

> construct a female framework for the analysis of women's literature, to develop new models based on the study of female experience, rather than to adapt male models and theories. Gynocritics begins at the point when we free ourselves

from the linear absolutes of male literary history, stop trying to fit women between the lines of the male tradition, and focus instead on the newly visible
world of female culture. (131)

In the same year, Sandra M. Gilbert and Susan Gubar published an equally important collection of essays titled *Shakespeare's Sisters: Feminist Essays on
Women Poets*. Through these concerted efforts of poets and scholars, many of
today's canonized female poets were discovered (or rediscovered) and gained
considerable critical attention.

   The search for the "female experience" and an authentic female voice, however, was contested from the very beginning on political as well as theoretical
grounds. Poets from diverse backgrounds critiqued the implicit ethnocentric,
middle-class and heteronormative assumptions of much early feminist discourse. Sonia Sanchez, a poet of the Black Arts Movement, wrote about the
double discrimination that black women face—both in and outside of the black
community—due to their combination of race and gender. Other poets, such as
Audre Lorde and Judy Grahn, fused their respective explorations of the black
and the "common" working-class woman with a celebration of homosocial and
lesbian desire. As Lynn Keller and Cristanne Miller note, 1970s and 1980s feminism was "full of internal division; feminist activists differed passionately on
their willingness to work with men, on their priorities for social change, on lifestyles and sexual identities, on the intersections of class or race and gender"
(2005: 88). Difference and diversity emerged as key concepts capable of uniting
a multiplicity of historically discriminated groups against the common foe of
white patriarchy—concepts that were further buttressed in the United States by
the rise of poststructuralist theory.

   The so-called "French feminists"—poststructuralist literary critics such as
Julia Kristeva, Luce Irigaray, Hélène Cixous, and Monique Wittig—complicated
early feminism's essentialist conception of the body and female identity. Drawing on Lacanian psychoanalysis, they emphasized the patriarchal nature of language predicated upon the child's separation from the mother and entry into the
symbolic order of paternal law at the moment of language acquisition. Proposing
an *écriture feminine* instead, women authors were to write in non-linear fashion,
disrupt grammar and turn to the cracks in language in order to replace male
logic with allusive signification, an emphasis on rhythm, process, and the fluidity of all being. Poetry obviously was considered particularly suitable for such
écriture feminine. And although their writings were in turn often criticized for
their seemingly essentialist take on the female body, Cixous and others maintained that theirs was a theory of text and subject, not self and life. Hence,
écriture feminine could be, and long had been, practiced by male writers as well.
In any case, French feminism and poststructuralist thought in general turned
the attention of many women poets away from content to focus on experimentation with form and language. Consequently, an important characteristic of contemporary feminist poetry has been to critique rationality and the demand for
clarity and legibility of language as tools to enforce social and patriarchal norms
(cf. Armantrout 1992). Important contemporary poets like Susan Howe, Lyn
Hejinian, Rae Armantrout, and Carla Harryman have understood their variation
of experimental Language poetry in decidedly feminist terms.

   Harryette Mullen belongs to this slightly younger and formally more experimental generation of feminist poets who take a quite different approach to ad-

dress social questions and gender politics. Rich and Mullen, in fact, are rarely discussed together in literary criticism, and when they are, it is to draw contrasts rather than to point out similarities. According to Astrid Franke, for instance, Rich and Mullen start from an assumption of poetic powerlessness, an awareness of their complicity in power structures through language, and an emphasis on individual responsibility. Yet for Franke, Mullen's poetry predominantly provides "awareness and diagnosis" while Rich's poetry calls out for "connection, even commitment and solidarity with others" (Franke 2008: 71-4). When an interviewer asks Mullen about the "subject-driven" poetry of June Jordan or Adrienne Rich, a certain distance between these two writers is palpable: It is a "good" and "necessary thing" for poetry to change political discourse, Mullen argues, but literature also has other "intentions," including a spiritual one dedicated to the future (Mullen 2012: 256). Together, Adrienne Rich's and Harryette Mullen's evolutions and poetic programs are then suggestive of the contradictions, complexity, and richness of contemporary women's poetry.

2. Adrienne Rich's "Diving into the Wreck" and the Revision of Patriarchal Myth-Making

Adrienne Rich's importance to the feminist movement and to women's poetry in general cannot be underestimated, and her critical interventions and achievements go far beyond the field of poetry. Rich was a prolific writer of essays on patriarchy, politics and poetics, heteronormativity and lesbian identity, motherhood, capitalist exploitation, and imperialist violence. Neither her upbringing nor her early poetry, which was informed by the Black Mountain School, were (as evidenced by Auden's introduction quoted above) indicators of her subsequent radicalism. Born in 1929 to a Jewish father and a Protestant mother, Rich grew up in a Southern Christian middle-class environment, married at age 23, and had given birth to three sons by the end of the 1950s. The conflicting pressures of marriage, motherhood, and her poetry career soon caused her to become dissatisfied and restless; the political turmoil of the 1960s radicalized her and prompted her to become active in the anti-war, civil rights, and feminist movements. Of course, her politicization showed in her verse. When Rich published *Diving into the Wreck* (1973), an uncompromising volume of feminist poetry, eminent poetry scholar Helen Vendler could look back to Rich's debut and ask with good reason, "what has happened to the girl in 1951 . . . what has become of her?" (Vendler 1980: 241).

Laying out Rich's poetic development, Vendler argues that there is a clear line of evolution in her work from the decorous (*A Change of World*, 1951) to filial homeless nostalgia (*The Diamond Cutters*, 1955) to a bitter exile-in-marriage that gives up rhyme and adopts free verse (*Snapshots of a Daughter-in-Law*, 1963). The next three volumes represent a transitioning to the radicalism of *Diving into the Wreck*. According to Vendler, Rich continues to mine the old questions animating her poetry: tradition, civilization, the mind and the body, woman, man, love, writing; but her vision has taken a much darker turn (cf. ibid.: 259). Probing the roots of the current patriarchal condition, one of Rich's strategies in *Diving* is to explore myths foundational to Western self-consciousness and civilization. Using a strategy shared by many other women writers, Rich re-writes these myths in order to reveal a history of injustice, to search for a new language, and to awaken the female reader to a new perception of the connection between women's sexual lives and Western political order.

Rich's contemporaneous, programmatic essay "When We Dead Awaken: Writing as Re-Vision" (1972) describes the women's movement as the collective awakening of "sleepwalkers" and calls on women to stop writing for men's approval. Rich urges women writers to instead expand and redirect the Western literary canon, re-create their own traditions, and engage in the "difficult and dangerous" yet promising task of exploring "a whole new psychic geography":

> Re-vision—the act of looking back, of seeing with fresh eyes, of entering an old text from a new critical direction—is for women more than a chapter in cultural history: it is an act of survival. Until we can understand the assumptions in which we are drenched we cannot know ourselves. And this drive to self-knowledge, for women, is more than a search for identity: it is part of our refusal of the self-destructiveness of male-dominated society. (Rich 1984: 35)

The title poem of *Diving into the Wreck* is a poetic rendering of women's "drive to self-knowledge" in the context of patriarchy's "self-destructiveness," a "re-vision" and re-writing of the traditional male hero's quest. The poem opens with the speaker preparing for a diving expedition, a journey that is at once mythical and dangerous, using vocabulary traditionally associated with male adventurers:

> First having read the books of myths,
> and loaded the camera,
> and checked the edge of the knife-blade,
> I put on
> the body-armor of black rubber
> the absurd flippers
> the grave and awkward mask. (Rich 2013: 14, ll. 1-7)

It is important to note that the gender of the lyrical I is never unambiguously identified in these and the following lines. The poem's deviation from the language and conventions of the traditional quest narrative, however, may lead one to provisionally assume that the speaker is female. The speaker is well-equipped with the traditional instruments of science and conquest, but unlike others before her, she is alone on this expedition into the "grave" of the wreck. Following a series of past participle verb constructions, the late arrival of the "I" in the shortest monosyllabic line of the first stanza, together with the repeated end-stopped line "I go down." (ll. 22, 28), signals a solitary, self-conscious move into one's own and to self-directed action, even if it is a tortuous process that takes up full three stanzas and is accompanied by anxiety ("I crawl like an insect down the ladder / and there is no one / to tell me when the ocean / will begin," ll. 30-3). Once the speaker has left the "blue light" and "clear atoms" of the air (ll. 25-6) for the "green" and "black" light of the ocean (ll. 35-6), she finds that the male instruments of power are not what will sustain her here:

> the sea is another story
> the sea is not a question of power
> I have to learn alone
> to turn my body without force
> in the deep element. (ll. 39-43)

The poem has slowly prepared the reader for a different medium where worldly power and force are without value or use, and where these concepts carry, at most, a faint echo in the "crenellated fans" (l. 48) of the sea inhabitants. The military connotation of "crenellated" castle towers is here transmuted into the harmonious way of fish moving in the water, which foreshadows the transformation of the speaker's body. Unlike the traditional quests of the male hero, there is no battle here; there is only a sense of effortlessness and ease. Almost getting lost in this new medium, the speaker seems to remind herself of the serious business she has set out for:

> I came to explore the wreck.
> The words are purposes.
> The words are maps.
> I came to see the damage that was done
> and the treasures that prevail. (ll. 52-6)

In these anaphoric, declarative sentences the "wreck" makes its first appearance, a wreck on which the diver shines her lamp in order to assess what has been damaged and what can possibly be salvaged. Here and throughout Rich's poem, the causes and circumstances of how this wreck occurred are never explained. This may be the wreck of the speaker's own past, or that of a collective past. But what does the wreck stand for in Rich's exploration? The inserted declarations that words are both "purposes" and "maps" seem to give us a first hint, although the stripped-down simplicity of these sentences, we should note, belies their enigmatic character. Of course, we use language for a multitude of purposes, but here the words themselves *are* purposes, seemingly without any human agency involved. It is easy to see how language acts as a guide in our lives, for instance, in the form of our commitments, goals, promises, and beliefs. But what are these words maps *of*? What exactly do they show? In what relation do they stand to the "book of myths" in the poem's first line? One could simply surmise that Rich speaks here of language's general representational function. Perhaps the alliterative conjunction of "wreck" and "words" suggests that language is the broken vessel Rich set out to inspect. Or does this poem's language enable the speaker to find the wreck in the first place?

    In the next few lines, the speaker's reiteration of her exploration's goal begins to answer these questions. She came for "the wreck and not the story of the wreck / the thing itself and not the myth" (ll. 62-3). The speaker's voyage thus serves to leave behind (skewed) representation and (traditional) narrativization, and to renew the poetic dream of approaching, seeing, and understanding for herself the hidden, material essence of things. At the same time, however, Rich immediately re-mythologizes the wreck by anthropomorphizing it as a "drowned face staring / toward the sun" (ll. 64-5) and by endowing the "ribs" of this "threadbare beauty" with assertive agency (ll. 67-9). However tentative the diver's approach to the wreck has been—taking up more than two thirds of the poem—the wreck now triggers a sudden and strong realization of arrival: "This is the place." (l. 71). Opening up the third-to-last stanza, the revelatory, epiphanic character of this encounter is expressed by its prominent position in the poem as well as by the end-stopped, punctuated brevity of the line. This construction is particularly noteworthy as it contrasts with the slow retreat of punctuation in the next, grammatically more complex sentence, and the last, long-winding sentence that fluidly runs through three stanzas and 18 lines to conclude the poem in a swirl of pronouns, identifications and transformations.

It is here that the poem's gender politics and its idealization of androgyny come to the fore. The lyrical I is both "mermaid" and "merman," an "I" that because of its double-gendered identity quickly morphs into a "We" exploring the wreck, and then, by way of a dramatic enjambment between two stanzas, *becomes* the wreck itself. Unlike the traditional male adventurer exploring a ship that in English is typically coded female, in Rich's poem both diver and the wreck are androgynous:

> I am she: I am he
>
> whose drowned face sleeps with open eyes
> whose breasts still bear the stress
> whose silver, copper, vermeil cargo lies
> obscurely inside barrels
> half-wedged and left to rot
> we are the half-destroyed instruments
> that once held to a course
> the water-eaten log
> the fouled compass (ll. 77-86)

The wreck, then, may be understood as the mythical site of the breaking of a whole into "halves," of its attendant symptoms of "lies," decay, dislocation, and death, and a separation of the sexes into self-contained units of "she" and "he." Crucially, through the diver's identification with the wreck, s/he, too, becomes an object of exploration. The intricate rhyming and rich sound patterning through alliteration, assonance, and consonance (e.g., eyes/lies; breasts/stress/ barrels; rot/log; course/compass) may point to the treasures that lie submerged in the depths of the psyche, the neglect of which has made us lose our ways. But if the words are maps, as the speaker declared earlier, the "fouled compass" that we have become has lost the capacity to navigate them properly.

"Diving into the Wreck" is an attempt to retrieve, critique, and again make whole that which had been separated and annihilated in the repression of the feminine in patriarchy's foundational myth-making. Crucially, the poem addresses and includes the reader in this androgynous union of multiplicities, whose breaking of the bonds of gender can only be approached by also eschewing standard grammar and coining a new language: "We are, I am, you are / . . . / the one who find our way / back to this scene" (ll. 87-90). This ending evokes a community that still uses the same instruments of knowledge, but this is a community without leaders, where each "one" will have to go on their own solitary journey to achieve a historically informed consciousness and new self-awareness. Interestingly, the poem ends without the speaker ever leaving the sea as a medium of alternative, female/androgynous knowledge. In this sense the journey is redemptive; at the same time, the wreck remains a wreck that cannot be repaired.

Because of its deployment of myth and invocation of the androgynous principle, Rich's poem has often been read in terms of Carl Gustav Jung's analytical psychology. At the beginning of the 20th century, Jung emphasized the importance of myths and archetypal images in the cultural unconscious and described the ego's quest for a wholeness of the self that includes the adoption of the opposite-sex principles of animus and anima. "Reevaluative myth quests," as Rachel Blau DuPlessis has called them, have consequently been a popular choice for feminist poetry because it provides the opportunity to simultaneously address consciousness and underlying social and cultural structures (DuPlessis 1979: 280). The key here lies in transcending the destructive nature of an ideological past and seeking reinvention through re-mythologizing. Rich's poem therefore echoes Virginia Woolf's call for the androgynous writer and also reflects H.D.'s lines in *Tribute to the Angels* attributed to the figure of "Psyche": "she carries a book but it is not / the tome of the ancient wisdom, // the pages, I imagine, are the blank pages / of the unwritten volume of the new" (H.D. 1983: 570).

Rich kept reinventing herself by shifting and widening her focus while remaining faithful to her belief in giving a voice to and building bridges between different silenced groups. In her next volume of poetry, *The Dream of a Common Language* (1978), she repudiated androgyny for its male bias and appropriation of the feminine and embraced a separatist lesbian identity. The late 1970s and early 1980s saw Rich at the climax of prestige and influence with a series of celebrated poetry collections and her groundbreaking (if controversial) essays such as "Compulsory Heterosexuality and Lesbian Existence" (1980). Going beyond narrow feminist concerns, Rich interrogated the interlocking systems of oppression involving race, ethnicity, class, gender, and sexuality, dealt with her Jewish heritage, and broadened the reach of her poetry to give testimony to wars and atrocities all over the globe, as in her volume *An Atlas of the Difficult World* (1991).

According to Charles Altieri, Rich's poetry is anchored and unified across its diverse subjects by three basic qualities: "its processes of defining and testing personal identity, its capacity to make private states serve as public political testimony, and her elaborating a discursive style that absorbs scenic moments into a dynamic process of self-consciousness capable of linking the poet to her community" (1984: 168). Altieri's last point merits elaboration, as Rich's discursive style of poetry has become the main bone of contention even for critics who do not mind her occasional essentialist tendencies, moral lessons, and Manichean politics. As "Diving into the Wreck" illustrates, Rich favors a plain style. She writes predominantly in the present tense, makes use of anaphoric and repetitive structures, and relies on mild forms of fragmentation, ellipsis, and a fluid syntax that nevertheless allow her images to remain understandable. Rich's project is indeed to write an engaged public poetry that largely rejects poetic experimentalism, abstraction, and formal innovation for the sake of accessibility and social impact. Her political radicalism is thus couched in a mainstream, conventionalist aesthetics—something that other feminist poets and scholars have deemed unsatisfactory and too limiting.

3. Harryette Mullen's "She Swam On from Sea to Shine" and the Utopian Potential of Alternative Meaning-Making

Adrienne Rich's reservation concerning avant-garde poetry that sets out to challenge society by attacking conventional meaning resides in her view that it can easily become ineffective. Indeed, Rich argues that "avant-garde" has historically denoted rebellions of mostly privileged younger white men. This is something, she claimed in 1993, that is not available for minority writers who have first to "repossess and revalue" lost traditions and styles:

The poetry of emerging groups—women, people of color, working-class radicals, lesbians and gay men—poetry that is nonassimilationist, difficult to co-opt, draws on many formal sources (ballad, blues, corrido, reggae, sonnet, chant, cuentos, sestina, sermon, calypso, for a few). But it doesn't pretend to abandon meaning . . . Those poetries can be highly complex, layered with tones and allusions, but they are also concerned with making it "as clear as possible" because too much already has been buried, mystified, or written of necessity in code. (Rich 1993: 227)

Harryette Mullen's poetry is an example that unmistakably contradicts Rich's conception of the "poetry of emerging groups." In fact, if Mullen's highly complex poetry is a project to "repossess and revalue" forgotten traditions and styles, it is often to the largely ignored experimental tradition in Black letters. Unwittingly perhaps, by pitting avant-garde against minority writing, Rich defines the "avant-garde" as white and ignores the enormous influence of African and African American art forms and improvisational modes on modernism and postmodernism itself. She also overlooks how easily the "black voice" and other identity discourses have been appropriated as marketable commodities. In her essay "Poetry and Identity" (1996), Mullen maintains that "representative 'black' poets are currently more assimilable into the 'mainstream' than 'formally innovative' poets of any hue" (2012: 9). The "avant-garde poet of color," however, faces the additional problem of threatening the cohesiveness of a literary group or movement, "whether it is a group 'of color' or a movement defined by its commitment to 'formal innovation'" (ibid.: 10). Falling into the gaps of what Mullen sharply terms "aesthetic apartheid" (ibid.: 12), the avant-garde minority writer does not appear to belong to any clearly identifiable poetic community, and her writing seems to lack a proper history of its own. Mullen however refuses to choose between deploying the "codes of oppressed peoples" and belonging to "so-called 'purely aesthetic schools'" (ibid.: 12).

Mullen's poetic career reflects these tensions. Her first volume of poetry, *Tree Tall Women* (1981), is still very much indebted to the search for a representative black voice in the Black Arts Movement. However, Mullen's interest in Language poetry soon let her abandon the idea of a unified black female subjectivity. Identity still informs her poetry, but only, as she writes, "insofar as identity acts upon language, and language acts upon identity" (ibid.: 3). Her next two books, *Trimmings* (1991) and *S*PeRM**K*T* (1992), consist of short prose poems that, in correspondence to the "Objects" and "Food" sections in Gertrude Stein's modernist classic *Tender Buttons* (1914), deal with female clothing and products at a supermarket. In poems as short as "Shades, cool dark lasses. Ghost of a smile" (Mullen 2006: 58), Mullen's puns and wordplays evoke female and black subjectivities—in this case, for example, "dark lasses" is suggestive of sunglasses, young black women, and perhaps the ghostly legacy of the triangular trade of slaves and molasses. But rather than presenting a unified self, Mullen is primarily interested in hybrid constitutions of contemporary/black/female subjects through language, history, and the trappings of consumer culture. Mullen found, however, that the audience of her experimentalist poetry was now almost exclusively white. Consequently, with *Muse & Drudge* (1995), a long poem written in quatrains reminiscent of the blues tradition, she combines a more recognizably black genre with her improvisational play with language, form, and decentered, multiple subjectivities.

Sleeping with the Dictionary (2002) and one of its longer prose poems, "She Swam On from Sea to Shine," continue Mullen's project of making use of black folk materials and participating in discourses of gender and race while experimenting with innovative forms and exploring the "linguistic quirks and cultural references peculiar to American English as spoken by the multiethnic peoples of the United States" (Mullen 2012: 6). In contrast to other contemporary women poets of color, Harald Zapf perceptively describes Mullen as "less concerned with representing blackness than with enacting otherness and difference, linguistic otherness and differences of sound, rhythm, and the vernacular" (2008: 179). The result is a highly complex poetry whose referential variety and richness is challenging for any reader to comprehend. Yet this complexity is part of the fun to be had with Mullen's playful poetry: her word riddles and language games invite discussion and exchange across diverse communities of readers where each can contribute their own associations concerning specific phrases. The focus, both in Mullen's rule-governed writing and in the decoding of her texts, is thus more on the process than on the product itself.

The children's game and constant motion that opens "She Swam On from Sea to Shine" is programmatic:

> Hide and seek, where the tree decided to sleep was where she ran. She ran away with a ruckus. The baby girl was stolen by a tipsy woman came to take her. Where they found her in the mud. She'd stolen a doll. Her doll got sick, she died. The brown doll from her father. The pink doll came from somewhere else. She had drowsy eyes like marbles. (Mullen 2002: 61)

In one of her interviews, Mullen explains that this poem "summarizes" her "life in language." It makes sense, then, that this hybrid mixture of "prose poetry, autobiography, folklore, and fiction" (Mullen 2012: 264) begins with what appears to be childhood memories. The memories, however, are hard to make sense of because of their impressionistic, almost surreal character, which emerges out of the interplay of paratactic, sometimes incomplete or grammatically broken sentences, and the referential instability of the pronouns. In this referential maze, the game of "hide and seek" also doubles as the writer's and the reader's playful activity in continuously encoding and decoding life experiences and meaning.

In paratactic structures like these, Bob Perelman has argued that "the internal, autonomous meaning of a new sentence is heightened, questioned, and changed by the degree of separation or connection that the reader perceives with regard to the surrounding sentences" (1993: 313). The 'problem' in running these standard cognitive operations while reading Mullen's text is that in each sentence there are elements pulling simultaneously in different directions. Initially we are prone to understand the repetition of "She ran" in the second sentence as referring to the same girl in the game of hide-and-seek. We may also note how "ruckus" contrasts with the "sleeping" tree, and then perhaps imagine how the girl, having been detected by the seeker, noisily runs away. However, the intimation of the "taking" or the kidnapping of "the baby girl" by a "tipsy woman" sheds a different light on the "ruckus": maybe the ruckus and the running away were not a part of the children's game but something more serious. Likewise, "Where they found her in the mud" connects to the girl hiding behind the fallen tree because that is "where she ran"; but at this point, "her" should actually refer either to the stolen "baby girl" or the "tipsy woman." Both possibilities, in turn, give a much more ominous tone to the incident of an anonymous group of people ("they") finding a female person in the "mud." The sense of threat or a crime scene is further exacerbated by the possible conflation of the stolen "baby girl" with a "doll" that gets sick and "dies." Perhaps this girl was so charming that people nicknamed her "doll." Or perhaps it is a real doll given to the girl by her "father," and the sickness and death of this "brown" doll occurs only in the child's imagination, whereas the "pink" doll with the "drowsy eyes" is apparently healthy and just as sleepy as the tree of the first sentence.

This speculative close reading of the poem's beginning illustrates how the syntactic and semantic slippages in Mullen's poetry continuously subvert all our efforts to read for stable identities and meanings. The surrealist effect of the illogical succession of actions and images held together by their repetition and gradual transformation may express one meaning of the volume's title of "sleeping with the dictionary": not only an intimacy with language but also the way in which dreams, altered states of consciousness, and the (collective) unconscious show in the cracks and gaps in language (cf. Henning 2011: 40). At once innocently playful and ominously violent, the poem's opening passage also subtly weaves in cultural associations and prejudices concerning race and ethnicity by way of the explicit reference to the brown and pink dolls of different origins, and even by the proximity of "tipsy" with "Gypsy," an implicit rhyme and a terrible pun that the poem never makes, but is nevertheless stereotypically called up in the context of a child-stealing woman.

Read on an autobiographical level, "She Swam On" chronologically follows Mullen's life growing up in Fort Worth, Texas, and evokes, for instance, the history of segregation: "We kept moving until we moved the neighbors out" (Mullen 2002: 63) references an actual event when Mullen's family were the first black people to move into an all-white neighborhood (Mullen 2012: 185). She pays homage to Fort Worth's rich musical tradition ("Those saxophone streets and scratchy sidewalks," ibid.: 62) and testifies to its multicultural and multilingual character: French appears as a language of refinement and education; Spanish dominates the food culture and is simultaneously rejected by the Catholic nuns (cf. ibid. 63); the nuns' religious language at Mullen's Catholic school is also satirized by the poem's vernacularized version: "hell merry fuller grays. . ." and "Anomie, dull party, dull filly, dull spitter shoo sanity" (ibid.: 63-4) parodies the prayer of Hail Mary ("Hail Mary, full of Grace. . .") and the Trinitarian formula ("In nomine Patris, et filii, et spiritus sancti").

In witty, anaphoric passages full of paradoxes, homonyms, alliterations, assonances, consonances, and near-anagrams, Mullen describes her uneventful high school years ("High school was hormones and hers were a moan, she wasn't a whore or a harmed one," ibid.: 64) and her time in college, when the girl who "was a poem" (ibid.) and "was always writing anyway" "found a tongue" (ibid. 65). Reminiscent of the girl playing hide-and-seek in the first sentence, the motif of running is taken up again ("She got that piece of paper and ran with it"; "instead of bursting, she ran. She got used to running," ibid.: 65) and carried over to her writing, described in terms of its accelerating and decelerating dynamics: "More paper, more pencils, more writing, she went everywhere she could. She went on a whim, on a limb, she limped and whimpered. She slowed down, she settled, she got stuck . . . She shook her groove thing and got it on" (ibid.).

The poem closes, however, not autobiographically but symbolically, not with running but with a shipwreck and an unbelievable feat of swimming. Despite the apparent danger, she is prepared ("she brought her suit") and extremely boastful of her survival skills and powerful capacities:

> She'd float like a jellyfish, sting like a man of war, or seaweed ain't salty. Water was her element, she swam on. Right through a tsunami, she cut with scissor kicks. She caught a wave, she got in a flap, she was flippant. From sea, she ran past shark teeth. Like shine, see. If I'm lying, I'm flying. From sea to shine, she swam on. The whales sang Celtic music, dolphins frisked her. She was worked over and under she let her mind wander. Let it roll and keep on rolling on and on. Revolution is a cycle that never ends. Rumors of May made mermaids murmur. Plato opens utopia to poets on opiates. (ibid.: 66)

Like Rich's diver in her body-armor, Mullen's protagonist combines both female and male elements, even if the "man of war" is in fact a venomous colony of zooids making up the marine animal of the Portuguese man o' war whose name, in turn, is derived from an early modern warship. The sea again figures as an entirely different, feminine element that she experiences as "her element," which she can choose to work with (passively "floating," catching a wave) or work against (aggressively cutting through). Swimming in the sea paradoxically incorporates the diverse bodily movements of flipping, "rolling," and "running." Even "If I'm lying, I'm flying"—the colloquial phrase to ascertain the truth of one's tale—contributes to this flow of bodily states. Crucially, the rolling motion of the body in the water first morphs into the unending movement of the mind before it is extended, via a geometric denotation of "revolution," into the historical and social realm. To better understand the poem's ending, however, we need to explore the poem's symbolic deployment of American folklore and African American traditions.

Mullen's title of the poem "She Swam On from Sea to Shine"—and particularly the passage, "From sea, she ran past shark teeth. Like shine, see"—signify on the popular song "America the Beautiful" and its lines that God may crown America's "good with brotherhood / From sea to shining sea." Mullen's retelling of her life taps into this patriotic reservoir but replaces it with the black folk legend of "Shine and the Titanic." In this traditional African American toast—a genre of long, witty, and sometimes obscene narrative poems that were publicly performed in black male working-class culture—the black stoker Shine is the first to notice water flooding into the *Titanic*, but his repeated warnings go ignored. Eventually, Shine jumps into the water and begins to swim. Those still on board, now realizing that the *Titanic* is sinking, offer him money and sex in return for his help, but Shine refuses them. He encounters a shark and a whale, but due to his superhuman strength he outperforms them and swims safely ashore. For the folklorist Roger Abrahams, who introduced Mullen to these toasts at the University of Texas, Shine's story is one of black rebellion: one of the few blacks on board a ship generally reserved for wealthy whites, Shine achieves transformation and rebirth in the ocean by defying the whites and relying on his own powers (cf. 1970: 83-4). Such legends of improbable black triumph were the typical subject of toasts, which make heavy use of parataxis and whose lines usually begin with personal pronouns. Typically, Abrahams adds, the narrators try to identify with their heroes by the technique of the "intrusive I," whereby they make their presence felt in the fictional worlds (cf. ibid.: 65, 102-3).

Mullen thus employs quite a few of the toast's narrative and formal conventions in the fictionalization of her life, although she significantly rewrites the genre. Her use of pronouns, for instance, does not allow stable identities to emerge. Most importantly, Mullen takes a traditionally male-centered performance practice and turns it into a prose poem about a black woman's trials and triumphs. Turning away from the patriotism of "America the Beautiful," "She Swam On from Sea to Shine" subtly registers the legacy of discrimination and oppression against people of color as it celebrates black, and especially female, agency and survival.

The definition of "revolution" as an unending cycle at the poem's end thus carries with it the history of continuous black struggle and rebellion. Shine's revolt is subtly woven into the poem's penultimate sentence: "Rumors of May made mermaids murmur" may obliquely refer to the erroneous dating of the *Titanic* disaster on April 14, 1912 in the toast's opening line: "It was a hell of a day in the merry month of May" (in Abrahams 1970: 105). (Incidentally, "hell" and "merry" in the toast's opening line may also inform Mullen's earlier rewriting of the Hail Mary prayer.) But what the poem's ending also suggests is that "revolution" always involves and requires the power of alternative meaning-making through the imaginative use of language. Turning over the soft /mər/- and /mād/-sounds into ever new configurations and cycling anagrammatically through the plosives, sibilants, and 'o'-sounds of the last sentence echoes the gender difference that "mermaids" and "Plato" make explicit. But aside from the question of gender, her word-play more fundamentally speaks to language's endless power of transformation. This "utopian" power may potentially be retrieved from the collective unconscious of language, which figured as the sea in both Rich and Mullen's poems, and may be achieved through altered states of consciousness ("opiates"), dreaming ("Asleep, diving into dreams. Salty and warm, like ocean, like broth," ibid.: 61), or the recourse to, and re-vision of, largely forgotten oral and textual traditions and myths (Shine). In "She Swam On from Sea to Shine," Harryette Mullen combines the latter approach with a belief in the liberating potential of humor and word-play.

4. Conclusion

Perhaps the primary benefit of reading Adrienne Rich and Harryette Mullen together is that it provides a first inkling of the breadth and variety of thematic, stylistic, and formal choices in contemporary women's poetry, even if the label is problematic since "women's poetry" is not, and never has been, a particular school or movement. In one of her interviews, Harryette Mullen stated: "I don't know that I'm setting up a specifically female or feminine poetics . . . There's a feminist attitude, let's say" (Mullen 2012: 192). The unfulfilled goal of gender equality, of course, still animates the thoughts and writing of many female poets, but as shown by Rich's poetic trajectory and Mullen's practice, for many poets gender has become just one analytical category in an intersectional exploration of hegemonic power and oppression. The main questions for a non-essentialist analysis of "contemporary women's poetry" thus concern the extent and level of openness with which feminist matters are negotiated as well as the choice, functions, and effects of different aesthetic and rhetorical strategies.

Studies of Rich's and Mullen's poetry will provide vastly different answers to these questions, and this is not the place to adjudicate which poetic choices may be more appropriate or effective in changing people's minds about gender issues or bringing about social change. In an age that some scholars have referred to as "postfeminist," women's poetry has become, if anything, even more diverse and eclectic. Lynn Keller and Cristanne Miller write:

> Young feminists now, often looking to the models offered by their immediate female precursors, are bringing together resources gleaned from significant female poets who have not been identified primarily as feminist writers—among them Jorie Graham, Maxine Kumin, Mary Oliver, Rita Dove, Louise Glück—as well as the divergent examples offered by more obviously feminist poets. (2005: 91)

Rich's thinking and poetry kept exploring different critical directions and new subjects, and Mullen, whose latest book *Urban Tumbleweed* (2013) is a "tanka diary" on the environment, continues her experiments in constrained writing and formal innovations. In light of Rich's and Mullen's deployments of mythical shipwrecks and survival, their shifting pronouns, their retrieval of forgotten traditions in new poetic forms, and their revisions of theoretical and political positions, Liz Yorke's take on Rich surely applies to both writers—and indeed to much of contemporary women's poetry: "Re-visionary mythmaking, in creating . . . transitional subjectivities, continually recenters itself, refusing to see any single ideology, any single point of location as the answer" (Yorke 1997: 138).

Bibliography

Selected Primary Literature

Grahn, Judy. 1978. *The Work of a Common Woman: Collected Poetry (1964-1977)*. New York: St. Martin's P.
Hacker, Marilyn. [1986.] 1987. *Love, Death, and the Changing of the Seasons*. London: Onlywomen P.
Hejinian, Lyn. 2002. *My Life*. Copenhagen: Green Integer.
Howe, Susan. 1990. *Singularities*. Middletown: Wesleyan UP.
Lorde, Audre. 1978. *The Black Unicorn*. New York: Norton.
Mullen, Harryette. 2002. *Sleeping with the Dictionary*. Berkeley: U of California P.
——. 2006. *Recyclopedia*: Trimmings, S*PeRM**K*T, *and* Muse & Drudge. St. Paul: Graywolf P.
——. 2013. *Urban Tumbleweed: Notes From A Tanka Diary*. Minneapolis: Graywolf P.
Rich, Adrienne. 2013. *Later Poems: Selected and New, 1971-2012*. New York: Norton.
——. 1963. *Snapshots of a Daughter-in-Law: Poems 1954-62*. New York: Norton.

Selected Secondary Literature

Frost, Elisabeth A. 2003. *The Feminist Avant-Garde in American Poetry*. Iowa City: U of Iowa P.

Presents a theory and historical lineage of feminist avant-garde poetry from Gertrude Stein and Mina Loy over Sonia Sanchez to contemporary writers Susan Howe and Harryette Mullen, and analyzes this body of writing in its ambivalent relation to other (male) avant-garde movements.

Gelpi, Barbara Charlesworth and Albert Gelpi (eds.). 1993. *Adrienne Rich's Poetry and Prose: Poems, Prose, Reviews and Criticism*. Second ed. New York: W. W. Norton.

Very useful volume bringing together some of Rich's most important poetry and essays until the early 1990s, as well as (selections from) thirteen review essays and interpretations of Rich's work, by Helen Vendler, Charles Altieri, Joanna Feit Diehl, and other important scholars.

Keller, Lynn. 2010. *Thinking Poetry: Readings in Contemporary Women's Exploratory Poetics*. Iowa City: U of Iowa P.

Keller analyzes "exploratory" writing by poets like Alice Fulton, Myung Mi Kim, Joan Retallack, Cole Swensen, and Susan Wheeler whose experiments with visual elements, page space, multilingualism or digital technology leads Keller to develop a range of instructive reading strategies.

Mullen, Harryette. 2012. *The Cracks Between What We Are and What We Are Supposed to Be: Essays and Interviews*. Introd. Hank Lazer. Tuscaloosa: U of Alabama P.

In the absence of a monograph dedicated solely to Mullen's work, this edition of her own critical essays and informative interviews is a good start to explore Mullen's contributions to scholarship and poetics.

Ostriker, Alicia Suskin. 1986. *Stealing the Language: The Emergence of Women's Poetry in America*. Boston: Beacon Press.

This classic study focuses on women's poetry since the 1960s and argues that women writers need to be "thieves" of the male "oppressor's language." Dealing with questions of identity, the body, erotics and violence, Ostriker also proposes the concept of revisionist mythmaking.

Further References

Abrahams, Roger D. 1970. *Deep down in the jungle . . . Negro Narrative Folklore from the Streets of Philadelphia*. Chicago: Aldine.

Altieri, Charles. 1984. *Self and Sensibility in Contemporary Poetry*. Cambridge: Cambridge UP.

Armantrout, Rae. 1992. "Feminist Poetics and the Meaning of Clarity." *Sagetrieb* 11.3: 7-16.

Beauvoir, Simone de. [1949] 2011. *The Second Sex*. London: Vintage.

DuPlessis, Rachel Blau. 1979. "The Critique of Consciousness and Myth in Levertov, Rich, and Rukeyser." In: Gilbert/Gubar 1979. 280-300.

Franke, Astrid. 2008. "The Powerless Power of Poets: Experimenting with the Self-in-Relation." In: Kornelia Freitag and Katharina Vester (eds.). *Another Language: Poetic Experiments in Britain and North America*. Berlin: LIT. 67-75.

Fridan, Betty. [1963] 2010. *The Feminine Mystique*. London: Penguin.

Gilbert, Sandra M., and Susan Gubar (eds.). 1979. *Shakespeare's Sisters: Feminist Essays on Women Poets*. Bloomington: Indiana UP.

H.D. 1983. *Collected Poems, 1912-1944*. Ed. Louis L. Martz. New York: New Directions.

Henning, Barbara. 2011. *Looking Up Harryette Mullen: Interviews on* Sleeping with the Dictionary *and Other Works*. Brooklyn: Belladonna.

Keller, Lynn, and Cristanne Miller. 2005. "Feminism and the Female Poet." In: Stephen Fredman (ed.). *A Concise Companion to Twentieth-century American Poetry*. Malden: Blackwell. 75-94.

Perelman, Bob. 1993. "Parataxis and Narrative: The New Sentence in Theory and Practice. In: *American Literature* 65.2 (June 1993): 313-24.

Rich, Adrienne. 1984. *On Lies, Secrets, and Silence: Selected Prose 1966-78*. London: Virago.

——. 1993. *What Is Found There: Notebooks on Poetry and Politics*. New York: Norton.

Showalter, Elaine. 1986. "Toward a Feminist Poetics." In: Elaine Showalter (ed.): *The New Feminist Criticism: Essays on Women, Literature, and Theory*. London: Virago. 125-43.

Vendler, Helen. 1980. *Part of Nature, Part of Us: Modern American Poets*. Cambridge: Harvard UP.

Yorke, Liz. 1997. *Adrienne Rich: Passion, Politics and the Body*. London: Sage.

Zapf, Harald. 2008. "An Othering of Language: Harryette Mullen's Experiments in Transpoetry." In: Kornelia Freitag and Katharina Vester (eds.). *Another Language: Poetic Experiments in Britain and North America*. Berlin: LIT. 173-86.

28.

Asian American Poetry

Cathy Song's "Beauty and Sadness" and Theresa Hak Kyung Cha's
"Edward Hopper's Western Motel, 1957"

Nassim W. Balestrini

1. Asian American Literary Studies and Asian American Poetry

The phrase Asian America(n) is replete with political implications and historical baggage and can be seen as a verbal marker that is either coalition-building (and thus empowering) or essentializing (and thus stereotyping and discriminatory). In addition to the insecurity about which of the Asian countries should be included in the purview of Asian American Studies, the positioning of Pacific Islands (and thus of Pacific Islanders living in U.S. territories or on U.S. soil) remains a contentious issue. The high potential for controversy notwithstanding, scholars agree that the academic field of Asian American Studies evolved in the United States out of the student protests on the West Coast in the late 1960s, particularly in San Francisco and Berkeley. Asian American Studies has come to encompass not only the histories and artistic representations of numerous countries of vastly heterogeneous cultural and linguistic traditions, but has gone beyond immigration studies to include trans-Pacific cultural, economic, and political relations. Within literary studies, the phrase Asian American originally designated works by immigrants and their offspring whose roots were found in China, Japan, Korea (cf. Huang 2006: 3), and—at least in the context of a groundbreaking literary anthology edited by Frank Chin and others—the Philippines (cf. Chin et al. 2012 [1974]: 30; Kim 2012 [1982]: 58). By the late twentieth century, South Asia and Southeast Asia assumed prominent positions within the field (cf. Huang 2006: 3). The continuing use of Asian/Pacific Studies for research on, for instance, Hawai'i indicates the ongoing parallel existence of terminology that may or may not include the Pacific Islands into the larger category of Asian American Studies. As recent scholarship indicates, a rising number of national backgrounds have joined the ranks of Asian American writers, among them "Hmong and Laotian American," "Tibetan American," and "mixed race" (Yu 2011: 844; regarding the inclusion of Pacific Islanders, see Sumida 2010).

Scholars have attempted to identify several phases in the development of Asian American literary studies. From the late 1960s and throughout at least the 1970s, cultural nationalism and activism (which owes much to the contemporaneous Black Aesthetic movement; see Li 1998: 36) dominated the field (most prominently, see Chin et al. 2012 [1974]). In response to the unfortunate dichotomies resulting from this school of thought in terms of a rift separating male and female writers and also in terms of reinforcing race-based mainstream vs. margins or majority vs. minority binary oppositions, critics arguing from the perspectives of more recently developed theoretical vantage points—such as third-wave feminist, poststructuralist, postcolonial, and queer thought—and critics acknowledging the changing demographics of Asian American communities have promoted approaches that celebrate Asian American literature's diversity regarding authors' origins as well as approaches that scrutinize diasporic and domestic creative contexts (cf. Cheung 2012 [1990]: 100; Lowe 2012 [1991]: 123; Wong 2012 [1995]: 138-9; Cheung 1997b: 1; regarding transnational features, also see Mai 2012; Tunc et al. 2012).

Consequently, when teaching anything subsumed under the subject heading of Asian American Studies, Americanists must first illustrate the diversity of coexisting cultural traditions and histories; second, they must convey the conflicted historiographies and cultural imaginaries within which specific Asian Americans have been depicted by others, particularly by the white mainstream; and third, they must foster awareness of the debates within Asian American circles regarding self-definition and self-presentation within larger socio-historical and cultural contexts. The study and teaching of Asian American poetry serves as a case in point.

While Asian American poetry first appeared in the late 1880s, it did not boom until the late 1960s and early 1970s (cf. Huang 2006: 21-3). Before this initial phase of relative prominence, Chinese immigrants detained at Angel Island Immigrant Station between 1910 and 1940 carved poems into the barracks walls. Their poetry—written in Chinese—has been collected, published, and studied by Asian Americanists with knowledge of the Chinese language (see Yao 2012 [2008]). Asian Americanists have thus opened up to works written in Chinese by people who did not necessarily ever settle in the United States. Others have acknowledged, however, that Asian American poetic culture has entered the English-language mainstream in various ways, one of which is the establishment of an American type of *haiku* by Japanese poet Yone Noguchi (1875-1947), who lived in the United States from 1893 to 1904 and whose efforts to popularize *haiku* preceded the work of Imagists like Ezra Pound (see Marx 2012 [2006]). A more recent example is found in English versions of the seventh-century Arabic lyric form of the *ghazal* by Kashmiri-American poet Agha Shahid Ali (1949-2001) (cf. Yu 2011: 839-40). While Japanese-American *nisei* (American-born second-generation Japanese Americans) began to publish literary works before the Second World War and continued to do so during and after the internment of Japanese Americans following the Japanese attack on Pearl Harbor, Japanese American poetry began to gain real visibility with the "activist writing" (Yogi 1997: 140) of *sansei* (third-generation Japanese Americans), most prominently with Lawson Fusao Inada's volume *Before the War* (1971).

According to Guiyou Huang, the link between activism and the publication of literature was rooted in the protest movement against the war in Vietnam, in the participation of Asian American university students in the civil rights movement, and in the uprising of students from so-called 'Third World' countries at West Coast universities (cf. 2006: 24). The first literary magazine focused on Asian American writing, *Aion*, was published in San Francisco in 1970 as a result of these events (cf. Yu 2009: 77). As of the 1980s, poets diversified their thematic and stylistic concerns to include topics such as "generational clashes, cultural differences, nostalgia for the homeland, racism, and sexism" (Huang 2006: 25). Beginning with the 1990s, Asian American poets became more widely recognized as participants in the highly heterogeneous arena of American literature. Although authors did retain earlier themes and forms that have been considered features of an Asian American poetic tradition, they also included postmodernist experiments with form and current sociopolitical topics regardless of the respective author's background (cf. ibid.). At the same time, Asian American authors, both immigrants and descendants of immigrants, have been reclaiming their language(s) of origin (particularly from the Modernist poets' appropriation) and have been integrating, for instance, Chinese ideograms into their poems (cf. Hsiao 2012; regarding modernist appropriations and current reclaiming efforts, also see Park 2008; Yao 2010). In this sense, Asian American poetry has come full circle in the last one hundred years.

The participation of Asian American poets in the production of postmodern poetry also sheds light on how ethnic poetry has been treated in classrooms and in academia in a broader sense. Time and again, poems by 'non-mainstream'— that is, non-white—authors have been read as ethnographic documents of specific ethnic sensibilities. Notions of 'authenticity' linked to ethnic roots have been projected onto Asian American literature with the detrimental effect of limiting the respective author's range of self-expression to issues of identity, personal experience, and representing specific cultural contexts (cf. Li 1998: 34). The very issue of representation as a phenomenon that must be treated with postmodern mistrust of ideological constructs is thus often excluded because the poems by 'minority' authors are supposed to open windows to an experience non-Asian American readers do not share, but want to access and understand.

In sum, the following central concerns dominate the current scholarly conversation regarding Asian American poetry: How can poets claim a particular Asian American form of subjectivity that counteracts racialized perceptions and their concomitant depictions imposed on Asian Americans by others? How do Asian American poets deal with the objectification of the racialized body and of other reifications of ostensible ethnic characteristics that perpetuate stereotypes about Asian Americans through repeatedly referencing specific objects (such as works of art, clothing, or food) that bear symbolic implications? What is the relation between what critics have characterized as American avant-garde poetry and Asian American poetry?

Regarding subjectivity and objectification, scholars have recently been contemplating whether Asian American poetry projects definitions of selfhood and otherness that must be read through non-Western lenses. Xiaojing Zhou argues, for instance, that understanding the contribution of Asian American poetry to postmodern American poetry requires a revised sense of what 'self' and 'other' mean and of how the lyric I functions (2006: 1). On the one hand, excluding autobiographical poems from the purview of postmodern poetry disallows recognizing a selfhood in the lyric I which is different from the Western tradition whose understanding of the individual self can be traced back to René Descartes (ibid.: 6). On the other hand, including such autobiographical self-expression, which redefines selfhood as relational rather than solipsistic, allows postmodern poetry to address in more varied forms "the social, political, ethical, and philosophical" (ibid.: 7). Zhou argues that instead of assuming that the postmodern self equals "fragmented subjectivity" (ibid.: 9), poets using this specific autobiographical lyrical mode develop a different concept of self and of otherness (cf. ibid.: 13). Yu's analysis of 21st-century Asian American poetry indicates that despite the emergence of an ever-expanding variety of poets in terms of background, theme, and style, critics do not agree to acknowledge diversity but rather continue in their contentious endeavor to define ostensibly shared traits or characteristics of Asian American poetry (cf. 2011: 818). Diversity of poetic self-expression comprises a broad range from the continuation of pre-1980 traditions in Asian American poetry to participation in all forms of experimentation associated with contemporary American poetry at large. Like Zhou,

Yu indicates that the more experimental a poet may be, the less she or he may have been categorized as Asian American (cf. ibid.: 823)—as if ethnic poetry were to follow an agenda dictated by outsiders in need of ethnographic texts for the sake of completing an American mosaic of literary texts. One example is the critical response to John Yau who, for the longest time, was seen only as a follower of John Ashbery; critics did not address his racial background at all (cf. Yu 2009: 147). The question that remains is whether such categorizations make sense and how doing so would help readers understand Yau's work.

The centrality of the relation between the visual and the verbal, between described objects and their political implications, becomes clear in Joseph Jeon's study of how avant-garde art pinpoints "the physical and visual oddness of racial constructs" (2012: xxxi) and thus pulls the rug out from under interpretations that take verbal descriptions of the palpable world in ethnic poetry at face value. I agree with Yu's conclusion that attempts to interpret Asian American poetry (and all poetry, especially by non-white writers) remain poised between "seeing Asian American poetry as a poetry of pure content" and "reading 'experimental' poetic techniques too abstractly" (2009: 159). In other words, poetry is always rooted in social contexts no matter how seemingly concrete or abstract its aesthetics. As this discussion of Asian American selves demonstrates, defining what constitutes Asian American poetry remains an aporia—and that may lead to more flexibility in thinking about individual authors and their works.

In order to avoid the intellectually stifling effect of ethnographic interpretations, I chose two poems that should be discussed not in isolation but rather in conjunction with the debates within the study of Asian American poetry. My hope is that these poems will come alive for students by making them aware of the difficulty of reading such works without essentializing the texts and their authors. As a result, students can also gain insight into current scholarly conversations within American literary and cultural studies, which may in turn enable them to transfer various ways of approaching and dealing with contentious issues to other areas within their fields of study. Both poems discussed here use *ekphrasis*, meaning that they include descriptions of pre-existing visual images. By reading the texts in light of how the verbally explored paintings participate in the respective poem's reception as a work by an Asian American author, students can contemplate the following issues: Are the discourses and semiotic systems of the visual and the verbal pitted against each other? Does each poem recontextualize the painting and thus reevaluate its meaning, its cultural significance, and its process of signification? Does the painting participate in making the poem a work subsumed under the category of Asian American poetry?

2. Cathy Song's "Beauty and Sadness" (1983)
and the Dilemma of Gendered Representation

Song's first volume of poetry, *Picture Bride* (1983), includes texts referencing visual art by Japanese printmaker Kitagawa Utamaro (1753-1806) and American painter Georgia O'Keeffe (1887-1986). The volume's title refers to women from various Asian countries who entered arranged marriages with Asian men who had emigrated to the U.S. mainland and the Hawai'ian islands before them; these women, like Song's Korean grandmother, knew and were known to their fiancés only through photographs. While Song, who was born in Hawai'i of Korean and

Chinese descent, received the prestigious Yale Series of Younger Poets Award (1982) for this volume, *Picture Bride* has also incited some controversy. A selection of Song's poems has been included in the prestigious *Norton Anthology of American Literature*; the introductory text vaguely links the poet's "ability to write about her own or another's experience as an acute observer" to "her multicultural background" (Baym et al. 2012: 1124), thus implying that multicultural writers may have heightened perceptive faculties which result in poignant descriptions. Yet Asian American scholars in particular have criticized Song's poems as evoking "static visualization[s]" through which the poet may practice "accidental compliance" with traditions of "racialization in the United States" (Jeon 2012: 119).

When teaching "Beauty and Sadness" (included in the *Norton Anthology*) students should be made aware of such contrastive assessments in order to allow them to contemplate the reasons for these views and to consider which view they may find more or less convincing. In order to let students think about the umbrella phrase Asian American and the national origins of poets subsumed under this phrase, I would encourage them to look into the poets' biographical data and to collect some information on the countries of origin, immigrant experiences, and the current situation of later generations in the United States that may apply to Song and that may or may not contribute to understanding her artistic œuvre. My assumption is that students will become rather intrigued by the difficulty of disentangling the multiple histories and historiographies involved in 'defining' Song's cultural background. They may thus begin to question, through their research experience, the validity of connecting ethnicity and artistic output in a mimetic, positivist, biographical, and ultimately essentializing manner. Another way of achieving a related effect is to confront the students with Song's poem or with both poems discussed in this essay without revealing the authors' names and, thus, without predisposing the students in their expectations as to the type of poem a specific 'kind' of author may produce.

Song's 56-line poem, dedicated to Kitagawa Utamaro, describes characteristics of the visual artist's works (to find examples of his prints, see the Wikipedia entry on Utamaro which provides links to websites featuring numerous images). While the women he depicted remain anonymous, they testify to their own and to their creator's legacy through the sheer number of prints and through their preservation by art lovers. How then, does Song's poem embody these anonymous women categorized as "Teahouse waitresses, actresses, / geishas, courtesans and maids" (ll. 4-5)? Does the portrayal of Japanese prints simply confirm ethnic and gender clichés, such as the stereotype of Asian American women as either excessively submissive or sexually aggressive? Does the poem buy into Orientalist tropes, or does it undermine them? In what ways does the subject-object relation between artist and painted figure reflect other such relations? How useful is Jeon's adaptation of W.J.T. Mitchell's "critical iconology"—which inquires into the conflicted links between the visual and the verbal, and which encourages us to scrutinize the way we visualize—into what Jeon calls "racial iconology [which] provides an alternative model of politicizing representation, [and] which responds to calls for a postidentity politics and to the increasingly antisubjective sensibilities of contemporary avant-garde poetry and art" (2012: 112)?

In order not to simply regard this poem as an example of confirming stereotypes of Japanese women as objects suffering under the male gaze or as objects frozen in time by the artist's brush, it is worth considering Song's use of verbs. These verbs, one could argue, create a partially dynamic give-and-take between the artist's model and the artist. Although the artist and the buyers of his works possess and ultimately control the physical object of the print, the final moments of the poem foreground light and visual perception, as if the artist paradoxically needed to reexamine his own work in order to grasp it. In the first stanza, the creative act ("He drew," l. 1) is not disturbed by the models' agency in posing ("They arranged themselves," l. 6); but to the viewer of the prints, the painter's act of preserving a brief moment in time remains etched into the painting. Thus, even the viewer, who is removed from the moment of creating the visual image, senses that an artist eternalizes an ephemeral impression. Although paintings or drawings are necessarily static rather than moving images, the implication of sensing the painter's "invisible presence" (l. 8) endows the print with a human dimension that, to employ Yu's idea, indicates the social grounding of the aesthetic that is inherent in the interaction between the artist and the person he or she represents.

Beyond the artist himself, the history of his art's reception inscribes the poem into processes of transculturality. Utamaro has been credited with creating a style that highlights the beauty of the female form, which he predominately rendered in images of courtesans and which art lovers particularly appreciated for their eroticism. This applies also to the way his works entered the Western world: Impressionist painters in particular studied Utamaro's *ukiyo-e*, i.e., his 'pictures of a floating world,' which thrive on semi-transparency and on effects of light and shadow, thus teasing the viewer with allusions to pleasures. Similarly, eroticism is central to Imagist poet Amy Lowell's 1919 *Pictures of the Floating World*. In other words, the sexual focus on the feminine form applies both to the original cultural context and to its adoption into European-American art. To my mind, extrinsic knowledge about this Japanese art tradition, and particularly about its reception in the West, is a countermeasure to characterizing an *ekphrastic* poem as simply reiterating and thus reifying the social relations inherent in historically circumscribed aesthetic practices. Utamaro has been a presence within Western art in at least two media since the second half of the nineteenth century, and Western adaptations of his works are complicit in potentially fostering images of Asian American women as sexually available passive beauties. Song's poem softly argues against this stereotype by endowing Utamaro's models with verbs that convey agency and motion in a way alien to a woodblock print.

The second stanza rather overwhelmingly lists images of women in multiple poses and locations. Their poses evoke "cats" (l. 14), "bath[ers]" (l. 17), "porcelain vases" (l. 20), and "beautiful iridescent insects, / creatures from a floating world" (ll. 25-6). The tension between moving bodies and lifeless vases, equipped with regalia of clothing and headdress, lends itself to discussing issues of objectification and non-human representation, particularly because "purr[ing]" (l. 15) cats evoke Orientalist clichés reminiscent of Madame Butterfly. The second stanza thus counterbalances the sense of agency indicated by the verbs discussed above.

The third stanza then raises the question as to whether Song wants to problematize emblematic depictions of Japanese women. Here, all verbs stress the artist's power, as he "absorbed" (l. 27), "captured" (l. 30), and "transposed" (l. 38) visual details of the women's "moments of melancholy / as well as of beauty" (ll. 28-9). Thus, the "Sadness" of the poem title recurs as melancholy and is, throughout the stanza, associated with the voyeurism of exposing a half-naked woman (ll. 31-2), of revealing "A private space" (l. 35), and of freezing the moment of a woman "catching a glimpse of her own vulnerable / face in the mirror" (ll. 37-8) by transforming her heavily rouged lips into a simile mixing violence and aesthetic appeal: "like a drop of blood / soaking up the white expanse of paper" (ll. 40-1). This stanza, which reverses the title's order when referring first to "melancholy" (l. 28) and subsequently to "beauty" (l. 29), rather brutally subverts the notion (which still seems a possibility in the first stanza) that Utamaro's models were able to assert themselves. This in itself is not surprising, given the social status of these women and the historical context in which these visuals were created. More importantly, the poem points at the multiple layers of perception and illustration that are the heart of the matter: The model's "trembling plum lips" (l. 39) quiver once the model has gazed at her mirror image and has become aware of the visibility of vulnerability. This moment of painful insight gives birth to a bright-red detail in the painting, an eye-catcher that the poem encourages us to read not only in aesthetic, but also in social (and thus politicized) terms. In other words, the sadness of the moment overshadows the aesthetic appeal of the sensual and sensitive female lips.

The fourth and final stanza switches from the model's emotion to the painter's "inconsolable / eye" (ll. 42-3). But why would the artist's eye/I be sad in light of the ephemeral and moth-like women (cf. ll. 43-7)? Does he suffer with them? Or is he pained by the fleeting quality of the moments in time that he tries to retain for posterity through visual representation? The final stanza exudes appreciation for the models and the painter. Whereas the moth-like women are revered "as ancestors reincarnated" (l. 49), thus counteracting the emphasis on death in the rather stale image of the moth consumed by a source of light, the artist is credited with granting them "immortality" (l. 50) through his prints. As in the opening lines of the poem, the final stanza describes his numerous prints as leaves and petals swaying in the breeze. The artist passes his works "into the reverent hands of keepers" (l. 52), but at the same time he returns to his endeavor to understand things through visual scrutiny. What exactly he scrutinizes in the closing lines remains a secret. Is it one of his drawings, or is it an idea for a new work of art? Although the poem does not deny the social power structures when it comes to gender relations at the time in which Utamaro produced his works, it does not completely objectify the female models. Instead it includes at least some stirrings of human emotion and life, albeit only those which underscore the sadness underlying the functionalization of female models as vehicles of aesthetic appeal.

As a Hawai'ian-born woman with Korean and Chinese ancestry who has also lived on the U.S. mainland, Song is situated among the ethnic poets who are anything but enamored with ethnic classifications of artists. One could argue that choosing to write a poem about a Japanese painter and his works entails the risk of implying that some kind of pan-Asian cultural identity may exist. But Song's poem transcends the issue of ethnic stereotyping because its thematic focus resides in depictions of an artist, his models, and acts of perception. Thus, I would encourage students to discuss this poem as a commentary on the possibilities and limits of art. Although Song has been characterized as a writer using mainstream techniques—and this poem is hardly experimental in form—it is worth considering the questions engendered by this poem in light of the postmodern crisis of representation. In what ways does this poem encourage readers not to accept *ekphrastic* details as givens but rather to probe more deeply into the historical dimensions of representational politics? How does the poem mirror the reader's normative perception of otherness? Such questions not only help students avoid the traps of reading poems by ethnic writers as if they were unmediated acts of documenting their psyche and their experience as representatives of a larger group, but also stress the centrality of the reader-interpreter in making sense of a textual construct.

3. Theresa Hak Kyung Cha's "Edward Hopper's Western Motel, 1957" and the Indeterminate Gaze

Born in South Korea in 1951, Theresa Hak Kyung Cha came to Hawai'i in 1962, where she lived with her family for two years before relocating to northern California. She studied at the University of California, Berkeley. After further studies in Paris, she returned to the U.S. West Coast. She is particularly known for her experimental novel *Dictee* (1982) and her multimedia performance art. Shortly after the publication of her novel, she was raped and murdered by a serial rapist in New York City.

The title of her 1981 poem "Edward Hopper's Western Motel, 1957" obviously invites the reader to view the eponymous painting alongside the poem. The *ekphrastic* element in Cha's poem verbalizes both the tension between the seemingly photographic quality of Hopper's style and his paintings' subtexts. He integrates multiple paradoxes into his images to make them initially appear straightforward, but then nurture doubts about their ostensibly unequivocal meanings. Most centrally, stasis and motion as perceived in "Western Motel, 1957" and diametrically opposed readings of what the painting depicts undermine any sense of epistemological security. This poem situates Cha within an experimental poetic mode that questions the nature of representation and perception through an intermedial attempt to determine—what? Meaning? Reality? The poem certainly denies the possibility of *ekphrasis* as simplistically focusing on the 'what'; it rather challenges readers to contemplate potentially unpleasant thoughts about the 'how' of perception and understanding. As a result, uncovering the process of perception reveals mechanisms of constructing meaning and thus demonstrates the multiplicity of meanings based on subjectivity.

The two opening lines question the subjecthood of the woman sitting on the bed in the painted coastal motel room: "If she be she / She be her" (ll. 1-2). The grammatical impossibilities of "be" instead of an inflected verb form (l. 1) and the confusing subject-object relation between "She" and "her" (l. 2) remain unsolved. Instead, the persona imagines the painting as if it were a film, transforming the static visual into something that is absurdly "On the image track / Moving across immobile" (ll. 3-4). As it is unclear whether the "image track" refers to the perceiver's eyes surveying the painting or whether the painting is imagined as contradictorily "Moving" while it is "immobile," the poem introduces the back and forth between object and viewer, between the what on the canvas and the how of taking it in and processing it cognitively. Cha may have wanted to evoke Hopper's life-long interest in the cinema as well as the frequent association critics have pointed out between his paintings and movie stills. In this sense, the motion of surveying the motel room scene could be caught in a still taken from a tracking or dolly shot, a technique dating back to the 1910s.

The female figure is hard to interpret because we cannot know whether she has just arrived or is about to depart (cf. ll. 8-9). As in a Puritan sermon that branches off into arguments and sub-arguments, the lyrical I then continues to contemplate how a viewer might imagine the woman's next move, depending on whether she has just sat down or is about to get up (cf. ll. 11-3). This triggers a reflection on the locale: "Such rooms / Were it motel hotel predestined tran-science" (ll. 14-5). Not only does the persona undermine Hopper's motel refer-ence by adding the internal rhyme with "hotel," but the persona also grandiosely juxtaposes the usually goal-oriented concept of predestination with a strangely misspelled reference to ephemerality ("transcience" instead of "transience"), which may be a pun that contrasts religious with scientific worldviews.

Further contrasts and contradictions follow: progressive unidirectional movement versus circularity, movement versus stasis, light versus shadow (ll. 16-20). Then the speaker returns to the woman in the painting, hypothetically imagining twice "If she be I" (l. 22, 24) and describing this experience of merging with Hopper's fictional woman in terms that repeat the contradictions and dichotomies of previous lines ("yes and no," l. 22; "knowing not knowing," l. 24; "Leave or stay," l. 25). More importantly, becoming the woman in the painting creates awareness of being looked at ("the gaze waiting," l. 22) and, because this merging unites the viewer and the viewed, creates movement that transcends the restrictiveness of the frame: "Came and went enters the frame like / As if only to remain in like / Anonymous / All the others before / Hence" (ll. 28-32).

The syntactic indeterminacy of these lines, which recalls e. e. cummings's poems, contributes to the open ending of the text. Not only is the poem devoid of any punctuation marks whatsoever, but the final lines evoke the notion of multi-ple nameless women who, like motel/hotel guests using the same premises, un-ceasingly enter and leave. The contrast between "before" and "Hence" strikes me as particularly humorous because one can read it in terms of chronology ('up to now' versus 'as of then') and in terms of a teasingly promising, yet unfulfilled "Hence" (in the sense of 'therefore') that hints at an explanation that is never pro-vided. As "hence" can also mean 'from here,' the word incorporates a spatial com-ponent that propels the painting and the poem into complex realms of space and time rather than retaining the flatness of painted canvas and printed words.

Cha's experimentation serves as a good example of Asian American poets who participate in American postmodernist poetic endeavors and who do so by connecting their own work with American art traditions, in this case, the poetry of e. e. cummings and the paintings of Edward Hopper. Hopper's work has in-spired myriad poets in the U.S. and abroad, including Joyce Carol Oates, James Hoggard, Edward Hirsch, John Updike, and the Catalan poet Ernest Farrés. As a painter of modern urban existence with its striking interiors featuring solitary figures or small groups not engaged in communication, Hopper provided visual blueprints for poetry concerned with the human condition in the twentieth cen-tury. "Western Motel," a painting from his late period, takes up a contemporary trend of the 1950s: the construction of motels in the American West, as well as the American propensity to travel by car as indicated by the automobile seen through the window of the motel room. More importantly for Cha's poem, "West-ern Motel" is said to be Hopper's only painting in which the subject makes direct eye contact with the beholder.

Cha's poem focuses on the activity of looking and probes into the ways in which one may try to derive meaning from one's perceptions of someone else's artistic renderings of what may, in turn, be perceptions themselves. The poem addresses the impression of cold anonymity found in the treacherous surface realism (or "New Realism") of Hopper's depictions of individuals in impersonal

environments. By including the lyrical I as the owner of the gaze, and by tres-
passing across the line between viewer and viewed, Cha's poem participates in
artistic experiments aimed at reevaluating the relationship between works of art
and their viewers, readers, and respondents in the widest sense. At the same
time, the fact that a woman—who is situated inside a room, possibly waiting for
her male partner who may have driven their vehicle—gazes directly at the viewer
puts emphasis on the theme of seeing and being seen. The painting's similarity
to a travel brochure advertisement finds its echo in the closing of Cha's poem,
making the woman a generic female traveler and, possibly, a generic woman of
the 1950s who fulfils the role of a passive beauty waiting for someone to carry
her bags and drive the car—although her direct and bold eye contact with the
beholder somewhat challenges this cliché.

Cha's use of stylistic features reminiscent of e. e. cummings's work is particularly fitting because cummings, as he expressed in his Harvard lectures of
1953, despised the generic features of advertisements and the spectacle of television and rather favored individuality in flux; in his poems he also endeavored
to focus on processes of becoming and learning rather than on anything fixed,
prefabricated, or expressive of common sense. Consequently, cummings's style
of indeterminacy and fluidity in itself contributes to exploring the subtext of
Hopper's seemingly static painting. Cha thus links her lyrical reflections on perception and understanding with two iconic twentieth-century American artists
whose works defy superficial or simple interpretations.

4. Conclusion

Selecting two poems to 'represent' Asian American poetry is as heartbreakingly
difficult as defining 'Asian American' and its implications. Nevertheless, it is
necessary to make students aware of poets and poetic traditions that may go
unnoticed unless they are presented with certain labels attached. As discussions of racism frequently dwell on visual perception—on the viewer and the
viewed, the one who sets a normative frame and the one framed within its
limits—poems that address visual perception can encourage students to consider how verbalized images allow us to contemplate the ways in which our perceptions are guided, influenced, or even determined through often discriminatory
ways of seeing and understanding.

The comparative study of two *ekphrastic* poems, one focused on an eighteenth-century Japanese visual art tradition and the other on a painting by a
twentieth-century Anglo American, demonstrates the centrality of the politics of
depicting and seeing. It also allows students to reflect on the facts that an
author's ethnic origin does not and must not necessarily determine the choice of
subject matter, and that poets may or may not see themselves as spokespersons
of their ethnic group(s)—whatever the concrete consequences of (not) being emblematic for a specific segment of the world's population may imply.

Cathy Song's "Beauty and Sadness" is not a poem focused on one particular
painting; it refers to an artist's entire œuvre. The speaker thus encourages us to
contemplate how the semiotic system at work in Utamaro's visuals evokes emblematic views on gender and ethnicity. While one can argue that interpreting
Song's poem may require knowledge of this particular Japanese art tradition,
another consideration may even override the necessity of such multidisciplinary

knowledge. I wholeheartedly agree with Werner Wolf, who points out that intermediality research carried out by trained literary scholars runs the risk of dilettantism if the literary scholar does not possess academic training in the discipline linked to the non-literary medium (cf. 2011: 3). But if one disregarded Japanese art history for a moment, one could argue that within the American context it is more crucial to convey that interpreting Song's poem requires awareness of how the kind of Japanese art represented in the text has been part of Orientalist views and reception contexts in the Western world. Even if we know nothing about the implications of Utamaro's works from an art-historical vantage point sensitive to Japanese cultural history, we can and should learn how nineteenth- and twentieth-century America responded to Japanese art and projected Westernized readings into this art at a time when the Japanese were discriminated against by anti-immigration and anti-naturalization laws.

As Valerie Robillard points out, interpreting *ekphrastic* poems requires consideration of the viewing mechanisms that are current in specific cultural contexts (see 2002). The realization that these viewing mechanisms—the methods with which viewers derive meaning from the semiotic code of a painting—keep changing confirms my concern with the reference to Utamaro's prints within the essentialist viewing traditions of Western eyes perceiving Asian art and, through it, Asian people. In this context, students can benefit from looking at images of early 20th-century Americans indulging in fashion statements such as the temporary craze for Japanese kimonos—a craze which, of course, does not acknowledge illicit pleasures associated with kimono-wearers like the teahouse waitresses and courtesans of Utamaro's woodprints (see, for instance, photographs of the American philanthropist and reformer Margaret "Molly" Brown available in the digital collection on the Library of Congress website). Another source of visuals portraying ethnic and gender stereotypes is the Library of Congress's online American sheet music collection.

Reading Song's intermedial reference within the context of American cultural transformations of Asian culture, in particular the popularity of Asian artifacts and their significance within the stereotypization and exoticization of Asian Americans, allows us to functionalize the paintings as markers of commercially promoted dilettantism when it comes to dealing with ethnicity. Song's intermedial reference to Japanese art thus becomes an emblem for the problematic umbrella terms that lump diverse cultures under categories such as "Asian American." A cultural studies-informed perspective on this intermedial text opens the possibility of interpreting the poem as arguing for the need to transcend ethnic labels and to reject the expectation that Asian American authors write ethnographic poems.

As shown, Cha's poem does not include anything identifiably Asian. The poem's participation in poetic experiments that reflect on the perceiver and the perceived, on subjecthood and objecthood as contemplated in the postmodern era, strikes me as a notable example of how authors categorized as 'ethnic' ignore specific national or larger ethnic markers that set them apart from the mainstream. Three decades before scholarly literature on Asian American poetry takes up this issue, Cha's poem showcases an oscillation between subject positions and thus denies fixed perspectives. Her poem is firmly rooted in the verbal and visual discourse of twentieth-century American culture. The ambiguity of Cha's poem comes across forcefully because, first, Hopper's painting has been associated with a double-edged New Realism that seems concrete at first sight but then crumbles because of its indeterminacies. Second, Cha's use of stylistic features associated with a poet like e. e. cummings, who frequently did his best to subvert cemented ideas about humankind's features and desires, emphasizes on the verbal level that perception is fluid, versatile, erratic, and not prone to result in intersubjectively shared interpretations.

Song and Cha rely on their readers' knowledge of American traditions of artistic production and reception. Both poems emphasize not only the centrality but also the ephemerality and unreliability of perception. Although Song provides images of ethnicity and femininity, her poem ultimately deals with the interplay between the artist's eye and what he beholds and then creatively transforms into art. In this sense, both Song and Cha contemplate the implications of seeing and being seen, albeit through different visual and verbal means. When considering these two poems as examples of an illimitable mass of writings by poets of Asian American descent, it becomes clear that the authors participate in American poetic traditions whether or not they evoke Asian America.

Bibliography

Selected Primary Literature

Banerjee, Neelanjana et al. (eds.). 2010. *Indivisible: An Anthology of Contemporary South Asian American Poetry.* Fayetteville: U of Arkansas P.
Cha, Theresa Hak Kyung. 1981. "Edward Hopper's Western Motel, 1957." In: Walter K. Lew (ed.), *Premonitions: The Kaya Anthology of New Asian North American Poetry.* New York: Kaya Production. 232.
——. 2001 [1982]. *Dictee.* Berkeley: U of California P.
Chang, Juliana (ed.). 1996. *Quiet Fire: A Historical Anthology of Asian American Poetry, 1892-1970.* New York: Asian American Writers' Workshop/Rutgers UP.
Chang, Victoria M. (ed.). 2004. *Asian American Poetry: The Next Generation.* Urbana: U of Illinois P.
Hongo, Garrett K. 1993. *The Open Boat: Poems from Asian America.* New York: Anchor Books Doubleday.
Lew, Walter K. (ed.) 1981. *Premonitions: The Kaya Anthology of New Asian North American Poetry.* New York: Kaya Production.
Lim, Shirley Geok-Lin et al. (eds.) 1989. *The Forbidden Stitch: An Asian American Women's Anthology.* Corvallis, OR: Calyx.
Song, Cathy. 1983. *Picture Bride.* New Haven: Yale UP.
——. 1988. *Frameless Windows, Squares of Light.* New York: Norton.
——. 1994. *School Figures.* Pittsburgh: U of Pittsburgh P.
——. 2001. *The Land of Bliss.* Pittsburgh: U of Pittsburgh P.
——. 2007. *Cloud Moving Hands.* Pittsburgh: U of Pittsburgh P.
——. 2012 [1983]. "Beauty and Sadness." In: Baym et al. 2012. 1126-7.

Selected Secondary Literature

"Cathy Song." 1999. In: Lawrence J. Trudeau (ed.), *Asian American Literature: Reviews and Criticism of Works by American Writers of Asian Descent.* Detroit: Gale. 421-37.

    Good sourcebook on numerous authors (including Cathy Song) that students can consult when gathering basic information on poets and the way their works have been received by critics and scholars.

Chin, Frank et al. 2012 [1974]. "Preface and Introduction." In: Li 2012, I: 30-57. Repr. from: Frank Chin et al. (eds.), *Aiiieeeee! An Anthology of Asian-American Writers*. Washington, D.C.: Howard UP. vii-xvi, xxi-xlviii.

This text is a manifesto of a rather masculinist and cultural nationalist school of thought that has been at odds with those who approach Asian American poetry from feminist and/or postcolonial perspectives.

Huang, Guiyou. 2006. *The Columbia Guide to Asian American Literature Since 1945*. New York: Columbia UP.

Introductory essay on Asian American literary studies and encyclopedia-style entries on post-World War II authors (residing in the U.S. and Canada), their works, and the critical response. Section 5 (173-211) focuses on poetry.

Li, David Leiwei (ed.). 2012. *Asian American Literature*. Vols. I and III. London: Routledge.

This up-to-date essay collection comprises four volumes, two of which are relevant to studying Asian American poetry. Vol. I presents scholarship on "Literary History: Criticism and Theory"; vol. III is devoted to poetry.

Lowe, Lisa. 2012 [1991]. "Heterogeneity, Hybridity, Multiplicity: Marking Asian American Differences." In: Li 2012, I: 115-37. Repr. from: *Diaspora* 1.1: 24-44.

A seminal essay in the development of Asian American studies which should be discussed in conjunction with Chin et al. and more recent reflections on Asian American studies, such as Wong 1995 and excerpts from Yu 2009.

Park, Josephine Nock-Hee. 2008. *Apparitions of Asia: Modernist Form and Asian American Poetics*. Oxford: Oxford UP.

Park traces the development of invoking the East from Whitman through Fenollosa, Pound, and Snyder in order to subsequently discuss the development of Asian American poetry since the late 1960s.

Sumida, Stephen H. 2010. "Immigration, Diaspora, Transnationalism, and the Native—The Many-Mouthed Bird of Asian/Pacific American Literature in the Early Twenty-First Century." In: *EurAmerica* 40.2 (June): 359-92.

Sumida argues that scholars should not ignore the Pacific Islands within Asian/Pacific American Studies and details the possible consequences of assimilation-based, diaspora-focused, and U.S.-focused approaches to the field.

Yao, Steven G. 2010. *Foreign Accents: Chinese American Verse from Exclusion to Postethnicity*. Oxford: Oxford UP.

Yao discusses Ezra Pound's definition of 'Chineseness' and Chinese poems etched into the walls of Angel Island barracks. He then contextualizes works by contemporary poets Ha Jin, Li-Young Lee, Marilyn Chin, and John Yau.

Further References

Baym, Nina et al. 2012. *The Norton Anthology of American Literature*. Vol E. New York: Norton.

Cheung, King-Kok. 1997b. "Re-Viewing Asian American Literary Studies." In: Cheung 1997a. 1-36.

——. 2012 [1990]. "The Woman Warrior versus the Chinaman Pacific: Must a Chinese American Critic Choose between Feminism and Heroism?" In: Li 2012, I: 97-114. Repr. from: Marianne Hirsch and Evelyn Fox Keller (eds.), 1990. *Conflicts in Feminism*. New York: Routledge. 234-51.

—— (ed.). 1997a. *An Interethnic Companion to Asian American Literature*. Cambridge: Cambridge UP.

Hsiao, Irene C. 2012. "Broken Chord: Sounding Out the Ideogram in Marilyn Chin's *Rhapsody in Plain Yellow.*" In: *MELUS* 37.3 (Fall): 189-214.

Jeon, Joseph Jonghyun. 2012. *Racial Things, Racial Forms: Objecthood in Avant-Garde Asian American Poetry.* Iowa City: U of Iowa P.

Kim, Claire Jean. 2012 [1999]. "The Racial Triangulation of Asian Americans." In: Li 2012, I: 301-35. Repr. from: *Politics & Society* 27.1: 105-38.

Kim, Elaine H. 2012 [1982]. "Preface." In: Li 2012, I: 58-66. Repr. from: *Asian American Literature: An Introduction to the Writings and Their Social Context.* Philadelphia: Temple UP. xi-xix.

Li, David Leiwei. 1998. *Imagining the Nation. Asian American Literature and Cultural Consent.* Stanford: Stanford UP.

Mai, Xiwen. 2012. "'Continental Drift': Translation and Kimiko Hahn's Transcultural Poetry." In: *Journal of Transnational American Studies* 4.1. Web. 21 Feb. 2013.

Marx, Edward. 2012 [2006]. "A Slightly-Open Door: Yone Noguchi and the Invention of English Haiku." In: Li 2012, III: 25-42. Repr. from: *Genre* 39: 107-26.

Okihiro, Gary Y. 2012 [1994]. "Is Yellow Black or White?" In: Li 2012, I: 255-77. Repr. from: *Margins and Mainstreams: Asians in American History and Culture.* Seattle: U of Washington P. 31-63.

Palumbo-Liu, David. 2012 [2001]. "Modeling the Nation: The Asian/American Split." In: Li 2012, I: 223-38. Repr. from: Kandice Chuh and Karen Shimakawa (eds.), *Orientations: Mapping Studies in the Asian Diaspora.* Durham, NC: Duke UP. 213-27.

Robillard, Valerie K. 2002. "On the Virtue of Hindsight: William Carlos Williams and the Abstract Expressionists." In: Erik Redling and Ulla-Britta Lagerroth (eds.), *Cultural Functions of Intermedial Exploration.* Amsterdam: Rodopi. 135-47.

Rody, Caroline. 2012 [2009]. "The Interethnic Paradigm and the Case of Asian American Fiction." In: Li 2012, I: 465-500. Repr. from: *The Interethnic Imagination: Roots and Passages in Contemporary Asian American Fiction.* New York: Oxford UP. 17-46.

Tunc, Tanfer Emin et al. 2012. "Special Forum: Redefining the American in Asian American Studies: Transnationalism, Diaspora, and Representation." In: *Journal of Transnational American Studies* 4.1. Web. 21 Feb. 2013.

Wolf, Werner. 2011. "(Inter)mediality and the Study of Literature." In: *CLCWeb: Comparative Literature and Culture* 13.3: 1-9. Web. 15 May 2013.

Wong, Sau-Ling C. 2012 [1995]. "Denationalization Reconsidered: Asian American Cultural Criticism at a Theoretical Crossroads." In: Li 2012, I: 138-59. Repr. from: *Amerasia Journal* 21.1/2: 1-27.

——. 1997. "Chinese American Literature." In: Cheung 1997a. 39-61.

Yao, Steven G. 2012 [2008]. "Transplantation and Modernity: The Chinese/American Poems of Angel Island." In: Li 2012, III: 1-24. Repr. from: Eric Hayot et al. (eds.), *Sinographies: Writing China.* Minneapolis: U of Minnesota P. 300-29.

Yogi, Stan. 1997. "Japanese American Literature." In: Cheung 1997a. 125-55.

Yu, Timothy. 2009. *Race and the Avant-Garde: Experimental and Asian American Poetry since 1965.* Palo Alto, CA: Stanford UP.

——. 2011. "Asian American Poetry in the First Decade of the 2000s." In: *Contemporary Literature* 52.4: 818-51.

Zhou, Xiaojing. 2006. *The Ethics and Poetics of Alterity in Asian American Poetry.* Iowa City: U of Iowa P.

29

Chicano/a Poetry

Rodolfo "Corky" Gonzales's *I am Joaquín/ Yo Soy Joaquín*
and Lorna Dee Cervantes's "Beneath the Shadow of the Freeway"

Astrid M. Fellner

1. Introduction: The Development of Chicano/a Poetry

With the flowering of the Chicano Movement in the mid-1960s, which brought
about an increased political awareness for many Mexican Americans, a body of
creative writing emerged on the literary scene. Initially poetry was "the chosen
form of expression" (Sánchez 1985: 17) because it met the needs for cultural
representation of the Chicano/a community. At a time when minority voices were
making themselves heard, poetry was a form of communication that built on the
popular oral tradition of Chicano/a culture as well as the Anglo poetics of the
Beats, the poets of the San Francisco Renaissance, and the New York poets. The
change in the style of writing poetry and the performative importance of public
poetry readings in the post-war period also fostered the literary creativity of cultural minorities (cf. ibid.: 18-9). Although there had been a long tradition of
poetry and oral ballads (*corridos*) dating back to the Spanish colonial era and
the period after the 1848 annexation of Mexican land by the United States,
which marked the beginning of the richly hybrid Mexican-American culture, it
was the political turmoil of the 1960s that inspired a new wave of writings. Despite its many internal disputes, the Chicano Movement was legitimized as a
unifying phenomenon, creating an oppositional consciousness against the dominant Anglo social order, which was expressed in artistic creations. The use of
the term 'Chicano,' which signifies both a specific ethnic as well as political
identity, stems from this period and gained popularity through the great variety
of performative practices. Most probably deriving from the sixteenth-century
pronunciation of *mexicano* as *meschicano*, which with the dropping of the *mes*
becomes *chicano*, the term underwent a shift in meaning from indicating a lower-
class Mexican to describing the hybrid identity of someone of mixed Spanish,
Indian, and Anglo descent. Referring to persons of Mexican descent residing in
the United States, this term is often used interchangeably with the less political
ethnic label "Mexican American." The term 'Chicano/a' is generally used as a
critical term to refer to literary production and is used within academic institutions to signal cultural affirmation and a critical stance toward Anglo-American
culture (cf. Pérez-Torres 1995: 19).

The "Chicano Renaissance," a concept coined by Philip Ortego in 1971,
gained its force and impetus from the civil rights movements and comprised a
series of art forms, many of which were created to strengthen the social and
political objectives of *El Movimiento*. Luis Valdez's formation of the Teatro
Campesino in Delano, California in support of César Chávez's United Farm
Workers Union in 1965 was one of the milestones in this flowering of the arts.
Poetry proved a powerful and passionate expression for social protest, and poems and songs were performed during the early years of the Chicano Movement.
The priorities of Movement poetry were clear: accessible language, bilingualism

and interlingualism, concrete imagery, a driving rhythm to highlight the performative quality of the work, and a linking of the personal experience of the poetic self to the social and the larger political cause. Grounding the oppositional struggle in the postulation of the mythic homeland *Aztlán*, Movement poetry is characterized by identification with the pre-Columbian indigenous past and the times of the Mexican Revolution, the glorification of heroic male role models, and female icons like the Virgen de Guadalupe. The concept of *la raza*, which was adopted from José Vasconcelos's concept of "cosmic race" to refer to the pluralistic heritage of the mestizo identity of Chicanos/as, also became an important feature in the conceptualization of Chicano/a identity during that time.

This period was noteworthy for the emergence of bilingual Spanish/English publications such as the landmark periodicals *Aztlán* (1967-present) and *El Grito* (1967-1974) and a series of alternative presses, all of which served as powerful outlets for emerging Chicano/a voices. Like Charles Olson and the *Black Mountain Review*, the founding editors of *El Grito*, Octavio Romano-V. and Nick Vaca, solicited hitherto unpublished writers and insisted on experimenting with poetic forms such as bilingual poetry before code-switching became recognized as a legitimate poetic form for Chicano/a writers (cf. Candelaria 1986: xii). Poets such as Abelardo ("Lalo") Delgado (1930-2004), Raymundo ("Tigre") Pérez (b. 1946), the early Sergio Elizondo (b. 1930), Alurista (b. 1947), José Montoya (1932-2013), Ricardo Sánchez (1941-1995), and Tino Villanueva (b. 1941) served as bardic spokesmen for the Chicano Movement and this first flourishing period of poetry.

In the early phase of the Chicano Movement, poetry, as Sánchez views it, fulfilled a similar communal role as the *corrido* of earlier decades in the Mexican Southwest (cf. 1985: 17). According to folklorist Américo Paredes, the *corrido* developed on the Lower Rio Grande Border Region and was influenced by border conflict and the cultural clash between Mexicans and Anglos (cf. 1958: 103-4). Recounting the exploits of a hero who surpasses all odds to prevail against those in power, the border ballad follows a strict stanzaic structure and rhyme scheme and is usually accompanied by a guitar. As a cultural poetic form that was brought to Mexico by the Spanish *conquistadores* and is related to the Spanish medieval *romance*, the *corrido* is generally seen as a precursor to many strains of contemporary Chicano/a literature. In his *Mexican Ballads, Chicano Poems*, José Limón argues that rather than being an antecedent to contemporary Chicano/a poetry, the Mexican *corrido* is a "master poem that, as key symbolic action, powerfully dominates and conditions the later written poetry" (1992: 2). Similarly, José David Saldívar establishes the cultural poetic form of the *corrido* as the most important sociopoetic Chicano paradigm (cf. 1986: 13) which functions as a social text that draws on the deepest levels of the political unconscious (cf. ibid.: 12). The argument that the *corrido* is a master poem serving as the paradigmatic form for all later Chicano texts can, however, also been seen as problematic as it posits this border ballad as the 'essential' folk base of the Mexican-American community. Furthermore, the heroic tradition of the *corrido* is a male form that perpetuates patriarchy, which accounts for the predominantly male-centered themes of many Chicano texts.

The gendered voice of the *corrido* was initially marginalized by the Chicano Movement when issues of racial discrimination and cultural nationalism took precedence over those of gender and sexuality. In 1973 an entire issue of *El Grito* (edited by Estela Portillo) was devoted to the creative expression of Chicanas. Angela de Hoyos (1940-2009) was one of the few Chicana voices whose collections

Arise Chicano! and Other Poems (1975) and *Chicano Poems: For the Barrio* (1975) contained social protest poetry that dealt with social and political issues concerning the plight of Chicanos/as living in an Anglo-dominated society. Bernice Zamora (b. 1938) is another woman poet who collected her writings between 1966 and 1976 in a book she titled *Restless Serpents* (1976), "a feminist manifesto written in thoughtfully crafted poems that proved instantly that Chicanas could write as well as, if not better than, Chicanos" (Bruce-Novoa 1990: 86). The success of Chicana poets in the 1960s and 1970s clearly paved the way for the vast output of Chicana novels in the following decades. Since the 1980s, most major Chicana writers have also published poetry, among them Sandra Cisneros, Ana Castillo, Alma Luz Villanueva, Gloria Anzaldúa, and Cherríe Moraga.

The markers *o/a* in the term Chicano/a reinscribe the female presence to the non-gendered 'Mexican American,' drawing attention to the exclusionary practices of the term 'Chicano' and the patriarchal character of much of Chicano literature. With its focus on the centrality of family, the communal cohesion of the *barrio* (neighborhood), and the concept of *carnalismo* (brotherhood), most Chicano Movement poetry was committed to a depiction of cultural conflict, yet it failed to give a critical examination of the patriarchal forces within Chicano culture. When Chicana women expressed their own sense of a lack of representation and inclusion in the Chicano literary canon, they were initially accused of being traitors. Their poetry was pejoratively called "adobe poetry" or "tortilla poetry" (Rebolledo 1985: 143). Lorna Dee Cervantes's poem "You Cramp My Style, Baby" can be seen as an early example of a Chicana writer who directly confronts the sexism in Chicano men, voicing her rage and bitterness at the exclusionary practices of the Chicano Movement:

> You cramp my style, baby
> When you roll on top of me
> Shouting, "Viva La Raza"
> At the top of your prick (1977: 39)

Criticizing the devaluation of women as social activists in the Movement, this poem shows how men sexualize women, 'conquering' them for the sake of the revolution. Many Chicano poems focus on hard-working, long-suffering, tired women who endure hardships and make sacrifices for their families. For instance, José Montoya's poem "La Jefita" (1972) idealizes this kind of stereotype of the loving, self-sacrificing Chicana wife and mother. "La jefita" (the dear little mother) works in the house all day and never rests and, as the husband says at the end of the poem, complains only in her sleep. Chicana poets, however, assert the positive difference of the female as an ethnic subject. They give voice to their vision of women as active, dynamic subjects, challenging the stereotypical view of 'the Chicana' as the 'docile, submissive and passive woman' who accepts her insignificant and subordinate position in the household.

Chicano/a culture is rich in oral tradition, popular beliefs, and folklore, and the stereotype of the passive and submissive woman has been long in the making. Three major cultural poetic figures can be identified that have helped construct Chicana cultural identity: La Malinche, La Llorona, and La Virgen de Guadalupe. These figures have essentialized Chicana identity into the binary categories of woman as either goddess/virgin or traitor/whore. La Malinche, or Malintzin to use her indigenous name, is the most controversial cultural poetic figure. As a historical person Malintzin Tenepal is the Indian woman who helped

Cortés to subjugate the Aztec people. Her name has since become identified with conquest. The portrayal of Malinche as a betrayer of her own people in Mexican as well as Chicano writings has come to serve as legitimation for the view of all Mexican women as traitresses. Very close to La Malinche is the figure of La Llorona, the weeping woman, a distinct relative of the Medea story, who, as legend has it, drowned her own children to elope with a lover and was therefore cursed by God to search permanently for them. She is said to appear near water, and especially young children fear the vision, for La Llorona might snatch them. Another negative mother image that has become an important figure in literature is La Virgen de Guadalupe, the Virgin Mary, who appeared to the Indian Juan Diego in 1531. Chicana writers' responses to these three mythical figures have been very complex. Feminist writers in particular have tried to demythologize these figures by showing their active, strong, and positive qualities, and the amended symbols of La Virgen, La Malinche, and La Llorona have become important sources of symbolic empowerment for Chicanas (cf. Fellner 2002: 12-5).

The two poems chosen for discussion here represent two different periods in Chicano/a poetry. In 1967—during the height of the Chicano Movement—Rodolfo "Corky" Gonzales, founder of the Denver-based civil rights organization The Crusade for Justice, published the epic poem *I Am Joaquín/Yo Soy Joaquín*, which was supposed to promote Chicano nationalism and self-determination. Lorna Dee Cervantes's poem "Beneath the Shadow of a Freeway," which appeared in her poetry collection *Emplumada* in 1981, is an example of a feminist poem that has moved away from the type of oppositional poetry against social and gender oppression to a more personal reflection on identity.

2. Rodolfo "Corky" Gonzales's *I Am Joaquín/Yo Soy Joaquín* (1967) and the Nationalist Paradigm of Chicano Identity

I am Joaquín is probably "the most famous of all Chicano poems" (Candelaria 1986: 42). Before its publication by Bantam Books in 1972, *I am Joaquín* was published in early 1967 as a leaflet, which was distributed and recited as a form of agitprop at rallies during the height of the Chicano Movement. Its full title was: *Soy Joaquín; an Epic Poem. With a Chronology of People and Events in Mexican and Mexican American History*. By early spring this epic poem had already been adapted to film by the Teatro Campesino. The poem was mimeographed and widely circulated, laying the foundation for all Chicano/a poetry to come. This consciousness-raising piece of literature served as the starting point of the 'Chicano Literary Renaissance' in that it not only generated a collective sense of identity that triggered future Chicano literary expression, it also created a historical consciousness, drawing attention to the long history of Chicanos in the Americas. Through this poem Chicano literature began its awakening and the whole history of Chicanos/as from the 1600s to the 1960s retroactively came into being. The poem, as George Hartley argues, serves as "the founding literary work for all previous Chicano literature" (2003: 276).

Corky Gonzales was born in Denver in 1928 to a migrant-worker family, founded The Crusade for Justice in 1966, and was the organizer of the Youth Liberation Conference in Denver, Colorado, a gathering that produced the 1969 *Plan Espiritual de Aztlán* (Spiritual Plan of *Aztlán*) and established the concept of *Aztlán*, located in the American Southwest, as a national homeland. *Aztlán*, ostensibly the mythical home of the Aztecs, tied Chicano identity to pre-Columbian roots. As an early figure of the movement for the equal rights of Chicanos, Gonzales was a boxer, an activist, and a politician. *I am Joaquín* is a performative piece that, albeit written in simple style and accessible language, produces artistic experience through its skillful combination of theme and structure. Evoking the oral tradition, it relies on repetition to ensure the listener's attention. Its content is relatively simple, and Juan Bruce-Novoa explains how "Mexican popular lore—including its commonest clichés—is utilized. Images, like Cuauhtémoc, Nezahualcoyotl, Cortés, the materialistic and cruel Spaniard, the long-suffering Indian, Madero, Díaz, Huerta, Zapata, Juárez, Villa, the Virgin of Guadalupe appear, with their standard signification within Mexican nationalism and popular tradition" (1982: 47). Structurally the poem is straightforward, representing the construction of identity in the form of a journey from the present to the past and back to the present. The epic quality of the poem comes from the detailed depiction of the journey of the 'Chicano Everyman' Joaquín into the world of pre-Columbian Meso-America and the many contradictions of the Chicano heritage. *I am Joaquín* has been called the "contemporary Chicano/a *ur-text*" (Neate 1998: 117) as the poem constitutes a rewriting of history, voicing the heterogeneity of the community. In his introduction to the 1972 edition of the poem, Gonzales summarizes the theme and structure of *I am Joaquín*:

> Writing *I Am Joaquín* was a journey back through history, a painful self-evaluation, a wandering search for my peoples, and most of all, for my identity. The totality of all social inequities and injustices had to come to the surface. All the while, the truth about our own flaws—the villains and the heroes had to ride together—in order to draw an honest, clear conclusion of who we were, who we are, and where we are going. (1972: 1)

Bruce-Novoa views the structure of *I Am Joaquín* as a continual dialectical movement from the present to the past and back to a more enriched and complicated present. He divides the poem into three sections: the poem begins with a lament and retreat into the people, *la raza* (ll. 1-37); the second section details the development of Mexican *mestizo* culture and effects a dialectical transformation of Mexican Americans through the interplay of past and present (ll. 38-462); the third section (ll. 463-502) constitutes the declaration of a new revolutionary identity—the Chicano—which will transform the future (cf. 1982: 50-68). The title line "I am Joaquín" appears five times in the poem, and the 'I' functions as the symbolic unity of the people. Much like the self of Walt Whitman's "Song of Myself," the 'I' in this poem is a collective self.

> I am Joaquín,
> lost in a world of confusion,
> caught up in the whirl of a
>   gringo society,
> confused by the rules,
> scorned by attitudes,
> suppressed by manipulation,
> and destroyed by modern society.
> (1972 [1967]: 6, ll. 1-8)

Following the conventions of the epic, *I am Joaquín* begins in medias res with the speaker stating the theme, but the poem "modifies the epic heroic model" (Candelaria 1986: 44). Contrary to El Cid, for example, Joaquín is an Everyman figure who represents his people and who also has to battle an enemy within his community, as he must come to terms with the socio-historical contradictions within Chicano history. The speaker is lost, caught up, confused, scorned, and ultimately destroyed by the oppressive, alienating, and racist structures of modern Anglo America. The speaker goes on to say: "My fathers / have lost the economic battle / and won / the struggle of cultural survival" (1972 [1967]: 6, ll. 9-12). The invocation of the fathers signals the poem's movement between present and past and the construction of a heritage that will ground the speaker's identity and, as such, provide refuge from the whirl of a gringo society. The name Joaquín is not chosen accidentally; it evokes the figure of Joaquín Murrieta, a legendary bandit of the California gold-rush days who was wrongfully driven from his land and became a fearsome outlaw. Joaquín Murrieta became a famous *corrido* hero, and Gonzales's poem honors him by evoking his name. The poem, however, does not deal with Murrieta, although, as José Limón has it, there are several "resemblances between Gonzales's self-stylized epic poem and the precursory corrido tradition" (1992: 116).

Gonzales's hero is caught in a paradox. His main dilemma is induced by the forced choice "between / the paradox of / victory of the spirit, / despite physical hunger, / or / to exist in the grasp / of American social neurosis, / sterilization of the soul / and a full stomach" (1972 [1967]: 9, ll. 15-23). Not only does the protagonist feel "unwillingly dragged" (ibid.: 10, l. 26), but the process of deculturation inherent in modernization and progress is coupled with "Anglo success" (ibid.:10, l. 30), which recalls the earlier reference to "gringo society." In order to overcome such a conundrum, the speaker must turn to his age-old cultural legacy for spiritual empowerment. He thus takes refuge in his community: "I withdraw to the safety within the / circle of life— / MY OWN PEOPLE" (1972: 12, ll. 35-7, original emphasis). The speaker's withdrawal into community is crucial for the development of Chicano cultural identity; without this historical continuity, the Chicano/a can easily lose the connection with traditions and customs. Joaquín's lineage is, however, conspicuous in that it begins with miscegenation and cultural hybridity. Initiating a narrative in which the *mestizo* Mexican nation, and therefore also Chicanos, are envisaged as the descendants of the hybrid offspring of the Mayas and Aztecs as well as Hernán Cortés, the speaker not only complicates any claims to cultural purity but also draws the attention to the violent history in which the Chicano is "both tyrant and slave" (ibid.: 19, l. 63).

> I am Cuauhtémoc,
> proud and noble
>   leader of men,
> king of an empire,
> civilized beyond the dreams
>   of the gachupín Cortés,
> who is also the blood,
>   the image of myself. (ibid.: 16, ll. 38-45)

Tracing a tradition constituted by racially hybrid existentiality or *mestizaje*, Gonzales's epic poem thus "identifies a dialectical Chicano/a experience" (Neate 1998: 118). By beginning the historical survey with the figure of Cuauhtémoc— the famous Aztec ruler who was known for resisting Spanish conquest— Gonzales grounds Chicano history in a culture of resistance. But the problematic figure of Cortés is also part of the speaker's legacy. And although the derogatory term "gachupín" (a term used for a Spanish settler in America who immigrated from Spain) establishes some distance from the Spanish *conquistador*, Joaquín is nonetheless compelled to include "the sword and flame" (1972 [1967]: 16, l. 49) of the conqueror who sacrificed his "Indian sweat and blood" (ibid.: 19, l. 57) while he "ruled with tyranny over man" (ibid.: l. 59). As the product of imperial conquest, Joaquín is both Indian slave and Spanish master. It is this genealogy that allows him to claim "THE GROUND WAS MINE" (ibid.: l. 62, original emphasis), and this "appropriation of land as a spatialization of identity—that is, as a space through which identity is both defined and reaffirmed—is crucial to the founding of *Aztlán* as the lost homeland of modern Chicana/os" (Gallego 2011: 55).

What follows is the enumeration of famous figures (among them Pancho Villa, Emiliano Zapata, Francisco Madero, and Benito Juárez), key moments of the Spanish colonial period, and Mexican history. The beginning of the Chicano era in this historical overview occurs with the signing of the Treaty of Guadalupe Hidalgo in 1848, which formalized the loss of Mexican territory to the United States:

> equality is but a word—
>   the Treaty of Hidalgo has been broken
> and is but another treacherous promise.
> My land is lost
>   and stolen,
> My culture has been raped. (1972 [1967]: 66, ll. 349-54)

As Joaquín is divided between different lineages, he "is at least able to establish a consistent relationship to the land via proprietorship, even if this claim ideologically reinforces a status quo mentality" (Gallego 2011: 55). The invocation of history and his descriptions of idealized moments of pre-Columbian and Mexican cultural and political development serve "to reinforce his subjectivity, and as such do[es] not concern [themselves] with factual accuracy as much as heroic grandiosity and romanticized nationalism" (ibid.: 55-6).

Disregarding historical truth, the personae celebrated in the poem are presented as pious: "I am / faithful / humble / Juan Diego, / the Virgen de Guadalupe, / Tonantzin, Aztec Goddess, too" (1972 [1967]: 42, ll. 213-8). "The inclusion of the popular religious myth surrounding the apparition of the Virgin Mary to an indigenous Juan Diego Cuauhtlatoatzin reinforces the 'profound piety' of Chicano/a ancestry" (Gallego 2011: 56). This view, however, also reflects the sexism inherent in the poem. While the poem represents the history of the community as an exclusively male enterprise, women are relegated to traditional and subservient roles. They are "the black-shawled / faithful women / who die with me" (1972 [1967]: 42, ll. 208-10). As Candelaria observes: "From its title's masculine name through its scores of examples of 'great men' in *history*," the poem "presents a male, often chauvinistically macho, view of the Chicano world" (1986: 43, original emphasis). The references to women are anonymous with the exception of "the poet's allusion to the Virgin of Guadalupe and the Aztec goddess Tonantzín—that is, to mythical as opposed to historical figures of idealized femininity" (ibid.).

Gonzales's eclectic use of historical, religious, and mythopoetical elements contributes to his project of the creation of a national iconography and the nationalistic idealization of Chicano culture. While Joaquín feels lost at the begin-

ning of the poem, he has become conscious of his agency in the middle of the
poem. The poem's second half begins:

> I stand here looking back,
> and now I see
>   the present,
> and still
>   I am the campesino,
>   I am the fat political coyote (1972 [1967]: 51, ll. 251-6)

The poem, as Bruce-Novoa puts it, "has educated the I to see differently. Also,
placing the present moment at midpoint causes a pendulum effect of swinging
from past to future through Joaquín, the center of the historical process" (1982:
60). In the present, however, Joaquín remains a split person, which is graph-
ically represented "in the mutilation of the title line" (ibid.):

> I,
>
> of the same name,
>
>   Joaquín (1972 [1967]: 51, ll. 257-9)

Bruce-Novoa explains that the "chaotic lack of identity is attributed to living in a
country that has obliterated Joaquín's history and stifled his pride, imposing
inferiority on him" (1982: 60). The contradictory nature of Joaquín's identification can also be termed in what Gloria Anzaldúa refers to as *Mestizo* consciousness, the construction of an identity that performs as the hybrid embodiment of
historically opposed forces joined by blood in the sense of both lineage and of
destruction (cf. 1999 [1987]). The multiplicity of experiences is underlined in the
poem in terms of the recurring motif of the shedding and mixing of blood. As
Neate states: "The spilling of blood marks the presence of difference yet, through
the flow of blood, differences are linked in such a way as to bond the opposed
factions in the series of struggles enumerated" (1998: 118).

> I am Joaquín,
> who bleeds in many ways.
> The altars of Moctezuma
>   I stained a bloody red.
> My back of Indian slavery
>   was stripped crimson
> from the whips of masters
> who would lose their blood so pure
> when revolution made them pay,
> standing against the walls of
>   retribution.
>   Blood
>   has flowed from
>   me
> on every battlefield
>   between
> campesino, hacendado,
> slave and master
>   and
> revolution. (1972 [1967]: 54-6, ll. 286-305)

The poem, as Bruce-Novoa shows, indicates that the process of *mestizaje* can
only be achieved through the spilling of blood: "One must be willing to spill

blood—a ritual hierophany according to the poem—for the good of the people"
(1982: 49).

> My blood runs pure on the ice-caked
> hills of the Alaskan isles,
> on the corpse-strewn beach of Normandy,
> the foreign land of Korea
>   and now
>   Vietnam. (1972 [1967]: 62, ll. 327-32)

Rafael Pérez-Torres argues that the poem "stakes a claim for self-identity based on
selfless sacrifice; and the right to be 'Chicano' is validated by this history of sacrifice, which mixes the blood of the Chicano with the histories from which 'he'
arises" (1995: 71). The rest of the poem then expresses the "significance of
struggle and sacrifice as a means of achieving political ends" (ibid.).

Turning to the future, the speaker then says: "I am Joaquín. / I must fight /
and win this struggle / for my sons, and they / must know from me / who I am"
(1972 [1967]: 82, ll. 434-9). The key to survival, the poem declares at the end, is
endurance, perseverance, fortitude, and revolutionary faith. Conspicuously, the
term 'Chicano' is not used until the last section of the poem. Here it appears in
a list of terms, all of which, the speaker claims, refer to the politicized subject:

> La Raza!
> Méjicano!
> Español!
> Latino!
> Hispano!
> Chicano!
> or whatever I call myself (ibid.: 98, ll. 479-85)

Joaquín's journey takes him from the present to the past and back, establishing
him as a collective hero: "I am the masses of my people" (ibid.: 100, l. 491). Although at the end of his journey he finds the same contradictions in his identity, his experience has imparted him with a new vision and a sense of hope,
which is expressed in the last two lines: "I SHALL ENDURE! / I WILL ENDURE!"
(ibid.: ll. 499-500, original emphasis). Bruce-Novoa suggests that the "shift from
shall to *will* signals a change from a simple statement of futurity to a declaration of determination to form a future through willful action" (1982: 66). The
poem, as Pérez-Torres summarizes, posits "Chicano history as one that moves
inexorably toward repossession and empowerment, one in which resistance
most firmly makes its presence felt in the rich cultural heritage bestowed by the
Mexican past to the Chicano present" (1995: 73). Although the concept of *Aztlán*
had not yet entered Chicano discourse in 1967 when the poem was written and
first performed, the central ideas that led to the formation of the concept of
Aztlán were already present in this poem: "self-determination, cultural empowerment, political action, geographic reclamation" (ibid.). The notion of *Aztlán*
emerged in 1969 when Gonzales organized the Chicano Youth Conference in
Denver where the *Plan Espiritual de Aztlán* was adopted. Since then the myth of
Aztlán has served as a common denominator, often providing a stable and continuous frame of reference for Chicanos. This nationalist paradigm of Chicano
identity was, however, soon challenged, and it was women writers in particular
whose cultural productions called into question the nationalist paradigm of Chicano identity. In Lorna Dee Cervantes's poems, for instance, *Aztlán* becomes a

"discontinuous region" (ibid.: 84), a "site of tension between possession and dis-
possession," and a "place where the dream of escape is perpetually confounded
by the blasts and outrage of historical violation" (ibid.: 87).

3. Lorna Dee Cervantes's "Beneath the Shadow of the Freeway" (1981) and the Multiplicity of the Chicana Self

In the late 1970s women started to break the silence imposed on them during the
Chicano Movement. Moving away from the collectivist, patriarchal, and nationalist rhetoric toward a more personalized expression of the female/feminist
self, female writers split up the monolithic construction of 'Chicano' into 'Chica-
no/a.' With this slash, "singular constructions of idealized, homogenous subjects of Chicano political identity have given way to a plurality of competing
identities" (Chabram-Dernersesian 1993: 39). As a consequence, a new paradigm of identity came into being, which not only suffused the identity politics of
the Chicano Movement with a feminist agenda, but also included a pluralist vision of identity that offered internal critique, entailing a problematization of aspects of ethnicity, language, history, and culture. The existence of multiple
selves, what Norma Alarcón calls "multiple voiced subjectivity" (1990: 366),
evolves from the fact that so many competing ideologies beckon to Chicanas.
Bernice Zamora's poem "So Not To Be Mottled" from *Restless Serpents* (1976) is a
good example of the textual practices characteristic of Chicana poetry. "You insult me / When you say I'm / Schizophrenic. / *My* divisions are / Infinite" (1976:
52, original emphasis). Enunciating the complexities of their struggle for representation, Chicana poets have affirmed a multiple consciousness, recognizing
that the Chicana 'self' is not unified, but indefinitely divided.

Lorna Dee Cervantes is probably the best known of all Chicana poets. Her
three volumes of poetry, *Emplumada* (1981), *From the Cables of Genocide: Poems
on Love and Hunger* (1991), and *Drive: The First Quartet* (2006) have received
much critical attention. Among the prizes Cervantes's works have garnered are
the American Book Award in 1982 and the Lila Wallace Reader's Digest Foundation Writer's Award in 1995. Her latest collection was awarded the Balcones
Poetry Prize and was placed second for the International Latino Book Award for
Best Book of Poetry in English. Cervantes's poetry has been reprinted in more
than 200 literary anthologies and textbooks, and her work has received critical
attention since the 1970s (cf. Rodríguez y Gibson 2012: x).

Cervantes was born in San Francisco in 1954 and spent her childhood in an
Anglo environment in San José, California. Of Mexican and Native American
ancestry, she grew up speaking English—"without language" (1981: 41, l. 5)—as
she states in her poem "Refugee Ship," which forms part of *Emplumada* (1981).
While working as a high school teacher, she became active in the Chicano
Movement and her writings first appeared in the mid-1970s. Cervantes founded
the literary magazine *Mango*, which she directed from 1976 to 1982, and established the small press Mango Publications in 1974. Suggesting an identity politics that mediates between issues of race, class, and gender, her works exhibit a
mixture of cultural concerns and gender-based criticism that explore the complexities of the positioning of Chicana writers within both an Anglo mainstream
and a Chicano literary tradition that hitherto had silenced their voices. The collection *Emplumada* was completed with the help of a 1978 grant from the Na-

tional Arts Workshop and later by her participation in the Fine Arts Workshop in Provincetown, Massachusetts. Cervantes was a professor of creative writing at the University of Colorado at Boulder until 2007.

Cervantes's debut collection *Emplumada* constituted "a watershed moment in Chicano/a literature" as it marked the emergence of a Chicana writer on the national literary scene (Rodríguez y Gibson 2012: x). The title of this collection reflects the author's mixed cultural inheritance: the term *pluma* conjures up the plumed serpent Quetzalcóatl, an Aztec symbol of fertility and creativity. *Pluma* translates as both feather and pen, so the title *Emplumada* can be interpreted as a fertile and creative combination of 'pen flourish' and 'feathered.' The collection is divided into three parts: While the first two parts of the book deal primarily with social change, the last part includes poetry that is more lyrical. In her study of Chicana poetry, Marta Ester Sánchez described Cervantes's poetry primarily as oscillating between the two subject positions of Cervantes being a poet and a Chicana, giving rise to two opposed poetic strategies (Sánchez 1985: 10). On the one hand, there is "the narrative, discursive, 'hard' mode to communicate the real, divisive world she knows as a Chicana," and on the other, "the lyrical, imagistic, 'soft' mode to evoke contemplative and meditative moods" (ibid.). Deborah Madsen has observed that this division is "a bit formulaic" (2000: 196), and her analysis of Cervantes's poems illustrates the ways in which Cervantes's work is "characterized by her angry use of language, her passionate expression of emotions, and a complex interweaving of imagery to represent a feminist view of Chicana life in contemporary America" (ibid.).

"Beneath the Shadow of the Freeway" (1981) is generally considered Cervantes's "richest and most complex poem" (Sánchez 1985: 88) in the collection. Focusing on physical and psychological displacement, this poem takes the freeway as its major symbol. As is the case in many big cities, freeways have changed the nation's landscape by cutting deeply into Chicano *barrios*. "Beneath the Shadow" is the only poem in the collection that captures two character voices that are juxtaposed throughout the poem, presenting an "exchange of statement and rejoinder, a pattern of thought demanding that in the end a choice must be made" (ibid.: 119).

Introducing an all-woman family of three generations, the household includes the grandmother, described as an "innocent Queen" (1981: 11, l. 9) who "believes in myths and birds" (1981: 12, l. 35) and trusts "only what she builds / with her own hands" (1981: 12, ll. 36-7); the mother, referred to as "the Swift Knight, Fearless Warrior" (1981: 11, l. 10) who teaches her daughter a more cynical worldview and warns her not to become "soft" like her grandmother (1981: 12, l. 50); and the daughter, who is caught in-between and "could never decide" (1981: 11, l. 14).

Using the metaphor of urban encroachment to capture the experience of living on multiple borders, the poem relies on the metaphorical opposition between the freeway and the natural imagery of the house with its geraniums, kitten, and birds. The narrator occupies an attentive in-between position, becoming the translator between the public space of the patriarchal world and the private space of her matriarchal home: "I became Scribe: Translator of Foreign Mail, / interpreting letters from the government, notices / of dissolved marriages and Welfare stipulations" (1981: 11, ll. 16-8). The mail stands for the patriarchal world, the dominant culture that neither the grandmother nor the mother understand. As translator, the daughter-narrator has to learn to cope with the new environment and learns to trust "only what I have built / with my own hands" (1981: 14, ll. 86-7). The Chicana, it seems, must learn to "function through language, and also through an understanding of the old ways" (Rebolledo 1985: 127). The daughter also witnesses tense relationships between men and her mother and grandmother. The grandmother has built her own house after sharing two years of her life "with a man who tried to kill her" (1981: 12, l. 41); the mother has also become a victim of violence, and in section 5 the poem shifts from the contemplative mode to the description of a violent and loud outburst:

> in the night I would hear it
> glass bottles shattering the street
> words cracked into shrill screams
> inside my throat   a cold fear
> as it entered the house in hard
> unsteady steps   stopping at my door
> my name   bathrobe   slippers
> outside a 3 A.M. mist heavy
> as a breath full of whiskey
> stop it   go home   come inside
> mama if he comes here again
> I'll call the police (1981: 13, ll. 51-62)

Although the "it" is not specified, it clearly refers to a threatening force that is likened to male intrusion (cf. 1985: 125-6) and although it probably refers, as Sánchez has stated, to the freeway, it evokes fighting and perhaps even physical abuse.

While oscillating, throughout most of the poem, between the "romantic-idealist voice of the grandmother and the pragmatic-realist voice of the mother" (Sánchez 1985: 122), the speaker comes to a resolution in the final stanzas, and a sense of harmony is achieved:

> Back. The Freeway is across the street.
> It's summer now. Every night I sleep with a gentle man
> to the hymn of the mocking birds,
>
> and in time, I plant geraniums.
> I tie up my hair into loose braids,
> and trust only what I have built
> with my own hands. (1981: 14, ll. 81-7)

Evoking her grandmother by referring to birds and by echoing her voice, the speaker now pictures a scene of order and harmony that stands in contrast with her mother's loud and noisy nights (cf. Sánchez 1985: 129). The hymn of the mockingbird at the end of poem is a powerful symbol of the natural rhythm of existence. "Envisioning an agrarian utopia with matriarchal overtones" (ibid.: 130), the speaker is in control and will rely only on herself, continuing her grandmother's tradition. The culminating moment in this poem is, as Sánchez stresses, "an inner one in which the protagonist expresses her utopian, lyrical sentiments" (ibid.: 131).

The images and symbols that Cervantes uses in this poem recur in the rest of the collection. Floral imagery is especially predominant, and the presence of nature often takes the form of birds. While the other poems in *Emplumada* are more overtly political, "Beneath the Shadow of the Freeway" plunges deeply into poetic creativity, showing the speaker's psychological and spiritual development that, while critical of the larger surrounding society, demands a validation of her culture and her personal existence as a Chicana.

4. Conclusion

The poems selected here testify to the growth of Chicano/a poetry into a body of writing concerned with aesthetic craft and skillful verse. Following Candelaria (1986: 39-42), Chicano/a poetry developed in three phases: The Chicano Movement poetry, the phase of strengthening Chicano poetics, and the efflorescence of *flor y canto* (flower and song poetry). The dominant characteristic of the first phase of Chicano/a poetry is the close connection to the ideological core of the Movement with its concern for the empowerment of *la raza* (ibid.). This phase of poetry exemplified four features: the traditional use of meter and rhyme, frequent employment of imperative verb constructions, stylistic extravagance suggestive of political propaganda, and the prosaic nature of poems, making them powerful and effective means of literary statement but weak aesthetic compositions (cf. ibid.).

The later phases in Chicano/a poetry are characterized by an increasing poetic lyricism in which theme, form, and structure are interrelated in a more complex manner (ibid.: 71-131). In terms of language, Chicano/a poetics comprise different linguistic elements including dialect, slang, code-switching, bilingualism, and a mixture of indigenous languages (ibid.). Although the second phase is also political in terms of themes and argument, it is nonetheless more lyrical and stylistically more complex than the poetry of the Chicano/a Movement (cf. ibid.). The third phase of poetry consists of an increasingly sophisticated and refined style (ibid.: 137-71). Characteristic of the *flor y canto* poetry is an inward focus and the individual involvement in the treatment of subject and theme, which involves personal experience and a focus on subjectivity (cf. ibid.).

While Candelaria's division of Chicano/a poetry into three phases seems very schematic, Pérez-Torres sketches a continual development of Chicano/a poetry from "classic" Chicano poetry to Movement Poetry to more recent poems (1995: 6). For Pérez-Torres, the classic poetic tradition connects with the *corrido* tradition and includes poems that focus on topics like discrimination and exploitation. Relying on the literary heritage as its source, classic Chicano/a poetry combines features of vernacular expression with indigenous cultural elements, forming "a residual culture that helps form an emergent culture" (ibid.). This poetry is oriented toward the past, which it attempts to rewrite. Pérez-Torres comes to a similar conclusion concerning Movement poetry: Since the 1970s and 1980s, the revolutionary quality of poetry and the political fervor have calmed down, giving rise to a personal poetics which evokes "political discourse crossed at the site of the individual" (ibid.: 13). "On a poetic level" he says, "Chicano imaginative response has been to examine the ways fragmented political practices influence specific localities: communities, families, individuals" (ibid.). While Gonzales's poem clearly falls within the period of Movement poetry, Cervantes's poem is characteristic of what Candelaria calls "third phase poetry": preoccupied with "capturing the manifold quality of personal experience," her "verse also reveals a powerfully evoked *chicanismo* comprehended as both a literal part of her self-identity and as an external source of metaphor" (1986: 156). Together, *I Am Joaquín* and "Beneath the Shadow of the Freeway" represent the wide spectrum of themes in Chicano/a poetry, testifying to the vibrant quality of this emerging body of literature.

Bibliography

Selected Primary Literature

Alurista. 1971. *Floricanto en Aztlan.* Los Angeles: Chicano Cultural Centre, University of California.

Cervantes, Lorna Dee. 1981. *Emplumada.* Pittsburgh: U of Pittsburgh P.

——. 1991. *From the Cables of Genocide: Poems on Love and Hunger.* Houston: Arte Público.

——. 1977. "You Cramp My Style, Baby." In: *El Fuego de Aztlán* I: 39.

——. 2006. *Drive: The First Quartet: New Poems, 1980-2005.* San Antonio: Wings P.

Gonzales, Rodolfo. 1972 [1967]. *I am Joaquín/Yo Soy Joaquín.* New York: Bantam.

Hoyos, Angela de. 1975. *Arise, Chicano! and Other Poems.* San Antonio, TX: M & A Editions.

——. 1975. *Chicano Poems for the Barrio.* San Antonio, TX: M & A Editions.

Zamora, Bernice. 1976. *Restless Serpents.* Menlo Park, CA: Diseños Literarios.

Selected Secondary Literature

Bruce-Novoa, Juan. 1982. *Chicano Poetry: A Response to Chaos.* Austin, TX: U of Texas P.

One of the early groundbreaking studies of Chicano poetry, which includes a detailed analysis on I Am Joaquín.

Candelaria, Cordelia. 1986. *Chicano Poetry. A Critical Introduction.* Westport, CO: Greenwood P.

Comprehensive survey of Chicano/a poetry.

Limón, José. 1992. *Mexican Ballads, Chicano Poems. History and Influence in Mexican-American Social Poetry.* Berkeley: U of California P.

An analysis of Chicano poetry in terms of Bloom's theory of anxiety of influence which argues that the corrido acts as a master poem to Chicano poetry.

Madsen, Deborah L. 2000. *Understanding Contemporary Chicana Literature.* Columbia, SC: U of South Carolina P.

Contains chapters on the poetry of Bernice Zamora, Lorna Dee Cervantes and also analyzes the poetry of Ana Castillo, Sandra Cisneros, and Alma Luz Villanueva.

Pérez-Torres, Rafael. 1995. *Movements in Chicano Poetry: Against Myths, Against Margins.* Cambridge: Cambridge UP.

Situates Chicano/a poetry in terms of theoretical debates on postmodernism and postcolonialism.

Rodríguez y Gibson, Eliza (ed.). 2012. *Stunned into Being: Essays on the Poetry of Lorna Dee Cervantes.* San Antonio, TX: Wings.

Collection of essays that include detailed analyses of Lorna Dee Cervantes's poems.

Sánchez, Marta Ester. 1985. *Contemporary Chicana Poetry: A Critical Approach to an Emerging Literature*. Berkeley and Los Angeles: U of California P.
First book-length study of Chicana poetry with a large chapter on the works of Lorna Dee Cervantes.

Further References

Alarcón, Norma. 1990. "The Theoretical Subject(s) of *This Bridge Called My Back* and Anglo-American Feminism." In: Gloria Anzaldúa (ed.), *Making Face, Making Soul. Haciendo Caras: Creative and Critical Perspectives by Women of Color*. San Francisco: Aunt Lute Foundation Books. 356-69.
Anzaldúa, Gloria. 1999. [1987]. *Borderlands/La Frontera. The New Mestiza*. 2nd ed. San Francisco: Aunt Lute Books.
Bruce-Novoa, Juan. 1990. *RetroSpace: Collected Essays on Chicano Literature*. Houston: Arte Público.
Chabram-Dernersesian, Angie. 1993. "And Yes . . . The Earth Did Part: On the Splitting of Chicano/a Subjectivity." In: Adela de la Torre and Beatriz M. Pesquera (eds.), *Building With Our Hands: New Directions in Chicana Studies*. Berkeley: California UP. 34-56.
Fellner, Astrid M. 2002. *Articulating Selves: Contemporary Chicana Self-Representation*. Wien: Braumüller.
Gallego, Carlos. 2011. *Chicana/o Subjectivity and the Politics of Identity: Between Recognition and Revolution*. New York: Palgrave.
Hartley, George. 2003. *The Abyss of Representation: Marxism and the Postmodern Sublime*. Durham: Duke UP.
Ikas, Karin Rosa. 2002. *Chicana Ways: Conversations With Ten Chicana Writers*. Reno: U of Nevada P.
Montoya, José. 1972. "La Jefita." In: Octavio Romano-V. and Herminio Ríos C. (eds.), *El Espejo—The Mirror. Selected Chicano Literature*. Berkeley: Quinto Sol Publications. 232-3.
Neate, Wilson. 1998. *Tolerating Ambiguity: Ethnicitiy and Community in Chicano/a Writing*. New York: Lang.
Ortego, Philip. 1982. "The Chicano Renaissance." In: Livie I. Duran and H. Russell Bernard (eds.), *Introduction to Chicano Studies*. 2nd ed. New York: Macmillan. 568-84.
Paredes, Américo. 1958. *With His Pistol in His Hand: A Border Ballad and Its Hero*. Austin, TX: U of Texas P.
Rebolledo, Tey Diana. 1985. "The Maturing of Chicana Poetry: The Quiet Revolution of the 1980's." In: Paula A. Treichler, Cheris Kramarae and Beth Stafford (eds.), *For Alma Mater: Theory and Practice in Feminist Scholarship*. Urbana: U of Illinois P. 143-58.
——. 1995. *Women Singing in the Snow: A Cultural Analysis of Chicano Literature*. Tucson: U of Arizona P.
Saldívar, José David. 1986. "Towards a Chicano Poetics: The Making of the Chicano Subject, 1969-1982." In: *Confluencia* I.2: 10-7.

30.

Disability Poetry

Jim Ferris's "Abecedarius Hospitaler"
and Cheryl Marie Wade's "Cripple Lullaby"

Marion Rana

1. Introduction: Disability Poetry and Crip Poetry

Disability poetry has only been recognized as a new genre relatively recently, with the first anthology of poems about disability, *Toward Solomon's Mountain: The Experience of Disability in Poetry*, published in 1983. This anthology was inspired by the editors' condemnation of the then current poetry about disability as overly sentimental, melodramatic, and self-pitying; instead, they called for a poetry that was tough-minded, socially challenging, self-assertive, and grounded in experiences of and with the body. The fact that this anthology has justifiably been called the birth of disability poetry as a genre points to its strong focus on social and political assertiveness. Disability poetry does not necessarily have to be, but in reality often is concerned with the exact issues called for by the editors: it is a self-asserted, self-confident, socially critical poetry grounded in experiences of and with the body. A comprehensive, widely accepted academic definition of what constitutes the genre is still in the making. Focusing on the genre discussion to date, this essay will therefore outline and critically comment on the various points of argumentation before proposing a tentative working definition.

The fact that some of the most prolific writers of disability poetry had already started their writing careers years before the publication of *Toward Solomon's Mountain* points to one of the conundrums of defining and analyzing the genre: If poets such as Vassar Miller and Josephine Miles published the poems now considered to be part of a growing corpus of disability poetry before that genre was in fact "born," as Northen puts it (2011: 18), how is disability poetry actually marked? One way of defining the genre is grounded in a biographical approach. In that sense, any poetry written by a disabled poet is disability poetry. By that definition, even the work of language poet Larry Eigner, whose disability has neither been part of his critical and academic reception nor openly surfaces in his poems, could be included in the canon (cf. Davidson 2011).

Grounding a definition of disability poetry in the poets' biographies, then, would allow us to include poets who do not address their disability in their work. Yet treating the genre in such a manner is also a dangerous road to take for a genre that is already under suspicion of being too political and not literary enough. Thus, the biological determinism behind such an attribution, i.e., the idea that disabled poets inherently write differently than non-disabled poets, and that this different style of writing is based on their somatic experiences of disability, is at best problematic and at worst detrimental to a socially grounded discussion of disability. On the one hand, Petra Kuppers claims that the acknowledgment of physical difference—the naming of the poet's disability rather than merely calling him or her a "disability" or a "crip poet"—pays tribute to the poets' "barrier-overcoming fights, pain, and creativity" in creating their work (2007: 94). Similarly, Jim Ferris believes that the mind is influenced by the body, and their different bodies will thus affect disabled poets' writings:

If the working of the mind/brain is changed by the difference in handedness, it is a reasonable extrapolation that the different embodiments that come with physical as well as mental disabilities will also change how the mind/brain works. And whether disability influences one's being-in-the-world through nature, nurture, or, inevitably, both—disability does affect how one experiences and responds to the world we find ourselves in. And so it cannot help but have an impact on the artistic production of the people so marked. (2011: 90-1)

By focusing on disabled poets as sole originators of the genre, the biographical determination also answers David Hevey's claim that the history of disability representation is one "that was not done by us but to us . . . Disabled people have been the *subject* of various constructions and representations throughout history but disabled people have not controlled the object—that is, the means of producing or positioning our own constructions or representations" (1993: 423; original emphasis).

On the other hand, the biographical fallacy looms over and limits the interpretation of disability poetry even more than it does poetry without that specific marker. As Kuppers argues: "Disability stereotypes are too, too powerful, and I have too often seen the glimpse of imagined understanding in students' eyes when they find out 'what's the matter with that one—what happened?'—an understanding that ratchets readings down rather than out and up, across and backwards, below and beyond" (2007: 94). Defining a piece of work as disability poetry based merely on the fact that it was written by a disabled poet can thus both enrich and endanger an insightful reading of it, and knowing the difference is a fine line to tread.

Basing the definition of disability poetry on the poets' (assumed) biographies also gives rise to another problem of definition: What, in fact, counts as disability? It is much more than a medical or physical set of conditions. While impairment is a physical reality, disability is socially constructed, and what does or does not count as disability greatly varies over time (cf. Shakespeare 2010; Barnes 2010; Linton 1998). Many deaf individuals, for instance, reject the label of disability, and many physical differences that once served as markers of disability are no longer considered such. Is someone with AIDS disabled, or are they "just" (on the verge of becoming) ill? Do psychological impairments count as disabilities? The writings of Walt Whitman, who suffered from the aftereffects of a stroke, T.S. Eliot, who was clinically depressed, even poets such as Robert Creeley, Robert Duncan, and Allen Ginsberg, all three of whom had some form of vision problems, can be read through the lens of disability (cf. Bartlett 2012: 17; Davidson 2012: 385); but this does not in fact turn their works into parts of the canon of disability poetry.

Another approach for defining the genre is based on effect. Jim Ferris, one of the foremost theoreticians of disability poetry and himself a "crip poet," explains, "I know [disability poetry] when I feel it" (2007: n. p.). His "Poems with Disabilities" follows this line of thought, tongue in cheek:

> You can't always tell
> just from looking at them either. Sometimes
> they'll look just like a regular poem
> when they roll in . . . you're reading along
> and suddenly everything
> changes, the world tilts
> a little, angle of vision
> jumps, your entrails aren't
> where you left them. (ll. 14-22)

According to this excerpt, disability poetry is not necessarily defined by form or content ("they'll look just like a regular poem") but by the effect it has ("suddenly everything changes"). The effect is disconcerting and uncomfortable, reminiscent of Emily Dickinson's definition of poetry as something that makes the readers so cold that no fire can warm them. To a non-disabled reader, the "everything" that changes might be his or her view of disability; more importantly, to a disabled reader, the "everything" that changes is more profound: an altered sense of self, of belonging and representation.

With this definition, disability poetry becomes what Ferris has labeled crip poetry: "a poetics that valorizes the wide range of ways of being in and respond-ing to the world, that claims space for alternative, non-normative experience, language, thought and feeling" (2011: 91). Fundamental to crip poetry is the recognition of disability as a social construct, the breaking-up of stereotypes and of the marginalization and discrimination that go along with them. As the self-assertive re-appropriation of the term "crip" suggests, crip poetry is often characterized by a strong political and social agenda:

> When society wants us to stay out of sight, to keep quiet, to accept the still-rampant disability discrimination with resignation, with good humor, with pluck—even when we ourselves may most want to be ordinary—crip poetry comes from the outside, it comes from the abnormal, it is centered in the expe-rience of being out of the ordinary. (Ferris 2007: n. p.)

Crip poetry, as the title of the 1997 anthology *Staring Back* suggests, centers around redirecting the gaze on disabled persons, on them taking charge of that gaze and articulating the terms under which they are viewed. Challenging the medical gaze that frustrates recognition of the disabled as anything beyond their disability, crip poets endeavor to reassert agency by challenging society's view of the disabled and redirecting the (assessing, pitying, dehumanizing) gaze on them (cf. Pafunda 2011: 313).

Crip poetry has been criticized as essentializing a shared experience of disabil-ity—an experience that disabled poets may or may not have had (Weise 2011: 139). Convoluting all disability poetry into crip poetry, i.e., into a more or less po-litically inspired, activist art form, also excludes those writers whose work is not held in high regard by most of today's crip poets: A number of literary works about disability, particularly some of the most commercially successful ones, are charac-terized by a sentimentalism and melodramatic tendency or a reliance on the figure of the supercrip—the "inspirational hero overcoming insurmountable odds" (Northen 2011: 20), characteristics which many disability artists and activists de-fine as alien to disability culture in general and to disability poetry in particular. Because the emancipation process of the disability community has centered on the rejection of the medical model and the embracing of the social model of dis-ability (the realization that impairment only turns into a disability through the way society accommodates and treats this difference), crip poets decidedly do not want their work "co-opted by people who want to feel pity" (Kuppers 2007: 91). The reason for excluding certain types of poetry dealing with disability from a dis-cussion of the genre as such then becomes political and aesthetic rather than terminological, a question of mainstream poetry vs. poetry on the margins. Ac-cordingly, in her discussion of which poems she and her fellow editors chose for the seminal anthology *Beauty Is a Verb* (2011), Jennifer Bartlett outlines the selec-tion process, which was centered on questions of definition, aesthetics, and affilia-tion with disability culture: "Mainstream writers tend to reflect the predominant view of disability as tragedy. We wanted to avoid this norm not because it isn't valid, but because we are interested in investigating an alternative" (2011: 16).

To Kuppers, a practitioner of disability poetry herself, the genre is "the place where performed language and bodies come together and apart, and where disability culture as a shared experience can challenge itself" (2007: 90). Similarly, Ferris's definition of disability poetry as "a challenge to stereotypes and an insistence on self-definition; foregrounding of the perspective of people with disabilities; an emphasis on embodiment, especially atypical embodiment; and alternative techniques and poetics" (2007: n.p.), while drawing attention to the poetic distinctiveness of disability poetry, focuses on the social and political agenda of disability writing. As such, Ferris's definition is much more valid for crip rather than disability poetry. In order to facilitate a focused discussion of the genre in the future, however, it is imperative to differentiate between crip poetry on the one and disability poetry on the other hand. Thus, as an umbrella term, disability poetry encompasses poetry *written by* poets with a (self-attributed or socially assigned) disability as well as poetic works *about* disability. In contrast, crip poetry can be defined as a subgenre, a decidedly activist, socially grounded manifestation of disability poetry. Since within disability poetry, crip poetry is not only the fastest growing but also the stylistically and theoretically most ambitious field, the following analyses will focus on two crip poets: Jim Ferris and Cheryl Marie Wade.

2. Jim Ferris's "Abecedarius Hospitaler": Agency and the Medical Gaze

Jim Ferris is one of the foremost practitioners of crip poetry. His Whitmanesque *The Hospital Poems* (2004)—the "first book of disability poetry that could reasonably be called a best-seller" (Northen 2011: 21)—treats the poet's experiences as a child subjected to the medical routine of "curing" his disability and the sense of powerlessness and loss of agency associated with it:

> You are a specimen
> for study, a toy, a puzzle—
> they speak to each other
> as if you were unconscious . . . ("The Coliseum", ll. 4-7)

On the level of content, Ferris's poetry is marked by his self-definition as a crip poet, by its immediacy, and his political mindedness. Kuppers points out that his poetic voice "does not reach out towards a political correctness that would stifle the poetic material that shapes Western thought patterns, police it, and set it in narrow tracks" (2006: n. p.). Rather, Ferris forcefully problematizes medical as well as social constructions surrounding disability as "his poetic universe is explicitly shaped by larger stories, and bodies are never just 'natural'" (ibid.).

"Abecedarius Hospitaler" is part of *The Hospital Poems* (2004) and narrates a child's experiences at, we may assume, a "Grand Round"—the meetings at which various medical professionals would discuss a patient's medical history and treatment with the patient present for examination and presentation (a practice that has largely been abandoned). To the boy of the poem, the Grand Round is a familiar routine, albeit one that has retained its frightening and dehumanizing aspects. Kuppers (2007: 96) notes that the term "hospitaler" in the title can signify the member of a religious order caring for the sick, and it can also describe a knight fighting in the crusades. The poem then either becomes a piece of instruction for those caring for the boy, or its title emphasizes the fact that the boy is in fact taking part in a battle, not so much against his disability but against institutionalized medicine. The term "hospitaler" can also refer to an inmate of a hospital, which is, perhaps, the most straightforward interpretation that brings the poem's central aspect into focus: The boy's experiences are not just his own and they are not just the doctors'; rather, they reflect a more generic experience of disabled people's treatment by medical institutions.

In the poem, the sea serves as an extended metaphor for the ambiguity of the boy's emotions:

> A small sea of white coats, mouths and eyeballs
> Bobs, waves, watches the specimen on stage,
> Chatters about the boy who would be so
> Durably cold if he were here, but he
> Enters the sea, dons a lab coat for style,
> For warmth, for safety on the sea, and the sea
> Gabbles on, boring into what's left of
> Him on the stage, washing away all down to all–
> Important bone, washing away shame, joy,
> Jealously, to get down to the driftwood (ll. 1-10)

The sea's binary set of associations highlights the contradictory evaluation and experience of the medical treatment of disability. Just as the sea can stand for both a positively connoted sense of freedom and power, and—in its more negative, frightening aspect—for a dangerous, uncontrollable and, above all, indifferent force, Ferris develops this ambiguous nature of the sea into a light-hearted, nearly joyful metaphor that then turns into a more brutal, physically threatening one: The sea in the beginning of the poem resembles the calm Mediterranean rather than the harsh Atlantic, it "[b]obs" and "waves" (l. 2), "chatters" (l. 3) and "gabbles on" (l. 7). In the beginning, the sea is thus a benevolent force, and it is only from line 7 onward that the good-humored "gabbling" turns into frightening, threatening activeness—the tide has turned, as it were, and the sea now endangers the boy by "washing away all down to all– / Important bone, washing away shame, joy, / Jealousy" (ll. 8-10). The danger is revealed as both physical and emotional: Bone is laid bare by the boring into of the sea, i.e., of the doctors' gazes, but it also wrests from the boy his "shame, joy, / Jealousy." The disruption in the semi-alliteration of this list of emotions ([ʃ] of "shame" vs. [dʒ] of "joy" and "jealousy") underlines the disparaged nature of the sentiments listed in this seeming unit. The appropriation of sounds links joy to jealousy more than it does shame to either joy or jealousy, and while the listing together of these nouns feels contradictory on a semantic level, the fact that joy and jealousy are phonetically marked as more congruent than the obviously linked shame and jealousy highlights the contradictory and ambiguous feelings the boy experiences.

The poem's other important extended metaphor is that of the doctors' gaze. Introduced explicitly for the first time in line 2 in the description of the "small sea of white coats" watching the boy, instances of gazing and watching pervade the whole poem. What is evoked here is the medical gaze that much disability writing (both literary and academic) is concerned with. First theorized by Michel Foucault and refined by Disability Studies scholars such as Rosemarie Garland-Thomson (2009; 2010), the medical gaze describes medicine's dehumanizing separation of the patient's body from his or her psyche. The medical model derived in part from this theorization is "a standard, shorthand term to indicate the depersonalization of the institutionalized medical industry that can result in stripping people of their most intimate internal identity" (Rose 2011: 178). In "Abecedarius Hospitaler" the medical gaze is first referenced in line 1 where it links the (passive) gaze to its active conclusion: What marks the doctors as such are their "white coats, mouths and eyeballs," that is, their professional insignia (the lab coats) and their behavior: they diagnose, recommend, evaluate, and, above all, watch. The coats, which are referenced repeatedly, allow the doctors to take their positions in the medical establishment; they are a symbol of power that the boy is allowed to borrow but not to keep. The contrasting, yet broken-up and incomplete anaphora of lines 18 to 20 and line 23 illuminate the difference in power and authority: The enjambed sentence describing the boy's loss of the coat is broken up over three lines, its inherent hopelessness juxtaposed by the dactylic rhythm ("whatever / Safety the white coat provides melts down / To nothing", ll. 18-20). In contrast, the reference to the doctors' coats not only opposes the former lines in meaning (unlike the boy, the doctors keep their coats), it also does so stylistically. The pentametrical line is end-stopped rather than enjambed and consists of more dynamic, iambic rhythm ("Whatever they decide they keep their coats," l. 23; emphasis added). The concluding alliteration of "keep" and "coats", brought into focus by the mid-line caesura, stresses the sense of power assigned to the coats; the fact that the doctors, in contrast to the boy, are not stripped of their insignia is hammered home.

An interesting conundrum manifests itself in lines 3 and 4 when "the boy who would be so / Durably cold if he were here" evokes the question of where the referenced "here" is located. The attribution of coldness does not logically follow a remote localization of "here" as different from the Grand Round but instead points to a greater immediacy of localization.

The evocation thus hints at a schism, a disassociating experience that began in line 5: The boy's "enter[ing] the sea" and disguising himself as one of the doctors by putting on a lab coat "for style, / For warmth, for safety" (ll. 5-6) is an imaginary experience. However, both the safety provided by the white coat and the disassociation from his body are illusions: The medical gaze, this time represented by "the mist / Roll[ing] in" (ll. 17-8), melts down the safety of the boy's pseudo-transformation into a doctor with the realization that "the sea is no safer than / Under the cold spotlight" (ll. 20-1). It is this realization that ends the boy's disassociation and brings the lyrical I back into his position within the poem: Having talked about himself in the third person ("the specimen," "the boy," and "he," ll. 2-4), and associating himself with the doctors in line 12 ("while we look," emphasis added), he comes to the realization that his safety is an illusion since "it still ends in / Vomit and pain" and brings about the final change of identification: "but for me, not for them" (l. 22). Resigning himself to his place and his job ("to be the / Zoo animal," l. 26), the boy does what is expected of him: "I pace, I shiver, I don't cry" (l. 26). Ironically, through the boy's acceptance of his role in the medical process, he reclaims his identity. In a way, he is above things—as indicated by the metaphor of his being gazed at while positioned on a stage—so detached from them that through his acceptance he achieves a form of transcendence. Kuppers summarizes the boy's painful process of identification and acceptance: "A boy comes back to himself, and knows that it is he who will suffer" (2007: 97).

Ferris, whose familiarity with disability is deeply connected to his writing, elaborates upon his experience in his seminal "The Enjambed Body" on a stylistic rather than textual level with a focus on meter:

> Early on I made an aesthetic decision: my nonmatching shoes, my uneven feet, did not matter. I was a born loser on that count, so I decided to pay it no heed. Ever since it has been difficult for me to concern myself with appearance in general, but especially with feet—as in wearing shoes and socks that match. Writing lines with even feet. (2004: 223)

He continues: "When I walk, I aim to get somewhere. If my meters are sprung, if my feet are uneven, if my path is irregular, that's just how I walk. And how I write" (2004: 227). Not surprisingly, the meter of "Abecedarius Hospitaler" is highly irregular. Most of the poem is free verse, and when metrical rhythm does appear, it is disrupted before it can gain momentum. One of these instances starts with a near-quote from *Hamlet*: "Cut / Or not cut—that's never the question—it's / Places to cut, which bones to saw first" (ll. 14-6), which is written in anapestic meter (interrupted only by the replacement of the first unstressed with a stressed syllable in the first and the replacement of the anapestic with an iambic rhythm in the sixth foot), rhythmically extending the metaphor of the sea and the mist rolling in (ll. 17-8). The same rhythmical imagery is supported in lines 18 through 21 after which the dactylic rhythm is forcefully interrupted by a spondee, cutting short not only the soothing nature of the rhythm but also, on a textual level, ending the boy's illusion of safety:

> Whatever
> Safety the white coat provides melts down
> To nothing, the sea is no safer than
> under the cold spotlight. (ll. 18-21, emphasis added).

With regards to poetic form, the abecedarius is highly crafted and artificial; clearly marking its content as mediated, "it foregrounds its construction, rather than the illusion of a direct experience or an unmediated access to a reality" (Kuppers 2006: 95). In their literary tradition, abecedarii are connected to pedagogy, utilized as a tool for teaching both literacy and moralism/theology. In the original Hebrew, some of the biblical Psalms are abecedarii, and to this day ABC-books are used to teach children the letters of the alphabet. Drafting his poem as an abecedarius, Ferris thus invokes several realizations: First, being disabled in our society is a learning process—and a cruel one at that. Second, as an abecedarius the poem draws attention to itself as a crafted, mediated art form, emphasizing the fact that physical experiences are never really transmittable or even communicable. Finally, on the level of the poem, the retreat into a subliminally manageable art form such as the highly structured abecedarius highlights the boy's attempt to escape his reality or, since escape is clearly not possible, to control his reality and keep it in check. Ferris's "Abecedarius Hospitaler" thus becomes a learning tool that is both sarcastic and sad, rebellious and defeatist. Disassociation is fruitless, wishful thinking useless. Yet the boy's defeat is not complete; rather, he exhibits grace in falling. The reminder—"You're up there, kid"—is not necessary because the boy knows exactly what is expected of him; in his submission to the hospital's rules, he both confirms and denies them. As Kuppers put it: "[T]he doctrines of church and medicine do not hold, and to stand, unsupported and yet assaulted, might be the last stand" (2007: 97).

3. Cheryl Marie Wade's "Cripple Lullaby": Crip Identity and Self-assertion

While Ferris's approach to poetry is influenced not only by his biography but also by his interest in and contribution to poetic theory, Cheryl Marie Wade's work is deeply rooted in her social activism. The highly acclaimed "Queen Mother of Gnarly," "crip culture queen" was, foremost, a performance artist (Kuppers 2007: 92), and most of her writing, though it often reads as and is received as poetry, is in fact (part of) a solo performance. The connection between disability and identity is one of the central aspects in her work and appears, perhaps, at its most striking in her widely discussed poem, "I Am not One of The" (2013 [1997]: 526). This poem, in which Wade negates all outside definition of the disabled (e.g., "I am not one of the physically challenged— / . . . / I am not one of the differently abled—," ll. 1 and 5), re-appropriating derogative terms ("I'm the Cripple," l. 19), and enforcing her identity as sexual, political, and active ("I'm The Woman With Juice," l. 21), portrays disability as timeless and multifaceted. Wade "presents herself as the subject, but not the medical subject. She is a sexual woman with a mature sexual identity, and a historically integrated citizen rather than a medically defective, peripheral component of the population" (Rose 2011: 171). This self-definition finds its continuation in "Cripple Lullaby" (2013: 527). Here, Wade recounts the different aspects of her identity, some of which resonate with common perceptions of disability while others contradict and negate those stereotypes, but all of which end in the self-assertive proclamation: "One thing I am not is a reason to die" (ll. 6, 12, 20); this line, slightly altered, also serves as the poem's culmination and endpoint.

In explaining both the relevance and the possible dynamics of disability culture, Wade states: "It's finding a history, naming and claiming ancestors, heroes. As 'invisibles,' our history is hidden from us, our heroes buried in the pages, unnamed, unrecognized. Disability culture is about naming, about recognizing" (1992: 16). Just like "I Am not One of The," "Cripple Lullaby" names and recognizes different aspects of disability identity. The trickster coyote referenced in the first line ("I'm trickster coyote in a gnarly-bone suit") negotiates the question of identity so central to the poem. In her discussion of the relevance of the Native American trope of the trickster to feminist philosophy and policy, Shane Pelan points out:

> Coyote stories challenge ideas of identity as they present a being with the ability to shape-shift, to embody aspects of other beings while remaining "itself." They suggest a world in which caution and care are called for, in which we cannot assume that we know who is who or what is what. (1996: 131)

The multiple identities presented in "Cripple Lullaby," most of which question common stereotypes of the disabled, can easily be read in line with this aspect of trickster mythology as alternative descriptions and self-definitions move from the aggressive to the sexual (e.g. "I'm the nightmare booga you flirt with in dreams," l. 3); clearly, "Wade's self-narration subverts and reclaims language that conventionally subjugates and objectifies, as well as the power dynamics of the gaze/stare" (Millet-Gallant 2010: n.p.).

The defeatist images drawn up in the poem are equally multidimensional. The first of them ("I'm homeless in the driveway of your manicured street," l. 7) sets the speaker apart from the presumably non-disabled Other addressed in the poem, creating an opposition both through address ("I" vs. "your") and on a level of content (homelessness vs. suburban cleanliness and middleclass wealth); the next stanza consists of two disillusioned exclamations of defeat ("I'm the girl in the doorway with no illusions to spare / I'm a kid dosed on chemo so who said life is fair," ll. 9-10). The hopelessness conveyed in these lines is repeated in line 15 where the wealth and theoretically carefree life of the financially affluent are contrasted with the psychological depression and psychosomatic stresses that wealth may cause ("I'm that Valley girl, you know, dying of thin"). Other negatively connoted lines are more ambiguous. The image of "Evening Magazine's SuperCrip of the Week" (l. 8) expresses an angry rebuttal of media and social practices that glorify and dramatize disabled experiences into inspirational life stories (cf. Northen 2011: 20), and the allusion to the (fictionalized) Inuit practice of senicide ("I'm the ancient remnant set adrift on ice," l. 14; cf. Kjellstrom 1974/75: 117-24) speaks not only of the injustice and pain of this (imagined) tradition, but also evokes the dignity and grace associated with it.

While gladiatorial self-definitions such as "I'm Earth's last volcano, and I am ready to blow" (l. 18) both express and strengthen agency and power, the more defeatist lines align the lyrical I with less fortunate disabled people. The range of ability, both in and of oneself and as allowed and determined by society, is explicated in stanza 8: "I'm the Wheelchair Athlete, I'm every dead Baby Doe / I'm Earth's last volcano, and I am ready to blow" (ll. 17-8). The wheelchair athlete—a symbol of disability power and pride, of independence and agency—is contrasted with Baby Doe, a helpless victim of (fatal) ableist action. Transgressing the disability community, there is also a sense of solidarity with other groups socially marginalized through their deviant embodiment: the physically and/or mentally ill, the "kid" undergoing chemotherapy (l. 10), the anorexic woman (l. 15), the poor (l. 7), the sexually marginalized ("the girl in the doorway," l. 9), and the elderly ("the ancient remnant," l. 14). This variety of identification refers to the more general human experience of social stigmatization, and at the same time it marks the poem's desire to speak for the disability community as a whole, "invit[ing] its audience to imagine disability as a dynamic, omnipresent, mythical force, instead of a static, docile, medical anomaly" (Rose 2011: 171).

As in "Abecedarius Hospitaler," disassociation also comes up in Wade's poem, although it is granted less space and appears with very different connotations. While the boy in Ferris's "Abecedarius Hospitaler" disassociates from his body as a means to escape reality, the acclamation in Wade's poem—"I'm all that is left of the Cheshire Cat's grin" (l. 16)—has a more menacing undertone. The allusion to Lewis Carroll's *Alice's Adventures in Wonderland* (1865) along with the consonance in "Cheshire" lends this line an air of playfulness. This cheerful atmosphere is infiltrated, however, by the slightly ominous, mischievous nature of the Cheshire cat in the Alice narrative. Its ability to make itself disappear at will, at times leaving visible only its grin, is referenced in the poem which even goes a step further by drawing up the image of the grin itself disappearing. On the one hand, this image speaks to the anger of disabled people about being invisible both in public life and on an interpersonal level, where their sexuality in particular is often overlooked or negated (cf. Garland-Thomson 2009; Köbsell 2010; Wendell 2010). On the other hand, the image references a willful disappearance—one inspired by a more critical, philosophical outlook on life—and accommodates a slightly menacing stance: Despite its playful nature, the Cheshire cat holds a considerable amount of power, both intellectual and physical, given its ability to make itself invisible.

Different (recurring) aspects of self-description hold central positions within the poem: "I'm a whisper, I'm a heartbeat" (l. 5), which is repeated in each refrain;

"I'm 'that / accident,' and goodbye" (l. 5); "I'm 'let's call it suicide,' and a sigh" (l. 11); "I'm a genocide survivor, and Why?" (l. 19). On a level of content, both the image of the whisper and that of the heartbeat draw on a mixture of physical and sensual components: their inherent acoustic nature and their origin in bodily actions—one willful, one involuntary and irrepressible. On a metaphorical level they can stand for differing ideas: The heartbeat is a sign of life, of endurance, of existence, while the whisper can signify intimacy, secrecy, even an act of opposition. Either of these interpretations would fit here, though the more obvious reading (given the lines that follow), is one that aligns the whispering with a sense of shameful secrecy: Disability is not something that is commonly discussed out loud, and neither are its repercussions: social stigma and ableism, i.e. discrimination against disabled people and resistance against their active inclusion. "That accident" then becomes not just the physical act that may have caused a disability—a car crash, the wrong medication during pregnancy—but the disabled person him- or herself, while "and goodbye" demonstrates how easily and quickly the non-disabled majority loses interest in the disabled.

The same attitude, though with clearly more malicious undertones, is evoked in the second refrain, which reads "I'm 'let's call it suicide,' and a sigh" (l. 11). Taking its cue from many disability activists' grief over the fact that the abortion of fetuses that may grow into disabled babies is legally and socially acceptable, this line proclaims invalidicide as a socially pardoned crime that elicits only a cover-up and a sigh. The last refrain, then, differs from the others in that it not only proclaims another part of disability identity ("I'm a genocide survivor"); it also asks the only question of the poem: "and Why?" (l. 19). As obvious as this last attribution might be—today's disabled may regard themselves not only as survivors of the historical genocide committed (not exclusively) in Nazi Germany but also by abortion practices of disabled fetuses or as survivors of assisted suicide (cf. Hubbard 1990: 179-98; Wade 1992: 16)—the question of causation can go in different directions. Does it reflect common stereotypes of disability, assuming that disabled individuals are most likely to be self-pitying ('why me?') or, otherwise, bravely accepting their 'fate'? Is the question directed toward the perpetrators of genocide, asking why the disabled are so often targeted for genocidal actions? Or does the question reflect the survivor syndrome experienced by many genocide survivors (cf. Blaser 2005: 792-3)?

"Cripple Lullaby" consists of ten stanzas, mostly comprised of rhyming couplets. Apart from the half rhymes at the end of lines 1 and 2 ("suit/boots"), 7 and 8 ("street/week"), and 13 and 14 ("eyes/ice"), all rhymes are pure. Every stanza consists of two lines, apart from the sixth, which has four, and the tenth (the last), which consists of only one line. The final line also stands apart from the other lines because, in contrast to the tetrameter pervading throughout the rest of the poem, it is trimetrical. The anapestic rhythm consistently held throughout the piece gives it not only a sense of momentum, but also lends it the anodyne quality already evoked by the word "lullaby" in the title. As a title, "Cripple Lullaby" lends itself to two opposing interpretations: Does the poem represent a lullaby sung to a "cripple" or sung *by* a "cripple"? Is it trying to get a "cripple" to sleep or trying to lull the audience to sleep? On a meta-level, the term "lullaby" could also be used as a semi-ironic fighting term, describing crip poetry as a genre. The reader might be expecting a melodramatic, romanticized poem—a pitiful or inspirational story of disability—or perhaps to be entertained by a story like "Evening Magazine's SuperCrip of the Week" (l. 8). What we get, however, is Wade's version of a fighting-stance lullaby in which the speaker "emphatically demonstrate[s]: It ain't what it seems" (l. 4). The meter works in the same manner: Written in anapestic lines, the poem has a decided flowing, relaxed feeling to it. The only significant disruption to the meter occurs in the last line, which serves as a wake-up call for even those who have been lulled by the soothing rhythm: "I am not a reason to die."

There are two ways of accentuating the last line from a metrical perspective: Reading it in concurrence with the original anapestic meter ("I am not a reason to die"; emphasis added) raises an interesting conundrum. On the one hand, the emphasis on "am" threatens to overshadow the "not," to (phonetically) let it disappear; what is stressed in that sentence then becomes "am," "rea(son)," and "die." This is, of course, the exact opposite of what the poem is saying on a content level. At the same time, however, the sentence that is appropriated ("I am a reason to die.") represents the reality for many "aborted" fetuses, for many victims of the genocide by the Nazis, and also those individuals who take their own lives due to obstacles in their paths or because of the way society deals with those with disabilities. On the other hand, reading the last line in accordance with the anapestic meter and thus placing the emphasis on "am" can also strengthen the central message of the poem: "I am," i.e., "I exist" despite all obstacles, despite all associations that disability raises. The message is one of life, of human existence, of self-assertion and pride. Breaking with the meter and reading the line in (near) trochaic rhythm as "I am not a reason to die" leaves little ambiguity on a level of content, supporting the message repeated several times throughout the poem. Through the slight rephrasing of the recurring line, however, the last line breaks with its melodious, soothing tone and is set apart from the remaining poem. Read in trochaic rhythm, there is not only a slight pause before the last line, but the rhythm itself also forcefully rehashes the implied message. The emphasis is on "I," further strengthening the centrality of the individual experience, the self-proclamation and awareness of the poem.

4. Conclusion

"[T]here's a new definition of disability and it includes power," Wade proclaims in "Disability Culture Rap" (1992: 15), and her call for disability artists to take the stage as "proud freedom fighters" and talk about disability "from the inside out" (18) has resulted in a thriving disability arts scene (cf. Layward 2011; Johnston 2012). Disability poetry is part of a larger academic interest in Disability Studies, a discipline on the rise, as evidenced by the surge of publications dealing with the subject. *The Journal of Literary and Cultural Disability Studies*, for example, makes a valuable contribution both to the field of literary studies and to Disability Studies as a whole; the ongoing success of the online journal *Wordgathering*, the publication and jubilant reception of *Beauty Is a Verb* (2011) as well as the inclusion of Michael Davidson's introduction to disability poetics in *The Oxford Handbook of Modern and Contemporary American Poetry* (2012) have shown that academic interest in disability literature in general and disability poetry in particular is growing.

Questions of definition and identity, of agency and self-determination, are central not only to disability poetry but to disability culture as a whole; and while, as we have seen, these issues determine the works of crip poets such as Wade and Ferris, they are also highly relevant to the field on a social and political level: Some better-known authors such as Josephine Miles, Vassar Miller, and Larry Eigner have been (re-)appropriated into disability poetry, but many writers remain obscure and outside poetic and, particularly, academic discourse. Jillian Weise asks: "Until we know who we are—who wants to be included and who does not—how can we further integrate disability studies in the field of poetry?" (2011: 144). While Weise's is a rhetorical question and she does not venture a solution to the problem, the question of choice and self-definition remains central to the field: Disability poetry is in the process of defining its borders. Regardless of how these borders are to be drawn and redrawn in the future, however, the analysis of Ferris's and Wade's work has shown the distinctive way disability poetry successfully explores and manipulates the formal means of poetic language in order to convey experiences and socio-political activist concerns of disabled people. The "third language" which, according to Jennifer Bartlett, is born from the intersection between disabled people's specific physical challenges and society's treatment of non-normative bodies (cf. 2010: 15) can be traced not only in those poets who, like Wade and Ferris, foreground their disability in their work. Rather, a sense of nonalignment, of subversiveness is present even in the works of poets who do not self-classify their writing as part of a disability poetry canon, such as Jillian Weise or, more prominently, the late Josephine Miles. All questions of political or activist concerns aside, the aesthetic range of the genre—from Sheila Black's confessionalism to Larry Eigner's language poetry, from Clayton Valli's performance-based ASL (American Sign Language) poetry to Norma Cole's experimentalism—reflects that of contemporary poetry as a whole. In its embracing rather than negating of difference, disability poetry is exemplary of contemporary poetry's democratic move from the center to the margins. In that sense, the genre not only contributes to disability culture and disability studies but also expands and enriches the diverse landscape of contemporary US poetry.

Bibliography

Selected Primary Literature

Ferris, Jim. 2011. "Poems with Disabilities." In: Bartlett/Black/Northen 2011. 96.
—. 2004. *The Hospital Poems*. Charlotte, NC: Main Street Rag.
—. 2004. "Abecedarius Hospitaler." In: Ferris 2004. 52.
—. 2004. "Coliseum." In: Ferris 2004. 42.
Wade, Cheryl Marie. 1994 [1992]. "The Disability Culture Rap." In: B. Shaw (ed.), *The Ragged Edge: The Disability Experience from the Pages of the First Fifteen Years of The Disability Rag*. Louisville: Advocado Press, 15-8.
—. 2013. "I Am not One of The." In: Davis 2013. 526.
—. 2013 [1993]. "Cripple Lullaby." In: Davis 2013. 527.

Selected Secondary Literature

Baird, Joseph L. and Deborah S. Workman (eds.). 1986. *Toward Solomon's Mountain: The Experience of Disability in Poetry*. Philadelphia: Temple UP.

   Overlooking early disabled poets such as Larry Eigner, this first collection of disability poetry nevertheless succeeded in establishing disability poetry as a genre.

Bartlett, Jennifer, Sheila Black and Michael Northen (eds.). 2011. *Beauty Is a Verb: The New Poetry of Disability*. El Paso: Cinco Puntos Press.
This most recent, very insightful collection of disability writing brings together poets' academic and literary texts of and about disability poetry.

Davidson, Michael. 2012. "Disability Poetics." In: Cary Nelson (ed.), *The Oxford Handbook of Modern and Contemporary American Poetry*. Oxford: Oxford UP. 581-601.
Concise outline of the development of disability poetics through literary history.

Davis, Lennard J. (ed.). 2013 [1997]. *The Disability Studies Reader*. 4th ed. New York and London: Routledge.
With a focus on sociological questions, this reader brings together the key texts of Disability Studies. Each edition varies quite significantly from its predecessors, with the fourth edition emphasizing the global, transgender, homonational, and posthuman conceptions of disability.

Ferris, Jim. 2004. "The Enjambed Body: A Step Toward a Crippled Poetics." In: *Georgia Review* 58.2: 219-33. Web. 20 Dec 2014. <http://www.cstone.net/~poems/essaferr.htm>.
Ferris merges poetics and academe in this highly influential text on the interplay of embodiment, disability, poetic writing, and analysis.

——. 2007. "Crip Poetry Or How I Learned to Love the Limp." In: *Wordgathering: A Journal of Disability Poetry* 1.2. Web. 20 Dec 2014. <www.wordgathering.com/past--issues/issue2/essay/ferris.html>.
This article details one possible definition of disability poetry and outlines several criteria and poetic characteristics.

Fries, Kenny. 1997. *Staring Back: The Disability Experience from the Inside Out*. Harmondsworth: Penguin.
A key collection of disability poetry, this anthology has been called a manifesto of disability poetry and is used widely as teaching material.

Miller, Vassar (ed.). 1985. *Despite this Flesh: The Disabled in Stories and Poems*. Austin: U of Texas P.
Bringing together various poets writing about their lives with a disability and thus trying to call attention to disabled people, this collection had a decided political agenda.

Northen, Michael. 2011. "A Short History of American Disability Poetry." In: Bartlett/Black/Northen 2011. 18-24.
This paper concisely outlines and comments on the history of disability poetry.

Saxton, Marsha and Florence Howe (eds.). 1987. *With Wings: An Anthology of Literature by and about Women with Disabilities*. New York: The Feminist P.
This collection of disability short stories and poems inspired by feminist policies was influential for the further development of (feminist) disability culture and poetry.

Further References

Barnes, Colin. 2010. "A Brief History of Discrimination and Disabled People." In: Davis 2010. 20-32.
Bartlett, Jennifer. 2011. "Preface." In: Bartlett/Black/Northen 2011. 15-7.
Blaser, Arthur. 2005. "Genocide". In: Gary L. Albrecht (ed.). *Encyclopedia of Disability*. London: Sage. 789-93.

Davidson, Michael. 2011. "Missing Larry: The Poetics of Disability in Larry Eigner." In: Bartlett/Black/Northen 2011. 27-32.

Davis, Lennard J. (ed.). 2010 [1997]. *The Disability Studies Reader*. 3rd ed. New York, London: Routledge.

Dolnick, Edward. 1993. "Deafness as Culture." In: *The Atlantic Monthly* 272.3: 37-53.

Ferris, Jim. 2011. "Keeping the Knives Sharp." In: Bartlett/Black/Northen 2011. 89-93.

Foucault, Michel. 2003 [1963/1973]. *The Birth of the Clinic: An Archeology of Medical Perception*. Oxford: Routledge.

Garland-Thomson, Rosemarie. 2009. *Staring: How We Look*. Oxford: Oxford UP.

——. 2010. "Integrating Disability, Transforming Feminist Theory." In: Davis 2010. 353-73.

Hevey, David. 1993. "From Self-Love to the Picket Line: Strategies for Change in Disability Representation." In: *Disability, Handicap & Society* 8.4: 423-9.

Hubbard, Ruth. 1990. *The Politics of Women's Biology*. New Brunswick: Rutgers UP.

Johnston, Kirsty. 2012. *Stage Turns: Canadian Disability Theater*. Montreal: McGill-Queen's UP.

Kjellstrom, Rolf. 1974/75. "Senilicide and Invalidicide among the Eskimos." In: *Folk: Dansk Etnografisk Tidsskrift*. 16/17: 117-24.

Köbsell, Swantje. 2010. "Gendering Disability: Behinderung, Geschlecht und Körper." In: Jutta Jacob, Swantje Köbsell and Eske Wollrad (eds.). 2010. *Gendering Disability: Intersektionale Aspekte von Behinderung, Körper und Geschlecht*. Bielefeld: transcript. 17-34.

Kuppers, Petra. 2006. "Disability Culture Poetry: The Sound of the Bones." *Disability Studies Quarterly* 26.4. Web. 20 Dec 2014. <http://dsq-sds.org/article/view/809/984>.

——. 2007. "Performing Determinism: Disability Culture Poetry." In: *Text and Performance Quarterly* 27.2: 89-106.

Lane, Harlan. 1995. "Construction of Deafness." In: *Disability and Society* 10.2: 171-89.

Layward, Mike. 2011. "Live Art and Disability Art." In: *Contemporary Theatre Review* 21.3: 362-4.

Linton, Simi. 1998. *Claiming Disability: Knowledge and Identity*. New York: New York UP.

Longmore, Paul K. 1995. "The Second Phase: From Disability Rights to Disability Culture." First published in *Disability Rag & Resource* Sept./Oct. Web. 20 Dec 2014. <http://www.independentliving.org/docs3/longm95.html>.

Millet-Gallant, Ann. 2010. *The Disabled Body in Contemporary Art*. New York: Palgrave Macmillan.

Pafunda, Danielle. 2011. "Meat Life." In: Bartlett/Black/Northen 2011. 313.

Pelan, Shane. 1996. "Coyote Politics: Trickster Tales and Feminist Futures." In: *Hypatia* 11.3: 130-49.

Peters, Susan. 2000. "Is There a Disability Culture? A Syncretisation of Three Possible World Views." In: *Disability and Society* 15.4: 583-601.

Rose, Lynn. 2011. "Gender, Generation, Aging and Disability: The Case of Cheryl Marie Wade." In: Hella Ehlers (ed.), *Geschlecht—Generation—Alter(n): Geistes- und Sozialwissenschaftliche Perspektiven*. Münster: LIT Verlag. 167-89.

Schweik, Susan. 2011. "The Voice of Reason." In: Bartlett/Black/Northen 2011. 67-80.

Shakespeare, Tom. 2010. "The Social Model of Disability." In: Davis 2010. 266-73.

Weise, Jillian. 2011. "*from* The Disability Rights Movement and the Legacy of Poets with Disabilities." In: Bartlett/Black/Northen 2011. 138-44.

Wendell, Susan. 2010. "Towards a Feminist Theory of Disability." In: Davis 2010. 336-52.

31

Twenty-first Century Poetry and Politics

Myung Mi Kim's *Commons* and Claudia Rankine's *Don't Let Me Be Lonely*

Angela Hume

1. Introduction: Forms of Political Poetry Today

"What *is* English now, in the face of mass global migrations, ecological degrada-tions, shifts and upheavals in identifications of gender and labor?" asks the con-temporary Korean-American poet Myung Mi Kim in her essay "Pollen Fossil Rec-ord," which appears in her book *Commons* (2002: 110; emphasis in original). "What are the implications of writing at this moment, in precisely this 'Amer-ica'?" (ibid.). In posing these questions, Kim suggests that the forms and content of American literature are necessarily bound up with the political, environmen-tal, and social conditions under which this literature is produced. As readers, it becomes our task to read literature for what it can tell us about these condi-tions. One might say that for Kim, all poetry written today is political poetry.

This essay considers the work of Myung Mi Kim along with that of the Afri-can American poet Claudia Rankine, two contemporary writers for whom poetry plays an important role in illuminating the nature of American political life in the 21st century. For Kim and Rankine, poetry lends form to the struggles of racial minorities, immigrants, the working class, women, and others for social legibility and a sense of cultural history. Some critics have noted how American literature published after the September 11, 2001 terrorist attacks on the World Trade Center has often focused on evoking the sense of loss that has permeated the culture in the new century (Baym/Klinkowitz/Wallace 2007: 3205). In line with what might be a turn to mourning in American literature, Kim's and Rankine's poetry also laments the various losses and historical erasures that constitute their respective cultural pasts and presents. For Kim and Rankine, however, poetry must do more than just grieve; in fact, poetry may have the capacity to incite resistance and the imagination of new, more democratic forms of relation.

Kim's and Rankine's poetry comes out of a rich tradition of activist writing in the United States that began after World War II. The wide range of innovation that occurred in the latter part of the century makes it difficult to generalize about American poetry's trajectory during this period. That said, one might ob-serve the ways in which poets writing about political issues have turned in-creasingly to nontraditional and hybrid forms. From poetry that experiments with meter and syntax, to poetry that rejects or re-imagines the lyrical "I," to poetry that blurs traditional genre distinctions, the last fifty years have seen the emergence of a wide range of innovative political poetries. As Cole Swensen notes, today's poets often draw from a number of different traditions when im-agining new forms (St. John/Swensen 2009: xxi). In an attempt to evoke the emotions of lived experience while also expanding the boundaries of poetry, a poet might draw from the Romantic tradition, for example, while also employing the techniques of Language poetry, a later 20th-century movement in which poets shifted their focus from the "meaning" of language to its surfaces, exposing how even language is a social construct (ibid.). "While political issues may or may not be the ostensible subject of hybrid work," Swensen adds, "the political is always there, inherent in the commitment to use language in new ways that yet remain audible and comprehensible to the population at large" (ibid.).

For example, poets have experimented with various formal constraints to communicate political messages. In "Cruelty and Conquest" (2006), an example of a "procedural" poem, Kristin Prevallet employs Oulipo, a technique that can involve systematically switching out words from a source text. By replacing language from a speech by George W. Bush with the word "oil," Prevallet suggests that former President Bush's Iraq War was not about protecting the Iraqi people but rather about securing access to the country's crude oil. In her recent work, activist and poet Brenda Hillman has adapted musical forms like the Korean p'ansori (folk opera) and the oratorio in order to write poems about environmental issues in California, from the pollution of the Pacific coast to the endangerment of wildlife species.

Kim's and Rankine's work is also exemplary of the poetic hybridization and innovation that have come to characterize some American political poetry in the 21st century. Both poets employ a formal technique that this essay will refer to as "documentary collage," one that draws not only from the post-World War II experimental tradition but also from earlier Modernist collage practices. Juxtaposing language from various sources—from medical and historical texts to individual accounts of famine, hard labor, war, and migration—Kim's work "translates" (to use the poet's own term) forms of violence, revealing the ways in which this violence mediates language and thought today. For Kim, translation is poetry's task—a practice that has the potential to foster new forms of social awareness and responsibility. In her essay "Pollen Fossil Record," Kim writes that the poem may be said to "mobilize the notion of our responsibility to one another in social space" (ibid.: 111). In her 2004 volume of prose-poetry, *Don't Let Me Be Lonely: An American Lyric*—a book that interrogates histories of violence against African Americans in particular—Claudia Rankine cites Kim's essay. Upon recounting an act of police brutality against a black man in New York in 1997, Rankine meditates on the embodied experience of loss. She writes:

> There is no innovating loss. It was never invented, it happened as something physical, something physically experienced. It is not something an "I" discusses socially. Though Myung Mi Kim did say that the poem is really a responsibility to everyone in a social space. She did say it was okay to cramp, to clog, to fold over at the gut, to have to put hand to flesh, to have to hold the pain, and then to translate it here. (2004: 57)

The poet observes that before mourning becomes a shared social experience, it is "something physically experienced" in the individual body. Working through Kim, Rankine suggests that the poem might serve as a space in which we can begin to do the difficult work of "translating" the body's pain, rendering it socially intelligible.

For both Kim and Rankine, the process of poetry—the making or reading and interpreting of a poem—can bring experiences of violence and subjugation to language and form. In their work the poets focus especially on the experiences of minorities—populations that have long stood on the sidelines of democracy. Both employ documentary collage, juxtaposing voices, languages, cultural documents, and images with moments of more traditional lyric utterance. This essay explores these innovative collage practices in order to show how politically engaged poetry is being transformed in the early 21st century.

2. Myung Mi Kim's Poetics of Translation

The author of five books—*Under Flag* (1991), *The Bounty* (1996), *Dura* (1999), *Commons* (2002), and *Penury* (2009)—Kim's poetry explores the relationships between language, subjectivity, politics, economics, and ecology. In particular, her poetry examines the effects of militarization and capitalist development on already disenfranchised populations—the colonized, the working class, the refugee, and the immigrant. Kim's book *Commons* employs documentary collage as a means to "translate" forms of violence that have occurred and continue to occur under the conditions of empire, global capitalism, and ecological degradation. Comprised of fragments from various sources, *Commons* enacts a "processural" poetics of transcription and rehistoricization (2002: 111). The poems embody language's gaps and between-spaces—that which occurs in the interstices, in and through processes of translation, or *failures* of translation. In these between-spaces, meaning becomes multiple, and the poems resist what is arguably the totalizing power of reified language systems. Kim suggests that allowing for such multiplicity might be a first step in the direction of realizing new forms of relation. Or, a practice of "responsibility to one another in social space" (ibid.).

In *Commons*, Kim points to the experiences of people living on the Korean peninsula leading up to, during, and after the Korean War, as well as toward the difficulties and contradictions that came with emigration from Korea. While the book does not focus exclusively on Korean history and culture, Kim repeatedly evokes the 20th-century Korean diaspora; millions of Koreans were forced to leave or left their country during Japan's colonial rule of the peninsula from 1910 to 1945, during the United States' occupation from 1945 to 1953 leading up to and through the Korean War, and in the aftermath of the Korean war under a continued American occupation from 1953 to the present (see Cumings 2005). Consider, for example, the following lines from Kim's series "Works," which appears in *Commons*:

> For the most part there is the smell of dried meat
> Detail of blood smears
> All at once the maggots were arrived
>
> Capital   .   wound fragrant
>
> Here are specimens   grit in the folds of greens
> Direct pillage
> Equal dispensation of dirt in the doorway
>
> Compelled for the rest of the year to feed on noxious shoots (2002: 81)

Here is a picture of the exhaustion of life and land under empire or a military invasion. The consequence of this violence is famine: "Compelled for the rest of the year to feed on noxious shoots." The poem may point in part toward the famine that resulted from American scorched-earth tactics during the Korean War, which were devastating for the peninsula's food and water supply (Cumings 2005: 294-6). The poem goes on to depict a dwelling space: "dirt in the doorway." The leveling of or disregard for human life by empire or enemy invaders is juxtaposed with the vulnerability of the body and the home: "Capital . wound fragrant." When we read the poem as incriminating the West for its involvement in the Korean conflict, we can read the single period as creating a caesura in the already fragmented line (one might almost read "wound *fragment*"), evoking the antihuman, death-driven nature of "capital" in contrast to the raw animality of a "wound." One could also read the period as linking the two terms, underscoring the way in which the first calls the latter into existence (i.e., the poem highlights the way in which capitalism is predicated upon the exploitability of the laboring body). While the relationship between capital, the destruction or deterioration of the food supply, and domestic life remains somewhat ambiguous, we might ultimately read the poem as registering the dehumanizing effects of the West's effort to institute a capitalist economic system in Korea at the outset of the Cold War, one that came at the cost of many civilian lives.

With regard to form, one might consider the sound structures and collage methods of Kim's "Works" as they relate to Modernist poetry. As Marjorie Perloff points out, experiments with sound, textual materiality, and the spatialization of time were hallmarks of Modernist innovation (see 2002). Perloff suggests that in poetry today we can see a return to a more Modernist approach to experimentation. In Kim, arguably, there is a foregrounding of sound and collage that is similar to that which Perloff identifies as so important for Modernist poetry. In "Works," Kim creates severe sound structures through the use of alliteration. The sibilance in the lines "Detail of blood smears / All at once the maggots were arrived" and "Here are specimens grit in the folds of greens . . . Equal dispensation of dirt in the doorway / Compelled for the rest of the year to feed on noxious shoots" contributes to the ominous mood of the images. The lines hiss and fade, giving way to caesura (as in "Here are specimens "), leaving much to the reader's imagination. Instead of creating a historical narrative, the lines collage the *sounds* of a historical moment, immersing readers in the unhealthy ecology of mid-century Korea.

Born in 1957 in Seoul, Kim emigrated from South Korea to the United States with her family when she was nine years old (Keller 2008: 335). Technically, English is her second language. As someone who grew up between two languages, Kim cites what she calls her "interrogative relationship with language," one that has helped foster for her a sense of the "*translative* space" that exists between languages (ibid.). In other words, for Kim, moving between two languages enables one to question everything about language and, moreover, to see oneself as an active participant in the determination of its meaning. She continues: "Poetry invites a practice of language/perception that embraces mutability, undecidability, the motion underneath and around what's codified in conventions of language, grammar, syntax, semantics, and so forth. Poetry produces new ways of participating in perception, thinking, historical being and becoming" (ibid.). As a practice situated to register those indeterminate and dynamic spaces in and around language, poetry, argues Kim, shapes the way we see and think about the world and our histories. Kim's poetic forms reflect this belief in that they are often fragmented, full of space and air, and comprised of more than one language, ambiguous marks (e.g., punctuation or other symbols), and cultural documents.

In "Works," Kim collages voices and testimonies of individuals living under a colonial power or foreign occupation with those of refugees and immigrants,

English with Hangul (the Korean alphabet), and traditionally legible marks with those that are not traditionally legible. In the series, Kim gestures toward the effects of the administration of the Korean people by both the Japanese and American governments during the 20th century. "Modernization" under Japanese colonial rule—with which both the American and British governments were largely complicit—often entailed the deracination, forced labor, and slavery of Korean men and women (Cumings 2005: 142). The title of the series itself may point toward this labor of Koreans leading up to and during World War II. While the end of the war in 1945 signaled the end of Japanese imperialism in Korea, it was not the end of foreign administration of the peninsula; later that same year, the United States instituted a full military government in Korea (ibid.: 185).

Because "Works" does not name a specific population, the fragments resonate with many different histories of colonization, impoverishment, and diaspora. Consider the first page of the series, an example of Kim's collage technique:

Aggregate

Placed onto the actual
As in tool, scraper, shaper

Operative   f fl

A bereft

aba . apa

A small number multiplied many times by itself (2002: 69)

The first word of the series, "aggregate," references its method: the collection of many parts or units into a single body or whole (OED Online 2013). An "aggregate" method is, of course, a kind of collage method in that collage involves the sticking together of unrelated parts in such a way that these parts constitute a new whole (Perloff 1998). Halfway down the page, the consonant sounds "f fl" bring the line to a stuttering halt, highlighting not only the materiality but also the difficulty of speech. The word "bereft," which follows in the next line, may gesture toward the repression and deprivation that have contributed to the silencing of certain individuals, populations, and histories. As Lynn Keller has noted, one might read the following "aba . apa" as mere consonant play, but in fact the two terms translate from Korean as "father" and "hurt[s me]" (2010: 167). The period between the two terms creates pause in the line. One could also read the period as an interruption of a caesura—a struggle for utterance in the midst of the silence and pain embedded in the page's negative space.

At times the poem, in all of its white space, feels to be hardly there at all. In this way, the form of the poem registers modern Korea's long history of erasure. Even today, millions of Koreans who labored under Japanese imperial rule from 1935 to 1945 cannot locate official records of that which happened to them (Cumings 2005: 139). In the absence of history, perhaps, a culture must assemble an "aggregate" of its individual traces—a sudden sense of a family member's grief ("A bereft"), the sound of a child calling out ("aba . apa"). Together, these traces comprise not a seamless whole but rather a "small number multiplied many times by itself." Of course, Kim's collage of consonant sounds, punctuation, words, and languages will mean different things for different readers. In light of the poem's reference to tools ("scraper, shaper"), one could read the poet as evoking the hard work of assembling, or "aggregating," personal and cultural histories while subject to a colonial power ("operative"), dearth, or diaspora. Kim's collage, or "aggregate," engenders a highly textured, visual, spatial poetics—one for which reading the white of the page, the caesuras and absences, becomes as important as reading the text itself. Drawing on contemporary trauma studies, critic Grace Cho offers a name for this aggregate: "diasporic vision." In and through its form, diasporic vision registers the "nonnarrativizable" and is characterized by its "scattered images, affects, and voices," the haunting of those pasts distributed across the multiple bodies of the diaspora (2008: 24).

Early in "Works" is a page titled "Siege Document" (see fig. 1). On this page are five tercets, each comprised of three variations on a single line. The first line of each tercet is in standard romanization of Korean; the second line is in Hangul characters; and the third line is Kim's own transliteration, or "what [I] might be said to be hearing," as Kim explains in her commentary on "Siege Document" in "Pollen Fossil Record" (2002: 110). Flanked by transliterations that make the Hangul characters more accessible to the English speaker, or that "find correspondence" with English (to use Kim's language), the Hangul characters themselves could be read as being under siege (ibid.). We might read each transliteration as evidencing histories of violence against Koreans and their culture in the 20th century. Notably, Hangul has its own fraught history. The alphabet was invented in the 15th century as an alternative to what had been the dominant writing system, Hanja, comprised of Chinese characters. It was systemized under the reign of King Sejong (1418 to 1450) of the Choson dynasty (Cumings 2005: 64-5). The official explanation for the new alphabet was that Hangul

Siege Document

sesang sarămdŭr-a
세상 사람 들아
sae sahng sah rham deul ah

i nae mal tŭrŏ poso
이 네 말 들어 보소
e nae mahl deul uh boh soh

naj-i myŏn-ŭn mur-i malkko
낮이 면은 물이 맑오
naht e myun eun nul e mahl ggo

pam-i myŏn-ŭn pur-i palga
밤이 면은 불이 발가
bahm e myun eun bul e bahl gah

ttae-nŭn mach'um onŭ ttae-nya?
때 는 말칩 어 느 때 냐?
ddae neun maht chim uh neu ddae nyah?

This time what time does it happen to be?

Fig. 1

offered Koreans a written language that enabled them to convey in writing the sounds of their own language, which were not easily conveyed in Chinese writing (ibid.: 65). The new script of only 28 letters made it easy for almost anyone to learn and use it (ibid.). Even so, the alphabet did not come into general use until the 20th century, since many texts continued to be written and published in Chinese (ibid.: 66). Under periods of colonization and occupation, Hangul has been altered, marginalized, and repressed. For example, during the Japanese rule of Korea, the Korean language was forcibly replaced by the Japanese language (ibid.: 141). While today Hangul is the official script of North Korea and a version of it is used in South Korea, Kim herself recalls leaving the language behind upon immigrating to America (ibid.: 66; Keller 2008: 354-5).

Kim's documentary collage illuminates ways that Hangul has been appropriated, distorted, and transformed. Her collage also conveys more broadly a condition of language itself—the way in which language comes alive in its transitions between various handlers and authorities, in and through the various processes by which it is realized. With regard to the practice of romanizing, Kim asks in "Pollen Fossil Record": "Whose ears are at work? Where does the authority of romanizing reside? How might it be entered into otherwise?" (2002: 110). Here the poet suggests that, despite what may be transliteration's inherently imperial nature, an experimental or improvisational (mis)transliteration might actually have the capacity to subvert this imperial nature from within, redistributing authority among those who have not traditionally held it. In this way the colonized or the immigrant gains access to the language of the country where he or she was born. Moreover, (mis)transliteration has the potential to be realized anew as constructive, collective practice—a means for sharing social space or, in the case of "Siege Document," a means for sharing the space of the page.

Importantly, Kim does not provide a translation of the Hangul in "Siege Document," nor does she attribute the text to anyone in particular. Around these facts, tensions and difficulties arise—both for those who can read Hangul and for those who cannot. The five lines of Hangul translate as follows:

> People of the world
> Please listen to what I have to say
> When it is day the water is clear
> When it is night the fire is bright
> What kind of time is this time? (ibid.: 76, translated by Yoo-hyun Oak)

Kim incorporates a strong appeal to readers ("Please listen to what I have to say"), knowing full well that many of her readers will not have the language skills to be able to heed this appeal. The text calls out from the page, but few readers will have the ability to "hear" it in any traditional sense. Readers who can read Hangul will experience the tension around this catch-22. Readers who cannot read Hangul will experience a different kind of difficulty: lacking access to Korean, they will be forced to imagine alternative methods for interpreting the text. For them, "reading" involves encountering the Korean variations in stark juxtaposition. The experience may leave readers with feelings of being alienated or excluded by language. Alternatively, it may also be one of raw encounter with the violence of language appropriation, evidenced by the visible contrast between alphabets. While the Korean characters and letters may not carry symbolic significance for these readers, the shapes and textures of the characters and letters in harsh contrast create their own powerful effects.

On another page of "Works" appears a hand-written page of Hangul (see fig. 2). Notably, this Hangul is ridden with errors, reflecting, perhaps, the limited Hangul available to whomever transcribed it. (We can assume this person is Kim, though we cannot know for certain.) Kim says as much in "Pollen Fossil Record" as she explains:

Fig. 2

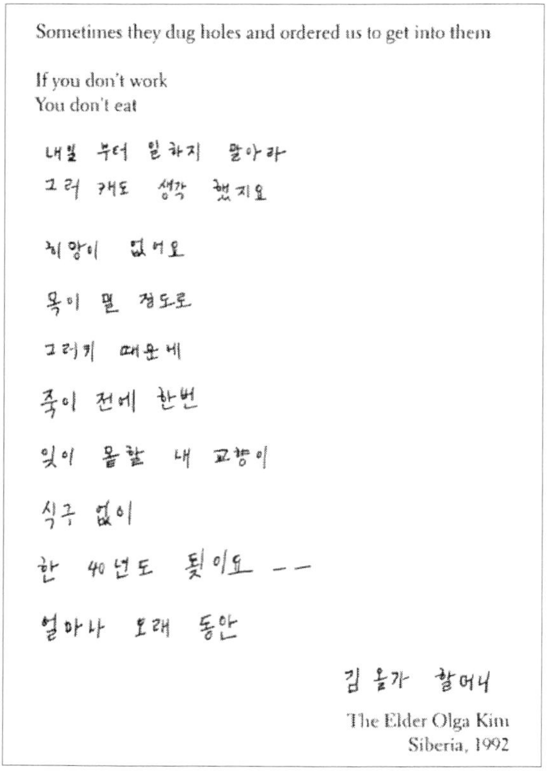

Sometimes they dug holes and ordered us to get into them

If you don't work
You don't eat

내일 누터 일 하지 말아라
그러 캐도 생각 했지요

희망이 없어요

목이 멜 점도로

그러키 때문에

죽이 전에 한번

잊이 못할 내 교향이

식구 없이

한 40년도 됫이요 ⸺

얼마나 오래 동안

김 울가 할머니
The Elder Olga Kim
Siberia, 1992

A further rehearsal: being compelled to write down as exactly as possible the words of Olga Kim, speaking about her forty years of living in Siberia, and knowing fully that an atrophied, arrested, third grade Korean writing is what was available. What was missing? What was forgotten? What was never learned in the first place? What was and was not written "correctly"? Each of these instances is enunciative. (2002: 110)

For Kim, the act of transcription is "rehearsal"—a practice that is tentative, not yet perfected. In its errors and failures, transcription has the capacity to reveal histories of language deracination—how language is depleted, even lost, in and through colonization and diaspora. A translation of the handwritten transcription, one that reflects the kinds of errors found in the Hangul, might read:

> Don't work from tomorrow
> I thought like dat
> There's no hop
> so much as my throat choked
> because of dat
> onetime before I am die
> my un forgetabl hom town
> without any family member
> fer about 40 years _ _
> so much long time (ibid.: 83, translated by Gowoon Noh and Kevin Smith)

Alternatively, a translation that reflects more closely the transcription's intended meaning might read:

> Starting tomorrow do not work
> I've thought that way
> There is no hope
> such that my throat chokes
> Because of all this
> Before death I've never once
> forgotten my hometown

Without family
for about 40 years
How long it was (ibid., translated by Yoo-hyun Oak)

Kim explains in an interview that Olga Kim is a "construction," an "allegorical figure inflecting the ways in which the Korean diaspora has taken place globally" (Keller 2008: 346). Both figures in the poem—Olga Kim and also she who attempts to transcribe Olga Kim's narrative in her "atrophied, arrested, third grade Korean writing"—reach toward their native Korea. Their attempts at storytelling and at language are incomplete, filled with gaps and errors. The effect of these two accounts is a picture of a Korea that is only partially intelligible. In the end, Kim's collage reveals how narrative, transcription, translation, and transliteration—however botched, partial, or contradictory—are necessary "rehearsals," a means for reimagining histories of language and culture and entering them into the historical register.

For Kim, poetry's processes are situated to do the work of "translating" individual experiences—of marginalization, repression, physical pain, and grief—rendering them accessible in and through their "aggregation." Moreover, Kim suggests, the "translative," "interruptive" work of poetic language has the capacity to undermine prevailing language systems (2002: 110). Drawing from the Modernist tradition, Kim's poetry attempts to glimpse history in and through a poetics of acute sound forms, merging lyric trace with documentary collage. While history may not be recoverable in any traditional sense, attention to the way the material conditions of the past have mediated and determined language and knowledge can help illuminate possible methods for relating to one another differently in the future.

3. Claudia Rankine and the Wasting of Life

Like Kim, Claudia Rankine is also not originally from the United States. Born in 1963 in Jamaica, Rankine was raised in Kingston and in New York City (Flescher/Caspar 2006). Today Rankine identifies herself as "a black woman who lives in America" (ibid.). The author of four poetry books—*Nothing in Nature Is Private* (1994), *The End of the Alphabet* (1998), *Plot* (2001), and *Don't Let Me Be Lonely: An American Lyric* (2004)—Rankine's most recent volume evokes in particular the sense of alienation that many minority populations experience living in America. In recent years, Rankine argues, the American government and economic system have been responsible for the proliferation of chronic disease, racial subjection, policing, and preventive warfare. Her poetry incites readers to look critically at these institutions that structure and in many ways determine people's lives. Arguing that "the poem is a process without resolution," Rankine advocates an "investigative poetics" that "takes race and class into account" (Flescher/Caspar 2006, n.p.). She explains that by "acknowledging who we are in the world" as poets, we can "keep the field reflective" (ibid.). For Rankine, the Language poets in particular model this kind of self-awareness—that language itself is "constructed around . . . certain sets of privileges" (ibid.). Rankine's co-editorship with Juliana Spahr of the 2002 volume *American Women Poets in the 21st Century: Where Lyric Meets Language* underscores her interest in the question of how innovative writing helps bridge the gap between the personal and the collective—between "private intimacies" and "public obligations," as Spahr puts it in her introduction

(Rankine/Spahr 2002: 11). Notably, while Rankine emphasizes the importance of Language poetry for her work, the forms of her poetry, like Kim's, employ collage techniques that draw from Modernism as well.

In *Don't Let Me Be Lonely*, Rankine employs documentary collage to interrogate the political, social, and environmental conditions under which people have lived and continue to live. The book is a series of prose meditations interspersed with images and documents: lists, drawings, media photographs, diagrams of the body, X-ray images, prescription labels, and others. Each prose section is separated by an image of a television with static on its screen, as if "reading" the sections were like switching from channel to channel. At times the book's lyric prose dwells on and mourns the experiences of contemporary life post-9/11, from living with chronic disease and addiction to standing witness, oftentimes daily, to racism, terrorism, and war. In collaging lyric language with documents—private with public—Rankine illustrates the way in which even personal experiences of grief are mediated by the ideologies of capitalism and empire.

In referring to her book as an "American lyric," Rankine invokes a contested genre history while also alluding to the question of whether there can even be such a thing as a distinctly American lyric genre. While today the term "lyric" is generally used to refer to poetry written in the first person, expressing personal feelings, or to poetry that foregrounds the musicality of language, these definitions, as Virginia Jackson and Yopie Prins point out, are actually relatively recent ones (2014: 1). In fact, the term has denoted different poetic forms at different points in time, often eluding critics as they have attempted to pin it down (Jackson 2012: 826-34). Contrary to popular belief, lyric is not an ancient genre that developed over centuries, but rather a modern idea that tends to collapse a wide range of disparate poetic practices and theories from centuries past. Simultaneously resisting and conforming to the modern idea of what a lyric is and has always been, *Don't Let Me Be Lonely* points not only to the amorphousness of the term "lyric," but also to that of its modifier, "American." In inviting the question, "What is it to be lyric?" Rankine prompts us in the same moment to ask, "What is it to be an American citizen?" The latter question is troubling in the context of Rankine's work, in which citizenship does not necessarily guarantee one rights (let alone equal rights) or humane treatment by society and the state. To be an "American lyric" is to be legible only to a certain point, and therefore always also to be at risk of historical erasure.

The tone of Rankine's *Don't Let Me Be Lonely* oscillates. Sometimes the speaker is sincere, almost sentimental: "I forget things too. It makes me sad . . . the sadness lives in the recognition that a life can not matter . . . I write this without breaking my heart, without bursting into anything" (2004: 23). At other times the speaker is cynical: "Now it is the twenty-first century and either you are with us or you are against us. Where is your flag?" (ibid.: 91). However tonally disparate, both of these moments gesture toward what Christopher Nealon has described as a central problem or question for the book: how to "give meaning to broken lives, or meaning to death, in a context where historical hope seems passé, and where its becoming passé is explicitly linked to its having ballooned into an empty spectacle" (2011: 148). Or in other words, how are we to hope for better lives when it is precisely in the name of this "hope" that the capitalist state has repeatedly made a mockery of equality, freedom, and democracy? How can we hope for better lives when "hope" has become the justification for making infinite war on just about anyone (from the African American to the non-western foreigner) who is perceived as threatening the coherence of the American "good life"? At the end of the book, Rankine includes an extensive "notes" section that details the sources for and stories behind her collaged images and further situates the book and its subjects historically. "Why do people waste away?" the poet asks (2004: 11). Arguably, the book itself is a chronicle of this wasting away (what the critic Lauren Berlant has named "slow death"), which for many people today, and in particular for African Americans, is definitive of their experience living under Western "democracy."

In her book, Rankine explores two forms of violence against African Americans that are the result of power structures in place. These forms of violence are chronic disease and police violence against black men. The section begins with a conversation between the speaker—a journalist—and her editor. The speaker explains:

> We are having lunch because I am writing a book on hepatotoxicity, also known as liver failure. In the public imagination, liver failure is associated with alcoholism, but the truth is 55 percent of the time liver failure is drug-induced . . . My editor asks me to tell her exactly what the liver means to me. She must not have read Laurie Tarkan's article in the *Times*, though she pulls it from her briefcase and places it in the middle of the table. I point to a paragraph and read aloud: *The liver is particularly vulnerable to drugs because one of its functions is to break down or metabolize chemicals that are not water-soluble . . . But sometimes the breakdown products are toxic to liver cells. Indeed it is surprising, given the noxious chemicals that the liver is exposed to, that more drugs do not damage it.* (ibid.: 53-4; original italics)

We cannot assume that the speaker is Rankine or even that the speaker is black. That said, at other points in the book Rankine's speakers do identify with African Americans or as African American. "Cornel West says this is what is wrong with black people today—too nihilistic. Too scarred by hope to hope, too experienced to experience, too close to dead is what I think," writes Rankine (ibid.: 23). For this reason we might also read Rankine's journalist as African American. Of course, liver disease is not a condition that affects only African Americans. However, both diabetes and obesity—two chronic conditions that African Americans are at higher risk of developing due to a variety of genetic, socioeconomic, and environmental factors—can lead to an increased risk of liver disease (US Department of Health and Human Services; Mayo Clinic). Furthermore, exposure to chemicals, toxins, and drugs can also contribute to liver problems (Mayo Clinic). Overexposure to any of these factors, Rankine's speaker suggests, can even lead to liver failure (Rankine 2004: 53). For all of these reasons, one could read Rankine as suggesting that liver disease is just one of the many chronic conditions that are associated with the wasting of African American life today.

In relating her own experience, Rankine's speaker defers to a document (Tarkan's article, a work of popular journalism), allowing it to speak for her. In deferring to the authority of the document, the speaker becomes empowered, asserting the way in which her own body is situated precariously amidst medication and noxious chemicals. Here is a key irony that Rankine's book distills: in order to care for one's body, to arm oneself with knowledge of the risks that one's body faces everyday, one must consume and internalize mediated forms of knowledge produced and circulated by institutions that in many cases are complacent with or even contributors to the production of these risks in the first place (e.g., the media, the government, pharmaceuticals, other corporations). The speaker continues:

> I understand that what she wants is an explanation of the mysterious connections that exist between an author and her text. If I am present in a subject position what responsibility do I have to the content, to the truth value, of the words themselves? Is "I" even me or am "I" a gearshift to get from one sentence to the next? Should I say we? Is the voice not various if I take responsibility for it? What does my subject mean to me? (ibid.: 54)

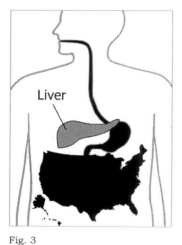

Why do I care about the liver? I could have told her it is because the word *live* hides within it. Or we might have been able to do something with the fact that the liver is the largest single internal organ next to the soul, which looms large though it is hidden.

Fig. 3

The speaker's question, "What does my subject mean to me?" ironically echoes her editor's earlier question ("My editor asks me to tell her exactly what the liver means to me"), in that when weighed against the conditions and interests that produce and reproduce subjectivity today, one's "subject" ultimately amounts to very little. Directly below the speaker's meditation appears a diagram of the body (see fig. 3). The speaker's confession, which appears next to the image, borders on sentimentality: "Why do I care about the liver? I could have told her it is because the word *live* hides in it" (ibid.: 54). But any sentimentality is quickly undermined when readers see that the "soul" to which the speaker refers, "which looms large though is hidden," is in the shape of the United States. What the image in juxtaposition with the text implies is that there is no "soul"; instead, there is only empire "looming large," penetrating every aspect of one's worldly, embodied, subjective experience. The image conveys a notion central to the book: that society's violence—whether in the form of the media, the commodity, or the police—is always experienced at the level of the physical body, violating it to its core.

The pages that follow, in which the speaker reflects on cases of police violence against young black men, drive home this idea. Before recalling the cases, the speaker confesses: "I get a sharp pain in my gut. And though heart disease is the leading killer of American women, the pain has nothing to do with that. I have had it all my life. Not quite a caving in, just a feeling of bits of my inside twisting away from flesh in the form of a blow to the body" (ibid.: 56). For Rankine, to live in today's world is to live with injury, and the line between emotional and physical injury has become increasingly blurred. Below the speaker's meditation is a television. On its screen is an image of Abner Louima, a New York City black man (see fig. 4). "It's been four years since he was sodomized with a broken broomstick while in police custody," Rankine writes bluntly (ibid.). On the next page she writes: "And the other: All the shots, all forty-one never add up, never become plural, and will not stay in the past. It felt wasteful to cry at the television set as Amadou Diallo's death was announced" (ibid.: 57). The book's "notes" tell us that Diallo was a West African immigrant and street vendor, shot dead in his New York City apartment building despite being unarmed (ibid.: 142). Also framed by a television screen, an image of a smiling Diallo appears below Rankine's text (see fig. 5).

Rankine's collage—lyric confession ("I get a sharp pain in my gut") juxtaposed with images of two victims of state-sanctioned violence—instills in readers a sense of horror. This horror intensifies as the speaker gestures toward the pain she experiences in her own body, the way she feels "loss to the point of being bent over each time" (ibid.: 57). The collage brings images of physical violence into close proximity with thoughts of the body in one of its most vulnerable states: "bent over." Readers begin to see that in a culture capable of violence that penetrates both physically (in the form of broomsticks and bullets) and psychologically (in the form of ideology and intimidation), the sentiments and suffering of individual bodies

Figs. 4 & 5

are rendered nearly insignificant. Even grief is highly mediated and administered; to condemn cultural violence is always also to consume this violence, as it has been repackaged by other parties and interests via channels like television and the Internet.

The poem, Rankine suggests, in its insistence on "[holding] the pain . . . [translating] it here," might come as a kind of refusal in the face of these conditions. Citing Kim, Rankine's speaker echoes the other poet's sentiment that "the poem is really a responsibility to everyone in a social space . . . what alerts, alters" (ibid.: 57). But it is unclear whether Rankine's speaker actually believes what she is saying. Can the restatement of shocking facts (the fact that Abner Louima was sodomized with a broken broomstick while in police custody) and the inclusion of images (the smiling face of the now-dead Amadou Diallo) really inspire social change? After all, as one of Rankine's speakers admits later in the book, "One observes, one recognizes without being recognized. One opens the paper. One turns on the television. Nothing changes" (ibid.: 117). It is this tension—between the impulse to "translate" one's embodied grief, a hopeful gesture; and the impulse to give in and give up in the face of so much wasted life, a kind of radical pessimism—that pervades the book. In the end, *Don't Let Me Be Lonely* reveals the way in which it is *this* tension, and not poetry's mourning, that may be what has the affective power to incite readers to fight for more democratic social structures and arrangements.

4. Conclusion: The Political Poet in the 21st Century

Continuing the 20th-century tradition of innovative political writing, Kim and Rankine employ documentary collage practices to register and interrogate the social, political, and environmental conditions under which people have lived and continue to live. They evoke in particular the experiences of minority populations that have long been vulnerable to subjugation by society and the state. Kim's and Rankine's hybrid forms are adapted not only from the post-World War II experimental tradition but also from Modernism and Modernist collage.

Importantly, both Kim and Rankine tarry with the question of whether politically engaged poetry can play a role in bringing about real social change, a question that has long been of concern to American activist poets. While Kim and Rankine both grapple with the relationship between personal experience and social relations and responsibility, their politics and poetics diverge in a number of essential ways. For Kim, the "translative," "interruptive" work of poetic language has the capacity to undermine prevailing language systems and "alert and alter" that which surrounds it (2002: 110). In and through this process, notions of social responsibility can be activated and histories can be realized anew (ibid.: 111). Ultimately for Kim, poetry plays an active role in the realm of the political. For Rankine, on the other hand, the conditions for social life under the capitalist state often render the modern subject, and in particular the black subject, "too scarred by hope to hope, too experienced to experience, too close to dead" (2004: 23). Power's unrelenting administration of knowledge has reduced subjectivity—the fact of the "I"—to nothing more than "a gearshift to get from one sentence to the next" (ibid.: 54). Rankine's work meditates on the ramifications of this fact for the lyric subject in poetry, ultimately questioning how and whether poetry can make a difference under these new pressures. In the end, Rankine weighs what might be the poem's ability to translate the body's pain—rendering it newly intelligible—against the fact that the poem is always already mediated by capitalism and the state. It is only in and through the poem's own realization of this tension, Rankine suggests, that poetry might become capable of inciting resistance and bringing about new forms of relation.

Together, Kim's and Rankine's projects foreground some of the most pressing questions for political poetry today. Their poetry registers the changing nature of social and political life in and through documentary collage practices, demonstrating how poetry's processes are uniquely situated to do the work of "translating" individual experiences of marginalization, repression, physical pain, and grief. What we know and how we know it, Kim's and Rankine's work shows, is a product of the material conditions and contradictions under which we live. In this way, regardless of whether the poet herself intends it, poetry takes on particular social and political significance.

Bibliography

Selected Primary Literature

Kim, Myung Mi. 1991. *Under Flag*. Berkeley: Kelsey Street Press.
——. 1996. *The Bounty*. Minneapolis: Chax Press.
——. 1999. *Dura*. Los Angeles: Sun & Moon Press.
——. 2002. *Commons*. Berkeley: U of California P.
——. 2009. *Penury*. Richmond: Omnidawn Publishing.
Rankine, Claudia. 1994. *Nothing in Nature Is Private*. Cleveland: Cleveland State University Poetry Center.
——. 1998. *The End of the Alphabet*. New York: Grove Press.
——. 2001. *Plot*. New York: Grove Press.
——. 2004. *Don't Let Me Be Lonely: An American Lyric*. Minneapolis: Graywolf Press.

Selected Secondary Literature

Cumings, Bruce. 2005. *Korea's Place in the Sun: A Modern History*. New York and London: W.W. Norton & Company.

Cumings provides an account of both North and South Korea's social, political, and economic history in the 20th century.

Jackson, Virginia and Yopie Prins. 2014. *The Lyric Theory Reader: A Critical Anthology*. Baltimore: Johns Hopkins UP.

Jackson and Prins gather 20th-century writings on the topic of lyric poetry, revealing that what we call the "lyric" is in fact a relatively recent invention of Western culture and criticism.

Jameson, Fredric. 2001. *Postmodernism, or, The Cultural Logic of Late Capitalism*. Durham: Duke UP.

Jameson examines postmodern aesthetics across a wide landscape, from architecture and film to painting and literature. Ultimately, Jameson argues, postmodern aesthetics register the developments of a particular moment in late capitalism.

Perloff, Marjorie. 2002. *21st-Century Modernism: The "New" Poetics*. Malden and Oxford: Blackwell Publishing.

Perloff traces the relationship between Modernist aesthetics and contemporary poetic forms, arguing that some new poetry is notable for its return to the experimentation of the early 20th century.

Rankine, Claudia and Juliana Spahr. 2002. *American Women Poets in the 21st Century: Where Lyric Meets Language*. Middletown: Wesleyan UP.

Rankine and Spahr examine forms of innovation in contemporary women's writing, challenging the lyric poetry-Language poetry binary.

Further References

"aggregate, n." 2013. *Oxford English Dictionary Online*. Web. 28 Aug. 2013.
Altieri, Charles and Daniel Herwitz. 2013. "Postmodernism." In: Micheal Kelly (ed.), *Encyclopedia of Aesthetics, Oxford Art Online*. Oxford: Oxford University Press. Web. 1 Apr. 2014.

Baym, Nina, Jerome Klinkowitz and Patricia B. Wallace. 2007. *The Norton Anthology of American Literature, Seventh Edition, Volume E.* New York and London: W.W. Norton & Company.

Berlant, Lauren. 2011. *Cruel Optimism.* Durham and London: Duke UP.

Cho, Grace M. 2008. *Haunting the Korean Diaspora: Shame, Secrecy, and the Forgotten War.* Minneapolis and London: U of Minnesota P.

Flescher, Jennifer and Robert Caspar. 2006. "Interview with Claudia Rankine." In: *Jubilat* 12: 14-28. Web. 1 Apr. 2014. <poems.com/special_features/prose/essay_rankine.php>.

Jackson, Virginia. 2012. "Lyric." In: Roland Greene and Stephen Cushman (eds.), *The Princeton Encyclopedia of Poetry and Poetics.* Princeton, NJ: Princeton UP. 826-34.

Kachur, Lewis. 2013. "Collage." *Grove Art Online, Oxford Art Online.* Oxford: Oxford UP. Web. 1 Apr. 2014.

Keller, Lynn. 2008. "An Interview with Myung Mi Kim." In: *Contemporary Literature* 49.3: 335-6.

——. 2010. "The Thing Seen Together With the Whole Space: Myung Mi Kim's Visual Poetics of the Aggregate." In: *Thinking Poetry: Readings in Contemporary Women's Exploratory Poetics.* Iowa City: U of Iowa P. 153-80.

Nealon, Christopher. 2011. "Bubble and Crash: Poetry in Late-Late Capitalism." In: *The Matter of Capital: Poetry and Crisis in the American Century.* Cambridge and London: Harvard UP. 140-66.

"obesity," "liver problems," and "type 2 diabetes." 2013. *Mayo Clinic.* Web. 1 Apr. 2014.

"Obesity and African Americans." 2013. *US Department of Health and Human Services Office of Minority Health.* Web. 1 Apr. 2014.

Perloff, Marjorie. 1998. "Collage and Poetry." In: Michael Kelly (ed.), *Encyclopedia of Aesthetics.* New York: Oxford UP. Web. 1 Apr. 2014.

——. 1999. "Language Poetry and the Lyric Subject: Ron Silliman's Albany, Susan Howe's Buffalo." In: *Critical Inquiry* 25.3 (spring): 405-34.

——. 2012. "Poetry On the Brink: Reinventing the Lyric." In: *Boston Review.* May 18. Web. 1 Apr. 2013.

——. 1996. "Poetry, Politics, and the 'Other Conscience': The Duncan/Levertov Correspondence." In: *PN Review* 112 (November/December): 33-8. Web. 1 Apr. 2014. <marjorieperloff.com.>

St. John, David and Cole Swensen. 2009. *American Hybrid: A Norton Anthology of New Poetry.* New York and London: W.W. Norton & Company.

Victor, Divya. 2013. "Eight discourses between Myung Mi Kim and Divya Victor." In: *Jacket2* (April). Web. 1 Apr. 2014.

Illustrations

Fig. 1: Kim, Myung Mi, *Commons.* © 2010 by the Regents of the University of California. Published by the University of California Press, p. 76.

Fig. 2: Kim, Myung Mi, *Commons.* © 2010 by the Regents of the University of California. Published by the University of California Press, p. 83.

Figs. 3, 4, 5: Rankine, Claudia, excerpts from *Don't Let Me Be Lonely: An American Lyric.* Copyright © by Claudia Rankine. Reprinted with Permission of The Permissions Company, Inc., on behalf of Graywolf Press, www.graywolfpress.org.

Index

Abstract Expressionism 275, 298, 327, 329, 339
Africa; African 39, 49, 52, 54-5, 223-4, 244, 246, 251, 253, 330, 391
African American 52, 56, 58-9, 66, 87, 90, 128, 215, 217-8, 220-7, 244, 250, 253, 329, 348, 385, 390-1, 393, 395, 405, 408, 458, 466-7; culture 215, 217-8, 220, 222, 245; identity 216, 218, 221, 224, 252; modernism 244-5, 247-8, 253; poetry 3, 49-61, 215-26, 243-56, 385-96; poets 2, 26, 38, 49-61, 66, 81, 215-26, 243-56, 385-96, 398, 457
Afro-Modernism *see* African American modernism
Afrocentric 254, 348
Aion (magazine) 414
Aldington, Richard 171, 201, 229-30
Alexander, Elizabeth 254, 395
Alexander, William 162, 364
Alexie, Sherman 341, 370, 374
Alighieri, Dante 41, 98, 176, 234, 316, 344; *Divine Comedy* 41, 176
allegory; allegorical 14-5, 85, 88, 91, 167, 289, 300-1, 465
Allen, Donald 276, 286; *The New American Poetry 1945-1960* 276, 286
Allen, Elizabeth Akers 125
Allen, Paula Gunn 370
alliteration; alliterative 11-2, 15-7, 43-4, 73, 85, 87, 165, 192, 219, 248, 267, 279, 285, 289, 302, 321, 350, 371, 380, 402-3, 407, 447-8, 460
Alurista 428
American English 277, 406
American Indian 66-70, 111-9, 121-2, 124, 128, 341, 369-80, 382, 427, 429-31, 433; Movement 369 *see also* Native American
American Renaissance 66
American Revolution 29, 35, 37-9, 45, 49, 50, 55, 61; poetry/poets of the 37-41, 45, 47-8, 50
Americas 1, 7, 25, 120, 251, 430; colonial 24-5, 27; early 3
Andrews, Bruce 356, 360, 365
Anglo-American 28, 68, 245, 427, 429; modernism 245, 248
Anglo-Saxon 68, 173-4, 182; modernism 174, 182
anonymity; anonymous 30, 37, 39-40, 96, 103, 262, 376, 407, 417, 421, 433
antebellum 79, 81, 85, 87, 91, 93, 390; poetry 65, 79, 93

Antin, David 351
antiquity: American 67-9; classical 8, 25, 28, 37, 40, 99, 193
antithesis; antithetical 12-3, 33, 43
Anzaldúa, Gloria 429, 434
Apollinaire, Guillaume 171, 232
Armantrout, Rae 356, 399 *see also The Grand Piano*
Ashbery, John 269, 273, 327-9, 332-40, 346-7, 416; "Self Portrait in a Convex Mirror" 332-8
Asian American 414-8, 423; poetry 3, 413-25; poets 2, 413-25; studies 413-4, 425
assonance; assonant 15, 16, 85, 175, 177, 192, 225, 267, 279, 289, 302, 350, 371, 380, 403, 407
Atlantic Monthly (magazine) 104, 128, 246
Auden, Wystan Hugh 249, 332, 397, 398, 400
Augustan age 25, 30, 35
autobiography; autobiographical 28, 51, 86, 111, 140, 178, 215, 218, 232-3, 269, 272, 276-7, 287, 318, 331, 344, 356-9, 363, 406-8, 415
Avantgarde/avant-garde 159, 171-2, 174, 180, 184, 187, 196, 201, 212, 249, 275, 298, 303, 308, 327-8, 338, 341, 343, 352, 357, 359-60, 366, 404-5, 416; poetry 294, 332, 355, 363, 365, 404, 410, 415, 417
Aztecs 430-3, 437
Aztlán (concept) 428, 430, 433, 435; (magazine) 428

ballad 24, 39, 96, 162, 222, 249, 405, 427; border ballad 428
Baraka, Amiri 58, 226, 228, 307-8, 346, 351, 385-92, 394-6; "Leadbelly Gives an Autograph" 385, 388-92, 395 *see also* Jones, LeRoi
Barlow, Joel 37-9, 41-4, 46-9, 86, 97; "The Hasty-Pudding" 40-4, 46-8, 97
Baroque 7-8, 12, 18, 25-7, 33, 36; colonial 8, 25
Baudelaire, Charles 80, 175-6, 246
Beat 283, 286, 293, 297-9, 302-4, 307-9, 350, 356, 427; poetry 196, 276, 297-309, 312; poets 276-7, 297-309, 311
Beauvoir, Simone de 398
bebop jazz 283, 385, 388-90, 392
belles lettres 25, 35-6, 41

Benjamin, Walter 239, 330, 340, 360-3, 366; "The Work of Art in the Age of Mechanical Reproduction" 361, 363
Benson, Steve 352, 356, 364 see also The Grand Piano
Bernstein, Charles 239, 242, 345, 347, 353-7, 360-5; A Poetics 362, 365; Islets/Irritations 360, 363; "The Klupzy Girl" 360-4
Berryman, John 151, 263, 311, 324
Bible; Biblical 10-4, 17-9, 51, 53-4, 56-7, 59, 69, 84, 98, 146, 222, 224, 237, 267, 290, 301, 315, 318-9, 323, 392, 394, 449; New Testament 12, 15, 237; Old Testament 15, 54, 99
Bishop, Elizabeth 211, 261-4, 269-70, 272-4, 312, 317, 325-6, 340; "At the Fishhouses" 261-2, 264, 269-73
Black Arts Movement 249, 254, 256-7, 364, 385-8, 391-2, 395-6, 399, 405
Black Mountain: College 275-6, 282, 286, 292-5; II 293; North Symposium 293, 295; poetry 275-95, 312; poets 196, 211, 275-95, 303, 356; School 211, 275-8, 291, 298, 312, 400
Black Mountain Review 275, 291, 428
Blackburn, Paul 275
Blast (magazine) 174, 182
Blue Cloud, Peter 370, 381
blues 222, 226-8, 254-5, 299, 308, 316, 385, 387-8, 391-2, 394, 405
Boccaccio, Giovanni 98
Bollingen Prize for Poetry 211, 282
Botticelli, Sandro 181-2
Bradstreet, Anne 7, 9-14, 16-21, 24, 27, 30, 34, 152; "Here followes some verses upon the burning of our house" 9-13, 17
Britain; British 19-20, 37, 39-41, 45-6, 53, 79-80, 85, 114, 120, 149, 229, 244, 262, 313, 315, 461; British-America/American 23-35
Bruchac, Joseph 370, 382
Bryant, William Cullen 46, 49, 65-72, 75-7, 84, 95, 99, 108-9, 130; "Forest Hymn" 67, 84; "Thanatopsis" 67, 99; "The Poet" 67, 72, 74; "The Prairies" 67-72, 75; "To a Waterfowl" 67, 70
Bunting, Basil 229, 241
Burke, Edmund 42, 82
Burns, Robert 98
Burroughs, William S. 297, 306
Byron, Lord (George Gordon); Byronism 80, 91, 98

caesura 11, 16, 42, 136, 233, 448, 460-2
Cage, John 275, 328, 338
Calvin, Jean 7, 20

Calvinism; Calvinist 7-8, 12, 14, 18-9, 70, 79
Cartesian 8, 129, 358 see also Descartes, René
Cary, Phoebe 66, 125
Cavalcanti, Guido 234-6
Cervantes, Lorna Dee 427, 429-30, 435-441; "Beneath the Shadow of the Freeway" 427, 430, 436-9; Emplumada 430, 436-8, 440; "You Cramp My Style, Baby" 429, 440
Cha, Theresa Hak Kyung 420-4; Dictee 420; "Edward Hopper's Western Motel, 1957" 420-2
Channing, William Ellery 66
Cherokee 113, 118-22, 128, 245, 370, 377-8, 380; nation 119, 121
Chesnutt, Charles 222, 387
Chicana/o 427-33, 435-41; poetry 427-41
Chinese 147, 173, 288, 298, 414-5, 417, 419, 425, 462-3
Christ 8, 12-3, 17, 29, 53, 237, 247, 290, 318
Christian; Christianity 7-8, 11-3, 17-9, 33, 49, 51-5, 58, 65, 66, 75, 84, 113, 116, 131, 147, 190-3, 202, 237, 247, 253, 289, 301, 305, 323, 390, 400
Cicero 40, 99
Cinquez, Joseph 247, 251
Cisneros, Sandra 429, 440
city 28, 33, 157-63, 168, 280, 305, 330, 332, 335-6, 339, 371, 373; poem 157, 159, 163, 168
civil religion 103
Civil Rights 385, 400, 430; Movement 247, 312, 324, 356, 369, 386-7, 392, 394-5, 414, 427
Civil War 49, 66, 79-81, 86-93, 96-7, 103, 105, 127, 129, 143-4, 151; poem/poetry 81, 93, 103, 129, 143
classical; Classicism 7, 24-6, 30-2, 38, 49, 51, 65, 68, 85, 88, 98-100, 119, 173, 175, 179, 221, 397
Cold War 263, 297, 299, 301-3, 306-10, 327-8, 460
Coleman, Wanda 351-2
Coleridge, Samuel Taylor 80, 82, 88, 149, 187, 323; "Kubla Khan" 80, 82, 88, 323
collage 19, 232, 251, 288, 458-63, 465-7, 469-70, 472
collective memory 96, 247, 250-1, 254
colonialism; colonialist 68, 113-4, 117, 120, 122-3, 215, 369
Columbus, Christopher 38, 88, 120-1, 358, 359
Colvin, Claudette 385, 392-95
communism; communist 263-4, 301

confession; confessional 138, 272, 356, 380, 469; poetry 2, 240, 269, 277, 311-25, 344
Connecticut Wits 39-40, 47
conservatism; conservative 67, 75, 129, 192, 263, 312-4, 397-8
Cook, Ebenezer 30, 34-5, 341, 345
Cortés, Hernán 430-3
cosmopolitan; cosmopolitanism 43, 172, 256, 385, 387, 392, 395-6
counterculture; countercultural 286, 298, 303-4, 307-8, 350, 356
Crane, Hart 91, 160, 172, 246, 252
creative writing 263, 312, 427, 436
Creeley, Robert 196, 275-7, 282-8, 290-1, 293-6, 303, 308-9, 360, 444; For Love 282, 284; "The Door" 282-6
crip poetry 443-6, 452-3, 455
Cullen, Countee 222, 226, 228, 249, 253
Cummings, E. E. 91, 232, 421-2, 424
Cunningham, Merce 275, 338

Dada 171, 341
dance 191, 218-21, 275, 278-9, 343, 360, 379
Deer Woman 377-9, 383
democracy; democratic 2, 66-7, 92, 102, 106, 142-3, 145, 149, 158, 172, 196, 223, 240, 243, 247-8, 363, 454, 457-8, 466-7, 470
Descartes, René 328, 415 see also Cartesian
diaspora, diasporic 40, 247, 252-3, 413, 425, 459, 461-2, 464-5
Dickinson, Emily 7, 13, 17-9, 66, 91-2, 125, 128, 134, 138-54, 212, 266, 273, 371, 397, 445; "I dwell in Possibility" (#466) 19, 144; "I like to see it lap the miles" (#383) 141, 145-48; "Tell all the truth but tell it slant" (#1263) 145; "The Railway Train" 146; "The Robin's my Criterion for Tune—" 7; "The Brain is wider than the Sky" (#598) 144
didactic; didacticism 65-6, 83, 103, 136, 167, 183, 249
disability: poetry 443-55; studies 447, 453-56 see also crip poetry
Doolittle, Hilda (H.D.) 159, 171-2, 174, 189, 199-204, 206, 210-2, 229, 244, 261, 287, 398, 404; "Epigram" 201; "Eurydice" 204; Helen in Egypt 211; "Hermes of the Ways" 159, 200-1; "Priapus" 201; Sea Garden 201-6, 212-3; "Sea Iris" 202; "Sea Lily" 202; "Sea Poppies" 202; "Sea Rose" 202-3; "Sea Violet" 199, 201-4; Trilogy 211
Dorn, Edward (Ed) 275, 291-3, 296; Slinger 292

Douglass, Frederick 102, 247, 291-4, 296
Dove, Rita 226, 254, 385, 387, 392, 394-6, 410; "Claudette Colvin Goes to Work" 385, 387, 392-5; On the Bus with Rosa Parks 392
Dryden, John 40
Du Bois, W.E.B. 59, 61, 217, 227-8, 385; 'African American double consciousness' 217-8, 249; The Souls of Black Folk 218, 222, 227
Duchamp, Marcel 172, 189
Dunbar, Paul Laurence 59, 221; "We Wear the Mask" 59, 221
Duncan, Robert 211, 275, 277, 282, 284, 286-91, 293-5, 444, 472; Bending the Bow 287-8; The H.D. Book 211, 287; "Often I am Permitted to Return to a Meadow" 286-9; "Passages" 287-8; "The Fire" 288; "The Homosexual in Society" 287; "The Structure of Rime" 287; "The Truth and Life of Myth: An Essay in Essential Autobiography" 287
DuPlessis, Rachel Blau 34, 217, 223, 403

Eady, Cornelius 395
ecology; ecological 69, 271, 372, 457, 459-60
economy; economic 30-1, 33, 37, 39, 43, 79, 96, 102, 116-7, 157, 160-1, 174, 239, 247, 252, 263-4, 314, 317, 357, 361, 413, 459-60, 465, 471
Eigner, Larry 275, 356, 365, 443, 454, 456
ekphrasis 104, 109, 332-4, 340, 416, 420
El Grito (magazine) 428
elegy; elegiac 7, 9, 24, 26, 32, 50-1, 54-5, 67, 128-32, 138, 250, 329, 330
Eliot, T. S. 2, 19, 80, 85, 92, 158-60, 168, 171-5, 177-8, 182-4, 187, 189, 196, 199, 205, 212, 229, 232, 234, 243-4, 246, 252-3, 261-2, 264, 267-70, 276, 303, 338, 444; "Ash Wednesday" 234; "Four Quartets" 19, 303, 338; Prufrock and Other Observations 174, 177; "The Love Song of J. Alfred Prufrock" 159-60, 174-7, 183; "The Metaphysical Poets" 199, 211; "The Waste Land" 19, 160, 232, 252-3, 255-6; "Tradition and the Individual Talent" 261, 268, 270, 273
Ellison, Ralph 52, 58, 387; Three Days Before the Shooting 58
emblem; emblematic 15, 17, 70, 86-7, 89, 91, 148, 226, 418, 422-3
Emerson, Ralph Waldo 18-9, 47, 49, 65-7, 71-7, 126, 141-2, 153, 173, 187, 197; "Divinity School Address" 73; "Experience" 73; "Terminus" 72; "The Lord's

Supper" 73; "The Poet" 72, 74; "The
  Rhodora" 71-5; "The Snow Storm" 72
Enlightenment 19, 25, 58, 120
epic 30, 37-41, 44, 68, 86, 97, 145, 160,
  189, 250, 430-2; mock epic 40, 97
epigram 9, 17, 24, 27, 201, 208
Erdrich, Louise 370, 374-5, 377, 381-2;
  "Jacklight" 374-7; Love Medicine 374
eroticism; erotic 95, 203, 218-9, 264,
  380, 411, 418
ethnicity; ethnic 61, 374-5, 404, 407,
  417, 422-5, 436; ethnic poetry 3, 415-6
Eurocentric 113, 254
Everett, Edward 85, 94, 395

Feldman, Morton 328, 338
feminism; feminist 89, 204, 212, 243,
  264, 312, 359, 377, 397-400, 403-4,
  409-11, 413, 425, 429-30, 436-7, 450,
  455; Second Wave Feminism 307, 356,
  359
Ferlinghetti, Lawrence 287, 297-304,
  306-9; "Horn on Howl" 303, 306, 308;
  "In Goya's Greatest Scenes" 299-303,
  306, 308
Ferris, Jim 443-7, 449-51, 454-6;
  "Abecedarius Hospitaler" 446-9, 451,
  454; "Poems with Disabilities" 444;
  "The Coliseum" 446; "The Enjambed
  Body" 449; The Hospital Poems 446
Fireside Poets 46, 66, 95-108
flor y canto (flower and song) poetry 439
folklore; folkloristic 39, 244, 248, 406,
  408, 429
Ford, Ford Madox 173, 180
formalism 26, 221-2, 230, 313, 365
Foucault, Michel 447
fragmentation 183, 210, 244-5, 355, 404
France; French 7, 24, 30, 42, 47, 79,
  80, 89, 114, 171-3, 232, 282, 298,
  369, 377, 399, 407
Franklin, Benjamin 31, 49, 51; "A receipt
  to make a New-England Funeral elegy"
  51
Free Speech movement 307, 356
free verse 92, 142-3, 145, 151, 157,
  161-2, 168, 202, 209, 225, 248, 283,
  313, 360, 371, 375, 378, 387, 389,
  392, 400, 449
Freedom's Journal (newspaper) 56-7
French Revolution 37, 89
Freneau, Philip 31, 37-9, 44-5, 47-9, 80,
  92; "House of Night" 80, 92; "The
  Rising Glory of America" 38, 47; "The
  Wild Honey Suckle" 38, 44-7
Freud, Sigmund 171, 199, 267, 287, 311
Frost, Robert 20, 157-8, 163-9, 172,
  266; "Design" 20; Mountain Interval
  163, 166-7; North of Boston 157, 163;

"Out, Out—" 163-7; "Provide, Provide!"
  20; "Talk California" 158; "The Black
  Cottage" 157-8; "The Gift Outright"
  168; "The Road Not Taken" 166-7, 266
Frye, Northrop 174, 176, 184, 350
Fuller, Margaret 66, 96, 106, 109
Futurism; Futurist 158, 171, 174, 341

Gaudier-Brzeska, Henri 173-4, 179
Gautier, Théophile 180-1
gender 1, 34, 119-20, 151, 200, 203,
  212, 278, 323, 348, 359, 373, 376,
  398-401, 403-4, 406, 409-10, 416-19,
  422-3, 428-30, 436, 457
genius 40, 51-2, 106, 282, 348
George, Phil 370, 374
georgic 31, 33, 40, 51
German; Germany 7, 18-9, 23, 26, 28-
  30, 33, 65, 79-80, 171-2, 232, 267,
  319, 321-2, 338, 375, 452; German-
  American 35, 264, 374-5
Germanic 15, 350
ghazal 414
Ginsberg, Allen 151, 196, 276, 286,
  297-9, 302-4, 306-11, 325, 350-1, 444;
  "Howl" 297-9, 303-8; Howl and Other
  Poems 299, 325; Notes Written on
  Finally Recording Howl 302-3
Giorno, John 341, 351
God 7-8, 10-8, 23, 38, 51-4, 58, 67, 69-
  70, 75-6, 84, 101-2, 130, 132-3, 144,
  147, 190, 204, 218, 236-7, 240, 268,
  285, 290, 311, 318, 321, 323-4, 385,
  390, 393-4, 408, 430
Gonzales, Rodolfo "Corky" 430-5, 439-
  40; "I am Joaquin," 430-6
Gothic: 41, 47, 80-4, 87-9, 91, 94, 261,
  315; Romanticism 80-1, 84, 89, 91,
  94; poetry 83-4, 88-9; American
  Gothic 47, 80
Goya, Francisco de 299-301
Graham, Jorie 20, 410
Grahn, Judy 399
Grainger, James 24
Graveyard poets 37, 83
Gray, Thomas 37, 83
Grenier, Robert 356
Griffitts, Hannah 38

H.D. see Doolittle, Hilda
haiku 371, 414
Hangul (Korean alphabet) 461-4
Harjo, Joy 370, 373, 377-8, 381-2;
  "Deer Dancer" 369, 377-80; In Mad
  Love and War 378, 381
Harlem Renaissance 215-27, 244, 247,
  253
Harper, Michael 254, 387
Harper's Magazine 66, 128

Harryman, Carla 307, 356, 365, 399
  see also The Grand Piano
Hawthorne, Nathaniel 47, 79, 96
Hayden, Robert 245, 248-57; "Middle
  Passage" 248-55
Hejinian, Lyn 307-8, 310, 355-65, 399,
  410; "As for we who 'love to be aston-
  ished'" 355, 357-60; *My Life* 357-60,
  363, 365, 410; *My Life in the Nineties*
  357, 359 *see also The Grand Piano*
Hemingway, Ernest 173, 187, 293
Henry, Gordon 370, 380
hexameter 27, 30, 33
High Modernism/Modernist 2-3, 107,
  158, 171-84, 200, 230, 246, 249, 252-
  3, 261-2, 267, 312, 324 *see also*
  Modernism
Hill, Geoffrey 20
hip-hop 342, 347-49, 380, 395
Hirsch, Edward 341, 349-50, 421
Hobson, Geary 370
Hogan, Linda 112, 123, 370, 372-3
Holiday, Billie 329-31
Holmes, John Clellon 297
Holmes, Oliver Wendell 46, 66, 95-8,
  107-8
Homer 24, 28, 50-1, 341
homiletics 9-10
Hopkins, Gerard Manley 270, 349
Hopper, Edward 420-3
Horace 24, 41, 49, 51, 99; *Ars poetica* 41
Horton, George Moses 49-52, 55-62;
  "Forbidden to Ride on the Street Cars"
  57; "Lines, on hearing of the intention of
  a gentleman to purchase the Poets
  freedom" 55-8; *Naked Genius* 19, 52;
  The Hope of Liberty 49, 57
Howe, Susan 152, 360, 399, 410
Hoyos, Angela de 428
Hughes, Langston 59, 159-60, 215-7,
  222-7, 245, 249; *The Big Sea* 215; "The
  Negro Speaks of Rivers" 222-6; *The
  Weary Blues* 222, 226
Hulme, T. E. 171, 174
humanism; humanist 8, 19, 26, 65, 120,
  122, 250, 387
Humphrey, David 38-9, 47
Hurston, Zora Neale 245, 387
hybridity; hybrid 327, 344, 364, 374,
  405-6, 427, 432, 434, 457-8, 470
hymn 9, 31, 51, 67, 84, 191, 251, 253,
  271, 306

Imagism; Imagist 150, 159, 171, 173,
  189, 293, 200-1, 203, 211, 213, 229-
  32, 242, 371, 418
immigration; immigrants 8, 66, 147,
  232, 236, 239, 264, 375, 413-4, 417,
  423, 425, 457, 459-60, 463, 469

Impressionism, Impressionist 189, 418
Indian *see* American Indian; Native
  American
intertextuality; intertextual 45, 48, 59,
  88, 99, 178, 233, 252, 255, 287, 292,
  347-8, 361
irony; ironic 41-2, 44, 106-7, 129, 132,
  135, 138-9, 141, 143-7, 149, 158, 167,
  174-8, 182-3, 190, 193, 240, 251, 253,
  261, 263, 266, 270-1, 283, 314, 322,
  338, 361, 363, 398, 448, 452, 467-8
Irving, Washington 47, 98
Italian; Italy 158, 171-4, 233-4, 332, 341

Jackson, Stonewall 105-6
Jarnot, Lisa 364
Jarrell, Randall 263
jazz 191, 225-8, 283, 298-9, 304, 306-9,
  329, 331, 377, 388-9, 392, 395-6
Jefferson, Thomas 37, 39, 58, 59
Johnson, Charles R. 254
Johnson, Charles S. 217
Jones, LeRoi/Amiri Baraka 58-9, 386
  see also Baraka, Amiri
Joyce, James 171, 174, 232
Juárez, Benito 431, 433

Keats, John 189, 335, 340
Kennedy, John F. 93, 168
Kerouac, Jack 297-9, 302-3, 306, 308-
  9, 345; "Belief and Technique for
  Modern Prose" 302, 309; "Essentials of
  Spontaneous Prose" 302, 308; *On the
  Road* 297, 304
Kettell, Samuel 46
Kim, Myung Mi 364, 411, 457-65, 469-
  70; *Commons* 457, 459-60; "Pollen
  Fossil Record" 457-8, 462-3; "Siege
  Document" 462-3
Klee, Paul 189, 362
Kline, Franz 275, 282, 327, 338
Koch, Kenneth 327, 329
Komunyakaa, Yusef 254, 395
Kooning, Willem de 275, 327, 338
Korean War 299, 435, 459-60
Kristeva, Julia 177, 399

La Llorona 429-30
La Malinche/Malintzin 429-30
la raza 428-9, 431, 435, 439
Language poetry/poets 2, 187, 272,
  293, 338, 352-3, 355-65, 399, 405,
  443, 454, 457, 465-6, 471; school
  307, 355-7, 360, 363-4
L=A=N=G=U=A=G=E (magazine) 356, 360
Latin 7, 24, 27, 30, 33, 41, 49, 54, 119,
  173, 188, 205
Lawrence, David Herbert 173, 232
Lejeune, Philippe 358, 366

Levertov, Denise 275, 291-3, 307, 377
Lewis, David Levering 216-7
Lewis, Richard 26, 30-5; "Food for
    Criticks" 31-3
Lewis, Wyndham 171, 173-4
Limón, José 428, 432
Lincoln, Abraham 97, 130, 162, 167,
    224-5
Locke, Alain 58, 216, 227, 247, 257,
    387; "The Obstruction of Genius" 52,
    60; *The New Negro* 58, 216, 227
Longfellow, Henry Wadsworth 46, 66,
    80, 91-2, 95-103, 106-10, 115, 132,
    142, 153; "A Psalm of Life" 95, 99-103,
    106; "The Singers" 99; *The Song of
    Hiawatha* 115
Lorde, Audre 399
Louis, Adrian C. 370, 380
Lowell, Amy 159, 201, 397-8, 418
Lowell, James Russell 46, 66, 95-8,
    107-8; *A Fable for Critics* 97-8; "To the
    Dandelion" 97-8
Lowell, Maria White 66
Lowell, Robert 196, 263, 269, 311-7, 324-
    6, 328; "Memories of West Street and
    Lepke" 328; "Skunk Hour" 312-7
Loy, Mina 172, 410
lyric poetry 14, 209, 398, 471

Mabbott, Thomas 84-5, 92
Mackey, Nathaniel 364, 395
Madero, Francisco 431, 433
Malcolm X 254, 386
Mandel, Tom 356 *see also The Grand
    Piano*
Manifest Destiny 79, 239
Marinetti, Filippo Tommaso 158, 168,
    171
Marx, Karl 233, 261
Marx, Leo 163, 170
Marxism; Marxist 230, 246
materialism 74, 233, 263, 360-1
materiality 193, 195-6, 343, 356, 363-4,
    460-1; of language 308, 343, 350
Mather, Cotton 24, 26, 34, 50
Maxwell, William 217, 220-2, 227-8
Mayer, Bernadette 356, 365
McCarthy, Joseph 226, 299
McClure, Michael 286, 297-8
McKay, Claude (Pseud.: Eli Edwards)
    59, 160, 216-22, 225-7; *A Long Way
    from Home* 218; "Invocation" 217-8,
    220-4; "The Harlem Dancer" 59, 216-
    22, 226
medieval 7-8, 80, 88, 166, 181, 428
meditation; meditative 9-11, 13-5, 17-20,
    24, 31, 70-5, 147, 150, 183, 209, 268,
    288, 332, 335, 360-1, 437, 466, 468
melodramatic 316, 443, 445, 452

Melville, Herman 19, 47, 66, 79-81, 85-
    94, 278, 281, 290; "America" 79, 81,
    85-91; *Battle-Pieces* 66, 81, 86, 88, 90-
    1, 93; *Clarel* 66, 86; *Moby-Dick* 80, 86,
    278, 290; *Typee* 86, 90
Mencken, H. L. 106
mestizaje 432, 434
metaphysical poetry/poets 25, 183, 199
métis 114-8
Mexican American 427-31
Middle Ages 8, 341
Miles, Josephine 443, 454
Miller, Vassar 443, 454
Milton, John 40, 49, 51, 88, 91, 209,
    316; *Paradise Lost* 88, 209, 316
minority 51, 276, 307, 374, 404-5, 413,
    415, 427, 457, 458, 465, 470
Modernism; modernist 1-3, 20, 107-8,
    124, 131, 151, 153, 159, 168-74, 178,
    182, 184-5, 187, 189, 198-200, 204,
    211, 226-7, 229-30, 232, 234, 242-9,
    252-7, 261-4, 269, 276, 291, 312, 324,
    326-7, 333, 339, 366, 397, 405, 466,
    470-1; depersonalization 261, 264,
    270, 324; poetry 3-4, 9, 92, 159, 189,
    199, 256-7, 267, 460 *see also* High
    Modernism
modernity 25, 84, 149, 153, 157-8, 160,
    163-4, 166-169, 173, 187, 195, 200,
    212-3, 217-8, 242, 245, 248, 301, 361,
    363, 426
Momaday, N. Scott 112, 369-71, 380-3;
    House Made of Dawn 112, 369-71;
    "The Gourd Dancer" 369
Monroe, Harriet 159, 174, 200-1, 232
Montoya, José 428-9; "La Jefita" 429
Moore, Marianne 172, 188, 194-6, 199-
    201, 204-5, 207-12, 261, 269-70, 398;
    "Marriage" 205, 209; *Poems* 201;
    "Poetry" 199; "The Fish" 194-6, 204-11
Motherwell, Robert 275, 327, 338
Mullen, Harryette 364, 397-400, 404-
    11; *Muse & Drudge* 405; *S*PeRM**K*T*
    405; "She Swam On from Sea to Shine"
    404-9; "Trimmings" 405; *Urban
    Tumbleweed* 410
music; musical 8, 101, 106, 147-50,
    173-4, 177, 180-3, 191-2, 204, 218-9,
    225-6, 235-6, 246-7, 275, 278, 280,
    286, 289, 291-2, 298-9, 306, 328-9,
    336-7, 339, 341, 343-6, 349, 352, 356,
    364, 371, 375, 377, 379, 385-6, 388-
    92, 394, 407, 458, 466
mysticism 8, 19, 268
myth; mythical 56, 67, 80-1, 85-7, 89-
    90, 114, 122, 202, 252, 261-2, 265-7,
    276, 287, 289-92, 371-2, 375, 377-80,
    386, 388, 390, 394, 398, 400-4, 409-
    11, 428, 430-1, 433, 435, 437, 451

mythology; mythological 43, 83, 89, 180, 190-1, 202, 204, 211, 290, 348, 377-8, 386, 391, 450

narrative 10, 26, 28-9, 51, 112-3, 122, 128, 133, 239-40, 252, 265, 283, 336, 357-9, 361, 372-3, 401, 409, 432, 437, 460, 465; poem/poetry 96, 292, 331, 372, 408

National Book Award 188, 269, 332

nationalism; nationalist 1, 24, 65-6, 76-7, 79, 86, 108, 130, 249, 253, 347, 374, 387, 413, 425, 428, 433, 436; black nationalism 385-7, 391; Chicana/o nationalism 430-1, 433, 435

Native American 8-9, 23-4, 47, 70, 111-3, 122, 128, 130, 268, 292, 369-74, 377-8, 380, 436, 450; culture 8, 119; literature 2, 111, 369-70; poetry 3, 111-24, 369-83; poets 66, 111-24, 369-83; Renaissance 2, 112, 369-70, 380, 382 see also American Indian

nature 30-3, 37, 40-1, 43-7, 51, 56, 66-76, 80, 83, 91, 113, 116, 125, 127, 135, 141, 143-4, 146-7, 150, 157, 163-7, 175-6, 188-9, 195, 204-5, 207-10, 264, 270-1, 277, 288, 371-2, 374, 376, 378, 438; poem/ poetry 30-1, 113, 175, 205, 209-10, 372, 377

Neal, Larry 249, 386

Negro 53-4, 215-6, 218, 222-6, 238, 244-9

Nemerov, Howard 263

Neo-Classicism; Neo-classical 25, 38, 40-3, 45, 51, 66

New Critics; New Critical 128, 196, 263, 277, 298

New World 7-8, 23, 120-1, 278, 281

New York Evening Post (newspaper) 66-7, 188

New York school 276, 311, 327-8, 339

Niatum, Duane 370

Niedecker, Lorine 229

nihilism; nihilistic 19, 467

noble savage 47, 113, 116

Noguchi, Yone 414

O'Hara, Frank 311-2, 325, 327-32, 334, 337-9; "The Day Lady Died" 329-32, 338

Objectivism; Objectivists 189, 229-33, 236-7, 239-42, 277, 355-6, 366

ode 9, 24, 28, 67, 120, 160, 178-9, 181, 209, 335

Odell, Margaretta Matilda 49

Olson, Charles 275-82, 284, 286-7, 289, 291, 293-5, 303, 309, 428; "Composition by Field" 277, 279; "Human Universe" 276-7; "I, Maximus of

Gloucester, to You" 278-81; Mayan Letters 276, 280; "Projective Verse" 275-8, 282, 284, 287, 291; The Maximus Poems 278, 287, 292

onomatopoeia; onomatopoeic 17, 43, 148, 191-2, 219, 225, 319

open form poetry 276-7, 293 see also projectivist poetry

Oppen, George 229, 236, 355

Opportunity (magazine) 217

orality; oral 111-2, 231, 238, 251, 281, 341-2, 345-7, 350-2, 354, 369, 409, 427, 429, 431; oral performance 112, 342

oratory 9, 12, 28

orientalism; orientalist 417-8, 423

Ortiz, Simon 370, 372-4; "Relocation" 373; "Smoking My Prayers" 372

Osgood, Frances Sargent 66, 125

Ostriker, Alicia 125, 204, 398, 411

otherness 171, 264, 333, 335, 337, 406, 415, 419

Others (magazine) 201

Ovid 40, 49

pantheism; pantheist 18-9, 67, 76

Paracelsus 235-6

parallelism 16, 248

paratext 232, 237

Paredes, Américo 428

Parker, Charlie 283, 388-9

Parks, Rosa 385, 392

Parks, William 30, 31

Parmigianino, Francesco 332-6, 338

parody; parodistic 41, 44, 103, 107, 178, 253, 372, 407

pastoralism; pastoral 31-3, 40, 44, 51, 66, 70, 87, 116, 157, 163, 166-8, 181, 219, 224, 332

Pastorius, Francis Daniel 23, 26-31, 33-6; "Epibaterium" 27-30, 34

Pearson, Ted 356 see also The Grand Piano

PennSound (audio archive) 346, 360

pentameter 127, 176-7; iambic 16, 73, 192, 371

Perelman, Bob 307, 356, 357, 365, 406 see also The Grand Piano

Pérez, Raymundo ("Tigre") 428

performance; performative; performativity 275, 298-9, 302-4, 306-8, 341-53, 357, 372, 388, 408-9, 420, 427-8, 431, 450, 454; performance poem/poetry 3, 192, 341-54, 395

Piatt, Sarah Morgan Bryan 66, 125, 127-9, 131-3, 135-40; "Descent of the Angel" 132, 140; "The Funeral of a Doll" 132-6; "The Palace-Burner" 129, 131

plain style 97, 404

Plath, Sylvia 138, 311-2, 317-9, 321-6;
  "Lady Lazarus" 317-24
Plato, Platonic 98, 289, 408-9
Poe, Edgar Allan 19, 47, 49, 51, 66, 79-
  87, 89, 91-3, 96, 106, 128; "Dream-
  Land" 80-6, 89; "The Philosophy of
  Composition" 85
Poetry: A Magazine of Verse 159, 168,
  174, 188, 200-1, 229
poetry slam see slam poetry
Pollock, Jackson 282, 327-8, 330, 338
Pope, Alexander 30, 32, 40, 49, 51, 58
Posey, Alexander 122-3
Posnock, Ross 387
postcolonialism; postcolonial 243, 257,
  264, 413, 425, 440
Postmodernism; postmodern 1-2, 184,
  196-7, 232, 240, 242-3, 264, 273, 276,
  288, 291, 327, 329, 333, 335, 338-9,
  343, 350-1, 355, 371, 375, 405, 414-5,
  419, 421, 423, 440, 471
Pound, Ezra 2, 107, 151, 158-9, 168,
  171-4, 177-84, 187, 189, 193, 196,
  199-201, 203, 205, 211-2, 229-30,
  232, 234, 242-4, 248-9, 252, 261-2,
  264, 267, 276-8, 280, 293, 299, 341,
  344, 355, 414, 425; "A Few Don'ts by
  an Imagiste" 159, 173; "E. P. Ode Pour
  L'Élection de son Sépulchre" 178-82;
  "Envoi" 178, 182; Gaudier-Brzeska
  179; Hugh Selwyn Mauberley 174,
  177-83; "In a Station of the Metro"
  159, 203; Personae 178-9; The Cantos
  171, 181-3, 205
Pre-Raphaelite; Pre-Raphaelites 173,
  178, 180
projectivist poetry 276-7, 287 see also
  open form poetry
prose 9, 26, 86, 111, 159, 163, 189,
  193, 232, 282, 302, 349, 360, 370,
  375, 378, 396, 466; poem/poetry 216,
  287, 338, 358, 371, 378, 380, 405-6,
  409, 458
providentialism; providential 8-9, 18-9,
  38, 70
psalm 51, 99-100, 103
Pulitzer Prize 167-8, 188-9, 211, 269,
  299, 332, 369, 387
Puritan, Puritanism 7-8, 10, 12-4, 19-
  21, 23-4, 36, 38, 97-9, 144, 420

Quaker 26-8, 33, 98, 105
Quintilian 88

race; racial 1, 27, 50, 53, 68, 70, 119,
  171-2, 217-9, 221-3, 225-6, 245, 248-
  50, 253, 264, 285, 299, 348, 364, 370,
  398-9, 404, 406-7, 413, 415-7, 428,
  432, 436, 457, 465
racism; racist 53, 238, 248, 250-1, 398,
  414, 422, 432, 466
Rakosi, Carl 229, 355
Rankine, Claudia 364, 457, 458, 465-
  71; Don't Let Me Be Lonely 458, 465-
  70; Nothing in Nature is Private 465;
  Plot 465; The End of the Alphabet 465
rap 8, 226, 344, 347-50, 352-4, 380,
  395, 453
religion; religious 7-9, 11-2, 15, 17, 19-
  20, 24, 26-29, 33, 38, 50, 52, 54, 56, 58-
  9, 67, 84, 88, 90-1, 98-9, 101, 113, 116,
  128-30, 137, 144, 146-8, 151, 190-1,
  237, 240, 270, 290, 292-3, 297-8, 301,
  305-6, 310-13, 316, 379, 390, 407, 421,
  433, 446; religious poetry 7-20, 292
Renaissance 8, 25, 181, 328, 332-3, 335
republican; republicanism 37, 40, 61,
  67, 97, 102
Revard, Carter 370-3
Rexroth, Kenneth 229, 306
Reznikoff, Charles 229, 231, 236-8, 240,
  242, 355, 366; Testimony: The United
  States, 1885-1890 (Recitative) 229,
  236-40
rhyme 8, 11, 13, 15-6, 72, 85, 87, 91-2,
  103, 136-8, 142-3, 145, 175, 177, 179-
  80, 183, 189, 192, 206, 218, 221, 225,
  233, 235, 266-8, 278, 285-6, 289, 291,
  312-6, 319, 321, 348-50, 375, 380,
  393, 400, 407, 439, 452; internal
  rhyme 12, 15-6, 177, 192, 266, 285,
  289, 319, 321, 350, 421; rhyme
  scheme 45, 66, 72, 99, 127, 129, 138,
  221, 225, 233-4, 302, 313, 350, 428
Rich, Adrienne 152, 211-2, 272, 397,
  398, 400-5, 408-11; A Change of World
  397, 400; "Diving into the Wreck" 211,
  400-4; Snapshots of a Daughter-in-Law
  400
Ridge, John Rollin (Yellow Bird) 66, 114-8,
  199, 124; "The Atlantic Cable" 118-22
Robinson, Kit 356, 365 see also The
  Grand Piano
Roethke, Theodore 261-70, 272-4; "The
  Lost Son" 261-2, 264-70
Romanticism; romantic 1, 3, 13, 18, 30,
  37, 40-2, 45-7, 49, 51, 61, 65-71, 73-4,
  76-7, 79-82, 84, 86-9, 91-3, 97-8, 113,
  116-7, 122, 125, 128-30, 141-2, 147,
  149, 173, 175, 176, 177, 187, 189,
  192, 195, 209, 230, 244, 249, 264,
  266, 273, 274, 277, 286, 298, 307,
  389, 457; American Romanticism 19,
  66, 73, 76, 77, 79-93, 187, 197, 244
Roosevelt, Franklin D. 276, 288
Rose, Wendy 370, 374

Rossetti, Christina 89
Rothenberg, Jerome 341, 351, 353
Rousseau, Jean Jacques 47
Russia; Russian 171, 226, 232, 236, 291, 341, 355, 365

San Francisco Renaissance 276, 286, 312, 427
Sánchez, Marta Ester 428, 437-8, 441
Sánchez, Ricardo 428
Sanchez, Sonia 341, 386, 399, 410
Sandburg, Carl 151, 157-60, 162-3, 167-70, 223, 225, 249; "Chicago" 157, 159-63, 168; *The People, Yes* 158, 162
Sappho 27, 202
satire; satirical 9, 24, 30, 39-40, 46, 58, 97, 292, 371, 374, 407
Schoolcraft, Jane Johnston 66, 111, 113-8, 122-4; "The Contrast" 114-8, 122
Schultz, Susan M. 338-9, 364
Sentimentalism; sentimental 26, 39, 44, 105, 125-30, 132, 138-40, 159, 200, 204-5, 231, 443, 445, 466; Poetry 125-7, 139
sermon; sermonic 9-10, 51, 65, 111, 386, 405, 420
Seven Arts (magazine) 217, 220, 222
Sexton, Anne 138, 311-2, 324
Shakespeare, William 19, 40, 89, 166, 217, 222, 232, 251-3, 290; *Macbeth* 89, 166; *The Tempest* 251-3
Shklovsky, Viktor 355, 365
Showalter, Elaine 398
Sidney, Philip 24, 98
Sigourney, Lydia Huntley 66, 75, 125-32, 136, 138-40; "Oracle for Seamen" 128; *Pocahontas* 128; "The Alpine Flowers" 75; "The Butterfly" 125, 130-2, 134, 136-8; "The Death of an Infant" 128; "The Unspoken Language" 128; "To a Shred of Linen" 128-9; "To the Ocean" 128; *Traits of the Aborigines of America: A Poem* 128
Silko, Leslie Marmon 370, 372, 375
Silliman, Ron 307, 356-7, 359, 365; 'new sentence' 357, 359, 365 *see also The Grand Piano*
simile 87, 191-2, 219, 289, 318-9, 321, 419
slam poetry; poetry slam 308, 341, 344, 352-4, 380
slavery 49-52, 54-7, 59, 66, 90, 96, 98, 105, 128-9, 224-5, 247-8, 252-4, 461; Middle Passage 52, 245, 251-2, 254
Smith, Elihu Hubbard 40
Snodgrass, W.D. 311, 324
Snyder, Gary 286, 297-8, 425
socialism; socialist 162, 169, 230, 397

Solomon, Carl 304-5
Song, Cathy 416-9, 422-4, 431; "Beauty and Sadness" 413, 416-20, 422; *Picture Bride* 416-7
sonnet 19, 24, 85, 217-22, 226, 252, 405
Sontag, Susan 329
sound 16, 85, 87, 106, 131, 143, 146, 148-9, 163-4, 175, 177, 187, 191-2, 194, 218-9, 225, 247, 277-8, 280, 288-9, 291, 308, 315-7, 322, 328, 331, 341, 349-50, 353, 403, 406, 456, 460-1, 465
Spahr, Juliana 364, 465
Spanish 251, 300, 407, 427-8, 432-3
Spenser, Edmund 51
Spicer, Jack 286, 298
Spinoza, Baruch 234, 236, 242
spoken-word poetry 227, 344, 347-8, 350, 352, 354
Stein, Gertrude 172-3, 187, 343-4, 356, 358, 360, 397, 405, 410
stereotype; stereotypical 51, 112, 116, 192, 291, 348, 374, 407, 413, 415, 417-9, 423, 429, 444-6, 450, 452
Stevens, Wallace 19-20, 172, 187-98, 212, 244, 249, 261, 270, 338, 371; "A High-Toned Old Christian Woman" 187, 190-4; *Harmonium* 188, 190, 193, 196; "Notes Toward a Supreme Fiction" 188, 190, 338; "Sunday Morning" 188, 190, 198, 371; *The Collected Poems of Wallace Stevens* 188; "Thirteen Ways of Looking at a Blackbird" 188, 198
sublime; sublimity 16, 37, 41-2, 67-71, 75, 81-5, 87, 91, 101-2, 178, 230, 254, 268
Surrealism; Surrealist 171, 298, 341
Symbolism; Symbolist 92, 173, 175, 178, 188, 190; French 173

TallMountain, Mary 370, 372
Tapahonso, Luci 370, 374
Taylor, Edward 9-10, 13-21; *Christographia* 10, 20-1; "Huswifery" 10, 14-8
Teatro Campesino 427, 430
technology; technological 120-1, 141, 143-4, 146-50, 157-60, 163-4, 167, 171-2, 300, 342, 363-4, 376
Terence 49
The Crisis (magazine) 217, 222
The Dial (magazine) 201
The Egotist (magazine) 201
The Grand Piano: An Experiment in Collective Autobiography 356, 364-5
The Little Review (magazine) 200, 397
The New Yorker (magazine) 262, 268
This (journal) 356, 364
Thoreau, Henry David 46, 66, 77

Tolson, Melvin B. 243, 245-9, 252-5; "Dark Symphony" 245-8; "Harlem Gallery" 246, 254, 277; *Libretto for the Republic of Liberia* 248, 253-5

Transcendentalism; Transcendentalist 19, 47, 65-6, 69, 72-5, 79, 81, 141-2, 153

transnationalism; transnational 1, 8, 48, 79, 200, 244, 387, 414

Trumbull, John 38-40; *M'Fingal* 40

Turner, Nathaniel (Nat) 247, 388-91

Utamaro, Kitagawa 416-19, 422-3

utopia; utopian 33, 68, 70, 85, 142, 404, 408-9, 438

Valéry, Paul 80, 371

vanitas 12, 45

Very, Jones 19, 66

Victorianism; Victorian 127, 129, 135, 171, 173, 192, 199, 203, 244, 285, 397

Vietnam War 288, 292, 356, 359, 414, 435

Villanueva, Alma Luz 429, 440

Villon, François 179

Virgen de Guadalupe 429-31, 433

Virgil; Virgilian 24, 31-2, 40, 49

Vizenor, Gerald 369-74, 380; *Bear Island* 372; 'survivance' 369, 380

Vorticism 171, 173-4, 211

Wade, Cheryl Marie 446, 450-4; "Cripple Lullaby" 450-3; "Disability Culture Rap" 453; "I Am not One of The" 250

Waldman, Anne 341-7, 350-2; "skin Meat BONES (chant)" 343-7, 351

Waller, Edmund 180, 182

Walsh, Marnie 370

Warren, Mercy Otis 38

Warren, Robert Penn 86, 90

Washington, George 38, 50, 130

Watten, Barrett 307-8, 310, 356, 365 *see also The Grand Piano*

Welch, James 370

Wheatley, Phillis 26, 33, 35, 38, 47, 39-56, 58-9, 61, 254, 397; "On Being Brought from Africa to America" 49, 52-5; "On the Death of the Rev. Mr. George Whitefield" 26, 35, 54-5, 128, 130; "To His Excellency General Washington" 38, 47

Whitefield, George 26, 50, 54-5

Whiteman, Roberta Hill 373; "Dream of Rebirth" 373

Whitman, Sarah Helen 66

Whitman, Walt 18-9, 66, 81, 88, 91-2, 120, 141-5, 148-53, 159, 161, 187, 189, 223, 225, 266, 298, 397, 425, 431, 444, 446; "Crossing Brooklyn Ferry" 143; *Drum-Taps* 81; *Leaves of Grass* 81, 92, 141-2, 151, 273; "Mannahatta" 143; *Sequel* 81; "Song of Myself" 142, 151, 431; "To a Locomotive in Winter" 145, 148-50

Whittier, John Greenleaf 46, 66, 81, 95-8, 103-7, 109; "Barbara Frietchie" 81, 95, 99, 103-6

Wieners, John 275, 293

Wilbur, Richard 263

Williams, Francis 49

Williams, Jonathan 275, 293

Williams, Roger 9

Williams, Saul 341-3, 347-50, 352; "Amethyst Rocks" 343, 347-50

Williams, William Carlos 14, 162, 172, 187-90, 193-7, 212, 229, 242, 249, 261-2, 268, 276-8, 280, 282, 291, 299, 343-4; *Spring and All* 189, 193-6; "The Red Wheelbarrow" 187, 190, 193-5, 262

Wittgenstein, Ludwig 355, 360

women poets 9, 66, 125-40, 199-212, 397-9, 406, 411, 465, 471

Woolf, Virginia 404

Wordsworth, William 67, 97, 208-10, 268; "Immortality Ode" 209-10, "Tintern Abbey" 209-10; "Preface" to *Lyrical Ballads* 97, 208, 268

World War I 19, 162, 171-2, 174, 177, 199, 216, 229-30, 240, 244

World War II 184, 261-3, 275, 298, 303, 309, 327-8, 338, 414, 425, 457-8, 461, 470

Wright, Jay 254

Wright, Richard 245, 249

Yau, John 416, 425

Yeats, William Butler 173, 190

Yellow Bird see Ridge, John Rollin

Young, Edward 37, 41, 83; *Night Thoughts* 41

Young, James 322, 326

Young Bear, Ray A. 370, 372, 382

Yu, Timothy 415-6, 418

Zamora, Bernice 429, 436; *Restless Serpents* 429, 436

Zapata, Emiliano 431, 433

Zitkala-Ša 122, 124, 369

Zukofsky, Louis 229-36, 240-2, 355-6, 366; *"A"* 229-36, 240-1

List of Contributors

Carsten Albers (Halle), carsten.albers@anglistik.uni-halle.de

Nassim W. Balestrini (Graz), nassim.balestrini@uni-graz.at

Michael Basseler (Gießen), michael.basseler@gcsc.uni-giessen.de

Helmbrecht Breinig (Erlangen), hbreinig@aol.com

Tanja Budde (Mainz), buddet@uni-mainz.de

Ludwig Deringer (Aachen), deringer@anglistik.rwth-aachen.de

René Dietrich (Mainz), dietricr@uni-mainz.de

Astrid M. Fellner (Saarbrücken), fellner@mx.uni-saarland.de

Astrid Franke (Tübingen), astrid.franke@uni-tuebingen.de

Kornelia Freitag (Bochum), kornelia.freitag@rub.de

Gudrun M. Grabher (Innsbruck), gudrun.m.grabher@uibk.ac.at

Gero Guttzeit (Gent), gero.guttzeit@ugent.be

Mirjam Horn (Gießen), mirjam.horn@anglistik.uni-giessen.de

Angela Hume (Davis), amlewandowski@ucdavis.edu

Heinz Ickstadt (Berlin), ickstadt@zedat.fu-berlin.de

Christian Kloeckner (Bonn), c.kloeckner@uni-bonn.de

Simone Knewitz (Bonn), sknewitz@nap-uni-bonn.de

Tim Lanzendörfer (Mainz), lanzendo@uni-mainz.de

Philipp Löffler (Heidelberg), philipp.loeffler@as.uni-heidelberg.de

Maximilian Meinhardt (Mainz), maximein@students.uni-mainz.de

Margit Peterfy (Heidelberg), margit.peterfy@as.uni-heidelberg.de

Marion Rana (Bremen), mrana@uni-bremen.de

Erik Redling (Halle), erik.redling@amerikanistik.uni-halle.de

Ulfried Reichardt (Mannheim), ulfreich@rumms.uni-mannheim.de

Oliver Scheiding (Mainz), scheiding@uni-mainz.de

Damien Schlarb (Mainz/Atlanta), schlarbd@uni-mainz.de

Clemens Spahr (Mainz), cspahr@uni-mainz.de

Julia Straub (Bern), julia.straub@ens.unibe.ch

Kathy-Ann Tan (Tübingen), kathy-ann.tan@es.uni-tuebingen.de

Harald Zapf (Erlangen), harald.zapf@amer.phil.uni-erlangen.de

WVT Handbücher zum literaturwissenschaftlichen Studium
Herausgegeben von Ansgar Nünning und Vera Nünning

18 A History of British Poetry. Genres – Developments – Interpretations

Ed. by Sibylle Baumbach, Birgit Neumann and Ansgar Nünning

This History provides a concise overview of the developments of British poetry from the Anglo-Saxon period to the present day. The volume brings together experts in the field and offers a series of introductions to key poetic genres, poetic conventions and recent debates. The 31 chapters trace major developments in the history of British poetry, featuring poets such as Geoffrey Chaucer, William Langland, William Shakespeare, Alexander Pope, William Wordsworth, Philip Larkin, Seamus Heaney, Carol Ann Duffy, David Dabydeen, and many more. Instead of presenting a 'comprehensive' survey of British poetry, this History provides in-depth analyses of selected poems, linking them to the multiple cultural, social and aesthetic contexts of their time. In addition to presenting an array of theoretical and methodological approaches to the study of poetry, each chapter assesses crucial generic changes and aesthetic concerns that had an impact on processes of production, distribution, and reception of poetry. As such, the handbook offers an essential guide to both teachers and students, to specialists and non-specialists of poetry alike.

ISBN 978-3-86821-578-6, 432 S., kt., € 37,50 (2015)

17 Dystopia, Science Fiction, Post-Apocalypse: Classics – New Tendencies – Model Interpretations

Ed. by Eckart Voigts and Alessandra Boller

Contents: *E. Voigts:* The Dystopian Imagination – An Overview · *R. Nate:* Dystopia and Degeneration: H. G. Wells, *The Time Machine* (1895) · *R. Tripp:* Biopolitical Dystopia: A. Huxley, *Brave New World* (1932) · *E. Voigts:* Totalitarian Dystopia: George Orwell, *Nineteen Eighty-Four* (1949) · *R. Heinze:* Anti-Humanist Dystopia: Ray Bradbury, *Fahrenheit 451* (1953) · *N. Wilkinson, E. Voigts:* Mechanistic Dystopia: E. M. Forster, "The Machine Stops" (1909) and K. Vonnegut, *Player Piano* (1952) · *R. Brosch:* Dystopian Violence: *A Clockwork Orange* (A. Burgess 1962/S. Kubrick 1971) · *C. Houswitschka:* Dystopian Androids: P. K. Dick, *Do Androids Dream of Electric Sheep* (1968) and R. Scott, *Blade Runner* (1982) · *R. Borgmaier:* Surrealist Dystopia: J. G. Ballard, *The Atrocity Exhibition* (1970) · *J. Cortiel:* Feminist Utopia/Dystopia: J. Russ, *The Female Man* (1975), M. Piercy, *Woman on the Edge of Time* (1976) · *R. Borgmaier:* Ambiguous Utopia: U. K. Le Guin, *The Dispossessed* (1974) · *J. Wilm:* Postcolonial Dystopia: J. M. Coetzee, *Waiting for the Barbarians* (1980) · *D. and M. Vanderbeke:* Graphic Dystopia: *Watchmen* (Moore/Gibbons, 1986-1987) and *V for Vendetta* (Moore/Lloyd, 1982-1989) · *L. Schmeink:* Cyberpunk and Dystopia: W. Gibson, *Neuromancer* (1984) · *K. Schmidt:* Religious Dystopia: M. Atwood, *The Handmaid's Tale* (1985) and its Film Adaptation (Schlöndorff/Pinter, 1990) · *S. Georgi:* Posthuman/Critical Dystopia: O. E. Butler's *Parable* Series (1993, 1998) and *Xenogenesis* Trilogy (1987-1989) · *V. Richter:* Dystopia of Isolation: W. Golding, *Lord of the Flies* (1954) and A. Garland, *The Beach* (1996) · *D. Mohr:* Eco-Dystopia and Biotechnology: M. Atwood, *MaddAddam*-Trilogy (2003, 2009, 2013) · *U. Horstmann:* Post-Nuclear Dystopia: R. Hoban, *Riddley Walker* (1980) · *N. Glaubitz:* Eugenics and Dystopia: A. Niccol, *Gattaca* (1997) and Kazuo Ichiguro, *Never Let Me Go* (2005) · *J. Petzold:* Dystopia of Reproduction: P. D. James, *The Children of Men* (1992) and A. Cuarón, *Children of Men* (2006) · *M. Pietrzak-Franger:* Virtual Reality and Dystopia: L. and A. Wachowski, *The Matrix* and D. Cronenberg, *eXistenZ* (1999) · *O. Lindner:* Postmodernism and Dystopia: D. Mitchell, *Cloud Atlas* (2004) · *J. Hollm:* Post-Apocalyptic Dystopia: C. McCarthy, *The Road* (2006) · *S. Domsch:* Dystopian Video Games · *E. Voigts, A. Boller:* Young Adult Dystopia: S. Collins' *The Hunger Games* Trilogy (2008-2010) **ISBN 978-3-86821-565-6, 436 S., kt., € 37,50 (2015)**

Wissenschaftlicher Verlag Trier · Bergstr. 27 · 54295 Trier
Tel.: 0651/41503 · Fax: 0651/41504 · www.wvttrier.de · wvt@wvttrier.de · www.facebook.com/wvttrier